INTRODUCTION TO COMMUNITY-BASED CORRECTIONS

McGraw-Hill Series in Criminology and Criminal Justice

Binder and Geis: Methods of Research in Criminology and Criminal Justice
Callison: Introduction to Community-Based Corrections
DeForest, Gaensslen, and Lee: Forensic Science: An Introduction to Criminalistics
Klockars: Thinking about Police: Contemporary Readings
Walker: The Police in America: An Introduction

INTRODUCTION TO COMMUNITY-BASED CORRECTIONS

Herbert G. Callison

Executive Director
The Villages, Inc.
Adjunct Assistant Professor in Criminal Justice
Washburn University

McGRAW-HILL BOOK COMPANY
New York St. Louis San Francisco Auckland Bogotá
Hamburg Johannesburg London Madrid Mexico Montreal New Delhi
Panama Paris São Paulo Singapore Sydney Tokyo Toronto

This book was set in Times Roman by Black Dot, Inc. (ECU).
The editors were Eric M. Munson and Claudia Tantillo;
the production supervisor was Charles Hess.
The cover was designed by Mark Wieboldt;
the cover photograph was taken by William Graham,
Photo Researchers, Inc.
R. R. Donnelley & Sons Company was printer and binder.

INTRODUCTION TO COMMUNITY-BASED CORRECTIONS

234567890 DOCDOC 89876543

ISBN 0-07-009637-6

Library of Congress Cataloging in Publication Data

Callison, Herbert G.
    Introduction to community-based corrections.

    (McGraw-Hill series in criminology and criminal justice)
    Includes indexes.
    1. Community-based corrections—United States.
I. Title. II. Series.
HV9304.C3 1983   364.6'8   82-9940
ISBN 0-07-009637-6   AACR2

TO MARY LOU, MICHAEL, AND
CHRISTINA

CONTENTS

FOREWORD   xvii
PREFACE   xix

1 GUILTY! NOW WHAT?   1

Chapter Objectives   1
Introduction   1
Guilty! Now What?   2
  *The Question / Retribution / Deterrence /
  Social Defense or Incapacitation /
  Reparation / Rehabilitation*
Current Sentencing Practices   5
  *Overview / Determinate versus Indeterminate
  Sentencing / A Curb on Discretion / Objections
  to Determinate Sentencing / Softening the Effects /
  Norwood Law / Determinate Sentencing Laws
  in 1980 / The California Law / The Indiana
  Law / Rationale for Determinate Sentencing /
  Results / Violent versus Nonviolent Offenders*
The Task of Corrections   13
  *The Criminal Justice System / The Task Stated /
  Punishment or Rehabilitation / Corrections Tools*
The Alternatives for Corrections   15
  *Closed Environment / Open Environment / Future
  Choices / An Eminent Decision / The Practical-
  ities of Rehabilitation*
Community-Focused Corrections   17
  *Past Experience / Redirecting the Offender /
  Reintegrative Model*
Conclusion   19
Exercises   20
Exercise References   21

2   HISTORY OF COMMUNITY-BASED CORRECTIONS   25

Chapter Objectives   25
Introduction   25
A Historical Overview   26
   The Nineteenth Century   /   Twentieth-Century
      Continuations
Jails   28
   The Gaol   /   Workhouses and Houses of
      Correction   /   Early Jails in the United States   /
      Early Conditions   /   Since the Civil War   /
      Twentieth-Century Jails
Probation   32
   John Augustus   /   Benefit of Clergy   /
      Recognizance   /   Judicial Reprieve   /
      Filing of Cases   /   Legality of Probation
Temporary Releases   36
   Work Release   /   The Huber Law   /
      Work Release for Felons   /   Study Release   /
      Furloughs and Passes
Community-Based Residences   40
   The European Beginning   /   Early Failures   /
      Success by Private Groups   /   Community-Based
      Residences Since 1950   /   The Federal
      Attempt   /   Community Correctional Centers
Parole   44
   The English Beginning   /   The "Irish System"   /
      Parole in the United States
Community-Based Corrections for Juveniles   46
   Parens Patriae   /   The First Juvenile Court
Recent Developments   47
Exercises   48
Exercise References   49

3   CORRECTIONS FOCUSING ON THE COMMUNITY: 1980   52

Chapter Objectives   52
Introduction   52
Rationale for Community-Based Corrections   53
   The Task of Corrections   /   Other Support   /   A Prac-
      tical Definition   /   Philosophical Justification   /
      Economic Justification
The Effects of Imprisonment on the Offender   55
   The Environment   /   Prisonization   /   Why
      Prisonization?   /   The Conditions of Imprisonment
Clients of Community-Based Corrections   58

*Prison Releasees / Court Releasees /
The Problems of Supervision*
Statewide Community-Based Corrections Programs 60
*National Overview / Minnesota / Oregon /
Kansas / The Results*
Public Reaction 63
*The General Public / Correctional Personnel /
Some Criticisms*
Success or Failure 65
*Favorable Statistics / The Critics' Response /
Unfavorable Statistics*
Conclusion 67
Exercises 68
Exercise References 69

4 JAILS 73

Chapter Objectives 73
Introduction 73
Rationale / An Overview / Specific Purposes
Jails Today 76
*Jail Administration / Jail Population /
Internal Conditions / Inmate's Reaction /
Hope for Improvement*
Jails as Institutions for Reintegration 82
*How to Use the Jail / Problems Encountered /
How to Prepare the Jail / Program
Rehabilitation / The Reintegration Program /
Diversion*
Alternatives to Jail 88
*Overview / Prebooking Release / Postbooking
Release / Two Early Programs / Evaluation /
The Des Moines Project / Evaluation*
Appraisal 93
*Continuing Problems / Hope for Reform /
Some Suggestions*
Conclusion 95
Exercises 96
Exercise References 97

5 PROBATION 100

Chapter Objectives 100
Introduction 100
Rationale 101

The Pros and Cons of Probation   101
    Advantages / Criticisms
Administration of Probation   102
    Structure / Methods of Assigning Cases
The Selection Process   104
    *Presentence Investigation / Statutory
    Limitations / Plea Bargaining*
Role of the Probation Officer   107
    Services / Techniques
The Probationary Relationship   108
    *Day-to-Day Tasks / Rule Enforcement /
    Revocation*
Trends in Probation   114
    *Centralized Organization / Probation Eligibility /
    Conditions of Probation / Professionalism*
Innovative Programs in Probation   115
    *Group Methods / Intensive Supervision /
    Sentencing Innovations / Probation Subsidy*
Evaluation   118
Appraisal   120
Conclusion   121
Exercises   122
Exercise References   122

6   PREPARING THE OFFENDER FOR THE COMMUNITY   125

Chapter Objectives   125
Introduction   125
    The Rationale for Prerelease Programs
The Prison Classification Process as Preparation for Release   127
Correctionalization   128
    *Community-Oriented Programs / Family
    Relations / Programs for Female Offenders /
    Family Home Evening Program*
Conjugal Visiting   133
    Appraisal
The Prison Work Experience   135
    *Inmate-Pay Experiment / Private Industry /
    Free Enterprise Systems / Appraisal*
Inmate Self-Government   140
    *Inmate Self-Management / Institutional
    Self-Government / Appraisal*
Prerelease Centers   145
    *Prerelease Center Programs / Models for
    Prerelease Centers*

Examination of Prerelease Programs 150
   Appraisal
Conclusion 153
Exercises 154
Exercise References 155

7 COMMUNITY ASSISTANCE FOR THE OFFENDER 158

Chapter Objectives 158
Introduction 158
Rationale for Preparing the Community for the Offender 158
Steps to Develop Community Assistance 160
Educating the Public 160
   The Problem Stated / Public to Be Educated /
     Methods of Public Education
Volunteers in Corrections 163
   Early Volunteerism / Use of Volunteers /
     Organizations That Use Volunteers / How Court
     Systems Use Volunteers / Problems in Volunteer
     Programs / Overcoming Problems / Appraisal
Creating Jobs for Offenders 171
   Rationale / Public Job Placement Programs /
     Private Job Placement Programs / Appraisal
Community Assistance for the Offender's Family 177
   Rationale / Friends Outside / A Model for Delivery
     of Community Services / Delancy Street
     Foundation / A Mental Health Service Delivery
     System
Conclusion 180
Exercises 181
Exercise References 182

8 THE TRANSITION TO THE COMMUNITY 185

Chapter Objectives 185
Introduction 185
Bridges to the Community 186
   Rationale / Supervised Trips / Temporary
     Releases / Work and Study Release
Goals 187
   Sentencing Options / Cost Reduction /
     Maintenance of Family and Community Ties /
     Positive Effect on Attitudes / Alternative to
     Incarceration / Period of Transition /
     Public Conception of Offender / Final Phase of
     Institutional Program

Selection of Candidates   189
    Selectors / Eligibility Requirements and
      Restrictions / Probationers and
      Misdemeanants / Questions Frequently Asked
Preparation of a Community-Based Corrections Plan   192
    Procedure / Housing / Employment /
      Transportation / Other Questions
Supervision of the Offender   194
    Carrying Out the Plan / Problems from Housing /
      Protecting the Public / Milwaukie Work Release
      Center
Evaluation of Bridges to the Community   198
    Temporary Releases / Work Release /
      Study Release
Other Benefits of Transitional Strategies   202
    Offender Earnings / Effect on Inmate Attitudes /
      Help in the Transition
Appraisal   204
    Recidivism Rates / Costs / Danger to the
      Community
Conclusion   207
Exercises   208
Exercise References   209

9 COMMUNITY-BASED RESIDENTIAL PROGRAMS   211

Chapter Objectives   211
Introduction   211
    Current Status
Types of Facilities   213
    Degrees of Freedom / Halfway House /
      Residential Housing Unit / Community
      Correctional Center
Residents of Community-Based Housing   214
    Preinstitutional / Postinstitutional
Development of the Community-Based Residence   215
    Site Selection / Sources of Assistance
Supervision of Residents   217
    Planning Supervision / Halfway House /
      Community Correctional Center / General
      Regulations / Staffing Pattern
Programs for Community-Based Residences   218
    Informal Relationships / Community Correctional
      Center / Residential Housing Unit /

Counseling / Representative Programs
Problems Encountered   222
    Community Resistance / Costs / Size of
    Population / Personnel Problems /
    Pressure to Use Existing Facilities
Appraisal   225
    Evaluation / Community Fears / A Response
Conclusion   228
Exercises   229
Exercise References   230

10 PAROLE   232

Chapter Objectives   232
Introduction   232
    Definition
Parole Today   234
    Overview / Advantages / Criticisms
Release from Prison   235
    Parolee's "Gate" Resources / Parolee's Expectations
The Parole Board   237
    Administrative Structure / Professional Parole Board
The Selection Process   239
    Standards for Granting Parole / Eligibility for
    Parole / Preparole Report / Parole
    Hearings / Greenholtz Decision */ Prediction*
    Techniques / Mutual Agreement Program
Parole Supervision   246
    Caseloads / Effect of Caseload Size / Parole
    Aides / Styles of Supervision / Parole
    Rules / The Interstate Compact
Release from Parole   250
    Overview / Variable Decision Making / Suggested
    Guidelines for Termination / Recommended
    Revocation Procedures / Morrissey v. Brewer
Evaluation of Parole   254
    Recidivism Defined / Effect of Supervision /
    Other Studies / Conclusions from Studies
Should Parole Be Abolished?   257
Appraisal   258
    The Criticism / The Response / The Future
Conclusion   261
Exercises   262
Exercise References   263

11 COMMUNITY-BASED PROGRAMS FOR JUVENILES 266

Chapter Objectives 266
Introduction 266
Juvenile Court 267
    Adjudication / "Get Tough" / Juvenile Rights
Status Offenses 269
    Definition / A Question of Jurisdiction /
      Deinstitutionalization
Delinquent Behavior 274
    California Youth Authority / School and Home /
      Self-Report Studies
Juvenile Community-Based Programs 275
Juvenile Diversion 276
    Overview / Police / Intake / Alternatives
      to Detention / Probation / Intensive
      Supervision / Foster Care / Intervention
      Programs / Youth Services Bureau / New
      Pride, Inc. / Outward Bound / Juvenile
      Restitution / Questions about Diversion
Community-Based Residences for Juveniles 284
    Halfway House or Group Home / Program
      Description / The Villages, Inc.
Parole or Aftercare 287
    Overview / Community Treatment Programs
Appraisal 288
    Evaluation / The Massachusetts Experience /
      Unresolved Questions
Conclusion 291
Exercises 292
Exercise References 292

12 REFLECTIONS FROM THE FIELD 297

Chapter Objectives 297
Introduction 297
Research 298
    The Problem / Past Attempts / Validation of
      Techniques
Cost-Benefit Analysis 301
    Rationale / Application / Accountability
Accreditation 304
    Historical Precedents / Accreditation Process /
      Standards Development / The Results
Corrections Reform 307
    Reform Process / Hindrances / "Selling" Change

Prevention of Crime and Delinquency   310
    Definition / Prevention Strategies /
    Macrosociological Programs / Community
    Programs / Individual Treatment Programs /
    School Programs / Government Agencies /
    Prevention of Child Abuse / Recommendations /
    Preventing the Criminal Act / Appraisal
Conclusion   315
Exercises   318
Exercise References   319

EPILOGUE   324

Introduction   324
"Practical" Approaches to Imprisonment   325
    Factorylike Prisons / "Real-Life" Solutions /
    Offender Aspirations
The Future of Incarceration   328
    Why Imprisonment?
Which Path to Take?   330
    The Choice Is Imminent
What Kind of Imprisonment?   332
    Incapacitation / Redirection / Restitution /
    Victim Compensation and Aid
The Future of Community-Focused Corrections   339
    Current Status / Potential Unrealized /
    Fiscal Concerns
Conclusion   341

BIBLIOGRAPHY   344
INDEXES   359
Name Index
Subject Index

FOREWORD

The author of this text, Herbert Callison, is a dynamic man. Energetic and forceful, he perceives what is in disarray in a situation and skillfully rearranges it. Impelled by inner forces, he tries to lighten the troubles of others. I have observed in his work as executive director of The Villages, Inc., in Topeka, Kansas, the adeptness with which he harmonizes conflicting trends and purposes. I have seen him react with admirable calmness, self-control, and imperturbability when frustration and disappointment interrupt the smooth course of an action; when carefully thought-out efforts are met with angry criticism.

He recognizes the inequalities in life and that some people react to disappointment, anxiety, and deprivation with angry outbursts or stealthy malice. He does not condone. But he has no instinct to reinforce the blow-for-a-blow formula which is society's usual answer to its dissident members.

The author shifted from the institutional penal care of convicted offenders to the noninstitutional home care of orphans and neglected children, in the belief (which is also mine) that crime is the delayed and misdirected revenge of a wounded child. It may be too late to correct the injury, but it is not too late to correct the child's vengeful reactions—or to aggravate them. Herbert Callison has devoted his life thus far to managing the care of people who lacked the standards, models, and supports which most of us had as children and as adults. He has been the kind, just, and wise father to thousands of youths who had none—or a bad one. (He is, incidentally, also a real father.) Hundreds of young people imitate him as they grow up. A few may emulate his leadership and dedication; many will continue to be his students; many more, his great admirers.

From such a man comes this book of guidance for those joining the ranks of a profession that tries to straighten and lighten our lives' paths by corrective attention to human protesters and attackers. It is a company who have dedicated their careers to correcting the mistakes of others, which affect us all and cause us to add more mistakes.

One of our mistakes lies in our conception and application of imprisonment. The National Advisory Commission on Criminal Justice Standards and Goals' January 1973 proclamation declared: "The prison, the reformatory, and the jail have achieved only a shocking record of failure. . . . There is overwhelming evidence that these institutions create crime rather than prevent it . . . !'' What, then, is the remedy?

Controlling and caring for dissidents, hated by the community, sullen, hostile, and potentially violent, requires training, skill, and knowledge not possessed by the types of persons traditionally hired for this task. It requires a revised philosophy of correcting misdeeds. The St. Georges of a new profession will change established ways of thinking and acting and will learn how to avoid the vast energy waste of our present system. They will acquire the art of using minimum power to control and redirect their bitter and desperate fellows whose aberrance can cause great public injury. Their clients are society's predators, its lawless ones, those who have exploded, wasted, hurt, and destroyed.

We have cast them out officially, but we want them returned to us as quickly and inexpensively as possible if they can live and let live in peace. Their families want them. Their friends want them.

At the right time, the touch of a skillful person with an idea can be a miraculous wand, awakening the miscreant to the new vision of life essential to transformation of character; arousing new hopes, new resolves, new dreams; stimulating ambition for ends to be attained not by force, stealth, or contrivance, but in peaceful, constructive ways.

For the most part, we still apply power clumsily to the difficult redirection of human outbursts. We contain them, but at such expense and waste! This is a book of better ways.

Herbert Callison presents clearly the details of the new idea for doing something with and for offenders. He proposes that the people most concerned with damage to property or person have a responsibility to participate in influencing the lives of the damagers. Hitherto, the so-called justice system has acted on the assumption that a person proven guilty of an offense should be taken for detention and punishment to some distant place—the more distant, the better. Contact between prisoner and community has been made as difficult as possible. When the time comes for the offenders to return, chastened and reformed, to earn livings, to reestablish friendships, perhaps to make redress for past sins, they go back almost as strangers to their communities; even, indeed, to their own wives or husbands and children.

The newer point of view, that of progressive criminology, which Herbert Callison systematically lays out, avoids taking offenders so far from the people they have lived with and even offended. His text is directly in line with the up-to-date conception of the transaction between offender and community. I envy the opportunity of teachers and ambitious students using it to follow in detail the logic and specifics presented by this brilliant teacher.

Karl A. Menninger, M.D., F.A.P.A.

PREFACE

For 7 years I worked in a prison (although it was called a reformatory). During that time I had the opportunity to review over 6000 inmates who were being considered for parole. Many returned to prison and gave me an opportunity to talk with them about their community experience; many did not come back to prison. For 3 years I was superintendent of a prerelease center—Riverview Release Center near Newton, Iowa—which gave me a chance to observe prisoners as they actually left the institutional setting and entered the community.

During those 10 years I reached a number of conclusions. First, that most offenders really want to stay outside the prison's walls. Second, that most correctional programs are designed to accommodate the state corrections department and not to help the prisoner. Third, that much could be done to assist the prisoner if the program were designed to help offenders resolve practical problems. Fourth, that accommodating the corrections department and helping offenders cope with practical problems are not incompatible.

Most of the offenders who did not return to prison and maintained contact with me indicated the basic reason they remained free had nothing to do with high school diplomas or vocational training certificates. The reason they did not commit any more crimes was that they became integrated into a community. They were reunited with loved ones; they established ties with friends and fellow employees; they believed they had a place in the community and a function to perform.

Many times, specific instances were cited—kindness shown by a fellow civilian employee, such as taking them fishing before they had means of transportation; an extra effort on the part of correctional personnel, especially correctional officers and probation and parole officers, to help them find a job or place to live; a member of a church or Alcoholics Anonymous group who invited them to dinner or otherwise encouraged their feeling part of the community.

Since 1965 I have been teaching in various colleges and universities in the midwest. Most of my students have been interested in occupations related to juvenile or adult corrections. It was obvious that most students would have to begin work before they could learn about the practical aspects of corrections. In general, textbooks and teaching methods provide an ideal view of corrections. The students learn the hypothetical assumptions and the theories upon which correctional programs are based but little about the actual programs. There is little opportunity for them to discuss both negative and positive aspects of an issue and little chance for appraisal or analysis during class time.

These two experiences resulted in a synthesis of purpose. To write a textbook that on one hand gave corrections students a practical view of corrections, and on the other hand gave them some theoretical knowledge. I hope that this purpose will be accomplished by this text, which is full of examples of programs as well as of the assumptions behind them. It contains a great deal of analysis and much opinion. The exercises are designed to stimulate discussion. The content is based on my experience as both teacher and practitioner.

Because of the long history of failure associated with correctional programs and especially with action labeled "rehabilitation," I have made some attempt to talk in other terms—*community-based corrections* is cited as an example of corrections focusing on the community. Corrections focusing on the community also includes programs that could be housed in jails and walled institutions. The term "redirection" is substituted in many instances for the term "rehabilitation." The philosophy of *reintegration* is evident throughout, even though the term may not be used on each page. At some points, the term "integration" is used, referring to those offenders who have not been incarcerated for extensive periods and, consequently, do not need to be *re*integrated. All these changes in terminology are not attempts to confuse the reader but to use terms that are not prejudiced by previous misuse or failure. They are also an attempt to use terms that encourage a more practical image on the part of the reader.

I hope that this book can be the basis for both correctional practitioners and students to learn enough about corrections focusing on the community to work in the field. It is my hope that it can serve as a basis for the practical application of theories they may learn from others.

It is certainly not intended to be *the answer* but to provide *some* ideas that can be applied to *some* offenders. It is intended to provide a few answers *for* a few offenders. More important, it is intended to answer some of the questions that are now being raised by politicians, correctional administrators, and the public. These questions are based on the failure of evaluations to show that many programs *succeed in rehabilitating the offender*; the discouragement of many people about the cost-effective use of correctional programs; and the hue and cry over high crime rates and increased violence in our society.

All these questions cannot be ignored by correctional administrators or teachers. Perhaps none of them will be answered in the near future. It is my hope, however, that this text will plant some seeds which can lead to further discussion, research, and conclusions that might be able, someday, to answer some of these questions.

Herbert G. Callison

GUILTY! NOW WHAT?

CHAPTER OBJECTIVES

- To discuss justifications for the alternative reactions to the criminal
- To present the current debate between proponents of determinate and indeterminate sentencing
- To discuss the differences in reactions to the violent and the nonviolent offender
- To outline the task of corrections
- To view the place of community-based corrections within the total scope of corrections

INTRODUCTION

John was one of two children who lived with his parents in a $90,000 home. His father, a banker, and his mother, a socially active member of a prominent family, provided him with many advantages, including piano lessons. After completing high school, John went on to college, earning Bachelor of Arts and Master of Arts degrees, both with majors in music.

After graduating from college he began teaching music at a private university in a state capitol and married his college sweetheart. Two children, a boy and a girl, were born within 3 years. Finding that his income from teaching music was inadequate to support his family in the way to which they were accustomed, he encouraged his wife to find employment. His wife's earnings were used to purchase property—with large mortgages.

Short on funds because of poor budgeting, John fraudulently sold the

1

properties. His crime consisted of the sale of approximately $200,000 worth of mortgaged property. He was convicted, and the business executives who were defrauded pressured the judge to sentence him to 5 years in prison without probation. After the minimum 18 months had been served for parole eligibility, he was released from prison on parole. Since he did not have tenure, his teaching job was gone. A parole officer who was encouraged by John's apparent potential for success, found him a job as a bookkeeper in an automobile dealership and a cheap hotel room in a small town 200 miles from his former home.

But 6 months after being released on parole, John was returned to prison for alleged embezzlement from his employer.

The parole violation report stated that the embezzled money was used to rent a home so that John could move his family the 200 miles to the community of his parole. The parole officer believed John impulsively "borrowed" the money for fear of losing his family. Unfortunately, John was shy and made no friends in the new community. Except for church attendance on Sunday, he remained alone in a rented room when he was not working. His wife and children visited him on two weekends after his release, but could not afford to stay in a motel more often, because they were saving money for the move. He had been released with $100 and a bus ticket. His job paid him $60 a week. He had hoped to give private piano lessons but found that few people wanted to come to a stranger for piano lessons in a small town. He failed to ask for help from his parole officer, employer, or minister. His parole officer saw him twice during the 6 months prior to his violation and return to prison. John's written reports were received by the parole officer on time each month.

John was not a typical offender. He came from a rather affluent family and had a good education and special skills. Nevertheless, his failure demonstrates why many offenders fail who lack a high school education or a vocation or an intact family. John was unprepared to cope with the loneliness, the need for quick successs, and the desire to make up for lost time immediately. What steps could have been taken to prevent his recidivism? Would he have succeeded on probation, where he might have remained at his job and lived with his family? Could he have saved enough money on work release to move his family to the community of parole before his release? Would he have sought advice if new friendships had been established? Could his parole officer have helped him deal with these problems? These questions are asked frequently by parole boards, prison counselors, and correctional administrators, who wonder how to deal with the 25 to 50 percent of released men and women who return to prison.

GUILTY! NOW WHAT?

The Question

What to do with men or women who do not behave according to the values of the majority has been a question since the beginning of group living. Some practices that have been used to discourage unacceptable behavior include public humiliation, fines, restitution, imprisonment, deportation, torture, dismemberment, corporal punishment, and capital punishment. The Babylonian code of monarch Hammurabi in 1700 B.C. prescribed "an eye for an eye and a tooth for a tooth." It was interpreted to mean that if anyone stole a loaf of bread with the right hand, the hand should be cut off; anyone who killed another should be put to death. As late as the sixteenth century A.D. a murderer who had killed with the right hand had the hand burned off with a red-hot iron, the flesh of the arm torn in six different places with pincers, the arm quartered and disconnected from the shoulder. Then, as a gesture of mercy, the criminal was killed.[1]

A society's form of response to deviation by an individual is a social creation. Various rationalizations have been offered to justify the forms of response within the criminal justice system. Historically, punishing the transgressor has been the most popular reaction. Punishment is the application of an unpleasantness or an evil to a convicted offender by an authority, as conferred through laws defining the offense committed.[2] Many reasons have been given to justify the punishment of some human beings by others. Even today, with ample legal authority, Supreme Court protection, and some emphasis on rehabilitation, representatives of the criminal justice system are often asked to explain why it is necessary to punish the offender.

Retribution

Hammurabi's code was an attempt to establish *retribution,* which implied that when an offense was committed the perpetrator deserved punishment, the natural or artificial consequences of the offense.[3]

Since the time of Italian criminologist Cesare Beccaria, retribution has been viewed as an effort "to make the punishment as analogous as possible to the nature of the crime."[4] A modern definition might say retribution creates a proportionate relationship between the offense and punishment or revenge. Retribution functions as a form of social barometer, reflecting the communal need to prohibit certain types of conduct. It is a natural human reaction. People who get hurt, hurt back, especially if the offense produces an emotional reaction from the public, as occurs after a mass murder or a rape. In retributive punishment, society seeks to "get even" with the offender for breaking the law.

---

[1]Herbert G. Callison, *Guilty! Now What?* Honors thesis, Parsons College, Fairfield, Iowa, 1960, p. 2.

[2]Edwin H. Sutherland and Donald R. Cressey, *Criminology,* J. B. Lippincott Company, New York, 1970, p. 4.

[3]Antony Flew, "Definition of Punishment," *Contemporary Punishment,* Rudolph J. Gerber and Patrick C. McAnany (eds.), University of Notre Dame Press, Notre Dame, Ind., 1972, pp. 32–33.

[4]A. C. Ewing, *The Morality of Punishment,* Kegan Paul, London, 1929, p. 13.

Deterrence

A second justification for punishment of the offender is *deterrence,* the restraint which fear of punishment puts on those likely to commit crime.[5] General deterrence may be defined as the preventive effect which punishment has on potential offenders. Special or individual deterrence aims to prevent the actual offender from relapsing into crime.

Criminal legislation is enacted in order to denounce acts which society abhors. Punishment is the sanction imposed on a wrongdoer in order to threaten others who may be thinking of committing the same act. Persons who were punished for their crimes, often with death, served as a symbol for the carrying out of justice. Thus, in the Middle Ages, the offender was put to death in public. English legal authority Sir Leon Radzinowicz estimates there were probably fifty crimes punishable by death in the nineteenth century, including poaching on royal land, theft, and certain religious offenses. These crimes, when added to seven groups of offender classes, totaled about 350 possible capital offenses.[6]

Social Defense or Incapacitation

A final justification for the punishment of an offender is to protect society. Called *social defense,* this view holds that, as a danger to society, the offender must be punished. Social defense argues that the offender's past criminal behavior is a prediction of future criminal acts which can be averted only by punishment.[7] Social defense recognizes the incapacitating function of imprisonment.

Although receiving little attention from criminologists, banishment was practiced even before the advent of Christianity in order to make a person incapable of transgressing. Later forms of banishment included sentencing offenders to terms of involuntary military servitude to fight battles for the ruling government, or to exile. Both Australia and America received some of their original immigrants from English courts.

Imprisonment is the current form of incapacitation or banishment. The justification of social defense is not concerned about preventing others from committing crimes in the future but only with protecting society from a proven dangerous person. Unfortunately, there are some dangerous offenders who do require quarantine to prevent the repetition of crime.

Reparation

Another reaction often considered by the court is based on the idea of *reparation.* Although it is a penalty often given as part of a sentence by a judge,

---

[5]Rudolph J. Gerber and Patrick C. McAnany (eds.) *Contemporary Punishment,* University of Notre Dame Press, Notre Dame, Ind., 1972, p. 93.

[6]Robert G. Caldwell, *Criminology,* Ronald Press Company, New York, 1965, p. 443.

[7]Marc Ancel, "New Social Defense," *Contemporary Punishment,* op. cit., p. 132.

reparation is not necessarily considered punishment by either the court or the public. It requires the offender to make amends by paying compensation to the victim or to society for the harm resulting from a criminal offense. The offender may return to the rightful owner what has been taken away or provide the equivalent in money or service. In community-oriented reparation, the community substitutes for the victim and receives compensation in the form of a fine or service. Compensating for social harm is supposed to provide healing for the criminal as well as repay the victim or the community for criminal actions.

Reparation came before incapacitation.[8] An early example is written in the "Laws of Alfred" from ninth-century England, which included a schedule of payments from criminal to victim: "For a wound in the head if both bones are pierced, 30 shillings shall be given to the injured man. If the outer bone is pierced 15 shillings shall be given."[9]

Rehabilitation

Punishment has not been society's only response to the offender. An alternative has been rehabilitation—the use of therapy, education, and training for managing prisoners. The hope is that rehabilitation will change their values and problem-solving abilities so that they will conform to the dictates of society (i.e., act within the accepted behavioral framework).

Rehabilitation is based on the belief that offenses are the result of emotional problems, social injury, or wrong learning. To reform offenders society must assist them to overcome a lack of education or job skills, neurosis or psychosis, or ineffective methods of solving problems. Rehabilitation is endorsed by professional behaviorists—psychiatrists, psychologists, and social workers—who believe that people can change. Instead of providing negative reinforcement, as in punishment, rehabilitation proposes that an offender can leave the criminal justice system a better person than when he or she entered.

CURRENT SENTENCING PRACTICES

Overview

One does not need a Gallup poll to conclude that the public has become concerned about crime. There is a general belief, and subsequent frustration, that despite all our social experimentation, crime—and particularly violent crime—continues to rise. Unfortunately, this belief is verified by statistical information. The most recent publication of *Uniform Crime Reports* indicated

---

[8]Clemens Bartollas, *Introduction to Corrections,* Harper & Row, Publishers, Incorporated, New York, 1981, p. 87.

[9]David C. Anderson, "A Judge Explores the Gap Between Theory and Practice," *Corrections Magazine,* vol. 6, no. 6, December 1980, p. 30.

that an estimated 13,295,339 offenses occurred throughout the United States in 1980, an increase of 6.9 percent per 100,000 inhabitants over 1979, a 12 percent increase over 1976, and a 41.7 percent increase over 1971.[10] Many people also think the costs of attacking the causes of crime and caring for lawbreakers are far too high.

In response to public concern, the concepts of retribution, deterrence, and incapacitation are popular in the legislative halls and legislatures have begun to debate the value of determinate and indeterminate sentences and reactions to the violent and nonviolent criminal.

Determinate versus Indeterminate Sentencing

One debate that has developed in the legislatures centers on the policies prescribing sentencing guidelines. The difference of opinion followed the realization that recidivism rates had not changed significantly in the 20 years since the 1970s, when rehabilitation programs were instituted in many prisons. Writers such as David Fogel and Alan M. Dershowitz, who endorse determinate sentencing, say that as long as prisons do not rehabilitate, criminals should be sentenced to humane prisons for definite periods of time, abandoning rehabilitation efforts except for programs that are small and entirely voluntary on the part of the offender. Other critics of the indeterminate sentence charge that inmates suffer anxiety from the uncertainty of their release date and that participation in rehabilitation programs is less effective because of the nonvoluntary involvement of the inmate ("to earn a parole").[11]

Andrew Von Hirsch, in *Doing Justice,* a report for the Committee for the Study of Incarceration, states that "severity of punishment should be commensurate with the seriousness of the wrong."[12] These penologists would abolish the entire structure of indeterminate sentencing, such as a 1-to-10-year sentence requiring the felon to be under sentence for the minimum time but leaving almost unlimited discretion to correctional and parole authorities for the maximum term.[13]

As a substitute, these writers would establish a legal code requiring the judge to impose a definite or determinate sentence. *Flat-time, mandatory,* and *presumptive* sentences are the forms of determinate sentencing proposed to replace indeterminate sentencing. A flat-time sentence of 3 years in prison means that the offender will serve no more and no less than 3 years. The judge may still choose between probation and imprisonment. A mandatory sentence specifies a certain required number of years of incarceration for a specific crime,

---

[10]*Crime in the United States,* U.S. Government Printing Office, Washington, D.C., September 1981, p. 38.

[11]Lynne Goodstein, "Psychological Effects of the Predictability of Prison Release," *Criminology,* vol. 18, no. 3, November 1980, pp. 364–365.

[12]Andrew Von Hirsch, *Doing Justice: The Choice of Punishments,* Hill and Wang, Inc., New York, 1976, p. 66.

[13]Michael S. Serrill, "Determinate Sentencing: The History, the Theory, the Debate," *Corrections Magazine,* vol. 3, no. 3, September 1977, p. 3.

such as 6 to 20 years for armed robbery. In presumptive sentencing, a judge is required to impose a selected sentence but is allowed to vary from that sentence where there are aggravating or mitigating circumstances.[14]

The determinate sentence would prevent sentencing practices like those found in a survey conducted by the *National Law Journal* and released in February 1981. This study revealed that prison time served for forcible rape varied from an average of 14 months in Alaska and Nevada to 119 months in Arkansas, 109 months in North Carolina, and 96 months in Missouri.[15]

A Curb on Discretion

Historical evidence has indicated a tradition of adherence to rule by law rather than rule by persons in the United States. Yet after conviction, nearly arbitrary and largely unsupervised discretion prevails. Guiding criteria are absent from the judge's sentencing; discretion is almost unfettered for the correctional administrator concerning prison conditions and disciplinary sanctions, and few barriers prevent the parole board from granting and revoking release at will.[16]

The general aim of those favoring determinate sentencing is to abolish or at least control discretion—the discretion of prosecutors to choose charges and bargain for pleas, the discretion of judges to impose any sentence within a broad range of time, the discretion of prison administrators to decide what kind of treatment is needed to make a prisoner law-abiding, the discretion of parole boards to release or not release prisoners without having to justify their decisions or make them consistent.[17]

Objections to Determinate Sentencing

Persons opposed to the determinate sentence believe there is no evidence that a new system would be better than the old. Rhode Island's John Moran and New York's Frank Hall predicted there would be a sizable increase in prison populations. Other critics, such as Franklin E. Zimring, believe it is impossible "to define in advance those elements of an offense that should be considered in fixing a criminal sentence."[18] When determinate sentencing is adopted, discretion is not being eliminated but merely transferred to the legislature.

Anthony P. Travisono, Executive Director of the American Correctional Association, believes such a system of sentencing should go no farther than it does in those states that have already legislated such changes. He suggests a 5-year moratorium in order to see what the results of determinate sentencing are.[19]

[14]Bartollas, op. cit., pp. 94–95.

[15]Lee Strobel, "Illinois: It's 'Short-Time' State for Felons," *Chicago Tribune,* Feb. 15, 1981.

[16]Gordon Hawkins, *The Prisoner: Policy and Practice,* University of Chicago Press, Chicago, 1976, p. 133.

[17]Serrill, "Determinate Sentencing," op. cit., p. 3.

[18]Bartollas, op. cit., p. 95.

[19]Edgar May, "Prison Officials Fear Flat Time Is More Time," *Corrections Magazine,* vol. 3, no. 3, New York, September 1977, p. 44.

Andrew Von Hirsch's suggestion of "commensurate deserts" has been criticized by psychiatrist Karl Menninger, author of *The Crime of Punishment,* who asks, "Why does the primitive obsession of punishment fill everyone's mind and freeze out consideration of constructive measures for social safety? Is it too much to expect that we might soon transcend the age-old evils of retaliation, intimidation, and dehumanizing restriction?"[20] The determinate sentence is a harsher system than the indeterminate sentence. It is a punitive reaction to crime, admitting the failure of rehabilitation.

This debate is not new to the American criminal justice system. Before the American Revolution, the repressive nature of punishment—particularly the frequency with which capital punishment was applied—brought strong protest from penological reformers such as the Italian Cesare Beccaria. As a result, the physical punishment adopted from the British legal system was reduced by state codes. American judges were restricted to determining guilt or innocence. Legal sanctions were applied uniformly without consideration of aggravating or mitigating factors. Within 10 years the widespread adoption of determinate sentences resulted in overpopulated prisons. By 1808 Newgate Penitentiary in New York and the prisons in Ohio were granting pardons to make room for newcomers.

Softening the Effects

Soon legislators began to modify the law to provide a systematic method to ameliorate determinate and fixed sentences. New York passed a "good-time" law in 1817 reducing prisoners' sentences as a reward for good behavior while incarcerated. By the end of the nineteenth century, most states had followed New York's example. American prison reformers like Zebulon Brockway began pushing for indeterminate sentences. In 1876 the first indeterminate sentence law was passed by the New York legislature. By 1922 thirty-seven states had followed the New York lead, enacting some form of indeterminate sentencing law. Most states established minimum and maximum sentences, and most added parole and good-time laws, permitting great discretion on the part of judges and correctional authorities.

Norwood Law

Not all state legislators were happy with indeterminate sentencing after its widespread enactment. By 1921 correctional conservatives in Ohio were criticizing the wide discretions allowed judges and other criminal justice officials. As a result, the Norwood Law, an experiment with fixed sentencing, was passed on March 31, 1921. During the 10 years the law was in effect, the prison population

---

[20]Karl Menninger, "Doing Justice: The Choice of Punishments," *Report of the Committee for the Study of Incarceration, Book Review,* 1977, p. 16.

in Ohio rose from 3686 to 9384 inmates. In April 1931, the Ohio legislature passed the Ackerman bill, which in effect repealed the Norwood Law.[21] By 1976 all states had adopted the indeterminate approach.

Determinate Sentencing Laws in 1980

After more than 40 years, during which judicial sentencing guidelines were dominated by indeterminate sentencing laws, critics again successfully demanded new legislation restricting human discretion over felons' terms within the criminal justice system. Maine, California, and Indiana had passed fixed or determinate sentencing laws by December 1977. Illinois and Arizona were added to the list in 1978 and Colorado in 1979 (see Table 1.1). Minnesota had passed two fixed-sentencing laws, but differences between them could not be reconciled.[22] The United States Congress proposed a bill that would establish determinate sentences as well as eliminate federal parole procedures. By January 1980, twenty-three states had substantial legislative action on fixed-sentencing proposals. Eighteen of those states had passed laws requiring minimum prison terms for specified crimes.[23]

The California Law

The California state legislature abolished its indeterminate sentencing laws by stating:

[21]*Let the Punishment Fit the Crime,* Contact, Inc., Lincoln, Nebr., May 1978, p. 1.
[22]Stephen Gettinger, "Fixed Sentencing Becomes Law In Three States; Other Legislatures Wary," *Corrections Magazine,* vol. 3, no. 3, September 1977, p. 16.
[23]*Criminal Justice Newsletter,* vol. 11, no. 2, Jan. 21, 1980, p. 3.

TABLE 1.1
STATES WITH DETERMINATE SENTENCING LAWS

State	Effective Date	Presumptive Sentence	Judge's Discretion	Good-Time Provisions	Parole
Maine	5-1-76	Upper limit only	Broad	⅓ of sentence	None
California	7-1-77	Moderate term	Narrow	⅓ of sentence	After term
Indiana	10-1-77	High term	Broad	½ of sentence	After term
Illinois	2-1-78	High range (no presumptive sentence)	Broad	½ of sentence	After term
Arizona	10-1-78	Moderate term	Moderate	None	Eligibility after ½ of term
Colorado	7-1-79	Moderate term	Narrow	½ of sentence	After term

Source: David Brewer, Gerald E. Beckett, and Norman Holt, "Determinate Sentencing in California: the First Year's Experience," *Journal of Research in Crime and Delinquency,* vol. 18, no. 2, July 1981, p. 202.

The legislature finds and declares that the purpose of imprisonment for crime is punishment. The purpose is best served by terms proportionate to the seriousness of the offense with provision for uniformity in the sentences of offenders committing the same offense under similar circumstances.

California adopted six sentencing categories. Within four categories, primarily property offenses, three sentencing prerogatives are available; for example, a 2-, 3-, or 4-year sentence for robbery.

Offenders found guilty under the two remaining categories are treated more harshly. Murder preceded by torture, and kidnapping in which the victim is harmed require a life sentence without possibility of parole. Convictions for kidnap/murder demand a death sentence. The judge must choose the middle term unless there are mitigating or aggravating circumstances, in which case either the minimum or maximum sentence is applied. In the case of multiple aggravating circumstances—previous records, violent crimes, or "excessive taking"—up to 10 years can be added to the sentence.

The California determinate sentencing law further restricted judicial discretion by declaring seven crimes or conditions for which probation may not be granted except in unusual cases. These include:

1 Crimes in which persons were unlawfully armed.
2 Attempting to use a deadly weapon other than a firearm on a human being.
3 Willfully inflicting great bodily injury or torture.
4 At least one previous conviction of a most serious felony.
5 Two previous convictions of any offense.
6 Previous conviction under the conditions listed in 1 through 5.
7 Crimes involving a public official or peace officer convicted of accepting or giving any bribe, embezzling public money, or extorting.

California's determinate sentencing law does not allow for early release except through accumulation of good time. Inmates can earn 4 months' good time for every 8 months served. At least one of these good-time months is granted for participation in prison programs. The state's parole board was abolished, but all prisoners, after serving their flat sentences, automatically serve 1 year on parole.[24]

The Indiana Law

Indiana, by contrast, established determinate sentences while continuing to allow substantial range for judicial discretion. For example, the sentence for noncapital murder is 40 years, with up to 20 additional years for aggravating circumstances or 10 years less for mitigating circumstances. For Class B crimes—rape, robbery with injury, minor narcotics dealing—sentences can be 10 years plus 10 years or minus 4 years; for Class C crimes—armed robbery,

---

[24]Michael S. Serrill, "California Turning to Fixed Sentences," *Corrections Magazine*, vol. 2, no. 6, December 1976, p. 55.

forgery, drug possession—5 years plus or minus 3 years. Indiana also retained good-time laws which permit inmates to earn back as much as half their sentence by good behavior.[25]

Rationale for Determinate Sentencing

According to Professor Henry R. Glick, the new mandatory sentencing policies represent a loss of confidence in the rehabilitative model of sentencing and a renewed public endorsement of retribution and deterrence. Glick does not believe these changes in sentencing policy alter the underlying purpose of the criminal justice system. Despite the moral tone of rehabilitation that has been endorsed by correctional reformers since the turn of the century, punishment has been the function of American jails and prisons. The loss of confidence in rehabilitation and the radicalism of American prisoners of the late 1960s and 1970s have only motivated a swing back to punishment.[26]

Unfortunately, the proof of the worth of determinate sentencing may be lost because of the vast difference between the states. In the constraints on judges regarding the decision whether or not to incarcerate, in the specificity of aggravating and mitigating factors, in the institutional use of good time, and in the range of possible penalties, there is a great variation. In addition, as sociology professors David Greenburg and Drew Humphries pointed out, the sentencing-reform legislation attempting to decrease the discretion allowed judges and correctional authorities has fallen short of its intended goals for the following reasons: (1) Essential features of criminal codes remain unchanged, (2) some legislation retains rehabilitative and predictive criteria, (3) prosecutors and judges keep substantial discretion under most of the new laws, and (4) the new legislation increases rather than reduces sentence lengths.[27]

Results

One thing is clear—the prediction that prisons would fill up has proved to be correct. In the 9 months prior to April 1, 1981, Illinois was forced to release 3878 prisoners—nearly one-third of the total number incarcerated in Illinois prisons—before they completed their sentences, in order to accommodate additional prisoners under the state's determinate sentencing law.[28] In New York, mandatory sentences for drug-related offenses have been influential in increasing the prison census from 14,387 to 20,400 since 1975. Florida's tough "felony-with-a-gun" law helped to create a sentencing mind-set which has

---

[25]Gettinger, op. cit., p. 30.

[26]Henry R. Glick, "Mandatory Sentencing: The Politics of the New Criminal Justice," *Federal Probation*, Vol. 43, no. 1, Administrative Office of the United States Courts, Washington, D.C., March 1979, p. 6.

[27]David F. Greenburg and Drew Humphries, "The Cooptation of Fixed Sentencing Reform," *Crime and Delinquency*, vol. 26, no. 2, April 1980, pp. 219–220.

[28]Michael Sneed and Lynn Emmerman, "Early Release Plan is in Chaos, Parole Official Says," *Chicago Tribune*, Apr. 6, 1981, p. 1.

resulted in an increase in its prison population from 11,400 in 1975 to 21,000 in 1980.[29] These increases prompted prison journal editor Caleb Foote to comment, "To eliminate discretionary release without doing anything significant about discretionary intake is likely to produce more injustice, not less."[30]

Other fears did not become realities. In California, contrary to expectations, despite a large increase in number of commitments, the overall length of terms was somewhat moderated. After the first year, data showed most offenders committed to prison received the middle base-term. Only 3.2 percent received additions to the base sentence for a prior prison term. Only 20 percent of the parole violators recommitted from parole with a new term received enhancements. The mean length of terms for prisoners newly received during 1977–1978 was 41.4 months, compared to a mean of 40 months served by men paroled for the first time between 1972 and 1976.[31]

Violent versus Nonviolent Offenders

With the loss of confidence in rehabilitation and the general belief that criminals should not be blatantly eliminated, the controversy has shifted to divergent views about the handling of violent and nonviolent offenders. Violent offenders should be dealt with harshly—thus the cry for capital punishment, determinate sentences, and less discretion for judicial and correctional authorities. At the same time, there is emphasis on avoiding harsh treatment of nonviolent offenders. Part of this emphasis has resulted from the fear of overcrowding prisons, which in turn produces conditions for riots and encourages court decisions ordering correctional administrators to lower prison populations. This controversy has been fueled by the persistent increase in violent crime (murder, assault, and rape). The Federal Bureau of Investigation's (FBI's) Index for 1980 indicated a 13 percent increase in violent crimes.[32]

Along with the increase in violent crimes and more determinate sentences, there has been the inflationary cost of housing criminals. Consequently, correctional program directors such as William Rentschler of the John Howard Association advocate the use of a wide range of less expensive alternatives to incarceration for nonviolent offenders, who comprise 40 to 70 percent of the prison population.[33]

Some of this emphasis is the result of a genuine concern for the nonviolent,

[29]William G. Nagel, "Prisonia: America's Growing Megalopolis," *Church and Society,* vol. 70, no. 3, March/April 1980, p. 11.

[30]Frederick Hussey, "Just Deserts and Determinate Sentencing: Impact on the Rehabilitative Ideal," *The Prison Journal,* vol. 59, no. 2, Autumn/Winter 1979, pp. 36–47.

[31]David Brewer, Gerald E. Beckett, and Norman Holt, "Determinate Sentencing in California: The First Year's Experience," *Journal of Research in Crime and Delinquency,* vol. 18, no. 2, July 1981, pp. 217, 225, and 227.

[32]Michael Hirsley, "Violent Crime Up: Court System Hit," *Chicago Tribune,* Apr. 1, 1981, sec. 1, p. 5.

[33]William H. Rentschler, "Reagan Has a Chance to Restructure Our Prisons," *Chicago Tribune,* Dec. 27, 1980.

apparently recoverable offenders. For them, correctional administrators, legislators, and academicians endorse a less expensive form of supervision—commonly called community-based corrections. However, the rehabilitation advocated for the nonviolent offender who serves his or her sentence in the community is a variation from the rehabilitation advocated for confined prisoners 20 years ago. Nonviolent offenders who are assigned to a community-based correctional program receive assistance in job hunting, money saving, or friend finding, rather than therapy for psychological ills or group counseling to overcome some social inadequacy.

THE TASK OF CORRECTIONS

The Criminal Justice System

The criminal justice system is America's method of coping with crime. The police and the courts are the segments of the system that attempt to apprehend and convict the offender, who, after sentence has been pronounced, becomes the responsibility of the corrections segment of the system. The deviant individual has legally become an offender, and all other participants in the system are released from direct responsibility. Corrections is that part of society's social control mechanism which attempts to rehabilitate offenders or neutralize their deviant behavior. It functions with legal authority only after a criminal court has determined an adult to be guilty of a violation of the law.[34]

Conceptually and practically, administration of the criminal's sentence generally follows two models simultaneously: punishment and rehabilitation. The criminal sentence is administered within a very general legal framework. Whether the sentence is considered punitive or rehabilitative, legal policy serves only as a guideline for its administration. Actual application of legal policy differs considerably from one jurisdiction to another, with differences in correctional practices related to the values regarding crime, criminals, and punishment held by respective jurisdictions.[35] In the United States the emphasis on rehabilitation has been the most significant development within the criminal justice system in the last 50 years. The use of probation and parole, the development of other community-based programs, and the establishment of rehabilitation programs within prisions all symbolize what Francis Allen has called the "rehabilitative ideal" in his often quoted 1959 essay.[36]

[34]Vernon Fox, *Introduction to Corrections,* Prentice-Hall, Inc., Englewood Cliffs, N.J., 1977, p. 1.

[35]Richard Quinney, *The Social Reality of Crime,* Little, Brown and Company, Boston, 1969, p. 17.

[36]Francis Allen, "Criminal Justice, Legal Values, and the Rehabilitative Ideal," *Journal of Criminal Law, Criminology, and Police Science,* vol. 50, no. 3, September/October 1959, pp. 226–232.

The Task Stated

The correctional apparatus is the part of the criminal justice system least known and understood by law-abiding citizens. This lack of familiarity is unfortunate, because the successful functioning of society is largely dependent on appropriate disposition of the criminal sentence. After all, the task of corrections is to minimize the frequency with which law violations are committed by persons who have prior records of criminality (i.e., to prevent the offender from committing another offense).

Punishment or Rehabilitation

Today corrections continues to apply methods of both rehabilitation and punishment, reflecting what James V. Bennett, former director of the Federal Bureau of Prisons, wrote in 1948:

> Even our modern prison system is proceeding on a rather uncertain course because its administration is necessarily a series of compromises. On the one hand, prisons are expected to punish; on the other, they are supposed to reform. They are expected to discipline rigorously at the same time that they teach self-reliance. They are built to be operated like vast impersonal machines, yet they are expected to fit men to live normal community lives. . . . And so the whole paradoxical scheme continues because our ideals and our views regarding the function of correctional institutions in our society are confused, fuzzy, and nebulous.[37]

Even if the offender is sentenced as punishment, correctional administrators cannot ignore the time when he or she is released from their control. Correctional administrators as well as legislators and the general public must believe that punishment alone is a short-sighted policy. Even when their part of the job is well done, society is protected only for the time the offender is under control of the criminal justice system. For long-range prevention of crime, it is necessary to have programs which focus on the reintegration of all offenders back into society, without their resorting to criminal behavior in the future.

Punishment means the inflicting of pain or suffering by one party on another as a reaction to an act of the recipient. It is vengeance on behalf of the "good" against the "bad."

Rehabilitation may also be painful, but it does not exact vengeance. The difference is significant, because during the rehabilitation process the person helping and the person being helped are working together to bring about a beneficial change, while in a punishment situation a dominance-submission relationship exists, even though the dominant party may be benevolent.[38]

---

[37]Negley K. Teeters, "The Alpha and Omega of the Prison," *Presidio,* vol. 37, no. 2, Iowa State Penitentiary, Fort Madison, May/June 1970, p. 10.

[38]F. Lowell Bixby, "Are We Applying What We Know?" *Federal Probation,* vol. 28, no. 1, Administrative Office of the United States Courts, Washington, D.C., March 1964, p. 16.

Corrections Tools

The tools employed in corrections consist of imprisonment and community-based corrections, including probation and parole. Imprisonment is, of course, incarceration in a penal institution. Theoretically, a penal institution is the locale of correction only for that period of time necessary for the protection of the community from offenders and the offenders from themselves, or for their rehabilitation.

Probation, parole, and community-based programs all involve a degree of supervised liberty in the community. Probation is used prior to incarceration, and is considered an alternative to imprisonment. Parole is granted to a prisoner and is applied as part of the prison term. Other correctional programs, including other community-based corrections programs, lie somewhere along this continuum. All forms of community-based corrections involve a threat of secure incarceration by a summary proceeding, far short of trial, for violation of the conditions of liberty. Each summary proceeding is preceded by an alleged violation of stated rules. The summary proceeding itself is a meeting during which a decision is made by a board or person (parole board, prison classification committee, or warden) whether or not to revoke privileges.

THE ALTERNATIVES FOR CORRECTIONS

Closed Environment

There are two environments which can be selected for the offender during his or her time served under sentence by the court. One is a restrictive, self-contained unit of no more than 64 acres (the largest being Stateville Prison in Illinois), where efforts by correctional officials are directed toward preventing inmates from escape and providing minimally humane surroundings.

Open Environment

A second environment is open, focusing on the free community as a structural model. The open environment encourages offenders to try to live as they would if they were free. All activities are focused on the community. Activities within the institution are patterned after those in the community. People from the outside community are invited to take part in the prisoners' daily routine. Inmates are expected to participate in various supervised programs conducted in the community outside the correctional institution. Before complete release, each offender must demonstrate an ability to manage his or her own behavior without direct supervision but under a monitoring agreement.

Future Choices

In the future the choice will remain between these alternatives: imprisonment or community-focused corrections. If the rise in the number of crimes continues and the trend toward less discretionary, more determinate sentencing continues, the public, legislators, and correctional administrators have two choices: They must expand the number of prison cells through construction of new prisons, as Senator Robert Dole's Criminal Justice Construction Reform Act proposes,[39] or they must expand community-focused corrections. The latter choice includes work release, prerelease centers, restitution, and noncustodial placement. The states of Minnesota, Iowa, and Kansas are attempting such corrections through state-subsidized, locally based correctional programs.

An Eminent Decision

The decision whether to build more prisons or expand community-based corrections must be made soon. The latest population census of prisons indicated that overcrowding is a national problem. The figures for January 1, 1981, revealed 320,583 offenders in United States prisons, an increase of 4 percent since January 1, 1980, and 42 percent since January 1, 1975. The increase in the year 1980–1981 took place despite the United States Bureau of Prisons' reduction of its prison population by 15 percent.[40] Six southern states—Alabama, Georgia, Louisiana, Maryland, Mississippi, and Tennessee— were under court order to lower their prison populations at that time.[41] Then, on October 4, 1981, the Bureau of Justice Statistics reported that state and federal prison populations swelled by more than 20,000 in the first 6 months of the year, more than were added in all 1980. This "unprecedented growth rate" left the national prison population at a record 349,118 on June 30, 1981.[42]

The Practicalities of Rehabilitation

The traditional rehabilitation program of the past (counseling, academic education, vocational training, and/or religion) did not inevitably prepare inmates to live in the free community successfully. They may have learned to control their emotions better or to resolve problems more reasonably, but as long as they lived in a closed institution their only experience in temper control or problem resolution occurred within the institution. Such experiences do not inevitably resemble those in the free community. Seeking a job in prison, where work is mandatory and work assignments are frequently decided by a counselor or a

---

[39]"State Corrections Directors Plead for Federal Aid to Build Prisons," *Criminal Justice Newsletter*, vol. 12, no. 11, May 26, 1981, p. 1.

[40]Kevin Krajick, "Annual Prison Population Survey: The Boom Resumes," *Corrections Magazine*, Vol: 7, no. 2, April 1981, p. 16.

[41]"How to Solve U.S. Prison Overcrowding," *Criminal Justice Newsletter*, vol. 12, no. 8, Apr. 13, 1981, p. 6.

[42]"Population of Prisons Hits Peak," *The Wichita (Kansas) Eagle-Beacon*, Oct. 5, 1981.

classification committee, is not the same as seeking employment competitively in a downtown metropolitan area. Factors such as the cost of meals, means of transportation, and proper dress must be considered. "Tools" such as a high school diploma or skill at operating a machine lathe can be acquired during incarceration in a closed institution. However, work schedules and academic class schedules are designed to fit into institutional routines. Sometimes this means that inmates work only 6 hours a day, with time off for school or counseling, or attend classes using outdated books and inmate tutors. Such "rehabilitation" cannot be expected to prepare them for successful living in the free community.

COMMUNITY-FOCUSED CORRECTIONS

Past Experience

The National Advisory Commission on Criminal Justice Standards and Goals stated: "The prison, the reformatory, and the jail have achieved only a shocking record of failure."[43] The most exhaustive review of research (231 separate studies) by Lipton, Martinson, and Wilks resulted in Robert Martinson's now famous conclusion in 1974: "With few and isolated exceptions, the rehabilitative efforts that have been reported so far have had no appreciable effect on recidivism."[44] Another review of studies noted:

> It is difficult to escape the conclusion that the act of incarcerating a person at all will impair whatever potential he has for a crime-free future adjustment, and that regardless of which "treatments" are administered while he is in prison, the longer he is kept there, the more deteriorated and recidivistic he will become.[45]

Over one-third (perhaps two-thirds) of those released from prisons and jails throughout the country commit additional offenses.

Despite these discouragements, some of these same persons offer more positive opinions (e.g., Robert Martinson hypothesizes that the prison experience or the kind of prison in which an offender is confined may have less to do with whether he or she commits other offenses after release than does interruption of normal occupational progress).[46] Prisons produce damage by interfering with the offender's life cycle—high school, college, marriage, first

---

[43]Bob Gross, "Why Imprisonment? Some Logical Considerations," *Alternatives to Prisons: Issues and Options,* Rodger O. Darnell, John F. Else, and R. Dean Wright (eds.), School of Social Work, Iowa City, Iowa, 1979, p. 37.

[44]Brewer, Beckett, and Holt, op. cit., p. 201.

[45]Lucien Zamorski, "Institutional Corrections: the State of the Art," *Alternatives to Prisons: Issues and Options,* Rodger O. Darnell, John F. Else, and R. Dean Wright (eds.), School of Social Work, Iowa City, Iowa, 1979, p. 55.

[46]Robert Martinson, "The Paradox of Prison Reform: The Dangerous Myth," *The New Republic,* vol. 166, no. 14, Apr. 1, 1972, p. 25.

job, bank account, next job, and so forth—at a time when the damage is most harmful (perhaps irreparable), between the ages of 15 and 25.

The same research findings also indicate that many offenders do not commit additional offenses no matter what kind of treatment they receive and that some offenders do commit additional offenses no matter what kind of treatment they receive. Those in between, those who do not *want* to commit more crime but do, may be harmed by processing them farther into the formal criminal justice system.

Redirecting the Offender

Today many correctional administrators realize offenders are not machines to be dealt with, as in physics or mathematics, or bad people who need only to be punished. These correctional personnel are attempting to understand the crime and the criminal and to help offenders redirect their lives away from unacceptable behavior. Evidence of this can be seen in the increased use of furloughs, self-help groups, and prerelease programs.

These same correctional administrators must realize that the "rehabilitative ideal" *is* an ideal, and rehabilitation must be sought with that in mind. Yet the failure of correctional officials to achieve an ideal does not mean that some offenders cannot be helped to prevent the reoccurrence of criminal behavior. Their lives can be redirected through practical programs aimed at permitting them to acquire the vocational and social skills, knowledge, and confidence that will enable them to reach modest goals. If it is true that most criminals are not on welfare when their crimes are committed, that most of them possess average intelligence and aspire to become law-abiding citizens, then it may be true that nonviolent, property offenders' crimes may be the result of ambition, not of psychosis or a maladjusted social environment or an accident of birth. These offenders should have an opportunity to voluntarily redirect their lives. For them, an opportunity to learn to weld or to earn a high school diploma, to understand how to apply for employment, to feel comfortable in church, or to learn how to resolve social conflicts with friends and family is a more logical choice than locking them away from the community where they live.

By using the community as a model for correctional practices, the focus is placed on learning those skills necessary to live in the community, not to survive in prison. In community-based corrections the emphasis is focused on the community outside the walls rather than on the structured life within the prison or jail. In this context community-based corrections includes activities in prisons and jails as well as activities outside institutional walls.

Reintegrative Model

Partly out of despair with the ineffectiveness of institution-based corrections programs, partly out of humane considerations, and partly out of the notion that the best place to learn how to live in the normal world is the normal world itself, advocacy of reintegrating the offender into the free community has increased.[47] This statement by the National Commission on the Causes and Prevention of Violence was used to introduce what textbook author George F. Cole calls the *reintegrative model.*

The reintegrative model is based on the assumption that offenders will obey the law if they are involved through personal and social ties with the normal institutions of the community—family, church, and work place. Incarceration is used primarily for diagnosis or to protect the public from uncontrollable or dangerous persons. Offenders should be returned as soon as possible, if they leave at all, to the community, where they can learn to adjust under guidance to normal community life.

Under the influence of the reintegrative model, the National Advisory Commission on Criminal Justice Standards and Goals recommended that no new institutions be built for 10 years. Instead, it endorses small correctional facilities placed in the community, with minimum emphasis on security. Correctional personnel would be less concerned with surveillance and more with helping offenders get jobs, serving as their advocates in dealing with authority, and assisting them in establishing positive relations with family and friends.

To develop such programs, corrections must be returned to the local community for management and support. For example, reformers such as Robert Cushman, president of the American Justice Institute, and Robert Smith, deputy director of the National Institute of Corrections, agree with Director of Corrections of Buck County, Pennsylvania, Art Wallensten. He says, "The jail should not be a warehouse but a community services center."[48] It should have a full range of programs and services—pretrial release, diversion, work release, counseling, alcohol and other drug therapy, school, job placement, and community supervision. Cushman, Smith, and Wallensten believe that all offenders, even long-term offenders, should be held in their home community program if they are not dangerous or escape risks. Yet broad-based local corrections are difficult to find. Eighty percent of the nation's 3101 counties have fewer than 50,000 residents and lack the financial resources to accomplish this goal.[49]

CONCLUSION

In asking the question, "Guilty! Now What?," many correctional administrators balk at dealing with the offender according to old-time instructions written by men now dead who knew nothing about the life of the present offender or the ethics of the newer generation. These administrators believe that the same society that has failed to successfully socialize offenders must attempt to help them. These leaders seek constructive, intelligent, purposeful change rather

[47]George F. Cole, *The American System of Criminal Justice,* Duxbury Press, North Scituate, Mass., 1975, p. 102.

[48]John Blackmore, "Can the Counties Succeed Where the States Have Faltered?" *Corrections Magazine,* vol. 7, no. 2, April 1981, p. 28.

[49]Ibid., p. 22.

than the present confusing duality of rehabilitation and punishment. They say a civilized society such as ours, with our knowledge and our progress, does not need to be driven to retaliatory actions based on outdated theories and practices. They are convinced that the present game of tit for tat and blow for blow can end. They are convinced that in its place a program can be developed aimed at *redirection of the criminal to useful citizenship.*

Corrections is the segment of the criminal justice system which is given the responsibility of redirecting the offender toward useful citizenship. Corrections focusing on the community is the result of some innovative correctional administrators' efforts to develop a better way of preventing offenders from repeating their criminal behavior.

The use of community-focused corrections is dependent on the continuance of sufficient legal discretion to allow officials to help each offender become assimilated within the law-abiding segment of the community. Efforts to increase the latitude of correctional officials which expand offenders' options for learning how to live in the free community will enhance the possibility that they will not commit more crimes.

As the American Congress of Corrections so well stated in 1970, in Principle III of their "Declaration of Principles,"

> Correction and Punishment are the presently recognized methods of preventing and controlling crime and delinquency. The strengthening and expansion of correctional methods should generally be the accepted goal.[50]

EXERCISES

1 In your opinion, is John, whose story introduces this chapter, a criminal who would be eligible for community-based corrections programs? Give reasons for your answer.
2 Which justification for punishment do you believe most acceptable? Explain.
3 Is "rehabilitation" of offenders a myth or a possibility? Give reasons.
4 Describe some situations you believe occurred among early peoples which might have precipitated the need for established rules.
5 Describe the process you think takes place when "expected behavior" is determined by members of a society.
6 Do you believe most citizens are successful in conforming to ideal behavior? Give reasons.
7 Describe your opinion of "plea bargaining." Give reasons for your conclusion.
8 "A society's response to crime is a social phenomenon." Agree or disagree with this statement.
9 Critically analyze the Von Hirsch concept of "commensurate deserts." Develop your analysis carefully.
10 Do you think judges, prosecutors, and correctional officials have too much discretion? Give reasons.

---

[50]"Declaration of Principles by the American Congress of Corrections," *American Journal of Correction*, vol. 32, no. 6, November/December 1970, p. 32.

11 Which system of determinate sentencing—California's or Indiana's—do you consider more appropriate? Defend your answer.
12 In your opinion, is capital punishment justifiable? Give reasons.
13 Explain the relationship between the values regarding crime, criminals, and punishment in various jurisdictions and their effect on the punishment/rehabilitation duality.
14 Do you agree with the task of corrections? Why or why not?
15 What determines the form of social pressure applied to the individual deviator?

EXERCISE REFERENCES

Allen, Francis: "Criminal Justice, Legal Values, and the Rehabilitative Ideal," *Journal of Criminal Law, Criminology, and Police Science,* vol. 50, no. 3, September/October 1959, pp. 226–232.

Ancel, Marc: "New Social Defense," in Rudolph J. Gerber and Patrick D. McAnany (eds.), *Contemporary Punishment,* University of Notre Dame Press, Notre Dame, Ind., 1972, pp. 132–139.

Andenaes, Johannes: *Punishment and Deterrence,* University of Michigan Press, Ann Arbor, 1974.

Anderson, David C.: "A Judge Explores the Gap Between Theory and Practice," *Corrections Magazine,* vol. 6, no. 6, December 1980, pp. 27–31.

Bartollas, Clemens: *Introduction to Corrections,* Harper & Row, Publishers, Incorporated, New York, 1981, chap. 4.

Becker, Howard: *Through Values to Social Interpretation,* Duke University Press, Durham, N.C., 1950.

Bixby, F. Lowell: "Are We Applying What We Know?" *Federal Probation,* vol. 28, no. 1, Administrative Office of the United States Courts, Washington, D.C., March 1964, pp. 16–18.

Blackmore, John: "Can the Counties Succeed Where the States Have Faltered?" *Corrections Magazine,* vol. 7, no. 2, April 1981, pp. 21–23, 27–31, 39–41.

Brewer, David, Gerald E. Beckett, and Norman Holt: "Determinate Sentencing in California: The First Year's Experience," *Journal of Research in Crime and Delinquency,* vol. 18, no. 2, July 1981, pp. 201–231.

Caldwell, Robert G.: *Criminology,* Ronald Press Company, New York, 1965, part II.

Carlston, Kenneth S.: *Law and Structure of Social Action,* Stevens & Sons Limited, London; Columbia University Press, New York, 1956.

Chambliss, William J., and Robert B. Seidman: *Law, Order, and Power,* Addison-Wesley Publishing Company, Reading, Mass., 1971.

Clear, Todd R., John D. Hewitt, and Robert M. Regoli: "Discretion and the Determinate Sentence: Its Distribution, Control, and Effect on Time Served," *Crime and Delinquency,* vol. 24, no. 4, October 1978, pp. 428–445.

Cohen, Albert K.: *Deviance and Control,* Prentice-Hall, Inc., Englewood Cliffs, N.J., 1966.

Cole, George F.: *The American System of Criminal Justice,* Duxbury Press, North Scituate, Mass., 1975, pp. 402–403.

Contact, Inc.: *Let the Punishment Fit the Crime,* Lincoln, Nebr., May 1978.

Davis, F. James, Henry H. Foster, Jr., C. Ray Jeffrey, and E. Eugene Davis: *Society and the Law,* Free Press of Glencoe, New York, 1962.

DeSilva, Bruce: "The Retarded Offender: A Problem Without a Program," *Corrections Magazine,* vol. 6, no. 4, August 1980, pp. 25–33.

Dickinson, George E., and Alban L. Wheeler: "The Elderly in Prison," *Corrections Today,* vol. 42, no. 4, July/August 1980, p. 10.

Dinitz, Simon, and Walter C. Reckless (eds.): *Critical Issues in the Study of Crime,* Little, Brown and Company, Boston, 1968.

Dressler, David (ed.): *Readings in Criminology and Penology,* Columbia University Press, New York, 1964, pt. IV.

Ewing, Alfred C.: *The Morality of Punishment,* Kegan Paul, London, 1929.

Faris, Robert E. L.: *Social Disorganization,* Ronald Press Company, New York, 1948.

Flew, Antony: "Definition of Punishment," in Rudolph J. Gerber and Patrick D. McAnany (eds.), *Contemporary Punishment,* University of Notre Dame Press, Notre Dame, Ind., 1972, pp. 31–35.

Garabedian, Peter G.: "Challenges for Contemporary Corrections," *Federal Probation,* vol. 33, no. 1, Administrative Office of the United States Courts, Washington, D.C., March 1969, pp. 3–10.

Gerber, Rudolph J., and Patrick D. McAnany (eds.): *Contemporary Punishment,* University of Notre Dame Press, Notre Dame, Ind., 1972.

Gettinger, Stephen: "The Death Penalty is Back—and So Is the Debate," *Corrections Magazine,* vol. 5, no. 2, June 1979, pp. 70–79.

———: "Fixed Sentencing Becomes Law in Three States; Other Legislatures Wary," *Corrections Magazine,* vol. 3, no. 3, September 1977, pp. 16–42.

Gibbons, Don C.: "Crime and Punishment: A Study in Social Attitudes," *Social Forces,* vol. 47, no. 4, June 1969, pp. 391–397.

Glaser, Daniel: *Adult Crime and Social Policy,* Prentice-Hall, Inc., Englewood Cliffs, N.J., 1972.

Glick, Henry R.: "Mandatory Sentencing: the Politics of the New Criminal Justice," *Federal Probation,* vol. 43, no. 1, Administrative Office of the United States Courts, Washington, D.C., March 1979, pp. 3–9.

Goodstein, Lynne: "Psychological Effects of the Predictability of Prison Release," *Criminology,* vol. 18, no. 3, November 1980, pp. 363–384.

Greenburg, David F., and Drew Humphries: "The Cooptation of Fixed Sentencing Reform," *Crime and Delinquency,* vol. 26, no. 2, April 1980, pp. 206–225.

Handerich, Ted: *Punishment: The Supposed Justifications,* Penguin Books, Baltimore, 1971.

Hartinger, Walter, Edward Eldefonso, and Alan Coffey: *Corrections: A Part of the Criminal Justice System,* Goodyear Publishing Company, Pacific Palisades, Calif., 1972.

Hawkins, Gordon: *The Prison: Policy and Practice,* University of Chicago Press, Chicago, 1976.

Homans, George C.: *The Human Group,* Harcourt, Brace and Company, Inc., New York, 1950.

Hussey, Frederick: "Just Deserts and Determinate Sentencing: Impact on the Rehabilitative Ideal," *The Prison Journal,* Autumn/Winter 1979, pp. 36–47.

———: "In Favor of 'Presumptive Sentences' Set by a Sentencing Commission," *Crime and Delinquency,* vol. 24, no. 4, October 1978, pp. 401–427.

Krajick, Kevin: "Growing Old in Prison," *Corrections Magazine,* vol. 5, no. 1, March 1979, pp. 33–46.

LaGoy, Stephen P., Frederick A. Hussey, and John H. Kramer: "A Comparative

Assessment of Determinate Sentencing in Four Pioneer States," *Crime and Delinquency,* vol. 24, no. 4, October 1978, pp. 385–400.

Lowie, Robert H.: *Social Organization,* Rinehart & Company, Inc., New York, 1948.

Martinson, Robert: "The Paradox of Prison Reform: the Dangerous Myth," *The New Republic,* vol. 166, no. 14, Apr. 1, 1972, pp. 23–25.

McGee, Richard A.: "California's New Determinate Sentencing Act," *Federal Probation,* vol. 42, no. 1, Administrative Office of the United States Courts, Washington, D.C., March 1978, pp. 3–10.

May, Edgar: "Prison Officials Fear Flat Time Is More Time," *Corrections Magazine,* vol. 3, no. 3, September 1977, pp. 43–46.

Menninger, Karl Augustus: "Verdict Guilty: Now What?" *Harper's Magazine,* August 1959, pp. 60–64.

———: *The Crime of Punishment,* Viking Press, New York, 1969.

Morris, Norval, and Gordon Hawkins: "Rehabilitation: Rhetoric and Reality," *Federal Probation,* vol. 34, no. 4, Administrative Office of the United States Courts, Washington, D.C., December 1970, pp. 9–17.

Nagel, William G.: "Prisonia: America's Growing Megalopolis," *Church and Society,* vol. 70, no. 3, March/April 1980, pp. 5–12.

Newman, Donald J.: "Pleading Guilty for Consideration: A Study of Bargain Justice," *Journal of Criminal Law, Criminology, and Police Science,* vol. 46, no. 6, March/April 1956, pp. 780–790.

———: *Conviction: The Determination of Guilt or Innocence Without Trial,* Little, Brown and Company, Boston, 1966.

President's Commission on Law Enforcement and the Administration of Justice, *Task Force Report: Corrections,* U.S. Government Printing Office, Washington, D.C., 1967.

Pound, Roscoe: *Law and Morals,* University of North Carolina Press, Chapel Hill, 1924.

———: *Social Control Through Law,* Yale University Press, New Haven, Conn., 1942.

———: *The Spirit of the Common Law,* Marshall Jones Company, Boston, 1921.

Proskauer, Joseph M.: "How Shall We Deal With Crime," *Harper's Monthly Magazine,* vol. CLIX, New York, June/November 1929, pp. 419–422.

Quinney, Richard: *The Social Reality of Crime,* Little, Brown and Company, Boston, 1970.

Rose, Arnold M., and Arthur E. Prell: "Does the Punishment Fit the Crime? A Study in Social Valuation," *American Journal of Sociology,* vol. 61, no. 3, November 1955, pp. 247–259.

Serrill, Michael S.: "Determinate Sentencing: The History, the Theory, the Debate," *Corrections Magazine,* vol. 3, no. 3, September 1977, pp. 3–13.

———: "California Turning to Fixed Sentences," *Corrections Magazine,* vol. 2, no. 6, December 1976, pp. 55–56.

Skolnick, Jerome H.: *Justice Without Trial,* John Wiley & Sons, Inc., New York, 1966.

Stone, Irving: *Clarence Darrow for the Defense,* Doubleday, Doran & Company, Inc., Garden City, 1941.

Sutherland, Edwin H., and Donald R. Cressey: *Criminology,* J. B. Lippincott Company, New York, 1970, chaps. 1, 14 and 15.

Thompson, T. M.: "The Criminal Justice System: A View From the Outside," *Crime and Delinquency,* vol. 18, no. 1, January 1972, pp. 23–29.

U.S. Department of Justice: *"Capital Punishment, 1978," National Prisoner Statistics*

Bulletin, Law Enforcement Assistance Administration, Washington, D.C., December 1979, pp. 1, 2, 6, and 7.

Von Hirsch, Andrew: *Doing Justice: The Choice of Punishments,* Hill and Wang, New York, 1976.

———— and Kathleen Hanrahan: "Determinate Penalty Systems in America: An Overview," *Crime and Delinquency,* vol. 27, no. 3, July 1981, pp. 289–316.

Wolfgang, Marvin E.: "Making the Criminal Justice System Accountable," *Crime and Delinquency,* vol. 18, no. 1, January 1972, pp. 15–22.

CHAPTER 2

HISTORY OF COMMUNITY-BASED CORRECTIONS

CHAPTER OBJECTIVES

- To present an overview of the history of community-based corrections
- To outline the history of probation, the jail, temporary release, the community-based residence, and parole
- To trace the historical precedents of juvenile corrections in the community

INTRODUCTION

Although the seeds for corrections focusing on the community were planted centuries ago, the concept of community-based corrections was not popularized until the 1960s. The initiators have included sheriffs, legislators, judges, business executives, and the idle wealthy, as well as correctional employees.

The beginnings were centered in Western Europe and England, but American reformers perfected the European ideas. Unfortunately, until recently, few attempts have been made to develop a coordinated system of programs. Most efforts have been piecemeal, localized, and lacking any long-term examination of the results. Despite these failings, however, judges, prosecutors, and correctional administrators can now look to many community-based corrections programs: pretrial release, diversion, probation, residential programs, and parole. Correctional practitioners who wish to recommend that an offender have regular contact with the community for at least part of a day now have an array of program options available. In this respect, corrections focusing on the community has expanded the answer to the question, "Guilty! Now What?"

A HISTORICAL OVERVIEW

The Nineteenth Century

The first attempts to establish community-based corrections in the United States occurred in the early nineteenth century. In 1817, after studying the state's prison system, a Massachusetts commission recommended to the legislature that a residence for offenders be organized in the community. The proposal met with public indifference and hostility, and the needed votes for passage failed to materialize. The same suggestion was disapproved in 1830, when the inspectors of the state prison feared that prisoners living together in a halfway house would contaminate each other.

Fifteen years later, the first residence for offenders, called the Isaac T. Hopper House, was opened in New York by a group of Quakers. It was managed entirely by private parties and is still operating. By 1864 a halfway house for women was begun in Boston. Within 30 years similar residences had opened in Philadelphia, Chicago, San Francisco, and New Orleans—all financed and managed by private parties.[1]

Another form of community-based corrections—probation—was initiated in this country when John Augustus approached the prisoner's bench in Boston police court in 1841 and requested that a guilty drunkard be released in his custody. Continuing this practice until his death 18 years later, Augustus accepted 1946 offenders "bailed on probation." Now more than half of all convicted offenders in the United States are placed on probation.

Parole was initiated in the United States in 1876 at the New York State Reformatory in Elmira. The law governing the reformatory, drafted by its first superintendent, Zebulon Brockway, provided a mark system that allowed prisoners to earn privileges. Early release on parole was the reward for offenders who maintained good conduct for at least 1 year and could show a satisfactory plan for employment. Parole legislation spread rapidly throughout the United States, and by 1900 it existed in twenty states. By 1922 it had been adopted in forty-four states, the federal system, and Hawaii.

The first attempt to provide inmates contact with the community while incarcerated also began in the nineteenth century when women prisoners were released in the custody of private families as indentured servants. No action was taken to authorize the practice until 1880, when the Massachusetts legislature passed a bill legalizing this form of work release. Twenty years later, a sheriff in

---

[1]Ronald L. Goldfarb and Linda R. Singer, *After Conviction,* Simon and Schuster, New York, 1973, p. 553.

New Hampshire began a similar practice with male prisoners. He released inmates to work in the community by day and serve nights and weekends in jail. As occurred with work release for female prisoners, the sheriff's action drew favorable publicity. Finally, after this century of experimentation, the Wisconsin legislature passed the Huber law in 1913, permitting jail inmates to support their dependents.

Twentieth-Century Continuations

Following the beginnings in the early nineteenth century, corrections officials have slowly but steadily adopted community-based corrections as a viable alternative to incarceration. By 1972, all fifty states of the United States, many European countries, and Canada had tried some form of community-based corrections. Thirty-seven states had adopted all forms of community-based corrections—probation, parole, temporary release, and community-based residences. Only thirteen states indicated they had no plans to follow suit. Twenty-one of the twenty-eight states which already possessed a complete community-based corrections program indicated they would expand their programs within the next 2 to 5 years.[2] Table 2.1 lists some of the states with a complete community-based corrections program and the type of housing facility used.

The first state to legislate the mechanisms for the development of a comprehensive statewide community-based corrections program was Minnesota. In 1974 the Minnesota legislature passed statutes which not only continued support for a state-operated program but allotted state money for financial grants to counties. The development of locally and regionally operated community-based corrections programs was designed to divert many offenders from the state-operated corrections system.

In 1977 the Minnesota Council of State Governments reported that from 1974 to 1976 there was a lower commitment rate of prisoners to Minnesota Corrections Department institutions from participating counties than from nonparticipating counties. The decline in juvenile commitments was so great that one juvenile training school was closed.[3]

By 1975 all but two states—Montana and Wyoming—permitted furloughs or work release to inmates. Offenders supervised on probation and parole in 1977 constituted 68 percent of all felons under federal supervision.[4]

---

[2]Bertram S. Griggs and Gary R. McCune, "Community-Based Correctional Programs: A Survey and Analysis," *Federal Probation*, vol. 36, no. 2, Administrative Office of the United States Courts, Washington, D.C., June 1972, pp. 9, 11.

[3]*A State-Supervised Local Corrections System: The Minnesota Experience,* Council of State Governments, St. Paul, Minn., 1977, p. 46.

[4]Jim McCafferty, Chief Statistical Research Analyst, Administrative Office of the United States Courts, Washington, D.C. (telephone conversation) November 1977.

TABLE 2.1
COMMUNITY-BASED CORRECTIONAL PROGRAMS: A SURVEY AND ANALYSIS.
(States with Community-Based Corrections Programs for Adult Felons, Prior to Release on Parole, 1972, Indicating the Type of Facilty in Which They are Housed)

| State | Capacity | Residents | | Type of facility | | |
		Male	Female	Hotel or apartment	Jail	State institution
Total	4143	27	19	20	9	16
California	437	X	X	X	X	X
Colorado	60	X	O	O	O	X
Connecticut	112	X	O	O	X	O
Florida	150	X	X	X	X	O
Georgia	138	X	X	X	X	O
Hawaii	145	X	O	X	O	X
Illinois	60	X	X	X	O	X
Indiana	214	X	X	X	O	X
Louisiana	150	X	X	X	X	X
Maine	10	O	X	X	O	O
Maryland	180	X	X	X	O	O
Massachusetts	72	X	X	O	O	X
Michigan	125	X	X	X	O	X
Minnesota	70	X	X	X	X	O
Nebraska	25	X	O	X	O	O
New Jersey	30	X	X	X	O	O
North Carolina	151	X	X	X	O	X
Oklahoma	48	X	O	X	O	O
Oregon	183	X	X	X	X	X
Rhode Island	50	X	O	O	O	X
South Carolina	311	X	O	X	O	O
Tennessee	50	X	X	X	O	X
Texas	350	X	O	O	O	X
Vermont	298	X	X	O	O	X
Virginia	105	X	X	O	X	X
Washington	25	X	O	X	O	O
Wisconsin	250	X	X	O	X	X
District of Columbia	335	X	X	X	O	O

Key: X represents yes,
O represents no.
Source: Bertram S. Griggs and Gary R. McCune, "Community-Based Correctional Programs: A Survey and Analysis," *Federal Probation*, vol. 36, no. 2, Administrative Office of the United States Courts, Washington, D.C., June 1972, pp. 9, 11.

JAILS

The Gaol

The jail is the oldest of all institutions in the criminal justice system. When people merged their small, family-related groups into larger units, social codes became more complex and punishment of serious violators became the responsibility of the larger unit rather than of the person or group whose rights were violated. As codes were written and public law was established, a system of criminal justice evolved, requiring a place where suspected offenders could be held. These confinement places performed the function of jails.[5] In fact, the first record of a jail appears in biblical times. As stated in the tenets of the Code of Justinian, confinement should never be used as punishment, but as a place of detention for the accused.

The American jail can trace its origins to the tenth-century gaol, whose principal function was to detain arrested offenders until tried. Later, jails resembled the fifteenth- and sixteenth-century houses of correction, whose special function was the punishment of minor offenders, debtors, vagrants, and beggars.[6] Jails became common in England in the twelfth and thirteenth centuries. Before that time there was little need for elaborate penal machinery, as free men atoned for their transgressions with fines, enslavement, mutilation, banishment, or death.[7]

By the twelfth century, a new legal system had evolved, in which the king administered justice through itinerate judges, sheriffs, and other officers. In order to keep prisoners in safe custody until the king's judges held the next court, places of detention were provided. There were no separate buildings for detention before the reign of Henry II. Any available facilities for detention were used, including towers, gatehouses, town hall cellars, and dungeons. All were operated by private keepers for profit.

In 1166 the Assize of Clarendon authorized the construction of jails. Inmates were charged fees for entrance and for discharge as well as for putting on and taking off irons. Prisoners with money could obtain special rooms and food and the services of the tap and brothel.[8]

Workhouses and Houses of Correction

Workhouses and houses of correction are listed frequently as jails in statistical compilations. However, they are of entirely different origins, beginning in England in the sixteenth century to deal with the unemployed and the growing number of untrained youths who neither knew how nor wanted to work.[9] Houses of correction were sometimes built next to jails or set up as part of jails.

The concept of punishment changed radically with the advent of the industrial

---

[5]J. M. Moynahan and Earl K. Stewart, "The Origin of the American Jail," *Federal Probation,* vol. 42, no. 4, Administrative Office of the United States Courts, Washington, D.C., December 1978, p. 42.

[6]Edith Elisabeth Flynn, "Jails and Criminal Justice," *Prisoners in America,* Lloyd E. Ohlin (ed.), Prentice-Hall, Inc., Englewood Cliffs, N.J., 1973, p. 49.

[7]Neil C. Chamelin, Vernon B. Fox, and Paul M. Whisenand, *Introduction to Criminal Justice,* Prentice-Hall, Inc., Englewood Cliffs, N.J., 1975, pp. 308–309.

[8]Lionel W. Fox, *The English Prison and Borstal System,* Routledge & Kegan, Ltd., London, 1954, pp. 19–21.

[9]E. M. Leonard, *The Early History of English Poor Relief,* Cambridge University Press, Cambridge, England, 1900.

revolution. Before this, keeping a person in jail was not popular, because governing bodies did not want to spend money to house and feed prisoners. The industrial revolution created a demand for labor, and convicts became the answer. It was discovered that sentenced offenders could be loaned to industry for a fee. In effect, governments found it economically advantageous to sentence convicted persons to jail for a period of time as punishment. Likewise, employers were eager to hire the less expensive convict labor rather than free men.[10]

Early Jails in the United States

Jails and houses of correction were established in the American colonies soon after settlement. The first jail was built in Jamestown, Virginia, in the early seventeenth century. In 1632 a small wood structure was erected in Boston as a jail for the entire Massachusetts Bay Colony. This building served for 18 years, until jails were built in other towns. In 1655 the general court of Massachusetts Bay Colony ordered that, "there shall be a house of correction provided in each county at the counties' charge," to house idle drunkards and other petty offenders.[11] Figure 2.1 shows the floor plan of an early jail.

Early Conditions

Conditions in these early jails and houses of correction were terrible. The following account describes the Walnut Street County Jail in Philadelphia at the end of the Revolutionary War:

> It is represented as a scene of promiscuous unrestricted intercourse and universal riot and debauchery. There was no labor, no separation of those accused, but yet untried, not even of those confined for debt only, from convicts sentenced for the foulest crimes . . . intoxicating liquors abounded and indeed were freely sold at a bar kept by one of the officers of the prison. Prisoners tried and acquitted were still detained til they should pay the jail fees to the keeper; and the custom of garnish was established and unquestioned; that is, the custom of stripping every new comer of his outer clothing, to be sold for liquor, unless redeemed by the payment of a sum of money to be applied to the same object.[12]

Inmates in early jails were largely dependent on their own resources or public charity for assistance. Even when money was provided for payment of the

---

[10]George T. Felkenes, *The Criminal Justice System: Its Functions and Personnel,* Prentice-Hall, Inc., Englewood Cliffs, N.J., 1973, p. 260.
[11]Edwin Powers, *Crime and Punishment in Early Massachusetts,* Beacon Press, Boston, 1966, p. 3.
[12]Francis Cadley Gray, *Prison Discipline in America,* J. Murray, London, 1848.

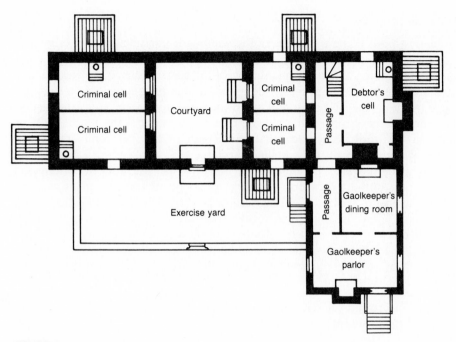

FIGURE 2.1
Diagram of an early jail in the United States. *(From Francis Cadley Gray, Prison Discipline in America, J. Murray, London, 1848, pp. 15, 16.)*

jailer's fees, the funds frequently were kept by the jailer. The early system of granting bail was managed by jailers. This greatly increased their manipulative power and augmented their unstable income, because jailers were left to their own devices to control the prisoners. The public's unofficial approval allowed jailers to use whatever systems of control they could invent. Fines, lashing, branding, and mutilation were common. Stocks, pillories, whipping posts, and dunking stools were often located near the jail so that offenders could receive their punishment.

The Quakers of Philadelphia were determined to change these conditions. In 1776 Richard Wistar, at his own expense, provided soup for some prisoners at the county jail after others died of starvation. In the same year, the Philadelphia Society for Alleviating Distressed Prisoners was formed. Although sidetracked by the Revolutionary War, the Society's activities were renewed in 1787. Its primary purpose was relieving the physical suffering of prisoners and substituting imprisonment for the death penalty.[13]

---

[13]Edwin H. Sutherland and Donald R. Cressey, *Criminology*, J. B. Lippincott Company, Philadelphia, 1970, pp. 483–484.

Since the Civil War

In the post-Civil War era, the increasing number of transient gangs of criminals, the lawlessness of the American frontier, and the migration of east coast colonists encouraged the transplantation of the eastern jails to the west. These early western jails were primarily designed to hold prisoners until an itinerant judge might try the case or until local townspeople took some concerted action on behalf of the victim of the alleged offense. Sometimes the local sheriff or marshall arbitrarily concluded that the length of the jail confinement was sufficient as punishment for the alleged offense.

Criminologist Walter Lunden states, "The first jail was built of cottonwood two-by-fours in the 1870's. In its confines of six by eighteen, as many as forty lawbreakers were kept at one time, largely cowboys who had shown too much exuberance upon reaching town."[14] Some western cities instituted rotary jails, also called human squirrel cages. These were set within a large brick and barred building. The cells were set in a permanent steel-bar cylinder with one opening on each floor. A revolving steel cylinder, also barred, moved past the opening until it became the door.

Twentieth-Century Jails

With the twentieth-century increase in urbanization, large high-rise city jails were built. Like their small rural counterparts, the city jails house misdemeanants, the poor, drunks, addicts, prostitutes, vagrants, and the mentally ill for whom no other holding facility exists. Today the original distinction between jails and houses of correction has been lost. Even by the last quarter of this century, jails contained a population of children, debtors, men, women, and the physically ill, a population similar to those confined in the Boston House of Corrections on May 1, 1837, as indicated in Table 2.2.

In fact, the workhouses and houses of correction have merged with the jail in all except name. Once prisons appeared, interest in jail reform disappeared and the focus was on prisons.[15]

PROBATION

John Augustus

The following was taken from the notes of John Augustus and reveals the first use of the term *probation*.

[14]Walter A. Lunden, "The Rotary Jail, or Human Squirrel Cage," *Journal of the Society of Architectural Historians,* vol. 18, no. 4, December 1959, p. 156.

[15]Law Enforcement Assistance Administration, *1970 National Jail Census,* U.S. Government Printing Office, Washington, D.C., 1971, p. 19.

TABLE 2.2
PRISON POPULATION, BOSTON HOUSE OF
CORRECTION, MAY 1, 1837

Confinement of males for:	Number
Common and notorious thieves	2
Felonious assault	1
Assault	1
Assault on a child 10 years old and attempt to rape	1
Adultery	1
Larceny	49
Larceny in a dwelling place	6
Common drunkards	64
Vagabonds	11
Common drunkards and vagabonds	5
Lascivious and common drunkard	1
Resisting constable	3
Forgery	1
Escape from house of correction	2
Lunatic	10
Total	158

Confinement of females for:	
Passing counterfeit money	1
Larceny in a dwelling house	1
Larceny	15
Wanton and lascivious	10
Common drunkards and vagabonds	3
Night-walkers	3
Common drunkards and night-walkers	5
Keeping a brothel	2
Vagabond	1
Common drunkards	23
Escaping from house of correction	1
Lunatic	4
Total	69

Source: Edwin Powers, *Crime and Punishment in Early Massachusetts*, Beacon Press, Boston, 1966, p. 3.

In the month of August, 1841, I was in court one morning, when the door communicating with the lockroom was opened and an officer entered, followed by a ragged and wretched looking man, who took his seat upon the bench allotted to prisoners. I imagined from the man's appearance, that his offense was that of yielding to his appetite for intoxicating drinks, and in a few moments I found that my suspicions were correct, for the clerk read the complaint, in which the man was charged with being a common drunkard. The case was clearly made out, but before sentence had been passed I conversed with him for a few moments, and found that he was not yet past all hope of reformation. . . . He told me that if he could be saved from the House of Correction, he never again would taste intoxicating liquor; there was such an earnestness in that tone, and a look of firm resolve, that I determined to aid him; I bailed him, by permission of the court. He was ordered to appear for sentencing three weeks from that time. He signed the pledge and became a sober man; at the expiration of this period of probation, I accompanied him back into the courtroom. . . . The judge expressed himself much pleased with the account we gave of the man and instead of the usual penalty—imprisonment in the House of Correction—he fined him one cent and costs amounting in all to $3.76, which was immediately paid. The man continued industrious and sober and without a doubt has been by this treatment, saved from a drunkard's grave.[16]

John Augustus's work in Boston eventually resulted in having 1946 men and women placed under his supervision—the first time probation services had ever been offered by a court.

Probation soon became a watchword for the state of Massachusetts, as others soon followed Augustus's lead and established formal services. In 1863, four years after Augustus's death, Rufus Cooke and L. P. Burnham organized the Children's Aid Society in Boston, offering probation to juveniles. Finally, in 1878, the state of Massachusetts authorized Boston to hire the state's first salaried probation officer, Lt. Henry C. Hemmenway, at a salary of $1500 a year. In 1890, the entire state of Massachusetts was permitted to appoint probation officers.[17]

Missouri was next to legislate probation, passing a law in 1897 authorizing all counties to establish these services. By 1910, twenty-one states and the District of Columbia had legislated enabling statutes. Twenty-nine years later, the federal government and forty-four states had enacted such legislation. However, not until 1957 had all fifty states and Puerto Rico authorized probation by statute. By that time, 91 percent of the 3082 counties and districts in the United States and Puerto Rico had some form of probation services.[18]

Benefit of Clergy

Despite the fact that a Bostonian coined the term *probation* and was the first to offer supervised suspended sentences to prostitutes, drunks, petty thieves, and felons, the idea of sparing certain deviates from the penalty authorized by law has existed for some time. The thirteenth-century practice of allowing benefit of clergy is considered the original antecedent to probation. At this time, many felonies were punishable by death under English statutory law. The church, in defense of its autonomy insisted that only ecclesiastical tribunals had jurisdiction over members of the clergy. In this way ordained clerks, monks, and nuns who were accused of crimes could escape the severity of secular courts.

[16]John Augustus, *A Report of the Labors of John Augustus for the Last Ten Years in Aid of the Unfortunate,* Wright & Hasty, Boston, 1852, pp. 4–5.

[17]George C. Killinger, Hazel B. Kerper, and Paul F. Cromwell, Jr., *Probation and Parole in the Criminal Justice System,* West Publishing Company, St. Paul, Minn., 1976, p. 14.

[18]Alan Coffey, Edward Eldefonso, and Walter Hartinger, *An Introduction to the Criminal Justice System and Process,* Prentice-Hall, Inc., Englewood Cliffs, N.J., 1974, p. 270.

By the middle of the fourteenth century, benefit of clergy was extended to other defendants, who pleaded benefit of clergy on the ground that they held membership in holy orders. The evidence of their membership was their ability to read a passage from the Bible. By 1487, this literacy test had become a fiction. Many accused defendants were being excused from secular courts even when illiterate, either by false statements from clerks or memorization of a passage from the Bible. Consequently, a law was passed stating that benefit of clergy could be claimed only once except by *bona fide* clerics. A brand of T for thief or M for murderer was placed on the thumbs of all others accused.

Recognizance

Another precedent for probation was recognizance. The word comes from the Latin *recognoscere,* meaning "recall to mind." Recognizance was a release from custody without bail while awaiting trial. It had been practiced in England for centuries, but the first recorded use of recognizance in the United States was in the case of *Commonwealth v. Chase,* decided in 1830 in the Municipal Court of Boston. Some of the accused posted a surety or bond to guarantee appearance in court, and thus the system of bail began.[19]

Judicial Reprieve

Judicial reprieve was another common practice used by early English judges who were not satisfied when a defendant was convicted. The judicial reprieve suspended the imposition or execution of the sentence in order to permit the defendant to apply to the Crown for a pardon. The practice was instituted at a time when there were no retrials or appeals and a defendant was allowed to remain at liberty until final disposition of the case. Neither supervision nor any conditions were imposed on behavior during suspension.[20]

Filing of Cases

Another innovation that preceded probation was the nineteenth-century practice in Massachusetts of the filing of cases when extenuating circumstances were discovered during the course of a trial. This filing took place after a verdict of guilty but before the imposition of a sentence. Sentencing was suspended but could be revived later by either the defense or the prosecution.

Legality of Probation

Despite the common law precedents, the legality of probation was not settled. In 1894, a New York district attorney challenged the judge's authority to suspend

[19]Killinger, Kerper, and Cromwell, op. cit., pp. 2–3.
[20]Goldfarb and Singer, op. cit., p. 210.

sentences, arguing that the New York Statute authorizing suspension of sentence was invalid and that a common law did not apply. The case, *People ex. rel. Forsythe v. Court of Sessions,* was settled by the New York Court of Appeals, which ruled in favor of the judge's right to suspend sentences.[21]

The final legal test ended on December 4, 1916, when the Supreme Court handed down a unanimous decision, *ex parte United States* 242 U.S. 27-53, commonly called the *Killits decision.* This stated that neither federal nor state courts possessed the inherent power to suspend sentences permanently or indefinitely. Common law did not apply. As a result, the Killits decision forced each state and the federal government to legislate the power of sentence suspension.[22]

TEMPORARY RELEASES

Work Release

From the beginning of the United States prison system, women had been placed informally in the custody of private families to serve as indentured domestics. However, a widely circulated report by the Wisconsin State Board of Charities and Reform encouraged a more sophisticated form of work release. This report, published in 1873, criticized the idle conditions of county jail inmates, as follows:

> Here are scores and hundreds of men, some of them young and in vigorous health, who are compelled to spend from a few days to a year, and sometimes two years, in absolute idleness, while the taxpayers of the various counties are supporting them. What a waste of labor! What an injury to the men themselves to keep them in a state of enforced idleness! What an unwise expenditure of public funds to support healthy, able-bodied men in such idleness.[23]

After the publication of the Wisconsin report, the first known attempt to release prisoners to work occurred in New Hampshire at the turn of the century. Although not authorized by law, a New Hampshire sheriff began releasing prisoners to work in the community by day and serve nights and weekends in jail. He received considerable public support for his bold action.

The Huber Law

Forty years after the original Wisconsin report was published, the Wisconsin legislature passed the Huber Law, establishing work release on a local level. This law authorized judges and magistrates to impose conditional sentences on misdemeanants, allowing offenders to remain employed while incarcerated.

[21]141 N.Y. 288, 36 N.E. 386 (1894).
[22]*Ex Parte United States,* 242 U.S. 27–53 (1916).
[23]Goldfarb and Singer, op. cit., p. 528. Reprinted by permission of Simon and Schuster, a division of Gulf and Western Corporation.

Until World War II, the Huber Law was applied only sporadically. The labor shortage created by the number of men in the armed forces during the war accelerated the use of work release. By 1956, fifty-two of seventy-one Wisconsin counties had work release programs and more than one-third (2654 of 7682) of all adult jail offenders in Wisconsin were sentenced under the Huber law.[24]

Work Release for Felons

The 1913 Wisconsin law applied only to misdemeanants. It was more than 40 years before any state adopted work release for felons. Finally, in 1957, a chain of circumstances created an unusual situation which induced the North Carolina legislature to consider releasing prison inmates to work in the community. For 24 years a 1933 law had allowed inmates to construct and maintain state roads; then mechanization forced the state to abandon the use of prison labor for road construction. The North Carolina state constitution required state penal institutions to be as nearly self-supporting as possible, and state finances were not available to expand prison industries to accommodate the influx from the disbanded road construction crews. In desperation, Governor Luther Hodges appointed a committee to study the work-release program in Wisconsin. The committee was impressed favorably and drafted a bill providing that any prison inmate could be granted work-release privileges after a recommendation from the sentencing court.

After viewing the committee's bill, the North Carolina legislature adopted a measure that restricted eligibility to felons with fewer than 6 months previously spent in prison. In the next 2 years, only sixteen inmates were recommended by North Carolina courts for part-time release. The law was then amended to include felons serving a 5-year sentence or less. Finally, in 1959, work-release eligibility was extended to any prisoner who received approval by the state parole board. These changes allowed more than 6000 North Carolina felons to be approved for work release during the next 5 years.

Other states quickly followed. The federal system initiated work release in 1965. The Federal Prisoner Rehabilitation Act allowed any federal prisoner selected at the discretion of the attorney general to "work at paid employment or participate in a training program in the community on a voluntary basis while continuing as a prisoner of the institution or facility to which he is committed."[25] One year after the beginning of federal work release, 1400 prisoners had earned $725,000, sending $134,000 to dependents, placing $254,000 in savings, paying $73,000 in taxes, and paying $12,000 to federal prisons as reimbursement for room and board.[26] Within 3 years after the federal work release law was passed by Congress, twenty-six states had enacted similar legislation. Work release was

---

[24]Ibid., pp. 529–530.

[25]P.L. 89–176, 89th Cong., 1st Sess., 1965, amending 18 U.S.C. Sec. 4082.

[26]Lewis A. Carpenter, "The Federal Work Release Program," *The Tasks of Penology,* Harry S. Perlman and Thomas B. Allington (eds.) University of Nebraska Press, Lincoln, 1969, p. 187.

available to females in women's prisons in twenty-five states by 1971.[27] According to the 1980 American Correctional Association *Directory,* all fifty states and the District of Columbia now permit correctional institutions to release offenders to work in the community.[28] Four European countries—Denmark, Sweden, Norway, and France—also have adopted work release.

Study Release

A survey published in 1974 revealed that inmates in forty states could be released to attend school. Thirty-eight of the study-release programs were started between 1966 and 1971. Of the offenders participating in 1970, 45 percent were in vocational school, 25 percent in college, and about 30 percent in high school and night school.[29]

Furloughs and Passes

The history of furloughs and passes from prison is similar to the history of work release. Since colonial times correctional officials have granted temporary special leave from prison, with an escort, for a funeral or illness. The first special leaves were not designed to reintegrate the prisoner but were simply humane acts at a time of personal crisis. They were granted by correctional administrators without legal authorization. The leaves were approved by a warden of a prison or sheriff of a county jail by virtue of his position as the custodian of the prisoner. The first legal sanction of temporary releases occurred in 1918, when the state of Mississippi voted approval of 10-day holiday furloughs for minimum custody inmates. The Arkansas state legislature enacted a similar law 4 years later. No other state followed the lead of Mississippi and Arkansas for more than 40 years.[30]

Finally, in 1964, a furlough law was passed by the Louisiana state legislature with the same snowball effect that followed the federal approval of work release. The next year, the Federal Bureau of Prisons, North Carolina, Utah, and the District of Columbia permitted temporary releases. Twenty-eight other state legislatures had approved furloughs and passes by 1974. Female offenders were permitted furloughs in seven states by 1971.[31] The number of furloughs granted by state and federal officials in 1974 are detailed in Table 2.3.

At least nine European countries and four Latin American countries use

---

[27]Edna Walker Chandler, *Women in Prison,* Bobbs-Merrill Company, Inc., Indianapolis, Ind., 1973, pp. 138–139.

[28]*Directory,* American Correctional Association, College Park, Md., 1980.

[29]Robert R. Smith, John M. McKee, and Michael A. Milan, "Study-Release Policies of American Correctional Agencies: A Survey," *Journal of Criminal Justice,* vol. 2, no. 4, 1974, pp. 357–363.

[30]Carson W. Markley, "Furlough Programs and Conjugal Visiting in Adult Correctional Institutions," *Federal Probation,* vol. 37, no. 1, Administrative Office of the United States Courts, Washington, D.C., March 1973, p. 20.

[31]Chandler, op. cit., pp. 110–111.

TABLE 2.3
NUMBER OF FURLOUGHS, 1974, BY STATE.

	Adults	
	Per month	Fiscal 1974
Alabama	90	1,805
Alaska	NA*	NA
Arizona	NA	77
Arkansas	14	170
California	93	1,121
Colorado	190	2,300
Connecticut	550	6,600
Delaware	25	450
District of Columbia	3,000	38,000
Florida	4,388	53,000
Georgia	230	2,800
Hawaii	Not permitted	
Idaho	21	200
Illinois	375	4,500
Indiana	38	425
Iowa	186	2,238
Kansas	25	302
Kentucky	45	500
Louisiana	NA	1,671
Maine	78	935
Maryland	500–700	5,000
Massachusetts	651	8,115
Michigan	400–500	5,282
Minnesota	33	393
Mississippi	40	490
Missouri	NA	934

	Adults	
	Per month	Fiscal 1974
Montana	Not permitted	
Nebraska	194	2,322
Nevada	Furlough programs just approved	
New Hampshire	Furlough programs just approved	
New Jersey	696	8,352
New Mexico	NA	135
New York	1,352	16,226
North Carolina	2,918	35,020
North Dakota	6	29
Ohio	Furlough programs just approved	
Oklahoma	Not permitted	
Oregon	3,716	27,000
Pennsylvania	350	1,506
Rhode Island	Furlough programs just approved	
South Carolina	753	9,877
South Dakota	1	10
Tennessee	105	1,300
Texas	Not permitted	
Utah	45	540
Vermont	778	9,340
Virginia	NA	4,500
Washington	239	2,865
West Virginia	Not permitted	
Wisconsin	Not permitted	
Wyoming	Not permitted	
Federal system	1,450	17,400

*NA-Figures not available

Source: Michael S. Serrill, "Prison Furloughs in America," *Corrections Magazine,* vol. 1, no. 6, July/August 1975, p. 5.

Copyright 1975, Criminal Justice Publications and Corrections Magazine, 116 West 32 St., New York, New York 10001.

temporary releases as part of their correctional programs. Sweden permits temporary releases from prison more routinely than any other country, granting 48- to 72-hour furloughs at regular 4-month intervals, beginning 6 to 10 months after admission.[32]

COMMUNITY-BASED RESIDENCES

The European Beginning

In 1817 the Massachusetts legislature appointed a commission to study its prison and recommend changes. The commission's report proposed that a building be

> erected of wood, at a small expense, as it is only recommended by way of experiment. The convicts who are discharged are often entirely destitute. The natural prejudice against them is so strong, that they find great difficulty in obtaining employment. They are forced to seek shelter in the lowest receptacles; and if they wish to lead a new course of life, are easily persuaded out of it, and perhaps driven by necessity to the commission of fresh crimes. It is intended to afford a temporary shelter in this building, if they choose to accept it, to such discharged convicts as may have conducted themselves well in prison, subject to such regulations as the directors may see fit to provide. They will here have a lodging, rations from the prison at a cheap rate, and have a chance to occupy themselves in their trade, until some opportunity offers of placing themselves where they can gain an honest livelihood in society. A refuge of this kind, to this destitute class, would be found, perhaps, humane and polite.[33]

Thus more than 160 years ago the first recommendation was presented by a governmental body in this country for a community-based residence. The idea was not originated by the Massachusetts legislature, however. It can be traced to eighteenth-century England. In 1788 the Philanthropic Society of London organized three small cottages for children who had been picked up for begging and stealing. Craftsmen and their wives lived in the cottages, caring for twelve children each. The couples taught their foster children gardening, tailoring, shoemaking, and other crafts. By the mid-nineteenth century, a large number of agencies provided similar shelters. The great British philanthropist, Dr. Thomas Bernardo, was responsible for opening 112 residences for children.[34]

In continental Europe, during the latter part of this century, probation hostels began to provide an alternative to incarceration for convicted felons placed on supervision in the community. Parolees were similarly housed in these small, homelike centers, both privately and publicly financed, with a home director and his wife. These residences provided the former prisoner with a place

[32]Markley, op. cit., pp. 20–21.

[33]Edwin Powers, "Halfway Houses: An Historical Perspective," *American Journal of Correction,* vol. 21, no. 4, July/August 1959, p. 35.

[34]Martin R. Haskell and Lewis Yablonsky, *Juvenile Delinquency,* Rand McNally College Publishing Company, Chicago, 1974, p. 467.

to eat and sleep but were of little assistance in dealing with unacceptable behavior.

Early Failures

In the United States the statement by the Massachusetts commission was the first recorded reference to a community-based residence for offenders. After carefully considering their recommendation of a lodging for offenders, the legislature discarded the idea. Rather than embark on a new program, they decided to improve prison conditions, inasmuch as the state penitentiary had been opened as an experiment only 11 years earlier and an insurrection had taken place just before the commission was appointed.

Interest in a community-based residence for released offenders was revived in the Massachusetts state legislature 13 years later. This time legislators asked the inspectors of the state prison to respond in the form of a report. Their report, filed in 1830, disapproved of the proposal. They argued that a temporary shelter would be a source of contamination for convicts, because discharged felons would be associating with each other in a "school of depravity."[35]

Success by Private Groups

The defeat in Massachusetts for legislative support ended government action for more than 100 years, but the push for community residences did not cease. Private groups began establishing housing for released felons a few years after the recommendation by the Massachusetts inspectors. The Quakers opened the first transitional residence for men—the Isaac T. Hopper Home in New York City—in 1845. A second pioneer effort originated in Philadelphia in 1889, when the House of Industry began receiving parolees from Pennsylvania state institutions. The first housing unit for women discharged from jails and prisons was established in Boston in 1864. This residence—the Temporary Asylum for Disadvantaged Female Prisoners—remained open for 20 years.[36]

Continual opposition to the community residence movement slowed progress throughout the early period. Criticism from the American Prison Association existed from the beginning. This organization believed that residences for offenders in the community would perpetuate the prison stigma and create a "permanent class of undesirable citizens." Police and parole authorities also resisted. Police argued that the housing units would become hangouts for criminals, while parole authorities simply stated that association with former prisoners was against regulations.

Despite this opposition, the first major effort to establish community-based residences for offenders throughout the United States began before the end of the nineteenth century. The movement was led by Maud and Ballington Booth.

[35]Ibid., p. 35.
[36]Goldfarb and Singer, op. cit., p. 553.

In 1896 they quietly rented a large building in the Washington Heights section of Manhattan, in New York City. With assistance from the Volunteers of America, a religious missionary society of which Ballington Booth was a coleader, the home began receiving released prisoners from Sing Sing prison. Harassment from the police prompted the Booths to seek help from the police commissioner of New York, Theodore Roosevelt. With his assistance the program flourished.

Two years later the Booths moved their residents to a second building on Long Island, named Hope Hall. This was more comfortably furnished and contained a piano, phonograph, and library. Another Hope Hall was opened in Chicago in 1903. Eventually, the Booths established Hope Halls throughout the United States, including San Francisco; New Orleans; Fort Dodge, Iowa; Columbus, Ohio; Waco, Texas; and Hampton, Florida. All the Booth-sponsored residences eventually ceased operations, but several functioned for many years, providing temporary shelter for thousands of released prisoners.

Despite early successes, the movement bogged down in the 1920s. Opposition from the American Prison Association, law enforcement personnel, and correctional officials continued. Advocates of parole maintained that community-based residences were not needed. Parole, they argued, would provide the necessary transition from the institution to the community.[37]

The Depression and World War II demanded the public's attention for the next 20 years, and residences for offenders in the community did not become an issue again until the 1950s.

Community-Based Residences Since 1950

The first step in the revival of the movement took place in London. Merfyn Turner, who had visited offenders in England's Pentonville Prison, concluded that in order to "settle to the acceptable mode of living which they had said they wanted," released prisoners needed a "home and family tailor-made for them where they would be accepted for what they were and supported, supervised, and directed into a satisfactory and satisfying way of life."[38] Turner persuaded the London Parochial Foundation to finance a housing unit for selected prisoners.

In 1954, despite discouragement from skeptics, he and his wife began living with ex-prisoners. Originally, the occupants of Norman House, as their residence was called, remained for only 4 months. Although their criminal activities ceased when they lived at Norman House, approximately half the residents drifted back into crime within a short time after moving out. In response to these statistics, the Turners opened a large boardinghouse, which allowed indefinite periods of housing, counseling, and friendship. The average length of stay was extended to 3 years, and the recidivism rate of their ex-residents became negligible.

[37]Benedict S. Alper and Oliver J. Keller, *Halfway Houses—Community Centered Corrections and Treatment,* Heath & Company, Lexington, Mass., 1970, p. 7.
[38]Goldfarb and Singer, op. cit., p. 555.

In the United States at about the same time, Father Charles Dismas Clark, a Jesuit priest, convinced that the only real rehabilitation of criminals could be accomplished in the community, established Dismas House in St. Louis. He persuaded Norris Shenker, an attorney, to raise enough money to buy an old school building and establish a nonprofit foundation. Operating expenses were paid from private contributions and a small fee collected from each resident. The released prisoners were given housing, a place of fellowship, and help in finding jobs. Within a short period after Father Dismas's resumption of community-based residences in the United States, more such houses were opened. Some of the more successful were the Crenshaw House in Los Angeles; St. Leonard's House in Chicago; and 308 West Residence in Wilmington, Delaware.

The Federal Attempt

The residential concept gained popularity in the 1960s, following the recommendation by the late Attorney General Robert F. Kennedy that funds be appropriated by Congress for an experimental residential program in urban communities for certain federal offenders. Several months later the first prerelease guidance centers were opened in New York and Chicago. They were designed for young prisoners who had been committed to federal jurisdiction under the Federal Juvenile Delinquency Act or the Federal Youth Correction Act. Each offender placed at a center was scheduled for release within 90 days to a home within 50 miles of the center.

In 1965 the program was expanded by the Prisoner Rehabilitation Act to include adult offenders. Two years later, three more prerelease guidance centers, renamed "community treatment centers," were opened for offenders between the ages of 20 and 40. Original plans called for as many as thirty-five such facilities. However, subsequent reports, including one by the President's Commission on Law Enforcement and Administration of Justice, advised that thirty-five facilities were not necessary for United States Bureau of Prison releasees. As an alternative, the federal government was advised to assist state agencies to develop community resources.[39] By 1976 there were fifteen community treatment centers being operated for federal prisoners.[40]

The prerelease guidance centers or community treatment centers are not designed in the same way as the original community-based residences. In contrast to the indefinite period that offenders lived in earlier housing units, the federally sponsored facilities keep offenders for approximately 90 days, while they prepare for release on parole or expiration of sentence. Designed to assist the prisoner through counseling and employment interview preparation, federal community treatment centers do not provide the homelike atmosphere of the halfway house.

[39]Paul Keve, *Imaginative Programming in Probation and Parole*, University of Minnesota Press, Minneapolis, 1967, pp. 223–225.
[40]*1976 Federal Prison System*, U.S. Department of Justice, Washington, D.C., 1976, p. 1.

Community Correctional Centers

After the federal government established prerelease guidance centers,many states began developing community-based residences. In addition to halfway houses and larger, short-term prerelease centers, some states offer another innovative residential program—community correctional centers—which are normally located near a metropolitan population area. Residents are assigned to a certain center because they intend to live in that geographic area. The population base needed for a community correctional center ranges from 250,000 to 300,000 people. The physical plant is located centrally in order to provide access to the widest range of community resources.

California and Kentucky pioneered the establishment of community correctional centers in 1965. California opened its center in Oakland under the administration of the state Parole and Community Services Division. It houses parolees, serves as headquarters for parole officers, and provides recreation and counseling for any offender in its geographic region. By June 1976, California had opened nine such centers, four of which offered space for women. The programs were supplemented by eighteen privately operated halfway houses under contract to the California Parole and Community Services Division. In these, fifty-three beds were available to women parolees exclusively.[41]

The Kentucky experiment was initiated at Harlan through a joint effort by the federal government (funds appropriated by the Economic Opportunity Act) and the Kentucky state government. The primary purpose, besides housing, was to provide vocational training for offenders from rural areas of the state who leave prison with no job skills.[42]

PAROLE

The English Beginning

Primitives dealt with their criminals by banishing them from the tribe; in a sense, when modern society sends a man or woman to a distant prison, that person, too, is banished. Parole originated from the same basic premise. As the number of criminals mounted in England, concern increased about what to do with them. The American colonies presented the solution, and for a century and a half, ending in 1776 with the Revolutionary War, England transported an estimated 15,000 to 100,000 convicts to the western world. When England no longer could send convicts to the colonies, prisoners again began to overcrowd local jails. Soon after the discovery of Australia in 1770, the English parliament had decided that England's convicts could be transported there, but none were

---

[41]Arlene Becker, Deputy Director, Parole and Community Services Division, Department of Corrections, Health and Welfare Agency, State of California (personal memorandum), 1976.
[42]Keve, op. cit., pp. 225–226.

sent until the loss of America as a transportation colony. On May 13, 1777, a fleet of 11 ships set sail from Spithead, England, bound for Australia with 552 male and 190 female criminals.

In 1840 Alexander Maconochie, a captain in the Royal Navy, was sent to the penal colony of Norfolk Island as governor. Located a thousand miles off the coast of Australia, Norfolk Island is sometimes called the colony of the "twice condemned," because criminals were sent there who had committed further crimes on the mainland.[43] At this penal colony, brutality, corruption, disease, and famine were the rule. Even cannibalism had been practiced. Here Maconochie, horrified by the depraved conditions and dispirited state of the convicts, had schools and churches built and instituted a program called the mark system, which enabled prisoners to earn a shortening of their sentences for good conduct. As they earned marks, prisoners passed through five stages: (1) strict custody upon entrance; (2) work with government gangs; (3) limited freedom within a prescribed area; (4) ticket of leave, which permitted the convict to choose a place of residence on the island; and (5) full restoration of liberty.[44] As Maconochie stated, "When a man keeps the key to his own prison, he is soon persuaded to fit it to the lock."[45]

The "Irish System"

Irish penologist Sir Walter Crofton had an even stronger influence on American penologists than Maconochie. Crofton initiated the "Irish System." When the free citizens of Australia protested that their country was being used as a dumping ground for England's convicts, it became necessary to institute a method whereby "convicts under sentence of transportation could be discharged at home on tickets of license."[46] A written permit allowed the convict to live at home in Ireland as a reward for good behavior. Crofton then initiated the "intermediate system," whereby the offender, after a period of good behavior in prison, was released into the community under the supervision of an agent of the state.

Parole in the United States

The first person to use the word *parole* in the sense of conditional release was a prison reformer, Dr. S. G. Howe of Boston. In a letter written to the Prison Association of New York in 1846, he stated, "I believe there are many prisoners who might be so trained as to be left upon their parole during the last period of

---

[43]Harry Elmer Barnes and Negley K. Teeters, *New Horizons in Criminology*, Prentice-Hall, Inc., Englewood Cliffs, N.J., 1959, pp. 296, 418–419, 422.

[44]Louis P. Carney, *Introduction to Correctional Science*, McGraw-Hill Book Company, New York, 1974, pp. 312–313.

[45]Frederick H. Wines, *Punishment and Reformation*, Crowell, New York, 1895, p. 209.

[46]Mary Carpenter, *Reformatory Prison Discipline as Developed by the Rt. Hon. Sir Walter Crofton in the Irish Convict Prison*, Longmans, Green, Reader & Dyer, London, 1872, p. 2.

their imprisonment with safety." *Parole* is from the French, *parole d' honneur,* "word of honor."[47] The implication was that offenders were released from prison on their word of honor.

Under superintendent Zebulon Brockway, New York's Elmira Reformatory opened in 1876 with the adoption of several new principles, one of which was the release of select prisoners on parole. To Brockway, parole was seen as the culmination of a course of institutional training whereby the inmate's capacity for reform would be developed. Parole was preceded by exemplary conduct and compulsory education and served as a test period to determine whether the offender had absorbed training.[48]

The use of parole was first extended throughout a state prison system by Ohio in 1884. By 1889 it had been adopted in twenty-five states. By 1922, parole laws had been passed by forty-five states. The last state to adopt parole was Mississippi in 1944.

COMMUNITY-BASED CORRECTIONS FOR JUVENILES

Parens Patriae

That portion of the criminal justice system responsible for dealing with children under the age of legal maturity is called the juvenile justice system. In the past it centered around a benevolent judge acting as a guardian of a youth's rights in the name of the state. The philosophical principle legitimizing this control was based on the old English concept of *parens patriae,* whereby the state assumed parental responsibility for children when their parents had failed to maintain their welfare. The organizational structure of the system was designed to keep the juvenile court (judge) in control at all stages of the procedure, whether it was intake, adjudication, or release into the community.

Originally the idea of protective custody of children through *parens patriae* was a part of the Crown's power in England. In 1562 Parliament passed the Statutes of Artificers, which transferred the protective custody of children from the Crown to statute. The statutes provided that children of pauper parents could be involuntarily separated from their parents and apprenticed to others. Similar laws were passed in America, and almshouses, workhouses, and poorhouses became the centers of poor relief. By 1856 New York state had fifty-five almshouses containing 4936 people. Among them were 837 "lunatics," 273 "idiots" of all ages, and 1037 children.[49]

Legislation in 1824 allowed the Society for the Reformation of Juvenile Delinquents to build and manage an institution exclusively for children. The

---

[47]"Parole," *The Attorney General's Survey of Release Procedures,* U.S. Government Printing Office, Washington, D.C., 1939, vol. IV, pp. 4–5.

[48]Zebulon R. Brockway, *Fifty Years of Prison Service,* Charities Publication Committee, New York, 1912, p. 324.

[49]Frank R. Prassel, *Introduction to American Criminal Justice,* Harper & Row, Publishers, Incorporated, New York, 1975, p. 33.

New York House of Refuge, as the Society's home was named, housed children convicted of crimes and children "taken up or committed as vagrants."[50]

The New York statutes were written without the phrase *parens patriae,* but the Latin phrase *in loco parentis,* "in place of the parents," was included. Soon thereafter, however, in 1839, the Pennsylvania supreme court did use the phrase *parens patriae* to justify statutory commitments to a residential institution for juveniles.[51] Following New York's example, Ohio, Massachusetts, Michigan, Wisconsin, Pennsylvania, Connecticut, Rhode Island, Maryland, New Hampshire, Indiana, and New Jersey passed legislation regulating the care of children in poorhouses.

The First Juvenile Court

The juvenile court, too, can trace its origin directly to pauper laws. The first one was established in Chicago in 1899 to protect children under the doctrine of *parens patriae.* Before that, they were tried for their crimes exclusively in criminal courts. Thirteen years later the Children's Bureau was founded. Under the leadership of social workers, it encouraged the development of juvenile courts throughout the United States, and by 1945 every state had passed laws providing for a separate jurisdiction for juveniles.

Today the juvenile court is a statutory court, i.e., its powers are provided for and limited by statute and its procedures are fixed by law or by the judges of the court. At least 1,252,700 delinquency cases were processed by the nation's juvenile courts in 1974.[52]

Historically, officials have used the same form of community-based corrections for juveniles as for adults: probation, parole, and community-based residences. Except for the use of community-based residences, this development came a short time after experimentation with adult offenders.

Juvenile detention centers play the same role for juveniles as jails do for adults. Unfortunately, however, many juveniles are still held in jails—an estimated 100,000 a year. In 1976 there were 328,854 juveniles on probation and 53,347 juveniles on parole or after-care status. Community-based corrections is as much a part of juvenile corrections as of adult corrections.

RECENT DEVELOPMENTS

By the 1960s all forms of community-based corrections had begun. Until then the term had not been popularized. During the late 1960s and early 1970s these programs captured the imagination and support of American citizens. Guided by reintegration philosophy, advocated by a number of blue-ribbon commissions,

---

[50]Frederic L. Faust and Paul J. Brantingham, *Juvenile Justice Philosophy: Reading Cases and Comments,* West Publishing Company, St. Paul, Minn., 1974, p. 82.

[51]4 Whart. 9, 11 (Penn. 1839).

[52]Faust and Brantingham, op. cit., p. 86.

and supported by federal dollars, community-based corrections programs sprouted in nearly every state. The new challenge, according to the Corrections Task Force of the President's Commission on Law Enforcement and Administration of Justice, was to keep offenders in the community and to help reintegrate them into community living.

Furthermore, the spirit of the times was one of reform. The turbulence brought on by the Vietnam War, disturbances on college campuses, urban riots, and the widespread questioning of traditional values and institutions fostered receptivity to new solutions.

The area of mental health had already gone through a period of deinstitutionalization in the 1960s. More and more mental health patients were kept in the community rather than being placed in large state hospitals. This, along with the bloody prison riots that frequently appeared in the news between 1971 and 1973, helped to support the inevitable conclusion that there must be a better way to deal with social problems. The result was an amazing proliferation of community-based programs throughout the country, funded primarily by federal grants. For example, from the inception of the Law Enforcement Assistance Administration (LEAA) in 1967 to July 1975, federal grants of $23,837, 512 authorized by the Safe Streets Act were bolstered by $12,300,710 from state and local funds for residential aftercare programs for adults.[53]

But community-based corrections began to decline in popularity even more rapidly than it had gained approval. Indeed, the mood of the country suddenly changed to the "get-tough-with-criminals" approach as publications of official statistics and media coverage of street crime convinced the public in the mid-1970s that the crime problem was out of hand. The permissive approach that kept offenders in the community became harder and harder to accept. Supporters of the punishment model were quick to recommend incarceration as a more fitting way of dealing with crime. Institutional populations climbed to an all-time high.

EXERCISES

1 The original concept of probation arose from an attempt to alleviate the severity of punishment. Do you believe this motive is still the major reason for judges' using probation? Explain your answer.
2 What similarities exist between the King's justice of the twelfth century and the county jails of today? Explain fully.
3 Both prisons and jails have developed from similar origins. Why are they now different?
4 The original reasons for releasing a prisoner temporarily to visit sick relatives or to work were based on humanitarian principles rather than a hope of rehabilitation. Do you believe these reasons are sufficient to justify temporary releases? Why or why not?

---

[53]Clemens Bartollas, *Introduction to Corrections,* Harper & Row, Publishers, Incorporated, New York, 1981, p. 110.

5 Early inmates approved for work release were assigned to employers as indentured servants or inexpensive labor. Do you think this practice should have been continued? Justify your answer.

6 What fallacy is present in the objection voiced by inspectors of the state prison who believed that halfway house inmates would contaminate each other?

7 Describe the image of prisoners held in this country by correctional officials in the nineteenth century.

8 Explain the London experience of the Turners and the insight they gained regarding the process of offenders' reentry into society.

9 Compare the mark system with modern theories of treatment. How effective do you think it might have been? Support your belief.

EXERCISE REFERENCES

Alper, Benedict S., and Oliver J. Keller: *Halfway Houses—Community Centered Corrections and Treatment,* D. C. Heath and Company, Lexington, Mass., 1970.

Augustus, John: *A Report of the Labors of John Augustus for the Last Ten Years in Aid of the Unfortunate,* Wright & Hasty, Boston, 1852.

Barnes, Harry Elmer, and Negley K. Teeters: *New Horizons in Criminology,* Prentice-Hall, Inc., Englewood Cliffs, N.J., 1963, chap. 35.

Bartollas, Clemens: *Introduction to Corrections,* Harper & Row, Publishers, Incorporated, New York, 1981, chap. 4.

Brockway, Zebulon R.: *Fifty Years of Prison Service,* Charities Publication Committee, New York, 1912.

Caldwell, Robert G.: *Criminology,* Ronald Press Company, New York, 1965, chaps. 22 and 26.

Carney, Louis B.: *Introduction to Correctional Science,* McGraw-Hill Book Company, New York, 1974, chaps. 10 and 13.

Carpenter, Lewis A.: "The Federal Work Release Program," in Harry S. Perlman and Thomas B. Allington (eds.), *The Tasks of Penology,* University of Nebraska Press, Lincoln, Nebr. 1969, pp. 185–197.

Carpenter, Mary: *Reformatory Prison Discipline as Developed by the Rt. Hon. Sir Walter Crofton in the Irish Convict Prisons,* Longmans, Green, Reader & Dyer, London, 1872.

Cavan, Ruth Shonle: *Criminology,* Thomas Y. Crowell Company, New York, 1958, chaps. 14 and 19.

Chamelin, Neil C., Vernon B. Fox, and Paul M. Whisenand: *Introduction to Criminal Justice,* Prentice-Hall, Inc., Englewood Cliffs, N.J., 1975, chaps. 2 and 3.

Chandler, Edna Walker: *Women in Prison,* Bobbs-Merrill Company, Inc., Indianapolis, 1973.

Children's Bureau, U.S. Department of Health, Education and Welfare: *Institutions Serving Delinquent Children: Guides and Goals,* U.S. Government Printing Office, Washington, D.C., 1957.

Coffey, Alan, Edward Eldefonso, and Walter Hartinger: *An Introduction to the Criminal Justice System and Process,* Prentice-Hall, Inc., Englewood Cliffs, N.J., 1974, chap. 12.

Council of State Governments: *A State-Supported Local Corrections System: The Minnesota Experience,* St. Paul, Minn., 1977.

Edwards, George: "Parole," in Sol Rubin (ed.), *The Law of Criminal Correction,* West Publishing Company, St. Paul, Minn., 1963, chap. 15.

Erjen, Victor H.: "The Federal Probation System: The Struggle to Achieve It and Its First 25 Years," *Federal Probation,* vol. 39, no. 2, Administrative Office of the United States Courts, Washington, D.C., June 1975, pp. 3–15.

Faust, Frederic L., and Paul J. Brantingham: *Juvenile Justice Philosophy: Reading Cases and Comments,* West Publishing Company, St. Paul, Minn., 1974.

Felkenes, George T.: *The Criminal Justice System: Its Functions and Personnel,* Prentice-Hall, Inc., Englewood Cliffs, N.J., 1973, chap. 15.

Fishman, Joseph F.: *Crucibles of Crime,* Cosmopolis Press, New York, 1923.

Flynn, Edith Elisabeth: "Jails and Criminal Justice," in Lloyd E. Ohlin (ed.), *Prisoners in America,* Prentice-Hall, Inc., Englewood Cliffs, N.J., 1973, pp. 49–88.

Fox, Lionel W.: *The English Prison and Borstal System,* Routledge & Kegan Paul, Ltd., London, 1954.

Fox, Vernon: *Introduction to Corrections,* Prentice-Hall, Inc., Englewood Cliffs, N.J., 1977, chaps. 5, 10, and 12.

Goldfarb, Ronald L., and Linda R. Singer: *After Conviction,* Simon and Schuster, New York, 1973, secs. IV, V, and VIII.

Gray, Francis Cadley: *Prison Discipline in America,* J. Murray, London, 1848.

Griggs, Bertram S., and Gary R. McCune: "Community-Based Correctional Programs: A Survey and Analysis," *Federal Probation,* vol. 36, no. 2, Administrative Office of the United States Courts, Washington, D.C., June 1972, pp. 7–13.

Johnson, Elmer Hubert: *Crime, Correction and Society,* Dorsey Press, Homewood, Ill., 1968, chaps. 17 and 26.

Keve, Paul: *Imaginative Programming in Probation and Parole,* University of Minnesota Press, Minneapolis, 1967, chaps. 6 and 8.

Killinger, George G., Hazel B. Kerper, and Paul F. Cromwell, Jr.: *Probation and Parole in the Criminal Justice System,* West Publishing Company, St. Paul, Minn., 1976, pt. II.

Leonard, E. M.: *The Early History of English Poor Relief,* Cambridge University Press, Cambridge, England, 1900.

Lunden, Walter A.: "The Rotary Jail, or Human Squirrel Cage," *Journal of the Society of Architectural Historians,* vol. 18, no. 4, December 1959.

Markley, Carson W.: "Furlough Programs and Conjugal Visiting in Adult Correctional Institutions," *Federal Probation,* vol. 37, no. 1, Administrative Office of the United States Courts, Washington, D.C., 1973, pp. 19–26.

Meeker, Ben S.: "The Federal Probation System: The Second 25 Years," *Federal Probation,* vol. 39, no. 2, Administrative Office of the United States Courts, Washington, D.C., June 1975, pp. 16–25.

Milosovich, John T., and Charles Megerman: "The Community Corrections Center Project," *Offender Rehabilitation,* vol. 1, no. 1, Fall 1976, pp. 33–43.

Moynahan, J. M., and Earle K. Stewart: "The Origin of the American Jail," *Federal Probation,* vol. 42, no. 4, Administrative Office of the United States Courts, Washington, D.C., December 1978, pp. 41–50.

"Parole," *The Attorney General's Survey of Release Procedures,* U.S. Government Printing Office, Washington, D.C., 1939, vol. IV.

Parker, William: *Parole: Origins, Development, Current Practices and Statutes,* Parole Correctional Project, Resource Document Number 1, American Correctional Association, College Park, Md., 1975.

Powers, Edwin: *Crime and Punishment in Early Massachusetts,* Beacon Press, Boston, 1966.

————: "Halfway Houses: An Historical Perspective," *American Journal of Correction,* vol. 21, No. 4, July/August 1959, pp. 20–22, 35.

Prassel, Frank R.: *Introduction to American Criminal Justice,* Harper & Row, Publishers, Incorporated, New York, 1975.

Robinson, Louis N.: *Jails: Care and Treatment of Misdemeanant Prisoners in the United States,* John C. Winston Company, Philadelphia, 1944.

Smith, Robert R., John M. McKee, and Michael A. Milan: "Study-Release Policies of American Correctional Agencies," *Journal of Criminal Justice,* vol. 2, no. 4, Winter 1974, pp. 357–363.

Sutherland, Edwin H., and Donald R. Cressey: *Criminology,* J. B. Lippincott Company, Philadelphia, 1970, chaps. 18, 21, and 26.

Turner, Merfyn: "The Lessons of Norman House," *The Annals of the American Academy of Political and Social Science—The Future of Corrections,* vol. 383, January 1969.

Wines, Frederick H.: *Punishment and Reformation,* Crowell, New York, 1895.

Wright, Roberts J.: "The Jail and Misdemeanant Institutions," in Paul W. Tappan (ed.), *Contemporary Corrections,* McGraw-Hill Book Company, New York, 1951, pp. 310–322.

CORRECTIONS FOCUSING ON THE COMMUNITY: 1980

CHAPTER OBJECTIVES

- To establish a rationale for community-based corrections
- To discuss the advantages and disadvantages of community-based corrections
- To present the possible effects of the other option: imprisonment
- To examine the community-based correctional client
- To review the status of statewide community-based corrections programs

INTRODUCTION

Even though the enthusiasm generated in the 1960s over corrections focusing on the community had begun to dampen by 1980, there was no question that community-based corrections had been established as a concept and a process of corrections. The use of probation had multiplied to the point where 60 percent of all convicted defendants were placed on probation by the courts.[1] For most state correctional departments, allowing inmates to enter the community temporarily, prior to release on parole or expiration of sentence, has become a routine part of the process of reintegration for adult felons.

---

[1]Clemens Bartollas, *Introduction to Corrections,* Harper & Row, Publishers, Incorporated, New York, 1981, p. 111.

By 1981 there were 18,151 inmates living in community-based residences such as halfway houses.[2] The 1980 edition of the Directory of the International Halfway House Association lists 1061 such residences in the United States and halfway houses solely for female offenders in twenty-nine states.[3] Each year a smaller number of inmates end their sentences without some form of supervision —parole, conditional pardon, or mandatory release.

RATIONALE FOR COMMUNITY-BASED CORRECTIONS

The Task of Corrections

Every time convicted felons leave the courtroom, society is confronted with the problem of assisting them in their quest for a law-abiding life. The task of corrections therefore includes building or rebuilding solid ties between offenders and the community, integrating or reintegrating them into community life, restoring family ties, and obtaining employment and education. In the larger sense, this means securing a place for the offender in the routine functioning of society.

In the 1960s, after years of futility, correctional administrators began to search for new methods to assist offenders. The Task Force on Corrections of the President's Commission on Law Enforcement and Administration of Justice stated in 1967:

It is clear that the correctional programs of the United States cannot perform their assigned work by mere tinkering with faulty machinery. A substantial upgrading of services and a new orientation of the total enterprise toward integration of offenders into the mainstream of community life is needed.[4]

Other Support

In their search for a replacement for the "faulty machinery" correctional administrators received support from other sources. The general public demanded increased effectiveness in rehabilitation because of the increased incidence of crime. Humanitarians, previously concerned with mental patients and juveniles, called for humane treatment of offenders. Behavioral scientists endorsed the concept that crime was a social phenomenon that originated in the community and could not be treated by removal from the community. Over the years attempts have been made to discover new techniques of rehabilitation which

[2]Kevin Krajick, "Annual Prison Population Survey: The Boom Resumes," *Corrections Magazine,* vol. 7, no. 2, April 1981, p. 19.
[3]*1979–1980 IHHA Directory,* International Halfway House Association, Cincinnati, 1980.
[4]John P. Conrad, "Corrections and Simple Justice," reprinted by special permission of *The Journal of Criminal Law, Criminology, and Police Science,* by Northwestern University Law School, vol. 64, no. 2, 1973, pp. 211–212.

correctional administrators could use to interrupt the cyclical pattern of criminality. Community-based corrections is one result of this effort.

A Practical Definition

Community-based corrections is the utilization of any community resource that can be beneficial to the socially acceptable adjustment of the offender. Such resources include community service centers, halfway houses, parole and probation officers, prerelease programs, and drug and alcohol clinics—all especially designed for the offender—as well as jails and other local correctional institutions. However, community-based corrections does not end with these obvious programs. On the contrary, it encompasses all community resources, including vocational and academic public education, vocational rehabilitation, community mental health services, churches, recreation facilities, service clubs, unions, employers, medical and dental clinics, citizen volunteers, and state and federal public assistance programs.

A model community-based correctional program is a comprehensive service-delivery system. The community provides needed services to the offenders being detained; or, where possible, the offender or the former offender should be guided to the resources within the community as a probationer, parolee, work furloughee, or inmate on educational furlough. The correctional system should not duplicate services available within the community. For example, if educational resources or drug counseling exist in the community and are available, they should be used rather than duplicating these services.[5]

Philosophical Justification

Community-based corrections is based on the belief that rehabilitation of offenders can be accomplished most efficiently in the community itself. Supporters argue that felons who have difficulty adjusting to society before conviction cannot be expected to resolve their problems by being isolated from society. In contrast, by remaining in the community, offenders assume the same responsibility for solving their personal problems and controlling their behavior as they will have after release from their sentences. The result is a more effective attempt at rehabilitation.

Supporters of community-based corrections state further that the experience of working through problems within the community can be a learning process. Offenders learn to live normally in the same neighborhood where they lived before conviction. Family ties are continued. Offenders associate with the same people. They work 8 hours a day. They assume their debts. They plan their own leisure time. They receive assistance from the local Alcoholics Anonymous

[5]M. Robert Montilla, "Environment for Community Corrections," *Corrections in the Community,* E. Eugene Miller and M. Robert Montilla (eds.), Reston Publishing Company, Inc., Reston, Va., 1977, p. 25.

group or employment office. A lifestyle can be developed by each offender that is identical to that required after completion of sentence.

Economic Justification

The efficiency of community-based corrections is substantiated by a better economic utilization of the tax dollar. The community already possesses schools, hospitals, and other resources, eliminating the need for their duplication in prison—hence a savings. Convicted felons living in the community are expected to be responsible for themselves for as many as 16 hours a day, removing the necessity to pay for 24-hour custodial care. Many personal needs, such as housing or food, are met by the offender and not the taxpayer.

One project conducted by the state of California demonstrated the monetary savings achieved. Beginning in fiscal 1966–1967, counties were given a $4000 subsidy for each felon not sent to a state correctional institution. As a condition of participation, the county had to have a base commitment rate of 40 to 49 persons per 100,000 of total population. Within 6 years, the California probation subsidy program saved an estimated $60 million of state funds.[6] State support through direct dollar subsidies to local governments will continue to be justified by a number of practical considerations—the increasing number of prisoners being sentenced to state institutions, the decreasing availability of federal funds—especially from the Law Enforcement Assistance Administration (LEAA)—the low budgetary priority of corrections for local governments, and the fiscal crises of many local governments.[7]

THE EFFECTS OF IMPRISONMENT ON THE OFFENDER

The Environment

The final justification for community-based corrections is the effect of the other option—imprisonment—on offenders. Within a prison, large groups live together 24 hours a day in a circumscribed space under a tightly scheduled sequence of activities imposed by a central authority. Inmates carry out sets of activities in one place, according to a timetable controlled by a single authority, in the company of others who are treated similarly. All are subjected to formal rules under a rationale intended to achieve the organization's official aim.

Unlike most people, inmates do not have the opportunity to sleep, play, and work in different places, with a different set of companions and different plans for organizing these sets of relationships. Prisoners are denied experiences taken for granted by free men and women—a spouse's kiss on returning home, a choice of food, a leisurely cup of coffee, an opportunity to withdraw from

---

[6]James McSparron, "Community Correction and Diversion," *Crime and Delinquency,* vol. 26, no. 2, April 1980, p. 230.
[7]Ibid., pp. 235–236.

unpleasant situations. They are subjected to social debasement resulting from the prison's lack of concern for personal dignity and individuality. They become numbers to be processed by prison employees.

From admission until release they are subject to a series of humiliations—fingerprinting, deprivation of personal belongings, standardized haircuts, wearing drab prison clothes, and constant invasion of privacy through shakedowns. Inmates are constantly aware of the threat of strongarm attacks from more aggressive inmates or gangs of marauders, yet they cannot withdraw from their association. The rules implement a control system which assign the prisoners to a status socially inferior to the keepers. In fact, inmates are expected to comply with a code of rules framed with only slight interest in meeting their personal needs.[8]

Prisonization

In Donald Clemmer's descriptive text, *The Prison Community,* the process that an immigrant experiences when entering America is compared with the process an inmate experiences when entering prison. Prisonization, as Clemmer describes it, is the "taking on in greater or lesser degree of the folkways, mores, customs, and general culture of the penitentiary."[9] Prisonization is a process of assimilation, a more or less unconscious process during which a person learns enough of the culture of a social unit to become typical of that unit. The definition implies that the assimilated individual begins to share the sentiments, memories, and traditions of the group.

Prisonization is an assimilation process that begins when a first offender, or "new fish," enters prison or a recidivist returns. The new inmate may attempt to remain aloof from other inmates, yet is inevitably subject to the conditions for prisonization described by Clemmer—acceptance of an inferior role; accumulation of facts concerning the organization of the prison; development of new habits of eating, dressing, working, and sleeping; the adoption of the local language; and the recognition that all needs are supplied without obligation. Even the most resistant prisoner, after a number of years, is affected by these segments of the prison culture.[10]

Why Prisonization?

Every offender experiences feelings of disgrace because of the social degradation associated with trial and arrest. Although feelings of disgrace may be acute in first offenders, experienced criminals may be irritated at "getting busted." All offenders undergo physical separation from and rejection by society.

---

[8]Erving Goffman, "On the Characteristics of Total Institutions: The Inmate World," *The Prison: Studies in Institutional Organization and Change,* Donald R. Cressey (ed.), Holt, Rinehart, and Winston, Inc., New York, 1961, pp. 16–17, 23–48.
[9]Donald Clemmer, *The Prison Community,* Christopher Publishing House, Boston, 1940, p. 299.
[10]Ibid., pp. 87, 300.

Inmates enter prison as former members of social groups. They may have been members of families, of neighborhood gangs, or of labor groups in shops. They may have been habitues of sundry hangouts where they shared common group experiences. Although there is a weakening of past relationships with family, friends, and fellow employees, each person retains strong inclinations toward being part of a social group.

Most penitentiaries are large institutions with populations overcrowding the facilities. Inside, there are many cliques and subgroups. Life becomes social during the first night, as each prisoner meets other inmates—maybe even a cell partner or partners. It gradually dawns on the "new fish" that this new world will eventually dominate their judgment or behavior. They must adjust to its praise or blame, its applause or ridicule.

New inmates soon learn that a prison environment has its own set of ethics, largely developed from the beliefs of the majority of those incarcerated and adopted as a code of prison living. Inmates learn new notions of how fast one should work, what nicknames to apply to guards, and what behaviors are approved or condemned. These notions may conflict with previous ideas. Individuals may separate themselves from the mass of prisoners and maintain private thoughts, but their overt behavior cannot disregard prison opinion.[11]

The Conditions of Imprisonment

The final factor is imprisonment itself. The reality of cell confinement with its restriction of mobility grinds deeply into the emotions of new inmates. Prison neurosis is no empty diagnostic term. Offenders often say they know every stone, every line, every cranny in their cells. They say they have stood many hours in a sort of hypnosis, just counting lines or stones or bricks. Others relate that night after night they have paced their cells and walked patterns, counting the steps.[12]

David Jones's study of the Tennessee State Penitentiary revealed that prisoners reported psychological distress at a rate 3.6 times higher than that reported for the general adult population in the United States.[13] Researchers Charles Thomas, David Petersen, and Rhonda Zingraff's study of 239 inmates in a maximum security federal penitentiary concluded that easy adoption of inmate social roles is based on a paucity of positive experiences before prison rather than on in-prison variables, the loss of inmate contact with outside society during confinement, and a negative perception of postprison life chances.[14]

[11]Donald R. Taft and Ralph R. England, Jr., *Criminology,* The MacMillan Company, New York, 1964, pp. 472–473.

[12]A. M. Kirkpatrick, "Prisons Produce People," *Federal Probation,* vol. 26, no. 4, Administrative Office of the United States Courts, Washington, D.C., December 1962, p. 28.

[13]David A. Jones, *The Health Risks of Imprisonment,* D. C. Heath and Company, Lexington, Mass., 1976, p. 85.

[14]Charles W. Thomas, David M. Petersen, and Rhonda M. Zingraff, "Structural and Social Psychological Correlates of Prisonization," *Criminology,* vol. 16, no. 3, November 1978, p. 391.

Yet these effects are minor compared to more serious consequences of imprisonment. Of the inmates who responded in David Jones's study of the Tennessee State Penitentiary ten percent estimated that four homosexual rapes took place in their prison each week, 30 percent estimated that there were two such rapes, and 37 percent estimated one such rape a week.[15]

Tom Murton's tenure as superintendent of the Cummins Prison Farm in Arkansas exposed rampant cruelty—use of the strap, chains, rubber hoses, and the Tucker "telephone" (an electronic generator taken from a crank-type telephone, which was wired to the inmates' bodies); forced homosexuality; and inmate extortion. Murton's story, which reached a grim climax in January 1968, when skeletons of three murdered prisoners were discovered, is vividly described in his book, *Accomplices to the Crime*[16] and the movie *Brubaker*.

Two of the most traumatic experiences in the United States took place in prisons. First was the riot in Attica, New York, on September 13, 1971. Then came the riot at the New Mexico State Prison in Santa Fe on February 2, 1980, during which 33 inmates were killed and 200 others beaten and raped. This riot, although probably planned, was not a controlled, calculated revolt similar to that in Attica, but an unpredictable, leaderless, and uncontrolled—almost berserk—explosion of torture and mutilation. New Mexico corrections officials had been warned for some time that the overcrowded, understaffed prison was ripe for a riot. The murders of the 33 inmates were not the result of drug overdoses or smoke inhalation or racial anger. The prisoners who exploded in a frenzy of violence were not intoxicated. There was no target for their murderous fury except that thirteen of the murdered had been labeled "snitches" by the inmate population.[17] This riot and the threat of similar disturbances in other prisons clearly demonstrate the emotional climate faced by offenders when they enter prison.

Ultimately, a new inmate has limited choices: psychological withdrawal; cooperation with the administration, at the risk of being considered a stool pigeon; or identification with the inmate population, with the feeling that this is the wisest and only practical solution.[18]

Considering these conditions, it is little surprise that the pain of imprisonment becomes less severe as the prisoner moves in the direction of prisonization.[19] After all, it is simply the offender's adoption of the prison culture and the rejection of the free-world culture.

CLIENTS OF COMMUNITY-BASED CORRECTIONS

Offenders who take part in community-based corrections emerge from two major sources—the prisons and the courts. They are felons or misdemeanants

---

[15]Jones, op. cit., p. 157.

[16]Tom Murton, *Accomplices to the Crime,* Grove Press, New York, 1970.

[17]Michael S. Serrill and Peter Katel, "The Anatomy of a Riot," *Corrections Magazine,* vol. 6, no. 2, April 1980, pp. 7–8.

[18]Kirkpatrick, op. cit., p. 27.

[19]Gresham M. Sykes and Sheldon L. Messinger, "The Inmate Social System," *Theoretical Studies in Social Organization of the Prison,* Social Science Research Council, New York, 1960, p. 16.

released from incarceration or placed in the community under some form of suspended sentence by a judge. In either situation, the influence of the community can be supportive or destructive. Offenders with suspended sentences are allowed to remain in the community because the people responsible for sentencing believe they are not dangerous enough to be removed. Released offenders leave prison because correctional personnel believe they do not need to be isolated from the community or because they are completing their sentences. In each case, the community has been selected as the most appropriate place for the convicted felon.

Prison Releasees

For each inmate, the change from institutionalized life to freedom is drastic and requires major adjustments. In fact, most inmates regard release with a degree of apprehension. Frequently, questions asked by the released prisoner include: "Where should I go?" "Who will help me?" "What should I do?" The released inmate's problems vary, depending on the nature of the individual, the length of incarceration, and the circumstances of release. Incarceration may weaken self-reliance and promote dependence on others. At the same time, relationships with friends and work associates have been interrupted and may have deteriorated. When a married man or woman leaves prison, release terminates public assistance for the waiting spouse, yet may result in immediate demands for payment of debts and a search for larger and more expensive living quarters.

The prison routine often creates habits inconsistent with patterns of community life. Frequently, former inmates are embarrassed by automatically stopping before a door, waiting for a guard to open it. After being isolated from the community, the inmate emerges to a world that appears strange. Techniques of work have changed. Routine skills such as driving a car or ordering a meal in a restaurant have been forgotten.

Court Releasees

Problems also confront the sentenced probationer. Following a lengthy wait in jail while guilt is being determined, probationers return to the community to discover that the same environment and responsibilities still exist. Their drinking friends meet in the tavern on Friday night. Bills need to be paid. Work is difficult to obtain. Offenders employed before indictment discover that they have been replaced during their absence. The problems that existed in interpersonal relations with spouse, family, or friends, are unresolved. In addition, public advertising of the offenders' deviant behavior encourages hesitancy in extending trust to them.

The Problems of Supervision

Community-based corrections offers an opportunity for correctional personnel to assist both ex-inmates and probationers with their problems. Administrators responsible for offenders in the community assume that all are eligible for the reintegrating or integrating process before final release, and their problems should be resolved before they are given total freedom.

Upon receiving offenders, administrators consider the recommendations of the placing parties but apply their own knowledge of the community in order to reintegrate or integrate them. After a short period of orientation, they are extended opportunities to work themselves into the community as law-abiding citizens. To accomplish this goal, questions are asked. How responsible is the offender? How much outside control or support will be needed? What privileges should be allowed?

Some probationers who lack internal behavioral controls, resulting in drug addiction or explosive behavior, may require extensive structure. If so, they are placed "halfway in" a halfway house. Members of the staff at the halfway house assist these probationers in their efforts to develop self-control. Still allowed time in the community through work release and furloughs, they are able to retain community ties that would have been broken if they had been incarcerated. Other probationers may be allowed to live with their families while receiving intensive support from a probation officer, from alcohol or drug treatment personnel, or from a counselor at a mental health center. On the other hand, an offender who has exhibited considerable self-reliance and personal control at a prerelease center may be placed on parole with minimum supervision (i.e., one visit a month and weekly reports mailed to the parole agent).

Whether the offenders have been released from incarceration or placed in the community with suspended sentences, correctional personnel responsible for their reintegration are aware of their previous problems and behavior. They use all the community resources available to effectively and efficiently redirect the offenders, who are encouraged to seek whatever assistance they need from the community.

STATEWIDE COMMUNITY-BASED CORRECTIONS PROGRAMS

National Overview

The greatest endorsement of corrections focused on the community is the development of statewide programs. In the 1970s Minnesota, Oregon, and Kansas approved legislation permitting statewide community-based corrections programs. A little later, California also passed a community corrections bill replacing the Probation Subsidy Act, but whether it will increase or decrease community-based corrections is debatable. Maryland has a dormant community corrections act. Many states—Arizona, Colorado, Connecticut, Florida, Iowa, Kentucky, Nevada, New Jersey, Ohio, Pennsylvania, Virginia, and Wisconsin—have adopted legislation either endorsing or authorizing community-based corrections but have failed to fully implement the intent of the legislation.

Minnesota

The first step in Minnesota was the formation in July 1972, of a study committee, composed of legislators and their staffs, police, judges, representatives of state and county agencies, local elected officials, and personnel from the department of corrections. This group drafted the Community Corrections Act and presented it to the legislature in February 1973. The act became law, with an appropriation of $1.5 million for three pilot areas. The 1975 legislature appropriated more than $7 million to continue the program in the pilot areas and expand it to an additional eighteen counties. The 1977 legislature provided further support with $13.6 million to maintain the program in all the previous counties and extend it into nine additional counties.

The establishment of a local community advisory board is basic to the implementation of the plan. This board identifies correctional needs and defines the necessary programs and services. A comprehensive plan is submitted to the county board for final approval. It is then sent to the commissioner of corrections 30 days before the expected starting date. When the commissioner approves the comprehensive plan, the county is eligible for a state financial subsidy.

Community corrections counties are charged $27.50 a day for any adult commitment to a state institution for less than 5 years, thus discouraging commitments to state institutions. On the basis of inmates per 100,000 residents in the state, Minnesota has the second-lowest commitment rate in the nation.

Oregon

Enacted in July 1977, Oregon's Community Corrections Act also provides a state subsidy to those counties choosing to participate. But for every felon who is convicted of a minor property offense (Class C crime) and committed to a state correctional institution, the county is required to return part of its grant money to pay the costs of care for the first year of incarceration.

Oregon's Community Corrections Act includes a central referral agency which consolidates services at the point of entry into the system. This 24-hour service includes pretrial release, medical screening, referral to community facilities for drug addicts, and information and other support systems for offenders. It has already reduced the number of individuals detained awaiting trial.

Kansas

In contrast to Minnesota and Oregon, the Kansas act was sponsored in the legislature by community interest groups. Although it was passed in 1978, the Community Corrections Act remains in the implementation stage. Counties involved in the plan are permitted to sentence defendants to a maximum 20-year prison term without a charge-back to their subsidy allotments, thus restricting effectiveness of the act in keeping offenders in community-based programs.[20]

The Results

As of May 1981, twenty-seven of Minnesota's eighty-seven counties, representing 70 percent of the state's population, were participating in the Community Corrections Act. They received a subsidy of $12 million in fiscal 1981. Two of the original objectives of the act have been clearly achieved—improved planning and administration in local corrections and improved services in the counties participating in the act.[21]

A third objective was to decrease prison population by retaining more offenders in the community. Juvenile commitments to state institutions were reduced first. Five counties experienced a 50 percent reduction in juvenile commitments, and the overall reduction in commitments is almost 30 percent. During the first 6 years after the inception of the Community Corrections Act, the average daily institutional population had been reduced by 15 juveniles.

The change in sentencing patterns for adult offenders in Minnesota, however, has been slight. In the beginning the reduction in adult commitments was about 3 percent, which amounts to an average *annual* population reduction of approximately fifty-one offenders. Since 1975 the trend has reversed. As a result, the adult inmate count has risen from about 1300 in 1975 to more than 2000 in 1980.

Even juvenile institutional populations have increased. From 1970 to 1978, populations declined from 800 to 170 inmates, but from 1979 to the end of June 1980, they increased to 255.

A criticism of the Minnesota experience has been its failure to reduce costs. A report released in January 1981 by Minnesota corrections authorities revealed that costs of community corrections had increased by 13 to 16 percent. Savings from decreased state prison populations were insufficient to offset higher overhead, program, and local incarceration costs associated with the Community Corrections Act.

Three factors were cited to explain the increased costs. First, the program was initiated in a state that already had a high level of community corrections, so the potential for additional impact was small. The second factor described by Minnesota authorities was that

> in Minnesota the alternative to prison has tended to be local incarceration. Moreover, judges tend to use local incarceration to a greater extent for types of offenders previously sentenced to the community. This increased use of a relatively expensive local alternative has reduced the savings that result from keeping offenders out of prison.

[20]Bartollas, op. cit., pp. 111, 112, 114, 115.

[21]*Minnesota Community Corrections Act Evaluation,* Minnesota Department of Corrections, St. Paul, January 1981, p. 76.

Finally, hardening of public attitudes happened at about the same time, encouraging judges to deal more harshly with offenders.

A look at the results of Oregon's Community Corrections Act revealed a clear reduction in prison population. Specifically, the rate of commitments for Class C felons—the group intended to be diverted from state prisons—dropped from 21 percent of all Class C felony convictions to 17 percent in fully participating counties. Of all burglars, 17 percent were sent to state prisons in 1979, compared to 40 percent in 1977.[22]

PUBLIC REACTION

The General Public

The establishment of some form of community-based corrections in all fifty states does not mean that public reaction has been favorable. There are still many correctional officials and many of the general public who disapprove of allowing the convicted felon access to the free community. Wherever community-based corrections has been established, supporting correctional administrators have been forced to convince those who disagree.

One major task is lessening the apprehension of the general public. To accomplish this, adequate preparation of the community is a prerequisite to the introduction of the program. A knowledgeable citizen advisory board can be an aid in ensuring continuous sympathetic dialogue with the community. Many states have mandated citizen advisory boards through legislation. Human interest stories in the newspaper, staff presentations to community groups, and rapid attention to unfavorable publicity that might create opposition from local residents are other methods of gaining public support.

Initially, many people are afraid of the consequences of the inevitable escapes and failures. Correctional personnel are frequently asked how they will protect the public from violent offenders. News releases and public presentations informing people of the elaborate selection process that screens participants in community-based corrections are used to alleviate this fear. The public is assured that offenders will be supervised and that they can be returned immediately to a walled institution if need be. The methods of continual supervision and follow-up are explained. Those inmates who are not ready for community living will have all privileges taken away, thus protecting the public from violent offenders.

Correctional Personnel

One problem that hinders public acceptance of community-based corrections is the lack of confidence expressed by some correctional personnel who are convinced that inmates should be confined primarily and helped secondarily.

[22]John Blackmore, "Oregon Has No Second Thoughts About the 'Minnesota Model,'" *Corrections Magazine,* vol. 7, no. 4, New York, August 1981, p. 38. Copyright 1981 by Criminal Justice Publications and Corrections Magazine, 116 West 32nd Street, N.Y., N.Y., 10001.

These correctional workers, especially custodial personnel, fear that the inmates will become uncontrollable without walls and prison routine. Correctional departments have faced this problem by using an in-service training program similar to the education program designed for the general public. As soon as community-based corrections programs are considered, the preparation of correctional personnel must begin. As a last .resort, terminating correctional workers who are recalcitrant is sometimes necessary. New personnel must then be recruited who are oriented to a philosophy of reintegration.

One way to convince members of the staff that community-based corrections has positive value is to explain how they themselves will benefit. A smaller client-staff ratio actually results in greater control of offenders, not less. Inmates are observed more closely and with greater frequency in community-based residences of twenty-five felons than they are in institutions with 1000 inmates.

Crime rates do not rise, as some citizens fear, when community-based residences open. Utah authorities found no difference in the reported crime rate in the primary impact area of the Bonneville Community Corrections Center in Salt Lake City for July, August, and September of 1980 compared to the same months in 1979. This contrasted with an increase of 3 percent in the reported crime rate citywide.[23] Intrainstitutional tensions are reduced, cutting down escapes and disciplinary reports. State, federal and local officials have reported an escape rate of less than 6.5 percent for inmates on work release.[24]

Some Criticisms

Another problem is the cost of building or managing community correctional centers or halfway houses. To the uninformed, the cost sometimes appears exorbitant. However, the costs of initial development of the programs and their management are actually less than those for walled institutions. Richard Rachin, in his 1972 article entitled "So You Want to Open a Halfway House," recommends approximately 9000 square feet for a twenty-five-bed halfway house.[25] The costs of construction have been estimated at $32.00 to $40.00 per square foot in 1980, bringing the total cost of building the halfway house to $360,000, or $14,400 a bed. The cost of constructing a maximum security prison is $70,000 or more per bed.[26] If these costs appear too high, correctional administrators can lease facilities. In Iowa a forty-bed work release center was leased for $24,000 a year.[27]

Correctional officials also answer their critics by referring to long-range

[23]*July–September 1980, Crime Statistics Bonneville Community Corrections Center,* Utah State Division of Corrections, Salt Lake City, September 1981, p. 2.

[24]William A. Ayer, "Work Release Programs in the United States: Some Difficulties Encountered," *Federal Probation,* vol. 34, no. 1, Administrative Office of the United States Courts, Washington, D.C., March 1970, p. 56.

[25]Richard L. Rachin, "So You Want to Open a Halfway House," *Federal Probation,* vol. 36, no. 1, Administrative Office of the United States Courts, Washington, D.C., March 1972, p. 35.

[26]Robert E. Taylor, "Life in Prison," *The Wall Street Journal,* Aug. 18, 1981, p. 10.

[27]Paul Muller, Superintendent, Riverview Release Center, Bureau of Adult Corrections, State of Iowa, personal correspondence, June 3, 1977.

expenditures. Daily costs of keeping an offender in a community-based residence are less than in a medium or maximum security institution. The average cost for maintaining a prisoner in state institutions in Colorado was $26.32 a day and in Iowa was $34.25 in 1980. The cost for keeping an inmate at a state community-based residence in Colorado was $20.18 a day and in Iowa, $21.00. The cost of supervising an offender on probation or parole was estimated at $362.71 a year in 1980 by the Florida State Probation and Parole Service.[28] Although costs have risen for all correctional programs, the relatively less expensive supervision offered by community-based corrections remains less expensive than institutional programs. By utilizing such programs, Iowa decreased its institutional population from 2365 in 1962 to 1032 in 1973, resulting in estimated annual savings of $3 million.[29]

A final criticism raised by skeptics addresses the application of the concept. The use of community resources is sometimes more complicated in practice than in theory. Locating willing and competent volunteers is difficult. Maintaining a sufficient number of cooperative agencies, such as schools and churches, who are willing to accept offenders is time-consuming. Salaries are frequently inadequate, discouraging contracts with specialists such as medical doctors and psychiatrists.

Correctional officials who answer this criticism point out the importance of careful planning. Before selection of locations for community correctional programs, careful screening can identify promising sites. Most frequently, successful programs are located near population centers. Here the Chamber of Commerce and service groups such as the Jaycees can offer invaluable aid in recruiting volunteers and supportive agencies. Similarly, local medical and mental health associations can assist in hiring medical doctors, dentists, and psychiatrists. The screening process requires that correctional personnel contact potential community resources prior to site selection.

SUCCESS OR FAILURE

Since 1960, correctional authorities have attempted to evaluate the success of community-based corrections, but the accumulated facts tend to be contradictory. Some statistical samples from all forms of community-based corrections appear favorable; other samples are less so.

Favorable Statistics

The California Department of Corrections, Parole, and Community Services Division released data in 1972 revealing that offenders who had been on work release had a recidivism rate of 8.4 percent, compared with a statewide overall

---

[28]*American Correctional Association Directory, 1981,* American Correctional Association, College Park, Md., 1981, pp. xvii, 29–30, 53–64, 101–102.

[29]*Institutional Planning Report,* Iowa Department of Social Services, Bureau of Adult Corrections, Des Moines, 1973, p. 21.

felon recidivism rate of 9.6 percent. Both sets of statistics were compiled 1 year after release. A study in Bucks County, Pennsylvania, revealed an 8 percent recidivism rate among releasees from the work-release program and a 15 percent recidivism rate among other releasees.[30] Probation revocation rates were reported at less than 10 percent for all states in 1977. This contrasted with 20 percent for most reporting states during this same year for inmates released from prison.[31]

The most significant statistics come from Massachusetts, which reported its rate of recidivism for offenders who participated in a prerelease program, including residence at a prerelease center, furloughs, and work release. The rate was 8 percent in 1977, compared with 25 percent for all releasees in 1971, before the adoption of the prerelease program. Furthermore, the prerelease recidivism rate of 8 percent (compiled from releasees representing 42 percent of the total inmate population from Massachusetts prisons) is 11 percent less than the recidivism rate for offenders released without an opportunity to use prerelease centers (see Table 3.1).[32]

The Critics' Response

Critics of community-based corrections question the validity of these favorable statistics, because of the criteria for the selection of participants. The offenders selected for probation or work release are generally better prospects for success than those released directly from prison. The criteria for selection in both

[30]*Graduated Release,* National Institute of Mental Health, Rockville, Md., 1971, p. 11.
[31]Herbert G. Callison, "Survey of United States Correctional Services," unpublished report, 1978.
[32]Daniel P. LeClair, *Community Based Reintegration: Some Theoretical Implications of Positive Research Findings,* Massachusetts Department of Corrections, Boston, November 1979, p. 7.

TABLE 3.1
RECIDIVISM RATES OF PRERELEASE PARTICIPANTS AND NONPARTICIPANTS (BY YEAR)

Year released	Number released	% population released from prerelease centers	Recidivism rate: prerelease participants (%)	Recidivism rate: prerelease nonparticipants (%)	Recidivism rate: total releasees (%)
1971	1,107	0	—	35	25
1972	1,550	1	—*	—*	22
1973	966	11	12	20	19
1974	911	25	12	21	19
1975	806	28	14	22	20
1976	925	40	9	21	16
1977	1,138	42	8	19	15

*Figures not available for subsamples in this year.
Source: Daniel P. LeClair, *Community Based Reintegration: Some Theoretical Implications of Positive Research Findings*, Massachusetts Department of Corrections, Boston, November 1979, p. 7.

programs is less criminality, more favorable work history, greater family stability, greater sobriety, and less addiction—all factors permitting a better chance for success.

Unfavorable Statistics

A federally funded research project by Albert Reiss, examining the first 4 years of Federal Pre-Release Guidance Centers, which utilized work release and temporary release, found contradictory figures. The recidivism rate for a 1962 group of releasees was 38 percent and for a 1969 group was 30 percent. Releasees in a control group who did not participate in the prerelease program had a failure rate of 32 percent.[33]

The National Institute of Mental Health Center for Studies of Crime and Delinquency has stated,

> The more rigorous the methodology used with research and experiments undertaken in regard to pre-release, work release, and halfway houses, the more ambivalent or negative are the findings regarding the efficacy of such programs.[34]

CONCLUSION

Since the beginning of community-based corrections in the nineteenth century, both professional correctional officials and the general public have voiced criticisms of its concept and application. Others from both the community and corrections have vehemently defended the concept. The final chapter has not yet been written. Arguments with considerable merit can be offered in both attack and defense. As community-based corrections becomes firmly established during the last quarter of this century, both prosecutors and defenders of its use undoubtedly will learn the truth.

The concept of reintegration suggests that after a short period of incarceration most offenders should be given the opportunity to rebuild ties to family and other social institutions; other offenders can be integrated into society as an alternative to incarceration. Yet evaluations of community-based corrections have not conclusively shown that probation, parole, work release, or halfway houses result in less recidivism for adult felons. The statistics cited earlier, based on a study by federal officials, revealed approximately the same recidivism rate for felons participating in community-based corrections and for offenders directly released from prison. On the other hand, those same studies do not show a *higher* recidivism rate for offenders who participate in community-based corrections.

The National Institute of Mental Health reached two conclusions regarding

---

[33]Albert J. Reiss, Correctional Research Associates, *Treating Youth Offenders in the Community,* U.S. Government Printing Office, Washington, D.C., 1966, p. 154.

[34]*Graduated Release*, op. cit., p. 23.

the future. First, evidence that many adult inmates can be safely released to work in the open community without any increase in recidivism implies that most offenders who are eligible for such programs could be safely and effectively retained in the community in the first place. Second, a vast number of offenders currently living in prison could be managed in the community at least as effectively and at much lower cost. They might even be diverted from the criminal justice system entirely, thus returning to the community the responsibility for dealing with behavior defined as antisocial or deviant.[35]

A similar conclusion was stated by the United States Chamber of Commerce:

> There is growing evidence that new programs making use of community approaches to corrections as alternatives to incarceration, and also a means of facilitating reintegration of the offender back into the community following release from an institution, can be more successful and less costly to society.[36]

If the conclusion of either organization is accepted, there is justification for community-based corrections as a better way and for encouraging more than a continuation of such programs. Efforts are necessary to constantly refute and reorder, using results of data derived from sophisticated evaluation. As this happens, community-based corrections will become preferred—not merely fashionable—as a part of the weaponry of corrections based on demonstrated importance.

EXERCISES

1 Can you envision an institutional setting within which an inmate could resolve community-oriented problems? If so, describe such a setting.
2 What advantages and disadvantages exist for a statewide community-based corrections program? Give reasons for both sides.
3 What hidden costs are present if the offender remains in the community on probation?
4 Why would state officials adopt probation and parole more quickly than other forms of community-based corrections?
5 What steps can be taken to minimize the probationer's problems created by the court appearance itself?
6 List reasons why so few offenders are placed in halfway houses.
7 Would you advise that a "halfway in" probationer be housed with a "halfway out" inmate? Give reasons.
8 What problems might arise for community-based correctional clients in their reaching-out process?
9 List methods of improving release procedures besides community-based corrections which might assist the offender in the transition from prison to the community.
10 What arguments for *and* against community-based corrections appear the most valid to you? Be specific.

[35]*Community-Based Correctional Programs,* National Institute of Mental Health, Rockville, Md., 1971, p. 33.

[36]George F. Cole, *The American System of Criminal Justice,* Duxbury Press, North Scituate, Mass., 1975, p. 423.

11 How would you prepare the public for community-based corrections before the initiation of the program?

12 What explanations are possible for the apparent lack of improvement in recidivism rates for community-based corrections participants?

13 Do you agree with the author's conclusion that even if recidivism rates do not improve, community-based corrections is a "better way"? Give reasons for your answer.

14 Should researchers continually scrutinize community-based corrections with more rigorous and demanding methodology in their examination of its "success"?

15 Compare and contrast the conditions leading to the process of prisonization with conditions of living in other total institutions such as schools or the military.

16 Agree or disagree with this statement: "The pains of imprisonment become less severe as the prisoner moves in the direction of prisonization." Explain your position.

17 How might a prison use rules and regulations to decrease the effects of prisonization? Give specific examples.

EXERCISE REFERENCES

Alonzo, Thomas M.: "The Transition Away From Traditional Incarceration: Community Based Corrections," *Criminal Justice Review,* vol. 4, no. 2, Fall 1979, pp. 1–6.

Ayer, William A.: "Work Release Programs in the United States: Some Difficulties Encountered," *Federal Probation,* vol. 34, no. 1, Administrative Office of the United States Courts, Washington, D.C., March 1970, pp. 53–56.

Banks, Jerry, Terry R. Siler, and Ronald L. Rardin: "Past and Present Findings on Intensive Adult Probation," *Federal Probation,* vol. 41, no. 2, Administrative Office of the United States Courts, Washington, D.C., June 1977, pp. 20–25.

Bartollas, Clemens: *Introduction to Corrections,* Harper & Row, Publishers, Incorporated, New York, 1981, chaps. 4 and 6.

Bird, Gordon: "Community Centered Treatment of Offenders," in Edward M. Scott and Kathryn L. Scott (eds.), *Criminal Rehabilitation . . . Within and Without the Walls,* Charles C Thomas, Publisher, Springfield, Ill., 1973, chap. 10, pp. 127–146.

Blackmore, John: "Evaluating the Minnesota Evaluation," *Corrections Magazine,* vol. 7, no. 4, August 1981, pp. 24–38.

Boesen, Povl G., and Stanley E. Grupp (eds.): *Standards and Goals for Community Based Corrections: Theory, Practice and Research,* Davis Publishing Company, Inc., Santa Cruz, Calif., 1976, pp. 9–19.

Bradley, H. B.: "Community Based Treatment for Young Adult Offenders," *Crime and Delinquency,* vol. 15, no. 3, July 1969, pp. 359–370.

Brown, Bailey: "Community Service as a Condition of Probation," *Federal Probation,* vol. 41, no. 4, Administrative Office of the United States Courts, Washington, D.C., December 1977, pp. 7–9.

Carlson, Norman: "Concern Shown—But Problem Goes Unsolved," *American Journal of Correction,* vol. 39, no. 4, July/August 1977, p. 28.

Carter, Robert M.: "The Diversion of Offenders," in Burt Galaway, Joe Hudson, and C. David Hollister (eds.), *Community Corrections,* Charles C Thomas, Publisher, Springfield, Ill., 1976, pp. 42–45.

Chaneles, Sol: *The Open Prison,* Dial Press, New York, 1973.

Clemmer, Donald: *The Prison Community,* Christopher Publishing House, Boston, 1940.

Conrad, John P.: "Corrections and Simple Justice," *The Journal of Criminal Law, Criminology, and Police Science,* vol. 64, no. 2, 1973, pp. 208–217.

"Diversion from the Criminal Justice System," in Povl G. Boesen and Stanley E. Grupp (eds.), *Community Based Corrections: Theory, Practice and Research,* Davis Publishing Company, Santa Cruz, Calif., 1976, pp. 33–44.

Estes, Marion M., and James S. New: "Some Observations on Prison Psychoses," *Journal of Medical Association of Georgia,* vol. 37, January 1958, pp. 2–3.

Farrington, David P., and Christopher Nuttal: "Prison Size, Overcrowding, Prison Violence, and Recidivism," *Journal of Criminal Justice,* vol. 8, no. 4, 1980, pp. 221–231.

Fishman, Robert: *An Evaluation of the Effect on Criminal Recidivism of New York City Projects Providing Rehabilitation and Diversion Services,* New York State Division of Criminal Justice, New York, 1975.

Fox, Vernon: *Community Based Corrections,* Prentice-Hall, Inc., Englewood Cliffs, N.J., 1977, Chaps. 3 and 4.

Goffman, Erving: *Asylums,* Anchor Books, New York, 1961.

Goffman, Erving: "On the Characteristics of Total Institutions: The Inmate World," *The Prison: Studies in Institutional Organization and Change,* Donald R. Cressey (ed.), Holt, Rinehart, and Winston, Inc., New York, 1961, pp. 15–67.

Goldfarb, Ronald L., and Linda R. Singer: *After Conviction,* Simon and Schuster, New York, 1973, sec. VIII.

Griggs, Bertram S., and Gary R. McCune: "Community Correctional Programs: A Survey and Analysis," *Federal Probation,* vol. 36, no. 4, Administrative Office of the United States Courts, Washington, D.C., June 1972, pp. 7–13.

Grosser, George H.: "The Role of Informal Inmate Groups in Change of Values," *Children,* vol. 5, no. 1, U.S. Superintendent of Documents, Washington, D.C., January/February 1958, pp. 25–29.

Hudson, Joe, Gerald Strathman, and Patrick McManus: "De-Centralizing Corrections: The Minnesota Community Corrections Act," in Burt Galaway, Joe Hudson, and C. David Hollister (eds.), *Community Corrections,* Charles C Thomas, Publisher, Springfield, Ill., 1976, pp. 188–198.

————, Burt Galaway, William Henschel, Jay Lindgren, and John Penton: "Diversion Programming in Criminal Justice: The Case of Minnesota," in Burt Galaway, Joe Hudson, and C. David Hollister (eds.), *Community Corrections,* Charles C Thomas, Publisher, Springfield, Ill., 1976, pp. 46–60.

Hushagen, James: "Pre-charge Habilitation Listed as Success in Pierce County, Washington," *American Journal of Correction,* vol. 39, no. 4, July/August 1977, p. 14.

Irwin, John: *The Felon,* Prentice-Hall, Inc., Englewood Cliffs, N.J., 1970.

Jeffery, Robert, and Stephen Woolpert: "Work Furlough as an Alternative to Incarceration: An Assessment of Its Effects on Recidivism and Social Cost," *Journal of Criminal Law, Criminology, and Police Science,* vol. 65, no. 3, September 1974, pp. 405–415.

Jones, David A.: *The Health Risks of Imprisonment,* D. C. Heath and Company, Lexington, Mass., 1976.

Kirkpatrick, A. M.: "Prisons Produce People," *Federal Probation,* vol. 26, no. 4, Administrative Office of the United States Courts, Washington, D.C., December 1962, pp. 26–33.

LeClair, Daniel P.: *Community Based Reintegration: Some Theoretical Implications of Positive Research Findings,* Massachusetts Department of Correction, Boston, November 1979.

Mabry, James: "Alternatives to Confinement," in George C. Killinger and Paul F. Cromwell, Jr. (eds.), *Penology,* West Publishing Company, St. Paul, Minn., 1973, pp. 359–382.

Martinson, Robert, Douglas Lipton, and Judith Wilks: *The Effectiveness of Correctional Treatment,* Praeger Publishers, New York, 1975.

McSparron, James: "Community Correction and Diversion," *Crime and Delinquency,* vol. 26, no. 2, April 1980, pp. 226–247.

Milosovich, John T., and Charles Megerman: "The Community Corrections Center Project," *Offender Rehabilitation,* vol. 1, no. 1, Fall 1976, pp. 33–43.

Montilla, M. Robert: "Environment for Community Corrections," *Corrections in the Community,* Reston Publishing Company, Inc., Reston, Va., 1977, pp. 5–27.

Murton, Tom: *Accomplices to the Crime,* Grove Press, New York, 1970.

National Institute of Mental Health: *Community Based Correctional Programs,* Rockville, Md., 1971.

National Institute of Mental Health: *Graduated Release,* Rockville, Md., 1971.

Palmer, John W.: "Prearrest Diversion: Victim Confrontation," in Burt Galaway, Joe Hudson, and C. David Hollister (eds.), *Community Corrections,* Charles C Thomas, Publisher, Springfield, Ill., 1976, pp. 221–234.

Pettibone, John M.: "Community Based Programs, Catching Up with Yesterday and Planning for Tomorrow," *Federal Probation,* vol. 37, no. 3, Administrative Office of the United States Courts, Washington, D.C., September 1973, pp. 3–8.

Potter, Joan: "The Pitfalls of Pretrial Diversion," *Corrections Magazine,* vol. 7, no. 1, February 1981, pp. 5–7, 10–11, and 36.

———: "Shock Probation: A Little Taste of Prison," *Corrections Magazine,* vol. 3, no. 4, December 1977, pp. 49–55.

Rachin, Richard L.: "So You Want to Open a Halfway House," *Federal Probation,* vol. 36, no. 1, Administrative Office of the United States Courts, Washington D.C., March 1972, pp. 30–37.

Richmond, Mark S.: "Measuring the Cost of Correctional Services," *Crime and Delinquency,* vol. 18, no. 3, July 1972, pp. 243–252.

———: "The Practicalities of Community Based Corrections," *American Journal of Corrections,* vol. 30, no. 6, 1968, pp. 12–18.

Rudoff, Alvin, and T. C. Esselstyn: "Evaluating Work Furlough: A Follow-up," *Federal Probation,* vol. 37, no. 2, Administrative Office of the United States Courts, Washington, D.C., June 1973, pp. 48–53.

Runyon, Tom: *In for Life, a Convict's Story,* W. W. Norton & Company, Inc., New York, 1953.

Serrill, Michael S., and Peter Katel: "The Anatomy of a Riot," *Corrections Magazine,* vol. 6, no. 2, Criminal Justice Publications, Inc., New York, April 1980, pp. 7–8, 24.

Sommer, Robert, and Humphrey Osmond: "Symptoms of Institutional Care," *Social Problems,* vol. 8, no. 3, Winter 1961, pp. 87–90.

Sykes, Gresham M.: "The Pains of Imprisonment," *The Society of Captives,* Princeton University Press, Princeton, N.J., 1958, pp. 65–78.

——— and Sheldon L. Messinger: "The Inmate Social System," in Richard T. Cloward (ed.), *Theoretical Studies in Social Organization of the Prison,* Social Science Research Council, New York, 1960, pp. 5–19.

Taft, Donald R., and Ralph R. England, Jr.: *Criminology,* Macmillan Company, New York, 1964.

Thomas, Charles W., David M. Petersen, and Rhonda Zingraff: "Structural and Social

Psychological Correlates of Prisonization," *Criminology,* vol. 16, no. 3, November 1978, pp. 383–393.

Wakefield, William, and Vincent Webb: "An Application of the Interorganizational Perspective to Community Based Corrections in an Urban Area," *Criminal Justice Review,* vol. 4, no. 2, Fall 1979, pp. 41–50.

Waldron, Joseph A., and Henry R. Angelino: "Shock Probation: A Natural Experiment on the Effect of a Short Period of Incarceration," *The Prison Journal,* vol. LVII, no. 1, Spring/Summer 1977, pp. 45–52.

Warren, Marguerite Q.: *Correctional Treatment in Community Settings,* National Institute of Mental Health, Rockville, Md., 1972.

————: "The Community Treatment Project," in Norman Johnston, Leonard Savitz, and Marvin E. Wolfgang (eds.), *The Sociology of Punishment and Correction,* John Wiley & Sons, Inc., New York, 1970, pp. 671–683.

Wheeler, Stanton: "Socialization in Correctional Institutions," in David A. Goslin (ed.), *Handbook of Socialization Theory and Research,* Rand McNally & Company, New York, 1969, chap. 25.

Zimring, Franklin E.: "Measuring the Impact of Pretrial Diversion From the Criminal Justice System," Povl G. Boesen and Stanley E. Grupp (eds.), *Community Based Corrections: Theory, Practice, and Research,* Davis Publishing Company, Inc., Santa Cruz, Calif., 1976, pp. 355–375.

CHAPTER 4

JAILS

CHAPTER OBJECTIVES

- To examine the present condition and status of jails
- To describe the jail resident
- To discuss jails as institutions for reintegration
- To review examples of reintegration programs in jails
- To examine alternatives to detention, including one exemplary project—the Des Moines project

INTRODUCTION

Community-based corrections is a correctional strategy whereby community resources are utilized in an effort to reintegrate offenders. This strategy is carried out in various ways: by diverting them into community-based programs prior to incarceration, by permitting them contacts with the community during incarceration, by preparing them for reentry into the community before release from incarceration, and by transferring them to community-based programs after incarceration. Although proponents of community-based corrections have been criticized for coddling prisoners and endangering free citizens, the programs offer correctional administrators a clear alternative to incarceration.

Rationale

From many points of view, the jail is the most important of all our institutions of imprisonment. The enormous number of jails is alone sufficient . . . to make one realize that the jail is after all the typical prison in the United States. . . . The part, therefore, which the jail plays in our scheme of punishment cannot be overestimated. Whether for good or for evil, nearly every criminal that has been apprehended is subjected to its influence.[1]

The reader might wonder what a chapter on jails is doing in a textbook on community-based corrections. The answer is simple—all jails are community-based correctional institutions. Jails are managed by law enforcement or correctional personnel responsible to city, county, or regional citizenry. Most jail inmates come from the metropolitan or rural area immediately surrounding the facility. The jail is the correctional institution most able to benefit from community resources. Each jail is a community-based correctional institution, whether correctional personnel use the resources of the community effectively or not.

Jails are in the local community and are community-related. They offer opportunities for inmates to seek professional and family assistance. When located in cities or suburban counties, jails can recruit a wide variety of competent people and helpful community resources. When they are in small counties, they are of manageable size and can give personal attention to inmate needs. In this context, jails can more easily develop reintegration programs. For example, in Pennsylvania some jails have up to one-third of their total population on work release.[2]

Because the jail is a locally administered institution that handles local offenders, jail managers have an advantage not allowed to most correctional administrators, i.e., the possibility of attaining local credibility with the public and maximizing use of local resources. The local jail official has a better chance of beginning reintegration programs than has an "outsider." If the community accepts the jail as a local institution, then the people confined are a local problem calling for local solutions.

There are approximately 10 times as many jails as prisons and several times as many prisoners serving jail sentences during a year than doing prison time.[3] This chapter deals with jails in a general way. Actually, there are different types of jails and jail inmates, with different problems. For example, suburban jails are overcrowded while rural jails are underutilized. Civil rights groups may be filing litigation to alleviate the crowded conditions and the problems created by mixing male and female offenders, juveniles and adults, the convicted and the unconvicted. At the same time, county commissioners in rural areas may be implementing regional jails to reduce the exorbitant expenses that result from maintaining lockups and hiring jailers for only a few inmates in each county and small town.

[1]Louis N. Robinson, *Penology in the United States,* John C. Winston Company, Philadelphia, 1921, pp. 32–33.

[2]"Editorial," *The Prison Journal,* vol. 61, no. 1, Spring/Summer 1981, p. 2.

[3]Clemens Bartollas, *Introduction to Corrections,* Harper & Row, Publishers, Incorporated, New York, 1981, p. 209.

An Overview

The jail is the port of entry to the criminal justice system for most suspected or accused felons. Confinement in jail is a crucial period because there is increasing evidence that the mere incarceration of a person, even when awaiting adjudication only, may increase rather than lessen the likelihood that the detained will remain in the system and continue posing a criminal problem to society.[4]

Prisons are places where local troublemakers are exiled at the expense of the state. Jails are places of confinement for persons not troublesome enough to be exiled. A prison is where an offender is placed if convicted of a felony, a crime with a sentence of 1 year or more. A jail is where he or she is placed if convicted of a misdemeanor, a crime with a sentence of 1 year or less.

The official definition of a jail is fairly simple:

A jail is a confinement facility administered by a local law enforcement agency, intended for adults but sometimes also containing juveniles, which holds persons detained pending adjudication, or persons committed after adjudication for sentences usually for a year or less or both.[5]

The jail exists primarily for what is known as *holding*. While other participants within the criminal justice system determine innocence or guilt, jails are those local facilities that hold misdemeanants or accused persons for 48 hours or longer. There are other institutions for shorter-term detention, such as stockades or lockups. Stockades are county facilities used like jails for persons who can work under minimum security. They may also be confinement facilities on military posts, or facilities that house accused offenders who have not been tried and who cannot be worked. Lockups are short-term detention facilities that are found in most police stations, where persons cannot legally be held for more than 48 hours.

Specific Purposes

The basic purposes of jails and other institutions of detention are (1) to hold accused persons awaiting trial who cannot be released on bail or their own recognizance; (2) to hold convicted persons awaiting sentence or execution of a long-term sentence, such as transfer to a prison; (3) to hold material witnesses who might otherwise disappear; (4) to detain for their own protection the insane or feeble-minded and others suffering from mentally or physically debilitating conditions until some other arrangements can be made for their care; and (5) to retain misdemeanants during their period of sentence.

In carrying out these purposes, most jails make little distinction between men and women, old and young. In addition, lockups are frequently used for

---

[4]L. T. Empey, *Studies in Delinquency: Alternatives to Incarceration,* U.S. Government Printing Office, Washington, D.C., 1967, p. 9.

[5]Timothy J. Flanagan, Michael J. Hindelang, and Michael R. Gottfredson, *Sourcebook of Criminal Justice Statistics—1979,* U.S. Government Printing Office, Washington, D.C., 1980, p. 630.

short-term interrogation of suspects and for holding vagrants and suspicious persons while verifying information about them.

JAILS TODAY

Jail Administration

In their administrative operation, jails present a variety of systems. Four levels of government in the United States—city, county, state, and federal—have their own jails. Of the total number of jails, 22 percent are part of city government, 73 percent are part of county government, and 4 percent are part of city-county joint management.[6] In six states jails are operated by state government, and in one state management of jails is a joint state-local effort. The Federal Bureau of Prisons has three jails, called Metropolitan Correctional Centers, in San Diego, Chicago, and New York. Many jails are under the direction of officials unprepared to perform the duties of jail administration, although this trend is changing as opportunities increase for correctional personnel to receive training. Approximately 85 percent of the jails are administered by sheriffs.

Usually the sheriff is an elected official and has duties in addition to managing the jail. Frequently he or she holds office for only a short period or is not permitted to remain in the position for two successive terms. In effect, this means that the ability to administer a jail is not considered an important qualification for the position. When the sheriff leaves office, he or she is succeeded by another untrained person who must also learn administrative skills by practicing them—a costly and inefficient procedure. Furthermore, the office of sheriff is often a patronage plum in county politics, sought after for the prestige and influence it brings to the party that holds it. For this reason, the revenue from the operation of a jail is considered as something incidental to its administration. As jail critic Roberts J. Wright has succinctly put it, "Jails mean jobs. Jails mean power. Jails mean influence. Jails mean patronage. Jails mean votes."[7]

Some jail officials are paid by the fee system. The fee system is a method of compensating sheriff, police, or jailer with fixed fees for different services performed for the prisoners, including the provision of food. The total amount the sheriff or jailer receives depends on the number of prisoners and the length of time they remain in jail. Consequently, there is an incentive to keep the jail full. For example, there is a food allowance—so much money each day for each prisoner. If the sheriff or jailer can feed prisoners for less, the unspent portion of the fee is profit.[8] Fortunately, the use of the fee system is steadily diminishing in the United States.

---

[6]The President's Commission on Law Enforcement and Administration of Justice, *Task Force Report: Corrections,* U.S. Government Printing Office, Washington, D.C., 1967, p. 163.

[7]Roberts J. Wright, "The Jail and Misdemeanant Institutions," *Contemporary Corrections,* Paul W. Tappan (ed.), McGraw-Hill Book Company, New York, 1951, p. 310.

[8]Robert G. Caldwell, *Criminology,* Ronald Press Company, New York, 1965, p. 552.

Jails surveyed in 1981 reported spending an average of $35.31 a day, or $12,888 a year, for each sentenced inmate. This figure should be compared with an average annual operating budget of $13,505 spent by federal prisons on each prisoner.[9] The nation's jails employed 44,298 persons in 1972, including 39,627 full-time and 4671 part-time employees.[10] The National Jail Census reported that jail employees were paid an average of $617 a month.[11]

Jail Population

In 1978 the national jail census recorded 3493 locally administered jails with authority to detain prisoners for 48 hours or longer, excluding the state-operated jail systems of Connecticut, Delaware, and Rhode Island. The number of lockups has been estimated as high as 41,000, depending on what definition is used. The jail census of February 1978, revealed 158,000 persons being held in the nation's jails, 58 percent of whom had been convicted of a crime and the other 42 percent were awaiting trial. Some 70 percent of the jail inmates were younger than 30. Blacks, who are 12 percent of the population of the United States, comprised 41 percent of the jail population. The median income for jail inmates during the year prior to arrest was only $3255.[12]

Many different types of people are housed in jails, including juvenile offenders, male and female offenders, drug addicts, alcoholics, mentally ill persons, suicide risks, handicapped prisoners, homosexuals, epileptics, and the medically ill. As stated before, half the jail's population has not been convicted of either a misdemeanor or a felony. Of those convicted, a great many are misdemeanants who have been sentenced for less than 1 year. Their misdemeanors include disorderly conduct, petty larceny, assault and battery, vagrancy, vandalism, gambling, prostitution, and family offenses.

The largest single group of misdemeanants (nearly 50 percent) are arrested for some form of drunkenness. Public intoxication is a crime in almost every jurisdiction in the United States. The more than 2 million arrests for drunkenness each year place a heavy load on the court system and the jail.

The jail population is a cross section of Americans. Most persons booked into jail are between 18 and 45 years old, with the largest single group between 18 and 24. The majority of jail inmates have less than an eleventh grade education, and approximately 10 percent have some college or other advanced education.[13] Most jail inmates have been incarcerated before. As one study indicated, only 49

[9]Jo Gustafson, National Institute of Corrections, National Information Center, Boulder, Colorado, personal conversation, Dec. 18, 1981.

[10]*The Nation's Jails,* U.S. Government Printing Office, Washington, D.C., May 1975.

[11]Law Enforcement Assistance Administration, *1970 National Jail Census,* U.S. Government Printing Office, Washington, D.C. 1971, p. 19.

[12]"158,000 Held in Local Jails Last Year," *Criminal Justice Newsletter,* vol. 10, no. 12, June 4, 1979, p. 4.

[13]Nick Pappas (ed.), *The Jail: Its Operations and Management,* United States Bureau of Prisons, Washington, D.C. 1971, pp. 153, 155.

percent of jail inmates were incarcerated for the first time. Twenty percent had been incarcerated 11 times or more. Many jails of the twentieth century have become the poorhouses of the correctional system. Many inmates are incarcerated only because they cannot afford bail or are unable to pay fines. Inmates of middle-class socioeconomic status or above do not remain in jails.

A study by the National Center on Institutions and Alternatives indicated that around 479,000 children were locked up in jails each year.[14] Most of these children did not need to be held anywhere, and those who did need detention could have remained only a day or two. In fact, 23 percent of boys and 70 percent of girls held in jail have not been convicted of a crime for which an adult could be convicted.[15] In 1974 a Congressional statute was passed requiring that juveniles and adults be totally separated in both jails and prisons. The Office of Juvenile Justice and Delinquency Prevention interpreted Section 223(a)(13) as "sight and sound" separation. As Deputy Attorney General Charles Renfrew has stated, the result is that "juveniles are often isolated in what are the most undesirable areas of the facilities such as solitary cells and drunk tanks." On April 22, 1980, the United States House of Representatives Education and Labor Committee approved a bill (HR 6704) requiring states to "remove juveniles from all pre-adjudication facilities (jails and lockups) holding adults within five years."[16]

Internal Conditions

Unfortunately, the condition of many jails continues to be similar to that of 50 years ago, as described by Joseph F. Fishman:

> Jails: an unbelievably filthy institution in which are confined men and women serving sentences for misdemeanors and crimes, and men and women not under sentence who are simply awaiting trial. With few exceptions, having no segregation of the unconvicted from the convicted, the well from diseased, the youngest and the most impressionable from the most degraded and hardened. Usually swarming with bedbugs, roaches, lice, and other vermin; has an odor of disinfectant and filth which is appalling; supports in complete idleness countless thousands of able-bodied men and women, and generally affords ample time and opportunity to assure inmates a complete course in every kind of viciousness or crime. A melting pot in which the worse elements of raw material in the criminal world are brought forth blended and turned out in absolute perfection.[17]

[14]"A Suicide a Day in the Nation's Jails National Center on Institutions Says," *Criminal Justice Newsletter*, vol. 12, no. 24, Dec. 7, 1981, p. 3.

[15]"Thousands of Youngsters Jailed for Noncriminal Acts," *American Journal of Correction*, vol. 37, no. 3, May-June 1975, p. 18.

[16]"Removal of All Youths From Jails Proposed," *Criminal Justice Newsletter*, vol. 11, no. 7, Mar. 31, 1980, p. 5.

[17]Joseph F. Fishman, *Crucibles of Crime*, Cosmospolis Press, New York, 1923, pp. 13–14.

TABLE 4.2
AMERICAN CORRECTIONAL
ASSOCIATION SURVEY, 1203
JAILS

Programs offered	Percent
Academic education	22.5
Vocational training	13.0
Counseling	53.0
Drug	45.1
Alcohol	54.8
Agriculture	3.8
Work release	55.4
Study release	19.5
General education	28.2
Furlough	17.2
Religious counseling	68.5

Source: American Correctional Association, *National Jail and Adult Detention Directory,* American Correctional Association, Rockville, Md., 1978, p. 14.

meager reintegration program contribute to inmate misery. In some cases, the institution is not staffed except when a police officer stops by the jail during a routine patrol. The result has been tragic loss of life from fire or smoke inhalation, beatings or rapes of inmates by other inmates, and undetected illness. Inmates still depend on benevolence—although now from public officials —for food and clothing. Many inmates suffer from extreme heat or cold and from feelings of degradation because of practices of strip searches by wardens or callous treatment.

The suicide rate for male jail inmates was discovered in a study by researcher Bruce L. Danto to be 57.5 per 100,000 population compared with 16.5 per 100,000 population in the national nonjail population. In fact, the successful male suicidal inmate, who can be white or black, is younger than the nonjail male suicide (under 30 compared with over 50). The suicide, usually by hanging, is induced most frequently by one of three conditions. First, the inmate's alleged criminal behavior is a source of embarrassment to himself and his family, especially if it is an act of violence or sexual abuse or a well-publicized financial fraud. Second, the inmate is overcome by persistent feelings of hopelessness and futility because of the length of his detention. Third, the suicidal behavior is used as an attempt to manipulate others, such as his family or law enforcement officials, without the actual desire to die.[22]

A study of 419 suicides in jails in 1979 confirmed the high suicide rate in

---

[22]Bruce L. Danto, *Jail House Blues,* Epic Publications, Inc., Orchard Lake, Mich., 1973, pp. 19–21, 34.

Even today nobody seems to like the jail. Richard A. McGee, a leading authority on jails, calls them sick. Jack Newfield, author of *Bread and Rose. Too: Reporting About America,* refers to them as "the ultimate ghetto." Richard W. Velde, former Administrator of the Law Enforcement Assistance Administration (LEAA) considers jails to be "brutal, filthy cesspools of crime— institutions which serve to brutalize and embitter men to prevent them from returning to a useful role in society."[18]

Jailed inmates throughout the nation continue to languish in filth, suffer from poor food, and receive inadequate health care. In many jails the cagelike atmosphere and barbarous facilities of the nineteenth century still exist. Almost half the jails in this country were constructed before 1951, and nearly 30 percent were built over 50 years ago (see Table 4.1). According to the 1978 American Correctional Association survey of 1203 jails, 47 percent offered no counseling, 71 percent had no educational classes, and 87 percent had no vocational training (see Table 4.2).[19] Lack of medical care (only 13 percent of the jails in another 1978 survey gave physical examinations upon admission) has resulted in 189 jails being embroiled in lawsuits or court orders.[20] This condition exists despite the fact that "cruel and unusual punishment" is prohibited by the United States Constitution, and the Supreme Court has ruled that the withholding of basic health care from jail inmates is cruel and unusual punishment.[21]

Inmates are exposed to guard and inmate brutality. All too often, low maintenance budgets, inadequate pay, nonexistent training programs, and a

[18]Bartollas, op. cit., p. 210.

[19]American Correctional Association, *National Jail and Adult Detention Directory,* American Correctional Association, Rockville, Md., 1978, p. 14.

[20]Joan Amico and Roderick O'Connor, *The American Jails in Transition: Proceedings of the Second National Assembly on the Jail Crisis,* May 17–20, 1978, National Association of Counties, Washington, D.C., 1978, p. 22.

[21]Lawrence J. Guzzard, G. Richard Braen, and K. David Jones, "Health Care in Jails: A New Approach to an Old Problem," *Corrections Today,* vol. 42, no. 2, March–April 1980, p. 41.

TABLE 4.1
AMERICAN CORRECTIONAL ASSOCIATION JAIL
SURVEY, 1203 JAILS

Year jail constructed	Before 1901	14.7%
	1901–1925	13.2%
	1926–1950	19.6%
	1951 and later	52.5%
Year of last renovation	Before 1950	4.9%
	1950–1965	10.3%
	1966–1970	5.1%
	1971 and later	79.7%

Source: American Correctional Association, *National Jail and Adult Detention Directory,* American Correctional Association, Rockville, Md., 1978, p. 13.

jails—16 times greater than the rate in a city of a size comparable to the daily jail population (200,000). On the average, in 1979 one jail inmate committed suicide each day. The rate of suicide among children in jail is 4 times that among the general population.[23]

Inmate's Reaction

The condition of the jails in the United States at the beginning of 1970 and the inability of inmates to represent themselves legally have resulted in a number of inmate disturbances. In the fall of 1971 alone, eight jails in this country experienced riots. One inmate who took part in the Manhattan Jail Riot of 1970 stated, "We have no mouth, and we must scream."[24] The jails where riots occurred in the fall of 1971 are located throughout the country—Civic Center Jail in San Jose, California; Dallas County Jail; Suffolk County Jail in Boston; Cumberland County Jail in Bridgeton, New Jersey; Bexar County Jail in San Antonio, Texas; and San Joaquin County Jail in California.[25]

Hope for Improvement

The type of inmates confined has a great deal to do with the conditions of the jails. Inmates have no constituency. Most are not capable of speaking for themselves and do not possess the financial capability to process complaints and/or demands for adequate care. Jails have become the outcasts of the correctional system. This is not to say that no attempts have been made to improve conditions. Since 1967 there has been a significant effort to improve jails throughout the United States.

Federal inspections have taken place since the middle of this century. Many states have instituted inspection programs; only twelve had no state jail inspections in 1981. In fact, when one reads the list of the states with jail inspection agencies and officials, it is hard to understand why so little improvement has occurred. However, in most cases jails run by local government do not need to comply with the recommendations of the state or federal inspectors. Only a minority of states have a program of mandatory inspection to which counties are held accountable.

Since 1967 national government and professional organizations have produced an abundance of standards for jails. It was hoped that these standards would be used as guidelines to measure the effectiveness of local correctional facilities. Among the groups that have written standards are The National Task Force on Corrections, The Presidential Commission on Law Enforcement and

---

[23]"A Suicide a Day in the Nation's Jails National Center on Institutions Says," *Criminal Justice Newsletter*, vol. 12, no. 24, Dec. 7, 1981, p. 3.

[24]Newfield, *Bread and Roses Too: Reporting About America*, Greenwood Press, Westport, Conn., 1970.

[25]Ronald Goldfarb, *Jails: The Ultimate Ghetto*, Anchor Press/Doubleday, New York, 1975, p. 15.

Justice, The National Advisory Committee on Criminal Justice Standards and Goals, The National Sheriff's Association, The American Bar Association, The American Correctional Association, The American Medical Association, and the United States Department of Justice. The most used standard has been the Federal Bureau of Prisons Manual of Jail Management. By 1981, only two jails—the Denver, Colorado, County Jail and New Haven, Connecticut, Community Correctional Center—had met accreditation standards of the Commission on Accreditation for Corrections of the American Correctional Association. Ninety-seven jails had complied with the medical standards of the American Medical Association.[26]

In 1976 the National Institute of Corrections established the Jail Center in Boulder, Colorado, in an effort to upgrade jail operations. The Jail Center offers training to jail managers, trainers, and county commissioners. Training programs have been conducted for approximately 2500 participants during fiscal years 1978, 1979, and 1980. Responses were given to 1032 requests for technical assistance during the same 3 years. A major function of the Jail Center is to supply informational materials about model programs, jail policy, standards, training curriculum, and research study results. The National Information Center for Corrections processes approximately 400 requests a month.[27]

A number of jail systems can be cited for having attempted to improve jail operations—Alachua County, Florida; Ingham County, Michigan; Montgomery County, Maryland; and Boulder, Colorado, for example. The Correctional Center in Boulder is part of an $8-million Boulder County Criminal Justice Center. Ten jail residents are housed in single rooms in eight individual units, each with a different level of custody. There is also a dormitory for fourteen inmates on work release and ten-room units for women prisoners. A well-stocked library, a full-size gymnasium, a game room, and a small dining area, are shared by men and women residents. Highly trained, informally dressed personnel contribute to the impression of a small residential school.[28]

JAILS AS INSTITUTIONS FOR REINTEGRATION

How to Use the Jail

As local institutions serving as centers for reintegrating offenders into the community, there are a number of ways jails could be used. Certain offenders, such as alcoholics and narcotics addicts who are "drying out" or going through withdrawal, could be helped by detoxification programs during jail confinement. Other incarcerates, because of their lack of abilities, could benefit from

[26]Dick Ford and Ken Kerle, "Jail Standards—A Different Perspective," *The Prison Journal*, vol. 61, no. 1, Spring/Summer 1981, pp. 23–24.

[27]Paul Katsampes and Thomas C. Neil, "A Decade of Improvement for Our Sick Jails," *Federal Probation*, vol: 45, no. 3, Administrative Office of the United States Courts, Washington, D.C., September 1981, pp. 45–46.

[28]Bartollas, op. cit., p. 213.

traditional correctional rehabilitation before their gradual release into the community. Some administrators believe that detention itself has advantages. Some argue that a jail sentence is superior to probation for cases not meriting a prison sentence. These people reject the belief that probation is too lenient, but they maintain that if a particular offender requires closer security than probation affords, jail is the best alternative. Others believe that the imposition of a period of jail confinement should be a condition of the granting of probation.

It has been suggested that if the jail is used for reintegration of the offender, the program must aim toward (1) developing jobs for the unemployed; (2) increasing educational opportunities for the undereducated; and (3) assisting with personal problems such as alcoholism, personality deficiencies, marital and financial difficulties, and other problems found among the social groups confined in jails.[29]

Problems Encountered

Some inherent problems have prevented jails from developing reintegration programs. First, the jail is for short-term offenders and there is much turnover. It is difficult to develop a reintegration program when inmates have little time to complete it. Second, unsentenced offenders may be found innocent. If so, the legality of involving them in programs may be questioned; in fact, it could be considered cruel and unusual punishment. Third, there is lack of adequate staff in local and county jails. A survey conducted in 1972 discovered only 2113—less than 5 percent—identifiable personnel in jails and local adult institutions who could be considered noncustodial staff.[30] Fourth, there is lack of money. In almost all jails throughout the country, funding is insufficient.[31]

These problems do not mean that reintegration programs are nonexistent in American jails. The number is small, but some have attempted to organize such programs. Sample studies estimate that approximately 42 percent of short-term institutions have work release, and 46 percent have weekend sentences, although small jails (fewer than 21 inmates) are less likely to initiate such programs.[32]

How to Prepare the Jail

Before the development of improved programs in jails can occur, two changes must take place—program rehabilitation and jail rehabilitation. These suggestions imply that a mutually dependent relationship exists between them. Any

[29]Alice Howard Blumer, *Jail Management: A Course for Jail Administration,* Book III, Jail and Community Corrections Programs, U.S. Bureau of Prisons, Washington, D.C. 1971, p. 1.

[30]Goldfarb, op. cit., p. 15.

[31]Blumer, op. cit., p. 1.

[32]Ronald L. Goldfarb and Linda R. Singer, *After Conviction,* Simon and Schuster, New York, 1973, p. 588.

attempts to reintegrate offenders will depend on the improvement of the jail itself. If the jail is to be functionally changed to a correctional institution rather than a warehouse, it must be reformed at the same time its improved programs are initiated. This involves improving the physical structure of the jail facility and changing the attitudes of personnel.

Jail rehabilitation can be accomplished much more easily than inmate reintegration into the community. Improvements can be made in the physical condition of the building, so that it meets nationally recognized standards. Steps to improve food service, general cleanliness, and sanitation, can be instituted in even the oldest facilities. Psychiatric evaluations and physical examinations can take place, so that inmates who require special assistance can be identified and unusually dangerous prisoners or prisoners with contagious diseases separated from the others.

Competent administration depends on the awareness of all jail personnel of the basic legal obligations owed to the public and to the prisoners. Thus, recruiting capable jail personnel is the beginning of good jail administration. The attitude of intake staff during the receiving process sets the tone for the prisoner's attitude toward the entire criminal justice system. Security, too, is primarily dependent on personnel. If they perform ineptly, "kangaroo courts" often take place, with inmates being judged and punished by other inmates.

Program Rehabilitation

The President's Commission on Law Enforcement and Administration of Justice recommended that the ideal jail would be located in or near the population center, so that its inmates could have maximum use of community resources. The ideal jail would receive newly committed defendants and carry out screening and classification. It would provide short-term intensive rehabilitation as well as long-term confinement for more difficult and dangerous inmates. The local detention complex would also maintain a number of small facilities in different parts of the metropolitan area to house inmates participating in community-based programs. The location of these satellite facilities would provide physical separation of totally confined inmates in the rehabilitation program from inmates permitted access to resources, jobs, and personal contacts in the community.

Jail personnel would attempt to minimize the harms of the super institution or outdated detention facility and maximize the use of small, informal settings. In addition, court personnel would try to minimize the number of defendants who were actually detained, by using forms of pretrial diversion.[33]

Some efforts have been made to reform the programs. One attempted reform is the community correctional center as developed by Vermont, Connecticut, Rhode Island, and Alaska. These are statewide detention facilities that replace

[33] *Task Force Report: Corrections,* op. cit., p. 82.

local jails and lockups. Other alternatives to jails have been initiated, including a state regional correctional center at Crookston, Minnesota, and detoxification centers throughout the United States. Similarly, the federal system has begun developing a series of regional detention centers, the first in San Diego in November 1974 and a second in the New York metropolitan area in July 1975. At the opening of the New York Center it was stated, "The swift processing and humane treatment of prisoners is of paramount importance; because most men and women incarcerated here will be awaiting trial and not be convicted, it is important that detention be brief, meaningful, and productive."[34] Included within the center are a multimedia educational program, recreation, library, and religious facilities. The center is designed to house 500 inmates with 389 private rooms and 111 dormitory beds. Each of the twelve stories has classrooms, staff office space, and counselors.

The Reintegration Program

Work release and educational release also have been recommended for the jail inmate. The original Huber Law, which established work release in Wisconsin in 1913, was designed to assist jail inmates rather than felons. Although there are a multitude of work release programs for the jail prisoner, it has been difficult to evaluate their success in terms of recidivism. A 4-year follow-up of work releasees from the San Mateo County, California, jail showed that the work release group received 2472 fewer days in jail sentences than a non-work release control group. This figure represented a reduction of 35 percent, or $17,000 in savings to the county.[35] A 3-year follow-up study of the Montgomery County, Maryland, work release program, financed by the LEAA and designated an "exemplary" project, showed that under 22.2 percent of the participants were rearrested after leaving the program.[36]

The cost savings from allowing work release has been obvious from the beginning. One of the more elaborate studies was conducted on the Bucks County, Pennsylvania, work release program. The study was extensive and provides a detailed overview of the financial advantages of work releases from jails. Between 1963 and 1973, work release privileges were allowed to 1263 jail inmates. Prisoner earnings totaled $811,509. Families of prisoners received $144,709. Reimbursements to the county including payment of fines amounted to $211,811 (see Table 4.3).

Other jail programs designated to help reintegrate the offender are similar to those in some state or federal correctional systems. Programs using volunteers

---

[34]Roberts J. Wright, "Federal Bureau of Prisons Opens New Detention Headquarters in New York," *American Journal of Correction,* vol. 37, no. 5, September–October 1975, p. 32.

[35]Robert Jeffery and Stephen Woolpert, "Work Furlough as an Alternative to Incarceration: An Assessment of Its Effects on Recidivism and Social Cost," *Journal of Criminal Law, Criminology, and Police Science,* vol. 65, no. 3, September 1974, p. 414.

[36]*Exemplary Projects,* Law Enforcement Assistance Administration, Washington, D.C. September 1977, p. 11.

TABLE 4.3
SUMMARY OF WORK-RELEASE
EARNINGS
(October 1963 to May 1973: Bucks County,
Pennsylvania)

	10-year-total
Wages earned	$811,509
Board to county	158,811
Court costs and fines	96,304
Support and arrears	57,866
Voluntary support	86,843
Restitution	14,162
Miscellaneous expenses	73,279
Travel	131,470
Canteen and savings	232,811
Federal board to county	181,494
Personal money	40,037

Source: John D. Case and James F. Henderson, "Community Corrections in a County Jail," *Corrections in the Community,* E. Eugene Miller and M. Robert Montilla (eds.), Reston Publishing Company, Inc., Reston, Va., 1977, p. 197.

have been popular for years. Job-finding and job-keeping programs with volunteer staff exist in Vanderburgh County (Evansville), Indiana, and Richmond, Virginia. Volunteer chaplains' services are available in Lee County (Auburn), Alabama, and Bexor County (San Antonio), Texas. A third-party custody for inmates released on recognizance or bail operates in Baltimore, Maryland. Elsewhere volunteers teach art classes, tutor, provide library services, conduct workshops, and share musical talents with prisoners.[37]

Probably the most ambitious program to recruit volunteers for jails was conducted by Offender Aid and Restoration, USA. The Citizen Involvement Project was begun in order to demonstrate that citizens can be effectively mobilized to participate in their community's correctional system. Fifty teams of civic leaders and jail administrators from thirty states enrolled in a 12-month training program on how to use volunteers in jail. Although the final evaluation is not yet completed, many local programs have been started by the community representatives.[38]

Jail social service programs include the provision of sufficient personnel to permit assistance to inmates after their detention. This could be accomplished either under probation supervision or following discharge. Such assistance

[37]Fahy G. Mullaney, "Citizen Volunteers Are Breaking Into Jail," *Corrections Today,* vol: 43, no. 4, July/August 1981, p. 58.
[38]Barbara Nobles Crawford, *Citizen Involvement Project 1979 Proceedings,* U.S. Department of Justice, Washington, D.C., December 1979, pp. 1–2.

would include assisting prisoners with job seeking and educational planning and working with their families.[39]

Diversion

The National Advisory Commission on Criminal Justice Standards and Goals published their standards for community-based corrections in 1973. They recommended that community-based corrections include all correctional activities that take place in the community, or "any activity in the community directly addressed to the offender and aimed at helping him to become a law-abiding citizen." One of their standards is a "Development Plan for Community-Based Alternatives to Confinement." Two of the alternatives recommended for inclusion in the plan were (1) diversion mechanisms and programs prior to trial and sentence and (2) nonresidential supervision programs, in addition to probation and parole.

The term *diversion* refers to the procedure of postponing prosecution, either temporarily or permanently, at any point in the judicial process. To qualify as diversion, such efforts must be carried out before adjudication and after a legally forbidden action has occurred. In terms of process, diversion implies halting or suspending formal criminal or juvenile justice proceedings against a person who has violated a statute, in favor of processing through a noncriminal disposition or means.[40]

This practice is based on the belief that the earlier offenders can be diverted from the criminal justice system the greater the chance they will not be involved in additional offenses. Or, as stated by the President's Commission on Law Enforcement and Administration of Justice:

> The deeper the offender has to be plunged into the correctional process and the longer he has to be held under punitive (though humane) restraints, the more difficult is the road back to the point of social restoration. It is logical, then, to conclude that the correctional process ought to concentrate its greatest efforts at those points in the criminal justice continuum where the largest number of offenders are involved and the hope of avoiding social segregation is the greatest.[41]

Although the reasons for diversion have been well-documented—dissatisfaction with the criminal justice system, to lessen the brutalizing conditions of incarceration, to lower the overload of the courts—there is a danger that diversion will only expand the number of persons involved in the criminal justice system rather than actually divert the accused. These concerns are based on the fear that those who are diverted might have had their charges dismissed anyway, because of weak evidence or some other reason. In view of this, guidelines must

[39]Louis B. Carney, *Introduction to Correctional Science,* McGraw-Hill Book Company, New York, 1974, p. 257.

[40]Povl G. Boesen and Stanley E. Grupp (eds.) *Community-Based Corrections: Theory, Practice and Research,* Davis Publishing Company, Inc., Santa Cruz, Calif., 1976, pp. 15 and 33.

[41]Bartollas op. cit., p. 216.

be established to determine eligibility for diversion and the selection of agencies to receive those diverted. The effectiveness of the diversion techniques should be examined, compared to the routine procedures of the criminal justice system.[42]

ALTERNATIVES TO JAIL

Overview

The problems connected with jail incarceration have prompted numerous attempts to provide pretrial release as an alternative to detention in jail. Pretrial release offers a series of options that provide varying levels of supervision and services. The programs have become popular for three reasons: (1) the expense of booking persons into jail ($24 a case) and keeping them there ($35 a day), (2) the crowded conditions in many jails (about 50 percent of the jail population are defendants awaiting trial), and (3) the large number of defendants who are unable to raise bail.

There are various forms of pretrial release (see Figure 4.1), which are generally divided into two groups: prebooking release and postbooking release.

Prebooking Release

An arresting officer has the option of releasing any misdemeanant who does not demand to be taken before a magistrate. Called a field citation, this is the most widely available informal, nonpenal technique of pretrial release. The field

[42]Robert M. Carter, "The Diversion of Offenders," *Alternatives to Prison: Community Based Corrections, A Reader,* Gary R. Perlstein and Thomas R. Phelps (eds.), Goodyear Publishing Company, Inc., Pacific Palisades, Calif., 1975, p. 21.

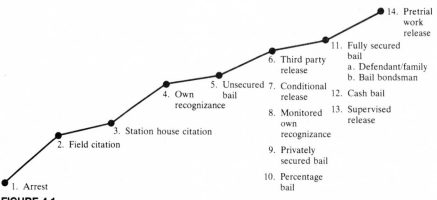

FIGURE 4.1
Forms of pretrial release. (From John L. Calvin et al., *Alternatives to Pretrial Detention,* Law Enforcement Assistance Administration, U.S. Government Printing Office, Washington, D.C., October 1977, p. 2.)

citation diverts some of the prearraignment population back into the community at the point of arrest.

After transporting a misdemeanant to a police station, the police officer can issue a stationhouse citation. The information provided by the arrested person is verified, permitting the officer to make a decision on the basis of valid information. The alleged misdemeanant is then released, avoiding prearraignment detention.

Postbooking Release

Figure 4.1 lists several options for pretrial release after booking. One distinction among them is the presence or absence of a requirement for cash security.

Bail is release of a prisoner upon delivery of a monetary security. There are a number of types of bail releases. Unsecured bail permits the alleged offender to be released without an actual monetary security but with the obligation to pay the established fee upon default. Cash bail is demanded when the charge is not serious and the bail is low. In some programs, a private organization provides bail for indigent defendants who meet certain eligibility requirements. The defendants or their families or professional bonding companies put up the security when fully secured bail is required, with the bonding company receiving a nonrefundable fee ranging upward from 10 percent. Percentage bail is a publicly managed bail program under which the alleged offender deposits a percentage of the bail amount, usually 10 percent with the court.

The most widely used pretrial release program is release on recognizance (i.e., without bail). Defendants are put on their honor to report when scheduled. Applicants are interviewed, judged on a point system by preestablished criteria, and approved by the court officials, usually the judge. Three frequently used methods of release on recognizance are (1) supervised release with certain conditions, such as having the accused person remain within the court's jurisdiction or at home with periodic check-ins; (2) release into custody of a willing third party; and (3) daytime release with return to jail at night, sometimes resembling work release.[43]

Two Early Programs

Two of the first innovative pretrial release programs were the Manhattan Bail Project, begun in October 1961 by retired businessmen Louis Schweitzer and Herbert Sturz, and the Illinois Ten Per Cent Plan. Some of the factors used to qualify inmates for release without bail in the Manhattan Project were length of employment, number of relatives in New York City, place of residence and persons with whom they were living, references, and previous criminal record. It

---

[43]Paul Wice and Rita James Simon, "Pretrial Release: A Survey of Alternative Practices," *Federal Probation*, vol. 34, no. 4, Administrative Office of the States Courts, Washington, D.C., December 1970, pp. 62–63.

was assumed that those offenders who had closer ties to the community would be more likely to reappear in court after their release on recognizance.

The Illinois Plan allows defendants to pay 10 percent of the total bail as cash security for release on their own recognizance. No professional bonding or surety company may pay the bail. When the defendant appears in court, 90 percent of the original cash security is refunded. In Illinois, percentage bail is the most common form of pretrial release.[44]

Evaluation

One study of pretrial release indicated that people released under less stringent practices neither jumped bail more often nor failed more frequently to show up at hearings or trials than did those under the traditional bail practice. Categories included in the study were (1) the traditional bail system; (2) the bail reform system, which used a standardized fact-finding mechanism to recommend to the judge whether or not a defendant should be released; and (3) the Illinois Ten Per Cent Plan.

Populations of the cities studied ranged from 30,000 to 75,000, with similar proportions of nonwhite persons, those engaged in manufacturing, those having medium income, and those with incomes under $3000. The survey indicated that there was little difference in effectiveness among the three programs. Of people released on bail under traditional bail practices, 17 percent jumped bail or were arrested, compared with 16 percent under bail reform plans and 18 percent under the Illinois Ten Per Cent plan. One statistic was more significant. Of those released on bail under the Illinois Ten Per Cent Plan, 91 percent did not require a bond, contrasted with 14 percent under the traditional bail practice.[45]

A twenty-city study by researcher Wayne Thomas found that the average failure-to-appear rate for felony defendants released on recognizance was 9 percent. The lowest rate was 4 percent in Des Moines, Iowa, and Peoria, Illinois; the highest was 17 percent in Boston and Chicago. Thomas found the rates for those released on bail and those released on recognizance to be similar. Dozens of other studies have confirmed his findings. In each case, the default rate for defendants released on recognizance is generally as good as or better than that for defendants released on bail.[46]

The jail alternative project in Pierce County, Washington, estimated a savings of $55.00 per misdemeanor and $650.00 per felony for each inmate diverted from jail incarceration. The project provided defendants with personal counseling, job placement, educational assistance, and financial support services.[47]

[44]Bartollas, op. cit., pp. 127–133.
[45]Wice and Simon, op. cit., pp. 62–63.
[46]Stephen Gettinger, "Has the Bail Reform Movement Stalled?" *Corrections Magazine*, vol. 6, no. 1, February 1980, pp. 31–32.
[47]James Hushagen, "Pre-charge Habilitation Listed as Success in Pierce County, Washington," *American Journal of Correction*, vol. 39, no. 4, July–August 1977, p. 14.

The Des Moines Project

One "exemplary" project using alternatives to jail is in Des Moines, Iowa. Its official title is the Fifth Judicial District Department of Court Services, but it is more commonly known as the Des Moines Project. Originally funded in 1970 by an LEAA grant, the project now encompasses four programs under one administration: pretrial release on recognizance (ROR), supervised pretrial release with services (RWS), presentence investigation and probation supervision, and residential alternatives to incarceration.

Release on recognizance is based on an objective point system which determines whether a person is a safe risk for release into the community while awaiting trial. Points are awarded if accused offenders are employed, if they have no previous criminal record, if they have family ties, and if they have resided for a period of time in Des Moines. Five points or more qualify a person for release. According to a 1973 study by the National Council on Crime and Delinquency, a point system was more effective than traditional bail practices, for only 1.3 percent of ROR people failed to appear in court, compared to 3.2 percent of those released on bail. The same study also indicated that 8 percent of ROR people were rearrested while awaiting trial, compared to 11 percent of the persons released on bail. In the Des Moines Project, a total of 1467 accused persons were released on recognizance during the 1975–1976 fiscal year. Over 80 percent of those released had been charged with nonviolent offenses. The RWS program provided various services for 488 accused offenders during the 1975–1976 fiscal year.

Generally, RWS is a sort of preparatory school for probation. Counselors work as resource brokers and channel alleged offenders into community-based programs. More than 150 community agencies are utilized, including job and drug counseling agencies. Counselors within the program do not talk about rehabilitating criminals but prefer the similar concept of "turnaround." Eleven probation officers of the Des Moines Project supervise about 900 offenders. In addition, four other staff members conduct approximately 40 presentence investigations a month. RWS makes 40 percent of the requests for presentence investigations, and another 30 percent come from the ROR program. The remainder of the presentence investigations are initiated while the offender is in jail or released on bail.

The final phase of the Des Moines Project is the Men's Residential Correctional Center. This fifty-four-bed facility is a converted army barracks formerly known as Fort Des Moines. Operating since 1971, it is designated as a jail according to a state law that existed at that time, although it seems more like a fraternity house. Each offender carries his own key to a cubicle-size room. Young men can be seen playing table tennis, pool, and cards or watching television in a large sunlit room. Most residents are sentenced to Fort Des Moines, where the average stay is 4 to 6 months, as a condition of probation. The main program of the center is work release. A residential facility for women was opened in 1972, with room for six females. During the fiscal year 1975–1976,

TABLE 4.4
ALLEGED NEW OFFENSES COMMITTED DURING
PRETRIAL PERIOD

	New offense	No new offense	Total
Pretrial release	50 (7.9%)	583	633
Bail	26 (8.8%)	268	294
Supervised release	45 (16.8%)	223	268

Source: David Boorkman, Ernest J. Fazio, Jr., Noel Day, and David Weinstein, *An Exemplary Project: Community Based Corrections in Des Moines,* U.S. Department of Justice, Washington, D.C., November 1976, p. 9.

there were 200 admissions to the two residential facilities and 120 offenders were paroled or discharged.[48]

Evaluation

The evaluations of the Des Moines Project have produced interesting results. Alleged offenders released under the pretrial release program were charged with fewer new offenses during the pretrial period than either those released on bail or those under supervised release (see Table 4.4). Pretrial releasees failed to appear for their trial less frequently than alleged offenders released on bail plus those under supervised release (see Table 4.5). An estimated $454,229 was saved county and state corrections programs through the Des Moines Project (see Table 4-6). The success of the project prompted LEAA officials to award grants for the purpose of replication to Clark County, Washington; San Mateo County, California; Salt Lake County, Utah; St. Louis County, Minnesota; and Orange County, California.[49]

[48]Rob Wilson, "Replicating LEAA's First Outstanding Project," *Corrections Magazine,* vol. 2, no. 5, September 1976, pp. 16–19.
[49]David Boorkman, Ernest J. Fazio, Jr., Noel Day, and David Weinstein, *An Exemplary Project: Community Based Corrections in Des Moines,* U.S. Department of Justice, Washington, D.C., November 1976, pp. 8 and 13.

TABLE 4.5
APPEARANCE RATES FOR PRETRIAL GROUPS

	Appeared	Failed to appear	Total
Pretrial release	625	8 (1.3%)	633
Bail	274	20 (6.8%)	294
Supervised release	254	14 (5.2%)	268

Source: David Boorkman, Ernest J. Fazio, Jr., Noel Day, and David Weinstein, *An Exemplary Project: Community Based Corrections in Des Moines,* U.S. Department of Justice, Washington, D.C., November 1976, p. 9.

TABLE 4.6

COST SAVINGS FROM HANDLING CLIENTS THROUGH THE DES MOINES
PROJECT RATHER THAN OTHER PROGRAMS

	Add'l clients	Cost each per day	Total add'l cost per day	Total add'l cost per year
Polk County jail	56	$10.49	$ 587.44	$ 214,415
Probation and parole	515	1.09	561.35	204,893
Men's institutions	133	17.55	2,334.15	851,965
Total additional costs				$1,271,273
1973 costs of the Des Moines Project*				817,044
Total cost savings				$ 454,229

*Costs include women's facility.

Source: David Boorkman, Ernest J. Fazio, Jr., Noel Day, and David Weinstein, An Exemplary Project: Community Based Corrections in Des Moines, U.S. Department of Justice, Washington, D.C., November 1976, p. 13.

APPRAISAL

Continuing Problems

Problems concerning the jail are many. Public apathy and the poor ranking of jails in public esteem are fundamental reasons for the lack of reform. Fiscal constraints and scarcity of professionally trained staff further discourage any improvements. In small jails 21 percent of the staff are part-time employees, including even 13 percent of jail administrators and 31 percent of custodial personnel. Control over local jails is given to a number of government bodies at the local and state level. Most of the small jails (78 percent) are located in the police station or sheriff's office, giving them a secondary role in the operational structure of the agency.[50]

Controlled by local government, the jail is subject to inconsistency of effort. Seldom are two jails operated identically. They are dependent on local conditions, employment situations, and the whim of county commissioners.[51] Adding to these problems is the fact that jail occupants are social outcasts, frequently transient, and the poverty of the majority of inmates offers little possibility that their circumstances will attract general public concern. As Huey Long said, "There ain't no votes in prison."[52]

Federal Bureau of Prisons Director Norman Carlson reported in 1977 that jails have come under close scrutiny by the courts in recent years. He quoted a survey reporting that 7 jails had been ordered closed by the courts, 28 were

[50]Roger Handberg and Charles M. Unkovic, "Corrections Policy in Rural and Small Town America: A Proposal for Change," The Prison Journal, vol. 61, no. 1, Spring/Summer 1981, pp. 3–5.

[51]Wright, "Jail and Misdemeanant Institutions," op. cit., p. 311.

[52]E. Eugene Miller, Jail Management, Lexington Books, Lexington, Mass., 1978, p. 17.

under federal order to carry out specific improvements, 144 were under administrative review, 95 were barred from receiving additional inmates, and 87 were cited for failing to meet state standards.[53] Obviously, the problems of jails are still complex and mainly unresolved. At present there is little enforcement of existing standards or legislative action to overcome the identified problems.

Hope for Reform

This does not mean that reform is not in the offing. One of the most encouraging developments during the 1970s has been the aforementioned involvement of the courts in directing that specific improvements be made in jail facilities, programs, and personnel staffing patterns. As noted in the Sheriff's Association *Training Manual for Jail Personnel,* published in 1980, during the 1970s courts have issued orders relating to jail programs and procedures in "matters such as adequate health, diet, right to practice religion, right to communicate with legal counsel and family, right to be free from cruel and unusual punishment, and the right to fresh air and exercise."

The efforts on the part of some local officials to meet recognized national standards prior to the issuance of a court order can be viewed as another hopeful sign of progress toward professionalism in local corrections. Other local law enforcement officials advocate the transfer of jails to state correctional control, a change which they believe would increase the likelihood of jail reform.[54]

Some Suggestions

Current suggestions for jail reform are based on three primary changes: First, remove the jail from politics; second, reduce the jail population; third, provide programs for the inmates that decrease their idle time and permit reintegration into the community.

By placing jails under a centralized agency, it would be possible to develop facilities that serve several government units. This is the so-called *metro-jail* which has a cooperative form of administration. In essence a regional or county-city jail, it is considered a substitute for total state control. Collaboration or state assumption of responsibilities for the administration of jails replaces the fee system with tax-supported financing. Grants from state or federal governments can subsidize some of the costs of enforcing operational standards. These steps would allow more uniform standards of operation and easier enforcement by the state or metro-agency that controls the facilities.

The jail population can be reduced by a number of methods. As stated

---

[53]Norman Carlson, "Concern Shown—But Problem Goes Unresolved," *American Journal of Correction,* vol. 39, no. 4, July/August 1977, p. 28.

[54]Theodore L. Heim, "The Jail in Historical Perspective," unpublished manuscript, Washburn University, Topeka, Kansas, 1980, chap. 1, pp. 12–13.

before, there are a great many alternatives to confinement—diversion from the criminal justice system through pretrial release, or postconviction procedures such as probation or other community-based correctional programs. The 1978 jail census revealed that 81 percent of unconvicted jail inmates were eligible for release on bail.

Author Ronald Goldfarb has suggested that another way to reduce jail population is to limit categories of offenders who can be held in detention. He suggests housing in jails only the following: the pretrial offender who might not otherwise show up for trial or is too dangerous to be released, the offender with a health or welfare problem who must be held while being examined or referred to an appropriate specialized institution, and the convicted offender who requires local institutional housing before being integrated into the community.[55]

Providing a program to reduce idle time and permit reintegration into the community has been continually suggested to improve the jail. Programs such as vocational education, academic education, medical services, recreation, religious services, temporary release, work release, and study release are the most frequently mentioned choices. With a lower jail population, programs are easier to initiate. Many cells can be replaced by classroom space. Functional grouping can be achieved, so that inmates who require special medical attention can be segregated. Even work release would be easier to institute under conditions permitting separation of inmates.

As psychiatrist Karl Menninger has said in *The Crime of Punishment:*

> Certainly jails should be secure. But security does not require austerity and physical discomfort. The city, the county, the law—none of them has been authorized or commissioned to force citizens to endure privation and discomfort without a trial, and without conviction of offense. But it is done even today in thousands of communities—*only to people too poor, too ignorant, or too intimidated to escape it legally.* All this in the name of justice.[56]

CONCLUSION

Jails are invisible institutions. People know where to find the school, the library, the museum, the basketball arena, the hospital, and the dog pound. But not the jail. Jails are institutions which even if not out of sight, are out of mind. Both the guards and the guarded are forgotten people.

Yet local incarceration holds the potential for having a significant positive effect on offenders, if a humane and helpful setting can be developed for them. Without jail programming, local incarceration is simply dead time. With the disruption of positive connections the offender may have had in the community,

[55]Goldfarb, *Jails,* op. cit., pp. 41, 419.
[56]Karl Menninger, *The Crime of Punishment,* copyright © 1966, 1968 by Jeanetta Lyle Menninger. Reprinted by permission of Viking Penguin, Inc., New York, 1966, pp. 44–45.

jail time as an end in itself can be counterproductive to the goal of encouraging noncriminal behavior.

Or, as O. D. Coffey said in a 1979 article: "Jail, as an entry point into the criminal justice system (can) ideally also be the beginning, the solid foundation of a continuum of offender services to be continued in the community after release."[57]

The primary goal of jail programming should be the reintegration of the individual into the community. In the past, the traditional objectives of the jail have been to enhance public safety by keeping in secure custody those believed a threat to other people or to property, to ensure that persons awaiting court action appear for trial, and to punish. But the jail population generally consists of young, uneducated, underemployed men with few positive connections with the community; thus, looking far beyond the point of incarceration and helping to establish these connections must now be paramount. There is a need to create a sense of positive community, of connectedness within the fabric of society, recognizing that these young men will soon return to their home communities.

In his book, *Jail Management,* Gene Miller stated that the role of the jail should be expanded because of its unique position in the local community. To achieve this goal, efforts should be made to implement community-based corrections services and seek public support for those services, based on the proximity of the local correctional system to the people which it serves.[58]

EXERCISES

1 In your opinion, to what extent should jail inmates work on county projects such as roads and farms or for private businesses? Give reasons for your conclusion.
2 Do you think jail management should be placed under state control, or should it remain under local control? Defend your decision.
3 What steps would you take to minimize the power, influence, and patronage associated with jail administration? Explain each step fully.
4 Review Figure 4.1. What could be done to divert certain categories of misdemeanants from jail detention?
5 What steps could be taken to reduce the jails' high suicide rate? Explain fully.
6 "Because most inmates are not capable of speaking for themselves and do not possess the financial capability to process complaints and/or demands for adequate treatment, jails have become the derelict of the correctional system." Agree or disagree with this statement. Give your reasons.
7 What would you do to improve the condition of the jails?
8 Some corrections officials have stated that "detention itself has rehabilitative advantages." What do you think? Explain your position fully.
9 Outline the steps you would take to institute reintegration programs in jails. Justify each step.

---

[57]O. D. Coffey and C. N. Louis, "Unemployment, Crime and the Local Jails," *Corrections Today,* vol. 41, no. 2, March/April 1979, p. 37.

[58]Arthur M. Wallenstein, "Chillon Castle Revisited or Removing the Moat Surrounding American Jails," *The Prison Journal,* vol. 59, no. 2, Autumn/Winter 1979, p. 69.

10 List the advantages and disadvantages of a regional or county-city metro-jail. Why have not more communities developed such a facility?
11 List your recommendations for diverting citizens from jail detention. Explain how each alternative would work.

EXERCISE REFERENCES

Bartollas, Clemens: *Introduction to Corrections,* Harper & Row, Publishers Incorporated New York, 1981, Chaps. 6 and 10.

Blumer, Alice Howard: *Jail Management: A Course for Jail Administration,* Book III, Jail and Community Corrections Programs, U.S. Bureau of Prisons, Washington, D.C., 1971.

Caldwell, Robert G.: *Criminology,* Ronald Press Company, New York, 1965, chap. 22.

Carlson, Norman: "Concern Shown—But Problem Goes Unresolved," *American Journal of Correction,* vol. 39, no. 4, July/August 1977, p. 28.

Census of State Correctional Facilities, 1974, Advance Report, U.S. Government Printing Office, Washington, D.C., July 1975.

Danto, Bruce L.: *Jail House Blues,* Epic Publications, Inc., Orchard Lake, Mich., 1973.

Downey, John J.: "Why Children Are in Jail—And How to Keep Them Out," *Children,* vol. 17, no. 1, Office of Juvenile Delinquency and Youth Development, Washington, D.C., 1971, pp. 21–26.

Empey, L. T.: *Studies in Delinquency: Alternatives to Incarceration,* U.S. Government Printing Office, Washington, D.C., 1967.

Fishman, Robert: *An Evaluation of the Effect on Criminal Recidivism of New York City Projects Providing Rehabilitation and Diversion Services,* New York State Division of Criminal Justice, New York, 1975.

Flynn, Edith Elisabeth: "Jails and Criminal Justice," *Prisoners in America,* Lloyd E. Ohlin (ed.), Prentice-Hall, Inc., Englewood Cliffs, N.J., 1973, pp. 49–88.

Ford, Dick, and Ken Kerle: "Jail Standards—A Different Perspective," *The Prison Journal,* vol. 61, no. 1, Spring/Summer 1981, pp. 23–35.

Friday, Paul C., and David M. Peterson: "Shock of Imprisonment: Short Term Incarceration as a Treatment Technique," *Corrections: Problems of Punishment and Rehabilitation,* Edward Sagarin and Daniel E. J. MacNamara (eds.), Praeger Publishers, New York, 1973, pp. 61–69.

Gettinger, Stephen, "Has the Bail Reform Movement Stalled?" *Corrections Magazine,* vol. 6, no. 1, February 1980, pp. 26–35.

Goldfarb, Ronald: *Jails: The Ultimate Ghetto,* Anchor Press/Doubleday, New York, 1975.

Guzzard, Lawrence J., G. Richard Braen, and K. David Jones: "Health Care in Jails: A New Approach to an Old Problem," *Corrections Today,* vol. 42, no. 2, April 1980, pp. 40–41, 46.

Handberg, Roger, and Charles M. Unkovic: "Corrections Policy in Rural and Small Town America," *The Prison Journal,* vol. 61, no. 1, Spring/Summer 1981, pp. 3–12.

Hushagen, James: "Pre-charge Habilitation Listed as Success in Pierce County, Washington," *American Journal of Correction,* vol. 39, no. 4, July/August 1977, p. 14.

Jeffery, Robert, and Stephen Woolpert: "Work Furlough as an Alternative to Incarceration: An Assessment of its Effects on Recidivism and Social Cost," *Journal of Criminal Law, Criminology, and Police Science,* vol. 65, no. 3, September 1974, pp. 405–415.

Johnson, Elmer Hubert: *Crime, Corrections, and Society,* Dorsey Press, Homewood, Ill., 1968, chap. 17.

Katsampes, Paul, and Thomas C. Neil, "A Decade of Improvement for Our Sick Jails," *Federal Probation,* vol. 45, no. 3, Administrative Office of the United States Courts, Washington, D.C., September 1981, pp. 45–48.

Lamb, H. Richard, and Victor Geortzel: "A Community Alternative to County Jails: The Hopes and Realities," *Federal Probation,* vol. 39, no. 1, Administrative Office of the United States Courts, Washington, D.C., March 1975, pp. 33–39.

Leonard, E. M.: *The Early History of English Poor Relief,* Cambridge University Press, Cambridge, England, 1900.

McMillan, David, R.: "Work Furlough for the Jailed Prisoner," *Federal Probation,* Administrative Office of the United States Courts, Washington, D.C., March 1965, pp. 33–34.

Malcolm, Benjamin J.: "The Changing Role of the Local Detention/Correctional Center," American Correctional Association, *Proceedings of the One Hundred and Fifth Annual Congress of Correction,* College Park, Md., 1976, pp. 172–176.

Miller, E. Eugene: *Jail Management,* Lexington Books, Lexington, Mass., 1978.

Mintzes, Barry: "Building Bridges Over Fences," *Corrections Today,* vol. 42, no. 4, July/August 1980, pp. 22–23.

Molosovich, John T., and Charles Megerman: "The Community Corrections Center Project," *Offender Rehabilitation,* vol. 1, no. 1, Fall 1976, pp. 33–43.

Moynahan, J. M., and Earl K. Stewart: "The Origin of the American Jail," *Federal Probation,* vol. 42, no. 4, Administrative Office of the United States Courts, Washington, D.C., December 1978, pp. 41–50.

Mullaney, Fahy G.: "Citizen Volunteers Are Breaking Into Jail," *Corrections Today,* vol. 43, no. 4, July/August 1981, pp. 54, 56, and 58.

National Sheriff's Association, Inc.: *Manual on Jail Administration,* Washington, D.C., 1970.

Palmer, John W.: "Prearrest Diversion: Victim Confrontation," *Federal Probation,* vol. 38, no. 3, Administrative Office of the United States Courts, Washington, D.C., September 1974, pp. 12–18.

Pappas, Nick (ed.): *The Jail: Its Operation and Management,* U.S. Bureau of Prisons, Washington, D.C., 1971.

Praedmore, Kenneth L.: "Role of the Local Jail in Corrections," American Correctional Association, *Proceedings of the One Hundred and Third Annual Congress of Correction,* College Park, Md., 1974, pp. 188–192.

Richmond, Mark S., and George W. Aderhold: *New Roles for Jails,* U.S. Department of Justice, Washington, D.C., 1969, pp. 1–26.

Shover, Neal: *A Sociology of American Corrections,* Dorsey Press, Homewood, Ill, 1979.

Sigler, Robert T., and William A. Formby: "The Necessity of Bail Reform," *Criminal Justice Review,* vol. 3, no. 1, Pergamon Press, Albany, New York, Spring 1978, pp. 1–7.

Smith, Talbot: "A New Approach to the Bail Practice," *Federal Probation,* vol. 29, no. 1, Administrative Office of the United States Courts, Washington, D.C., March 1965.

Steiner, Jessee F., and Roy Brown: *The North Carolina Chain Gang,* Negro Universities Press, Westport, Conn., 1970.

Sturz, Herbert: "An Alternative to the Bail System," *Federal Probation,* vol. 26, no. 4, Administrative Office of the United States Courts, Washington, D.C., December 1962, pp. 49–53.

Wallenstein, Arthur M.: "Chillon Castle Revisited or Removing the Moat Surrounding American Jails," *The Prison Journal,* vol. 59, no. 2, Autumn/Winter 1979, pp. 58–70.

Weisberg, Susan: *Cost Analysis of Correctional Standards: Alternatives to Arrest,* American Bar Association, Washington, D.C., October 1975.

Wheeler, Gerald R.: "Federal Court Intervention in Pretrial Release: the Case for Nontraditional Administration," *Federal Probation,* vol. 45, no. 2, Administrative Office of the United States Courts, Washington, D.C., June 1981, pp. 18–25.

Wice, Paul, and Rita James Simon: "Pretrial Release: A Survey of Alternative Practices," *Federal Probation,* vol. 34, no. 4, Administrative Office of the United States Courts, Washington, D.C., December 1970, pp. 60–63.

Wilson, Rob: "Replicating LEAA's First Outstanding Project," *Corrections Magazine,* vol. 2, no. 5, September 1976, pp. 13–24.

Wright, Roberts J.: "The Jail and Misdemeanant Institutions," *Contemporary Corrections,* Paul W. Tappan (ed.), McGraw-Hill Book Company, New York, 1951, pp. 310–322.

Zimring, Franklin E.: "Measuring the Impact of Pretrial Diversion from the Criminal Justice System," *University of Chicago Law Review,* vol. 41, no. 1, Fall 1973, pp. 224–241.

Zoet, Thomas H.: "Treatment Programming: A New Role for Jails," *Corrections Today,* vol. 43, no. 1, January/February 1981, pp. 62–68.

PROBATION

CHAPTER OBJECTIVES

- To discuss the advantages and disadvantages of probation
- To view the status of probation today, including the use of presentence investigations
- To outline the services provided by the probation officer
- To examine supervisory techniques used by the probation officer
- To discuss the probation officer-probationer relationship
- To present current trends in probation
- To examine the evaluations of probation

INTRODUCTION

Jails are local prisons. Prisoners incarcerated in jails suffer the same loss of self-esteem, contact with family, and economic stability as prisoners incarcerated in reformatories. Prisonization can take place just as easily in jails as in penitentiaries. Offenders can be instructed by other offenders regarding crime skills just as readily in jails as in long-term institutions. The same is true about positive aspects of correctional institutions. Creative therapy, recreation, and religious instruction can be offered in jails, as well as work release, furloughs, and prerelease programs. In fact, in some ways, the jail is in a better position to reintegrate the offender into the community than are state or federal institutions. After all, the jail is a local correctional institution, located within the community and serving local residents.

RATIONALE

For some offenders, a period of adjustment with supervision can resolve problems without the need of institutionalization. For other offenders, deeply ingrained habits cannot be ended without a period of institutionalization followed by a period of supervision in the community. As a result, alternative methods of releasing offenders have originated—the suspended sentence, probation, parole, pardon, unconditional release of felons at the end of their sentences, and unconditional release of misdemeanants after a short jail term or payment of a fine. The most widely known method of releasing offenders is *probation.*

Probation is a disposition that is administered to individuals instead of sending them to prison. It is justified by inherent drawbacks in the criminal justice system which hinder the adjustment of criminals in the community. Offenders whose life habits are firmly set in a delinquent or criminal pattern and inexperienced offenders whose situations prompt desperate behavior to alleviate problems may both find difficulty in adjusting to conventional life. Those who have dealt with such offenders over a period time believe that they would probably continue in their old patterns of misconduct if left to their own devices and that, consequently, some form of supervision is necessary during the period of community adjustment.

The word "probation" is derived from the Latin *probare,* meaning "to try or prove." In corrections, probation is a form of criminal sanction imposed by a court on an offender after a verdict, finding, or plea of guilty. It provides a period of proving or trial in lieu of incarceration and allows the offender to serve his or her sentence under supervision in the community.[1] Probation as a method of reintegration is designed to facilitate the social adjustment of offenders in the community rather than in correctional institutions. Probation evolved from antecedent practices all intended to lessen the severity of the penal code. In English common law, the courts were presumed to have power to suspend sentence for specified purposes and periods.

THE PROS AND CONS OF PROBATION

Advantages

The advantages of probation are many. Those most frequently cited by correctional administrators are as follows:

1 Offenders are spared the experience of imprisonment and isolation from normal community contacts. Consequently, they are not labeled convicts in the minds of family, friends, and potential employers.

2 Offenders benefit from professional supervision, counseling, and guidance

---

[1]George G. Killinger, Hazel B. Kerper, and Paul F. Cromwell, Jr., *Probation and Parole in the Criminal Justice System,* West Publishing Company, St. Paul, Minn., 1976, p. 14.

which is available in the community. Needed resources, such as schools, mental health clinics, and vocational training courses, are readily available. An offender who fails to adjust to supervised freedom can always be placed in a correctional institution with a greater degree of control.

3 Probation is more economical than imprisonment, for offenders continue to support themselves and their dependents. Moreover, the cost of administering probation is 13 times less expensive per offender than the cost of incarceration. Offenders also continue to pay taxes, and their families do not need public assistance.

4 Offenders who remain in the community maintain employment, live with their families, and do not associate with the anticommunity culture that exists in prison. There is no disruption of their lives.

5 Offenders are in a position to make financial reparations for their offenses. They can pay court costs, fines, and restitution.

6 Minor offenders are supervised rather than merely being dismissed.

Criticisms

The practice of probation has not been without its critics. Probation to many has appeared to be soft on criminals and is sometimes referred to as a "bleeding heart" approach. Critics believe probation pampers offenders by enabling them to avoid punishment and, moreover, does not protect the community, for the offender is still at large and may repeat crimes. "Going soft" does not serve as a deterrent. If the goal is the elimination of criminal behavior, probation is not the answer, because it permits offenders to return to the same families and community environment that contributed to their previous crimes. Offenders may not believe any change in their behavior is necessary; probation may reinforce that belief. Even if all the claims about probation are true, in actuality probation does not operate efficiently. Presentence investigations are inadequate. Caseloads are too large for effective supervision. Personnel are poorly trained. Judges make inappropriate selections of cases.[2]

ADMINISTRATION OF PROBATION

Structure

Today legislation has established probation on the local, county, state, and federal levels. Both juveniles and adults of both sexes are eligible for probation, which is available to both misdemeanants and felons. In addition, probation is considered a useful tool in both the administration of justice and the reintegra-

---

[2]Ruth Shonle Cavan, *Criminology,* Thomas Y. Crowell Company, New York, 1948, pp. 531–532; and Robert G. Caldwell, *Criminology,* Ronald Press Company, New York, 1965, pp. 468–471.

tion of the offender. The use of probation has increased to the point that in 1980, of all adults within the criminal justice system, 60 percent were on probation and only 40 percent were incarcerated.[3] A survey by staff of Improving Victim Services Through Probation in 1976 indicated that there may be as many as 36,000 probation officers engaged in federal, state, and local probation services.[4]

Although the current application of probation follows a number of general guidelines, each state as well as the federal government has legislated an individualized structure for its administration. In eleven states adult probation is a county-operated system; in thirty-nine, it is a statewide system operated by a state agency. This latter group includes thirteen states in which there is some combination of county and state services.[5]

Two questions have been asked concerning who should administer probation: Should it be administered by the judicial or the executive branch of government? Should it be within a state or local administrative structure?

Both questions really stem from the same argument. Since probation is a judicial disposition and a local program for local offenders, should not the administration be the same? Furthermore, citizens and agencies of the community will more easily support programs if they have input and believe the programs are responsive to local wishes. Locally operated probation has a better opportunity to be flexible, to adjust more quickly to change and be less encumbered by bureaucratic rigidity.

Yet state policymakers have convinced the legislatures of thirty-six states that state-administered probation systems offer more consistent standards, make more effective use of funds, and use resources and manpower more efficiently. Even locally administered programs in California, New York, Michigan, and Illinois have sought state subsidies.[6]

Methods of Assigning Cases

As a result of the structural differences, cases are assigned to the probation officer by various methods. Some probationers are assigned by district. This means that all probationers within a certain geographic area are placed with one probation officer. Another method is based on individual characteristics of the offenders. Under this system all who meet certain criteria, such as being of the same sex, race, or religion, are assigned to a specific probation officer. A third method is based on the offenders' particular problems. For example, alcoholics may be assigned to a certain probation officer and heroin addicts to another.

[3]Clemens Bartollas, *Introduction to Corrections,* Harper & Row, Publishers Incorporated, New York, 1981, p. 146.

[4]Scotia Knouff, Co-Director, Improving Victim Services Through Probation, Aberdeen, North Carolina, telephone conversation, June 24, 1980.

[5]Robert M. Carter, Richard A. McGee, and E. Kim Nelson, *Corrections in America,* J. B. Lippincott Company, Philadelphia, 1975, p. 22.

[6]Bartollas, op. cit., p. 149.

This method is applied in the more elaborately organized probation depart-ments.[7]

A valid statistically based risk-prediction scale has been implemented by the federal probation system and the state of Wisconsin's Bureau of Community Corrections. The Risk Prediction Scale (RPS-80) was adopted by the federal probation system in January 1981. Based on a 1978 study of a number of similar scales (Revised Oregon, California, United States District Court 75), the RPS-80 appears valid in classifying offenders on probation in terms of revocation risks.[8] The Wisconsin system uses a risk assessment to classify offenders placed on probation into four levels of supervision—maximum, medium, minimum, and mail-in. The level-of-supervision classification determines the number and nature of the contacts between probationer and probation officer. A maximum supervision probationer must see the probation officer—face to face—twice a month; a mail-in supervision probationer merely mails in a monthly report. A 24-month follow-up concluded that the number of probations revoked *did* correspond with the original risk assessment (see Table 5.1).[9]

THE SELECTION PROCESS

Presentence Investigation

One of the methods used to decide the eligibility of an offender for probation is the presentence report, mandatory in more than one-quarter of all states.[10] The

[7]Don J. Hager, "Race, Nationality, and Religion—Their Relationship to Appointment Policies and Casework," *National Probation and Parole Association Journal,* vol. 3, April 1957, pp. 129–141.

[8]James B. Eaglin and Patricia A. Lombard, "Statistical Risk Prediction as an Aid to Probation Caseload Classification," *Federal Probation,* vol. 45, no. 3, Administrative Office of the United States Courts, Washington, D.C., September 1981, p. 32.

[9]S. Christopher Baird, "Probation and Parole Classification: The Wisconsin Model," *Corrections Today,* vol. 43, no. 3, May/June 1981, p. 36.

[10]Edwin H. Sutherland and Donald R. Cressey, *Criminology,* J. B. Lippincott Company, Philadelphia, 1970, p. 467.

TABLE 5.1
INITIAL RISK CLASSIFICATION AND SUBSEQUENT OUTCOMES

Risk assessment scores	Number assessed	Number revoked
Low risk	3153	94 (3.0%)
Moderate risk	2664	267 (10.0%)
Moderately high risk	1827	495 (22.2%)
High risk	607	225 (37.1%)

Source: S. Christopher Baird, "Probation and Parole Classifi-cation: The Wisconsin Model," *Corrections Today,* vol. 43, no. 3, May/June 1981, p. 38.

judge relies on a presentence report to arrive at a decision regarding sentence suspension. This report is written following the probation officer's investigation of the probationer. The investigator talks with police officers, welfare workers, and others who have knowledge about the offender and also interviews the offender, his or her family, and friends. Tests may be requested and school or employment records acquired. The end result is a recommendation by the investigator about the advisability of probation for the offender.

The presentence investigation is designed to select offenders who are most likely to succeed, not to guarantee noncriminal behavior of all those released. Those considered most likely to succeed may include offenders who already identify with law-abiding citizens, those who require guidance and supervision but are favorable prospects, and questionable candidates requiring intensive therapy. Also, it is inevitable that both judges and probation officers appraise the feelings of the people in the community and compare the effect of imprisonment with the benefits of the probationary process in regard to public support for correctional programs.[11]

The impact of the probation officer's recommendation on the judge's final decision is monumental. In fact, Professors Robert M. Carter and Leslie T. Wilkins discovered that probation officers' recommendations are followed in more than 94 percent of all cases (see Tables 5.2 and 5.3).[12]

In addition to aiding the judge in sentencing, the presentence report serves four other functions: (1) assists correctional institutions in classifying and providing services for offenders, (2) guides probation officers in designing and implementing a plan for individuals placed on probation, (3) furnishes the parole board information relevant to its decision making, and (4) serves as a source of

[11]Elmer Hubert Johnson, *Crime, Correction, and Society,* Dorsey Press, Homewood, Ill., 1968, pp. 671–672.

[12]Robert M. Carter and Leslie T. Wilkins, "Some Factors in Sentencing Policy," *Journal of Criminal Law, Criminology, and Police Science,* vol. 58, no. 4, December 1967, p. 505.

TABLE 5.2
PERCENTAGE OF PROBATION OFFICER
RECOMMENDATIONS FOR PROBATION
FOLLOWED BY CALIFORNIA SUPERIOR
COURTS

1959	95.6%
1960	96.4%
1961	96.0%
1962	96.5%
1963	97.2%
1964	97.3%
1965	96.7%

Source: State of California Department of Justice, *Delinquency and Probation in California,* 1964, p. 168; and *Crime and Delinquency in California,* 1965, pp. 98–99.

TABLE 5.3
PERCENTAGE OF PROBATION OFFICER
RECOMMENDATIONS FOR PROBATION
FOLLOWED BY TEN JUDICIAL CIRCUITS,
FISCAL YEAR 1964

First circuit	99.4%
Second circuit	96.0%
Third circuit	93.2%
Fourth circuit	93.3%
Fifth circuit	95.2%
Sixth circuit	93.9%
Seventh circuit	89.9%
Eighth circuit	95.0%
Ninth circuit	93.5%
Tenth circuit	97.8%
Overall	94.1%

Source: Data furnished by the Administrative Office of the
United States Courts, Washington, D.C.

information for research and evaluation. For these reasons, the presentence report may be the most important single document completed during the corrections process.[13]

Statutory Limitations

Many states have imposed statutory limitations on offenders eligible for probation. Those who are ineligible usually fall into categories which include crimes of violence, crimes involving use of a deadly weapon, sexual crimes, crimes against government, and crimes carrying certain penalties, such as life imprisonment. Other states do not specify particular offenses but require a thorough investigation of offenders convicted of certain crimes.

Plea Bargaining

Unfortunately, the selection process for probation and the plea bargaining which accompanies adjudication place the probation officer in a quasi-judicial role. Plea bargaining is a procedure whereby the prosecution and the defense discuss a case and work out a "deal," which does not bind a judge but is usually followed. A reduction of the charge is frequently the result of the negotiations. The granting of probation is sometimes one part of the deal. In a classic study of plea bargaining, Donald J. Newman found that 93.8 percent of convictions were the result of bargained pleas.[14] Free administrative decision making based on

[13]E. Eugene Miller and M. Robert Montilla, *Corrections in the Community,* Reston Publishing Company, Inc., Reston, Va., 1977, pp. 48–49.
[14]Sue Titus Reid, *Crime and Criminology,* Holt, Rinehart and Winston, Inc., New York, 1979, pp. 321–322.

individual characteristics of the offender has given way to the offender's relative success at plea bargaining. Today's probation officer has become a part of this process. Nowadays it is likely that the prosecutor has communicated the plea bargaining agreement to the probation officer, and the latter's recommendation takes into consideration the prosecutor's agreement with the offender.

ROLE OF THE PROBATION OFFICER

Services

The probation officer is charged with the responsibility of offering many services to the probationers, including helping them to change their life situations to improve the available behavioral choices, discovering and maintaining a list of community resources, and providing guidance and counseling. In performing these services, the probation officer utilizes home visits, volunteers, office contacts, and one-to-one relationships.

Even the application of authority need not be an obstacle to providing effective probation services. Although its clumsy and arbitrary use by the probation officer lessens the potential of reintegration, proper use can make authority an instrument that encourages the probationer to face reality and overcome personal problems. Contacts between officer and probationer generally are made at either the officer's office or the probationer's home. Home visits are effective because they enable the officer to view the offender's environment, making better understanding possible. Also, since the attitudes of the probationer's family and other intimate associates are important in determining whether criminal or noncriminal behavior is likely to take place in the future, contacts with these people can assess their effect on the probationer.

Most probationers are required by court order to report at regular intervals to the probation officer. Sometimes these reports are made once a week, sometimes once a month, and sometimes less frequently. The procedure varies widely. In some places the officer merely checks a card that the probationer hands through a window. In slightly less perfunctory systems, the officer questions the probationer about work, companions, recreation, legal problems, personal habits, and financial status and may give advice on these topics. Probationers frequently are required to bring written reports from school or employers and receipts for support payments and reparation.[15]

Techniques

Textbook author David Dressler suggests four techniques of supervision to be employed by probation officers to help offenders:

1 Manipulative techniques involving the modification of the offender's envi-

[15]Sutherland and Cressey, op. cit., p. 473.

ronment. This means that the officer may help the offender obtain a job, find a residence, be admitted to school, or establish welfare eligibility. More specifically, he may help the probationer fill out an employment application, prepare a résumé, or anticipate the questions of a job interview.

2 Executive techniques employing resources of the community. This is accomplished through referrals to public and private welfare agencies, medical and dental care organizations, legal aid societies, recreational programs, churches, employment services, Alcoholics Anonymous groups, county mental health associations, educational and vocational services, family service agencies, and recreational facilities.

3 Guidance techniques, giving advice not requiring a high degree of specialized training. The agent endeavors thus to help offenders mobilize resources to meet their problems realistically.

4 Counseling techniques applying a level of skill usually not possessed by the probation officer. This requires referral to community resources where counseling is available.

It is hoped that by applying these four techniques of supervision the probation officer can help offenders to develop strength enabling them to resolve their own problems with little assistance from others.[16]

THE PROBATIONARY RELATIONSHIP

Day-to-Day Tasks

Probation officers are responsible for providing many services to the probationers. Theoretically, the techniques suggested by Dressler would be valuable tools in carrying out this responsibility. Equally important are the day-to-day tasks that officers must complete. They keep up-to-date case files, compiling required statistical reports for the court and state probation offices. They write presentence reports, notice-of-violation reports, and violation-of-probation reports for revocation hearings. In some jurisdictions periodic progress reports are required on each probationer. Officers must make certain that each probationer complies with the conditions of probation and does not break the law.

Although probation officers may actually give advice on financial affairs, job seeking, or interpersonal problems, most of the time they function as resource managers or brokers. In this task, they must assess the situation, refer the probationers to the available resources, and follow up the referrals. There is little time or effort spent on counseling.

An important element is the relationship between probationer and probation officer. The relationship is a continuing one, allowing an outside person with skills in dealing with behavioral problems an opportunity to assist the potential

---

[16]David Dressler, *Practice and Theory of Probation and Parole,* Columbia University Press, New York, 1969, pp. 216–235.

incarcerate. It is a last attempt before incarceration when it is believed that all other alternatives have been exhausted.

The relationship between officer and probationer is an eclectic one. The officer applies his or her skills in an expedient manner, changing the plan or strategy as the direction of the probationer's progress becomes apparent. Correction of deviant behavior is a creative process; the probationer's needs and potentialities vary from case to case, and the officer's techniques cannot be neatly fitted to prearranged specifications.

Throughout the probationary period, the officer must create an individualized program, applying community resources as needed, cajoling, coercing, pleading, assisting, suggesting, and commanding, as the requirements of the individual case dictate. The probation officer must be a leader, always in control of the situation, whose discretion is applied most decisively in choosing what techniques are needed and how and when they should be used.

Probation officers are patient listeners. Although at times they take command, there are other times, especially at the beginning of the probation period, when the offender wants someone to talk to. The officer does not prejudge or stereotype the offender according to the type of offense committed or method of operation used. The alcoholic does not always need to join Alcoholics Anonymous; drinking may be only a symptom of feelings of insecurity which will take more than an A.A. membership to resolve. The check writer does not always need to avoid accumulating debts; check writing may be the result not of excessive debts but of poor management, which could better be resolved by a class in money management than a cash system of spending.

Regardless of the plan, the desire for change must exist within the probationer, who must actually struggle with problems before gaining insights and a sense of personal responsibility. He or she must learn to discover personal weaknesses in order to correct them and must bow to certain limitations and learn to adjust to them or be confronted with the possibility of more restrictive ones.

In actuality, caseloads of probation officers sometimes run as high as 500 probationers. Most caseloads fall between 75 and 150. Most officers have barely enough time to conduct required investigations of those who are rearrested. With a caseload of 160, on a 40-hour workweek without interruptions, each probationer would receive 15 minutes a week.

Most of the officer's time is spent on paperwork. Another large segment of time is wasted waiting for court hearings and meetings with law enforcement personnel. A presentence investigation could take as long as 20 hours to complete. Fewer than one-third of all persons committed to prisons have been the subject of a presentence investigation, partly because of excessive workloads.

Concerned judges, correctional administrators, and even law enforcement personnel have long realized that the practical demands made on probation officers leave insufficient time for personal contacts between officers and offenders. Most officers do not have time to individualize solutions to cases. In

IN THE DISTRICT COURT OF SHAWNEE COUNTY
THIRD JUDICIAL DISTRICT

STATE OF KANSAS,   Plaintiff,

    vs.

JOHN DOE,   Defendant.

ORDER OF PROBATION

In accordance with Kansas Statutes Annotated, Section 21–4603/20–2302/20–1935 you are placed on probation this _____ day of _____ , 19 _____ , for a period of _____ by the Honorable _____ , Judge.

THE COURT ORDERS THAT YOU SHALL COMPLY WITH THE FOLLOWING CONDITIONS:

(1) You shall at all times conduct yourself as a peaceful and law–abiding citizen and contact your proba-tion officer at once if arrested or questioned by a law-enforcement officer for any reason.

(2) You shall maintain reasonable hours as directed by the probation officer.

(3) You shall work regularly at a lawful occupation and support your dependents to the best of your ability and obtain approval from the probation officer before changing employment.

(4) You shall not leave Shawnee County, Kansas, with-out authorization.

(5) You shall reside at such place as shall be desig-nated by the probation officer and obtain his approval be-fore changing residence.

(6) You shall report to the probation officer as di-rected in person and in writing or permit him to visit you and supply full and correct information at all times.

(7) You shall seek counsel from the probation officer before entering into marriage and obtain his approval be-fore buying a car or incurring indebtedness.

(8) You shall not associate with persons having a

FIGURE 5.1
Order of probation. *(Court Services, Third Judicial District Court, Shawnee County, Topeka, Kansas, December 1981.)*

criminal record or bad reputation and you shall not visit
any jail or penal institution or correspond with inmates
thereof without approval of the probation officer.

(9) You shall pay court costs, restitution, and fine
as directed below:

                Item   Amount   Payable by

        Court Costs
        Restitution
        Fine

(10) You shall comply with all additional conditions
which may be imposed by the court and all reasonable orders, including any treatment program, prescribed by the
probation officer.

        Special Condition(s):

/s/_____   /s/_____
District Attorney   Judge

I understand the above conditions and agree to abide
by them. I also understand that the conditions and the
term may be modified, and that probation may be revoked if
I present myself, by work or deed, as unwilling or unable
to comply with these conditions.

I further understand that I may be arrested by the
probation officer without a warrant or by a law-
enforcement officer with written authorization from the
probation officer, without warrant for any alleged violation as provided by K.S.A. 62-224 -45.

/s/_____   /s/_____
Probation Officer   Defendant

FIGURE 5.1
(Continued)

addition, the complexities of offenders' problems may require special training—
training too costly in time and money to be justified when the rapid turnover of
probation personnel demands that training be limited to preparing replace-
ments.

The resource-broker concept of delivering services to probationers is the
result. The brokerage technique is economical in terms of both finances and
conservation of staff time. Spared the need to personally provide services to

each probationer, the officer has the opportunity to spend more time with each person on the caseload.[17]

Rule Enforcement

The probationary relationship is also affected by conditions imposed by the court. Although discretion is granted in applying supervisory techniques, the officer must enforce certain rules (see Figure 5.1).

In most states, probationers are required to pay restitution, support their families, pay court costs, avoid further criminal behavior, report periodically to an officer, maintain employment, and remain within a specific geographic area.

John Koontz, a supervising federal probation officer, suggests that a probation officer should apply the rules governing probation pragmatically, taking into consideration the probationer's specific needs as well as the legality of the decisions, the clarity of the expectations for the probationer, and the effect of the application of rules on the probationer's future adjustment.[18]

The advisory committee on sentencing and review of the American Bar Association recommends that whatever the conditions of probation, they must be clear and definite to be effective. They must not violate the probationer's right to expression, association, or religious freedom and must not involve cruel or inhumane punishment. They must not violate the individual's constitutional protection against self-incrimination or waive his or her right to privacy. Other probation policymakers believe that administrators should set specific, enforceable probation conditions to limit the probationer's opportunity for further crime.[19]

Revocation

If the conditions imposed by the court are violated, the probationer may be subject to a hearing and returned to the judge's chambers. Ultimately, a refusal to abide by these conditions will result in orders that the probation be revoked and the sentence served.

Unfortunately, the criteria for revoking probation are not uniform in district courts throughout the country and at times not even among judges in the same district court. Some judges and probation officers believe that infractions of the conditions of probation are sufficient justification for revocation, particularly when such violations are committed by an indifferent probationer who is unwilling to cooperate with the probation officer and the court. Others contend

[17]Kevin Krajick, "Probation: The Original Community Program," *Corrections Magazine,* vol. 6, no. 6, December 1980, pp. 7–10.

[18]John F. Koontz, Jr., "Pragmatic Conditions of Probation," *Corrections Today,* vol. 42, no. 1, January/February 1980, pp. 14, 34, 42, and 44.

[19]Stevens H. Clarke, "What is the Purpose of Probation and Why do we Revoke it?" *Crime and Delinquency,* vol. 25, no. 4, October 1979, pp. 420–423.

that the circumstances of the violation; the probationer's adjustment with family, in the community, and on the job; and his or her previous efforts to comply with the conditions should also be considered.

Probationers differ in their ability to comply. Violations of the conditions of probation do not always reflect a poor probation adjustment. The conditions imposed may have been unrealistic. Perhaps too much was expected of the probationer. The customs, feelings, attitudes, habits, and moral values of the social group of which a probationer is a part should be considered in assessing noncompliance.

Some judges and probation officers insist that convictions for new offenses should be the only basis for revocation. Most believe that no violation, especially failures to keep appointments, submit monthly reports, observe a curfew, or remain within a geographic area should result in automatic revocation.[20]

The revocation of probation is clearly a critical matter for probationers, for it can send them to prison. The United States Supreme Court ruled in *Mempa v. Rhay* (339 U.S. 128, 2d Cir., 3023, 1968) that legal counsel should be provided when the probationer claims not to have committed the violation and when the reasons for the violation are complex or otherwise difficult to present. Because Mempa did not have counsel at his revocation hearing, the Court reversed the decision of the lower courts and ordered his release from prison. In another case, *Gagnon v. Scarpelli* (411 U.S. 788, 1973), the Supreme Court reversed a lower court's decision on the grounds that a probation revocation without a hearing and counsel violated Scarpelli's due process rights.[21]

Common sense dictates that a probationer should not be regarded as a violator until convicted. There is always the possibility of an acquittal. Neither should probation be revoked only because a probationer fails to participate in a planned program. Also, to prevent the probation officer from being guilty of usurping the power of the court, all unfulfilled conditions of probation should be brought to the court's attention, because the decision to revoke or continue is not the officer's alone. To assist the court in revocation hearings, the probation officer should prepare a formal report containing details of any alleged violation, factors underlying the violation, the probationer's attitude toward the violation, and a summary of his or her conduct during supervision and general attitude and outlook. Recommendations for a course of action should be included in the report. The probationer should always attend any revocation hearing. In the end, revocation should serve a constructive purpose and not be used merely for punishment.[22]

[20]Eugene C. Dicerba, "When Should Probation be Revoked?" *Probation, Parole, and Community Corrections,* Robert M. Carter and Leslie T. Wilkins (eds.) John Wiley & Sons, Inc., New York, 1976, pp. 448, 457.

[21]Bartollas, *op. cit.,* pp. 150–151.

[22]Rolando V. del Carmen, "Legal Responsibilities of Probation and Parole Officers: Trends, General Advice and Questions," *Federal Probation,* vol. 45, no. 3, Administrative Office of the United States Courts, Washington, D.C., September 1981, pp. 21–24.

TRENDS IN PROBATION

Centralized Organization

Probation has become a vital part of the total correctional process. As this has happened, a number of trends have emerged. First, there is a trend toward a centralized state organization. Initially, most state probation officers were hired by local jurisdictions—counties and cities. Later, as states realized the vast differences in the quality of probation services offered by different jurisdictions, there was a tendency for the state to consolidate all probation services into a statewide system. As was said earlier, probation in thirty-nine states is now operated by a centralized state organization. In twenty-six states, the state manages both adult misdemeanant and felony probation supervision.

Probation Eligibility

A second trend is the extension of eligibility for probation services to more people, including both men and women. Originally the court granted probation only to offenders who appeared to offer little risk that future criminal behavior would result from their remaining in the community. Misdemeanants were the original recipients. As probation practices became more efficient, states gradually lifted restrictions and felons were added to the list of eligible offenders.

The increase in the use of probation is obvious. The most recent statistics available indicate that 923,064 adult offenders were on probation status as of September 1976.[23] The inmates of California state prisons in the same year were only 22 percent of all persons under correctional supervision (not including local detention), compared with 30 percent in the 1960s.[24]

Conditions of Probation

A third trend is the use of wider discretion in the conditions of probation. Both judges and probation officers are learning how to adapt probation conditions to accommodate the individual. As the rights of probationers are acknowledged formally, rules are relaxed, making technical violations fewer; hearings are established; and lockup is minimized. From restitution to driving instructions, from marriage counseling to lectures on budgeting, probation conditions have become more individualized. Many judges require the probationer to perform a community service as a condition of probation. Probationers have been assigned to work at Boys Clubs, public libraries, the Salvation Army, hospitals, runaway houses, state and national parks, and Head Start projects.[25]

---

[23]United States Department of Justice, *State and Local Probation and Parole Systems,* Law Enforcement Assistance Administration, U.S. Government Printing Office, Washington, D.C., 1978, p. 1.

[24]*Crime and Delinquency in California, 1976,* Department of Justice, Division of Law Enforcement, Bureau of Criminal Statistics, State of California, Sacramento, 1976, p. 39.

[25]Bailey Brown, "Community Service as a Condition of Probation," *Federal Probation,* vol. 41, no. 4, Administrative Office of the United States Courts, Washington, D.C., December 1977, p. 8.

Professionalism

A fourth trend involves a change in the caliber of probation officers. The first persons who assumed the duties of probation officers were volunteers. Early salaried probation officers were approved by a politically responsive judge. Skills in probation practices were not necessarily a prerequisite to an officer's employment. Currently, probation is considered as "moving from a politically oriented to a professional career oriented service."[26] Today most states require a bachelor's degree in the social sciences, merit examination, detailed social history, previous related work experience, and adequate references. More important, the preferred probation officer candidate is an understanding, mature, empathetic person, rather than a judge's political supporter or a former public official who was not reelected.

INNOVATIVE PROGRAMS IN PROBATION

Group Methods

The state of Missouri has applied group counseling to the intake process for new probationers. Each new probationer is required to attend six group counseling sessions. The first is set aside for the probation officers and felons to get acquainted. The second meeting is devoted to a thorough presentation and discussion of the rules of probation. The third is used to introduce the probationers to the counseling technique of their probation officers. The fourth session is used to identify the problems of the probationers in the group. The final two sessions are reserved for developing a behavioral plan for each probationer. The plan is an informal contract which outlines what behaviors the probationer must engage in, in order to complete the probation period.[27]

McLennan County in Texas uses family therapy with probationers. Through a contract with Baylor University in Waco, doctoral students in the clinical psychology program serve as therapists and consultants for probationers and their families. As of March 1978, research was being done to evaluate the program. Preliminary results were favorable.[28]

Some probation departments use a treatment team composed of all the professionals who participate in the probation process in addition to the probation officers themselves. Caseloads are assigned according to individual problems rather than probationer-officer ratio. Treatment teams exist throughout the United States, most frequently on the county level. In some instances where treatment teams exist, probationers are referred to private community resources. Treatment team members help offenders to seek employment. They

---

[26]Lloyd E. Ohlin, *Sociology and the Field of Corrections,* Russell Sage Foundation, New York, 1956, p. 45.

[27]Paul Hotfelder and A. Dwain Sachs, "Intake Group Counseling," *Federal Probation,* vol. 43, no. 2, Administrative Office of the United States Courts, Washington, D.C., June 1979, pp. 52–53.

[28]Donald J. Wendorf, "Family Therapy: An Innovative Approach in the Rehabilitation of Adult Probationers," *Federal Probation,* vol. 40, no. 1, Administrative Office of the United States Courts, Washington, D.C., March 1976, p. 48.

utilize community resources to deal with alcohol- or drug-related problems as well as for counseling, the development of leisure time activities, and assistance in obtaining additional education.[29]

Intensive Supervision

Multnomah County, including Portland, Oregon, uses probation teams to provide intensive services to probationers. Each team is composed of a maximum of two secretaries and five counselors, a mental health specialist, and an unlimited number of volunteer aides. The mental health specialist has a caseload not to exceed 50 persons, and counselors counsel no more than 100 probationers. The teams assume responsibility for intake and case development, assessment of needs, case classification, probation plan development, probation plan application, and identification and solicitation of specialized services.[30]

One intensive probation project uses outreach methods, rapport-building incentives, negotiated treatment contracts, and financial incentives to maintain contact with "complex offenders" or reluctant probationers. For the purposes of this project, complex offenders were defined as probationers between the ages of 18 and 30 who had prior convictions; a history of psychological or psychiatric difficulty; and poor adjustment in the community, as indicated by chronic unemployment, dependence on public subsidy, and absence of a stable living situation. Over a period of 3½ years, statistically significant results were achieved with sixty randomly selected probationers. Recidivism was reduced, and psychiatric hospitalization was virtually eliminated. Increased employment and better educational achievements facilitated independent living.[31]

Beginning in 1960, intensive services were provided probationers in Royal Oak, Michigan, by volunteers. Court services there combine salaried personnel and volunteers, providing an elaborate support system for probationers. Two full-time professional staff members, and thirteen part-time paid employees (including five retired persons) supervise volunteers who are assigned to individual cases. The volunteers' efforts permit the caseloads of the professional counselors to remain small, intensive, and comprised of probationers who demand special skills. In October 1977, the recidivism rate for all probation cases under the jurisdiction of the 44th District Court of Royal Oak was estimated at 10 percent.[32]

[29]Rob Wilson, "Probation/Parole Officers as 'Resource Brokers,'" *Corrections Magazine*, vol. 4, no. 2, June 1978, p. 48.

[30]William T. Wood, "Multnomah County Probation Teams," *Federal Probation*, vol. 42, no. 3, Administrative Office of the United States Courts, Washington, D.C., September 1978, pp. 8–9.

[31]James D. Klass and Joan Karan, "Community Intervention for Reluctant Clients," *Federal Probation*, vol. 43, no. 4, Administrative Office of the United States Courts, Washington, D.C., December 1979, pp. 38, 42.

[32]Charles J. Grisdale, Director of Probation and Psychological Services, 44th District Court, State of Michigan, personal correspondence, Oct. 4, 1977.

Sentencing Innovations

Some innovations have also occurred in the administration of probation. In many states judges have the option of combining incarceration and probation. Two types of judicial sentencing combinations are most common, the *split sentence* and *shock probation*. Under the split sentence, used by Massachusetts, Maine, Delaware, and the federal government, at the time of sentencing the judge combines incarceration and probation. In some states, such as California, jail confinement is seen as a desirable condition of probation, but the maximum period of confinement is limited to 30, 60, or 90 days; 6 months; or 1 year.[33]

The other refinement, shock probation, is suspending the sentence after the offender has been confined in a correctional institution. Since 1970, seven states (Ohio, Idaho, Indiana, Kentucky, North Carolina, Maine, and Texas) have passed laws giving judges this option.[34] South Dakota adopted this form of suspension in 1960. The law that applied in this case simply stated, "Courts and the judges thereof . . . shall have and retain jurisdiction for the purpose of suspending any such sentence or granting any such parole for a period of one year from the effective date of the judgement of conviction."[35] Between 1960 and 1967, there were 327 suspended sentences granted from the South Dakota State Penitentiary. Of this number, 93, or 30.88 percent, were violated and the offenders returned to the penitentiary.

Two reasons have been stated for this high violation rate. Courts did not request information from prison officials regarding the inmate's adjustment, and the suspended offenders were not placed under the jurisdiction of a probation officer. Similarly, a study in Ohio concluded that shock probation is not especially effective. The number of post-shock-probation convictions amounted to 33 percent of the men after 4½ years, and 23 percent of the women after 3½ years.[36] Despite these results, Ohio judges continue to release offenders under the 1965 law. During the calendar year 1978, releases were granted to 1247 offenders. The number of offenders released over the 13 years between 1965 and 1978 amounted to 11,859.[37]

Probation Subsidy

Beginning in 1965, as mentioned in Chapter 3, California subsidized local counties that chose to retain offenders in the community on probation rather

[33]Nicolette Parisá, "Combining Incarceration and Probation," *Federal Probation*, vol. 44, no. 2, Administrative Office of the United States Courts, Washington, D.C., June 1980, pp. 6–10.

[34]Joan Potter, "Shock Probation: A Little Taste of Prison," *Corrections Magazine*, vol. 3, no. 4, December 1977, p. 50.

[35]Victor Batista, Assistant Director, South Dakota Probation and Parole Department, Sioux Falls, South Dakota, unpublished correspondence, October, 1976.

[36]Joseph A. Waldron and Henry R. Angelino, "Shock Probation: A Natural Experiment on the Effect of a Short Period of Incarceration," *Prison Journal*, vol. LVII, no. 1, Spring/Summer 1977, p. 49.

[37]Ohio Department of Rehabilitation and Correction, Division of Parole and Community Services, *Annual Report*, Columbus, 1978, p. 9.

than sentence them to a prison. As a result, a decrease in the number of offenders sentenced to prison began in 1966 and continued to 1970. By that time, actual commitments had dropped off by 200 persons and total commitments had decreased by 11,654 persons. The decrease was 16 percent in 1966 and 38 percent by 1970 (see Table 5.4).[38] Although it was replaced in 1978 by another act, most of the fifty-eight counties participated.

The state of Washington has a similar probation subsidy plan. New York reimburses local communities up to 50 percent of their operating costs if they are willing to conform to staffing patterns. From 1965 to 1972, probation staff was increased from 1527 to 1956. Michigan simply assigns state-paid probation officers to local units of government. A 1979 Illinois law mandates officer training and minimum standards of operation in return for a $400-a-month subsidy for each probation officer.[39]

EVALUATION

The most elaborate evaluation of the effectiveness of probation is conducted by the Administrative Office of the United States Courts. The 1974 annual report of

[38]Kenneth E. Kirkpatrick, "Probation Subsidy: Impact on Los Angeles County," *Proceedings of the One Hundred and Third Annual Congress of Corrections,* American Correctional Association, College Park, Md., 1974, p. 252.

[39]Bartollas, op. cit., pp. 155–156.

TABLE 5.4
COMPARISON OF STATE AND COUNTY SUCCESS IN REDUCING COMMITMENTS IN CALIFORNIA SINCE 1966

Year	Base expected commitments	Actual commitments	% decrease in rate	Subsidy
State				
1966–1967	8,757	7,359	16.1	$ 5,675,815
1967–1968	9,620	7,205	25.4	9,819,625
1968–1969	11,309	7,992	29.3	13,747,910
1969–1970	11,982	8,425	29.7	14,200,160
1970–1971	11,654	7,159	38.5	18,145,142
1971–1972	12,087			
Los Angeles				
1966–1967	4,418	4,369	1.1	$ 104,615
1967–1968	4,466	3,841	14.0	2,415,625
1968–1969	4,509	3,244	28.0	5,060,000
1969–1970	4,446	3,150	29.1	5,184,000
1970–1971	4,444	2,478	44.3	7,864,000
1971–1972	4,461	2,141	52.0	9,276,000

Source: Kenneth E. Kirkpatrick, "Probation Subsidy: Impact on Los Angeles County," *Proceedings of the One Hundred and Third Annual Congress of Corrections,* American Correctional Association, College Park, Md., 1974, p. 252.

the cases of 17,360 offenders who had been placed on probation concluded that only 15.2 percent were removed because of unsatisfactory completion of probation.[40] Revocation rates were reported at less than 10 percent for all reporting states in 1977.[41] Earlier studies have shown a similar percentage of success. Ralph England's classic study of 490 ex-probationers in 1950 revealed only 17.7 percent revocation.[42] Only 25 percent of Wisconsin male probationers violated probation between 1954 and 1959.[43]

Researchers Jerry Banks, Terry Siler, and Ronald Rardin examined findings of intensive adult probation studies and concluded that the effects of probation supervison are controlled more by quantity and quality of contact time than by caseload reduction.[44] Robert Martinson, Douglas Lipton, and Judith Wilks, in their *Effectiveness of Correctional Treatment,* compared three kinds of supervision—"intensive" (15-person caseload), "ideal" (50-person caseload), and "minimal" (client-initiated contact). These researchers found that there were no statistically significant differences in the rates of new crimes by adult federal probationers under the three types of supervision. However, "intensive" probationers had a substantially higher rate of technical violations (i.e., violations of rules governing probation rather than commitment of acts of criminal behavior). The implication is that the closer surveillance made possible by "intensive" probation increased the discovery of technical violations.[45]

Another advantage of probation has been lower costs. The national average per capita cost for 1 year of institutionalization of adult felons is more than $10,000, compared to less than $1000 for probation services for adults per year.[46] A special study commission in California concluded that in 1956 alone, 84,100 probationers paid $2,747,000 toward the support of their families and $902,000 in reparation and restitution.[47]

The effect of probation services was measured in another way by Dorothey Greenwood, Laurence Lipsett, and Robert A. Norton. They concluded, after comparing probationers who received help finding employment and those who

[40]*National Prisoner Statistics, 1974,* Administrative Office of the United States Courts, Washington, D.C., 1977.

[41]Herbert G. Callison, "Survey of United States Correctional Services," unpublished report, 1978.

[42]Ralph W. England, "A Study of Post Probation Recidivism Among 500 Federal Offenders," *Federal Probation,* vol. 19, no. 3, Administrative Office of the United States Courts, Washington, D.C., September 1955, p. 16.

[43]Dean V. Babst and John W. Mannering, "Probation Versus Imprisonment for Similar Types of Offenders," *Journal of Research in Crime and Delinquency,* vol. 2, no. 2, National Council on Crime and Delinquency, Hackensack, N.J., July 1965, p. 67.

[44]Jerry Banks, Terry R. Siler, and Ronald L. Rardin, "Past and Present Findings on Intensive Adult Probation," *Federal Probation,* vol. 41, no. 2, Administrative Office of the United States Courts, Washington, D.C., June 1977, p. 25.

[45]Robert Martinson, Douglas Lipton, and Judith Wilks, *The Effectiveness of Correctional Treatment,* Praeger Publishers, New York, 1975, p. 59.

[46]Timothy Harper, "Probation: Justice System's Troubled Hope," *Lawrence (Kansas) Journal-World,* May 15, 1981, p. 12.

[47]Special Study Commission, *Probation in California,* Department of Corrections, Sacramento, 1957, p. 117.

did not, that there were no statistically significant differences in revocation rates. However, almost 75 percent of the experimental group (those probationers receiving help) had increased their level of employment during the 6 months of the study (see Table 5.5).[48]

APPRAISAL

Newly hired probation officers usually begin their jobs with enthusiasm. They are dedicated to their probationers. They become involved in their work, expending a great deal of physical and emotional energy. They work long hours.

Before long, the problems and frustrations of the job wear them down. They begin to feel overworked, underpaid, inadequately trained, and unsupported by others in the community. Turnover is high. They are faced with legal challenges regarding the disclosure of information in their presentence reports *(Williams v. New York State)* and the procedure of the revocation review *(Mempa v. Rhay* and *Gagnon v. Scarpelli)*. County sheriffs become unhappy if the allocation of funds to probation departments lowers their appropriations. The press and the public protest if a probationer commits a crime. Peace officer organizations join in the efforts to get criminals off the streets.

A summary of a nine-volume report on probation sponsored by the federal LEAA stated:

> With few notable exceptions, the state of research relating to probation is quite poor. . . . Very little research has been attempted. . . . Most of what has been undertaken . . . has not met the minimum standards and this does not materially contribute to our knowledge. . . . It is nearly impossible to attempt to draw any conclusions . . . about the effectiveness of probation compared to alternative

[48]Dorothey Greenwood, Laurence Lipsett, and Robert A. Norton, "Increasing the Job Readiness of Probationers," *Corrections Today,* vol. 42, no. 6, November/December 1980, p. 82.

TABLE 5.5
EMPLOYMENT OR EDUCATIONAL IMPROVEMENT
(6 MONTHS)

Employment or educational status	Control group	Experimental group
No improvement	23 (56.1%)	15 (29.4%)
Improvement	18 (43.9%)	36 (70.6%)

NOTE: Differences between the experimental group and the control group were significant to a degree that would occur by chance not more than 5 times in 100 as determined by the Chi Square statistical test.

Source: Dorothey Greenwood, Laurence Lipsett, and Robert A. Norton, "Increasing the Job Readiness of Probationers," *Corrections Today,* vol. 42, no. 6, November/December 1980, p. 82.

dispositions. . . . Nearly all . . . innovative programs . . . have one factor in common: they have not been sufficiently analyzed or evaluated. . . . The state of the art can only be poorly represented.[49]

There is little evidence that smaller caseloads result in a reduction of crime by probationers. Not only do studies fail to reveal that intensive probation is superior to conventional procedures, but they indicate that many probationers do not require supervision at all.

Yet revocation statistics show that most probationers complete their period of supervision successfully. Studies confirm that costs of probation are significantly less than those of incarceration. Even though many people criticize probation and say they are disappointed at its disarray, few correctional administrators argue in favor of abolishing it. At a time of diminishing fiscal resources, probation will prevail. As Anthony Travisono, head of the American Correctional Association has said, "Every time prison population booms, probation gets rediscovered. It's got to be. When people are pressed financially, they may discover the potential of a cheap alternative."[50] The probation of the future may be different, however. The probation officer may oversee payment of fines or restitution, or followup mandated service to the community or the victim. The probation officer may be only a resource broker—and only for a few offenders. Most probationers—that is, that large class of offenders who are no risk to society with or without supervision—will obtain their own services.

CONCLUSION

All in all, it appears that probation is one correctional program focusing on the community that continues to be endorsed by criminal justice personnel. The courts continue to impose this stipulation on 60 to 80 percent of the offenders who come before them. Most persons on probation are released by discharge, generally meaning that they have successfully completed the period of probation.

Martinson, Wilks, and Lipton, after their exhaustive efforts to evaluate all reasonably scientific rehabilitative projects, concluded that a larger proportion of offenders who are now imprisoned could be placed on probation without any change in the reconviction rates as a whole.[51] In 1973 this belief was first put forth by the Board of Directors of the National Council on Crime and Delinquency, who stated that "confinement is necessary only for offenders who, if not confined, would be a serious danger to the public. For all others, who are not dangerous and who constitute the great majority of offenders, the sentence of choice should be one or another of the wide range of non-institutional dispositions."[52] Probation is one of those dispositions.

[49]Krajick, op. cit., p. 7, copyright 1980 by Criminal Justice Publications and Corrections Magazine, 116 West 32nd Street, N.Y., N.Y., 10001.
[50]Krajick, op. cit., p. 12.
[51]Martinson, Lipton, and Wilks, op. cit., p. 563.
[52]Board of Directors, National Council on Crime and Delinquency, "The Nondangerous Offender Should Not Be Imprisoned," *Crime and Delinquency,* vol. 21, no. 4, October 1975, p. 315.

EXERCISES

1 If releasing harmless offenders prior to incarceration is successful, why waste money for supervisory personnel? Support your answer with reasons.

2 Write a paragraph responding to the objections to probation.

3 The original antecedents of probation arose from an attempt to alleviate the severity of punishment. Do you believe this motive is still the major reason judges use probation? Explain.

4 Should the structure of probation be made uniform throughout the United States? Give reasons.

5 Outline a method you would use to assign probationers to probation officers.

6 Compare and contrast each service provided by the probation officer with the techniques of supervision suggested by Dressler.

7 Examine the utilization of authority as a supervisory technique, using those techniques of supervision suggested by Dressler as a guide. Explain fully.

8 Agree or disagree: "The relationship between probation officer and probationer is an eclectic one." Give your reasons.

9 How would you apply the results of the presentence investigation to the probationary relationship, subsequent incarceration, and parole? Examine each separately and add other ways the presentence investigation might be used.

10 Do you believe it is best to have a definite list of rules for the probationer, covering all aspects of community adjustment, or a short list of rules, with the probation officer given wide discretion in setting guidelines for the probationer's behavior? Support your belief with reasons.

11 Examine each trend in probation. Which do you believe will continue? which will end? which will reverse itself? Give reasons for your conclusions.

12 Do you believe that the California subsidy program is an appropriate tool to encourage the use of probation? What other methods would you use? Explain.

13 Today, probation officers have great discretion in reporting violations of probation to the courts. Examine this discretion and develop arguments for and against its use.

EXERCISE REFERENCES

Ankersmit, Edith: "Setting the Contract in Probation," *Federal Probation,* vol. 40, no. 2, Administrative Office of the United States Courts, Washington, D.C., June 1976, pp. 28–33.

Babst, Dean V., and John W. Mannering: "Probation Versus Imprisonment for Similar Types of Offenders," *Journal of Research in Crime and Delinquency,* vol. 2, no. 2, July 1965, pp. 61–69.

Baird, S. Christopher: "Probation and Parole Classification," *Corrections Today,* vol. 43, no. 3, May/June 1981, pp. 36, 38–41.

Bartollas, Clemens: *Introduction to Corrections,* Harper & Row Publishers, Incorporated New York, 1981, chap. 7.

Board of Directors, National Council on Crime and Delinquency: "The Nondangerous Offender Should Not Be Imprisoned," *Crime and Delinquency,* vol. 21, no. 4, October 1975, pp. 315–322.

Carter, Robert M., and Leslie T. Wilkins: "Some Factors in Sentencing Policy," *Journal of Criminal Law, Criminology, and Police Science,* vol. 58, no. 4, December 1967, pp. 503–514.

Clarke, Stevens H.: "What Is the Purpose of Probation and Why Do We Revoke It?" *Crime and Delinquency,* vol. 25, no. 4, October 1979, pp. 409–424.

Czajkorski, Eugene H.: "Exposing the Quasi-Judicial Role of the Probation Officer," *Federal Probation,* vol. 37, no. 3, Administrative Office of the United States Courts, Washington, D.C., September 1973, pp. 9–13.

del Carmen, Rolando V.: "Legal Responsibilities of Probation and Parole Officers: Trends, General Advice, and Questions," *Federal Probation,* vol. 45, no. 3, Administrative Office of the United States Courts, Washington, D.C., September 1981, pp. 21–24.

Dicerbo, Eugene C.: "When Should Probation Be Revoked?" *Probation, Parole, and Community Corrections,* Robert M. Carter and Leslie T. Wilkins (eds.), John Wiley & Sons, Inc., New York, 1976, pp. 448–458.

Division of Probation, Administrative Office of the United States Courts: "The Selective Presentence Investigation Report," *Federal Probation,* vol. 38, no. 4, Administrative Office of the United States Courts, Washington, D.C., December 1974, pp. 47–54.

Eaglin, James B., and Patricia A, Lombard: "Statistical Risk Prediction as an Aid to Probation Caseload Classification," *Federal Probation,* vol. 45, no. 3, Administrative Office of the United States Courts, Washington, D.C., September 1981, pp. 25–32.

England, Ralph W.: "Post Probation Recidivism," *Federal Probation,* vol. 19, no. 4, Administrative Office of the United States Courts, Washington, D.C., September 1955, pp. 10–16.

Eskridge, Chris W.: "Issues in VIP Management: A National Synthesis," *Federal Probation,* vol. 44, no. 3, Administrative Office of the United States Courts, Washington, D.C., September 1980, pp. 8–18.

Fisher, H. Raymond: "Probation and Parole Revocation: The Anomaly of Divergent Procedures," *Federal Probation,* vol. 38, no. 2, Administrative Office of the United States Courts, Washington, D.C., September 1974, pp. 23–29.

Fitzharris, Timothy L.: "The Impact of Diminishing Fiscal Resources on Probation," *Proceedings of the One Hundred and Tenth Annual Congress of Corrections,* American Correctional Association, College Park, Md., 1980, pp. 150–157.

Greenwood, Dorothey, Laurence Lipsett, and Robert A. Norton: "Increasing the Job Readiness of Probationers," *Corrections Today,* vol. 42, no. 6, November/December 1980, pp. 78–79, 82–83.

Hager, Don J.: "Race, Nationality, and Religion—Their Relationship to Appointment Policies and Casework," *National Probation and Parole Association Journal,* vol. 3, April 1957, pp. 129–141.

Havenstrite, Al: "Case Planning in the Probation Supervision Process," *Federal Probation,* vol. 44, no. 2, Administrative Office of the United States Courts, Washington, D.C., June 1980, pp. 57–66.

Imlay, Carl H., and Charles R. Glasheen: "Standards of Probation," *Introduction to Correctional Rehabilitation,* Richard E. Hardy and John G. Cull (eds.), Charles C Thomas, Publisher, Springfield, Ill., 1973, pp. 88–108.

Imlay, Carl H., and Elsie L. Reid: "The Probation Officer, Sentencing and the Winds of Change," *Federal Probation,* vol. 39, no. 4, Administrative Office of the United States Courts, Washington, D.C., December 1975, pp. 9–17.

Ives, Jane K.: "The Essential Task of the Probation/Parole Officer," *Federal Probation,* vol. 26, no. 1, Administrative Office of the United States Courts, Washington, D.C., March 1962, pp. 38–43.

Kirkpatrick, Kenneth E.: "Probation Subsidy: Impact on Los Angeles County," *Proceed-*

ings of the One Hundred and Third Annual Congress of Corrections, American Correctional Association, College Park, Md., 1974, pp. 250–263.

Koontz, John F., Jr.: "Pragmatic Conditions of Probation," *Corrections Today,* vol. 42, no. 1, January/February 1980, pp. 14, 34, 42, and 44.

Krajick, Kevin: "Probation: The Original Community Program," *Corrections Magazine,* vol. 6, no. 6, December 1980, pp. 7–12.

————: "Probation Subsidy: Behavior Modification for Bureaucracies," *Corrections Magazine,* vol. 6, no. 6, December 1980, pp. 19–22.

Latessa, Edward, Evelyn Parks, Harry C. Allen, and Eric Carlson: "Specialized Supervision in Probation: Implications, Research, and Issues," *The Prison Journal,* vol. 59, no. 2, Autumn/Winter 1979, pp. 27–35.

Latta, Robert M., and Jack Cocks: "Management Strategies for Federal Probation Officers in Metropolitan Areas," *Federal Probation,* vol. 39, no. 3, Administrative Office of the United States Courts, Washington, D.C., September 1975, pp. 10–17.

Lichtman, Cary M., and Sue M. Smock: "The Effects of Social Services on Probationer Recidivism: A Field Experiment," *Journal of Research in Crime and Delinquency,* vol. 18, no. 1, January 1981, pp. 81–100.

McSparron, James: "Community Correction and Diversion," *Crime and Delinquency,* vol. 26, no. 2, April 1980, pp. 226–247.

Miles, Arthur P.: "The Reality of the Probation Officer's Dilemma," *Federal Probation,* vol. 29, no. 1, Administrative Office of the United States Courts, Washington, D.C., March 1965, pp. 18–23.

Miller, E. Eugene, and M. Robert Montilla: *Corrections in the Community,* Reston Publishing Company, Inc., Reston, Va., 1977, pp. 45–82.

Ohlin, Lloyd E., Herman Piren, and Donnell M. Pappenfort: "Major Dilemmas of the Social Worker in Probation and Parole," *National Probation and Parole Association Journal,* vol. 2, July 1956, pp. 211–223.

Paresi, Nicolette: "Combining Incarceration and Probation," *Federal Probation,* vol. 44, no. 2, Administrative Office of the United States Courts, Washington, D.C., June 1980, pp. 3–12.

Schoen, Kenneth F.: "PORT: A New Concept of Community Based Corrections," *Federal Probation,* vol. 36, no. 3, Administrative Office of the United States Courts, Washington, D.C., September 1972, pp. 35–40.

Smith, Robert M.: "The Problem Oriented Record Used in a Probation Setting," *Federal Probation,* vol. 39, no. 1, Administrative Office of the United States Courts, Washington, D.C., March 1975, pp. 47–51.

Special Study Commission: *Probation in California,* Department of Corrections, State of California, Sacramento, 1957.

Sullivan, James O., Jr.: "Probation Caseload Management Programs: Prescriptions for Implementation," *Federal Probation,* vol. 45, no. 2, Administrative Office of the United States Courts, Washington, D.C., June 1981, pp. 31–37.

Tomaino, Louis: "The Five Faces of Probation," *Federal Probation,* vol. 39, no. 4, Administrative Office of the United States Courts, Washington, D.C., December 1975, pp. 43–45.

Wice, Paul, and Rita James Simon: "Pre-trial Release: A Survey of Alternative Practices," *Federal Probation,* vol. 34, no. 4, Administrative Office of the United States Courts, Washington, D.C., December 1970, pp. 60–63.

PREPARING THE OFFENDER FOR THE COMMUNITY

CHAPTER OBJECTIVES

- To define Donald Clemmer's process of "correctionalization"
- To examine methods used to prepare offenders for total release
- To present techniques used to make prisons more "communitylike"
- To discuss inmate self-government
- To outline the structure and program of a prerelease center
- To offer alternative models for prerelease programs

INTRODUCTION

Probation may be the most commonly recognized form of community-based corrections. Used at an early stage in the criminal justice process, it is a preventive strategy that diverts the offender from the negative effects of incarceration. Probation is used prior to incarceration, whether the conviction is for a felony or a misdemeanor. The offender is sentenced to jail if convicted of a misdemeanor—a crime with a sentence of 1 year or less—and to prison if convicted of a felony—a crime with a sentence of 1 year or more. Whether incarcerated in jails or in prisons, inmates suffer the same losses of self-esteem, contact with their families, and economic stability. "Prisonization" takes place in both jails and penitentiaries. Offenders can be instructed in crime skills by other offenders just as easily in jails as in institutions for persons convicted of felonies.

The same is true about the positive aspects of correctional institutions.

Realistic work experiences and contacts with the community can be offered both jail and prison inmates. Creative therapy, recreation, and self-help groups can be made available to offenders in either jails or prisons, as can work release, furloughs, and prerelease programs. However, in some ways, the jail is in a better position to prepare the offender for the community than are state or federal institutions, because the jail is a local correctional facility, located within the community, and housing primarily local residents.

The Rationale for Prerelease Programs

The justification for jails as part of community-based corrections also demands that inmates incarcerated in federal, state, and local prisons be prepared for their return to the community. Community-based corrections means that the focus of the prerelease program is the community. The accompanying inmate activity is focused on the offender's community rather than institutional adjustment, even though he or she may be incarcerated. The importance of prerelease preparation is especially pertinent when one realizes that in some states, such as New York, as few as 3 percent of all incarcerated felons actually remain in prison until the maximum expiration dates of their sentences.[1]

Both correctional officials and prisoners generally agree that the gradual integration of offenders is preferable to an abrupt return to community living. As Charles Rowe, former director of the Illinois Department of Corrections, expresses it, "It makes no sense . . . to keep someone in maximum security for a number of years where he's told when to go to bed and when to get up and what to do every minute of the day and then throw him out in the street and expect him to function as a model citizen."[2]

A similar fear is expressed by former prisoners in the book *An Eye For An Eye:*

> Upon arriving in the city (following release from prison) the pedestrians scared me almost as much as the traffic. They seemed to flow along the street in a controlled hysteria, determined, set upon goal and destination, and when one of them approached, I didn't know whether to jump to one side, freeze, or keep right on walking toward the inevitable collision. You didn't have all this confusion in prison. There everyone walked in neat, orderly lines in a sort of half-shuffle. The noise of the traffic, the horns, the whistles, the music coming from somewhere, coupled with the clatter of high heels and the chatter of voices welled up, a cacaphonous crescendo. Hey! I'm free![3]

More than 100,000 offenders are released each year from federal and state prisons alone. The number released from jails each year is much larger. Some return to the community where they were living before arrest, and others move

[1]Susan Sheehan, "Annals of Crime," *The New Yorker,* Oct. 24, 1977, p. 56.
[2]Clemens Bartollas, *Introduction to Corrections,* Harper & Row, Publishers, Incorporated, New York, 1981, p. 166.
[3]H. Jack Griswold, Mike Misenheimer, Art Powers, and Ed Tromanhauser, *An Eye For An Eye,* Holt, Rinehart and Winston, Inc., New York, 1970, p. 235.

to different communities. For 50,000 offenders released from prison there are no homes to go to. At least one in ten leaves prison with no particular destination in mind. Ex-prisoners tend to be detached and rejected, without spouse, skill, job, or close friends. The more time one spends incarcerated the more likely is exclusion to occur from husband or wife, employer, or friends. Thirty-seven percent of the parolees in a Canadian study of 423 male offenders described themselves as married when admitted to prison, but only half this number were living with their wives 5 weeks after release. Significantly, it was routine for the ex-prisoner's wife to have to change residence as a result of the husband's imprisonment. For six of ten released felons, there are jobs, but frequently they are temporary jobs to earn eligibility for parole. Of the prisoners released during a study of Ontario, Canada, penitentiaries, 80 percent began unskilled or semiskilled jobs. After release, nearly half these prisoners' prospective employers turned them away on discovering they had been incarcerated.[4]

For most ex-prisoners, lack of money is a greater problem than managing money. Depending on prison policies and the length of incarceration, felons may leave prison with as little as $50.00. Inmates may leave jail with no money. One of three ex-prisoners from Ontario penitentiaries had spent all his release money within a week and a half and had borrowed money within 5 weeks. A national survey in 1970 revealed that only ten states offered loans to prisoners. Small loans were available from some private sources, such as the Osborne Association of New York, The Salvation Army, and Volunteers of America. An alternative would be to grant the released prisoner immediate eligibility for unemployment insurance, as is done in Great Britain, but no states in the United States have established an automatic policy to this effect.[5]

THE PRISON CLASSIFICATION PROCESS AS PREPARATION FOR RELEASE

The Sam Houston Institute of Contemporary Corrections in Huntsville, Texas, concluded after a national survey of prerelease programs that prerelease preparation should begin as early as possible in the sentence.[6] This preparation can be accomplished through classification. Over 100 years ago, the American Prison Association declared that the main purpose of prisoner classification "is to fit the treatment program of the correctional institutions to requirements of the individual as determined by appropriate diagnostic procedures."[7] Unfortunately, the classification process in most institutions is used to benefit the institution rather than the inmate—for segregating inmates according to age, sex, or potential for violence; for filling work assignments; or for keeping the size

---

[4]Sol Chaneles, *The Open Prison*, Dial Press, New York, 1973, p. 161.

[5]Lamar T. Empey, *Alternatives to Incarceration*, U.S. Government Printing Office, Washington, D.C., 1967, pp. 57–58.

[6]"Graduated Release," *Contemporary Corrections*, Benjamin Frank (ed.), Reston Publishing Company, Inc., Reston, Va., 1973, pp. 224–226.

[7]*Handbook on Prerelease Preparation in Correctional Institutions*, American Prison Association, New York, 1950, p. 13.

of cellhouse populations manageable. Classification could, however, be used as a tool to assist the inmate to prepare for release.

Through the intake classification process, the resources available within the correctional institution could be offered to the individual offender on entry into prison. Emphasis should be on resources that will counteract the problems which precipitated the criminal behavior. When classification team members recommend work assignment, custodial rating, academic education, vocational training, types of counseling, and extracurricular activities, they are taking the first step in preparing the offender to reenter the community.

The classification process continues throughout the offender's confinement. Through reclassification, his or her progress is reviewed periodically. Subsequent program recommendations could be made in response to changes in the inmate's attitudes and capacities and suspected errors in intake classification.

Release classification is the final step in this process before an inmate leaves an institution. At this time, recommendations must be developed to assure that any problem-solving techniques which have been adopted by the offender will be continued and that any skills acquired will be utilized in his or her release plans, whether in auto mechanics, computer programming, reading, or mathematics. Each offender must be prepared to apply these tools in an effort to solve problems without reversion to criminal behavior.

Even a comprehensive leisure-time program can play a vital role in the resocialization of an incarcerated individual by including activities that can be continued in the community, such as camping, dancing, card games, table games, drama, music, art, and hobbies. The program should include classroom instruction as well as actual activity experience.[8]

CORRECTIONALIZATION

Twenty-five years after author Donald Clemmer introduced the term *prisonization,* based on his work experience inside an Ohio prison, he originated another word, *correctionalization.* Prisonization, according to Clemmer, is the "taking on in greater or less degree of the folkways, mores, customs, and general culture of the penitentiary."[9] Correctionalization refers to a process designed to combat and counteract prisonization. The process of correctionalization utilizes prison programs to improve an inmate's personality, character, and work skills and also encourages reciprocal relationships and communication between inmates and members of free society.[10] Preparing the offender for the community is one goal of correctionalization.

The correctional administrators who hope to create a process of correctionalization seek to develop an institutional environment as much like that of the

---

[8]Raymond L. Arjo and Lawrence R. Allen, "The Role of Leisure Time in Corrections," *Corrections Today,* vol. 42, no. 1, January–February 1980, p. 41.

[9]Donald Clemmer, *The Prison Community,* The Christopher Publishing House, Boston, 1940, p. 299.

[10]Thomas R. Sard, "Contact With the Free Community Is Basic If Institutional Programs Are to Succeed," *Federal Probation,* vol. 31, no. 1, Administrative Office of the United States Courts, Washington, D.C., March 1967, p. 3.

community outside prison as possible. Correctionalization brings the community into the institution. For example, the District of Columbia Department of Corrections utilized seventeen different forms of community activities within the Lorton institution, including a fair, a jazz festival, educational classes, special interest groups led by Small Business Administration personnel, and visits by volunteers. In each case, bringing the outside community into the institution was considered a technique for creating a communitylike institution.

Another suggestion is the addition of an institutional social service program that maintains or increases interpersonal relations between inmates and free citizens. It appears that the less rejected offenders are, the less likely they are to be in the penitentiary in the first place, the more likely they are to be paroled, and the less likely they are to be back in prison after release.[11]

A large number of private organizations, including Alcoholics Anonymous, Toastmasters, Jaycees, and the Dale Carnegie Institute, visit prisons in an effort to establish communication between inmates and free citizens. Visits are also made by specialized associations, clubs, and persons sharing such avocational interests as chess, bridge, writing, and art. In addition, various church groups, such as the Home Mission of the Episcopal Church and members of the Society of Friends, have begun prison-visiting programs.

Community-Oriented Programs

It has been suggested that a correctional rehabilitation program be designed to make the institutional program community-oriented. A rehabilitation program should be realistic; each of its facets should be centered on the community rather than on the institution. Vocational training should provide offenders with skills that match anticipated employment opportunities after release. Researcher Daniel Glaser found that only 10 percent of the released inmates in his sample used prison work experiences in postrelease jobs, and of these, about half had had preprison jobs related to their prison training. However, the statistics showed that those using prison-acquired skills were twice as likely to become parole successes. Glaser's study implies a need for job training with high probability of use by offenders after release from prison, based on the capabilities and interests of the inmates themselves.[12] To be realistic, job training in prison should take into account increases or decreases in occupational demand, as determined by employment trends in the community. In reality, two-thirds of all prison work assignments are in occupational categories in least demand in the community, i.e., unskilled maintenance jobs and semiskilled assembly-line tasks in industries.

Author Harris Chaiklin suggests that correctional rehabilitation programs should be designed to minimize disruption of a person's ability to handle the

---

[11]Irvin Waller, "Rejection and Recidivism: The Experience of Men Released From Prison." *Corrections: Problems of Punishment and Rehabilitation,* Edward Sagarin and Donal E. J. MacNamara (eds.), Praeger Publishers, New York, 1973, pp. 134–143.

[12]Daniel Glaser, *The Effectiveness of a Prison and Parole System,* The Bobbs-Merrill Company, Inc., Indianapolis, 1969, pp. 167–168.

affairs of everyday living. In most prisons, offenders become dependent on their keepers to accomplish the most trivial transactions. To achieve the goal of permitting as much independence as possible to inmates while they are in prison, they must be held responsible for managing their lives throughout their incarceration. This means creating a communitylike environment where an offender-employee applies to the institution-employer for work and accepts responsibility for the organization and management of self-help groups. Creative therapy or self-help groups in subjects such as drama, art, music, writing, and crafts can be used for this purpose quite readily during leisure time.

One form of self-help which has maintained consistent popularity among prisoners is art therapy. In 1977 Project Culture, funded by the Law Enforcement Assistance Administration (LEAA), initiated twenty-one different art projects in sixteen states. By mid-1980, $1.9 million had been given to thirty-five art programs.[13] One of the more successful art therapy programs, Prisoners Accelerated Creative Exposure. Inc., began in New York City. By 1981 it had produced twenty-five major exhibits and claimed 263 prisoner artists, some selling their work for nearly $5000 apiece.[14]

Another highly successful form of creative therapy is drama. One such program is the Theatre for the Forgotten (TFTF). Beginning in 1967 at the New York City Correctional Facility on Rikers Island, by 1973 its workshops were being presented in all fifteen of New York City's correctional facilities. Initially funded privately and relying on community volunteers and prison actors, TFTF was approved in 1978 for a $675,000 grant under the Comprehensive Employment and Training Act (CETA). That grant permitted fifty actors, dancers, musicians, directors, playwrights, and technicians to present workshops and give performances in colleges, community centers, hospitals, and senior centers as well as in prisons.[15]

Some self-help projects have been initiated to benefit others. In Kansas two such projects exist. At the Kansas State Penitentiary in Lansing, 148 inmates participated in the Second Annual Run-A-Thon to Prevent Child Abuse. Each runner earned $6.00 from an outside sponsor to support programs of the Johnson County (Kansas) Coalition for the Prevention of Child Abuse.[16] Across the state in Hutchinson, Kansas State Industrial Reformatory inmates read textbooks into tape recorders to help mildly mentally retarded or visually handicapped children learn to read. Since June 1980, more than 250 hour-long tapes have been produced on subjects as diverse as driver's training, history, and literature.[17]

[13]Philip B. Taft Jr., "The Alchemy of Prison Art," *Corrections Magazine,* vol. 5, no. 3, September 1979, pp. 13–19.

[14]Kay Bartlett, "Inmates' Art Their Escape Routes," *Wichita (Kansas) Eagle-Beacon,* July 5, 1981, p. 1c.

[15]J. Wandres, "Presenting Theatre for the Forgotten," *EXXON USA,* Exxon Corporation, New York, 1981.

[16]Warren T. Liston, "Inmates Run to Battle a Childhood Evil They Recall," *The Kansas City Star,* May 17, 1981, pp. 33a–34a.

[17]"Inmates Tape Textbooks for Handicapped Youths," *The Salina (Kansas Journal),* June 9, 1981, p. 5.

Family Relations

Family ties are especially important. Almost no one in prison is totally without relatives. Contact or lack of contact with relatives significantly affects the manner in which offenders handle the institutional experience. Success or failure after release is often determined by the maintenance of family relationships.

Maintaining contact with relatives outside prison can be encouraged through liberal visiting and mail policies.[18] A study published in September 1978 examined prison visiting regulations in forty-five states. Survey questionnaires were mailed to 230 state correctional facilities for adult offenders, and responses were received from 168. The number of visits a month allowed each inmate was unlimited for all institutions in Idaho and Iowa. Some institutions in Colorado, Kentucky, Michigan, New Jersey, and Washington also permitted an unlimited number. At the other extreme, only two visits a month were allowed in Texas and some institutions in Arkansas, Ohio, Oklahoma, and South Carolina. More than half the respondents (59 percent) reported that prisoners are permitted visitors at least 8 times a month. Nearly one-quarter (24.7 percent) permit twenty or more monthly visits for each resident. Visits were limited to 1 hour in Delaware and in some institutions in Connecticut, Hawaii, Illinois, Indiana, Maine, Massachusetts, Minnesota, New Jersey, North Carolina, Oklahoma, Virginia, and Vermont. In Michigan, Pennsylvania, and New York some institutions permit twelve-hour visits, and a maximum of forty-eight hours is allowed in California.[19]

Marriage counseling or family therapy can be offered as a routine part of the institutional social service program. Historically, very few social service agencies —governmental or voluntary—have identified families of incarcerated individuals as needing services. However, criminal justice consultant Judith Weintraub urges that departments of corrections establish a coordinating committee to match existing services to families. She recommends providing free transportation for families to correctional institutions, initiating institutional programs to deal with family problems, and developing social service units trained in family work.[20]

Programs for Female Offenders

Some special family problems are experienced by women offenders. One of the most difficult adjustments for women who are mothers is coping with the separation from their children. Nationally, as many as 80 percent of incarcerated women have children—an average of two each, or a total of 155,000 children

---

[18]Harris Chaiklin, "Developing Correctional Social Services," *Correctional Treatment of the Offender,* Albert R. Roberts (ed.), Charles C Thomas Publisher, Springfield, Ill., 1974, pp. 299–302.

[19]N. E. Schafer, "Prison Visiting: A Background for Change," *Federal Probation,* vol. 42, no. 3, United States Courts, Washington, September 1978, p. 48.

[20]Judith F. Weintraub, "The Delivery of Services to Families of Prisoners," *Federal Probation,* vol. 40, no. 4, Administrative Office of the United States Courts, Washington, D.C., December 1976, p. 30.

throughout the country. Yet, except for a few innovative programs, the children are left homeless, with only limited visiting opportunities, or placed in foster care. A 1974 Junior League of New York survey of eighty-one federal and state prisons found that of the 727 children identified under 5 years of age, 70 percent were being cared for by relatives, 14 percent were in foster homes, and 16 percent were in institutions or released for adoption.[21]

A few exceptions do exist. In San Jose, California, local authorities place twenty-four jail inmates in an apartment complex with their children, where they work, drive cars, attend school, have bank accounts, and take care of their children. Costs of the program are $24.00 a day, compared with $55.00 a day for women inmates in the county jail. Four years after the Santa Clara County Women's Residential Center opened in 1976, only four escapes had occurred and only two women were rearrested on new charges after release. In Downey, California, the California Institution for Women maintains two-bedroom trailers where women are permitted weekend visits with their families. At the Dwight, Illinois, Correctional Institution for Women, a "Sesame Street" nursery school has been built to permit twice-a-week visits in an informal atmosphere. The Chicago-based Mothers in Prison Project provides counseling for families of prisoners and transports children to the Dwight Correctional Institution to visit their mothers.[22]

The Nebraska Center for Women allows children to remain with their mothers up to 5 days a month. At the same time, mothers are enrolled in child care classes. The visitation program is housed in a building equipped with a nursery school, day care center, and kindergarten. The Purdy Treatment Center in Washington also supports the mother-child relationship. Each prisoner has her own private room. About 70 percent of the residents have children. Each of the six living units is equipped with children's books, toys, and a small play area for visits. A nursery school is operated by the institution for the community— and serves as a training tool for offenders as well. One day a week the nursery school is set aside for children of prisoners.[23]

Family Home Evening Program

For offenders who have severed ties with family, friends, and former acquaintances, programs can be worked out to encourage new interactions with people in the community. The volunteer Family Home and Evening Sponsorship Program operated by the Utah Division of Corrections is an example. At the Utah State Prison in Draper, Utah, volunteer families are assigned to inmates. Each family visits an inmate and encourages friendship. An inmate who is classified in minimum custody is allowed to visit the home of the Home Family. The program is designed to continue after release, thus giving each inmate an opportunity to

[21]*Female Offenders: Problems and Programs,* American Bar Association, Washington, D.C., 1976, p. 2.
[22]Eileen Ogintz, "If Mom's in Prison, Where Are Her Kids?", *Chicago Tribune,* Aug. 4, 1980, sec. 2, pp. 1–2.
[23]*Female Offenders,* pp. 12–13, 62.

have friends in the community after leaving the institution. In fact, Home Families often voluntarily assist inmates to obtain employment and to carry out other postrelease planning. Since the program was initiated in 1956, volunteer families have established ties with 700 inmates, including 50 convicted murderers. In September 1973, 80 percent of all Utah felons released in conjunction with the Home Family program were believed to be successful, contrasting with a 49 percent rate of recidivism for those not in the program.[24] Former Utah convicts have praised the program:

> It gave me somebody on the outside to keep in contact with. It gave me a lot of strength to keep me going in there. It gave me some trust in people when the family came to visit. . . . The way I see it . . . the big thing is being accepted by somebody in the community, having somebody you can turn to, to talk to—not being an outcast.[25]

CONJUGAL VISITING

A key strategy in preparing offenders for the community is structuring a prison environment where they can practice the behavior they will engage in after release. Administrators have attempted to develop communitylike prisons by creating institutional experiences similar to community experiences. Conjugal visits permit the marital relationship to retain a semblance of normality. They are an attempt to help inmates retain family ties which might sustain them after release to the community.

Conjugal visits for prisoners began in the United States as early as 1918 at Parchman Prison Camp in Mississippi. There the conjugal visit is still part of a general visiting and leave program. Offenders meet their wives and other members of the family in the "red houses." Each wife must be legally married to the prisoner she visits. After 3 years of good behavior and successful participation in conjugal visits, prisoners are permitted home visits for reasons other than emergencies. Approximately 300 ten-day furloughs are granted each winter to Parchman prisoners.[26]

In California, prison administrators have initiated "family visiting aimed at preserving the family relationship and helping families grow stronger."[27] In contrast to Mississippi, Minnesota, and New York, inmates in California are encouraged to include children, parents, and siblings in their conjugal visits, which for this reason are called family visits. Inmates' eligibility for family visits depends on their having attained their minimum parole dates and completed 6 months with good conduct. At the Tehachapi prison, where the program began

[24]James B. Horlacker, Division of Corrections, Utah State Prison, Draper, unpublished correspondence, September 5, 1973.

[25]Michael White, *The Times-Mail* (Bedford, Ind.), Associated Press Release, July 24, 1981, p. 8.

[26]Norman S. Hayner, "Attitudes toward Conjugal Visits for Prisoners," *Federal Probation,* vol. 37, no. 1, Administrative Office of the United States Courts, Washington, D.C., March 1973, p. 48.

[27]Lawrence E. Wilson, "Conjugal Visits and Family Participation in California," *Proceedings of the One Hundred and Third Annual Congress of Corrections,* American Correctional Association, College Park, Md., 1970, p. 263.

in 1968, visits are conducted at two-family visiting cottages. Each cottage has three bedrooms, a bathroom, a kitchen-living room, a service porch, and a fenced-in recreation yard for children. Meals are prepared in the cottages. Food is brought by the visiting family. Most family visits are for 48 hours. Some, however, last as long as 72 hours, depending on such factors as frequency of visits, distance visitors travel, and the length of waiting lists for visits.

As late as 1971, California was the only state that permitted conjugal visits for women. To be eligible for 48-hour visits from her family, a female inmate must be within 6 months of parole consideration, in minimum custody, and without disciplinary reports for 6 months.[28]

By 1977 there were ninety family visiting units on the grounds of the state's twelve institutions. An estimated 15,000 visits took place that year, half of them involving family members other than the inmate's wife or husband. Until the first legislative appropriation ($300,000) in 1976, family visits were reserved for minimum- or medium-custody inmates. At that time, however, facilities were added for protective custody inmates.[29]

Appraisal

The Mississippi and California programs were primarily designed to preserve marriages and strengthen family relationships. Increased contact with a prisoner's family is also believed to reduce homosexuality within prison, boost inmate morale, and relieve tensions for both the inmate and the inmate's family.

Despite enthusiastic support from some prison officials, especially from those who administer conjugal or family visits, criticisms of the program are frequent. Objections include the following: Conjugal visits offer no solution to the sexual tension of single male or female prisoners; pregnancies among wives create additional problems for both the state and the prisoner; inmates with sexual problems are the least likely to receive permission for conjugal visits. It is also argued that married inmates who earn conjugal visiting privileges are the ones who can best adjust to prison life without sexual relations.

The chief objection, however, has been that conjugal visits are incompatible with existing mores, because the visits seem to emphasize primarily the physical satisfactions of sex.[30] Lawrence Wilson, an administrator of the California program, has responded to this criticism by stating, "The fact that husbands and wives engage in sexual intercourse is incidental to our main objectives: the preservation and strengthening of the family."[31]

To quote a San Quentin prisoner and his wife:

---

[28]Edna Walker Chandler, *Women in Prison,* The Bobbs-Merrill Company, Inc., Indianapolis, 1973, p. 43.

[29]*Family Visiting in California Prisons,* California Department of Corrections, Sacramento, 1977.

[30]Columbus B. Hopper, "The Conjugal Visit at Mississippi State Penitentiary," *Journal of Criminal Law, Criminology, and Police Science,* vol. 53, no. 3, September 1962, p. 341.

[31]Wilson, op. cit., p. 263.

The sex and intimacy are wonderful, the food is wonderful, but the greatest thing is just—Vivian has an expression for it—'laying down hugs.' That's the comfort you derive from comforting each other, from holding each other, an intimacy that you don't have here, a closeness that people on the outside probably take for granted.[32]

As with other prison programs that can be community-oriented, prison administrators have been more likely to initiate conjugal visits as a way to relieve prisoners' tensions than as a way to prepare offenders for release. Again, that does not negate the potential for conjugal visits to be used as a way of strengthening family ties in preparation for an offender's release. Keeping family ties strong helps ease the transition between life inside and outside the prison walls. And a continuity of family life means that once prisoners get out, they are less likely to go back in.

THE PRISON WORK EXPERIENCE

The prison work experience has long been considered a factor contributing to the high recidivism rate of released American prisoners. The unproductive nature of most prison work robs it of value as preparation for postrelease employment. Prison officials have viewed inmate labor as a tool to help operate the institution, e.g., plumbing, cooking, and cleaning—or as a surplus commodity to dispose of without disturbing other functions of the institution. Outside prison, the wage an employer is willing to pay an employee depends on the latter's performance, measured according to units of production and the value of the goods produced. Not only does this wage system provide a living income for the employee, but it greatly affects his or her self-concept. Traditional prisons do not duplicate the incentives of a living income, attractive working conditions, and the prospect of future promotion and wage increases. Such benefits would oppose department of corrections' policies of holding costs to a minimum. Consequently, prison work programs usually have limited value in training inmates for successful postrelease employment. Thus programs that are acceptable from the correctional administrator's standpoint are unlikely to contribute to a lowered recidivism rate.[33]

The big push in the 1960s toward rehabilitation further aggravated the problem. Prisoners were encouraged to attend school, seek counseling, or enroll in vocational training. The idea of involving inmates in a realistic work experience—where inmate-employees were expected to work 8 hours a day, arrive on time, and achieve a certain productivity level—fell into neglect.

Most attempts at equating the prison work experience with work in the outside community have emphasized two factors: creating working conditions that simulate a community job and increasing wages to a level comparable to

[32]Lisa Levitt, "Conjugal Visits Brighten Inmate's Life in San Quentin Prison," *The Kansas City Star,* Associated Press Release, July 19, 1981, p. 2b.

[33]Neil M. Singer, "Incentives and the Use of Prison Labor," *Crime and Delinquency,* vol. 19, no. 2, April 1973, pp. 201–206.

TABLE 6.1

INMATE WAGES FROM INSTITUTIONAL EARNINGS*—1971

Wage range	Number of states	States
No institutional earnings	6	Alabama, Florida, Georgia, Maine, Mississippi, Texas
Less than $.50 a day	17	Colorado, District of Columbia, Illinois, Indiana, Kansas, Louisiana, Massachusetts, Michigan, Montana, Nevada, New Jersey, North Carolina, North Dakota, Oklahoma, Virginia, West Virginia, Wyoming
$.50 to $1.00	21	California, Connecticut, Delaware, Idaho, Iowa, Kentucky, Maryland, Minnesota, Missouri, Nebraska, New Hampshire, New York, North Dakota, Ohio, Pennsylvania, Rhode Island, South Carolina, South Dakota, Tennessee, Utah, Vermont
$1.00 or more a day	9	Alaska, Arizona, Arkansas, District of Columbia, Hawaii, Illinois, New Mexico, Oregon, Washington
Total	53†	

*Institutional earnings are derived from jobs connected with prison maintenance or prison industries. Crafts and hobby items sold at a piece rate and blood donations are not included.

†Illinois and the District of Columbia are included in two categories because they have two distinct wage ranges.

Source: Kenneth J. Lenihan, "The Financial Resources of Released Prisoners," *Proceedings: Second National Workshop on Corrections and Parole Administration,* American Correctional Association, 1974, p. 121.

community employment. As late as 1971, only nine states paid the working prisoner more than $1.00 a day. As Table 6.1 indicates, at that time few states were paying even a "living wage" in prison. The situation has not changed drastically in most prisons since then (see Table 6.1).[34] As a result, most inmates have little opportunity to practice money management in prison, a skill they will need for good budgeting after release.

Inmate-Pay Experiment

Some experiments have attempted to create a prison pay scale similar to that of community employment. At the federal reformatory in Reno, Oklahoma, an

[34]Kenneth J. Lenihan, "The Financial Resources of Released Prisoners," *Proceedings: Second National Workshop on Corrections and Parole Administration,* American Correctional Association, College Park, Md., 1974, p. 121.

TABLE 6.2

SICK-CALL USE BY INMATES

	In performance-pay program (%)	In industry program (%)
February 1971 (T1)	62	66
June 1971 (T2)	64	78
October 1971 (T3)	53	82

TABLE 6.3
AVERAGE NUMBER OF INMATE JOB TRANSFERS

	In performance-pay program	In industry program
February 1971 (T1)	4.2	4.2
June 1971 (T2)	3.3	3.8
October 1971 (T3)	2.9	3.8

inmate-pay demonstration project began on February 1, 1971. The maximum amount paid for each work classification ranged from $10 to $25 a day. The pay was contingent on the performance of each inmate and the skills and responsibilities required for each job. A competitive atmosphere prevailed, because the number of job seekers exceeded the number of paid positions. Several indices were used to determine whether the higher pay scale actually increased work motivation. It was found, for example, that inmates involved in the program visited the outpatient clinic less often than did a comparable group in the regular industrial program. The experimental group also showed an improvement in job stability. The most dramatic statistic was that inmates in the experimental program received approximately half as many disciplinary reports as those in the regular industrial program. Tables 6.2, 6.3, and 6.4 present findings from the comparison between the two groups.

Private Industry

Zephyr Products, Inc., Leavenworth, Kansas, employs 30 inmates of the Kansas Correctional Institution, both men and women. At first, the men lived in the minimum security dormitory at the state prison and the women at the women's prison. But in 1980 Kansas officials decided to move some men to the women's institution, and the Zephyr employees were the first men to be transferred. Each prisoner works 8 hours a day for minimum wages. Although all pay the institution for their room and board, buy their own lunches, and pay for transportation to and from their quarters, they are able to save a considerable

TABLE 6.4
INMATES RECEIVING DISCIPLINARY REPORTS

	In performance-pay program (%)	In industry program (%)
February 1971 (T1)	6.0	10.8
June 1971 (T2)	8.0	11.6
October 1971 (T3)	6.2	13.0

Source: Ernst A. Wenk and Colin Frank, "Some Progress on the Evaluation of Institutional Programs," *Federal Probation,* vol. 37, no. 3, Administrative Office of the United States Courts, Washington, D.C., September 1973, pp. 32–33.

portion for the date of release. Only up to $100 a month can go into the inmate's current spending account.

Fred Braun, the owner of Zephyr, believes prisoners are more dependable employees than those from the free community, because of the lack of alcohol-related absences and "sick-leave" vacations. Prison officials screen inmates, who must have gained minimum security status, and Zephyr hires those with a year or more left on their sentences, trying to keep a mix of long-term and short-term inmates. Braun, a successful businessman, opened Zephyr in 1979 with little help from state officials. He was appalled by the idleness at the state penitentiary. He puts it this way: "I hate idleness. It's almost sinful. That was the biggest waste of time and talent I'd ever seen. And there's nothing more rehabilitative than work."[35]

Cudahy Foods Company meat packing plant in Phoenix employs sixty inmates from the Arizona prison system. The Arizona Pork Producers Association supplies the hogs, leases the plant and equipment, and markets the products. The Arizona Department of Correction provides inmate labor from its Correctional and Training Center in Perryville, 26 miles west of Phoenix.[36]

Since 1973 Minnesota has allowed private entrepreneurs to set up shop *inside* the state's penal facilities. Stillwater Prison Data Processing Systems, Inc., began operations in 1976. Five years later sixteen inmates were working as computer programmers for a company with $200,000 in sales. Minnesota, with the help of Free Venture Prison Industries Program, an LEAA-funded project, established a bus repair business and a farm machinery plant. In addition, Lino Lakes medium security inmates can subcontract their labor to outside firms. Free Venture has also helped Illinois, Connecticut, South Carolina, Iowa, Colorado, and Washington contract with private business for prison industry programs.[37]

Free Enterprise Systems

At La Mesa Penitentiary in Mexico a combination of a private enterprise economy and arrangements for conjugal visits has operated since the early 1960s. Conjugal visits and open family visits are regularly permitted. Quantities of food, clothing, and money are legally given to prisoners during these visits. A market system is permitted, with special sleeping quarters; bartering for bedding; and the operation of stores, restaurants, and small manufacturing firms. The La Mesa prison society is thus similar to the social realities outside prison and draws inmates into daily economic decisions. On busy visiting days the large, open prison yard appears to be a bustling Mexican village. Children chase each other across the yard. A jukebox blares from a privately managed restaurant. Craftsmen and ice cream vendors peddle their wares.[38]

[35]Michael Fedo, "Free Enterprise Goes to Prison," *Corrections Magazine,* vol. 7, no. 2, April 1981, pp. 10–13.

[36]Len Ackland, "Prison Inmates Will Report to Cudahy Plant," *The Wichita (Kansas) Eagle Beacon,* Aug. 30, 1981.

[37]Michael Fedo, op. cit., pp. 5–10.

[38]John A. Price, "Private Enterprise in a Prison," *Crime and Delinquency,* vol. 19, no. 2, April 1973, pp. 222–227.

A similar experiment was attempted at the Maine State Prison, located a few hundred feet from busy highway U.S. 1, the main highway for New England tourists. Since before World War II, Maine prisoners have been encouraged to work at hobbycrafts—leather, jewelry, wood carvings, and novelties. Correctional administrators allowed inmates to use prison industrial machinery to make their own products for private sale in lieu of receiving wages. In the 1950s the maximum any inmate could earn was $600 a year. By the early 1970s the gross revenue ceiling had increased to $4500 a year per inmate, with a stipulation that one person could own no more than four handicraft patterns. By 1978 the ceiling on individual earnings had been raised to $15,000. By that time each inmate could own ten patterns. Between half and three-quarters of the approximately 370 inmates either had their own hobbycraft operations or worked for other inmates who did. In 1979 the gross hobbycraft revenue reached $538,000. Then on April 6, 1980—despite inmates being busy at work they enjoyed, with disciplinary reports down to a minimum and profits mounting—the prison was locked down and the hobbycraft program reorganized. State Director of Corrections Donald Allen believed the action was necessary because the inmates had taken over the prison—earning more money than correctional employees and exploiting other inmate-employees. He believed the "novelty kings" were in a position to corrupt prison civilian employees and convert the prison to a "fee-for-service" economy, where the washing of personal laundry had a price, as did styled haircuts and television set rentals.[39]

Appraisal

Despite work experiences that would appear to be superior to the costly idleness that exists in most prisons, and the opportunity for prisoners to pay taxes and social security, support families, make restitution, and repay the state for their room and board, criticism of realistic work experience programs has been frequent. Union officials have accused Arizona corrections personnel of "union busting" and exploiting convicts for a profit. They claim prison industries should not be allowed to improve at the expense of displacing civilian employees. These arguments are similar to those voiced in the early twentieth century, which persuaded Congress to ban inmate-made products from interstate commerce.

Even the initial evaluation of Free Venture-sponsored programs showed no clear evidence that inmate-employees developed better work habits or had greater opportunities for employment or higher wages after release. However, there was evidence that inmates who participated in the program 6 months or longer returned to prison less quickly and held employment for longer periods.[40] To date no one has seriously questioned the economic benefits to the prison system and the community in general or the reduced tension within the prison which results from these programs.

[39]Edgar May, "Maine: Was Inmate Capitalism Out of Control?", *Corrections Magazine,* vol. 7, no. 1, February 1981, pp. 18–21.
[40]"Free Venture Concept Evaluated," *Criminal Justice Newsletter,* vol. 12, no. 20, Oct. 12, 1981, p. 7.

INMATE SELF-GOVERNMENT

Many offenders do not have an opportunity to participate in activities that most citizens take for granted. In fact, a felon's preincarceration leisure-time activities are frequently deviant or bordering on deviancy, such as drinking, gambling, walking the streets, or "hitting up" with drugs. While incarcerated, offenders have a severely limited number of alternatives for recreation, social functions, and interpersonal relations. Prison conditions force them to operate like robots, not like decision-making human beings. Consequently, offenders leave the institution unprepared to manage their daily lives. The use of self-government in corrections can give them a supervised opportunity to learn to do so.

Inmate Self-Management

To permit inmates to assume responsibility for their own behavior, some institutions eliminate so-called Mickey Mouse rules which encourage routinization: 10:00 P.M. curfews, regulated hair lengths, and restricted intrainstitution movement. Those who endorse self-management for offenders believe most inmates do not require compulsory locks, rigid rules, or constant supervision. In a correctional institution permitting self-management, inmates are informed of the established times to eat and to report to work. Prisoners not at work on time may lose their jobs or have their pay reduced. If meals are missed, they may go hungry. Inmates are also encouraged to organize their own institutional programs, apply for institutional jobs, and enroll in school and other activities.

One of the most advanced systems designed to permit prisoners to manage their own affairs has been proposed by correctional administrator David Greenburg. He suggests a voucher system for incarcerated prisoners. Each prisoner would receive a voucher representing money, the amount to be proportional to the length of his or her sentence. The voucher could be used to purchase a wide variety of rehabilitation services. Prisoners would decide for themselves how to use the vouchers, which would be valid as fees for psychiatric, psychological, or religious counseling; vocational training, educational classes, or correspondence courses; books, newspapers, and magazines; musical instruments, arts and crafts supplies, or athletic equipment. The choices would be as unrestricted as possible.

Administrators might consider a prisoner's choice foolish or irrational but would not interfere, because the purpose of the voucher program is to allow prisoners to make choices based on their own preferences. Under Greenburg's system, a number of prisoners could pool their funds, so that resources too costly for a single prisoner to purchase could be available to a cooperative group of inmates. Individuals whose choices were not shared by other prisoners could purchase what they wanted, if someone was willing to supply the item at sufficiently low cost. Organizations concerned with the welfare of prisoners would be permitted to help inmates who have little money. Time payments could even be used, if providers of goods and services were willing to accept such terms.[41]

Institutional Self-Government

The highest degree of self-government is prisoner participation in the administration of correctional residential facilities. Institutional self-government by inmates is not new. The earliest reference to its use in America, according to author J. E. Baker, was in 1793 at the Walnut Street Jail in Philadelphia. Here prisoners established rules to provide "harmonious living with each other." Since then, more elaborate systems of self-government have been attempted at various correctional institutions throughout the country. Some of the more famous include the New York City House of Refuge (1824), Michigan State Penitentiary (1888), and the Massachusetts State Prison Colony (1927). One of the most zealous advocates of self-government was Warden Thomas Mott Osborne, who originated a mutual welfare league at New York's Auburn prison in 1913 and at Sing Sing 1 year later. By 1964, thirteen states reported some form of inmate self-government.[42]

One form of inmate self-government is the inmate council, or an elected or appointed body of inmates, usually representing work assignments or cellhouses, who serve as representatives of the entire population. The council may hear inmate grievances and present them to the salaried correctional administrators or may be given the authority to recommend minor rule changes or the use of specified funds. In all instances, inmate council decisions are subject to salaried administrators' approval.

In 1974 a survey of 113 correctional institutions with some form of inmate council revealed the following: 81 percent of respondents stated that the inmate council's membership was composed of both salaried personnel and inmates, 89 percent reported that inmate representatives were elected, and 88 percent reported some changes in the institution as a result of council action or recommendations.[43]

Many offenders have never voted, held public office, or even expressed an opinion on community matters. Some do not understand the democratic process. All can learn from the experience of assisting correctional personnel in the management of a correctional community. In many institutions practicing self-government, convicted felons participate in a "town meeting" and democratically elect representatives for inmate councils and special task committees or select group activities.

Although self-government within prison encourages individual thinking, staff

[41]David F. Greenburg, "A Voucher System for Corrections," *Crime and Delinquency,* vol. 19, no. 2, April 1973, p. 214.

[42]J. E. Baker, "Inmate Self-Government," *Journal of Criminal Law, Criminology, and Police Science,* vol. 55, no. 1, 1972, pp. 40–42, 45.

[43]Tom Murton, "Shared Decision Making as a Treatment Technique in Prison Management," *Offender Rehabilitation,* vol. 1, no. 1, Fall 1976, pp. 26–28.

guidance is always provided. If an inmate council is elected, a staff member serves as sponsor. If actual governing responsibilities are given inmates, a staff member is assigned as advisor. If a cellhouse or galley conducts weekly town meetings, salaried personnel are always present. Town meetings allow personnel to communicate to inmates information regarding the financial or administrative state of the institution. The meetings also provide an acceptable time and place for residents to air complaints, to make suggestions to prison personnel regarding activities, or to participate in institutional decision making.

In some institutions prisoners are allowed to assume partial responsibility for disciplinary action or program decisions through elected representatives on classification committees. In this way, inmates participate to some degree in the daily operation of the institution. They organize and maintain committees to assist with public relations, inmate loan funds, and community improvement projects. They supervise recreation activities, such as softball, volleyball, or pool. They serve with prison personnel on committees responsible for rule changes and institutional maintenance standards. Table 6.5 illustrates the variety of activities in which inmate groups participate.

Waupun (Wisconsin) Correctional Institution education director George Smullen suggests that natural groups within prison be used in a form of "participation management." He believes prison administrators can utilize these groups as (1) channels for complaints from inmates to staff members, (2) mechanisms for problem solving, (3) models for rehabilitation programs, (4) opportunities to teach management concepts, (5) tools to illustrate the importance of planned rather than impulsive behavior, (6) barometers to determine the daily "climate" of the institution, and (7) channels for prison personnel to transmit their points of view.

To encourage inmate groups to form in prison, the administrator can offer staff assistance and opportunities for service activities (lobbying for legislation) and business ventures (selling products such as soft drinks or sandwiches). At

TABLE 6.5
ACTIVITIES IN WHICH INMATE GROUPS PARTICIPATE

Activities	Number of institutions
Recreational programs	4
Entertainment programs	5
Holiday programs	5
Blood bank	3
Charity drives	2
Tours or visits by service clubs, student groups, industrial representation groups	1
Other: eye bank, postage fund, sanitation drive, safety drive, self-improvement, talent show, TV-radio-movies, and curio program	1

Source: J. E. Baker, "Inmate Self-Government," reprinted by special permission of *Journal of Criminal Law, Criminology, and Police Science,* Northwestern University School of Law, vol. 55, no. 1, January 1964, p. 43, Table I.

Waupun in 1981 there were eleven groups, their formation most frequently based on ethnic backgrounds (Black Culture Group) or a common concern (Alcoholics Anonymous). They each prepare a constitution and solicit a staff advisor. Two meetings a week are allowed, continuing about an hour and a half. Individual advisors usually spend 5 to 10 hours a week with their groups, or 55 to 110 staff hours a week for the total institution.[44]

Appraisal

The 1977 Autumn-Winter issue of *The Prison Journal* is devoted to the topic of "Democracy in Prison." The editor, Rendell Davis, states:

> To establish a democratic process in a prison is no easy matter . . . when one realizes that democracy is never easily achieved in a free society, it should not be surprising that it faces great obstacles in the closed setting of a correctional institution. . . . But . . . the effort must go on.
>
> In the absence of a sanctioned system of self-government, informal unregulated power structures among inmates will continue to govern day-to-day living within the institutions.[45]

Extensive inmate self-government, or, as correctional practitioner Seth Bloomberg calls it, "participatory management," has been disregarded by correctional administrators for two main reasons: the lack of a structural replacement for the traditional prison order and the fear of losing control of institutional decision making.[46] Furthermore, past attempts to permit offender participation in administration revealed some potential problems: manipulation of programs by inmates, brutality in discipline, failure to understand the operation of self-government, and lack of general support from salaried correctional personnel.

Most problems resulted from correctional personnel's failure to participate properly in institutional self-government. Members of the staff were either inadequately prepared to assist offenders, or they did not believe in the concept and so refused to support the program. In other instances, institutional self-government was given to inmates as a result of administrative or inmate pressures, sometimes following a period of inmate unrest and as a result of prisoner demands or grievances. Allowing the inmates to manage the institution was easier than trying to manage the inmates. Inmate councils and other forms of self-government or self-management were gestures to keep peace within the institution or provide opportunities for inmates to expend energy. When self-government was permitted as a result of pressures and without proper

---

[44]George J. Smullen, "Recognizing Inmate Groups: The Participation Management Model," *Corrections Today,* vol. 43, no. 5, September–October 1981, pp. 58, 60, 62.

[45]Rendell A. Davis, "Democracy in Prison," Preface, *The Prison Journal,* vol. LVII, no. 2, Autumn-Winter 1977, p. 2.

[46]Seth Allan Bloomberg, "Participatory Management," *Criminology,* vol. 15, no. 3, August 1977, p. 150.

preparation of personnel, "kangaroo courts" and gangs of marauders frequently gained control of the institutions. Many programs of self-government have failed because of poor leadership on the part of correctional advisors and supervisory personnel.

The Washington State Prison at Walla Walla is an example. Beginning in 1970 the penitentiary was a laboratory for a prison self-government program for 4 years. The conversion to self-government was initiated by psychiatrist Dr. William Conte, then director of institutions. Prison personnel were unprepared and had little part in the planning. An eleven-man Resident Government Council (RGC) was the center. Inmate members were elected by the entire prison population for a 6-month term. They had little formal power but could make recommendations at regularly scheduled "agenda meetings" with the superintendent. Council representatives sat in on disciplinary committees and classification hearings. They had contact with outside media, held press conferences in prison, lectured around the state, organized social events for outside visitors, managed a budget, and endorsed other inmates for work release or furlough. The principal changes which took place after recommendations from the RGC were liberalized hair and dress codes, abolition of censorship, increased contact with the outside world, and recognition of ethnic and special interest clubs. Some of the clubs provided work opportunities for inmates: tape-recording books for the blind, repairing appliances for the poor, conducting handicraft courses for children, and upholstering furniture.

At the same time that some apparently positive changes took place, problems also emerged. The arbitrary reforms resulted in resignations and requests for transfer by correctional personnel. Some clubs became centers for smuggling of contraband, extortion from inmates, and bargaining for control of the institution. Political squabbles developed among correctional administrators, judges, and elected officials over the advisability of continuing the program. Conte resigned as director of institutions in mid-1971. The Resident Government Council was replaced by a resident advisory council in 1974. By 1979 all remnants of the experiment were gone. Even so, at that time the last warden of Walla Walla, an avowed opponent of the reforms, stated that the reforms "may have got us through the 70s without a major riot. It only came when we tried to regain control."[47]

As with other methods existing within prison walls that can prepare offenders for return to the community, self-government techniques can be organized to maximize the value to the prisoner. Most problems can be remedied by three steps. First, prison personnel must constantly assist inmates, working with them and being willing to intervene with outside controls when necessary. Second, inmate self-government, to be effective, must be applied only within a correctional model in which all salaried personnel—not just the warden—are supportive of self-government. Third, all prison personnel must be adequately educated and trained in institutional management before attempting to assist offenders.

---

[47]Gabrielle Tyrnauer, "What Went Wrong at Walla Walla?", *Corrections Magazine,* vol. 7, no. 3, June 1981, pp. 37, 38, and 41.

Encouraging offender participation in the administration of correctional institutions does not mean relaxation of security. On the contrary, there is always the necessity to establish rules outlining limits to behavior, just as there are rules establishing limits within the free community. Limits within the prison community are based on general principles of acceptable behavior, common decency, and the experience of the decision makers. There are times, of course, when inmates are not able to assume responsibility for themselves and must lean upon the established authority in the institution. This is also consistent with the free community.

The ultimate goal of incarceration is to prepare offenders to assume full responsibility for their community behavior. First, it is hoped that self-management can help them learn how to conduct personal affairs so that they no longer depend on correctional personnel to make decisions. Many adult offenders learn for the first time the process of selecting a single behavioral choice from the vast number of available alternatives. Second, participation in institutional administration provides an opportunity to be a contributing member of a self-governing community in prison. Inmates thus gain confidence in their ability to function as part of the self-governing free community—a valuable asset in a society which places community goals over individual goals.

A review of past applications of inmate self-government encouraged Bloomberg to state that "participatory management has been utilized in the past by several prison administrators who have reported improved institutional management, reduced recidivism, and increased self-esteem as a result."[48]

PRERELEASE CENTERS

In 1950 the American Prison Association (APA) published a handbook on prerelease preparation in correctional institutions. The authors stated that "adequate preparation for release and helpful supervision . . . represent two very important features for the protection of the public."[49] The basis for APA emphasis on prerelease preparation was the knowledge that the highest percentage of postprison failures occur within 90 days after release. Most inmates have many anxieties and fears about their return to the community. Prerelease programs attempt to ready inmates for life in a normal community situation. The goal is to assist them with mundane decisions such as job seeking, apartment hunting, and money management as well as to minimize the interpersonal problems created by isolation that sometimes result in emotional maladjustment and faulty judgment. Many offenders act out childish urges, overreact to ordinary setbacks, and become defeated by everyday decision making, if they are unprepared for the routine of daily living, especially during the first 3 months after release.[50]

[48]Bloomberg, "Participatory Management," op. cit., p. 150.
[49]*Handbook on Pre-release Preparation,* op. cit., p. 11.
[50]John J. Galvin, "Progressive Development in Pre-Release Preparation," *Correctional Classification and Treatment,* Leonard J. Hippchen (ed.), The W. H. Anderson Company, Cincinnati, 1975, p. 223.

As a result of research conducted by the Federal Bureau of Prisons after World War II, the Department of Justice secured passage of legislation setting aside separate wings as prerelease centers for prisoners at six federal correctional institutions.[51] The idea of a prerelease center for inmates who were being released from federal correctional institutions was stimulated when United States military authorities realized that many World War II veterans experienced difficulty in adjusting to civilian life after serving within the regimented structure of the military. The result was the development of a prerelease program to gradually "muster out" military personnel. Within a few years, prisoner separation centers patterned after military prototypes appeared at such widely scattered places as Chino, California; Seagoville, Texas; and Louisburg, Pennsylvania.

Prerelease Center Programs

From these early efforts three principles emerged which are now recognized as essential to a program of release preparation for inmates: (1) to provide inmates before release with information which will help them carry out their release plan; (2) to provide each prerelease inmate the opportunity, in a nonthreatening situation, to discuss fears and anxieties relating to release and future social adjustment; and (3) to provide a system of evaluating the effectiveness of release planning procedures.[52]

Both correctional administrators who have operated prerelease centers and inmates who are leaving prison agree that prerelease centers are effective only if they deal with specific problems of inmates returning to the community; for example, inmates learn more about job interviews from either a mock or a real job interview than from a lecture about employment practices.

David and Barbara Duffee conducted an intensive study of the perceived needs of offenders in prerelease centers. Their results supported the belief that inmates preparing for release are primarily concerned with daily decision making after they leave the institution. After interviewing 148 male offenders and their counselors they concluded that money- and employment-related problems were of greatest concern to the inmates. The counselors rated significantly higher than did inmates personal problems and family problems that would require "fixing the person rather than the world in which the person lives."[53] Table 6.6 details the findings of the Duffees.

A 1978 study of federal releasees would tend to support these findings. After 12 months of release, the parolees studied showed an unemployment rate of almost 25 percent (compared with 6 percent nationally), an average of 184 days

[51]Benedict S. Alper, *Prison Inside-Out,* Ballinger Publishing Company, Cambridge, Mass., 1974, pp. 113–114.

[52]J. E. Baker, "Preparing Prisoners for their Return to the Community," *Federal Probation,* vol. 30, no. 2, Administrative Office of the United States Courts, Washington, D.C., June 1966, p. 43.

[53]David E. Duffee and Barbara W. Duffee, "Studying the Needs of Offenders in Prerelease Centers," *Journal of Research in Crime and Delinquency,* vol. 18, no. 2, July 1981, pp. 247–248.

TABLE 6.6
FREQUENCY OF PROBLEMS CLAIMED BY 148 HALFWAY HOUSE RESIDENTS
AND THEIR COUNSELORS

Frequency with which problems mentioned by residents	Rank	Problem or need	Frequency with which problems mentioned by counselors	Rank
72	1	Help in finding job	79	2
70	2	Money to get started	101	1
60	3	Transportation	57	6
51	4	Training/education to get job/better job	61	4.5
35	5	Getting a wardrobe together	13	19
32	6	Seeing family often enough	37	8
31	7	Problems with family after return from prison	62	3
29	8	Help with legal matters	29	10
26	9	Dental or medical problem	32	9
23	10	Putting together a parole plan	38	7
21	11.5	Establishing credit	10	23
21	11.5	Advice or counseling on an emotional problem	61	4.5
16	13	Paying for meals	15	16
14	14	Center rules about spending own money	5	26
13	15	Alcohol problem	26	11.5
12	16	Feeling out of place on the job because of being a center resident	8	24
10	17.5	Finding housing for family or self on parole	23	13
10	17.5	What to do with spare time	26	11.5
8	19.5	Type of work required on job	14	17
8	19.5	Center rules about curfew	2	28
7	22	Problems with co-workers	19	14
7	22	Center rules about rent	11	21.5
7	22	Problem with another resident	18	15
6	24	Dealing with people	13	19
5	25	Finding friends outside the center	13	19
4	26	Drug problem	11	21.5
3	27.5	Center rules about week-end furloughs	5	26
3	27.5	Day care for children	5	26
605*				

*Total exceeds number of respondents because most respondents cited more than one problem.
Source: David E. Duffee and Barbara W. Duffee, "Studying the Needs of Offenders in Prerelease Centers," *Journal of Research in Crime and Delinquency,* vol. 18, no. 2, July 1981, pp. 248–249.

worked (full-time employment is considered to be 240 days a year), and median earnings of $6025 (the poverty level for a family of four was considered to be $6700 in the city and $5700 in rural areas).[54]

Initially, prerelease programs were conducted within penitentiaries. Applicants were eligible for participation if they anticipated parole or expiration of sentence within ninety days. Information-giving and problem-solving discussions took place regarding detainers, parole rules, marital and family problems, race relations, credit installment buying, employment interviews, job selection, community resources, drugs, and clothing selection. In some cases, offenders were required to attend these sessions before their release.

Social education classes were frequently included in these early prerelease programs. The Texas Prerelease Program included an extensive 5-week classroom study of 24 different topics—one each day. Using instructors from the state prison department, the community, and other areas of state government, courses such as communication skills, social and family relationships, budgeting, law, social etiquette, current news events, citizenship, and basic economics were offered.

Models for Prerelease Centers

In the late 1950s designs were begun for special facilities planned to deal with prerelease problems of inmates. By 1965 three models for prerelease centers had been established. In 1959 Colorado began operating a prerelease center at Canon City which was a self-contained unit designed expressly for the purpose it fulfilled. It was a minimum security place without walls or fences; movement within the center was unrestricted. Each Monday a new group arrived, each remained for a 5-week course designed to deinstitutionalize the offender.

The Canon City program consisted of twenty-three phases, with one day given to each. Guest speakers came from city, state, and federal agencies; from private industry; and from the general public. Lectures were supplemented by films and other visual aids. Topics included programs previously initiated in prison prerelease programs plus such subjects as buying new and used cars, leisure-time activities, and veterans' rights. Two evenings a week were reserved for open group discussions.[55]

In 1961 Robert Kennedy, attorney general of the United States, recommended to Congress that funds be appropriated to the Bureau of Prisons for the establishment of prerelease guidance centers as an experimental project. Later in the year, after careful study, the decision was made to establish centers only in metropolitan areas where the number of inmates to be released would justify the cost of such facilities. By 1976 the Federal Bureau of Prisons operated fifteen

---

[54]James L. Beck, "Measuring the Impact of Community Treatment Center Placement on Post-Release Employment and Recidivism," *Proceedings of the One Hundred and Tenth Annual Congress of Correction,* American Correctional Association, College Park, Md., 1980, p. 248.

[55]J. E. Baker, *Colorado's Preparole Release Center,* State of Colorado, Canon City, Colo., 1959, pp. 1–3.

prerelease centers—renamed community treatment centers. Each federal center serves as a hub for a specific geographic area.

Three to four months before their parole dates, inmates are transferred from a federal institution to a treatment center. Also, offenders waiting release at expiration of sentence or completion of diagnostic study or by mandatory release are scheduled for a 30-to-180-day program in one of the federal centers. Residents are given the opportunity to complete their institutional sentence under conditions of minimum security, while still legally and administratively in the custody of the Bureau of Prisons.

YMCAs have been favorite locations for several of the first community treatment centers, with activities occupying one floor or a block of rooms on a floor. Programs have also been housed in a former children's home, a former college administration building, and in the staff quarters of prison officers attached to a penitentiary. The centers provide cooking and dining facilities, informal counseling, educational and occupational placement assistance, and community adjustment follow-up.[56]

A third model was established by the South Carolina Department of Corrections. In October 1964, a process was initiated at Watkins, South Carolina, designed to reintegrate inmates gradually into their home communities. The first prerelease center was established to enable inmates to work at paid employment for a period of 90 days to 1 year prior to expiration of sentence. The program has since been extended to prospective parolees as well. It was believed that working in the community during the last few months of confinement would have a stabilizing effect on the inmates. They would be able to establish themselves in employment situations which could be retained after release, support their dependents while serving the final portion of their sentences, and deposit money in trust for use after their release. Thus they would be able to assume much of the financial burden of their subsistence while incarcerated, providing relief for the taxpayers. By 1979, eight such prerelease centers were in operation throughout South Carolina.[57]

In addition to state and federally operated pre-release programs, a county-operated center is located in Montgomery County in Rockville, Maryland. The inmate participants of this LEAA-initiated program are federal and state correctional offenders (11 percent) and residents of the County Detention Center (89 percent). This program has been designated as an exemplary project by LEAA. It offers work and educational releases, weekly counseling, and the opportunity to participate in community social service programs (family counseling, Alcoholics Anonymous, and pastoral counseling). Seminars are held on money management, housing selection, family planning, and similar topics relevant to problems facing the inmate after release. From August 1972 to December 1976, there were 538 inmates assigned to the center. Of these, 141 (26

[56]Benedict S. Alper and Oliver J. Keller, *Halfway House: Community Centered Correction and Treatment,* Raytheon and Heath Publishing Company, Lexington, Mass., 1970, pp. 96–97.

[57]*Annual Report 1972–1973,* South Carolina Department of Corrections, Community Programs Division, Columbia, S.C., 1973, pp. 1–3.

percent) had their participation in the program revoked, but only 22 (4 percent) of them were reincarcerated.[58]

EXAMINATION OF PRERELEASE PROGRAMS

Some research has been conducted to determine the effect of prerelease courses on inmates who have completed them. One survey indicated that 66 percent of those interviewed believed the course had been worthwhile. However, the researchers concluded that the program had sought to meet the needs of inmates as a group rather than as individuals and, consequently, had met the needs of no one in particular.[59] A 1969 study of the California prerelease program by researchers Norman Holt and Rudy Renteria revealed that inmates derived only a meager amount of learning from classes and little change of attitude.[60]

Even though the conclusions from studies examining the value of prerelease preparation have not been encouraging, there is evidence that recidivism rates in some states have been favorably affected. The Texas Department of Corrections witnessed a drop in their recidivism rate from 33.3 percent to 9.8 percent within 5 years after the introduction of a prerelease program.[61]

A similar recidivism rate (9.5 percent) was discovered by the state of South Carolina for inmates participating in its prerelease program. The study divided the inmates released through the state's centers according to the number of days they had actually participated in the program (30 to 120 days). As Table 6.7 shows, the highest percentage of success was among those who remained at the release center 120 days.[62]

A study released in November 1979 by the Massachusetts Department of Corrections indicated that offenders released through a prerelease program in 1977 had only an 8 percent recidivism rate. This compares with a 19 percent recidivism rate for offenders not in the program. The effect of such a program in Massachusetts is also reflected in an overall recidivism decrease from 25 percent in 1971 to 15 percent in 1977 for all released offenders.[63]

However, statistics regarding recidivism rates for offenders who complete prerelease programs have not all been favorable. An elaborate study conducted on 1000 federal prisoners from prerelease guidance centers in Detroit, Chicago, Los Angeles, and New York during fiscal year 1964 revealed that 57 percent had

---

[58]Robert Rosenblum and Debra Whitcomb, *Montgomery County Work Release/Pre-Release Program: An Exemplary Project,* U.S. Government Printing Office, Washington, D.C., June 1978, pp. 2, 3, and 81.

[59]Baker, "Preparing Prisoners," op. cit., p. 48.

[60]Norman Holt and Rudy Renteria, "Prerelease Program Evaluation: Some Implications of Negative Findings," *Federal Probation,* vol. 33, no. 2, Administrative Office of the United States Courts, Washington, D.C., June 1969, p. 43.

[61]Jesse E. Clark, "The Texas Pre-release Program," *Correctional Classification and Treatment,* Leonard J. Hippchen (ed.), W. H. Anderson Company, Cincinnati, Ohio, 1975, pp. 240–241.

[62]*Annual Report, 1972–1973,* South Carolina Department of Corrections, Community Program Division, Columbia, S.C., 1973, p. 41.

[63]Daniel P. Le Clair, *Community-Based Reintegration: Some Theoretical Implications of Positive Research Findings,* Massachusetts Department of Corrections, Boston, Mass., November 1979, p. 7.

TABLE 6.7
COMMUNITY PRERELEASE PROGRAMS, RECIDIVIST
STATISTICS

120-day accelerated prerelease program	
Inmates paroled or released	870
Recidivists to date	83
Recidivism rate	9.5%
Successful readjustment rate to date	90.5%
30-day prerelease program	
Inmates released from prerelease center	5190
Recidivists to date	843
Recidivism rate	16.2%
Successful readjustment rate to date	83.8%
Consolidated recidivist report—all centers	
Released or paroled	6540
Recidivists to date	961
Recidivism rate	14.7%
Successful readjustment rate to date	85.3%

Source: Annual Report 1972–1973, South Carolina Department
of Corrections, Community Program Division, Columbia, S.C., 1973,
p. 41. (Data current 6–30–72)

been recommitted for 1 day or more or had had a parole violation warrant issued in their names.[64]

A second study of 974 parolees released in the first half of 1978 revealed that Community Treatment Centers (CTC)—the current name for the federal prison system's prerelease guidance centers—had little overall effect on recidivism. The rate for 1 year was 22 percent for CTC releasees and 23 percent for non-CTC releasees. Among nonwhite offenders, however, CTC releasees had a rearrest rate of 22.4 percent compared to 32 percent for non-CTC releasees (see Table 6.8).

A more interesting statistic revealed that CTC releasees were helped signifi-

[64]Reis H. Hall, Mildred Milazzo, and Judy Posner, *A Descriptive and Comparative Study of Recidivism in Pre-release Guidance Center's Releasees,* U.S. Department of Justice, Bureau of Prisons, Washington, D.C., 1968, p. 11.

TABLE 6.8
REARREST OR WARRANT ISSUED AT 12 MONTHS AFTER
RELEASE
(Adjusted for Background Differences)

	White	Nonwhite
Offenders released through a CTC	22.5%	22.4%
	(N=336)	(N=305)
Offenders not released through a CTC	19.0%	32.1%
	(N=229)	(N=101)

cantly in acquiring employment, number of days employed, and money earned—as Table 6.9 indicates.[65]

Appraisal

Obviously evaluations of prerelease center programs indicate mixed conclusions. Some studies tend to verify the value of prerelease preparation for inmates in reducing the recidivism rate; others do not show any significant decrease. It is important to realize, however, that *none* of the studies show a significant *increase* in rearrest rates.

Even if the studies were unanimous in their endorsement of the prerelease center concept, they would be questioned because of the difficulties in carrying out the evaluations. And many questions have been raised. Few studies have compared prerelease inmates with other groups. No method has been devised to successfully isolate the effect of prerelease preparation from other release factors. Many prerelease programs serve only volunteers or especially selected inmates and do not represent a random cross section of the offender population leaving prison.

Despite the failure of research to unequivocally justify prerelease centers, there are sufficient favorable results to defend their continuance. Massachusetts

[65]James L. Beck, "Measuring the Impact of Community Treatment Center Placement on Post-release Employment and Recidivism," *Proceedings of the One Hundred and Tenth Annual Congress of Corrections,* American Correctional Association, College Park, Md., 1980, p. 255.

TABLE 6.9
COMMUNITY ADJUSTMENT
(Excluding Those With a "Legitimate" Reason for Being Unemployed)

Adjustment criteria	Results (N)
Mean days employed at 6 months after release	95.1 days (N=864)
Mean days employed at 12 months after release	183.6 days (N=853)
Median money earned at 6 months after release	$3000 (N=860)
Median money earned at 12 months after release	$6025 (N=846)
Percent unemployed at release	25.0% (N=907)
Percent unemployed at 6 months after release	18.3% (N=864)
Percent unemployed at 12 months after release	23.5% (N=856)

Source: James L. Beck, "Measuring the Impact of Community Treatment Center Placement on Post-Release Employment and Recidivism," *Proceedings of the One Hundred and Tenth Annual Congress of Corrections,* American Correctional Association, College Park, Md., 1980, p. 255.

and South Carolina officials are convinced of the value of gradual reintegration of the offender. Daniel Le Clair, deputy director of research in Massachusetts stated: "These findings provide striking support for the recently enacted community-based correctional network of programs in Massachusetts: pre-release centers, halfway houses, work and education release programs. . . ."[66] There appears to be the potential for a substantial decrease in costs of institutional care and tax dollars. By removing inmates close to release, they offer an alternative to overcrowded prisons and jails.

Correctional administrators who, like this author, have been responsible for the operation of prerelease centers would not discard them without a lengthy trial, if for no other reason than that they offer an opportunity to rehumanize the offender.

CONCLUSION

Preparing the offender for the community is not simply educational training in prison or jail, a visit with a family member, work release, or prerelease centers; it is all of these—making a whole greater than its parts. To eliminate criminal problem-solving techniques and the effects of prisonization, correctional person-nel must begin at the moment of the offender's initial commitment. Classifica-tion ensures that programs are available to suit the specific needs of each offender. Opportunities to improve skills are offered to inmates through educational classes, vocational training, leisure-time activities, and creative therapy. They are thus given the wherewithal to achieve socially acceptable community adjustment. Both individual and group counseling assist offenders to understand better how to deal with problems as they occur. Encouraging free citizens to carry on a dialogue with inmates, coupled with liberal visiting and mailing privileges for family members, permit constant contact with the outside community.

At the same time, a sense of community is brought into the institution by the creation of a communitylike environment. Allowing inmate involvement in institutional government and self-help groups, encouraging individual responsi-bility for both behavior and program participation, and developing structured programs which permit prisoners to behave as if they were in the outside community are all factors which allow them to remain community-oriented.

As a felon adjusts to the institution and shows ability to successfully accept responsibilities, he or she is extended privileges which permit entry into the outside community. Supervised community visits, furloughs, and day passes allow the offender to bowl, attend movies, or visit family and friends.

As the time approaches when the offender is nearing community release, prerelease programs prepare for the actual removal of institutional structure. Classes assist with clothing selection, driver's license examinations, job selec-

---

[66]Daniel P. Le Clair, *Rates of Recidivism: A Five Year Follow-up,* Massachusetts Department of Corrections, Boston, Mass., October 1981, p. 16.

tion, and educational planning. Counseling deals with the anxieties and fears developed during the days behind bars.

Finally, a transfer is processed to a prerelease center, halfway house, work release center, or similar facility. This allows the offender to live in a relatively unstructured setting in the community for an indefinite period while being given assistance by correctional personnel. His or her lifestyle is now similar to that expected after complete release into the community, except for not yet having established an independent residence. During this time, work release privileges and extended furlough privileges permit more contact with family members, friends, and the public in general. As the offender exhibits ability to resolve problems in a responsible, socially acceptable manner, further privileges are extended and more freedom is permitted. Parole followed by expiration of sentence or an expiration of sentence without parole is the ultimate goal.

If at any time an offender demonstrates either incapability of handling unrestricted freedom or potential for crime or violence, the privileges are removed and more structure is imposed. In either instance, the total correctional program, including counselors and correctional officers, provides constant and immediate support with efforts to resolve the identified difficulties that caused the reversion to unacceptable behavior.

Each offender is given continual opportunity to achieve success. Problems are viewed not as failures but simply as setbacks. During subsequent periods of incarceration, opportunities continue for learning new ways of coping with difficult situations, for practice in dealing with them, and for growing in the ability to use new methods and skills. There is no pressure to "bust" inmates in an effort to return them to prison or jail for punishment; instead, all efforts are concentrated on assisting them to deal with problems in the community in a socially acceptable manner.

Ninety-six percent of all incarcerated felons eventually return to the community. Consequently, preparing them for this return is both economical and wise. Leaving an institution is something like being born; if left to one's own resources, death is almost inevitable. Just as children are incapable of meeting their own needs, many newly released offenders are incapable of solving their own problems. Preparing them for the community involves a carefully planned series of helping steps necessary to assure maturation.

EXERCISES

1 Agree or disagree: Preparing an offender for the community begins at the time of judicial commitment. Give reasons for your answer.
2 List reasons why you believe corrections administrators have not made institutions similar to the community.
3 What steps would you take to increase the likelihood that married inmates would not be divorced while incarcerated? Explain each step fully.
4 If the federal minimum wage law were applied to inmates in prison, what additional steps could be taken to make the prison like the community?
5 Compare and contrast the bartering system of La Mesa Penitentiary and the labor

market system of Reno Reformatory. List advantages and disadvantages of each system.

6 In 1960, the Warden's Association of America reportedly went on record that they were against inmate advisory councils. Why do you believe they opposed them? Explain your reasons fully.

7 What specific activities do you believe inmates can manage by themselves (e.g., program decisions, job applications, daily intrainstitutional movements)? Give reasons for your answer.

8 Critically examine Greenburg's voucher system. Present both positive and negative points regarding this proposal.

9 Which model of prerelease centers do you believe would be most successful? Give reasons for your conclusion.

10 Why might a prerelease program which does not have a mandatory release date or a minimal residence period for prereleasees be more successful than other programs?

11 How would you apply furloughs, day passes, and work release in a program preparing an offender for the community?

12 What advantages and disadvantages can you see in bringing the community into the institution by means of jazz festivals, Alcoholics Anonymous meetings, etc.? Explain.

13 Why do you believe that corrections administrators have not based institutional vocational training on current occupational demands in the community?

14 The author believes that the value of gradual reintegration for offenders has never really been tested because no state has "put it all together." Agree or disagree with this belief.

EXERCISE REFERENCES

Arjo, Raymond L., and Lawrence R. Allen: "The Role of Leisure Time in Corrections," *Corrections Today,* vol. 42, no. 1, January-February 1980, pp. 36–37, 40–41.

Baker, J. E.: "Inmate Self-Government," *Journal of Criminal Law, Criminology, and Police Science,* vol. 55, no. 1, 1972, pp. 39–47.

———: "Preparing Prisoners for Their Return to the Community," *Federal Probation,* vol. 30, no. 2, Administrative Office of the United States Courts, Washington, D.C., June 1966, pp. 43–50.

———: *The Right to Participate: Inmate Involvement in Prison Administration,* Scarecrow Press, Inc., Metuchen, N.J., 1974.

Beck, James L.: "Measuring the Impact of Community Treatment Center Placement on Post-release Employment and Recidivism," *Proceedings of the One Hundred and Tenth Annual Congress of Corrections,* American Correctional Association, College Park, Md., 1980, pp. 247–256.

Bloomberg, Seth Allan: "Participatory Management." *Criminology,* vol. 15, no. 3, August 1977, pp. 149–166.

Brayshaw, R. D.: "Investment Counseling—A Function of Correctional Recreation," *Corrections Today,* vol. 42, no. 4, July-August 1980, pp. 92–93.

Chaneles, Sol: *The Open Prison,* Dial Press, New York, 1973.

Clark, Jesse E.: "The Texas Pre-release Program," *Correctional Classification and Treatment,* Leonard J. Hippchen (ed.), W. H. Anderson Company, Cincinnati, Ohio; 1975, pp. 240–244.

Committee on Classification and Casework of the American Prison Association: *Handbook on Pre-release Preparation in Correctional Institutions,* American Prison Association, New York, 1950.

Committee on Classification and Casework of the American Prison Association: "Democracy in Prison," *The Prison Journal,* vol. LVII, no. 2, Rendell A. Davis (ed.), Autumn-Winter 1977.

Duffee, David E., and Barbara W. Duffee: "Studying the Needs of Offenders in Pre-release Centers." *Journal of Research in Crime and Delinquency,* vol. 18, no. 2, July 1981, pp. 233–253.

Empey, Lamar T.: *Alternatives to Incarceration,* U.S. Government Printing Office, Washington, D.C., 1967.

Fedo, Michael: "Free Enterprise Goes to Prison," *Corrections Magazine,* vol. 7, no. 2, April 1981, pp. 5–15.

Glaser, Daniel: *The Effectiveness of a Prison and Parole System,* The Bobbs-Merrill Company, Inc., Indianapolis, Ind., 1969, chaps. 13, 14, and 15.

Greenburg, David F.: "A Voucher System for Corrections," *Crime and Delinquency,* vol. 19, no. 2, April 1973, pp. 212–217.

Hayner, Norman S.: "Attitudes Toward Conjugal Visits for Prisoners," *Federal Probation,* vol. 37, no. 1. Administrative Office of the United States Courts, Washington, D.C., March 1973, pp. 42–49.

Helfman, Harold M.: "Antecedents of Thomas Mott Osborne's Mutual Welfare League in Michigan." *Journal of Criminal Law and Criminology,* vol. 40, no. 2, May–April 1949–1950, pp. 597–600.

Holt, Norman, and Rudy Renteria: *Prerelease Program Evaluation: How Effective Are Prerelease Programs?* Research Report Number 30, California Department of Corrections, Sacramento, October 1968.

————: "Pre-release Program Evaluation: Some Implications of Negative Findings," *Federal Probation,* vol. 33, no. 2, Administrative Office of the United States Courts, Washington, D.C., June 1969, pp. 40–45.

Hopper, Columbus B.: "The Conjugal Visit at Mississippi State Penitentiary," *Journal of Criminal Law, Criminology, and Police Science,* vol. 53, no. 3, September 1962, pp. 340–343.

Le Clair, Daniel P.: *Community-Based Reintegration: Some Theoretical Implications of Positive Research Findings,* Massachusetts Department of Corrections, Boston, Mass., November 1979.

Lenihan, Kenneth J.: "The Financial Resources of Released Prisoners," *Proceedings: Second National Workshop on Corrections and Parole Administration,* American Correctional Association, College Park, Md., 1974, pp. 109–135.

Lewis, O. F.: "Inmate Self-Government a Century Ago," *The Delinquent,* vol. 8, no. 1, January 1918, pp. 9–15.

McCarty, Joseph H.: "Inmates Fatten Pay Outside Walls," *KCCD Newsletter,* vol. 7, no. 3, Kansas Council on Crime and Delinquency, Kansas City, May 1980, p. 7.

May, Edgar: "Maine: Was Inmate Capitalism Out of Control?" *Corrections Magazine,* vol. 7, no. 1, February 1981, pp. 17–23.

Miller, Michael J.: "Vocational Training in Prisons: Some Social Policy Implications," *Federal Probation,* vol. 36, no. 3, Administrative Office of the United States Courts, Washington, D.C., September 1972, pp. 19–21.

Murton, Tom: "Shared Decision Making as a Treatment Technique in Prison Management," *Offender Rehabilitation,* vol. 1, no. 1, Fall 1976, pp. 17–31.

Powers, Sanger B.: "Off-Ground Activities Present an Opportunity for Correctional Institutions," *Federal Probation,* vol. 31, no. 2, Administrative Office of the United States Courts, Washington, D.C., June 1967, pp. 11–15.

Price, John A.: "Private Enterprise in a Prison," *Crime and Delinquency,* vol. 19, no. 2, April 1973, pp. 218–227.

Rosenblum, Robert, and Debra Whitcomb: *Montgomery County Work Release/Prerelease Program: An Exemplary Project,* U.S. Government Printing Office, Washington, D.C., June 1978.

Sard, Thomas R.: "Contact With the Free Community Is Basic If Institutional Programs Are to Succeed," *Federal Probation,* vol. 31, no. 1, Administrative Office of the United States Courts, Washington, D.C., March 1967, pp. 3–8.

Schafer, N. E.: "Prison Visiting: A Background for Change," *Federal Probation,* vol. 42, no. 3, Administrative Office of the United States Courts, Washington, D.C., September 1978, pp. 47–50.

Singer, Neil M.: "Incentives and the Use of Prison Labor," *Crime and Delinquency,* vol. 19, no. 2, April 1973, pp. 200–211.

Smullen, George J.: "Recognizing Inmate Groups: The Participation Management Model," *Corrections Today,* vol. 43, no. 5, September–October 1981, pp. 58–60, 62–63.

Taft, Philip B., Jr.: "The Alchemy of Prison Art," *Corrections Magazine,* vol. 5, no. 3, September 1979, pp. 13–19.

Tyrnauer, Gabrielle: "What Went Wrong at Walla Walla?", *Corrections Magazine,* vol. 7, no. 3, June 1981, pp. 37–41.

U.S. Department of Labor: "Making Prison Training Work," *Manpower,* vol. 3, no. 1, Washington, D.C., January 1971.

Waller, Irvin: "Rejection and Recidivism: The Experience of Men Released from Prison," *Corrections: Problems of Punishment and Rehabilitation,* Edward Sagarin and Donal E. J. MacNamara (eds.), Praeger Publishers, New York, N.Y.: 1973, pp. 135–144.

Weintraub, Judith F.: "The Delivery of Services to Families of Prisoners," *Federal Probation,* vol. 40, no. 4, Administrative Office of the United States Courts, Washington, D.C., December 1976, pp. 28–31.

Wilson, Lawrence E.: "Conjugal Visiting and Family Participation in California," *Proceedings of the One Hundred and Third Annual Congress of Corrections,* American Correctional Association, College Park, Md., 1970, pp. 261–264.

COMMUNITY ASSISTANCE FOR THE OFFENDER

CHAPTER OBJECTIVES

- To present techniques used by correctional personnel to assist the offender after release
- To discuss methods of public education
- To outline the roles of volunteers in corrections
- To examine some volunteer organizations
- To describe some public and private job placement programs
- To present some suggested models that can be used to help the offender

INTRODUCTION

The process that Donald Clemmer called "correctionalization" begins within the correctional institution when administrators create a setting that is community-like, with conjugal visiting, work opportunities patterned after private industry, and inmate self-government. Correctionalization continues in a prerelease program when inmates are made aware of solutions to practical problems such as acquiring car insurance, filling out a job application, and balancing a budget.

RATIONALE FOR PREPARING THE COMMUNITY FOR THE OFFENDER

Regardless of how well prepared offenders are for the community, or whether or not they have actually been incarcerated, all efforts toward reintegration can be wasted unless the community is ready to integrate them. Norval Morris believes there are only three factors correlated with success after a prisoner's release: the availability of a family or other supportive social group, the availability of a reasonably supportive job, and the maturation that accompanies aging itself.[1] Daniel Glaser's research concluded that prisoners who did not continue to see prison acquaintances succeeded at an 81 percent rate, while those who did see former prisoners succeeded at rates ranging from 79 to 68 percent.[2] Inmates who made new friends reported that friendships began at work or places of commercial recreation, such as taverns, restaurants, or pool halls.

Allen Hess and Raymond Frank studied predictors of success (defined as parole or release from custody) in community-based preparole corrections centers in Michigan. They concluded that older residents had a higher rate of success. Full-time employment, too, was correlated with a higher success rate. In fact, a combination of age and employment appeared to predict success.[3]

Authors Richard Schwartz and Jerome Skolnick stated in their article, "Two Studies of Legal Stigma," that prospective employers refused to hire a hypothetical employee who had had contact with the criminal justice system. According to the employers, once contact with the system had occurred, the individual was contaminated, even though official agents of control had completed their work with the offender. The study involved preparing four employment folders which were shown to twenty-five individual prospective employers. A 32-year-old single male applicant was described with the same qualifications in all four folders, except that in one he had been convicted and sentenced for assault; in another he had been tried for assault and acquitted; in the third he had been tried for assault and acquitted, with a letter from a judge included confirming the not-guilty finding; and in the fourth no mention of any criminal record was made. The same "employment agent" approached each employer. Nine employers agreed to hire the applicant with no record; six agreed to hire the acquitted applicant with the letter from the judge; three agreed to hire the acquitted applicant without the letter from the judge; only one would hire the convicted applicant.[4]

Unfortunately, the criminal justice system perpetuates the offender's criminal stigma. Inmates placed on probation or parole are visibly displayed under the conditions of their supervision. In some jurisdictions a convicted felon must register as a criminal. In most states, the offender's police and court records are public documents available on request.[5]

[1]Norval Morris, *The Future of Imprisonment,* University of Chicago Press, Chicago, 1974, pp. 35–36.

[2]Daniel Glaser, *The Effectiveness of a Prison and Parole System,* The Bobbs-Merrill Company, Inc., Indianapolis, 1969, p. 257.

[3]Allen K. Hess and Raymond L. Frank, Jr., "Predictions of Success in Community Based Preparole Corrections Centers," *Offender Rehabilitation,* vol. 2, no. 2, Haworth Press, New York, 1977, p. 125.

[4]Richard D. Schwartz and Jerome H. Skolnick, "Two Studies of Legal Stigma," *Social Problems,* vol. 10, no. 2, Fall 1962, p. 137.

[5]John P. Reed and Dale Nance, "Society Perpetuates the Stigma of a Conviction," *Federal Probation,* vol. 36, no. 2, Administrative Office of the United States Courts, Washington, D.C., June 1972, p. 27.

STEPS TO DEVELOP COMMUNITY ASSISTANCE

The tools of community-based corrections—work release, furloughs, probation, and parole—are effective only if the offenders are accepted within the community. The general public as well as employers, friends as well as family, and politicians as well as government employees must be aware of the offenders' problems and be willing to assist them to cope with these problems. In this context, community activities of correctional personnel include the following steps: (1) educating the public, including prospective employers and the community power structure, about the process of reintegration into the community; (2) recruiting volunteers and private agencies to assist in reintegration; (3) assisting offenders in the maintenance of relationships with family and friends; (4) developing educational and occupational opportunities; and (5) creating and operating private and public agencies that can offer assistance to offenders.

Preparing the community for offenders also involves informing community members about the problems of nonincarcerated offenders and describing the steps that can be taken by the public to provide assistance.

The President's Commission on Law Enforcement and Administration of Justice stated:

> The task of corrections therefore includes building or rebuilding solid ties between offender and community, integrating or reintegrating the offender into community life—restoring family ties, obtaining employment and education, securing in the larger sense a place for the offender in the routine functioning of a society. This requires not only efforts directed toward changing the individual offender, which has been almost the exclusive focus of rehabilitation, but also mobilization and change of the community and its institutions.[6]

EDUCATING THE PUBLIC

The Problem Stated

Correctional administrator Ellis MacDougal, in his presidential address to the Ninety-Ninth Congress of Corrections, summarized a public opinion survey thus:

> Only 48 per cent of those questioned felt that our prisons emphasize rehabilitation. Only 1 in 5 say corrections is helping the ex-offender; only 31 per cent said "Yes, we are committed to spend more for corrections;" only 13 per cent said they would recommend careers in corrections to their children, and only 1 per cent of the teenagers are interested in coming into the field.[7]

[6]The President's Commission on Law Enforcement and Administration of Justice, *Task Force Report: Corrections*, U.S. Government Printing Office, Washington, D.C., 1967, p. 7.

[7]Gary Hill, "How to Improve Our Public Image," *American Journal of Correction*, vol. 32, no. 6, November/December 1970, p. 44.

The poor image of corrections represented by these statistics confirms the necessity of educating the public.

For too many years, correctional administrators have been content to tolerate the public's attitude, "out of sight, out of mind." The activities of correctional departments seldom attract public interest except in times of crisis. Given a prison riot, or an alleged error in judgment by probation or parole administrators, the public becomes incensed. Criticism or advice is offered; investigations are threatened and instituted—often by those who have no basic knowledge of corrections.[8]

Educating the public is a long-term, day-to-day task. It requires assistance from all levels of agency personnel and direction by skilled public relations practitioners. Public education in corrections involves interpreting its philosophy and program to all segments of the public. Two tasks must be completed before a public education program is begun: first, identifying the public to be educated; second, designing the methods to be used.

Public to Be Educated

"Publics" that need to be educated about corrections are those which can provide both financial and psychological assistance. Three separate classifications can be distinguished: supporting, operating, and receiving publics.

The *supporting public* comprises the relevant political authorities, legislative bodies, and other groups who actively assist in correctional programs. Taxpayers and voters are members of the general public and thus part of the supporting public. The general public is often educated through influential special interest groups—civic, service, and volunteer organizations. Among these are local mental health associations, parent-teacher associations, Jaycee groups, women's church circles, and various other "in groups" of middle class America.

Local opinion molders who compose the community power structure must also be educated. It is a common mistake to minimize the influence of the press, radio, and television and to maximize that of person-to-person communication or vice versa. In actuality, use of both the mass media and individual communication is necessary to achieve a successful public education program.

The *operating public* refers to the correctional agency's own employees and personnel. Included also are supplementary agencies that assist offenders but are not part of a government corrections department. Regardless of whether the agency's employees are clinical staff, maintenance personnel, or custodial officers, they must possess an understanding of and sympathy for its goals and methods of operation. Others outside the corrections department—such as teachers, court and welfare personnel, and physicians—who directly or indirect-

[8]Garrett Heyns, "What the Public Should Know About Adult Corrections," *Federal Probation*, vol. 28, no. 1, Administrative Office of the United States Courts, Washington, D.C., March 1964, p. 11.

ly provide services to offenders, must also possess a clear picture of objectives and procedures.

The *receiving public* is composed of recipients and potential recipients of correctional services and their families. They need to know when, how, and where to seek help. Efforts to educate the receiving public should not be deferred until after the felon is incarcerated; they should begin with his or her first contact with the criminal justice system.[9]

Methods of Public Education

Public education about corrections is initiated through a variety of programs. Recruiting a citizen's advisory board can ensure initial and continuing dialogue with the community. Using the mass media for sympathetic human interest stories and rapid, direct attention to unfavorable publicity can minimize the antipathy of local residents.[10]

Each correctional department should appropriate funds for a public relations officer, who is responsible for periodic news releases as well as replies to questions about crises. Techniques must be developed to deliver the message. Examples of the various possible approaches are: (1) printed vehicles— newspapers, newsletters, professional journals, community periodicals, church bulletins, shopping guides, posters, pamphlets, brochures, outdoor advertising; and bumper stickers; (2) audiovisual vehicles—radio, television, motion pictures, video cassettes, sound filmstrips, slide tapes, and cable television; and (3) speakers' bureau: public hearings; demonstrations or open houses; personal letters, telephone calls and meetings; structured contact between groups; public forum groups; coalition-building groups; workshops; consultations; door-to-door visits; special events; one-to-one visits; and small group meetings.

When direct contact between the public and offenders is possible, an equally effective tool is created. Narcotics rehabilitation units like the Odyssey and Phoenix Houses in New York have conducted neighborhood cleanup campaigns in an effort to educate people living near their facilities. The District of Columbia's Youth Crime Control project enlisted private citizens who lived near their halfway house and involved them regularly in the planning and operation of the facility.[11]

One agency, Crofton House in San Diego, has developed some elaborate programs of public education using direct personal contact. Both agency personnel and residents have made significant efforts to include neighbors and citizens in their project. Easter egg hunts for neighborhood children were conducted on the Crofton House lawn. Halloween and Christmas parties were

---

[9]H. P. Halpert, *Public Relations in Mental Health Programs,* pp. 1–4.

[10]William A. Ayer, "Work-Release Programs in the United States: Some Difficulties Encountered," *Federal Probation,* vol. 34, no. 1, Administrative Office of the United States Courts, Washington, D.C., March 1970, p. 54.

[11]Ronald Goldfarb and Linda Singer, *After Conviction,* Simon and Schuster, New York, 1973, p. 579.

held, an open house for the entire community was organized, and a wedding ceremony open to the public was performed at the House. Many neighbors who initially found Crofton House threatening became involved and subsequently supported the program enthusiastically.[12]

An inmate panel or a single speaker can present a vivid picture of the corrections system and the problems of offenders as effectively as any salaried correctional personnel. At least twenty-five states have used inmate speakers. Colorado began an inmate panel program in 1966 called the Crime Prevention Teen Program, Inc. Its members, all graduates of the Dale Carnegie course, had traveled approximately 200,000 miles by October 1970. As stated by one correctional administrator, "Inmate speakers . . . may dispel erroneous stereotypes and help create attitudes favorable to corrective methods."[13]

The operating public is most commonly educated by a continuous diet of information about corrections activities during each correctional agency's preservice and in-service training sessions. Both written and oral material can be presented at these sessions.

As regards the receiving public, as soon as an indictment has been filed, families and friends of alleged offenders can be invited to attend group educational sessions conducted by the court having jurisdiction of the case. Such sessions will inform them about the general operational procedure of the criminal justice system as well as helping the alleged offender to maintain ties with the community.

VOLUNTEERS IN CORRECTIONS

Early Volunteerism

One method used to generate community assistance for the offender is the development of a volunteer program. The education received by volunteers in the course of recruitment, training, and providing services prepares them to be advocates for offenders.

The idea is not new. As early as 1822, a group of volunteers, "The Philadelphia Society for Alleviating the Misery of Public Prisoners," supervised men released from penal institutions. John Augustus, called "the father of probation," was a Boston shoemaker who volunteered to take misdemeanants from Boston police court.[14]

Volunteerism decreased considerably in the early 1900s because of an effort to professionalize correctional services. The result was that probation officers

---

[12]Bernard C. Kirby, "Crofton House: An Experiment With a County Halfway House," *Federal Probation*, vol. 33, no. 1, Administrative Office of the United States Courts, Washington, D.C., March 1969, p. 55.

[13]Albert Morris, *The Involvement of Offenders in the Prevention and Correction of Criminal Behavior*, Massachusetts Correctional Association, Boston, October 1970, pp. 7–8.

[14]Frank P. Scioli and Thomas J. Cook, "How Effective Are Volunteers?" *Crime and Delinquency*, vol. 22, no. 2, April 1976, p. 194.

assumed many functions previously handled by volunteers. The Citizen's Participation Committee was organized within the American Prison Association after World War II, but its impact was minimal. In the 1960s, however, emphasis on citizen participation in the criminal justice system rejuvenated volunteerism. By 1972, more than 200,000 volunteers were assisting in approximately 2000 court jurisdictions.[15] In 1980, according to Fahy Mullaney, Executive Director of the National Office for Offender Aid and Restoration, "250,000 citizens give time every week as volunteers in criminal justice."[16]

The importance of volunteers was stressed by the National Institute of Corrections and The Lilly Endowment, Inc., when they jointly awarded a $200,000 grant to the National Association on Volunteers in Criminal Justice, a national membership organization, for the purpose of creating a set of guidelines for volunteers. The Guidelines Project was begun on April 1, 1980, and a short time later a national advisory committee was named.[17]

Use of Volunteers

Originally, volunteers served corrections as a way of "doing good." Religious organizations were prime movers in this undertaking. The Quakers of Philadelphia and other religious groups converted offenders to Christianity while assisting them. Today, although the motivation to do good endures, volunteers have replaced their religious preaching with the provision of professionally supervised services. Table 7.1 illustrates the primary reasons for volunteering. As a result, today's volunteers may be friends or acquaintances of correctional personnel; members of service organizations; college-educated people (especially employees of universities and colleges); and professionals such as attorneys,

---

[15]*Volunteers in Law Enforcement Programs,* Law Enforcement Assistance Administration, Division of Program and Management Evaluation, Washington, D.C., 1972, p. 17.

[16]Fahy G. Mullaney, "Citizen Volunteers Are Breaking Into Jail," *Corrections Today,* vol. 43, no. 4, July/August 1981, p. 56.

[17]David Gooch and William W. Wright, Jr., "Volunteer-Established Guidelines for Volunteers," *Corrections Today,* vol. 43, no. 4, July/August 1981, p. 52.

TABLE 7.1
THE THREE PRIMARY REASONS FOR VOLUNTEERING

Personal humanitarian goals	78%
Personal interest in corrections	36%
Personal sense of community responsibility	27%

Source: Vernon Fox, "A Handbook for Volunteers in Juvenile Court," *Alternatives to Prison,* edited by Gary R. Perlstein and Thomas R. Phelps, Goodyear Publishing Company, Inc., Pacific Palisades, California, 1975, p. 335.

teachers, insurance agents, personnel and sales people.[18] One study of volunteers in a misdemeanor program showed recruitment from a variety of sources (see Table 7.2).

The John Howard Association of Illinois believes volunteers can perform a number of community services for the offender, including job finding or acting as "big brothers," "big sisters," or friendly advisers. Volunteers can accompany offenders to sporting events and social activities and assist them in finding a residence, usable clothing, suitable reading material, and secondhand furniture.

In some instances when correctional agencies need money to implement programs not funded by state or federal appropriations, volunteers aid fundraising efforts. In addition, they seek scholarships, provide transportation to work, and make referrals to other sources of assistance. Professionally trained volunteers give valuable counseling and guidance to understaffed communitybased programs. Many serve as tutors or provide special education expertise. Others assist in the operation of craft or leisure-time programs. Some volunteers improve an agency's physical appearance by brightening the decor or otherwise providing a homelike touch.

Volunteers are a valuable source of community education, informing other citizens about corrections. They also operate as mediators, bringing together correctional personnel and offenders to resolve a common problem. Finally, volunteers serve as sources of information for correctional officials regarding community opinion.[19]

In at least one instance a volunteer program became a planned method of public education. Labor union officials in Minnesota began learning about corrections in 1969 through volunteer contacts with inmates and prison personnel. The AFL-CIO assigned union officials in four industrial cities as "buddies" to inmates at the Stillwater Penitentiary in Minnesota. As buddies, union officials met offenders shortly before release and continued assistance while they adjusted to community living. The result was that union members served as

---

[18]Ivan H. Scheier and Leroy P. Goter, *Using Volunteers in Court Settings: A Manual for Volunteer Probation Programs,* Office of Juvenile Delinquency and Youth Development, Department of Health, Education and Welfare, U.S. Government Printing Office, Washington, D.C., 1969.

[19]*Volunteer Services for Offenders,* John Howard Association of Illinois, Chicago, 1969, pp. 1–2.

TABLE 7.2
SOURCES OF VOLUNTEERS IN A MISDEMEANOR PROGRAM

Friends and relatives of volunteers	27%
Newspapers, magazines, or pamphlets	23%
Clubs, business groups, and organizations, including churches	22%
The organization needing the volunteers (the courts)	28%

Source: Vernon Fox, "A Handbook for Volunteers in Juvenile Court," *Alternatives to Prison,* Gary R. Perlstein and Thomas R. Phelps (eds.), Goodyear Publishing Company, Inc., Pacific Palisades, Calif., 1975, p. 335.

educators of the general public through their own involvement in the prison program.[20]

Organizations That Use Volunteers

There are many organizations that use volunteers. The Salvation Army has a division of corrections which provides housing, food, and clothing and helps offenders to find jobs, counseling, and legal assistance. The Volunteers of America have similar programs. The John Howard Association, founded in 1866 in Chicago, attempted to create a nationwide corps of volunteers. Prisoner-aid associations have been prominent throughout the United States, providing job counseling and financial aid. Similar organizations are the Jewish Community for Personal Service, established in 1921 in Los Angeles; the Northern California Service League, established in 1948 in San Francisco; Prisoners Aid by Citizens Effort, Inc., organized in 1960 in Indianapolis; the Correctional Association of New York, founded in 1844; and paraprofessional organizations such as the National Council on Crime and Delinquency, the American Society of Criminology, and the American Civil Liberties Union.

Some organizations that use volunteers have been established to assist a specific correctional institution. Job Therapy, Inc., for example, focused on assisting felons in their transition to the community from the Washington State Reformatory in Monroe. Inmates were assigned to individual businessmen sponsors who, along with their wives and children, visited inmates twice a month for about a year prior to their release. At the time of the felons' reentry into the community, sponsors served as friends, aiding in specific tasks such as job seeking. In 1970, three hundred companies were actively cooperating with the job-placing service of this project.[21] Since its inception, Job Therapy, Inc., has spread to fifteen other states, Canada, and Mexico. In Kansas City a similar program called Man to Man Service was originated in 1971. By 1981, Man to Man, Woman to Woman, had matched 1000 inmates and sponsors and boasted of a 10 percent recidivism rate.[22]

Job Therapy, Inc., was terminated at the Washington State Reformatory in 1974, following the loss of state and federal monies and a review of program participants' recidivism rates. A "one-to-one" program continues, however, relying on private funds. Volunteers from churches throughout the state are recruited. In October 1977, sixty-nine sponsors from this organization were assisting offenders.[23]

Two nationally recognized organizations were founded by ex-prisoners. The Seven Steps Program, started by ex-offender Bill Sands, has branches throughout the United States and several foreign countries.

[20]Sol Chaneles, *The Open Prison,* Dial Press, New York, 1973, pp. 195–196.
[21]Arthur Gordon, "M-2: New Formula for Wasted Lives," *The Rotarian,* August 1970, p. 50.
[22]Kris Hansen, "Outsider-to-Inmate Sponsorship Helps Ex-Cons Find a New Start," *The Wichita* (Kansas) *Eagle Beacon,* June 23, 1981, p. 4C.
[23]Roger Button, Community Resource Coordinator II, Washington State Reformatory, Department of Social and Health Services, State of Washington, personal correspondence, 1978.

Many ex-offenders have been helped by the Seven Steps program. Yet some professionals in corrections resist efforts by ex-convicts to help their fellows. Professionals working in prerelease guidance centers seem to fear interference with their relationship to the inmates. Nevertheless, because of its popularity among offenders, Seven Steps chapters have mushroomed since the program's inception. By 1980, there were 130 chapters. The program is similar to that of Alcoholics Anonymous in that it includes seven steps that the offender must follow to successfully remain free.

1 Facing the truth about ourselves, we decided to change.

2 Realizing that there is a power from which we can gain strength, we decided to use that power.

3 Evaluating ourselves by taking an honest self-appraisal, we examined both our strengths and weaknesses. Admitted to God (as we understand him), to ourselves, and to another human being the exact nature of our weaknesses.

4 Endeavoring to help ourselves overcome our weaknesses, we enlisted the aid of that power to help us concentrate on our strengths.

5 Deciding that our freedom is worth more than our resentments, we are using that power to help free us from those resentments. Made us a list of all persons we had harmed and became willing to make amends to them all. Made direct amends to such people wherever possible, except when to do so would injure them or others.

6 Observing that daily progress is necessary, we set an attainable goal toward which we can work each day. Continued to take personal inventory, and when we were wrong promptly admitted it.

7 Maintaining our own freedom, we pledge ourselves to help others as we have been helped.

Source: "Championing the Ex-Offender," *Corrections Magazine,* vol. 1, no. 5, May/June 1975, p. 19. Copyright 1975, by Criminal Justice Publications and Corrections Magazine, 116 West 32nd. St., New York, New York 10001.

A second volunteer program established by ex-convicts is the Fortune Society, organized in 1967. This organization sends out teams of former offenders to speak in schools, churches, and civic groups and to make presentations on radio and television. In addition, they offer a multitude of helping services to offenders who voluntarily appear at their offices. The society serves the largest group of ex-offenders in the country; between 4000 and 5000 persons come for help each year.[24]

How Court Systems Use Volunteers

The Department of Court Services of the Hennepin County, Minnesota, court system uses volunteers in a variety of ways. Since 1969, volunteer probation

[24]Vernon Fox, *Introduction to Corrections,* Prentice-Hall, Inc., Englewood Cliffs, N.J., 1977, pp. 394–395.

officers have established a one-to-one volunteer-recipient relationship. In the first 4 years after it began, 320 volunteer probation officers were recruited, screened, and matched with juveniles. The volunteers provided more than 100,000 hours of direct services, estimated at a value of over $500,000. Since 1971, Hennepin County Court Services has used volunteers to supplement juvenile probation diagnostic functions. By 1973, forty-nine volunteers had been trained and forty-one were active. They had written 568 predisposition reports, working 12,000 hours. During the 1972–1973 school term a volunteer teacher program was started in the County Home School (a residential treatment facility for youth) and the Juvenile Detention Center. Twenty volunteer teachers participated, and fifteen remained active for the entire school year, contributing approximately 6000 hours of direct services to students.[25]

In Royal Oak, Michigan, a similar program was designed by volunteers in 1959 at the request of a municipal court judge who discovered upon election that there were no probation officers assigned to his court. In 1965 the city of Royal Oak provided a budget of $17,000 and private donors contributed about $8000. Approximately 20 percent of all probationers were assigned to volunteers. By October 1977, fifty-one volunteers were assigned to individual cases as support personnel for probationers. Retirees and volunteer psychiatrists and psychologists were doing presentence investigations. The judge, Keith J. Leenhouts, convinced that volunteers offer an alternative to overworked probation officers, founded an organization called Volunteers in Probation, which is dedicated to promoting and professionalizing volunteerism.[26]

Problems in Volunteer Programs

The recent increase in the use of volunteers does not mean problems do not exist. Correctional personnel frequently perceive volunteers as tampering with duties that should be under the control of paid employees. In fact, some correctional personnel fear that volunteers may relate to prisoners more effectively than staff members do, eventually replacing them. Other personnel consider that the time required for training and supervising volunteers is not justified by the services they offer.

Other problems stem from the volunteers themselves. They are subjected to a variety of subtle pressures by prisoners to aid them illegally. They are exposed to prisoners' attempts to obtain money, drugs, sex, and early release from correctional supervision. Some offenders cannot accept the volunteer because of their own basic mistrust of anyone who is helping them. Often volunteers overidentify with offenders and act out of sympathy rather than giving objective

[25]John Stoeckel, "The Use of Volunteers in Juvenile Probation," *Corrections in the Community,* E. Eugene Miller and M. Robert Montilla (eds.), Reston Publishing Company, Reston, Va., 1977, pp. 61, 66, 68, and 70.
[26]Charles J. Grisdale, Department of Probation, State of Michigan, 44th District Court, Royal Oak, Michigan, personal correspondence, October 4, 1977.

assistance. Volunteers who become impatient with the normal procedures of the correctional program may try to circumvent them.

Problems are also created by the motives of some volunteers. Persons frequently offer to aid offenders because of a desire to see the inside of a prison or to say that they have helped an offender. After the curiosity is satisfied, such persons lose interest and drop from the program. This unreliability creates suspicion and hurt on the part of the offender.[27]

Overcoming Problems

It is doubtful that the conflict between correctional personnel and volunteers will ever be completely resolved. However, if correctional personnel provide input into the volunteer program and a full-time volunteer coordinator is responsible for recruiting, training, and supervising volunteers, conflicts are minimized.

Recruitment of volunteers should be approached similarly to the recruitment of salaried personnel. Announcements of open volunteer positions can be handled through the usual procedures: public media releases, speeches at organization meetings (college classes, professional associations, and service organizations), and use of the local volunteer recruitment bureau. Selection of volunteers can follow the same procedure as for salaried personnel, using selection criteria, application forms, references, interviews, and security checks.

Training of volunteers should be complete. They should be introduced to all employee positions within the agency, receiving on-the-job role descriptions by employees performing the tasks. At least 20 hours of preservice training should be required and a like amount of in-service training made compulsory during each year of service. Volunteers should be thoroughly acquainted with all community resources used by the supervising agency. If assigned to assist specific employees, they should be considered paraprofessionals, and given all duties and privileges assigned to those jobs. Volunteers should not be allowed to come and go at their discretion but should contract with the agency for a specific amount of time each week for a specific period, such as 1 year.

Gordon Grindstaff, a volunteer at the Cook County Jail in Chicago, has offered a number of practical suggestions for the beginning volunteer that should also be heeded by the volunteer coordinator: (1) Set a goal for the volunteer for each period on duty, (2) do not allow a volunteer to attempt a task he or she is not qualified to perform, (3) do not prevent volunteers from using their unique knowledge or abilities, and (4) vary the pace of the tasks to be performed.[28]

Author and former practitioner Vernon Fox has also recommended some "basic principles" for volunteers to remember in their relationship with offend-

[27]Leo H. Bowker, "Volunteers in Correctional Settings: Benefits, Problems, and Solutions," *Proceedings of the One Hundred and Third Annual Congress of Corrections,* American Correctional Association, College Park, Md., 1974, pp. 299–301.

[28]Gordon Grindstaff, "Practical Help for the Beginning Volunteer," *Corrections Today,* vol. 42, no. 4, July/August 1980, pp. 82–83.

ers: (1) Listen to the offenders, (2) accept the offenders as they are without being judgmental, (3) give the offenders a trusting relationship, (4) develop the capacity to withstand provocative behavior, and (5) do not give advice.[29]

Appraisal

Statistics indicate varied results from volunteer programs. Some, such as Project Re-Entry in Massachusetts, claim a reduction in recidivism and less serious crime as a result of their efforts.[30] Job Therapy, Inc., reports a reduction of about 75 percent in recidivism rates among its participants.[31]

However, another review of more than 250 reports, monographs, and memos evaluating volunteer programs did not demonstrate that they were more successful than other alternatives. However, the review did not examine a report challenging any conclusions that volunteer programs were less successful than alternatives. The reviewers, Frank Scioli and Thomas Cook, stated, "If there is any kind of trend or tendency in the volunteer research literature, it is that volunteer programs performed as well as, or better than, the program alternatives with which they were compared."[32]

Most problems in volunteer programs are the result of poor management. Too many times the volunteer program is considered an adjunct to the main function of the agency and receives little time or money. Personnel assigned to supervise volunteers are often people who have failed at other jobs or staff members who are already overworked.

The development of an effective volunteer program requires a clear decision by correctional administrators that volunteers have an important function to perform within the correctional agency. Administration must exhibit a willingness to invest them with the power to use their skills and resources. All agency personnel who work with volunteers must be trained and supportive. In addition, a commitment of funds and correctional personnel is a prerequisite for an adequate system of recruitment, screening, training and supervision.[33] After all, the volunteer supervisor can continually evaluate each volunteer, and anyone found wanting can be fired the same as salaried personnel.

In times of fiscal limitations, volunteers are increasingly needed to perform a variety of services to enhance the effectiveness of staff members. The investment of time and money will be rewarded by increased productivity of the agency and greater understanding by the community. Public confidence will be bolstered by the knowledge that respected members of the community think enough of the program to give their time, energy, and expertise.

[29]Vernon Fox, *Community-Based Corrections,* Prentice-Hall, Inc., Englewood Cliffs, N.J., 1977, pp. 255–256.

[30]Marie Buckley, "Enter: The Ex-Con," *Federal Probation,* vol. 36, no. 4, Administrative Office of the United States Courts, Washington, D.C., 1972, p. 26.

[31]Hanson, op. cit.

[32]Scioli and Cook, op. cit., p. 198.

[33]Vincent O'Leary, "Some Directions for Citizen Involvement in Corrections," *The Annals of the American Academy of Political and Social Science,* no. 381, January 1969, p. 102.

CREATING JOBS FOR OFFENDERS

Rationale

Offenders' work assignments while incarcerated are not related to employment opportunities after leaving prison. The majority leaving prison do not have prearranged jobs; most accept unstable employment; most experience extended periods of unemployment. These statements have been confirmed by research time after time.

A study conducted by the Federal Bureau of Prisons in 1979 revealed that 54 percent of former federal prisoners aged 24 or under and 35 percent of those older than 36 were unemployed. For those working, the average annual salary was less than $7,000 a year.[34] These statistics do not mean that offenders leave prison without employment. In most instances, a prerequisite for parole release is a confirmed job. However, as Daniel Glaser discovered, many offenders obtain jobs to facilitate their release, with the intention of quitting a short time after leaving the institution. In fact, the majority of unemployed ex-felons were not discharged but actually quit their jobs. Most left because of dissatisfaction with pay or with the nature of the work; others agreed to unsatisfactory jobs with little intention of retaining them.[35] One program, financed by the LEAA, was called the Ex-Offender Coordinated Employment Lifeline. An analysis by this organization disclosed that 236 of 506 job placements made during the project's first year were no longer active by August 1, 1972.[36]

Incarceration does create job problems for some offenders. According to the United States Department of Labor, many state employment agencies refuse to refer any applicant with an arrest record to job interviews. A recent survey of former federal prisoners disclosed that only 10 percent obtained their first postrelease job through state employment services. More than 80 percent of the jobs were obtained through the help of family and friends.[37] These statistics reveal an unfortunate truth, because state employment counselors have a unique advantage. They can serve inmates from their placement in an institutional work assignment or vocational training position to the work release or parole job. By using standard evaluative techniques, such as the general aptitude test battery, they can match offenders with the right jobs.

Even today many offenders are still barred from a myriad of licensed trades and occupations. Excluded are inmates convicted of specified crimes or types of crimes, men and women who do not to possess "good moral character," and those who had committed a crime involving "moral turpitude."[38] Some employers resist hiring ex-prisoners because of perceived security risks. More often than

---

[34]"Employment and Ex-Offender," no. 20, Unitarian Universalist Service Committee, Washington, D.C., 1980, p. 10.

[35]Glaser, op. cit., pp. 235–236.

[36]*Excel in Indiana,* Palmer-Paulson Associates, Inc., Chicago, 1973, pp. 16–17.

[37]Goldfarb and Singer, op. cit., p. 646.

[38]Andrew D. Gilman, "Legal Barriers to Jobs Are Slowly Disappearing," *Corrections Magazine,* vol. 5, no. 4, December 1979, p. 70.

not, an offender cannot be bonded by the private bonding industry. The standard blanket bond is the only type of bonding acceptable to many large corporations, because it is available at a price they can afford. Employers' insurance coverage is specifically void if they knowingly hire any person with a criminal record. Finally, under statutes enacted to protect the public from criminal depredations, offenders are excluded from service in many government positions.[39]

Public Job Placement Programs

Vocational Rehabilitation is one federal program that does help offenders to obtain employment. A 1965 amendment to the Vocational Rehabilitation Act of 1920 provided for the rehabilitation of persons handicapped by cultural, economic, or social disadvantages. Subsequent interpretations broadened the intention of the amendment to permit persons convicted of crimes to be eligible for vocational rehabilitation services because of behavioral disorders.

In 1976 there were 1070 offenders referred to job placements in the community by vocational rehabilitation counselors working in correctional institutions or court services. Another 16,766 clients were accepted, many of whom had been incarcerated because of alcoholism or other drug addiction. Some had character, personality, or behavioral disorders.[40] At least 257 local programs designed to find jobs for ex-offenders were established as a result of the Comprehensive Employment and Training Act (CETA). About half have been in operation 4 years or more. Approximately 80 percent of the programs averaged one staff-offender contact a week. As with vocational rehabilitation job placements, referrals by parole officers were the usual way for prison releasees to come into the program, with referral by prison officials the next most common. Unfortunately, federal spending cutbacks in the 1980s threaten the existence of both federally funded programs.[41]

A number of other federal agencies have backed job placement programs. Since 1968, the Department of Labor and the National Alliance of Businessmen (NAB) have cosponsored JOBS (Job Opportunity in the Business Sector). JOBS is designed to encourage private businesses to employ disadvantaged people, including felons. By July 1974, the program involved 137 metropolitan offices of NAB and had placed more than 6000 persons.[42]

Before its demise, the LEAA developed correctional programs designed to assist offenders seeking employment. In North Carolina, where state employment services reported that there were no job opportunities, an LEAA-financed

---

[39]Mitchell W. Dale, "Barriers to the Rehabilitation of Ex-Offenders," *Crime and Delinquency,* vol. 22, no. 3, July 1976, pp. 323–329.

[40]Larry Mars, Rehabilitation Services Administration, United States Department of Health, Education and Welfare, telephone conversation, August 1977.

[41]Mary A. Toborg, *The Transition From Prison to Employment: An Assessment of Community-Based Assistance Programs,* U.S. Government Printing Office, Washington, D.C., 1978, pp. 3–4.

[42]David T. Stanley, *Prisoners Among Us: The Problem of Parole,* Brookings Institute, Washington, D.C., 1976, p. 163.

program recruited private contractors, who located 3200 jobs in a 3-month period. Even though contractors used only 200 of the jobs for offenders, the experience of utilizing public and private cooperation in a viable program was important.

Another program funded by the LEAA is the Parole and Pre-release Employment Program (PREP). Beginning in June 1974, PREP had placed 1500 offenders a year through May 29, 1977. Of inmates referred to PREP counselors before release, 97.5 percent have been employed in full-time, permanent jobs, compared with 77 percent placed by state agencies. In addition to job finding, PREP has a bonding program and offers offenders job counseling and cash loans to enable them to renew drivers' licenses, purchase clothes, or receive medical and dental treatment.[43] PREP discovered that 60 percent of those offenders who completed the orientation program obtained the jobs they sought, while only 40 percent who did not complete the orientation obtained the desired jobs.[44]

The state of Iowa began a unique experiment in 1978 with the purpose of creating jobs for offenders. The Prisoners Employment Program is a combined effort of the Department of Social Services and the Department of Transportation. According to a proposal submitted to the state legislature, selected inmates, both male and female, would receive 6 months of training at the Riverview Release Center near Newton in such fields as drafting, printing, vehicle body repair, sign painting, and keypunch operation. Following the completion of their training, they would be given employment for 1 year by the Department of Transportation. At the end of the year offenders would be expected to obtain work in private industry.[45]

One successful job-creating program is New Careers, established in the mid-1960s when labor statistics revealed a lack of jobs for skilled and semiskilled workers in spite of an increased demand for human services. Those who endorsed New Careers believed many of the duties ordinarily performed by professionals could be delegated to nonprofessionals or paraprofessionals. They believed that offenders could make important contributions toward the reintegration of other offenders, as is done by Alcoholics Anonymous. The first New Careers training program in corrections began in 1964, under J. Douglas Grant of the California Department of Corrections Medical Facility at Vacaville. Eighteen inmates were trained by teams of correctional personnel as program development assistants. After a 4-month training program, they performed tasks such as planning a project to use indigent people as teaching assistants in an elementary school summer program, conducting a survey to determine the possibilities of developing a New Careers program in state government, and training community organizers for work with the poor.[46]

[43]News Release, U.S. Department of Justice, Law Enforcement Assistance Administration, May 29, 1977.

[44]Henry R. Cellini, John Giannini, Debra L. Wright, and Dan Coughlin, "The Probation Rehabilitation and Employment Program," *Federal Probation,* vol. 41, no. 3, Administrative Office of the United States Courts, Washington, D.C., September 1977, p. 46.

[45]Prisoner Employment Program, State of Iowa, Newton, 1978, pp. 3 and 5.

[46]Goldfarb and Singer, op. cit., pp. 648–659.

Even though the inmates selected for the program were carefully screened, the results of the New Careers experiment are extraordinary. In 1971, twelve of the original eighteen inmates trained were still working in the welfare field as executives or consultants. Only one was returned to prison for a crime. The other five were employed and free but not in the welfare field. The far-flung activities of New Careers include work in New York State and the District of Columbia; in the City-Community Relations Division of Richmond, Virginia, and Los Angeles, California; and in the Probation and Parole Department of Los Angeles County.

One of the Fall 1980 issues of *Youth Alternatives* gave an account of Larry Dye, a former New Careers trainee. Serving as an administrator in the Department of Health, Education and Welfare, he was mentioned as a possible candidate for the director's position in the Office of Juvenile Justice and Delinquency Prevention.[47]

Private Job Placement Programs

One privately operated job placement program for offenders is Project Second Chance in New York City. This organization endeavors to help offenders find employment and to counsel them during their initial period of employment. Beginning in 1972, personnel of Project Second Chance made presentations explaining their program to prisoners. Application forms were passed out at several of the largest prisons in New York State, including Sing Sing, Elmira, Green Haven, and Rikers Island. At first, most prisoners were suspicious and skeptical. However, within a few months applications began to come in, and within 2 years 1000 inmates had applied. Eight hundred ex-inmates actually appeared at the Project Second Chance offices.

Personnel at Project Second Chance discussed job plans with the offenders and evaluated their plans in terms of feasibility. If the plans were impractical, a specific program of school, job training, or patient waiting was designed for each offender. During the first 2 years of operation, Project Second Chance placed about 450 ex-convicts on jobs, at a cost of $400,000. At last report in 1975, more than half these men were still working and only seven had returned to prison.[48]

A similar program for female offenders began in Oklahoma in 1976. Women Offenders Resource Center (WORC) placed 80.5 percent of the 387 female offenders referred to the program. The AFL/CIO serves as a sponsor when WORC counselors seek jobs in nontraditional fields.[49]

In 1972, the Vera Institute of Justice of New York began a supported employment program for heroin addicts. By the end of 1975 the Wildcat Service

[47]Nancy Hodgkins, "New Careers for Ex-Convicts," *London Times,* Furnival Press, London, January 8, 1971.

[48]Sol Chaneles, "A Job Program for Ex-Convicts that Works," *Psychology Today,* vol. 9, no. 10, March 1975, p. 45.

[49]Jana Mooney, Director, Women Offenders Resource Center, Oklahoma City, Oklahoma, personal correspondence, June 20, 1978.

Corporation, a nonprofit corporation which directed the program, had employed more than 1300 addicts and offenders. For Wildcat employees, working conditions and expectations are similar to those for nonsupported work, but greater emphasis is placed on employee motivation, the teaching of good work habits, and assistance with personal problems. Data collected on program participants showed that the number of arrests for the first year after entry into the program was 0.37 arrests per person-year compared to 0.43 arrests per person-year for a comparable control group. This indicated savings of about $207,000 for the New York City criminal justice system.[50]

One noteworthy private job placement effort was developed in Columbia, South Carolina. The Austin-Wilkes Society was organized for the express purpose of finding employment for persons released from prison or jail. This society offers offender-aid programs in many cities. Its activities include (1) helping the individual offender prepare for release from incarceration and readjustment to community life, (2) operating a job placement program for ex-inmates, and (3) securing support from the local business community for the job placement program. Other services include managing a halfway house, assisting families, and conducting one-to-one volunteer work. It has a staff of thirty-four and a membership of 6000. Since nearly all members perform some activities, a large amount of volunteer work is accomplished.[51]

Assistance in placing offenders on jobs can also be obtained from churches and other religious groups, mental health associations, women's clubs such as the Junior League, local chambers of commerce, the Small Business Administration offices, and civic clubs such as Rotary or Jaycees. In Illinois a statewide employment program for ex-prisoners is sponsored by the Illinois Jaycees. It coordinates private prisoner-aid groups, employment-service staff, private employers, and trade associations, for the purpose of educating the public and planning and implementing methods of developing jobs for offenders. The Illinois Jaycees program uses sales kits and other paraphernalia in order to persuade employers to hire offenders. In North Carolina the Jaycees Prison Reform Commission works to enlighten citizens about the need for prison reform and the problems of ex-prisoners.[52]

Appraisal

A report by the Pennsylvania Prison Society issued in December, 1979, stated: "Programs which simply aim to provide jobs for ex-offenders will have negligible

[50]Steven R. Balenko and Lucy N. Friedman, "The Impact of Supported Work on Arrest Rates of Ex-Addicts," *Federal Probation,* vol. 41, no. 2, Administrative Office of the United States Courts, Washington, D.C., June 1977, pp. 14, 19.

[51]Richard E. Hardy, George R. Jerrell, and John H. Wallace, "Developing Employment Opportunities for the Public Offender," *Introduction to Correctional Rehabilitation,* Richard E. Hardy and John G. Cull (eds.), Charles C Thomas Publisher, Springfield, Ill., 1973, p. 259.

[52]Jerome M. Rosow, "The Role of Jobs in a New National Strategy," *Federal Probation,* vol. 35, no. 2, Administrative Office of the United States Courts, Washington, D.C., June 1971, p. 17.

impact on criminal behavior."[53] This report confirmed the necessity for correctional officials to develop a variety of forms of community assistance for the offender. Great effort should be made to assure offenders an opportunity to work, but equally great efforts should be expended to educate the public, to recruit volunteers, to seek housing, to encourage acceptance by citizens, and to remove barriers complicating the offender's reintegration. As shown by the examples in this chapter, prisoner-aid organizations should be more than job placement agencies if they are to be successful. Both public and private agencies should carry out these activities. The private agency has the function of filling gaps in government services. Private agencies are the innovators, embarking on new ideas and services while government agencies tend to use "tried-and-true" techniques.

The use of ex-offenders as correctional personnel is an example. They served first as links between community service agencies and prisoners living in a neighborhood for private agencies—Seven Steps and the Fortune Society. Finally, beginning in 1969, they were hired in appreciable numbers by government agencies.[54] In 1977, forty-eight correctional systems reported no prohibitions against the hiring of ex-offenders and had employed a total of 315 (290 men and 25 women). Table 7.3 indicates the positions they held. More than half the ex-offenders (55 percent) were employed in offender contact positions (line staff,

[53]"Employment Research Project, Executive Summary," *The Prison Journal,* vol. LX, no. 1, Spring/Summer 1980, p. 5.
[54]Vernon Fox, *Community Based Corrections,* Prentice-Hall, Inc., Englewood Cliffs, N.J., 1977, p. 168.

TABLE 7.3
POSITIONS HELD BY EX-OFFENDER EMPLOYEES IN
AMERICAN CORRECTIONAL AGENCIES

Positions held by ex-offender employees	Number of ex-offenders employed
Line Staff (correctional officers)	103
Counselors	36
Teachers	2
Administrators	25
Clerical staff	26
Maintenance staff	70
Other:	
Parole officers	10
Parole case aides	6
Medical staff	5
Dental technician	1
Librarian	1
Physician	1
Total	286

Source: Robert R. Smith and Charles M. Petro, "An Updated Survey of Four Policies and Practices in American Adult Corrections," *Journal of Criminal Justice,* vol. 8, no. 2, 1980, p. 125.

counselors, and teachers). Today the ex-offender is hired because he or she has the best credentials and capabilities for the job.

Finally, private and public prisoner-aid organizations can learn from successful job placements. Nearly all effective company programs for hiring and training offenders are characterized by careful assignment, an inclusive orientation program, and unwavering confidentiality. Indispensable are competent management staff and a comprehensive follow-up program, operating even after the offender has been accepted as a permanent employee. Companies that have failed to work out a successful program exhibited a lack of commitment or real concern for the offender and offered insufficient training and job opportunity. General employer pessimism, even before the program started, was a significant factor in its failure.[55]

COMMUNITY ASSISTANCE FOR THE OFFENDER'S FAMILY

Rationale

Traditionally, emphasis on the offender's family as a special problem has been only through crisis intervention. However, studies exploring the inmate's community relationships have discovered that the prisoner's family is an important link in preparing the community for the offender.

Lloyd Ohlin, a criminologist, studied the connection between family ties and parole success. Using a sample of inmates released between 1925 and 1935, he found that 75 percent of the inmates classified as maintaining "active family interest" while in prison succeeded after release. This can be contrasted with 34 percent considered loners, who failed on parole.

In a similar study of 1956 offenders released from federal prisons, Daniel Glaser found 71 percent of the "active-family-interest" group successful on parole, compared with only 50 percent of the "no-contact-with-relatives" group. In an earlier study of Illinois State Penitentiary prisoners released between 1940 and 1949, Glaser found a 74 percent parole success rate in the "active-family-interest" group and a 43 percent success rate for those parolees without in-prison family contacts.

Using more definite criteria, California researchers Norman Holt and Donald Miller conducted a similar study, called "Exploration in Inmate-Family Relationships." Of the men studied, 70 percent of those with three or more continuing visitors experienced no parole difficulty. Those with no visitors were 6 times more likely to be sent back to prison during the first year of parole.[56]

Yet, despite the encouraging findings in these studies, the criminal justice system hinders the relationship between offenders and their families. Throughout arrest, trial, and incarceration, the families do not receive sufficient information to interpret these occurrences. Lawyers are inaccessible, jail visits

[55]Gopal C. Pati, "Business Can Make Ex-Convicts Productive," *Harvard Business Review,* vol. 52, no. 3, May/June 1974, pp. 75–78.

[56]Eva Lee Homer, "Inmate-Family Ties, Desirable But Difficult," *Federal Probation,* vol. 43, no. 1, Administrative Office of the United States Courts, Washington, D.C., March 1979, pp. 48–49.

are inconclusive, and even some sentencing procedures (indeterminate sentences) make it impossible for families to know when their loved ones will be home. Frequently, visiting regulations and the distant location of many state and federal prisons make visiting itself difficult. The obvious communication problems, the lack of and uncertainty about financial resources, and the need to concentrate on caring for themselves at the expense of the offender's welfare contribute to the unsatisfactory situation. Social services specifically designed to assist offenders' families are nonexistent. Thus the offender's family constitutes a real dilemma for correctional personnel working in the community.

Friends Outside

One way of keeping prisoners in contact with their families is to create organizations like Friends Outside, founded in California in 1954. Friends Outside is based on a California Department of Corrections research report that concluded, "There is a strong and consistently positive relationship between parole success and the maintenance of strong family ties while in prison." The group provides outreach to families (crisis intervention, information about prison life), hospitality centers offering overnight lodging and child care, transportation, prerelease and postrelease counseling, and family support groups.[57] By 1981, Friends Outside had thirty-four satellite offices, including twenty county chapters and six prison representatives, located throughout California and Nevada. More than 1000 volunteers work in the program.[58]

In Kansas there are three similar organizations—Leavenworth-Lansing's Outside Connection, Topeka's Friends and Families of Offenders, and Wichita's Friends and Families of Prisoners. A Hartford, Connecticut, volunteer program assists offenders by creating a support system for their families. Known as Women in Crisis, the group uses volunteers as the key "professionals." Families of offenders are identified the day of court sentencing and are provided with information about prison rules and routines. They are accompanied to the prison for visits, assisted in coping with residence and financial problems, and offered friendship.[59]

Comparable organizations have been formed for families of inmates in jails. The Service League of San Mateo County, California, is an example. The League, which began in 1961, operates an information table in the jail lobby. Volunteers or personnel interview new admissions to learn of the families' needs. The League sponsors a message program at the jail, each day picking up and acting on inmates' requests for family assistance. Other services are equivalent to those offered families of prison inmates.[60]

[57]"Services for Inmates' Families," *Criminal Justice Newsletter,* vol. 12, no. 15, July 20, 1981, pp. 6–7.

[58]*Annual Report, 1980,* Friends Outside, Salmos, Calif., 1981.

[59]Susan Hoffman Fishman and Albert S. Alissi, "Strengthening Families as Natural Support System For Offenders," *Federal Probation,* vol. 43, no. 3, Administrative Office of the United States Courts, Washington, D.C., September 1979, p. 17.

[60]"Services for Inmates' Families," op. cit., p. 7.

A Model for Delivery of Community Services

Correctional practitioners Joanne Sterling and Robert Harty have suggested a model for delivery of community services to offenders and their families. They propose that a physical facility be centrally located and used as a program center. Such a facility may be a halfway house or a drop-in center similar to that in a drug treatment program. It can serve as the hub for a vast number of direct services available to offenders, both felons and misdemeanants. Other program components are prerelease preparation of the offender, a volunteer program, transitional living facilities, vocational counseling, job placement, social outreach services, a loan fund, therapeutic recreation, and special assistance for wives and families of prisoners.[61]

Delancy Street Foundation

The Delancy Street Foundation in San Francisco is a self-help, residential, therapeutic community founded in 1971 by John Maher. Its purpose is to help ex-convicts, drug addicts, and anyone else who seeks assistance in the community. Each person enters the Delancy Street project "cold turkey." The use of "games" is central to the program. These are group techniques whereby peers attack members of the foundation and visitors for behaviors they feel are self-destructive. Members attend college, vocational school, an accredited in-house high school, or private schools. Participants may work for one of the businesses operated by the Delancy Street Foundation, including a flower and terrarium delivery service, a sidewalk café and restaurant, an automobile garage, a moving company, an advertising specialties sales force, and a construction business. Members of Delancy Street take part in many community services, including counseling young children and consulting with prison administrators. Members are encouraged to form volunteer political clubs and to take part in various community advocacy programs.[62]

A Mental Health Service Delivery System

The field of mental health offers another valuable model. In 1968, under the sponsorship of the Missouri Institute of Psychiatry at the St. Louis State Hospital, a foster-community project was established. Following a period of public education about the project and other mental-health-related issues, programs were begun in New Haven and Troy, Missouri, to place long-term hospital patients in the community. The foster community served as a total supportive environment, with mental patients living with other townspeople or on their own in rented houses or apartments. A voluntary, nonprofit corporation

---

[61]Joanne W. Sterling and Robert W. Harty, "An Alternative Model of Community Services for Ex-Offenders and Their Families," *Federal Probation,* vol. 36, no. 3, Administrative Office of the United States Courts, Washington, D.C., 1972, pp. 32–33.

[62]Charles Hampden-Turner, *Sane Asylum,* San Francisco Book Company, Inc., San Francisco, 1976, pp. 7–8, 16, and 27.

in each town and a psychiatric hospital team (psychiatrist, social worker, and psychiatric nurse) shared responsibility for the patients in a novel partnership arrangement. Women's clubs, church groups, the Rotary, and Kiwanis all assisted in the conversion of New Haven and Troy into foster communities. Within 3 years, sixteen patients who had spent 6 to 12 years in the state hospital moved to Troy. Townspeople served as community sponsors and organized group activities to welcome mental patients to their community and encourage their relationship with community members. Troy celebrated the third anniversary of its program on May 13, 1974. During that time 153 patients had been hosted by sixty-one families in thirty-one houses.[63]

CONCLUSION

Just as offenders should be helped to integrate themselves into the community, so the community should be prepared to receive the offenders.[64] The fundamental idea upon which corrections focusing on the community is based is to provide offenders with the assistance they need by utilizing the services that already exist in the community. It requires delivering the offender to the service or, if necessary, delivering the service to the offender. This means that correctional personnel, community agency personnel, and volunteers work cooperatively to this end. It also requires public insistence that community agencies provide the same services to offenders as they do to the rest of the population.

Offenders have historically encountered difficulty in achieving success goals through legitimate means because of the restrictiveness of the opportunity structure. They lack both access to social institutions which control chances for achievement and the high degree of social integration necessary in order to use legitimate opportunities. An offender who is married, has social ties in the community, participates in social organizations, and has employment has a better prognosis for not relapsing into crime than has one without these ties.[65]

The first and most significant level of correctional decision making lies in the degree of citizen, family, and community agency tolerance of the offender. The second most significant occurs when the offender is brought into contact with the formal helping agencies in the community. Through the creation of certain helping agencies and the exclusion of others, each community defines for itself those kinds of offenders which it is willing to accept.[66]

The mobilization of community assistance for the offender plays a strategic part in his or her integration. Civic clubs and fraternal organizations can provide a forum. Unions can play a central role by breaking down employment barriers

---

[63]Suzanne Fields, "Foster Communities for the Mentally Ill," *Innovations,* vol. I, no. 3, Fall 1974, pp. 4, 7, 8, and 10.

[64]Robert G. Caldwell, *Criminology,* Ronald Press Company, New York, 1965, p. 671.

[65]George W. Knox, "Differential Integration and Job Retention Among Ex-Offenders," *Criminology,* vol. 18, no. 4, February 1981, p. 483.

[66]E. Eugene Miller and M. Robert Montilla, *Corrections in the Community,* Reston Publishing Company, Reston, Va., 1977, p. 7.

and encouraging industry to accept a philosophy of integration. Churches can perform a vital function by inviting offenders to become part of church life (e.g., potluck suppers, Sunday services, and other church-related programs). The employers in industry must be apprised of offenders' special problems and then be willing to employ and otherwise assist them. Government agencies can help by reinforcing the various community resources.

A total community effort must also include wide participation by individual citizens. Each member of the community has a stake in the offender's integration. All helping agencies diminish in significance when compared to the importance of citizen participation. Consequently, all members of the community should be prepared to assist each offender to build a firm foundation for community living. Integration, to be effective, must begin the moment he or she has contact with the criminal justice system. A favorable environment must be established in which the cultural expectation is that the offender has a chance to be integrated. In the final analysis, extensive citizen involvement will provide the pillars of support for successful integration, and developing community assistance for the offender will be a wise investment of the professional's time.

EXERCISES

1 What steps would you take to minimize the effect of practices within the criminal justice system which perpetuate the criminal stigma of the ex-offender?

2 Which of the "publics" do you believe is most vital for a successful public education program? Support your answer with evidence.

3 You have been given the task of educating the public in an area proposed for a new community program in corrections. Design an education program, placing segments in chronological order.

4 "In many cases, an inmate panel or speaker presents a more salable story than salaried correctional personnel." Do you agree or disagree with this statement? Give your reasons.

5 With the difficulties encountered in volunteer programs clearly in mind, what functions do you believe volunteers could perform most profitably for the corrections department? Give reasons for your answer.

6 How could you minimize "the subtle pressures" placed on volunteers by offenders or ex-offenders? Explain fully.

7 List advantages and disadvantages of volunteer programs operated by ex-offenders. Conclude with your opinion of their overall applicability.

8 Obviously, research has not conclusively proven volunteer programs to be successful. Do you believe they should be continued? Why or why not?

9 List steps you would take to create a more successful job placement program for persons released from prison. Include suggestions to increase the percentage of offenders who remain on release jobs and the percentage of those assisted by state employment services.

10 Could the problem of prisoners seeking employment in the community be partially resolved by a more efficient prison vocational training program? Explain.

11 You are a parole officer and you must "sell" parolees to private business. What

advantages and disadvantages would an ex-offender offer a company? Explain each one fully.

12 Using suggestions by Sterling and Harty as a guide, recommend a plan which would prepare the community for the offender. Where would you start? Is it an ongoing or a temporary program?

13 Who should assume responsibility for the prisoner's wife—prison personnel, local social welfare agencies, volunteer groups? Defend your answer.

14 Compare and contrast the Delancy Street Foundation with the Foster Community project. Conclude with your recommendations and your preference.

EXERCISE REFERENCES

Balenko, Steven R., and Lucy N. Friedman: "The Impact of Supported Work on Arrest Rates of Ex-Addicts," *Federal Probation*, vol. 41, no. 2, Administrative Office of the United States Courts, Washington, D.C., June 1977, pp. 14–20.

Bowker, Leo H.: "Volunteers in Correctional Settings: Benefits, Problems and Solutions," *Proceedings of the One Hundred and Fourth Annual Congress of Corrections*, American Correctional Association, College Park, Md., 1975, pp. 298–322.

Buckley, Marie: "Enter: The Ex-Con," *Federal Probation*, vol. 36, no. 4, Administrative Office of the United States Courts, Washington, D.C., December 1972, pp. 24–30.

Cellini, Henry, John Giannini, Debra L. Wright, and Dan Coughlin: "The Probation Rehabilitation and Employment Program," *Federal Probation*, vol. 41, no. 3, Administrative Office of the United States Courts, Washington, D.C., September 1977, pp. 42–46.

Chaneles, Sol: "A Job Program for Ex-Convicts That Works," *Psychology Today*, vol. 9, no. 10, March 1975, pp. 43–46.

Dale, Mitchell W.: "Barriers to the Rehabilitation of Ex-Offenders," *Crime and Delinquency*, vol. 22, no. 3, July 1976, pp. 322–337.

Fields, Suzanne: "Foster Communities for the Mentally Ill," *Innovations*, vol. 1, no. 3, Fall 1974, pp. 3–10.

Fishman, Susan Hoffman, and Albert S. Alissi: "Strengthening Families as Natural Support Systems for Offenders," *Federal Probation*, vol. 43, no. 3, Administrative Office of the United States Courts, Washington, D.C., September 1979, pp. 16–21.

Gilman, Andrew D.: "Legal Barriers to Jobs Are Slowly Disappearing," *Corrections Magazine*, vol. 5, no. 4, December 1979, pp. 68–72.

Gooch, David, and William W. Wright, Jr.: "Volunteers Establish Guidelines for Volunteers," *Corrections Today*, vol. 43, no. 4, July/August 1981, pp. 48, 52.

Gordon, Arthur: "M-2: New Formula for Wasted Lives," *The Rotarian*, August 1 970, pp. 36–38, 40, and 50.

Grindstaff, Gordon: "Practical Help for the Beginning Volunteer," *Corrections Today*, vol. 42, no. 4, July/August 1980, pp. 82–83.

———: "Volunteers: An Invaluable Resource at Cook County Jail," *Corrections Today*, vol. 42, no. 4, July/August 1980, pp. 86–87.

Hampden-Turner, Charles: *Sane Asylum*, San Francisco Book Company, Inc., San Francisco, 1976.

Hess, Allen K., and Raymond L. Frank, Jr.: "Predictors of Success in Community-Based

Preparole Corrections Centers," *Offender Rehabilitation,* vol. 2, no. 2, 1977, pp. 111–126.

Heyns, Garrett: "What the Public Should Know About Adult Corrections," *Federal Probation,* vol. 2, no. 1, Administrative Office of the United States Courts, Washington, D.C., March 1964, pp. 11–15.

Hill, Gary: "How to Improve Our Public Image," *American Journal of Correction,* vol. 32, no. 6, November/December 1970, pp. 44–46.

Holt, Norman, and Donald Miller: *Explorations in Inmate-Family Relationships,* Report Number 46, Department of Corrections, Sacramento, Calif., January 1972.

Homer, Eva Lee: "Inmate-Family Ties, Desirable But Difficult," *Federal Probation,* vol. 43, no. 1, Administrative Office of the United States Courts, Washington, D.C., March 1979, pp. 47–52.

Kiersh, Ed: "A Private California Agency Likes to Keep Prisoners and Their Families Together," *Corrections Magazine,* vol. 5, no. 3, September 1979, pp. 39–42.

Kirby, Bernard C.: "Crofton House, An Experiment With a County Halfway House," *Federal Probation,* vol. 33, no. 1, Administrative Office of the United States Courts, Washington, D.C., March 1969, pp. 53–58.

Leenhouts, Keith J.: "Royal Oak's Experience with Professionals and Volunteers in Probation," *Federal Probation,* vol. 34, no. 4, Administrative Office of the United States Courts, Washington, D.C., December 1970, pp. 45–51.

Margolin, Reuben J.: "Post Institutional Rehabilitation of the Penal Offender: A Community Effort," *Federal Probation,* vol. 31, no. 1, Administrative Office of the United States Courts, Washington, D.C., March 1967, pp. 46–50.

Morris, Norval: *The Future of Imprisonment,* University of Chicago Press, Chicago, 1974.

O'Leary, Vincent: "Some Directions for Citizen Involvement in Corrections," *The Annals of the American Academy of Political and Social Science,* no. 38, January 1969, pp. 99–108.

Palmer-Paulson Associates, Inc.: *Excel in Indiana,* Chicago, 1973, pp. 16–17.

Pati, Gopal C.: "Business Can Make Ex-Convicts Productive," *Harvard Business Review,* vol. 2, no. 3, May/June 1974, pp. 69–78.

Pownall, George A.: "Employment Problems of Released Prisoners," *Manpower,* vol. 3, no. 1, U.S. Government Printing Office, Washington, D.C., January 1971.

Reed, John P., and Dale Nance: "Society Perpetuates the Stigma of Conviction," *Federal Probation,* vol. 36, no. 2, Administrative Office of the United States Courts, Washington, D.C., June 1972, pp. 27–31.

Rosow, Jerome M.: "The Role of Jobs in a New National Strategy," *Federal Probation,* vol. 35, no. 2, Administrative Office of the United States Courts, Washington, D.C., June 1971, pp. 14–18.

Scheier, Ivan H.: "The Professional and the Volunteer in Probation: Perspectives on an Emerging Relationship," *Federal Probation,* vol. 34, no. 2, Administrative Office of the United States Courts, Washington, D.C., June 1970, pp. 12–18.

Schwartz, Mary C., and Judith F. Weintraub: "The Prisoner's Wife: A Study in Crisis," *Federal Probation,* vol. 38, no. 4, Administrative Office of the United States Courts, Washington, D.C., December 1974, pp. 20–26.

Schwartz, Richard D., and Jerome H. Skolnick, "Two Studies of Legal Stigma," *Social Problems,* vol. 10, no. 1, Fall 1962, pp. 134–138.

Scioli, Frank P., and Thomas J. Cook: "How Effective Are Volunteers?" *Crime and Delinquency,* vol. 22, no. 2, April 1976, pp. 192–200.

Shields, Linda F.: "Developing a Volunteer Program," *Corrections Today,* vol. 43, no. 4, July/August 1981, pp. 24–26.

Sterling, Joanne W., and Robert W. Harty: "An Alternative Model of Community Services for Ex-Offenders and Their Families," *Federal Probation,* vol. 36, no. 3, Administrative Office of the United States Courts, Washington, D.C., September 1972, pp. 31–34.

Stoeckel, John: "The Use of Volunteers in Juvenile Probation," *Corrections in the Community,* E. Eugene Miller and M. Robert Montilla (eds.), Reston Publishing Company, Inc., Reston, Va., 1977, pp. 52–73.

Treger, Harvey: "Reluctance of the Social Agency to Work With the Offender," *Federal Probation,* vol. 29, no. 1, Administrative Office of the United States Courts, Washington, D.C., March 1965, pp. 23–28.

Unitarian Universalist Service Committee: "Employment and Ex-Offender," no. 20, Washington, D.C., Spring 1980, p. 10.

Unkovic, Charles E., and Jean Reiman Davis: "Volunteers in Probation and Parole," *Federal Probation,* vol. 33, no. 4, Administrative Office of the United States Courts, Washington, D.C., December 1969, pp. 41–45.

Weintraub, Judith F.: "The Delivery of Services to Families of Prisoners," *Federal Probation,* vol. 40, no. 4, Administrative Office of the United States Courts, Washington, D.C., December 1976, pp. 28–31.

THE TRANSITION TO THE COMMUNITY

CHAPTER OBJECTIVES

- To explain the meaning of "bridges to the community"
- To describe work release, study release, temporary releases, and supervised trips
- To discuss the administration of community-based corrections
- To explain the process of selection and supervision of offenders for community-based corrections
- To examine evaluations of work release and temporary releases

INTRODUCTION

Preparing the offender for the community can be accomplished by "community-like prisons" and prerelease classes. Equally important is creating resources within the community. Public education can develop a receptive climate. Volunteers can serve as friends and mentors. Jobs can be found through public and private job placement programs. In fact, a total-service delivery system can be set up in the community. However, regardless of the extent of the offender's preparation for unsupervised living and the number of community resources available to assist him or her, all efforts can be wasted if successful transition from correctional supervision to unsupervised community living is not achieved.

Many correctional officials realize the debilitating effects of prisonization and make an effort to build "bridges" from correctional institutions to the community. Within the past 20 years, more than half the states in the United States have developed various forms of intermediate steps between confinement, parole, and expiration of sentence. Some of these bridges are work release, furloughs, day passes, and supervised trips. Each is a constructive activity designed by correctional administrators to help offenders adjust to the lessening of correctional supervision. Each bridge allows closer observation and control than probation or parole, yet permits relatively normal contact with the community.

BRIDGES TO THE COMMUNITY

Rationale

All forms of bridges have the common objective of giving an offender the opportunity to practice law-abiding behavior. Correctional officials hope that practicing acceptable behavior during supervised release will encourage continuation of such behavior after complete release. The offender becomes gradually accustomed to life in the community and reestablishes family ties and other appropriate relationships, lessening the culture shock of going from total incarceration to complete freedom on release. In this sense, supervised trips, temporary releases, work release, and study release are classified as techniques of reintegration.

Although few states have tried to apply these techniques in a coordinated program, it is possible to apply them as a system of gradual release. Felons can be released more safely and successfully if each step in the process is closely scrutinized by correctional personnel. During each trip into the community, staff members retain the option of withdrawing offenders from participation in the program or of increasing the degree of freedom. Careful observation allows immediate help to be offered to offenders who appear to be having difficulty adjusting to community living. If they behave in a manner indicating a potential for violence, they are removed from the community; when they exhibit socially responsible behavior, they are allowed more frequent and less structured community contact for longer periods.

Supervised Trips

For many prisoners, the first contact with the free community is through trips under direct supervision. Inmates are transported by correctional personnel, who stay throughout the visit. The supervised trips supplement institutional programs by permitting attendance at church and vocational and academic classes. Some states allow supervised trips for recreation and social purposes, with inmates attending such activities as a church potluck supper, service club luncheon, sports event, or movie. Twelve states even allow inmates to pursue college degrees while accompanied by correctional personnel.[1]

---

[1]Bertram S. Griggs and Gary R. McCune, "Community Correctional Programs: A Survey and Analysis," *Federal Probation,* vol. 36, no. 1, Administrative Office of the United States Courts, Washington, D.C., June 1972, p. 10.

Temporary Releases

Another form of community contact is a temporary release. There are two types—day passes and furloughs. The day pass is a 1- to -24-hour pass allowing an offender to leave correctional supervision for a specific period, accompanied by a responsible person (spouse, friend, employer, or volunteer). While absent from the place of residence, he or she remains with the approved companion and is subject to the same rules of behavior as when under direct supervision of correctional personnel.

The furlough is an approved absence of an inmate from correctional supervision for a specified period without the accompaniment of any other person. A furlough may last for a few hours, for 1 day, or for 10 days, with the maximum time limit determined by law. The felon is subject to the same regulations as those remaining at the correctional residence.

Work and Study Release

A final form of bridge to the community is work release or study release, which can best be defined by this excerpt from a work release law:

> The department of corrections shall establish a work release program under which inmates sentenced to an institution under the jurisdiction of adult authorities may be granted the privilege of leaving actual confinement during necessary and reasonable hours for the purpose of working at gainful employment in this state. Under appropriate conditions the program may also include release for the purpose of attendance at an institution (vocational or academic). Inmates may also be allowed to be self-employed or perform housekeeping in their domicile.[2]

Work release and study release are designed to assist in total community adjustment. In contrast to the short periods of release time allowed by a furlough or pass, the offenders enter the community on each work or school day, leaving correctional supervision in the morning and returning to supervision in the evening. During the time of absence there is no direct supervision, and the offenders assume complete responsibility for their behavior.

GOALS

Correctional administrators and designers of correctional strategy have advocated a number of possible goals for transitional techniques of offender reintegration. Although most advocacy has resulted from their perceived need to justify the offender's temporary release from prison, all forms of bridges to the community are just as applicable for jail inmates and residents of halfway houses or community correctional centers.

---

[2]*The Work Release Program,* Bureau of Adult Corrections Services, Des Moines, Iowa, 1969, p. 2.

Sentencing Options

The use of bridges gives flexibility to the sentencing practices of judges. For both felons and misdemeanants, judges can offer alternatives to the orthodox prison or jail sentence. Placing probationers "halfway in" a community-based residence with the stipulation that they be granted work release reduces the potential harm of total disruption of a person's life.

Cost Reduction

The use of bridges decreases the financial burden on the taxpayer. The work releasees pay some of the costs of their imprisonment. They partially support their dependents, who might otherwise require public assistance. They pay income taxes, fines, and court costs. They make restitution to the victims of their crimes or to the community.

Maintenance of Family and Community Ties

When offenders support their dependents, they are continuing their status as heads of families, retaining their affection and respect as breadwinners, parents, and spouses. They are also permitted a sensitive and practical way to have conjugal visits. Friends and acquaintances continue their ties to the offenders. Attendance at church and civic organizations is uninterrupted. They are not seen as absent from their neighborhoods.

Positive Effect on Attitudes

Bridges have a positive effect on offenders' attitudes and behavior. They have an opportunity to lessen the feelings of frustration, anger, and helplessness that accompany absorption into the criminal justice system. They have a chance to test their perceptions of the environments in which they will live after release.

Alternative to Incarceration

Reformers have been appalled at the debilitating effects of incarceration on the initiative, self-respect, and value system of confined offenders. Contact with the community, even for only part of the day, can diminish the negative effects. This factor is especially important in a country that has one of the highest rates of imprisonment per 100,000 population in the world, i.e., 200 per 100,000 population, compared with 59 for the United Kingdom and 63 for Sweden.

Period of Transition

For prison and jail inmates temporary releases, work release, and study release become transition periods between the place of total confinement and the community. The half-free status of the inmate can serve as a bridge between life in prison and life after release or before confinement. For the incoming prisoner, jobs can be retained. For the outgoing prisoner, jobs can be obtained. The transition period is used by correctional administrators to determine the inmate's readiness for parole or expiration of sentence.

Public Conception of Offender

The public's attitudes can be reshaped by having felons and misdemeanants in their midst. The offender's image as a totally evil and dangerous being can be tempered. Notions of retribution can be counteracted by offender participation in community life. Employers, friends, and acquaintances become advocates for corrections.

Final Phase of Institutional Program

Bridges complement the educational, vocational, and therapy program of the correctional institution. Work release can be a valuable alternative to a work assignment in prison industry. Study release can increase an offender's aptitude for the "paper chase." Furloughs can permit offenders to confirm their career aspirations, leisure-time interests, and family plans.[3]

SELECTION OF CANDIDATES

Selectors

The first step in the administration of community-based corrections is the selection of offenders who will participate. Applicants requesting temporary releases must generally be approved by correctional employees, usually an institutional staff committee, with a review by the institution's superintendent. Selectors of work releasees vary from state to state. Three government bodies have most frequently been given the responsibility for determining which offenders will be allowed to participate in work release: the sentencing court, the parole board, and the department of corrections. In some states a combination of the three is used to approve work release applicants. In Pennsylvania, for example, legislation restricts correctional authorities from approving an applicant for work release over the objection of the sentencing court. The New York legislature has placed the responsibility for approval jointly on the divisions of corrections and parole. The warden of each institution gives final approval after the chairman of the board of parole has established preliminary eligibility.[4]

---

[3]Elmer H. Johnson, "Work Release: Conflicting Goals Within a Promising Innovation", *Canadian Journal of Corrections,* vol. 72, no. 1, 1970, pp. 67–77.

[4]Lawrence S. Root, "Work Release Legislation," *Federal Probation,* vol. 36, no. 1, Administrative Office of the United States Courts, Washington, D.C., March 1972, p. 39.

Eligibility Requirements and Restrictions

Most state legislatures have not attempted to enact eligibility requirements for community-based corrections; they prefer to give this responsibility to the government bodies designated to select the candidates. Consequently, state legislation is worded in general terms to provide considerable discretion. "Not a high security risk," "trustworthy," "likely to be rehabilitated by such a program," are typical statements from work release laws. However, there are exceptions: Illinois prohibits participation of offenders convicted of kidnapping, treason, and murder; South Dakota, those convicted of rape, mayhem, and assault with intent to commit great bodily harm; and Massachusetts, those convicted of robbery and lascivious acts. In a 1973 survey, twelve states excluded individuals whose offenses were accompanied by heavy media coverage or notoriety. Other restrictions are listed in Table 8.1.

TABLE 8.1
CRITERIA FOR EXCLUSION FROM WORK RELEASE
PROGRAMS BY OFFENSE OR BACKGROUND, 1973

	Violence	Sexual crimes	Narcotics sale	Narcotics use	Notoriety	Organized crime
California	X	X	X			
Connecticut	X	X	X	X	X	X
Florida		X	X			X
Georgia	X				X	X
Illinois	X	X	X	X	X	X
Indiana	X	X	X	X	X	
Louisiana	X		X	X		
Massachusetts	X	X				
Maryland	X	X	X	X	X	
Michigan	X	X	X			X
Minnesota	X	X	X	X		
Montana	X				X	
New Jersey	X	X	X		X	X
New Mexico	X					X
New York	X	X	X	X		
North Carolina		X	X	X	X	
South Carolina		X	X	X	X	
South Dakota	X	X				
Texas	X	X	X	X		X
Virginia		X	X	X		
Washington	X				X	
Wisconsin	X	X				
Totals	20	18	16	12	12	10

Source: Lawrence S. Root, "Work Release Legislation," *Federal Probation,* vol. 36, no. 1, Administrative Office of the United States Courts, Washington, D.C., March 1972, p. 39.

Parole eligibility is a prerequisite in some states. Minnesota requires the offender to be under parole consideration when approved for community-based corrections. Tennessee requires that the work release candidate be a "first term inmate without a prior record of thirty days (30) or more detention upon a conviction for a felonious crime."[5] A number of legal restrictions include length of time remaining on sentence, opposition by local police, proximity to parole release date, and conviction of major crimes.

In some states criteria for selection of work releasees have consistently included a lengthy institutional stay. A report released by California officials in 1976 revealed that the median time spent in correctional institutions by work releasees was 31 months; only 17 percent of those approved during 1975–1976 served 18 or fewer months in prison.[6] New York requires that applicants be within 1 year of parole review or sentence expiration.[7] In most states, however, approval for work release, study release, or temporary releases is judged solely on individual need and the qualifications of the applicant.

Probationers and Misdemeanants

Although work release, study release, and temporary releases were originally established for incarcerated offenders, probationers can also benefit from them. Assigning a probationer to a halfway house with an opportunity to be released on furlough or work release is a viable alternative to imprisonment. It prevents some offenders from being sent to prison because judges are faced with only two choices—prison or probation.

Many states and cities are developing release programs from jails and halfway houses for misdemeanants who appear to need close supervision. Wisconsin and North Carolina were pioneers in this phase of community-based corrections, allowing the judge to recommend placement at the time of sentencing.

Unfortunately, many state legislatures have eliminated probationers and misdemeanants from such programs, because participation is limited to felons near final release. New Jersey, for example, limits furloughs to offenders who are within 3 months of parole or 1 month from expiration of sentence.[8]

Questions Frequently Asked

When candidates are being considered for placement on work release, study release, or temporary release, these six questions are most frequently asked:

[5] *Tennessee Code*, 1970, chap. 41–1802.

[6] *Demographic Characteristics of Male Felons Placed on Work Furlough Program: Institution Based Community Correctional Center Fiscal Years 1974–1975 and 1975–1976*, Department of Corrections, Health and Welfare Agency, State of California, November 22, 1976.

[7] Susan Sheehan, "Annals of Crime" (Prison Life-Part I) *The New Yorker*, October 24, 1977, p. 50.

[8] Carson W. Markley, "Furlough Programs and Conjugal Visiting in Adult Correctional Institutions," *Federal Probation*, vol. 37, no. 1, Administrative Office of the United States Courts, Washington, D.C., March 1973, p. 23.

1 Does community-based corrections fit the needs of the applicant? Each applicant's needs are evaluated individually to determine which form of contact with the community is most appropriate or if reintegration can be more efficiently accomplished by another method.

2 Is the state wasting its time in the offender's reintegration process by placing him or her in the community? Will the offender attempt to beat the system? Is a longer period of incarceration needed to develop better controls?

3 Can the applicant be classified as a nondangerous offender? Is there likely to be any harm or threat to anyone in the community either accidentally or intentionally? It may be advisable to seek a professional evaluation for an offender with a history of rape, child molestation, or violent behavior.

4 Does the applicant's prearrest history, probation records, and institutional adjustment imply readiness for community-based corrections? Does his or her current adjustment justify a further extension of freedom? What is the likelihood that the offender will remain crime-free during absence from direct supervision?

5 Did the applicant volunteer for the program? In almost all states, the participant in community-based corrections volunteers. However, in the case of a person who prefers incarceration and will be ending a sentence, correctional personnel occasionally initiate community-based corrections on his or her behalf.

6 Is the applicant in good physical and mental health? Through examination by either physicians, correctional diagnostic teams, or community-based residence staff, the applicant is confirmed as having a healthy mind and body, capable of functioning in the community.

PREPARATION OF A COMMUNITY-BASED CORRECTIONS PLAN

Procedure

After the eligibility of an offender—whether an incarcerated felon, probationer, or misdemeanant—for community-based corrections has been established, actual entrance into the community takes place only after a specific plan has been approved by correctional officials. The procedure for approval of a work release, study release, or temporary release plan follows a similar pattern in all states. A request is submitted in writing to correctional officials. When furloughs or passes are being considered, the plan states the purpose of temporary release, method of transportation, place of residence, and date and time of departure and return. An offender eligible for work release or study release submits a plan that specifies employer or school, method of transportation, place of residence, and a proposed budget.

Work or study releasees are allowed to attend vocational or academic classes, perform housekeeping in their domicile, maintain self-employment, or obtain a job. Correctional authorities permit temporary releases for home visits, job interviews, school interviews, medical care, an illness or death in the family, volunteer work, short-term training, specialized treatment, family counseling, recreation, civic or social activities, residence interviews, driver's license examinations, insurance applications, religious services, Alcoholics Anonymous or other drug group attendance, panel discussions, and radio or television interviews.

Housing

Regardless of the purpose of work release, study release, or temporary release, many factors are considered before correctional officials approve an individual community-based corrections plan. Housing, particularly, receives careful deliberation. Before approving housing, correctional officials consider the amount of supervision available, proximity to place of work, physical condition of housing, neighborhood of residence, and nearness to community resources. Places most frequently accepted as residences for both work or study releasees and temporary releasees are state institutions, county jails, residential housing units, community correctional centers, and contracted housing. In addition, temporary releasees are allowed to reside in the private homes of family members. Contracted housing might include an alcoholic or other drug treatment center, a YMCA or YWCA, or a hotel.

Employment

Correctional officials consider the type of employment for the work releasee as another key factor. Approval of a job in the work release plan is preceded by the establishment of a number of prerequisites: (1) The work releasee is not to be placed in skill areas where there is a surplus of labor or where replacement of another worker would occur. (2) The offender may be placed only in jobs where conditions and pay are equal to those for ordinary citizens. (3) The offender must not become a strike-breaker.[9] Fortunately, problems with employment appear to be more the exception than the rule. In a few instances employers have attempted to exploit the work releasee, but this is infrequently. However, potentially stressful situations do arise around company social functions such as office parties and picnics in which employees typically participate and bring their families. Most jurisdictions prohibit participation by the offender in these activities, although a few states have considered company social functions beneficial and have accepted the responsibility for authorizing an offender's involvement.[10]

---

[9]Root, "Work Release Legislation," op. cit. p. 42.

[10]William A. Ayer, "Work Release: A Pre-Release Program," *Introduction to Correctional Rehabilitation,* Richard E. Hardy and John G. Cull (eds.), Charles C Thomas Publisher, Springfield, Ill., 1973, p. 66.

Transportation

Transportation is another important factor. It is usually available by public conveyance or offered by the offender's family. Yet the means of traveling to and from their places of employment or school has been a consistent problem for some work or study releasees. In most instances, the problem has been resolved through use of state vehicles, personal cars, or participation in car pools. Occasionally, transportation has been provided by hiring residents as drivers for state vehicles, which has the advantage of creating additional jobs for work releasees at the same time the transportation problem is solved.[11] In some rural areas where transportation is not available, offenders may be permitted to remain away from the correctional residence during the workweek, staying in a hotel or private home, but required to return to the institution or community-based residence on holidays and weekends.

Other Questions

Many other questions are asked. Some of these are: How long can the offender remain in the community without being overwhelmed by anxiety? (Massachusetts limits the number of days an inmate may be on furlough to 14 days in any 1 year.) Does the offender possess sufficient capabilities to achieve the proposed vocational or academic goals? How responsible are the people who are assisting with transportation? Will the offender have sufficient funds to finance the proposed plan? These questions are frequently answered by probation officers, social workers, teachers, work supervisors, correctional officers, or parole officers. A telephone call or letter often helps to determine the appropriateness of the proposed plan.

SUPERVISION OF THE OFFENDER

Carrying Out the Plan

After being approved for a specified plan, the offender enters the community. While absent from correctional supervision, he or she is expected to carry out the plan, usually outlined in a "contract." This document specifies the terms of the plan, its duration, basic rules of conduct, any special conditions, and any necessary information, such as the phone number of the institution of origin.

At this point, administration by correctional officials is concerned primarily with helping the offender and protecting the public. A number of services are provided, of which counseling is one. Many state departments of correction and the Federal Bureau of Prisons employ correctional counselors, social workers, or work release coordinators to help the offender resolve marriage and family problems, employer-employee difficulties, and other interpersonal conflicts. If

---

[11]Paul Muller, Superintendent, Riverview Release Center, Bureau of Adult Corrections, State of Iowa, personal conversation, June 13, 1977.

emotional or interpersonal problems require counseling from a psychiatrist or psychologist and neither is available through the department of corrections, a referral is made to a community mental health agency. Other assistance is provided by various correctional specialists and noncorrectional agencies. The Federal Bureau of Prisons assigns employment placement specialists to prerelease guidance centers to help offenders obtain work. State and private employment offices provide placement and testing services, both vocational and academic. Financial assistance and guidance is obtained from vocational rehabilitation counselors, social security officers, and other federal agencies. If difficulties with alcohol are anticipated or experienced, referrals to an Alcoholics Anonymous group can be processed.

Problems from Housing

Assistance is frequently required to lessen emotional pressure. Work releasees find that for 8 hours a day they live as free citizens in the community and then return to the institution to become "just inmates." Their frustration is increased by the fact that they are paying for their own room, board, and transportation; buying their own clothes; and paying taxes and yet are confined when not working or on a temporary release (see Table 8.2).

Correctional officials who recognize these offenders' half-free status generally try to isolate them from other inmates. New York City and State officials both recommend that work release participants be housed in separate quarters within an institution. New York State even specifies that housing should be "on an easily accessible gallery,"[12] in order to encourage unfettered movement in and out of the institution and to reduce contacts with totally confined inmates. Separation also encourages the development of community-based programs for nonworking hours. Ultimately, most states seek to place participating offenders in community-based residences, thus minimizing the contrast between freedom and return to correctional supervision.

Protecting the Public

Public protection is accomplished by careful supervision, conducted primarily by correctional field staff such as work release coordinators, community coordinators, and community-based supervisory personnel using various methods. In addition, correctional officials seek assistance from local law enforcement agencies and probation or parole staff. Many states require home and job visits by correctional personnel. Offenders are asked to report periodically to the local law enforcement agencies and to probation or parole staff who have agreed to assist in supervision. Letters to county and city officials inform them of

---

[12]Lawrence S. Root, "State Work Release Programs: An Analysis of Operational Policies," *Federal Probation*, vol. 37, no. 4, Administrative Office of the United States Courts, Washington, D.C., December 1973, p. 55.

TABLE 8.2
PRIORITIES ESTABLISHED BY STATUTE FOR DISBURSEMENT OF WORK RELEASE WAGES

State	Room and board	Transportation and other incidental expenses	Support of dependents	Payment of fines and debts	Savings for release
California	1	2	3	4	5
Connecticut	1	2	3		4
Georgia	1	2	3		
Illinois	1	2	3		
Louisiana	1	2	3	4	5
Maryland	1	2	3		4
Montana	1	2	3		
New Jersey	1	2	3	4	5
New York	1	2	3	4	5
New York City	1	2	3	4	
North Carolina	2	1	3	4	5
North Dakota	1	2	3	4	5
Oregon	1	2	3	4	5
Pennsylvania	1	2	3	4	5
South Dakota	1	2	3	4	5
Tennessee	1	2	3	4	
Texas	1	2	4		
Vermont	1	2	4		3
Washington	2	1	3	4	5
Wisconsin	1	2	3	4	5

Source: Lawrence S. Root, "State Work Release Programs: An Analysis of Operational Policies," *Federal Probation,* vol. 37, no. 4, Administrative Office of the United States Courts, Washington, D.C., December 1973, p. 55.

offenders' community-based corrections plans and ask assistance in observing their behavior. Telephone calls are made to determine if offenders are where they are supposed to be. Saline and alcoholizer tests are conducted to detect illegal consumption of drugs. Follow-up contacts are made with prospective employers and family members to evaluate the offenders' community adjustment.

There are some common regulations governing the temporary release, work release, or study release plan. They forbid the use of alcohol or other drugs, restrict the offender to a specific geographic area, demand obedience to state and federal laws, forbid signing of contracts without permission, ban the use of firearms, and demand obedience to community-based residence rules.

The importance of protecting the public cannot be overestimated. When offenders become a threat to the public while temporarily released, there is an immediate outcry. An example is United States Attorney General William B. Saxbe's reaction to the haphazard administration of the furlough system in Washington, D.C. In October 1974, Saxbe said, "I want to get criminals off the streets."[13] For this reason, establishing efficient and functional administrative policies is the key to an effective program. Progressive legislation regarding temporary releases, work release, and study release does not assist in the reintegration of offenders unless regulations are enforced. The support of legislatures and of the public can be quickly lost by inefficient management, because of increasing the danger of criminal behavior and wasting money.

Milwaukie Work Release Center

One example of an effort to utilize all forms of community contact in a system of gradual release exists at the Milwaukie Work Release Center, Milwaukie, Oregon. The center, housing a maximum of forty-six men, is located in a small urban community near Portland. The 5-acre facility accepts only men who are within 6 months of expiration of sentence or parole. They are transferred to the center from the Oregon State Penitentiary or Oregon State Correctional Institution. Milwaukie Center personnel have established five goals for persons in their program: (1) They should function effectively with authority, (2) they should develop internal controls, (3) they must try to acquire more constructive means of coping with reality, (4) they should be helped to develop genuine feelings of self-worth, and (5) they should learn to use their potential effectively.

To accomplish these goals a program using supervised trips, passes, and work release was developed. During the first week after arrival, each man is restricted to the center except when accompanied by a staff member or a correctional aide. This allows personnel to observe each individual and evaluate his reactions to new situations, including the rules and regulations governing the center.

---

[13]"Furor Over Furloughs," *Newsweek,* October 28, 1974, p. 54.

After a week, if his behavior warrants approval, the enrollee is allowed to leave the center on a social pass for 4 hours a day or for 12 hours on a weekend. If he is able to behave satisfactorily while in the free community for a short period, additional 12-hour passes, occasional overnight passes, and finally home leaves of longer duration are permitted. Eventually each man is given temporary release privileges to attend school or seek employment but is expected to return to the center from school or job within the allotted time. He is accountable for keeping his sleeping area in order within the facility and continues to use social passes.

An enrollee who abuses his privileges by returning late from work, drinking on a pass, or breaking other rules is brought before a unit team for disciplinary action. The team conducts a hearing that includes listening to the offender's explanation for his unacceptable behavior. The team has many options, which include recommending that no action be taken or that the offender's passes be restricted for 1 or 2 weeks. In this way, he is made aware that he has behaved inappropriately, yet continues to profit from his placement.

Sometimes an enrollee is unable or unwilling to alter unacceptable behavior and continues to defy or break the rules. In such a situation, he might receive a substantial restriction and a warning that similar behavior in the future would result in his return to the state penitentiary or correctional institution. In more serious cases the unit team may recommend immediate return.[14]

EVALUATION OF BRIDGES TO THE COMMUNITY

Temporary Releases

In a 1972 study no state using passes and furloughs reported enough violations to warrant curtailment or termination of the program. In fact, only three states— California, Utah, and Washington, in addition to the District of Columbia— reported serious problems. These included escapes, drug use, and crimes committed by offenders on temporary release.[15] Since then California has decreased the number of furloughs granted, and United States Attorney General Saxbe halted federal furloughs in 1974 but reinstated them 1 year later. Both decisions followed some serious violations and a subsequent public outcry.

Most states have indicated successful experiences with temporary releases. Maine managed 1 full year with only three escapes and no new crimes among its 1576 inmates on furlough.[16] In Illinois, during one 2-year period, 6400 prisoners were issued passes and furloughs and less than 1 percent were accused of new crimes.[17] The Federal Bureau of Prisons granted 22,391 3-to-7-day furloughs

---

[14]Gordon Bird, "Community Centered Treatment of Offenders," *Criminal Rehabilitation . . . Within and Without the Walls,* Edward M. Scott and Kathryn L. Scott (eds.), Charles C Thomas Publisher, Springfield, Ill., 1973, pp. 129–136.

[15]Markley, op. cit. pp. 22, 24.

[16]Steve Gettinger, "Profile/Maine," *Corrections Magazine,* vol. 1, no. 6, July-August 1975, p. 18.

during 1976 and experienced only one violation for every 100 furloughs.[18] In the 10 years preceding 1977 in South Carolina, 8758 furloughs were approved; less than 1 percent failed to abide by rules.[19]

A survey of furlough programs in 1972 revealed that no reporting state had an abscondence rate exceeding 2 percent (see Table 8.3). During 1977, fifteen correctional systems reported no abscondence, seven estimated from one to five abscondences, six estimated from six to fifteen, three estimated from sixteen to twenty-five, and four reported twenty-six or more.[20]

E. Eugene Miller, former Alaskan correctional facilities administrator, believes that an escape or abscondence rate from furloughs is likely to be from 2 to 4 percent. If the rate is 1½ percent or less, the screening process is too severe; if the rate is 5 percent or more, the screening process is too liberal or something is seriously wrong with the administration of the program.[21]

Since the first use of temporary releases, correctional officials have debated their value. For the most part this debate has not lessened their popularity. As of December 31, 1977, forty-two state correctional systems, the District of Columbia and the Federal Bureau of Prisons allowed offenders to leave supervision on temporary release.[22] In 1974, more than 250,000 furloughs were granted to incarcerated offenders.

[17]Michael S. Serrill, "Prison Furloughs in America," *Corrections Magazine,* vol. 1, no. 6, July-August 1975, p. 54.

[18]*1976 Federal Prison Systems,* U.S. Department of Justice, Washington, D.C., 1976, p. 10.

[19]*Division of Community Services Consolidated Report Since Inception of Program,* South Carolina Department of Corrections, Columbia, S.C., October 1977.

[20]Robert R. Smith and Charles M. Petro, "An Updated Survey of Four Policies and Practices in American Adult Corrections," *Journal of Criminal Justice,* vol. 8, no. 2, 1980, p. 124.

[21]E. Eugene Miller, "Furloughs as a Technique of Reintegration," *Corrections in the Community,* E. Eugene Miller and M. Robert Montilla (eds.), Reston Publishing Company, Inc., Reston, Virginia, 1977, p. 206.

[22]Smith and Petro, op. cit., p. 124.

TABLE 8.3
ABSCONDENCE RATES IN FURLOUGH PROGRAMS

Maximum days of release permitted in home furlough program	No. of agencies reporting home furlough program in operation	Abscondence rates reported (%)
1	2	2
2	8	4
3	4	4
4	1	1
5	2	1
10	4	4
30	4	2

Source: Vernon Fox, *Community-Based Corrections,* Prentice-Hall, Inc., Englewood Cliffs, New Jersey, 1977, p. 95.

Work Release

The foregoing discussions are interesting to correctional administrators, but historically the most common gauge of success or failure of any correctional program is recidivism. Results of studies have varied. A study of Canadian felons indicated a 24 percent lower recidivism rate for released inmates who had been on work release. In 1971, California completed a 24-month follow-up comparing nonwork releasees with work releasees. It was discovered that 18.8 percent of former work releasees returned to prison—a figure 7.8 percent lower than the recidivism rate of nonwork releasees. Furthermore, work releasees who returned to prison were free 44 days longer than comparable nonwork releasees.[23] Four years later, in the same state, 173 of 978 inmates on work release (18 percent) were returned to California prisons—only 10 because of a new felony or other criminal act.[24]

Studies from the state of Indiana showed 5 percent less and from Bucks County Prison in Pennsylvania, 7 percent less recidivism among work releasees.[25] A 1-year study of ninety-nine federal prisoners who successfully completed a work release program concluded that "maximum benefit was apparently derived by those men falling into the poorer risk categories. Men who were good risks succeeded at or near the rates expected. Those offenders who were poorer risks succeeded at much higher than their expected rates."[26] At the end of the year's study, 84 percent of the federal prisoners involved in the work release program had maintained themselves in the community without additional serious convictions.

Early data from an Alabama evaluation project show that "work releasees have worked more, earned more, and at three months past release, have been involved in fewer undesirable law encounters than offenders in comparison groups."[27]

All studies have not been favorable, however, as proved by 1965 figures from the District of Columbia Reformatory. Work releasees had a 76 percent success rate and nonwork releasees, an 85 percent rate. Researchers concluded that the higher rate of failure among work releasees was due to the practice of assigning higher risk inmates to the community-based corrections program.[28] A 4-year study of 201 men who participated in a work release program in a county jail revealed that the men accumulated more than 32 years in jail sentences and 27

---

[23]Alvin Rudoff and T. C. Esselstyn, "Evaluating Work Furlough," *Federal Probation,* vol. 37, no. 2. Administrative Office of the United States Courts, Washington, D.C., June 1973, p. 52.

[24]Management Information Section, Research Unit, Policy and Planning Division, State of California, Health and Welfare Agency, Department of Corrections, November 22, 1976.

[25]*Graduated Release,* National Institute of Mental Health, Rockville, Md., 1971, p. 11.

[26]Ronald L. Goldfarb and Linda R. Singer, *After Conviction,* Simon and Schuster, New York, 1973, p. 546.

[27]*Final Interim Report on Phase IV,* Rehabilitation Research Foundation, Experimental Manpower Laboratory for Corrections, Montgomery, Ala., 1974, p. 60.

[28]*Graduated Release,* op. cit., pp. 12–13.

TABLE 8.4
PERCENT OF INMATES NOT ARRESTED OR CONVICTED OF A
CRIME IN EACH OF THE YEARS FOLLOWING RELEASE FROM
JAIL

Time period	% not arrested		% not convicted	
	Work furlough	Control	Work furlough	Control
Year 1	51	25	61	35
	n = 109	n = 91	n = 109	n = 91
Year 2	68	51	77	61
	n = 106	n = 87	n = 106	n = 87
Year 3	65	59	79	72
	n = 105	n = 83	n = 105	n = 83
Year 4	70	60	90	67
	n = 105	n = 89	n = 106	n = 89
4-year total	23	13	43	23
	n = 109	n = 92	n = 109	n = 92

Source: Robert Jeffery and Stephen Woolpert, "Work Furlough as an Alternative to Incarceration: An Assessment of Its Effects on Recidivism and Social Cost." *Community Corrections,* Burt Gallaway, Joe Hudson, and C. David Hollister (eds.) Charles C Thomas Publisher, Springfield, Ill., 1976, p. 112.

years in prison terms. Only 38 men (19 percent) avoided arrest and only 68 (34 percent) were not convicted of a new offense. However, when compared to a control group, the work releasees had nearly double the number of men with no arrests and no convictions (see Table 8.4). The work furlough program appeared most beneficial to those having the highest risk of failure, i.e., the unskilled, unmarried men under 35 with three or more prior convictions.[29]

Study Release

In 1977, forty-three correctional systems reported having a study release program. Georgia, Iowa, Illinois, Michigan, and New Hampshire have done away with study release since 1971. As Table 8.5 shows, 3717 offenders participated in 1977, only a slight increase since 1971 when 3087 offenders participated. The abscondence rate was approximately 1 percent in 1977. Thirty correctional systems report that the study release program helped in rehabilitation. No administrator said it did not help.[30]

Several reasons have been given to explain why study release is used less frequently than work release: (1) Many inmates cannot qualify for college-level

[29]Robert Jeffery and Stephen Woolpert, "Work Furlough as an Alternative to Incarceration: An Assessment of Its Effects on Recidivism and Social Cost," *Community Corrections,* Burt Gallaway, Joe Hudson, and C. David Hollister (eds.), Charles C Thomas Publisher, Spring field, Ill., 1976, pp. 117–119.
[30]Smith and Petro, op. cit., p. 124.

TABLE 8.5
NUMBER OF MEN AND WOMEN REPORTED
PARTICIPATING IN STUDY-RELEASE, BY TYPE
OF EDUCATION

Type of education	Men	Women
College	594	119
State vocational school	644	151
Federal vocational school	20	0
Regular high school	133	49
Adult basic education	66	15
Other		1722*
Total		3717†

*District of Columbia Department of Corrections report-
ed 1722 on education furlough but did not break down by
sex or education program.
†Figure includes men and women and the District of
Columbia Department of Corrections figure.
Note: Florida reported that individuals were attending a
private vocational school, without further explanation.
Source: Robert R. Smith and Charles M. Petro, "An
Updated Survey of Four Policies and Practices in American
Adult Corrections," *Journal of Criminal Justice,* vol. 8, no. 2,
1980, p. 124.

work because they are not high school graduates, (2) college courses are offered within the prison, (3) television and correspondence courses are available to interested inmates, (4) correctional institutions are often located a great distance from college campuses, and (5) there is greater acceptance of work release than study release.[31]

OTHER BENEFITS OF TRANSITIONAL STRATEGIES

Offender Earnings

In 1977 South Carolina published accumulated statistics based on offenders' work release participation since the inception of the program 10 years earlier. These figures revealed: 6,526 work releasees earned $13,163,009.64, a total of $2,198,920.30 was disbursed to dependents, $3,085,455.70 was returned to the state for room and board, and $1,672,332.29 was paid in state and federal taxes.[32]

A survey compiled by the American Correctional Association indicated that only nine states provided more than $60.00 release money to offenders being discharged or paroled. Vermont allowed the maximum limit of $200 "gate"

[31]Clemens Bartollas, *Introduction to Corrections,* Harper & Row, Publishers Incorporated, New York, 1981, p. 173.
[32]*Division of Community Services Report,* op. cit.

money.[33] These figures have not changed significantly since the survey. In contrast, Oregon reported that offenders discharged from the Milwaukie Work Release Center possessed savings averaging $500 and some left with as much as $1500.[34] A 1974 study concluded that "most men who have savings usually have accumulated their money from jobs on work release."[35]

Effect on Inmate Attitudes

A number of researchers have tried to determine the effect of work release on inmate attitudes. Correctional officials generally have assumed that temporary releases into the community do improve attitudes, reduce institutional tensions, and decrease disciplinary reports and escapes. California witnessed an escape rate of less than 1 percent from an unlocked institution of 1500 prisoners in a single year while using temporary releases into the community.[36] Proponents of this assumption state that the progress of potential parolees is easily observed, and that inmates believe they have greater control over their fate in institutions using temporary releases, work release, or study release.

Norman Holt conducted a study in California of 795 three-day furloughs. The inmates' reactions were varied, but 78 percent believed the furlough turned out "better than expected," 57 percent believed the furlough made incarceration "easier," and 68 percent believed "being with family and friends" was the most pleasant part of the furlough. Only 7 percent of the men studied had any known trouble—one was arrested and two absconded.[37]

In contrast, at least one study downgraded the value of work release on inmate attitudes. A Florida study by Gordon Waldo, Theodore Chiricos, and Leonard Dobrin indicated a decrease in perception of legitimate opportunity, achievement motivation, self-esteem, and self-concept. These researchers concluded that work release did not improve inmate attitudes; in fact, the only attitude change was unfavorable.[38]

Help in the Transition

The use of furloughs and work release to obtain and accept jobs eases the "employment shock" suffered by discharged prisoners who go from a period of total or partial idleness to a job in the community. Work release exposes

---

[33]*Proceedings: Second National Workshop on Corrections and Parole Administration,* American Correctional Association, College Park, Md., 1974, pp. 111–113.

[34]Bird, op. cit., p. 131.

[35]*Proceedings,* op. cit., p. 123.

[36]Kenyon Scudder, "The Open Institution," *Readings in Criminology and Penology,* David Dressler (ed.), Columbia University Press, New York, 1972, p. 555.

[37]Norman Holt, "Temporary Prison Release," *Correctional Institutions,* Robert M. Carter, Daniel Glaser, and Leslie T. Wilkins (eds.), J. B. Lippincott Company, New York, 1977, p. 433.

[38]Gordon P. Waldo, Theodore G. Chiricos, and Leonard E. Dobrin. "Community Contact and Inmate Attitudes," *Criminology,* vol. 11, no. 3, 1973, pp. 369–373.

offenders to the work pace, working conditions, and social environment they will encounter after release.

Employers, too, have praised work release. In the North Carolina program, most employers of work releasees considered their work to be as good as or better than that of other workers. In an annual report from Indiana, employers indicated that work releasees exhibited lower absenteeism than other workers, less alcoholism, and less garnishment of wages or other court actions.[39]

California Department of Corrections officials believe that one benefit of work release is the guarantee of a job upon release. According to a state employment survey conducted in 1975, no work releasee was released without a job but 29 percent of institutional parolees did not have jobs. Also, after 1 month on parole, 95 percent of parolees released from a community correctional center using work release were employed, compared with 57 percent of parolees from institutions.[40] These figures agree with Martinson, Wilks, and Lipton's conclusion that releasing offenders to jobs developed by parole officers is much more likely to be associated with failure than is releasing offenders to jobs developed by family or friends.[41]

APPRAISAL

"I consider work release as the most humane and economical method of 'handling' a select group of public offenders. I strongly endorse work release."

"Man, get me off this work program. I'm going to blow it. The pressure is starting to get to me."[42]

These remarks, the first from a former director of corrections and the second from an inmate, demonstrate the divergency of opinions about bridges to the community. Although based on the experiences of the speakers, the statements are representative of the public as a whole. For the most part judgments about programs permitting offenders to be in the community while still under custody of institutional personnel focus on recidivism rates, costs, and the danger to the public.

Recidivism Rates

The studies here discussed are not conclusive. While they do not show positively that supervised trips, work release, study release, and temporary releases into the community are valuable tools, neither do they show conclusively that bridges into the community increase the likelihood of return to prison. Martinson,

---

[39]Root, "State Work Release Programs," op. cit., p. 56.

[40]Jack Burris, "Arguments Pro and Con to Work Furlough," Parole Agent III, Parole and Community Services Division, Department of Corrections, Health and Welfare Agency, State of California.

[41]Robert Martinson, Judith Wilks, and Douglas Lipton, *The Effectiveness of Correctional Treatment,* Praeger Publishers, New York, 1975, p. 149.

[42]Bartollas, op. cit., pp. 171–172.

Wilks, and Lipton stated that although it has shown promise of being a worthwhile program alternative, claims for and assumptions underlying work release remain largely untested.[43] At worst, the recidivism rate of offenders remains the same. The critics of both the favorable and unfavorable recidivism rates use the same arguments. Some say the rates are unfairly negative because the worst risks are permitted release. Others apply the same rationale to the results of research indicating a *higher* success rate among work releasees. The implication is that the high success rate occurs because offenders placed on work release are better risks.

Some states have tried to counter these accusations by making public careful reviews of what happens to all offenders permitted the use of bridges. Nebraska released information revealing reasons for termination of offenders on work or study release. Forty percent were placed under parole supervision, 31 percent were discharged or transferred to mandatory release status, 18 percent were returned to prison for rule violation, 6 percent were returned to prison at their request, 4 percent escaped, and less than 1 percent committed new crimes.[44] The hope is that this information will show that proper supervision of offenders approved for work or study release reduces the risk of failure on parole or after expiration of sentence.

Costs

There are obvious favorable aspects that appear to be factually observed. Offenders can accumulate savings during work release. They become tax producers, not tax consumers. The money they earn can be applied to board and room in the prison or in community-based residences, to travel expenses, support of dependents, payment of personal debts, and payment of court costs or restitution. During 1974, a total of $988,701.43 was earned by 1352 offenders on work release in Georgia. Of this, $575,641.75 (58 percent) reduced state expenses. Some money was returned to the Georgia state treasury directly through state income taxes or rent. Some was paid to dependents, thus reducing state welfare payments. During the same year the operating expenses for the work release program, including expenses incurred at two community-based residences (the Atlanta Advancement Center and Andromeda Drug Center) were only $802,538.72.[45]

Even these apparent benefits have been questioned. Critics have asked if all the direct costs of administering these programs are being considered. They include counseling services, selection procedures, interviewing, testing, record-keeping, case investigation, field supervision, housing, and feeding. Others ask about indirect expenses. Is there an increase in costs for apprehension of

[43]Martinson, Wilks, and Lipton, op. cit., pp. 277–278.

[44]*Third Annual Report,* July 1, 1976–June 30, 1977, State of Nebraska, Lincoln, 1977, p. 94.

[45]*Georgia Department of Corrections and Offender Rehabilitation: Annual Report 1974,* Georgia Correctional Industries Print Shop, Stone Mountain, 1974, pp. 64, 65, and 82.

absconders? What is the effect of a high rate of turnover on administrative costs? How many families of work release inmates actually would receive public assistance? Do work releasees displace non-work release employees?

Danger to the Community

Most of the criticism is focused on the potential danger to the community. These concerns reach gigantic proportions after a work releasee or an inmate on furlough escapes, commits a crime, or otherwise creates a furor while in the community. Most rule violations are a product of the participants' accommodation to the half-free status. The sudden change from the rigid discipline of an institution to the relative freedom of the community results in tension for the offender, who frequently goes from unstructured to structured living in the course of an 8-hour period. Resulting unorthodox behavior takes the form of drunkenness, traffic violations, difficulties with employers and fellow employees, poor money management, and absconding.

The main danger is sometimes what is referred to as the "honeymoon effect." Once the novelty of the program has worn off, there is a risk that the program will be taken for granted and there will be a tendency to take some liberties with the rules. A honeymoon effect occurs after several successful furloughs have been completed; with work release, it has been shown statistically to occur after persons have been in the program for 6 months.[46]

Violations resulting from the honeymoon effect are apparently a product of the half-free status rather than of opposition to the social order. Acceptable levels of conduct can no longer be maintained by authoritarian rules alone. The inmate must rely on self-discipline, the habits incidental to regularity of employment, and systems of social relationships. All but a few of the offender population realize this and take steps to ensure the success of their participation. Correctional officials can assist in this effort by careful selection of participants, adequate preparation, and available support personnel in the community. Clear-cut rules overseeing inmate conduct should be established.

Supervised trips, work release, study release, and temporary releases should not be granted as a way to buy peace within an institution. Deals should not be made with inmate leaders as a means of gaining their support. Hope is a primary instrument by which inmates survive, and it should not be misused. Unfortunately, most serious problems in these programs result from poor screening of candidates, lax supervision, or inadequate follow-up.

Offenders are more likely to behave like criminals if convinced that the community defines them as unreliable, violent, or larcenous. Many correctional employees and law enforcement personnel present an equally difficult roadblock. The problems associated with supervised trips, work release, study release, and temporary releases represent "extra work." A frequent reaction by the uninformed, both citizens and law enforcement personnel, is to agree with

---

[46]Miller, "Furloughs as a Technique of Reintegration," op. cit., p. 207.

the opening of a program as long as it is not located in their community. An effective community relations campaign can encourage citizens to characterize the offender less adversely, thus increasing opportunities for jobs and social acceptance. Including correctional employees and law enforcement personnel in an advisory capacity from the planning stages can provide a basis for a set of social relationships between them and the offender. Administration should not forget that the success or failure of any correctional program is dependent on community receptivity.

CONCLUSION

Properly applied bridges to the community can be positive incentives to confined offenders. Supervised trips, work release, study release, and temporary releases can be used to successfully reintegrate the offender into the community if viewed as part of a total community-based correctional effort, i.e., "a structured, planned and well-coordinated effort to interrupt criminal careers and restore the inmate's faith in, and contact with, society."[47]

Some marriages are salvaged. Offenders become active in the community through attendance at service clubs or church. Positive recreation habits are developed. The primary value of community-based corrections is not the long-range decrease in costs or in token visits to the inmate's family or the YMCA, but the offender's need to achieve acceptable social adjustment. Most behavioral disorders of offenders are characterized by a pattern of behavior unacceptable to society. The source of the deviant behavior is often traced to dysfunctional interpersonal relationships with family and community.

Before release from supervision, offenders must experience social situations by themselves if they are to learn to handle them in a socially acceptable manner without the assistance of correctional personnel or institutional structure. As one offender said,

> It is an exceptionally hard thing to readjust to the free society when you have little or no contact with it. In my opinion, the passes that we are permitted to have encourage our getting involved for short periods of time. I think of these periods as training. For instance, a football player does not engage in his first game without first getting gradually into shape. I'm afraid that if he tried to play without preconditioning, he would not last long. So it is with those of us who are incarcerated. It is a most difficult transition to the free world. I feel that passes are part of our preconditioning before being released to the free society. I think I'll be ready, upon my release, for society, and that they will be ready for me.[48]

Supervised trips, work release, study release, and temporary releases serve as stepping stones into the offender's community. In the community, correctional staff can observe the persons in an uncontrolled environment, not one protected

---

[47]Johnson, "Conflicting Goals," op. cit., p. 247.

[48]"Report to the Legislature," unpublished report, State of Iowa, Des Moines, October 1971, p. 1.

by the correctional structure. In this setting offenders can be dealt with as persons, not stereotypes, numbers, typologies, or "cons." No matter how well or poorly they adjust to a structured setting, the real test takes place when offenders "hit the streets" on their own. The streets are where they must really adjust. This is where their hopes lie, their fears exist, and their failure or success is to be accomplished.

EXERCISES

1 How could a supervised trip be structured to maximize its value for the offender?
2 Should temporary release privileges be restricted to white-collar offenders, who may have more "responsible" family members? Explain.
3 What is the value to inmates in requiring them or family members to assume responsibility for their behavior on a temporary release? Why not send members of the correctional staff?
4 What criteria should be used to limit work release privileges to certain offenders?
5 Examine the questions answered by correctional staff when selecting participants for temporary releases into the community. What additional questions would you suggest? Comment on each question relative to its value.
6 Based on social background, what type of offender would benefit most from work release, study release, and temporary releases? Consider social and economic status, education, and marital status of parents.
7 Evaluate the application process which an offender follows to gain permission for work release, study release, or temporary releases. Emphasize the positive and negative aspects of the process.
8 Which factor—employment, housing, or transportation—do you believe is most crucial in a work release plan?
9 What steps can be taken by correctional personnel to prepare the employer for supervising the work releasee?
10 At least one correctional administrator refers to community-based corrections as the "yo-yo theory," meaning that correctional staff members control the strings of the yo-yo, i.e., the inmate. Do you believe the ability to control the degree of inmate freedom is beneficial or detrimental? How does it affect inmates, their relatives, the correctional staff, and the public?
11 Do you agree or disagree with the argument that there is no program conducted in a walled institution which cannot be conducted in the community with greater value to the offender? Give reasons.
12 Which form of temporary release into the community do you think is most valuable for the offender? Why?
13 Which limitations to community-based corrections do you think are the most damaging and least likely to be eliminated? Why? Which limitations do you think are the least damaging and most likely to be eliminated? Why?
14 Do you believe that any of the research regarding work release, study release, and temporary release is too negative to justify continuance? Give reasons for your answer.
15 Many correctional administrators have stated that temporary release into the community decreases inmate anxiety within community-based residences. Yet the study by

Waldo, Chiricos, and Dobrin implies that temporary release may not improve inmate attitudes. Explain this apparent discrepancy.

16 Do you agree with the inmate who makes the analogy between a football player preparing for a game and himself? Justify your decision.

17 Corrections officials have been criticized for "coddling inmates." Do you believe temporary release into the community is coddling? Explain.

EXERCISE REFERENCES

American Correctional Association, *Proceedings: Second National Workshop on Corrections and Parole Administration,* College Park, Md., 1974.

Ayer, William A.: "Work Release: A Pre-release Program," *Introduction to Correctional Rehabilitation,* Richard E. Hardy and John G. Cull (eds.), Charles C Thomas Publisher, Springfield, Ill., 1973, chap. 5, pp. 59–71.

———: "Work Release Programs in the United States: Some Difficulties Encountered," *Federal Probation,* vol. 34, no. 1, Administrative Office of the United States Courts, Washington, D.C., March 1970, pp. 53–56.

Bartollas, Clemens: *Introduction to Corrections,* Harper & Row Publishers, Incorporated, New York, 1981, chap. 8.

Bird, Gordon: "Community Centered Treatment of Offenders," *Criminal Rehabilitation . . . Within and Without the Walls,* Edward Scott and Kathryn L. Scott (eds.), Charles C Thomas Publisher, Springfield, Ill., 1973, chap. 10.

Carpenter, Lewis A.: "The Federal Work Release Program," *The Tasks of Penology,* Harry S. Perlman and Thomas B. Allington (eds.), University of Nebraska Press, Lincoln, 1969, pp. 185–196.

Case, John D.: "Doing Time in the Community," *Federal Probation,* vol. 31, no. 1. Administrative Office of the United States Courts, Washington, D.C., March 1967, pp. 9–17.

Cooper, W. D.: "Employers and Employees in the Work Release Program in North Carolina," *Crime and Delinquency,* vol. 16, no. 4, October 1970, pp. 427–433.

Dunlavey, Dub: "Work Release in Minnesota," *American Journal of Correction,* vol. 31, no. 4, 1968, pp. 28–29.

Fox, Vernon: *Community-Based Corrections,* Prentice-Hall, Inc., Englewood Cliffs, N.J., 1977, chap. 6.

Gardner, Eugene J.: "Community Resources: Tools for the Correctional Agent," *Crime and Delinquency,* vol. 19, no. 1, January 1973, pp. 55–60.

Goldfarb, Ronald L., and Linda R. Singer: *After Conviction,* Simon and Schuster, New York, 1973, sec. VIII.

Grupp, Stanley E.: "Work Furlough and Punishment Theory," *Community-Based Corrections: Theory, Practice, and Research,* Povl G. Boesen and Stanley E. Grupp (eds.), Davis Publishing Company, Inc., Santa Cruz, Calif., 1976, pp. 65–77.

Holt, Norman: "Temporary Prison Release," *Correctional Institutions,* Robert M. Carter, Daniel Glaser, and Leslie T. Wilkins (eds.), J. B. Lippincott Company, New York, 1977, pp. 422–441.

Jeffery, Robert, and Stephen Woolpert: "Work Furlough as an Alternative to Incarceration: An Assessment of the Effects on Recidivism and Social Cost," *Community Corrections,* Burt Gallaway, Joe Hudson, and C. David Hollister (eds.), Charles C Thomas Publisher, Springfield, Ill., 1976, pp. 105–122.

Johnson, Elmer H.: "Report on an Innovation-State Work Release Programs," *Crime and Delinquency,* vol. 16, no. 4, October 1970, pp. 417–426.

————: "Work Release: Conflicting Goals Within a Promising Innovation," *Alternatives to Prison,* Gary R. Perlstein and Thomas R. Phelps (eds.), Goodyear Publishing Company, Inc., Pacific Palisades, Calif., 1975, pp. 247–257.

Kozol, H.: "The Diagnosis and Treatment of Dangerousness," *Crime and Delinquency,* vol. 18, no. 3, July 1972, pp. 371–392.

Lenihan, Kenneth J.: "The Financial Condition of Released Prisoners," *Crime and Delinquency,* vol. 21, no. 3, July 1975, pp. 266–281.

McMillan, David R.: "Work Furlough for the Jailed Prisoner," *Federal Probation,* vol. 29, no. 1, Administrative Office of the United States Courts, Washington, D.C., March 1965, pp. 33–34.

Markley, Carson W.: "Furlough Programs and Conjugal Visiting in Adult Correctional Institutions," *Federal Probation,* vol. 37, no. 1, Administrative Office of the United States Courts, Washington, D.C., March 1973, pp. 19–26.

Miller, E. Eugene: "Furloughs as a Technique of Reintegration," *Corrections in the Community,* E. Eugene Miller and M. Robert Montilla (eds.), Reston Publishing Company, Inc., Reston, Virginia, 1977, pp. 201–208.

National Institute of Mental Health: *Graduated Release,* Rockville, Md., 1971.

Newsweek, "Furor Over Furloughs," October 28, 1974, p. 54.

Powers, Sanger B.: "Off Grounds Activities Present an Opportunity for Correctional Institutions," *Federal Probation,* vol. 31, no. 2, Administrative Office of the United States Courts, Washington, D.C., June 1967, pp. 11–15.

Richmond, Mark S.: "Measuring the Cost of Correctional Services," *Crime and Delinquency,* vol. 18, no. 3, July 1972, pp. 243–252.

————: "The Practicalities of Community-Based Corrections," *American Journal of Correction,* vol. 30, no. 6, 1968, pp. 12–18.

Root, Lawrence S.: "State Work Release Programs: An Analysis of Operational Policies," *Federal Probation,* vol. 37, no. 4, Administrative Office of the United States Courts, Washington, D.C., December 1973, pp. 38–43.

Rudoff, Alvin, and T. C. Esselstyn: "Evaluating Work Furlough," *Federal Probation,* vol. 37, no. 2, Administrative Office of the United States Courts, Washington, D.C., June 1973, pp. 48–53.

Sard, Thomas R.: "Contact With the Free Community Is Basic If Institutional Programs Are to Succeed," *Federal Probation,* vol. 31, no. 1, Administrative Office of the United States Courts, Washington, D.C., March 1967, pp. 3–8.

Smith, Robert R., John B. McKee, and Michael A. Milan: "Study-Release Policies of American Correctional Agencies: A Survey," *Journal of Criminal Justice,* vol. 2, no. 4, Winter 1974, pp. 357–363.

Smith, Robert R., and Charles M. Petro: "An Updated Survey of Four Policies and Practices in American Adult Corrections," *Journal of Criminal Justice,* vol. 8, no. 2, 1980, pp. 123–128.

Waldo, Gordon P., Theodore G. Chiricos, and Leonard E. Dobrin: "Community Contact and Inmate Attitudes," *Criminology,* vol. 11, no. 3, 1973, pp. 345–381.

Zalba, Serapio R.: "Work Release," *The Sociology of Punishment and Correction,* Norman Johnston, Leonard Savitz, and Marvin E. Wolfgang (eds.), John Wiley & Sons, Inc., New York, 1970, pp. 693–698.

COMMUNITY-BASED RESIDENTIAL PROGRAMS

CHAPTER OBJECTIVES

- To describe the physical plants used in community-based corrections—halfway houses, work release centers, and community correctional centers
- To outline the uses of community-based residences
- To provide information on the process of establishing a community-based residence
- To discuss the environment of community-based residences
- To present hints on the administration of community-based residences

INTRODUCTION

As explained earlier, bridges to the community assist offenders in their transition from a correctional institution to the community. Supervised trips permit them to maintain contact with the community while incarcerated, minimizing the trauma accompanying actual release. The prisoner can use furloughs and day passes to seek employment, a place to live, and the reestablishment of a relationship with family and friends. Work and study release provide opportunities to actually begin the process of release from supervision—working or attending school but remaining under correctional supervision at other times.

Bridges to the community are often associated with placement in a community-based residence. Inmates live in halfway houses, work release centers, or community correctional centers while carrying out their plans. Community-based residences are small, local facilities designed for offenders who do not need to be in maximum custody prisons. In this context, they are "decompression chambers" between the hyper-regimented world of the prison, in which the exercise of genuine self-responsibility is likely to violate the rules, and the freedom of the street. Such residences provide a clean and comfortable place to live, wholesome meals, counseling, and help in preparing for a complete release.

Current Status

Today state and federal government agencies as well as many private agencies are operating a multitude of community-based residences for offenders throughout the United States. The private organizations may be religious groups, private foundations, nonprofit corporations, or ex-offender groups. In both England and Northern Ireland, residences for released felons have proliferated since 1950. All these facilities in the United States and Great Britain provide a variety of services, ranging from vocational training and counseling to places to live without additional services.

In 1964 the operators of community-based residences in the United States and Canada organized the International Halfway House Association (IHHA), which 5 years later became a part of the American Correctional Association. This step—official recognition by professional correctional administrators—symbolized the acceptance of community-based residences as a valid correctional tool. The 1979–1980 edition of the IHHA Directory lists 1061 halfway houses in the United States and 152 in Canada, including twenty-nine states that reported halfway houses solely for female offenders.[1]

Today many community-based residences still hold to the original conception of a homelike atmosphere with a simulated family relationship, serving about twenty residents each. At the same time, the prerelease centers, community correctional centers, and some residential housing units have expanded services to accommodate as many as 100 felons at once. Regardless of size, administrators have not forgotten their original purpose. Merfyn Turner said this of his experiences:

> The homeless men . . . who come to Norman House . . . need to learn to live with their fellow men. In the past, the process of learning has not proceeded far because they had no anchorage, nobody to help protect them from their own immature reactions to simple situations which well-integrated members of society take in their stride. Norman House offers that anchor. Living in a state of belonging, accepted as members of the family and not . . . as society's rejects and objects of charity, they see for the first time in their lives, the true nature of "going straight".[2]

[1]*1979–1980 IHHA Directory,* International Halfway House Association, Cincinnati, 1980.
[2]Ronald Goldfarb and Linda R. Singer, *After Conviction,* reprinted by permission of Simon and Schuster, a division of Gulf and Western Corporation, New York, 1973, pp. 555–556.

TYPES OF FACILITIES

Degrees of Freedom

During the nearly 200 years since the first community-based residence for offenders was opened, correctional administrators have developed different models and policies. Professor Stanley Swart has identified six different community residential settings, using the offender's degree of freedom as a criterion for the division. These settings include (1) private family placement of individuals, with unlimited access to the community; (2) homelike settings for a small number of offenders, such as "mom and pop" halfway houses, with ready access to the community, (3) quasi-institutional settings with some degree of privacy but still ready access to the community, such as work release programs housed in YMCAs; (4) quasi-institutional settings with impersonal living arrangements (dormitory) and controlled access to the community, such as work release centers; and (5) quasi-institutional settings with impersonal living arrangements (dormitory) and controlled access to the community, with access often denied to new residents, such as those in prerelease centers utilizing a therapeutic community.[3]

Currently the three most common types of community-based residences are the halfway house, the residential housing unit, and the community correctional center. Despite some differences, these three types do conform to one basic definition: each is a temporary residential facility for offenders, located in the community and offering various programs designed to assist in the reintegration of offenders into a society that has excluded them.[4]

Halfway House

The halfway house continues to be the most popular form. Most of the forty-nine states having halfway houses locate them in former private residences that accommodate fewer than twenty offenders. Some buildings that have been converted into small residences by correctional administrators include an Odd Fellows Hall, a nursing home, a beach club, a school, and a former parish house.[5]

Residential Housing Unit

The residential housing unit provides sleeping quarters for work releasees or preparolees. As many as 100 offenders may reside in a unit at one time. Twenty states and the federal government utilize hotels or apartments for this purpose.

---

[3]Stanley L. Swart, "Conceptualizing Community Residential Programs—Variety in Unity," *Proceedings of the One Hundred and Ninth Annual Congress of Corrections,* American Correctional Association, College Park, Md., 1980, p. 84.

[4]*Graduated Release,* National Institute of Mental Health, Rockville, Md., 1971, p. 15.

[5]Benedict S. Alper and Oliver J. Keller, *Halfway Houses—Community Centered Corrections and Treatment,* D. C. Heath and Company, Lexington, Mass., 1970, p. 2.

The most obvious examples are the prerelease guidance centers of the federal government. Located in metropolitan areas of the country such as Kansas City, Los Angeles, Chicago, and New York, they lease space from YMCAs and churches. Other examples of residential housing units are Florida's converted motel in Ft. Lauderdale and Iowa's leased thirty-three-bed apartment building in Des Moines. Some halfway houses, such as Dismas House in St. Louis, have increased their bed capacity and become residential housing units.

Community Correctional Center

The community correctional center is a multipurpose building that is frequently a converted jail. States that have developed this form of housing include Kentucky, Vermont, and California. In addition to released felons, such centers house misdemeanants, accused felons awaiting trial, and other inmates normally placed in county jails. The center provides all levels of supervision, from maximum to minimum. Sometimes diagnosis and classification for the state is done here. Both walled institutional programs and community-based programs for offenders are administered within the building.

RESIDENTS OF COMMUNITY-BASED HOUSING

Preinstitutional

It seems paradoxical to expect to correct criminal behavior by sending individuals to prison, where they will associate with other criminals. For this reason community-based residences have been used for "halfway-in" offenders. The court may consider an individual too much of a risk to release on probation. Yet he or she may not require incarceration. The court may therefore stipulate that the offender, as a condition of probation, must reside in a halfway house or community correctional center. Probationers who may be experiencing adjustment problems may profit more from placement in a community-based residence than by having their probations revoked.

Offenders can be committed to a community residential center for "study and observation," during which their presentence investigation is completed and a battery of psychiatric or psychological tests administered. Other offenders, such as those released on bail or on their own recognizance prior to final disposition and those charged with victimless crimes, can be housed in such residences in lieu of jail. In this sense, community-based residences assist in diversion from the criminal justice system.

Halfway houses (also called community treatment centers) are sometimes used for individuals with special difficulties such as drug abuse (including alcoholism) or psychiatric problems. These residences have programs especially designed to deal with the specific problems of offenders, who are placed in them both before and after incarceration.

Postinstitutional

The vast majority of community-based residences provide housing for offenders "on the way out" of prison, serving as transitional places for inmates transferring to mandatory release or parole. They buffer offenders from the negative effects of the stress accompanying the sudden change from incarceration to freedom. Other parolees or mandatory releasees may return to community-based residences because of problems after release from prison. Placement is an alternative to revocation and return to prison.

Other offenders are housed in community-based residences to permit their participation in work release or study release. Transfer is regarded as administrative from one "institution" to another "institution," with consideration for mandatory release or parole not yet given. The period "prerelease" status ranges from 30 days to 6 months.

DEVELOPMENT OF THE COMMUNITY-BASED RESIDENCE

Site Selection

Community-based residences are located in rural settings, small towns, and metropolitan areas. They are placed in slum and skid-row districts, commercial areas, working-class neighborhoods, or middle-class suburbs. The area selected is crucial to the success of the reintegration program. More than one study of a successful community-based residence reintegration program has concluded that its success was based on acceptance by the community and location of the residence in a low-delinquency area.[6]

A successful program is dependent on effective use of community resources. Consequently, the housing unit must be accessible to those resources necessary for the reintegration program. The facility must be close to businesses, schools, public transportation, and particularly to leisure-time activities. Locations in skid-row districts may provide opportunities for recreation only in deviant avocations such as drug consumption including alcohol, gambling, and prostitution. Wholesome leisure-time activities popular with offenders include pool, bowling, spectator sports, auto racing, and dancing.

While striving to obtain a residence within easy walking distance of sufficient community resources, correctional administrators have discovered that multiple-occupancy dwellings are frequently suitable. Small hotels, motels, and apartment buildings are usually close to public transportation, job opportunities, shopping areas, and leisure-time activities. Leasing or purchasing buildings already designed for multiple occupancy also lowers the initial cost of establishing residences. YMCA buildings are often used because they are usually near community resources and contain equipment for leisure-time activities. Sometimes dances and other social activities are available within the building.

The community correctional center provides activities within the facility and

[6]Derek Miller, *Growth to Freedom,* Indiana University Press, Bloomington, 1965, pp. 200, 212.

also allows offenders to use community resources. For example, gymnasiums, lounges, recreation rooms, vocational and academic classes, and counseling are available within such centers for medium security offenders. Minimum security offenders are allowed to seek similar services in the community.

A description of a typical community-based residence and its site is contained in the Halfway House Manual for the state of Iowa:

> The structure consists of eleven, three-man apartments, a television room, a lounge, and an office. Each apartment consists of a kitchen, dining area, living area, bedroom and bathroom. All apartments are furnished.
>
> The three men share apartment housekeeping duties at their own discretion. Meals may be taken in the community or prepared in the living quarters. A laundry (coin operated) is maintained in the basement. Recreation at the facility consists of television, radios, card playing, weight lifting, and social visits from friends and relatives. The bulk of recreation activity is taken in the community.
>
> The community surrounding the facility is made up primarily of large apartment buildings. It is located near the business district, which makes things as stores, theaters, bowling, hospitals, employment offices, and other services readily available.[7]

In considering site location, correctional administrators recommend that at least 6 months to a year be set aside for planning. In some places, the search is restricted to areas with certain zoning classifications. Especially important is the selection of a site where offenders can come and go as they please without ostracism by neighbors. A racially, culturally, and economically diverse community offers advantages to similarly mixed offender populations. An apartment house district is frequently within walking distance of commercial services, such as those offered by barbers, shoe repair shops, snack shops, and cleaners, without placing the residents in an unwelcome area.

Sources of Assistance

There are three major sources of assistance in selecting appropriate sites for community-based residences: real estate brokers, community leaders, and public agencies. Real estate brokers are familiar with the property available in most communities. With their assistance, a house or apartment building in an area near commercial and industrial districts can be purchased or leased. Most community leaders are also informed about available real estate, and securing their help also assures their proper education as the program is planned. Public agencies such as the police or welfare department—although not familiar with real estate—are knowledgeable about the positive and negative characteristics of specific geographic locations. Local agency directors can provide information regarding high-crime areas, community resources, and drug use areas.[8]

---

[7]*Halfway House Manual,* State of Iowa Publishing, Des Moines, 1970, pp. 1–2.

[8]Rachin, Richard L., "So You Want To Open a Halfway House," *Federal Probation,* vol. 36, no. 1, Administrative Office of the United States Courts, Washington, D.C., March 1972, pp. 31, 33–34.

SUPERVISION OF RESIDENTS

Planning Supervision

The decision recommending the development of a particular type of residence is undertaken by a planning group, a correctional administrator, or a program manager. A volunteer group usually plans for residences operated by private agencies, while an individual administrator or program manager is given the responsibility for developing a state of federal facility. In both public and private residences the amount of staff control over offenders is determined before the opening of the facility. Both residents and personnel are informed of the conditions of their living arrangements before beginning their group living. The number and nature of the rules and the necessary complement of supervisory staff to implement the rules are decided during the planning period.

Halfway House

Personnel of community-based residences, regardless of size or type of administration, maintain supervisory control over the offenders. The extent of staff supervision depends on the type of sponsoring agency and the purpose of the residence. In a halfway house, the structure may be informal, using peer group pressure as a means of control. Rules are simple and few, based on the requirements for successful interpersonal relations. In a small facility the informal structure and lack of rules minimize the need for personnel. In halfway houses operated by private agencies, a husband and wife may be in charge. Sometimes a member of the clergy, assigned by the religious organization sponsoring the housing unit, may be the only full-time house manager. In both cases, state regulations specifying the ratio of staff to residents and limited finances may require the recruitment of volunteers as the chief method of expanding the number of personnel.

Community Correctional Center

In contrast, large residences such as community correctional centers or residential housing units may incorporate the structure of the walled institution in its entirety. The center utilizes the rules and routine of the traditional correctional institution as a means of controlling movements of large numbers of residents. Most staff are supervisory personnel. The federal government names their supervisory personnel "correctional counselors," but their primary task is supervising residents. Government-sponsored residences provide supervisory personnel 24 hours a day, their number depending on the number of residents. For example, one staff member may be available on each shift for every twenty residents, but fewer supervisory personnel are necessary during hours when the offenders are working or attending school.

General Regulations

Common to all community-based residences are some rules designed to ensure orderly operation of the residence and provide for public safety. Some areas of staff control common to all residences include forbidding drug consumption, including alcohol; controlling unauthorized absences from the residence; and maintaining standards of acceptable behavior for offenders at the residence and legally absent. Other areas of staff control vary greatly. For example, personnel at most residences housing work releasees maintain some control over the amount of money each offender spends and the purposes for which it is spent. In some, rent is charged, ranging from $15.00 to $25.00 a week.[9] Rent may be the only financial obligation required. However, some states insist that debts be paid, restitution be made, funds be given to the offender's family, or a percentage of the offender's wages be placed in savings. The amount of money offenders are allowed to have in their possession also varies.

Staffing Pattern

In housing units where staff control is greater, additional personnel are employed to ensure that goals are met. Usually, an administrative director and a caseworker are regular staff members. In federally operated programs, an employment specialist is maintained. Cooks and housekeepers are employed in some residences. Some agencies have added a community resources developer, a community coordinator, or an activities coordinator to their roster. Such a person's primary responsibility is to prepare the community by establishing job banks, developing necessary community resources, and distributing pertinent information to the public. In addition to salaried personnel, many of the larger residences also recruit volunteers, accept student interns from colleges and universities, or contract with local businesses for food service or cleaning.

PROGRAMS FOR COMMUNITY-BASED RESIDENCES

Informal Relationships

Each type of residence has developed a reintegration program suitable to its particular environment, as explained by the Reverend J.T.L. Jones, a pioneer in the halfway house movement in Canada:

> Some administrators see their work as a continuation of the treatment begun in the institution; they may describe their houses as 'community residential treatment centers.' Others repudiate the concept of 'treatment' in a clinical sense, contending that the inmate has been subjected to professional treatment before in various forms and it has proven ineffective. Thus they offer . . . as natural and home-like an environment as possible. Both types of houses could be termed 'therapeutic communi-

---

[9]Paul Keve, *Imaginative Programming in Probation and Parole,* University of Minnesota Press, Minneapolis, 1970, p. 7.

ties,' one involving professionally trained persons in that community, the other comprising only persons occupying the role and status of family members.[10]

Correctional administrators of halfway houses have traditionally made use of the informal relationship between personnel and residents as a tool to help offenders. The constant interpersonal contact associated with living together in a small group setting is the main aid to reintegration. The interdependence that results from close living arrangements encourages offender and staff reactions simulating those of the free community. As the interpersonal relationship becomes important to each person, concern is demonstrated about the other's reaction. Consequently, when either expresses approval or disapproval of a specific act, the other's reaction influences the direction of future behavior.

Correctional personnel are available to residents with adjustment problems. They maintain limits of behavior and are always there to help when an offender falters. Members of a peer group help each other by reinforcing acceptable behavior and discouraging unacceptable behavior, while salaried correctional personnel are ready to assist with individual problems.

Community Correctional Center

Other residences offer more formal corrections programs. The community correctional center has the greatest variety. The offender has access to all the resources of the community as well as to institutional services such as gymnasium, kitchen, visiting area, infirmary, library, lounge, and laundry. Designed as an institution within the community, it is endorsed by many correctional administrators because it combines traditional correctional controls with an opportunity for the decision making of the free community. Depending on their performance, offenders are given increased or decreased responsibility for managing their own behavior.

California, one of the states that pioneered the use of community correctional centers, uses a three-step process of reintegration. Phase I involves confinement at all times in a secure unit for approximately 1 month. During this phase the inmate is allowed to participate in activities within the institution. Programs available include counseling, vocational or academic education, and classes designed to prepare for release.

Phase II, which lasts approximately 3 months, consists of residence in the secure unit and access to the outside community for work, school, or other activities, supervised and unsupervised. The type of activities offenders are allowed to attend depends on the amount of responsibility demonstrated. They may include academic or vocational classes, job seeking, and entering an Alcoholics Anonymous group. During Phase II the center is functioning as a community-based residence.

Phase III, which lasts approximately 20 months, permits offenders to live in

---

[10]*Graduated Release* op. cit., p. 18.

the community outside the correctional center but requires that they return periodically for group meetings and special services. The center functions as headquarters for probation and parole personnel during this phase. In each case, the number of times offenders must return depends on their adjustment in the free community. Visits are frequent at first but occur less often as they prove that they are responsible.[11]

Residential Housing Unit

Although most community-based residences provide a minimum number of services, the residential housing unit concentrates on basic services to the exclusion of both the informal atmosphere of the halfway house and the great variety of program alternatives of the community correctional center. Basic services are employment placement, counseling, and residence placement. The federally funded prerelease guidance centers or community treatment centers are examples of residential housing units. By allowing offenders to be personally accountable for their behavior in the community, the amount of supervision is minimized. They are encouraged to seek employment, work out personal problems, and organize their own release plan. However, if problems become evident, counselors assist. In connection with employment problems, services may range from helping a resident to fill out job applications to advising him what to wear, how to act, or what to say during an interview. A job bank is maintained for offenders' use, and employment placement specialists are available to administer tests to determine individual aptitudes.

Counseling

Counseling can be sought in the prerelease guidance center on a 24-hour basis. Although the caseworker may not be on duty at night, someone who can listen and respond is always present. The offender is encouraged to seek counseling for personal problems related to family or marriage, interpersonal relations, or internal conflicts. Periodically, classes are conducted on topics such as sex education, money management, federal aid programs, leisure-time activities, and clothes selection.[12]

In an effort to provide greater assistance, correctional personnel at many residences have established support programs. In addition to obtaining help from employment placement specialists or counselors, personnel may conduct regular group meetings to allow staff members and residents an opportunity to exchange views. The meetings may be similar to either New England town meetings or therapeutic group sessions.

---

[11]*Community Based Correctional Programs,* National Institute of Mental Health, Rockville, Md., 1971, pp. 30–31.

[12]Alpert and Keller op. cit., pp. 93–103.

Correctional personnel also maintain complete records on each resident. Every offender is evaluated at regular intervals, and many agencies systemically follow up to determine the degree of success or failure of each person after release.

Representative Programs

Typically, the programs developed at community-based residences show evidence of creativity and diversification. One example exists at the Chittenden Community Correctional Center in South Burlington, Vermont. With consultation from *Gardens For All* staff and the University of Vermont, funds were received from the Comprehensive Employment and Training Act (CETA). Four paid inmate workers raised enough vegetables on a 3½ acre plot to feed 130 inmates and 50 correctional personnel. The plot yielded produce with a retail value of $17,110.93, up about $2000 from the previous year. In 1980 another half acre of a fifty-resident correctional center was added to the project. The half acre brought forth 5089 pounds of produce with a retail value of $3340.87.[13]

Probational Offender Rehabilitation and Training (PORT) operates from a live-in facility on the grounds of the Rochester (Minnesota) State Hospital. It is designed to house males who require more assistance than is given by probation. Both juveniles and adults are accepted, with some twenty offenders in the house at any given time. They remain about 8 months. An average of one out of three juvenile offenders goes on to a juvenile institution, but only one out of nine adults has been institutionalized after residing at PORT.

The program provides real-life experiences and makes much use of existing community resources. Newcomers start at the bottom level of a classification system with categories ranging from 1 to 5. Working from minimum freedom (Level 1) to freedom equal to that of an individual of the same age in the community (Level 5) is accomplished through a combination of earned points and group evaluation.[14]

In Washington, D.C., therapeutic community techniques have been altered to serve the population of a halfway house. Euclid House is operated by the Psychiatric Institute Foundation as one of thirteen halfway houses in the District of Columbia correctional system. The two brownstone houses comprising Euclid House have beds for fifty-five residents. Personnel include a psychiatrist, a clinical director, and thirteen male and female mental health technicians—four of whom are ex-offenders. It is an example of a "halfway out" house.

The program is centered around meetings—6 A.M. meetings 5 times a week, two 1-hour meetings a week with members of the neighborhood, and open confrontations. Authority roles are not restricted but rotate among personnel and residents. Confrontation deals with topics such as irresponsible behavior,

[13]"Prison Gardens Yield Super Harvest," *Gardens For All News,* March–April 1981, p. 39.
[14]Vernon Fox, *Community-Based Corrections,* Prentice-Hall, Inc., Englewood Cliffs, N.J., 1977, pp. 66–67.

fears of independence, intolerance of anxiety, and how to "free up" the house community. Personnel and offenders make program changes together. Obstacles are deliberately created to intensify the residents' need to confront staff members.[15]

PROBLEMS ENCOUNTERED

Community Resistance

In 1978 the United States Bureau of Prisons conducted a survey of approximately 400 private and local government halfway houses. It found that 75 percent rated moderate-to-severe community opposition as their worst problem. The opposition was in the form of public protest by citizens and organizations, letters to various elected officials, passage of prohibitive zoning regulations, and lawsuits.

The objections almost always stem from two issues: fear of the residents and the effect on the neighborhood. Fear of escaping inmates attacking people and burglarizing homes is seldom well-founded, but when it is, it can be disastrous. In Pascagoula, Mississippi an inmate escaped from a work release center in 1977 and raped the daughter of a state senator. The center closed for a few months. In April of the same year, a rape, a murder, and an armed robbery were committed by residents of three separate New York City work release centers. A law was quickly passed reserving the centers for property offenders with few convictions. Available beds stayed empty for lack of eligible prisoners.

Neighbors of prospective community-based residences frequently assume that property values will go down and the number of crimes will increase. One neighbor of a Milwaukee halfway house, a state probation agent, demanded that the director of the house write him a check for $500.00, the amount by which the neighbor estimated the halfway house had lowered the resale value of his home.[16] Although occasional instances of crimes occur, studies measuring the effect of community-based residences on neighborhoods have failed to substantiate these fears. Studies in 1966 in Los Angeles; in 1970 in Washington, D.C.; and in 1979 in Wisconsin failed to find an increase in crime rates or a decrease in property values.

A study of this type was done in Utah and released in March 1980. It revealed that crime rates in the area of the Central Community Corrections Center in Salt Lake City increased 7 percent in 1979–1980, while citywide crime increased 17 percent. The study, which examined twenty-eight housing sales, concluded:

---

[15]Steward L. Aledort and Morgan Jones, "The Euclid House: A Therapeutic Community Halfway House for Prisoners", in Burt Galaway, Joe Hudson, and C. David Hollister (eds.), *Community Corrections,* Charles C Thomas, Publisher, Springfield, Ill., 1976, pp. 134, 135, and 137.

[16]Kevin Krajick, "Not on My Block," *Corrections Magazine,* vol. 6, no. 5, New York, October 1980, pp. 16–18.

"There is no evidence that the presence of a community center increased or decreased property values."[17]

Costs

Halfway houses are expensive to operate. In a prison, operational costs are distributed among many inmates, thus reducing per capita costs. In a halfway house, the costs may be distributed among only fifteen to twenty-five residents. It is hard to sell elected officials the need to appropriate large sums of money to initiate new programs when prisons are already overcrowded and in disrepair. The cost of operating a halfway house may range from $50,000 to $175,000 a year, depending on the economy near the site location, the type of management selected, and the services provided.

To counteract this problem, correctional officials have sought private funds to supplement state money. In many instances, state officials contract services for a fee from private organizations, who in turn seek private monies as additional income. Residents are charged for room and board; volunteers are recruited; college interns are used.

Size of Population

One problem is caused by correctional departments' "overuse" of community-based residences. If a program is successful, there is a tendency to increase the number of residents beyond the program's optimal operational size. This is especially true in times of overcrowded prisons. Managers of community-based residences are then forced to recommend release of inmates before the scheduled time or to become over concerned with security. A supportive environment changes into a taut atmosphere. Rules are borrowed from the prison. Time is spent keeping track of residents. The setting becomes impersonal.

Personnel Problems

Selection of personnel for community-based residences is crucial. If employees are transferred from other institutions, they must be able to function in a nonauthoritarian environment. They must be capable of establishing rapport with offenders; otherwise, they may feel insecure and threatened and resort to mere enforcement of rules and regulations. Preventing rapid turnover of personnel is also important in order to avoid program inconsistency resulting from new rule interpretation and lack of continuity in interpersonal relations with inmates. "Burnout" among correctional personnel in community-based

[17]*Crime Statistics and Property Values: Central Community Corrections Center Primary Impact Area,* Utah State Division of Corrections, Salt Lake City, March 1980, p. 2.

residences is a constant danger, because of the close contacts with inmates and the fear of loss of public acceptance of their jobs.[18]

Pressure to Use Existing Facilities

From the beginning, correctional administrators have been exposed to demands that offenders be housed within existing correctional facilities. Critics argue that the exorbitant costs of development are decreased by converting existing county jails or state and federal correctional institutions. In 1972, twenty states had succumbed to these demands and were using state institutions and jails for community-based residences (see Table 9.1).[19]

Advocates of separate facilities contend that the development of a community-based correctional program within a walled institution does not reduce the effects of prisonization. They argue that unless offenders are segregated completely, they are still exposed to the routinization of a large institution. The inmate code still influences their actions and thinking. This belief is substantiated by information released by the California Department of Corrections. During 1975–1976, of those male felons on work release who resided in prison, 38.5 percent were removed from work release status, compared with 14.9 percent of male felons on work release who resided in county jails or community correctional centers.[20] One reason for this discrepancy could be the tension arising from their half-free status. The experience of being free during the day and confined at night creates anxiety that results in escapes, the use of drugs, and other rule violations.

Another study concluded that much of the "therapeutic work of the unit" consisted of dealing with problems created by the offender's experience in a correctional institution, such as disregard for the feelings of others, exaggerated suspiciousness, and a lack of caring for others.[21] Supporters of community-based residences conclude that if a government agency is willing to spend the time and money to construct segregated facilities within a walled institution in order to eliminate prisonization, it would be better to build or lease a housing unit in the community.

States that have met resistance from the public or from legislatures are using other remedies. Contracts are signed with social service agencies in the community, such as alcoholic treatment centers, for the residential placement of eligible offenders. Many states encourage private groups to operate such residences and help them to apply for funds from the federal government or

[18]E. Eugene Miller, "The Halfway House: Correctional Decompression of the Offender," in E. Eugene Miller and M. Robert Montilla, (eds.), *Corrections in the Community,* Reston Publishing Company, Inc., Reston, Virginia, 1977, pp. 222–223.

[19]Bertram S. Griggs and Gary R. McCune, "Community Correctional Programs: A Survey and Analysis," *Federal Probation,* vol. 36, no. 2, Administrative Office of the United States Courts, Washington, D.C., June 1972, p. 9.

[20]California Department of Corrections, Policy and Planning Division, Management Information Section, November 22, 1976.

[21]Miller, op. cit., pp. 200, 212.

TABLE 9.1
FACILITIES IN COMMUNITY-BASED CORRECTIONAL PROGRAMS

State	Type of facility		
	Hotel/Apt.	Jail	State institution
California	X	X	X
Colorado			X
Connecticut		X	
Florida	X	X	
Georgia	X	X	
Hawaii	X		X
Illinois	X		X
Indiana	X		X
Iowa	X	X	X
Louisiana	X	X	X
Maine	X		
Maryland	X		
Massachusetts			X
Michigan	X		X
Minnesota	X	X	
Nebraska	X		
New Jersey	X		
North Carolina	X		X
Oklahoma	X		
Oregon	X	X	X
Rhode Island			X
South Carolina	X		
Tennessee	X		X
Texas			X
Vermont			X
Virginia		X	X
Washington	X		
Wisconsin		X	X
District of Columbia	X		

Source: Bertram S. Griggs and Gary R. McCune, "Community-Based Correctional Programs: A Survey and Analysis," *Federal Probation,* vol. 36, no. 2, Administrative Office of the United States Courts, Washington, D.C., June, 1972, p. 9.

from their own state crime commission. Unfortunately, in 1980 one major source of funds, the LEAA, greatly curtailed its funding activities, eliminating future funds for adult programs.

APPRAISAL

Evaluation

How do you determine the effect of community-based residences on offenders? That question has not been answered satisfactorily, mainly because it is nearly impossible to separate the effect of such residences from that of work release, temporary releases, family interest, or community involvement. Even in cases where actual studies have been conducted comparing the success of offenders residing in community-based residences and in prisons, researchers have been unable to show conclusively that the housing itself, as part of a complete community-based corrections program, was the cause for the difference in recidivism rates.

Usable data has not been available to justify either the continuation of community-based residences or their closing, although most advocates of these residences have some good hunches. Most of the advocates, including this writer, believe community-based residences can satisfy the community's need for safety at a lower cost than can incarceration. A 1975 study examining the costs of twenty-two representative halfway houses across the country concluded that the average cost per resident per day was $14.18 for the eleven least expensive and $22.26 for the eleven most expensive. These figures were based on a resident capacity of eighteen. In general, the daily per capita cost of operating a halfway house is equal to the per capita cost of a medium security prison.

Cost-effective policies can improve these figures in almost all instances. The most notable change in costs follows the increased use of community resources. Other changes can be made by requiring offenders to assume more responsibility for the cost of their care and allowing private organizations to assist in management.

There are other indirect benefits of community-based residences that contribute to cost-effectiveness. Residents who are working pay taxes, further offsetting costs of care. If an offender is not a recidivist, expenses of the criminal justice system and costs of reincarceration are decreased.

Community Fears

One can expect some apprehension on the part of the public when there is any change to the environment in which they live. The construction of a church or school, the introduction of a residence for mentally retarded adults or the physically handicapped, or the rezoning of an area to "commercial" are examples. In each instance, "What dangers will affect me as a citizen?" is always the question. When offenders are involved, even though the risks may be minimized, the public is harder to satisfy, because the potential threat is so serious—death, assault, or loss of property.

Some community corrections advocates believed public opposition would decrease after a substantial number of community-based residences had been established. Not so, says Richard Vernon, assistant director for community corrections in the Washington Department of Corrections, who wrote that there is "a whole new phenomenon—professional resistance. . . . A few years ago, people used to just pass around petitions. Now it's like war games. You've got the mayor, the city council, new zoning rules, complex litigation, environmental impact statements."[22]

A Response

There are two schools of thought for approaching the community: "Move in the dark of the night" or "Organize the community to befriend you." Citizens believe they are buying protection when they build prisons. Allowing offenders to live in the community is a highly visible contradiction that cannot be overcome by discussing risk factors. Sneaking into a community only delays the confrontation. After all, self-determination by neighborhood groups has been given a bigger and bigger role by city administrators.

The best way to convince citizens is to give community leaders some say in the planning of the residence. A board of trustees or an advisory board which includes community representatives can make the site selection. Open houses allow citizens to view the residents and their housing. Permitting neighborhood organizations to use a room for meetings improves community relations. Employing persons from the neighborhood is a means of educating the public as well as promoting good will.

A public information campaign is essential—before the opening of the residence—to inform the public of the careful screening process used before an offender is placed. Wisconsin releases statistical information annually on residents in community correctional centers. Of special importance to the community in this report is the percentage of residents (73.6 percent) whose offenses were nonviolent (forgery, burglary, or robbery) (see Table 9.2).[23]

The public should be informed that the residence has the advantage of helping offenders cope with stressful situations under real-life circumstances. If an offender has difficulties with heroin addiction, alcohol, family problems, or job-related stress, correctional personnel can respond immediately. Even probation and parole do not have such advantages as close supervision and opportunity for quick response. If an offender fails to go to work, it is known immediately. If a person is using drugs, it can be observed. The community-based residence offers a unique opportunity for corrections personnel to be responsive to an offender's problems.

Another part of the public information campaign outlines the methods used in supervision. Community members should be informed of the various procedures used to monitor offenders' behavior: telephone calls, letters, searches, breathalyzer, marijuana detection kits, and urine sampling. The campaign should describe the system of privileges and how they are earned. Offenders generally are not permitted any more freedom of movement than is appropriate to their demonstrated self-discipline.

[22]Krajick, "Not on My Block," op. cit., p. 16.
[23]*Residents in Wisconsin in Adult Correctional Institutions and Community Correctional Residential Centers on June 30, 1979,* Division of Corrections, Madison, Wisconsin, April 1980, p. 23.

TABLE 9.2
OFFENSES OF RESIDENTS IN COMMUNITY CORRECTIONAL
CENTERS IN WISCONSIN ON JUNE 30, 1979

Offense	Percentage of residents (%)
Murder (1st degree)	0.8
Murder (2d and 3d degree)	4.7
Attempted murder	0.8
Manslaughter	2.3
Negligent homicide	0.8
Robbery (armed)	14.7
Robbery (unarmed)	10.1
Assault	3.9
Injury by conduct regardless of life	1.5
Burglary	17.8
Theft, except auto	6.2
Auto theft	2.3
Fraud or embezzlement	1.5
Forgery or worthless checks	9.3
Sexual assault (1st degree)	3.9
Sexual assault (2d degree)	1.5
Rape (including attempt)	3.9
Other sexual offenses	0.8
Drug violations	6.2
Arson	0.8
Kidnapping, abduction	1.5
All other	4.7
Total	100.0

Source: Residents in Wisconsin Adult Correctional Institutions and Community
Correctional Residential Centers on June 30, 1979, Department of Health and
Social Services, Madison, Wisconsin, April 1980.

CONCLUSION

Community-based residences should be included when developing a statewide
or federal correctional system. When a new institution is planned, pre- and
postinstitutional mechanisms for release should be a major consideration in site
location and program determination.

Offenders must be selected with respect to public safety, balanced against the
knowledge that in 96 percent of the cases, the sentences will terminate and the
offenders will be released. Public safety demands that they be released through
the least dangerous method at the least dangerous time. Maximum security
institutions should be used only for dangerous offenders. Others should be
housed in community-based residences: residential treatment centers, halfway
houses, detoxification units, reintegration centers, and restitution centers.

Since the first community-based residence for offenders was established in
1788, correctional planners have endeavored to develop housing to serve a
variety of needs, including varying degrees of supervision and alternative
programs. In the last quarter of the twentieth century, there is no guarantee that

one type of residence will be superior to another. Whether it is a halfway house operated by a husband and wife or a community correctional center with a large professional staff, results are unpredictable.

The success of each type depends heavily on a site location near community resources essential to reintegration into the community. Thus the major task in establishing a successful program is selection of the site for the housing unit. Without careful planning, the application of a well-developed philosophy and good intentions may be doomed to failure.

The structure of the residence is another key component, because it depends on the purpose for which it is constructed. If the residence is specifically designed to assist the offender by simulating free community living as closely as possible, controls are minimal. If the residence is a large facility designed to help many offenders, the structure is similar to that of a traditional correctional institution, but with less supervision for those who are preparing for release.

One fact has been determined: The only true test of a reintegration program of any community-based residence is the ability of the offender to leave the residence, enter the community, and refrain from further criminal behavior. Ultimately the success or failure of any reintegration program can be judged only by the offender's adjustment after complete release from supervision by correctional personnel.

EXERCISES

1 In what way is the prerelease guidance center like a prerelease center? Like a halfway house? How would you classify the prerelease guidance center?

2 How can the necessary community resources be available for a community-based residence located in a rural community or a small town?

3 Compare and contrast the advantages and disadvantages of the halfway house, residential housing unit, and community correctional center for the offender and for the corrections department.

4 Compare and contrast various residences based on the following criteria: type of offender, degree of supervision, program availability, and use of community resources.

5 What problems and advantages can be anticipated when housing is contracted with private groups or helping agencies?

6 What advantages and disadvantages would there be if ex-offenders and noncorrections personnel were included in planning groups preparing the structure of community-based residences?

7 What factors need to be considered by a planning group before a decision can be reached regarding the number and nature of rules, number of residents, and size of staff?

8 If you were going to design a staffing pattern for a community-based residence, what positions would you request? What special knowledge should the staff possess? What volunteer staff could be utilized from community resources?

9 List in order of preference which staff members you believe would be necessary for a successful community-based residence. Give reasons.

10 Present a statement endorsing or criticizing the reintegration program of each type of

community-based residence. Then defend the specific reintegration program you prefer. One question needs to be answered: Does each type of residence offer a reintegration program?

11 What determinants should state correctional officials use to decide what categories of inmates (parolees, work releasees, probationers, discharged prisoners) should be placed in a halfway house?

12 What type of offenders would benefit most from each form of community-based residence?

13 Could community correctional centers replace all other forms of community-based residences?

14 What kind of problems would result for the offender if the community-based residence were bypassed?

15 Why are programs such as vocational training or academic education insufficient to prevent recidivism?

EXERCISE REFERENCES

Aledort, Stewart L., and Morgan Jones; "The Euclid House: A Therapeutic Community Halfway House for Prisoners," in Burt Galaway, Joe Hudson, and C. David Hollister (eds.), *Community Corrections,* Charles C Thomas Publisher, Springfield, Illinois, 1976, pp. 134–140.

Alper, Benedict S., and Oliver J. Keller: *Halfway Houses—Community Centered Corrections and Treatment,* D. C. Heath and Company, Lexington, Mass., 1970.

The American Correctional Association and the United States Chamber of Commerce: "Community Corrections: A Cheaper and More Humane Approach," George G. Killinger and Paul L. Cromwell, Jr., (eds.), *Penology,* West Publishing Company, St. Paul, Minn., 1973, pp. 382–389.

Anderson, Carol Staples, Barbara Nease, and Taduesz Griygles: "An Exploratory Study of Halfway Houses," *Crime and Delinquency,* vol. 16, no. 3, July 1970, pp. 280–291.

Baker, J. E.: "Preparing Prisoners for Their Return to the Community," in Robert M. Carter, Daniel Glaser, and Leslie T. Wilkins (eds.), *Correctional Institutions,* J. B. Lippincott Company, New York, 1972, pp. 365–380.

Bird, Gordon: "Community Centered Treatment for Offenders," in Edward M. Scott and Kathryn L. Scott (eds.), *Criminal Rehabilitation . . . Within and Without the Walls,* Charles C Thomas Publisher, Springfield, Ill., 1973, chap. 10.

Bradley, H. B.: "Community-Based Treatment for Young Adult Offenders," *Crime and Delinquency,* vol. 15, no. 3, July 1969, pp. 359–370.

Breslin, Maurice, and Robert G. Crosswhite: "Resident After-care: An Intermediate Step in the Correctional Process," *Federal Probation,* vol. 27, no. 1, Administrative Office of the United States Courts, Washington, D.C., March 1963, pp. 37–46.

Burdman, Milton: "Realism in Community-Based Correctional Services," *The Annals of the American Academy of Political and Social Sciences—The Future of Corrections,* vol. 383, January 1969.

Fahey, Frank, and Robert Vasoli: "Halfway Houses for Reformatory Releasees," *Crime and Delinquency,* vol. 16, no. 3, July 1970, pp. 292–304.

Flinn, Nancy: "Prisoners' Good Time, Plus Six Tons of Vegetables," *Corrections Today,* vol. 42, no. 3, May–June 1980, pp. 22, 60, and 74.

Fox, Vernon: *Community-Based Corrections,* Prentice-Hall, Inc., Englewood Cliffs, N.J., 1977, chap. 5.

Galliher, John F.: "Change in a Correctional Institution: A Case Study of the Tightening-up Process," *Crime and Delinquency,* vol. 18, no. 3, July 1972, pp. 263–270.

Griggs, Bertram S., and Gary R. McCune: "Community Correctional Programs: A Survey and Analysis," *Federal Probation,* vol. 36, no. 1, Administrative Office of the United States Courts, Washington, D.C., June 1972, pp. 7–13.

Hall, Reis, Mildred Milazzo, and Judy Posner: *A Descriptive and Comparative Study of Recidivism in Pre-release Guidance Center Releasees,* Bureau of Prisons, United States Department of Justice, Washington, D.C., 1966.

Krajick, Kevin: "Not on My Block," *Corrections Magazine,* vol. 6, no. 5, October 1980, pp. 15–21, 24–27.

Mabry, James: "Alternatives to Confinement," in George G. Killinger and Paul L. Cromwell (eds.), *Penology,* West Publishing Company, St. Paul, Minn., 1973, pp. 359–381.

McCart, John M., and Thomas J. Mangogna: "Overview of Issues Relating to Halfway Houses and Community Treatment Centers," in Robert M. Carter and Leslie T. Wilkins (eds.), *Probation, Parole, and Community Corrections,* John Wiley & Sons, Inc., New York, 1976, pp. 548–567.

Miller, Derek: *Growth to Freedom,* Indiana University Press, Bloomington, 1965.

Miller, E. Eugene: "The Halfway House: Correctional Decompression of the Offender," in E. Eugene Miller and M. Robert Montilla (eds.), *Corrections in the Community,* Reston Publishing Company, Inc., Reston, Virginia, 1977, pp. 213–230.

Nackman, Nathan S.: "A Transitional Service Between Incarceration and Release," *Federal Probation,* vol. 27, no. 4, Administrative Office of the United States Courts, Washington, D.C., December 1963, pp. 43–46.

Powers, Edwin.: "Halfway Houses: An Historical Perspective," *American Journal of Correction,* vol. 21, no. 4, July–August 1959, pp. 20–22, 35.

Rachin, Richard L.: "So You Want To Open A Halfway House," *Federal Probation,* vol. 36, no. 1, Administrative Office of the United States Courts, Washington, D.C., March 1972, pp. 30–37.

Richmond, Mark S.: "Measuring the Cost of Correctional Services," *Crime and Delinquency,* vol. 18, no. 3, July 1972, pp. 243–252.

———: "The Practicalities of Community-Based Corrections," *American Journal of Correction,* vol. 30, no. 6, December, 1968, pp. 12–18.

Schoen, Kenneth F.: "PORT: A New Concept of Community-Based Correction," *Federal Probation,* vol. 36, no. 3, Administrative Office of the United States Courts, Washington, D.C., September 1972, pp. 35–40.

Scudder, Kenyon: "The Open Institution," in David Dressler (ed.), *Readings in Criminology and Penology,* Columbia University Press, New York, 1964, pp. 550–562.

Swart, Stanley L.: "Conceptualizing Community Residential Programs—Variety in Unity," *Proceedings of the One Hundred and Ninth Congress of Corrections,* American Correctional Association, College Park, Md.; 1980, pp. 81–89.

Turner, Merfyn: "The Lessons of Norman House," *The Annals of the American Academy of Political and Social Science—The Future of Corrections,* vol. 383, January 1969.

U.S. Bureau of Prisons: *The Residential Center: Corrections in the Community,* Washington, D.C., 1971.

CHAPTER 10

PAROLE

CHAPTER OBJECTIVES

- To review methods of release after incarceration—parole, pardon, and mandatory release
- To present the status of parole today
- To examine the parole board
- To discuss the processes of selecting the parolee
- To examine the supervision of the parolee
- To describe the conditions of release from parole
- To present evaluations of parole

INTRODUCTION

Preparation for the offender to reenter the community begins with the classification process. For most convicted felons who complete an institutional program, such as vocational and academic education and counseling, authorities use many techniques to ease the transition to the free community. These include prerelease classes, furloughs, work release, and transfer to a community-based residence.

The entire correctional process is designed to help the offender cope with the stresses of living in the world outside the prison. In addition, a multitude of community resources are available to assist the offender after release. However, the final determination whether or not the correctional process has been successful in preventing further criminal behavior cannot be known until the offender's complete release. Parole is the last step in a correctional process designed as preparation for living in the free world.

Definition

Parole is a reintegration program in which an offender is conditionally released under supervision of and with assistance by a parole officer.[1] It is unlike probation, because the offender released on parole has served part of a term in a correctional institution. The release is contingent upon satisfactory behavior. The state retains control of the parolee until he or she is dismissed from parole.

Not all persons released from correctional institutions are under parole. Some are released by pardon, by commutation, by executive order, by discharge at the completion of sentence, or by mandatory or conditional release. A pardon is defined as an act of mercy or clemency—ordinarily by the chief executive officer of the jurisdiction—by which a criminal is excused from a penalty that has been imposed.[2] The pardon may be conditional or not. If it is conditional, release from prison is dependent on the performance of the felon.

A commutation is a reduction of the penalty by executive order. A sentence frequently is commuted so that it expires at once. Death sentences are often commuted to life imprisonment. Ohio governors, for instance, had commuted 38 percent of death sentences according to a 1961 report.[3]

A mandatory or conditional release is the release of a prisoner who is serving a term of commitment less good-time or work-time credit, under parole conditions and under supervision until the expiration of the maximum term of the sentence. Several states have mandatory release laws that provide for release of all prisoners prior to expiration of their sentences. Other states release only those prisoners designated by prison officials. Some mandatory release laws require release for a specified period, such as 6 months. This allows a short period of supervision in the community, similar to a parole.[4]

The various methods of exit from prison create a difference between the permissible sentence for an offense (the minimum and maximum sentences set by statute and imposed by judge and jury) and the sentence actually served (after good-time reductions and early release from prison). Although a statute may provide for a maximum sentence of 20 years, the offender may serve only 6 years. The real sentence is the result of the statutory penalty minus good-time allowances, parole, and other release procedure regulations.

The Ohio state legislature passed a statute authorizing shock parole. Begin-

---

[1]George G. Killinger, Hazel B. Kerper, and Paul F. Cromwell, Jr. *Probation and Parole in the Criminal Justice System,* West Publishing Company, St. Paul, Minn., 1976, p. 12.

[2]Edwin H. Sutherland and David R. Cressey. *Criminology,* J. B. Lippincott Company, Philadelphia, 1970, p. 578.

[3]Ohio Legislative Service, *Capital Punishment,* Staff Research Report no. 46, Columbus, 1961, p. 46.

[4]Killinger, Kerper, and Cromwell, op. cit., pp. 7, 11.

ning January 1, 1974, first offenders were eligible for release on parole after serving a minimum of 6 months. Restrictions excluded offenders convicted of aggravated murder, murder, felony of the first degree, narcotic drug offense, hallucinogen offense, felony drug-abuse offense, or adjudication as a psychopathic offender. In 1978, the Ohio parole board conducted 1751 shock parole hearings, releasing 574 inmates.[5]

PAROLE TODAY

Overview

Parole is the result of an administrative act by a statewide authority, usually called the board of parole, which is responsible for the decision to grant or to revoke parole and for parole supervision. Parole may be for a specified period or until the termination of the felon's sentence. In some states, the parole authority also has certain responsibilities regarding review and revocation of pardons or probation.

The parole system has two purposes: to reintegrate the convicted prisoner so that he or she will be able to live a useful life in society, and to protect society from the criminal behavior of some of its members.[6]

Advantages

The advantages of parole are many:

1 The cost of supervising offenders on parole is less than that of keeping them in an institution. The National Institute of Corrections National Information Center found that the average cost of imprisonment in 1981 was $29.10 a day per offender, compared with $1.67 for supervision of a person on parole. The range of costs was $13.73 to $66.67 a day per offender for imprisonment and $0.51 to $3.77 for parole supervision.[7]

2 Paroled offenders can support their families and assume other personal responsibilities, which must be performed by others when they are incarcerated.

3 Parole is an ego builder for most inmates, especially if administered as a positive reward for good behavior within correctional walls.

4 Parole gives convicted persons assistance during the transition from routinized institutional life to acceptance of social responsibilities outside the prison walls.

5 Parole lessens the negative effects of prisonization by shortening prisoners' dependence on institutional structure.

---

[5]*Annual Report,* Ohio Department of Rehabilitation and Correction, Division of Parole and Community Services, Columbus, 1978, pp. 13–14.

[6]Hazel B. Kerper, *Introduction to the Criminal Justice System,* West Publishing Company, St. Paul, Minn., 1972, p. 367.

[7]Jo Gustafson, National Institute of Corrections, National Information Center, telephone conversation, Dec. 18, 1981.

6 Well-informed correctional administrators, working closely with parole boards, can recommend the optimum release time for each offender. The community then can receive each offender at a time when he or she is most likely to succeed.

Criticisms

A number of criticisms have been leveled at the parole process: (1) The parole decision itself is sometimes considered inappropriate. When violent or other forms of antisocial behavior occur, the paroling authorities are criticized for their failure to have recognized the potential problem when they released the perpetrator. (2) Some parole personnel do not receive the training required to interpret information properly or to provide necessary assistance to the parolee. (3) Even if parole officers are properly trained, the number of cases assigned to them is sometimes so high that they are unable to exercise their professional responsibility properly.

The use of parole is further complicated by the legal issues confronting parole boards, which are often in a state of uncertainty. Many procedural questions have not been clearly answered by the United States Supreme Court. One example is the legal circumstances associated with parole revocation. Does the promise of immunity from criminal prosecution for testimony given bar the use of such testimony in a parole revocation hearing? May evidence seized in violation of the Fourth Amendment be used at a revocation hearing? Under what circumstances may criminal court procedures be used in lieu of the preliminary revocation hearing?[8]

RELEASE FROM PRISON

Parolees' "Gate" Resources

In 1979, there were 120,100 prisoners (39 percent of the total number incarcerated) released from state and federal institutions under some form of conditional supervision. Less than 3 percent of the total number of departures were due to death. There were 81,811 prisoners paroled and an additional 24,416 released from confinement under supervised mandatory release. Only 30,025 were released following expiration of sentence.[9]

There were an estimated 196,500 parolees and 25,000 mandatory releasees under the jurisdiction of fifty-five paroling authorities as of December 31, 1979, bringing the estimated total of conditional release population to 221,500.

Inmates can expect that if they are conditionally released, it will probably be under parole conditions. They can further anticipate being on parole for an

---

[8]Eugene N. Barkin, "Legal Issues Facing Parole," *Crime and Delinquency,* vol. 25, no. 2, April 1979, p. 219.

[9]*Parole in the United States 1979,* U.S. Department of Justice, Washington, 1979, pp. 28 and 34.

average of 29 months, although the length of time varies in different areas of the country. The average length of parole is 21 months in the midwest and Plains states and 37 months in the south. There is further discrepancy within individual states, ranging from 12 to more than 84 months.[10] There has also been a tendency to lengthen parole since the start of the "get tough" policy in the 1970s.

Most prisoners will be released from prison with no more than $134.00, including both savings and "gate money"; a ticket home; and a new suit (see Tables 10.1 and 10.2).[11] The average federal releasee in 1974 received $45.00 plus clothing and transportation.[12] Upon returning home, the releasee will probably be required to report to a parole officer, to notify the local law enforcement agency, to begin work on the first working day following arrival, and to find a residence. The average parolee can expect the parole officer to be supervising sixty-seven other parolees.

Offenders released from prison without parole receive a suit of clothes, a ticket home, and approximately the same amount of money, but no assistance from a parole officer in obtaining employment, seeking a residence, or dealing with personal problems. Felons who are discharged from prison are alone, a condition that frequently results in their return to a correctional institution. For

[10]The President's Commission on Law Enforcement and the Administration of Justice, *Task Force Report: Corrections,* U.S. Government Printing Office, Washington, D.C., 1967, p. 187.

[11]Kenneth J. Lenihan, "The Financial Resources of Released Prisoners," *Proceedings: Second National Workshop on Corrections and Parole Administration,* American Correctional Association, College Park, Md., 1974, pp. 114, 122.

[12]United States General Accounting Office, *Use of Statutory Authority for Providing Inmate Release Funds,* U.S. Government Printing Office, Washington, D.C., Aug. 16, 1974, p. 3.

TABLE 10.1
SUMMARY OF GATE MONEY AMOUNTS—1971—BY NUMBER OF STATES

Amount	Gate money regardless of savings	Gate money as a supplement to savings	Neither
Less than $20	9	1	
$20 to $29	13	6	
$30 to $39	2	–	
$40 to $49	3	–	
$50 to $59	6	2	
$60 or more	3	4	
Neither gate money nor a supplement			2
	36	13	2

Source: Kenneth J. Lenihan, "The Financial Resources of Released Prisoners," *Proceedings: Second National Workshop on Corrections and Parole Administration,* American Correctional Association, College Park, Md., 1974, p. 114.

TABLE 10.2
SAVINGS OF ALL INMATES RELEASED FROM
MARCH 1, 1972, TO FEBRUARY 28, 1973
(One Eastern State)

Savings		Percentage
$20 or less		17% (475)
$21 to $50		39% (1115)
$51 to $100		18% (523)
	Subtotal	74%
$101 to $150		7% (212)
$151 to $200		3% (97)
$201 to $300		4% (126)
$301 to $400		3% (77)
Over $400		8% (221)
	Total	100% (2850)

Source: Kenneth J. Lenihan, "The Financial Resources of Released Prisoners," *Proceedings: Second National Workshop on Corrections and Parole Administration,* American Correctional Association, College Park, Md., 1974, p. 122.

this reason, except for sentencing, no decision in the criminal justice process has more impact on the convicted offender than the release decision.

Parolees' Expectations

Studies of offenders released from prison reveal that criminals have high aspirations but little means of achieving them. Most criminals grew up in areas where crime and delinquency were prevalent, and have known other criminals most of their lives. They have few ties with the "straight" social world. Their choice of criminal behavior as a means of fulfilling middle-class aspirations seems reasonable.

Few criminals have known lives free from want of basic needs: job, money, car, and a place to stay. Criminals must be integrated into the straight social world, with opportunities to be legitimately self-sufficient. What "regular citizen" could exist today with less than a high school education, no job, $50.00, and no close personal ties or other resources and "make it"? To respond to these apparent discrepancies between aspirations and ability to achieve them, opportunities should be developed to maintain marital and other family relationships while creating ties with the larger social structure.

THE PAROLE BOARD

Administrative Structure

The parole board is an administrative body appointed by the governor which determines when certain inmates will be released under parole supervision.

Parole boards are of three principal types, although various combinations exist. One type limits its decision making to inmates in one institution; it sometimes includes institutional personnel or the warden. A second type is part of the state department of corrections, with authority to release inmates from any state institution. A third type is independent of the state department of corrections but has authority to release prisoners from any state institution.

According to a 1980 survey made for the American Correctional Association (ACA), which examined state and federal parole boards, eleven parole boards are autonomous, thirty are within the state department of corrections, and ten are part of a larger state agency.[13] In no jurisdiction is the final power to grant or deny parole given only to personnel who operate correctional institutions. States that have passed determinate sentencing laws (Arizona, California, Illinois, Maine, New Mexico, and Indiana) are eliminating their parole boards.

The number of members on a parole board may vary from three to eleven, depending on the size of the state. Twenty-five jurisdictions have five members; twelve have three. The model penal code of the American Law Institute recommends a 6-year term for parole board members, with the chairman designated by the governor. It stipulates that all members serve full time, engage in no other business or profession, and hold no other public office. In forty-five states, the governor appoints the parole board. Wisconsin and Ohio are the only states where members come from a civil service list.[14] In 1980 there were thirty-one states with full-time parole boards. Some states pay only the expenses of parole board members; others pay salaries as well.

The model penal code states: "No member shall, at the time of his appointment or during his tenure, serve as a representative of any political party, or any executive committee or governing body thereof, or as an executive officer or an employee of any political party, organization, association, or committee."[15] Despite this recommendation, parole board members often are selected as a reward for service to a political candidate or party. It is not unusual for new parole board members to be appointed each time there is a change of political parties in state administration.

Professional Parole Board

The President's Commission on Law Enforcement and Administration of Justice suggests a merit system for parole board members. It recommends requirement of a college degree—preferably in the field of criminology, education, psychology, psychiatry, social work, or law—plus experience. In addition, the commis-

---

[13]*American Correctional Association Directory, 1981,* American Correctional Association, College Park, Md., 1981, p. xx.

[14]William Parker, *Parole: Origins, Development, Current Practices and Statutes,* Parole Corrections Project, Resources Document no. 1. American Correctional Association, College Park, Md., 1975, pp. 53–54.

[15]Copyright 1962 by the American Law Institute. Reprinted with the permission of the American Law Institute.

sion recommends that a board of experts assist in making appointments from a list of candidates nominated by committees of qualified persons, similar to the appointments of judges in some jurisdictions. Parole board members should be persons of integrity, intelligence, and good judgment, with personal qualifications equal to those of the highest judicial officer in the state, so as to command public confidence.[16]

Another suggestion is the use of professional examiners to conduct hearings and interviews for the parole board. According to this suggestion, the board would delegate to these examiners only the power to make certain decisions. The board would concern itself with policy questions, unusual cases having public impact, and guidelines for parole fieldworkers. It also would act as an appellate body on the decisions of its examiners. Proponents of this system state that it would permit the development of professional examiners with the background and skills necessary to perform the complex tasks involved in parole decision making. At the same time, it would free the parole board to carry out the functions that should not be delegated. Another argument for this system is that professional examiners with training and experience in the correctional field would communicate more effectively with parole board members, institutional personnel, and inmates.[17]

THE SELECTION PROCESS

Standards for Granting Parole

The formal parole process begins when the parole board decides to consider release of a prisoner under parole supervision. A favorable decision is based on positive answers to a series of questions: (1) Is the inmate a fit risk for parole? (2) Will he or she be able to benefit from parole supervision? (3) Does he or she have a favorable attitude toward society? (4) Does he or she want parole? (5) Will the prisoner agree to abide by the rules and regulations? (6) Was the crime committed by the prisoner nonviolent?

Some states have established lists of specific factors to be considered by their parole boards in their decision making, which serve as standards for granting parole. Connecticut has such a list as part of its Statement of Organization and Procedures (see Figure 10.1).

Eligibility for Parole

In sixteen states an inmate is eligible for parole after completing the minimum sentence. Ten states deduct "good time" from the minimum. New York, for example, reduces all minimum terms by a period of 10 days per month for

[16]President's Commission on Law Enforcement and Administration of Justice, *Task Force Report: Corrections,* op. cit., p. 67.

[17]F. Lowell Bixby, "A New Role for Parole Boards," *Federal Probation,* vol. 34, no. 2, Administrative Office of the United States Courts, Washington, D.C., June 1970, p. 27.

FIGURE 10.1

STANDARDS FOR GRANTING PAROLE

Parole is not granted merely as a reward for good conduct or efficient performance of duties. There are many factors involved in the decision of the board as to the "reasonable probability" that an inmate will not violate the law and that his or her release is compatible with the welfare of society. Most inmates, but not all, are afforded at least one parole prior to the expiration of their sentences.

Among the factors considered by the board's panels in the parole decision process are:

1 The nature and circumstances of the inmate's offense and his or her current attitude toward it.

2 Prior criminal record and parole adjustment if the inmate has been paroled previously.

3 The inmate's attitude toward family members, the victim, and authority in general.

4 The inmate's institutional adjustment, including participation and progress in the areas of the institutional program important to self-improvement.

5 The inmate's employment history, occupational skills, and employment stability.

6 The inmate's physical, mental, and emotional health.

7 The inmate's insight into the causes of his or her past criminal conduct.

8 The inmate's efforts to find solutions to personal problems such as addiction to narcotics, excessive use of alcohol, and need for academic and vocational education, and use of resources related to such problems in the institutional program.

9 The adequacy of the inmate's parole plan, including the environment to which he or she will return, the character of those with whom he or she will associate, and his or her residence and employment program.

Source: From Statement of Organization and Procedures, Board of Parole, State of Connecticut. Appeared in George F. Cole's: The American System of Criminal Justice, Duxbury Press, North Scituate, Mass., 1975, pp. 407–408.

satisfactory behavior, although this time may be forfeited for serious misbehavior. In the District of Columbia, the federal system, and ten states, an inmate is eligible for parole after one-third of the maximum sentence. Other states set eligibility according to the length of the sentence or the number of previous felony convictions. In some states, such as Minnesota, there is no required minimum period; at a preliminary meeting shortly after the inmate's arrival at an institution; the parole board determines the eligibility date at which it will consider parole.[18]

[18]Parker, op. cit., pp. 60–66.

Although most parole systems do not have special conditions prerequisite to parole eligibility, there are exceptions. In 1978 the Florida legislature passed a bill requiring all inmates to declare their income and assets, with parole eligibility revoked for anyone refusing. Each inmate is assessed the cost of prison room and board. This amounts to $14.64 a day, or less if the inmate does not earn enough to pay this much. By the end of September only 843 inmates had refused to declare. At that time, however, the state had collected only $3103 of the total assessed $43,000.[19]

Preparole Report

While asking the questions listed earlier, parole board members use a number of techniques in an effort to determine the answers. Individual reports are requested from institutional personnel familiar with the inmate. In this preparole report his or her institutional adjustment is described in detail, including a behavior summary, programs attended, personal accomplishments, and a current problem assessment. At the same time, information is sought from the inmate concerning parole plans.

A feasibility study of the parole plan is sometimes conducted. Frequently this includes a field investigation within the community to which the inmate wishes to go. In many states parole authorities request information from the presentence investigation conducted by the probation officer.

Parole Hearings

Another means of obtaining information is the parole hearing, which is conducted in a number of ways. Some jurisdictions have the entire board interview inmates; in others only part of the board interviews. In some states boards are split into smaller working panels, each of which conducts hearings on its own, with the power to grant or deny parole. In the case of denial, a requirement often exists that the case be referred to the full board if the vote is less than unanimous. A few jurisdictions use hearing examiners to interview inmates. Some states do not interview inmates at all; they make their decisions solely on information from written reports. Other states permit counsel to represent inmates and allow witnesses to testify in some instances as well. Thirty-seven states and the District of Columbia request a recommendation from prison personnel regarding the inmate's readiness for parole.[20]

Parole interviews allow board members to view inmates as persons. Questions raised by the written reports are resolved, and the inmates frequently have the opportunity to plead their cases. Although the impression an inmate creates during the interview has a bearing on whether or not parole is granted, most

[19]Marc Levinson, "'Pay as You Stay' or Stay Longer," *Corrections Magazine,* vol. 5, no. 4, December 1979, pp. 22–23.

[20]Vincent O'Leary and Joan Nuffield, "Parole Decision-Making Characteristics: A Report of a National Survey," in Burt Galaway, Joe Hudson, and C. David Hollister (eds.), *Community Corrections,* Charles C Thomas Publisher, Springfield, Ill., 1976, pp. 155–156.

board members attempt to see each prisoner objectively. As of January 1972, inmates in twenty-three states were interviewed by the full parole board. In all others (except Texas, Georgia, and Hawaii, and also the District of Columbia and the Federal Bureau of Prisons, which have no parole hearings) from one to three members of the board interview potential parolees. Forty-three percent of the parole boards inform inmates of their decision. In the remainder, inmates are informed by someone other than a parole board member after the hearing has been completed.[21] Table 10.3 lists parole hearing practices.

Greenholtz Decision

Inmates sometimes challenge the practices of parole boards as being arbitrary and capricious. The Nebraska Eighth Court of Appeals ordered the state to provide a full hearing, with at least 3 days advance notice, whenever an inmate came up for review and to provide the inmate with a statement of the evidence used in parole denial. The Supreme Court, by a five-to-four vote in the *Greenholtz v. Inmates* case, held that due process is not a guarantee in parole board hearings. States are free to administer parole systems as they wish and are under no requirement to interview prisoners or inform them of the reasons for denial of parole.[22]

---

[21]Neal Shover, *A Sociology of American Corrections,* The Dorsey Press, Homewood, Ill., 1979, pp. 203–204.

[22]Fred Cohen, "Parole Release Decision Making and Constitutional Requirements—The *Greenholtz* Decision," *Criminal Law Bulletin,*vol. 17, no. 4, Warren, Gorham & Lamont, Inc., Boston, July–August 1981, pp. 344–348.

TABLE 10.3
SELECTED PAROLE HEARING PRACTICES OF 51
STATE* AND FEDERAL PAROLE BOARDS
(Felony Offenders, January 1972)

	Number of boards	
Selected practices	**Yes**	**No**
Counsel permitted at hearing	21	30
Inmate permitted to present witnesses	17	34
Reasons for decision recorded	11	40
Verbatim record of proceedings made	20	31
Inmate informed of decision directly	22	29

*States of Georgia, Hawaii, and Texas not included, because no hearings are conducted in these jurisdictions.
Source: Vincent O'Leary and Joan Nuffield, "Parole Decision-Making Characteristics: Report of a National Survey," Burt Galaway, Joe Hudson, and C. David Hollister (eds.), in *Community Corrections,* Charles C Thomas, Publisher, Springfield, Ill., 1976, p. 156.

Chief Justice Warren Burger, who wrote the majority opinion, said:

> That the state holds out the possibility of parole provides no more than a mere hope that the benefit will be obtained. To that extent the general interest asserted here is no more substantial than the inmate's hope that he will not be transferred to another prison, a hope which is not protected by due process.[23]

In response to these challenges the National Advisory Commission on Criminal Justice Standards and Goals recommended that parole hearings should be scheduled with inmates within 1 year after they enter the institution, that they should appear personally at the parole hearing and that parole decisions should be based on the quality and pertinence of program objectives agreed on by the inmate and institution personnel and completed by the inmate. The commission also recommended that if parole is denied, an interview date within 1 year should be set; that a parole board member or examiner should hold no more than twenty hearings a day; that an inmate should have access to parole-denial appeal procedures; that the inmate should be notified of the parole decision before the parole board leaves the institution and if denied, should be informed in writing of the reasons for denial; and that parole procedures should permit representatives of offenders to appear at hearings.[24]

Prediction Techniques

Over the years, correctional practitioners and theorists have endeavored to incorporate objective techniques of predicting future behavior of inmates into the parole selection process. Norval Morris suggests that there are three types of predictions of human behavior: (1) anamnestic, based on observations of past behavior in identical or similar situations; (2) categoric, based on statistical compilations which predict repetition of certain behavior for certain people; and (3) intuitive, based on purely intuitive or subjective information.[25]

Many states provide parole board members with actuarial tables designed to predict behavior of potential parolees. These tables analyze past experience to predict an offender's future behavior.[26] However, only in Wisconsin and Illinois have formal parole prediction tables routinely been used. Wisconsin used a base-expectancy-type table, and Illinois used a synthesis of several tables until 1979, when parole was abolished.[27]

[23]*Greenholtz v. Inmates of Nebraska Penal and Correctional Complex*, 99 S. Ct., 2100 (1979).

[24]National Advisory Commission on Criminal Justice Standards and Goals, *Corrections*, U.S. Government Printing Office, Washington, D.C., 1973, p. 422.

[25]Norval Morris, *The Future of Imprisonment*, The University of Chicago Press, Chicago, 1974, pp. 31–32.

[26]Daniel Glaser, "Prediction Tables As Accounting Devices for Judges and Parole Boards," *Crime and Delinquency*, vol. 8, no. 3, July 1962, p. 240.

[27]Vernon Fox, *Introduction to Corrections*, Prentice-Hall, Inc., Englewood Cliffs, N.J., 1977, pp. 318–319.

Parole prediction tables have been used since the 1920s, when sociologists W. Lloyd Warner (1923) and Ernest W. Burgess (1928) developed the first ones. The table by Burgess, using only existing records, has become the prototype for most parole prediction methods.

Criminologist Ferris Laune made a study based on analyses of the hunches of fellow inmates. Some of the statistical material used in developing the "Truth Group" was allegedly done by "Inmate X" (Nathan Leopold, the convicted murderer of young Bobby Franks in 1924.)[28]

The United States Parole Commission uses an actuarial device to predict the likelihood of a favorable outcome upon release. Termed a "salient factor score," it is based primarily on items indicating the absence of criminal behavior patterns (higher age at first conviction, no heroin or opiate dependence, and 6 months' employment during the last 2 years before conviction) and of previous instability (see Table 10.4).[29]

The creators of parole prediction tables believed that based on records of behavior of similar offenders, the likelihood of success for a given group could be predicted. Information is gathered from presentence investigations, previous community supervision reports, and classification summaries by correctional personnel. The information may include type of offense, marital status, age, and prior criminal record.

Studies of prediction tables have indicated that offenders most likely to be successful on parole are mature married persons, well-behaved during incarceration, who began criminal careers late in life, who have had little or no previous criminal history, and who have good work habits and capabilities. Obviously, parole board confidence in the staff members preparing the prediction table is a prerequisite to its effective development and use.

One Israeli study compared an early-release committee composed of correctional experts with a computer using the same criteria for release. A 5-year follow-up showed that 75.4 percent of the inmates released by the committee were reconvicted but only 30.3 percent of those recommended by the computer.[30]

However, most studies of predicting offender behavior on parole have not demonstrated any particular advantages of prediction tables. Researcher John Stanton concluded that the crucial question facing the parole board member "is not so much whether or not a parolee is classified as being in a poor risk group, it is: when is the best time to release the inmate? No parole prediction device has been yet developed which will answer that question."[31]

---

[28]Ferris Laune, *Predicting Criminality*, Northwestern University Press, Evanston, Ill., 1937.

[29]Peter B. Hoffman and Sheldon Adelberg, "The Salient Factor Score: A Nontechnical Overview," *Federal Probation*, vol. 44, no. 1, Administrative Office of the United States Courts, Washington, D.C., March 1980, p. 49.

[30]Yale Hassin, "Early Release Committee for Prisoners versus Computer," *Criminology*, vol. 18, no. 3, November 1980, p. 385.

[31]John M. Stanton, *Success Rates of Male Parolees*, State of New York, Division of Parole, Albany, 1970, p. 9.

TABLE 10.4
PAROLEES DECLARED VIOLATORS, AS RELATED
TO VARIOUS TYPOLOGIES

Typologies and their categories	Violators	
	Number	Percentage
Social development pattern		
Respected citizen	117	6
Fairly conventional	403	14
Inadequate	739	40
Ne'er-do-well	826	44
Dissipated	180	54
Floater	135	49
Socially maladjusted	287	61
Age at first leaving home or foster home for 6 months or more		
15 or under	710	52
16	362	44
17	447	41
18	401	32
19	267	31
20 or over	489	27
Seven-factor prediction table score		
−11 to −9	23	87
− 8 to −5	364	62
− 4 to −2	607	49
− 1 to 1	734	40
2 to 4	535	31
5 to 7	267	12
8 to 10	107	6
All cases*	2637	39

*Cases for which information on all seven factors was available in the files.
Source: Peter B. Hoffman and Sheldon Adelberg, "The Salient Factor Score: A Nontechnical Overview," *Federal Probation*, vol. 44, no. 1, Administrative Office of the United States Courts, Washington, D.C., March 1980, p. 49.

Mutual Agreement Program

One of the more innovative methods of parole selection is called Mutual Agreement Program (MAP), which allows an inmate to negotiate face to face with the parole board shortly after entrance into prison, regarding both institutional program and release date. The inmate contracts to complete certain segments of the program, such as obtaining a high school diploma or taking a vocational training course. The parole board agrees to parole the convict when the contract is completed. In most cases a date by which the agreement will be fulfilled is decided on. That date is also the inmates release date.

MAP was developed by the Parole Correction Project of the ACA in 1974, although Minnesota had begun to offer similar contracts to inmates in 1971, before the ACA project was started. By 1975 Maryland, Florida, Georgia, Maine, Massachusetts, Michigan, Minnesota, North Carolina, Wisconsin, and the District of Columbia used MAP-like contracts, in which about 4000 inmates were involved.[32] In Wisconsin nearly half of the MAP contracts were for 6 to 12 months. The total term of incarceration for MAP participants averaged 19 months.

The first of four intended follow-ups of MAP participants subsequently released on parole by Wisconsin officials indicated no significant difference in parole adjustment between MAP and non-MAP parolees. Approximately 75 percent of both groups maintained their paroles.[33]

In 1975 Massachusetts Half-Way Houses, Inc., opened 699 House, using the MAP process. 699 House is operated under a three-party agreement between the state department of corrections, state parole board, and Massachusetts Half-Way Houses, Inc. Inmates are placed in the house after receiving their parole dates. A contract is negotiated between inmate and house personnel for the completion of certain performance goals. Each resident is paroled after the sixth week if the contract performance goals are completed. At the time of parole the contract is updated to include a release plan and give the residents more control over their lives.

Forty-nine residents (71 percent) successfully completed their contracts in 1976. Table 10.5 shows the percentage of residents who achieved individual MAP contract goals. The highest percentage was the the 30- to 39-year-old group (94 percent); the lowest was the 17- to 19-year-old group (67 percent).[34]

PAROLE SUPERVISION

Caseloads

The average parolee is assigned to an officer responsible for supervising 68 offenders, as well as for investigating release plans and developing future employment opportunities for inmates still in prison. In thirty states, the same officer also conducts presentence investigations. The recommended caseload is 50 persons or fewer, but the actual size of caseloads varies from 20 in intensive supervision experiments to 200 or more in areas where probationers and parolees are supervised together. Obviously, releasing authorities must take into account probable caseload size in considering an offender for parole.[35]

---

[32]Stephen Gettinger, "Parole Contracts: A New Way Out," *Corrections Magazine,* vol. 2, no. 1, New York, October 1975, p. 4.

[33]*Mutual Agreement Program Practical Outcome Evaluation,* Division of Corrections, Madison, Wisc., July 1977, p. 28.

[34]J. Brian Riley, "Mutual Agreement Programs: Contracting for Client Change," *Community Corrections Institute,* Montana Board of Crime Control, Helena, 1978, pp. 190, 198.

[35]Ronald L. Goldfarb and Linda R. Singer, *After Conviction,* Simon and Schuster, New York, 1973, p. 287.

TABLE 10.5
MAP PARTICIPANTS—699 HOUSE: CONTRACT GOAL
COMPLETION

Contract goals	Percentage of participants completing
Full-time vocational placement	100
Employed	97
School	2
Vocational training	4
Accepted for vocational training by state vocational rehabilitation agency	37
Participated in upgrading vocational skill while in program	37
Savings (average $442)	100
Established monetary credit	35
Participated in outside therapy	50
Did volunteer work in community	47
Participated in out-residency	63
Relocated to new neighborhood on program completion	82

Source: J. Brian Riley, "Mutual Agreement Programs: Contracting for Client Change," *Community Corrections Institute,* Montana Board of Crime Control, Helena, 1978, p. 198.

Effect of Caseload Size

The importance of the quality of parole officer supervision and assistance has been demonstrated by a study of juvenile cases in California. In forty-four instances juveniles who received services beyond the minimum requirements of the agency were judged as 72.7 percent successful after 18 months. Success was determined by favorable discharge during that time or favorable adjustment up to that time. For the fifty-three cases receiving no more than minimal supervision, only 32.1 percent were judged successful.[36] In contrast, a review of caseload research by M. G. Neithercutt and Don M. Gottfredson, of the United States Probation Division, concluded that caseloads of fifteen do no better than caseloads of thirty. Furthermore, narcotics users in thirty-person caseloads do no better than those in seventy-person caseloads.[37]

During the 1950s California carried out a number of experiments examining the relationship between caseload size and parole success. The project, named the Special Intensive Parole Unit (SIPU), was divided into four phases. Phase I,

[36]Bertram M. Johnson, *An Analysis of Predictions of Parole Performances and Judgment of Supervision in the Parole Research Project,* Department of Youth Authority, Report no. 32, Sacramento, Calif., December 1962.

[37]M. G. Neithercutt and Don M. Gottfredson, "Caseload Variation and Difference in Probation/Parole Performance," Administrative Office of the United States Courts, Washington, D.C., 1973, processed.

begun in 1952, compared caseloads for 90 days prior to the parolee's scheduled release. Phase II, conducted between January 1956 and June 1957, compared caseloads of 30 persons and 100 persons for 6 months. Phase III measured the effectiveness of 35- versus 90-person caseloads from July 1957 to June 1959. Phase IV added an attempt to match specific types of parole agents with specific types of parolees. Phase III was the only experiment showing positive results; the other three phases indicated no differences between the experimental and control groups, or the results were inconclusive.

Parole Aides

In an effort to assist parole officers with excessive caseloads, a number of parole departments have hired nonprofessional aides. A 1975 survey revealed sixteen states using ex-offenders as parole officer aides: Alaska, California, Florida, Idaho, Illinois, Iowa, Kentucky, Michigan, New Jersey, Ohio, Pennsylvania, Utah, Vermont, Virginia, Washington, and Wisconsin. The aides perform tasks similar to those of parole officers—interviewing, counseling, job development, and follow-up—thus enabling the officers to provide more intensive services. The ex-offenders were especially effective, sometimes appearing better able to communicate with parolees than were the parole officers.[38]

Styles of Supervision

Parole supervision can be examined from a number of points of view. If supervision itself is considered a reintegration strategy, the knowledge and skills used by the parole officer encourage reduction of criminality through the solution of problems. The officer, in fact, serves as a diagnostic arm of the parole board and as a community organization specialist mobilizing agencies to resolve problems of specific offenders. However, the sympathy of some parole officers for offenders gets in the way of viewing objectively their problems and their potential for acceptable social behavior.

At the other extreme is the policing strategy, in which the duties of supervision emphasize protection of the community. The parole officer serves only as a police officer, communicating to the offender the fear that parole will be revoked.[39]

The most difficult task for parole officers is balancing these contradictory roles. As the enforcers of rules, they are given the power to restrict many aspects of the parolees' lives and to revoke release at will. In many states, officers can even search the parolees' houses without warning, arrest them without bail for suspected violations, and suspend parole pending a hearing.

Parole officers must be helpers—helping parolees to find jobs and residences and to restore family ties. They may be resource brokers as well, channeling

[38]Bartollas, Clemens, *Introduction to Corrections,* Harper and Row Publishers, Incorporated, New York, 1981, pp. 195, 198.

[39]Elmer Hubert Johnson, *Crime, Correction, and Society,* The Dorsey Press, Homewood, Ill., 1968, pp. 677–678.

parolees to the social agencies that can aid them. They must establish enough trust with the parolees that they confide their frustrations and concerns to the officers.

It has been suggested that these two roles should be separated. The parole officer could perform the supervisory function, and others could be the helpers. Or the reverse could happen: the officer could be the helper and others, such as the police, could check for parole violations. Both of these suggestions have been rejected in modern times. In fact, parole officers have performed both roles quite effectively. Although officers are required to supervise parolees like police, there are frequent instances of parolees praising an officer as a helper:

> I had what I feel everyone should have. I had a coach and that was my parole agent. He and his supervisor gave me a lot of basic confidence. They believed in me, and I can't say enough about them. He used to say that it was in me to succeed, but he made it a lot more comfortable.[40]

Parole supervision is difficult. Because release on parole is based on a mutual agreement, offenders are released conditionally and restrictions are placed on them. These conditions must be obeyed or the parolee is subject to return to the institution. In this respect, parole release is a contract—a contention that courts have consistently upheld when affirming parole revocations for breach of conditions attached to the parole.[41]

Parole Rules

The conditions of the contract are defined by statutes and set by parole boards. Sometimes parole conditions seem to control all facets of the releasee's behavior, including some areas of life and conduct totally unrelated to reintegration. A typical list of restrictions might include requirements that the parolee must proceed directly, within a period of 24 hours, to the place to which he or she has been paroled and report upon arrival to the area officer or the parole officer; must not leave the state or the community to which the parole has been granted; must carry out instructions of the parole officer; must make every effort to maintain gainful employment; must avoid excessive use of alcoholic beverages and abstain from use of unprescribed drugs; must not live as husband or wife with anyone to whom not legally married; must not carry firearms of any kind; and must not sign a written release relinquishing extradition rights.

A review of parole regulations in 1939 by Joseph B. Fishman and Vee Perlman revealed some problems that may prevent many parolees from successfully adjusting in the community: (1) There were an excessive number of regulations in most states, actually weakening parole board policy. (2) General conditions of parole needed to be clearly distinguished between state and federal laws, in order to avoid imposing a regulation on conduct already governed by

---

[40]Bartollas, op. cit., p. 194.

[41]George Edwards, "Parole," in Sol Rubin (ed.), *The Law of Criminal Correction,* The West Publishing Company, St. Paul, Minn., 1963, p. 556.

another criminal code. (3) Many parole regulations were not realistic and did not lend themselves to practical enforcement. For example, the complete prohibition of the use of liquor in some states forced the parolee into a position which bred rule violations and contempt for the value of parole supervision. (4) Parole regulations lacked uniformity. Fishman and Perlman suggested that parole regulations be standardized to fit all fifty states, the federal government, and the District of Columbia.[42]

Unfortunately, parole regulations still suffer from the same problems. In hopes of rectifying them, the National Advisory Commission on Criminal Justice Standards and Goals recommended that parole rules be reduced to an absolute minimum and that specific parole conditions be established for each individual offender. In addition, parole personnel should be able to request the parole board to change rules to fit the needs of each offender.[43]

The Interstate Compact

In 1937 several states signed the Interstate Compact for the Supervision of Probationers and Parolees. By 1951 all the states had signed. The compact guarantees supervision of probationers and parolees who leave one state and go to another for employment, family, or health reasons. The state of original jurisdiction retains authority over the offender.

The compact was created so that felons could not leave one state and go to another without the second state's being aware of their arrival. The state of reception investigates and approves a plan of residence and employment before the offender relocates there.

Problems have occurred because of differences in parole rules among states. There are also different approaches to supervision—some states interpreting rules rigidly while others are rather permissive. Some states accept only low-risk offenders; others merely delay approval in hopes that the parolee will become discouraged.

For the most part, the Interstate Compact has worked successfully. Before its inception cooperation between states was nonexistent, with few attempts to coordinate supervision of offenders who relocated across state lines.[44]

RELEASE FROM PAROLE

Overview

Termination of parole occurs by discharge or by revocation. Persons may not be kept on parole beyond the end of a maximum prison sentence. In some states they cannot be discharged before the end of the maximum period, while in others discharge can take place after a shorter period specified by legislation or

---

[42]Joseph F. Fishman and Vee Perlman, "In the Name of Parole," *Yale Review,* New Haven, Conn., 1939, p. 150.

[43]National Advisory Commission, *Corrections,* op. cit., p. 433.

[44]Bartollas, op. cit., p. 192.

parole board regulations. In still other states, the parole board has complete authority to arbitrarily determine, within the limits of the maximum sentence, how long parole should continue.[45]

Parole revocation is a formal procedure whereby the parole officer recommends to the board that a parolee be returned to prison. Usually violations of parole are cited. They may be either technical (referring to prescribed conditions of parole, such as a prohibition against the use of alcohol) or criminal.[46] The revocation is sometimes approved by the parole board in executive session. The parolee can request a public hearing, in which the board hears the officer, the parolee, and the parolee's counsel, then determines whether or not to revoke parole.[47] In contrast to probation revocation, the decision to revoke parole is an administrative procedure.[48]

Variable Decision Making

In 1965, California researchers collected data from 318 parole officers and supervisors of the parole and community service division of the state department of corrections. All participants were given summaries of ten actual case histories of parolees. In each, the officer was asked to recommend either return to prison or continuation on parole. The responses varied greatly, ranging from one agent who chose to continue nine of ten cases on parole to five agents who recommended returning all ten to prison. Half the agents chose to return either six or seven of the cases to prison. However, those agents who continued the same number of cases on parole frequently disagreed about which cases to continue.[49]

The study demonstrated obvious inconsistencies in judgment among parole agents. Their recommendations appeared quite susceptible to outside influence. An agent's personal background—education and prior employment—has a bearing on the judgment. The agent's supervisor has the greatest influence on the final recommendation. How the agent perceives the supervisor's orientation affects the decision to revoke or continue parole. In some states, these inconsistencies are encouraged by statutes which open the door to great discretion on the part of the agent. A New York statute allows the parole agent to ask for arrest of the parolee if the agent has "reasonable cause to believe that such [parolee] has lapsed, or is probably about to lapse, into criminal ways or company, or has violated the conditions of his parole in an important respect."[50]

[45]Sutherland and Cressey, op. cit., p. 596.

[46]Henry Burns Jr., *Corrections—Organization and Administration,* West Publishing Company, St. Paul, Minn., 1975, p. 308.

[47]Killinger, Kerper, and Cromwell, op. cit., p. 285.

[48]H. Raymond Fisher, "Probation and Parole Revocation: The Anomaly of Divergent Procedures," *Federal Probation,* vol. 38, no. 3, Administrative Office of the United States Courts, Washington, D.C., September 1974, p. 24.

[49]Robison and Tokagi, *Case Decisions in a State Parole System,* California Department of Correction, Research Report no. 31, Sacramento, November 1968.

[50]George F. Cole, *The American System of Criminal Justice,* Duxbury Press, North Scituate, Mass., 1975, p. 417.

The variation among parole officers and their recommendations for revocation suggests that boards should exercise careful, independent judgment in determining whether a violation occurred and the appropriate disposition of the offender took place. The size of the parole officer's caseload and the subsequent degree of surveillance provided could, of course, affect the rate of revocation. Parole departments with smaller caseloads and more diligent parole agents could show higher rates of failure than other programs.

Even in states where parole boards have introduced elements of due process of law into revocation hearings, the parolee often has little opportunity to refute the charges and participate in the board's decision. Parolees are often young, inarticulate, and frightened—totally unable to defend themselves in a formal hearing if legal counsel is not present.[51]

Suggested Guidelines for Termination

In addition to the possible variations among parole agents in their use of revocation, there has been concern about their judgment of the length of time offenders should remain on parole before discharge. At least one study indicated that early discharge could increase parole efficiency. An examination of national statistics clearly shows that parolees who complete their first year under supervision with no or minimal difficulty have a 90 percent probability of satisfactorily completing the second and third years without serious difficulty. Consequently, if parole authorities adopt a policy of discharge at the end of 1 year of arrest-free parole, considerable resources (approximately $10.5 million annually plus officer time and effort) could be made available for parolees remaining under the board's jurisdiction.[52]

Professor Vernon Fox has suggested that a good parole officer not only enforces rules, but judges the progress of each parolee on response to supervision and success in reintegration into the community—including good job adjustment, educational achievement, and money management. When it becomes obvious that the parolee is unresponsive or in danger of getting into further criminal difficulty, the parole officer recommends revocation on the basis of violation of rules, using the rules as a gauge rather than as limits.[53]

Recommended Revocation Procedures

The National Advisory Commission on Criminal Justice Standards and Goals recommends that each parole jurisdiction implement a system of revocation procedures that will permit prompt confinement of parolees exhibiting behavior

---

[51]Goldfarb and Singer, op. cit., p. 307.

[52]Lawrence A. Bennett and Max Ziegler, "Early Discharge: A Suggested Approach to Increased Efficiency in Parole," *Federal Probation*, vol. 39, no. 3, Administrative Office of the United States Courts, Washington, D.C., September 1975, p. 30.

[53]Fox, op. cit., pp. 329–330.

that poses a threat to others. It recommends that at the same time each jurisdiction provide careful controls, methods of fact finding, and alternatives to reincarceration, in order to keep as many offenders as possible in the community. Warrants for arrest and detention of alleged parole violators should be issued and signed by parole board members. A parolee alleged to have committed a new crime should be eligible for bail or another form of release, pending the court's determination of the outcome of new charges.

A preliminary hearing conducted by a person not directly involved in the case should be held promptly on all alleged parole violations. At revocation hearings, the parolee should have written notice of the alleged infraction of rules or conditions and access to official records regarding the case, the right to be represented by counsel (including, if indigent, the right to court-appointed counsel), the opportunity to be heard in person, and the right to subpoena witnesses or otherwise challenge allegations or evidence held by the state. Each jurisdiction should develop alternatives to parole revocation, such as warnings, short-term local confinement, varying the intensity of supervision, fines, and referral to other community resources. If returned to a correctional institution, the offender should be scheduled for subsequent parole consideration when appropriate.[54]

Morrissey v. Brewer

Many of these recommendations were affirmed on June 29, 1972, by a decision of the United States Supreme Court. The case of *Morrissey v. Brewer* originated when two parolees appealed their revocations and subsequent appellate court decision on the ground that their paroles were revoked without a hearing and that they were thereby deprived of due process. The appellate court had reasoned that parole is only a "correctional device authorizing service of sentence outside a penitentiary" and that a parolee is still "in custody." In reversing the court of appeals decision, the Supreme Court stated that "the liberty of a parolee, although indeterminate, includes many of the core values of unqualified liberty and its termination inflicts a 'grievous loss' on the parolee. . . . Its termination calls for some orderly process, however, formal." The decision in *Morrissey v. Brewer* affirmed the right of a parolee to a prerevocation hearing and extended unprecedented rights to accused parole violators. The court made it clear that parole was not an act of mercy but rather "an established variation on imprisonment of convicted criminals."

There must be prompt, informal inquiry by an impartial hearing officer, proximate to the place of parole violation, to determine whether there are reasonable grounds to conclude that a violation has indeed occurred. Procedural protection must be extended to the parolee, including the right to receive written notice of the proceedings and to summon witnesses in his or her behalf.[55]

[54]National Advisory Commission, *Corrections,* op. cit., pp. 425–426.
[55]*Morrissey v. Brewer,* 408 U.S. 471, 33 L. Ed. 2d 484 (1972).

EVALUATION OF PAROLE

Recidivism Defined

The annual reports of parole departments interpret the violation rate as a ratio between the paroles granted and those violated during the same year. Calculated by this method, parole violation rates cluster around 25 percent, with a range of 10 to 40 percent. Only those violations known to parole officers and serious enough to result in revocation are included. In many states the number of parole personnel is not sufficient to obtain reliable and complete information regarding the behavior of parolees. Therefore, considerable uncertainty regarding stated violation rates has developed.[56]

Another difficulty in evaluation is the inability to compare inmates released under parole supervision with those discharged unconditionally. One early study compared subsequent careers of prisoners on parole with those of a group of men discharged without supervision. Of the 345 men released from the Minnesota State Reformatory at St. Cloud between July 1, 1944, and June 30, 1945, 110 were discharged at expiration of sentence, 183 on parole, and 52 by other kinds of release. Five years later, 30 percent of the men discharged at expiration of sentence and 21 percent of those released on parole had been convicted, sentenced, and returned to custody or had paroles revoked for felonies. Also, 7.3 percent of those discharged at expiration of sentence and 2.2 percent of those released on parole had been fingerprinted for felonies, but there was no record of conviction. Among those discharged at expiration of sentence, 6.4 percent had been convicted and sentenced for misdemeanors, compared with 5.4 percent of the parolees (see Table 10.6).

Effect of Supervision

Although the differences in the St. Cloud study tend to favor release on parole rather than discharge at the expiration of sentence, the favorable statistics are not necessarily the result of assistance received from parole supervision. Traditionally, inmates least likely to commit new crimes are selected for parole, while those most likely to commit crimes remain until expiration of their sentences.[57]

Researcher Peter Hoffman compared adult male offenders under indeterminate sentences for robbery, burglary, or manslaughter released on parole with offenders under mandatory release. He concluded that parolees do better, even though a majority of mandatory releasees also completed the first year of supervision without delinquency.[58] Another researcher, Jay Lerner, concluded

---

[56]Sutherland and Cressey, op. cit., p. 697.

[57]Stanley B. Zuckerman, Alfred J. Barron, and Horace B. Whittier, "A Follow-up Study of Minnesota State Reformatory Inmates," *Journal of Criminal Law, Criminology, and Police Science,* vol. 43, no. 1, January–February 1953, p. 632.

[58]Peter B. Hoffman, "Mandatory Release: A Measure of Type II Error," *Criminology,* vol. 11, no. 1, August 1977, pp. 220–221.

TABLE 10-6
LATER ADJUSTMENT OF ST. CLOUD INMATES RELEASED ON PAROLE
OR EXPIRATION

Later adjustment	183 parolees	110 expirations
Convictions or revocations for felonies	21.3%	30.0%
Fingerprinted for felonies	2.2%	7.3%
Convictions or revocations for misdemeanors	5.4%	6.4%
Fingerprinted for misdemeanors	2.2%	2.7%
Returned as parole violators	25.1%	0.0%
Wanted by law enforcement officials	.6%	2.7%
Other infractions	1.1%	3.6%
Subtotal: involved in later offenses	57.9%	52.7%
At large, no offenses reported	42.1%	47.3%
Total	100.0%	100.0%

Source: Stanley B. Zuckerman, Alfred J. Barron, and Horace B. Whittier, "A Follow-up Study of Minnesota State Reformatory Inmates," reprinted by special permission of *Journal of Criminal Law, Criminology, and Police Science,* by Northwestern University School of Law, vol. 43, no. 1, January-February 1953, p. 632.

that parole supervision reduces subsequent criminal behavior to a greater degree for persons released from local correctional institutions than for those discharged at expiration of sentence.[59]

Other Studies

Using the customary method of determining parole violation rates, a number of studies over the years have gained national attention. The Attorney General's Survey of Release Procedures reported an analysis of the case histories of 90,664 adult male felons whose paroles began and terminated between January 1, 1928, and December 31, 1935. Results showed that less than 28 percent of these parolees violated their paroles.[60] Criminologists Eleanor and Sheldon Glueck, in their famous study of 500 criminal careers, found that 55.3 percent were officially known to have violated their paroles.[61] In a comparison of violation rates among jurisdictions in the 1960s, Daniel Glaser and Vincent O'Leary discovered a range of 35 to 44 percent.[62]

A nationwide examination by the federal government of 1972 parolees 3 years after their release revealed a recidivism rate of 26 percent for males and 18

[59]Mark Jay Lerner, "The effectiveness of a Definite Sentence Parole Program," *Criminology,* vol. 15, no. 2, August 1977, p. 547.
[60]"Parole," *Attorney General's Survey,* op. cit., pp. 311, 312, and 541.
[61]Sheldon Glueck and Eleanor T. Glueck, *500 Criminal Careers,* Alfred A. Knopf, Inc., New York, 1930, pp. 167–169.
[62]Daniel Glaser and Vincent O'Leary, *Personal Characteristics and Parole Outcome,* U.S. Government Printing Office, Washington, D.C., 1966, p. 14.

percent for females. Nineteen percent of male and 13 percent of female violations took place in the first year, 15 percent of the males and 10 percent of the females were returned to prison as technical violators; 4 percent of the males and 5 percent of the females were listed as absconders, and 7 percent of the males and 3 percent of the females were returned to prison following a new conviction. Male parolees with prior prison sentences violated rules at a 33 percent rate—the highest single category of recidivists.[63] During 1976 there were 89,128 offenders released on parole or conditional release. Of these, 22,374 men and women (24 percent) were returned to prison as violators from parole and conditional release.[64]

More recently the federal government released new statistics following long-term studies of parolees. In a 3-year study by the Bureau of Justice Statistics, the parole experience of the 64,000 people paroled during 1974 and 1975 was examined. It was found that only 25 percent had had their paroles revoked or were returned to prison before their paroles ended.[65] Another study by the Federal Bureau of Prisons' research staff found that the recidivism rate for federal offenders declined in terms of new arrests between 1970 and 1978. The study shows that the proportion of offenders with no arrests or warrants issued during the first year after release increased from 67.8 percent for 1970 releasees to 75.7 percent for those released in 1978.[66]

Conclusions From Studies

Although it is difficult to determine actual violation rates or to estimate whether parole is a success or a failure, statistical studies are consistent in some of their conclusions. For example, most parole violations occur during the first few months of supervision, depend a great deal on individual parole officers' discretion, and happen less frequently among offenders who commit crimes against the person. Violations take place most frequently among offenders with a high number of previous arrests, irregular previous work habits, and frequent contacts with associates from the institution. Older offenders succeed on parole more often than younger ones and white offenders more often than black. Success increases as the age at the time of the first delinquency increases.[67]

One review of seventy-one studies of parolees concluded that the most stable predictors in regard to recidivism were the presence or absence of prior convictions, age at first arrest, stability of employment, living arrangements,

---

[63]*Newsletter,* Uniform Parole Reports of the National Probation and Parole Institutes, National Council on Crime and Delinquency, Davis, Calif., 1979.

[64]Steve Dienstfrey, United States Department of Justice, Law Enforcement Assistance Administration, National Criminal Justice Information and Statistics Service, telephone conversation, Sept. 21, 1977.

[65]*Parole In the United States, 1979,* National Council on Crime and Delinquency, Hackensack, N.J., 1980.

[66]*On the Line,* vol. 4, no. 3, American Correctional Association, College Park, Md., March 1981, p. 6.

[67]Sutherland and Cressey, op. cit., p. 600.

current income, history of opiate use, and history of alcohol abuse. The degree of predictability was determined by one offense—auto theft. In this instance, a first arrest before age 18 is consistently related to recidivism, and a first arrest after age 21 is consistently related to nonrecidivism.[68]

SHOULD PAROLE BE ABOLISHED?

Unfortunately, problems associated with the administration of parole frequently discourage both its administrators and its observers. Problems of evaluating parole, violent acts by parolees, and the difficulty of predicting parole success have disheartened many people. Today there is a vocal group who say that the only solution to these problems is to do away with parole altogether, replacing it with relatively short fixed sentences, graduated according to the seriousness of the crime. Offenders should know exactly how long their sentences are and when they will be released. As stated in more detail in Chapter 1, state legislators in Maine, Indiana, California, and Illinois had passed fixed-sentence laws by 1976. Legislatures of five states—Alaska, Connecticut, Colorado, Washington, and Ohio—had bills pending at that time which would establish similar laws.[69] In addition, a bill was under consideration in Congress in 1979 which would have eliminated federal parole procedures and established determinate sentences. Maine, Indiana, California, and Arizona abolished parole in 1977. Illinois and New Mexico did so in 1978.

David Stanley, in his book on the problems of parole, concluded that parole boards are attempting to do something impossible—predict the future behavior of human beings. He argues that sentences should be set only by judges, based on standard penalties specified for each crime and determined by the median time actually served. Parole boards and supervision of the releasee should be abolished. Releasees should be left alone, except for making help available through a reentry facility.[70]

Martinson and Wilks in their article, "Save Parole Supervision," reached a different conclusion. After a survey of eighty categories, comparing inmates who were paroled and inmates who served until expiration of sentence, the authors concluded that "the data . . . should give pause to those policymakers and legislators who have been operating on the unexplained assumption that parole supervision makes no difference." These authors discovered that in seventy-four of the eighty comparisons, the mean of the recidivism rates was lower for parole than for expiration of sentence.[71]

[68]David A. Pritchard, "Stable Predictors of Recidivism: A Summary," *Criminology,* vol. 17, no. 1, May 1979, pp. 17–19.

[69]Joseph R. Tybor, "No Parole, Fixed Sentences Growing Trend in Penology," *Topeka (Kansas) Capital-Journal,* Oct. 3, 1976, p. 24.

[70]David T. Stanley, *Prisoners Among Us,* The Brookings Institution, Washington, D.C., 1976, pp. 185–186, 190–191.

[71]Robert Martinson and Judith Wilks, "Save Parole Supervision," *Federal Probation,* vol. 41, no. 3, Administrative Office of the United States Courts, Washington, D.C., September 1977, pp. 26–27.

Former parole officer John Conrad accepts the elimination of parole for surveillance but believes the released prisoner will continue to need assistance. He suggests two forms of help: (1) a referral service, independent of the prison administration, to steer parolees to agencies that assist with specific problems and (2) a revival of volunteerism.[72]

A number of alternatives have been suggested in view of the controversy. The John Howard Association recommended that parole not be abolished, but that the decision-making process be made more objective.[73] Norval Morris suggests that parole dates be determined earlier in the incarceration. They could be part of the classification at the reception and diagnostic center, to be changed only by poor behavior during imprisonment.[74]

A number of states (Maryland, Florida, Maine, Georgia, Massachusetts, Minnesota, North Carolina, Tennessee, and Wisconsin) have adopted mutual agreement programming, or contract parole, in part as a response to critics. Michigan, Arizona, and California passed legislation favoring contract parole but later dropped it.

The federal prison system, Florida, Georgia, Oregon, Hawaii, Louisiana, Minnesota, New York, Missouri, North Carolina, New Jersey, Virginia, and Washington have adopted parole-release guidelines. The guidelines of the Federal Parole Commission, which have been in effect since 1974, influenced the development of many of those in the states.[75]

The Oregon legislature adopted a modified "just deserts" model, which requires the parole board to establish ranges of terms within the maximum limits prescribed by Oregon statutes. The principle of "commensurate deserts" is applied, because the parole board is required to consider the harm created by the offense.[76] Oregon established a "matrix" which bases time to be served on the seriousness of the crime, the prisoner's past criminal history, and the perceived risk of repetition. All felonies are categorized within seven severity ratings. The degree of severity determines the length of time a convict will spend in prison before being considered for parole.[77]

APPRAISAL

The Criticism

The capricious and arbitrary manner in which some parole boards decide when an inmate is ready for release has drawn strong criticism from prison reformers

[72]John P. Conrad, "Who Needs a Door-Bell Pusher? The Case for Abolishing Parole," *The Prison Journal,* vol. 49, no. 2, Autumn–Winter 1979, p. 25.

[73]*Let the Punishment Fit the Crime,* Contact, Inc., Lincoln, Nebr., May 1978, pp. 2–3, 4, 6, 21–22, 41, and 57.

[74]Morris, op. cit., pp. 31–32.

[75]Bartollas, op. cit., pp. 189 and 196.

[76]Elizabeth L. Taylor, "The Parole Board and Public Policy," *Proceedings of the One Hundred and Eighth Annual Congress of Corrections,* American Correctional Association, College Park, Md., 1979, p. 134.

[77]Ibid., "In Search of Equity: The Oregon Parole Matrix," *Federal Probation,* vol. 43, no. 1, Administrative Office of the United States Courts, Washington, D.C., March 1979, p. 56.

and practitioners. The apparent unfairness of parole boards is legendary among inmates. Stories about how attendance at Alcoholics Anonymous meetings and church services favorably affected parole recommendations have been told among both prisoners and prison officials. The haphazard way the parolee has been supervised after release has also been criticized. Both the courts and public officials have rejected the belief that parole officials need not pay attention to due process during revocation proceedings.

The criticisms are based on facts. Parole boards have released the wrong persons at the wrong time for the wrong reasons. The interviews with inmates are purposeless. Hearings are often ineffective, lasting sometimes less than 10 minutes. One study indicated that the average time for the parole hearing in more than 50 percent of the states was only 15 minutes (see Table 10.7).[78]

Most parole boards rely on "progress reports" from institutional officials for most of their information. Many board members do not have time to read these reports or the expertise to interpret them. Their decisions are based on subjective judgments, such as a sympathy or dislike for "drug addicts."

Parole supervision is justly criticized too. Many officers who have 100 or more parolees to supervise are ill-trained and poorly paid. They receive scant praise for their work. Their day-to-day routine is hectic, with little private life, and the rate of turnover is high. Many times the parolee and parole officer come from two different worlds, and the officer does not have time to learn about the parolee's neighborhood and his or her family and job.

The rules the parolee must follow are frequently unrealistic. Few ordinary citizens would or could follow all the usual conditions of release on parole. Some, such as "cooperate" or "live a clean, temperate, and honest life," are sufficiently vague to allow enforcement at the subjective whims of the officer and

---

[78]O'Leary and Nuffield, op. cit., p. 155.

TABLE 10.7
FELONY OFFENDER CASES HEARD PER DAY
DURING PAROLE-CONSIDERATION HEARINGS
(51 Jurisdictions*)

Average number of cases heard per day	Number of parole boards
1–19	11
20–29	15
30–39	15
40 and over	13

*States of Georgia, Hawaii, and Texas not included, because no hearings are conducted in these jurisdictions.
Source: Vincent O'Leary and Joan Nuffield, "Parole Decision-Making Characteristics: Report of a National Survey," Community Corrections, Burt Galaway, Joe Hudson, and C. David Hollister (eds.), Charles C Thomas Publisher, Springfield, Ill., 1976, p. 155.

to create confusion on the part of the parolee. Revocation procedures have been unsupported by due process and pay little attention to the parolee's side of the story.

The Response

The granting of parole is an administrative act, with the parolee still legally under the jurisdiction of a state or federal department of corrections. In a sense it is an act of mercy—granted under such conditions and procedures as the releasing authority decides. The parolee contracts with the parole board for release and voluntarily agrees to all the conditions.

With this in mind, the procedure for the granting and carrying out of parole is appropriate. The parole board is a neutral body that can balance the rights and needs of the community and the offender. It is certainly in a better position to make a release decision than are institutional officials. The parolee can benefit from the supervision and helping services offered by parole officers, even with the restrictions. Somebody or some mechanism must be in a position to oversee the releasee, if for no other reason than to protect the community.

In terms of the overall operation of the criminal justice system, a parole board distributes the sentencing power. Abolishing parole would only increase the power of the legislature, prosecutor, and judge. The legislature is too far removed from the inmate population to make decisions about release and would more than likely react to political pressures instead. If parole were abolished, discretion would be given to prosecutors and judges who by the very nature of their positions would resist monitoring.

Cecil B. McCall, chairman of the United States Parole Commission, believes that individual judges do not possess any greater wisdom than parole boards or commissions regarding the optimum time for convicts to be released. He states that requiring offenders to serve to the expiration of their sentences although they could safely be released, is a misapplication of tax dollars and that judicial determination of expiration dates would increase the overcrowding of prisons. It would also encourage the abandonment of the search for successful institutional programs.[79]

The Future

One cannot deny the close scrutiny that the concept of parole has experienced. It is not unlike the arguments that rehabilitation of offenders is unrealistic and that indeterminate sentencing has a detrimental effect on the inmate. These pressures will probably continue to influence a number of changes in the criminal justice system, such as shorter and fixed sentences, assistance rather than

---

[79]Cecil C. McCall, "The Need for a Viable Parole System: A Rebuttal to S. 1437," *Proceedings of the One Hundred and Eighth Annual Congress of Corrections,* American Correctional Association, College Park, Md., 1979, pp. 125–126.

supervision in the community, and mandatory release. However, it will not affect the emphasis on the reintegrative model. The necessity of reintegrating the offender will continue to require that something like parole be available for the prisoner returning to the community.

The major discovery of the work-unit program in California (SIPU) was that prison return for technical violations can be reduced without an increase in serious criminal behavior as measured by new felony prison commitments. It resulted in California's evaluating its parole cases with the hope of dividing them into three categories: (1) control only, for those who need no supervision or services; (2) service emphasis for those who require supporting services; and (3) minimum supervision for those who require supervision. In late 1980, of the 14,000 parolees in California, 84 percent were classified as control cases and only 8 percent as minimum supervision cases.[80]

Another alternative was proposed by David Fogel, executive director of the Illinois Law Enforcement Commission. He devised the "Illinois Plan," which would abolish parole and indeterminate sentences. During the term of incarceration, if the inmate's conduct met certain criteria, he or she would be credited with one month time off per year served. Convicts would be released when their sentences were completed—minus accumulation of time off for good behavior. Parole officers would be available to each inmate requesting help upon release— for job finding, counseling, referral to community resources.[81]

Todd Clear, of the School of Criminal Justice, Rutgers University, believes that community supervision of the offender can be changed so that the clamor for its elimination would be abated. He argues that (1) there should be clarification of the purposes of community supervision, emphasizing the legitimate aims of the criminal law; (2) the use of discretion by supervisory officers should be controlled; (3) bonds should be established between the parolee and the community; and (4) a concerted effort should be made to increase the positive influence of community supervision on the offender. If these changes are effected, Todd Clear is convinced, parole supervision can be altered to benefit the offender.[82]

CONCLUSION

Parole is under attack. Some say it is in its twilight. Yet on the average, more than 60 percent of adult felons are released on parole before expiration of the maximum term of their sentence. At the end of December 31, 1979, parolees numbered 196,500.[83]

---

[80]Stephen Gettinger, "Separating the Cop From the Counselor," *Corrections Magazine,* vol. 7, no. 2, April 1981, p. 35.

[81]E. Eugene Miller, "Is Parole Necessary," in E. Eugene Miller and M. Robert Montilla (eds.), *Corrections in the Community,* Reston Publishing Company, Reston, Virginia, 1977, p. 260.

[82]Todd R. Clear, "Three Dilemmas in Community Supervision of Offenders," *The Prison Journal,* vol. 49, no. 2, Winter 1979, pp. 12–13.

[83]Bartollas, op. cit., p. 185.

For these offenders, the problems of reentry are stressful. Most parole violations occur relatively soon after release—nearly half during the first 6 months and more than 60 percent within the first year. Parolees' personal and material problems are overwhelming when they first come out of prison. In most states they are given only a change of clothes, a token amount of money, a list of rules governing their release, and the names and addresses of their parole supervisors. They must report to their parole officers within 24 hours. Although the promise of a job is often a condition for release, becoming employed in reality may be another matter. Most ex-convicts are unskilled or semiskilled, and parole rules may prevent movement to areas where jobs might be available.

For years we have complained about recidivism rates. Yet few people talk about the high success rates. After all, if the recidivism rate is 35 percent or 25 percent, then the success rate for parolees is 65 percent or 75 percent. It has been assumed that one reason for the high recidivism rates of parolees has been the failure to establish a method for gradually reintegrating them into the community after a term of incarceration. By the same reasoning, the high success rate is achieved because the majority of offenders *are* reintegrated into the community. In either case, parole is justified.

If parole is justified, then so is the method of parole release. Maurice Sigler, chairman of the United States Board of Parole, adds:

> The fairness of the parole process depends almost directly upon the fairness of the sentencing process. . . . To those who say 'let's abolish parole,' I say that as long as we use imprisonment in this country, we will have to have someone, somewhere, with the authority to release people from imprisonment.[84]

EXERCISES

1 Compare and contrast the advantages and disadvantages of probation and parole. Explain each similarity and difference.

2 What cultural factors might determine why one state might keep offenders on parole 12 months and another state might keep them 84 months?

3 It has been said, "Except for sentencing, no decision in the criminal justice process has more impact on the convicted offender than the parole decision." Agree or disagree with this statement and give reasons.

4 List advantages and disadvantages of having parole board structure consistent in all fifty states. Give reasons for each.

5 What characteristics do you believe most important for a parole board member? With these characteristics in mind, do you think a parole examiner could be just as effective for parole decision making? Explain your answer fully.

6 List in order of value each method a parole board member uses in making parole decisions. Support each ranking with reasons.

7 Do you believe parole prediction tables should be routinely used in all states? Give advantages and disadvantages.

[84]Maurice H. Sigler, "Abolish Parole?", *Federal Probation,* vol. 39, no. 2, Administrative Office of the United States Courts, Washington, D.C., June 1975, p. 48.

8 Compare and contrast MAP with the parole decision-making process used by most states. Examine each side closely.

9 Some critics of parole supervision have stated that there should be no rules. The offender should only have to abide by state and federal laws, as do other citizens. Agree or disagree with this opinion, and give reasons.

10 Outline a revocation procedure you believe would protect the public yet guarantee the offender's legal rights.

11 Explain your approach to parole supervision in comparison with the suggestions in Chapter 5 on probation.

12 If the statistics from the Minnesota study indicate a lower recidivism rate for inmates released under parole supervision, why not release all inmates under parole supervision? Support your answer with reasons.

13 Discuss the advantages and disadvantages of replacing parole with short, fixed sentences. Explain fully.

14 How would you determine the length of parole for an offender? Support your opinion with reasons.

EXERCISE REFERENCES

Barkin, Eugene N.: "Legal Issues Facing Parole," *Crime and Delinquency,* vol. 25, no. 2, April 1979, pp. 219–235.

Bartollas, Clemens: *Introduction to Corrections,* Harper & Row, Publishers, Incorporated, New York, 1981, chap. 9.

Beless, Donald W., William S. Pilcher, and Ellen Jo Ryan: "Use of Indigenous Non-Professionals in Probation and Parole," *Federal Probation,* vol. 36, no. 1, Administrative Office of the United States Courts, Washington, D.C. March 1972, pp. 10–15.

Bennett, Lawrence A., and Max Siegler: "Early Discharge: A Suggested Approach to Increased Efficiency in Parole," *Federal Probation,* vol. 39, no. 3, Administrative Office of the United States Courts, Washington, D.C. September 1975, pp. 27–30.

Berecochea, John, Alfred Himelsos, and Donald F. Miller: "The Risk of Failure During Early Parole Period: A Methodological Note," *Journal of Criminal Law, Criminology, and Police Science,* vol. 63, no. 2, March 1972, pp. 93–97.

Bixby, F. Lowell: "A New Role for Parole Boards," *Federal Probation,* vol. 34, no. 2, Administrative Office of the United States Courts, Washington, D.C. June 1970, pp. 24–28.

Burkhart, Walter R.: "The Great Parole Experiment," in E. Eugene Miller and M. Robert Montilla (eds.), *Corrections in the Community,* Reston Publishing Company, Inc., Reston, Virginia, 1977, pp. 240–252.

Clear, Todd R.: "Three Dilemmas in Community Supervision of Offenders," *The Prison Journal,* vol. 49, no. 2, Winter 1979, pp. 2–16.

Cole, George F.: *The American System of Criminal Justice,* Duxbury Press, North Scituate, Mass., 1975, pp. 402–419.

Conrad, John P.: "Who Needs a Door-Bell Pusher?: The Case for Abolishing Parole," *The Prison Journal,* vol. 49, no. 2, Winter 1979, pp. 17–26.

Contact, Inc.: *Let the Punishment Fit the Crime,* Lincoln, Nebr., May 1978, pp. 2–3, 4, 6, 21–22, 41, and 57.

"Decisions! Decisions! Decisions!" *Federal Probation,* vol. 34, no. 1, Administrative Office of the United States Courts, Washington, D.C. March 1970, pp. 27–32.

Dressler, David: *Practice and Theory of Probation and Parole,* Columbia University Press, New York, 1970.

Erickson, Rosemary J., Wayman J. Crow, Louis A. Zurcher, and Andrew V. Connett: *Paroled But Not Free,* Human Sciences Press, New York, 1973.

Fishman, Joseph F., and Vee Perlman: "A Critique of Parole Boards," *Yale Review,* vol. 28, no. 1, 1939, pp. 150–163.

Galvin, James L., and Kenneth Polk: "Parole Guidelines: Suggested Research Questions," *Crime and Delinquency,* vol. 27, no. 2, April 1981, pp. 213–224.

Gettinger, Steve: "Parole Contracts: A New Way Out," *Corrections Magazine,* vol. 2, no. 1, September–October 1975, pp. 3–8, 46–50.

————: "Separating the Cop From the Counselor," *Corrections Magazine,* vol. 7, no. 2, April 1981, pp. 34–38.

Glaser, Daniel: *The Effectiveness of a Prison and Parole System,* The Bobbs-Merrill Company, Indianapolis, Ind., 1969.

————: "Prediction Tables as Accounting Devices for Judges and Parole Boards," *Crime and Delinquency,* vol. 8, no. 3, July 1962, pp. 239–258.

————: and Vincent O'Leary: *Personal Characteristics and Parole Outcome,* U.S. Government Printing Office, Washington, D.C., 1966.

Goldfarb, Ronald L., and Linda R. Singer: *After Conviction,* Simon and Schuster, New York, 1973, sec. V.

Hoffman, Peter B., and Sheldon Adelberg: "The Salient Factor Score: A Nontechnical Overview," *Federal Probation,* vol. 44, no. 1, Administrative Office of the United States Courts, Washington, D.C., March 1980, pp. 44–52.

————: and Lucille K. Degoston: "Parole Decision Making: Structuring Descretion," *Federal Probation,* vol. 38, no. 4, Administrative Office of the United States Courts, Washington, D.C., December 1974, pp. 7–15.

Hussey, Frederick A.: "Parole: Villain or Victim in the Determinate Sentencing Debate," *Crime and Delinquency,* vol. 24, no. 1, January 1978, pp. 81–88.

Ives, Jane K.: "The Essential Task of the Probation-Parole Officer," *Federal Probation,* vol. 26, no. 1, Administrative Office of the United States Courts, Washington, D.C., March 1962, pp. 38–42.

Johnson, Bertram M.: *An Analysis of Predictions of Parole Performance and Judgment of Supervision in the Parole Research Project,* Research Report no. 32, Department of Youth Authority, Sacramento, Calif., December 1962.

Kassebaum, Gene, David A. Ward, and Daniel Wilner: *Prison Treatment and Parole Survival,* John Wiley & Sons, Inc., New York, 1971.

Laune, Ferris: *Predicting Criminality,* Northwestern University Press, Evanston, Ill., 1937.

Lenihan, Kenneth J.: "The Financial Resources of Released Prisoners," *Proceedings: Second National Workshop on Corrections and Parole Administration,* American Correctional Association, College Park, Md., 1974, pp. 109–135.

Lerner, Mark Jay: "The Effectiveness of a Definite Sentence Parole Program," *Criminology,* vol. 15, no. 3, August 1977, pp. 211–224.

Levinson, Marc: "'Pay as You Stay' or Stay Longer," *Corrections Magazine,* vol. 5, no. 4, December 1979, pp. 22–23.

McCall, Cecil C.: "The Need for a Viable Parole System: A Rebuttal to S. 1437," *Proceedings of the One Hundred and Eighth Annual Congress of Corrections,* American Correctional Association, College Park, Md., 1979, pp. 119–129.

Martinson, Robert and Judith Wilks: "Save Parole Supervision," *Federal Probation,* vol.

41, no. 3, Administrative Office of the United States Courts, Washington, D.C., September 1977, pp. 23–27.

Miller, E. Eugene: "Is Parole Necessary?", in E. Eugene Miller and M. Robert Montilla (eds.), *Corrections in the Community,* Reston Publishing Company, Reston, Virginia, 1977, pp. 253–261.

Morris, Norval: *The Future of Imprisonment,* The University of Chicago Press, Chicago, 1974.

Ohlin, Lloyd E.: *Selection for Parole,* Russell Sage Foundation, New York, 1951.

O'Leary, Vincent, and Joan Nuffield: "Parole Decision-Making Characteristics: Report of a National Survey," in Burt Galaway, Joe Hudson, adn C. David Hollister (eds.), *Community Corrections,* Charles C Thomas Publisher, Springfield, Ill., 1977, pp. 150–164.

Powers, Sanger B.: "Wisconsin's Mutual Agreement Program," *Proceedings: Second National Workshop on Corrections and Parole Administration,* American Correctional Association, College Park, Md., 1974, pp. 5–11.

Pritchard, David A.: "Stable Predictors of Recidivism: A Summary," *Criminology,* vol. 17, no. 1, May 1979, pp. 15–21.

Prus, Robert C., and John R. Stratton: "Parole Revocation Decision Making: Private Typings and Official Designations," *Federal Probation,* vol. 40, no. 1, Administrative Office of the United States Courts, Washington, D.C., March 1976, pp. 48–53.

Robison, James, and Paul T. Takagi: "The Parole Violator as an Organizational Reject," in Robert M. Carter and Leslie T. Wilkins (eds.), *Probation, Parole, and Community Corrections,* John Wiley & Sons, Inc., New York, 1976, pp. 347–372.

Shover, Neal: *A Sociology of American Corrections,* The Dorsey Press, Homewood, Ill., 1979.

Sigler, Maurice H.: "Abolish Parole?", *Federal Probation,* vol. 39, no. 2, Administrative Office of the United States Courts, Washington, D.C., June 1975, pp. 42–48.

Stanley, David T.: *Prisoners Among Us,* The Brookings Institution, Washington, D.C., 1976.

Taylor, Elizabeth L.: "In Search of Equity: The Oregon Parole Matrix," *Federal Probation,* vol. 43, no. 1, Administrative Office of the United States Courts, Washington, D.C., March 1979, pp. 52–59.

————: "The Parole Board and Public Policy," *Proceedings of the One Hundred and Eighth Annual Congress of Corrections,* American Correctional Association, College Park, Md., 1979, pp. 129–140.

Warner, Eric, and Ted Palmer: "Psychological Characteristics of Successful and Unsuccessful Parolees: Implications of Heteoscedastic and Norlinear Relations," *Journal of Research in Crime and Delinquency,* vol. 13, no. 2, July 1976, pp. 165–178.

Zuckerman, Stanley B., Alfred J. Barron, and Horace B. Whittier: "A Follow-up Study of Minnesota State Reformatory Inmates," *Journal of Criminal Law, Criminology, and Police Science,* vol. 43, no. 1, January–February 1953, pp. 622–636.

CHAPTER 11

COMMUNITY-BASED PROGRAMS FOR JUVENILES

CHAPTER OBJECTIVES

- To introduce the juvenile justice system and its clients
- To discuss two controversial issues—juvenile rights and the inclusion of the status offender within the jurisdiction of the juvenile court
- To provide information on the philosophy and practice of diversion from the juvenile justice system
- To examine residential facilities
- To describe The Villages, Inc., a community-based program for juveniles

INTRODUCTION

The objective of adult corrections is to minimize the frequency with which law violations are committed by persons who have prior records of criminality. Whether offenders are placed on probation or incarcerated, the goal is to prevent them from committing more offenses. Many different techniques are used to accomplish this goal—academic and vocational education, creative therapy, counseling, temporary releases, and parole. Similarly, the aim of juvenile corrections—including community-based corrections—is to minimize the frequency with which juvenile offenders and status offenders commit crimes.

The most dramatic change in the nature of crime within the last century is the decrease in the age of offenders. According to the 1980 Uniform Crime Reports, youths age 18 and 19 were arrested most frequently. Young people under 18 were arrested for more than 20 percent of all reported offenses. In 1980 there were 2,025,713 arrests of persons under 18.[1]

JUVENILE COURT

Adjudication

Today all states possess some form of juvenile court, usually as part of a circuit court, district court, county court, probate court, or municipal court. In a few states, separate juvenile courts exist, especially in larger communities.

If the child is not dismissed at any time between the offense and appearance before a judge, then the judge must decide how to classify the youth, usually after reviewing the probation department's social investigation. If he or she is formally adjudicated as delinquent, truant, wayward, dependent, neglected, incorrigible, miscreant, a child in need of supervision, or otherwise labeled, recommendations are made for disposition of the case.

The term applied to crime committed by young people is *juvenile delinquency*. However, "juvenile" means different ages in different states and "delinquency" has been given a broader interpretation than simply the commission of a crime. Juvenile court jurisdiction is initiated for juveniles 18 and under, but in seven states, once it is established, the juvenile court can continue jurisdiction to age 20. In forty-one states jurisdiction can be continued to age 21, and in three there is no limit on the maximum age.[2]

"Get Tough"

In 1980 Illinois passed a law which permits a juvenile to be locked up until age 21 after committing a third felony if that third crime is one of eleven specified offenses (mostly violent). Once a youth is charged under this law, the judge has no option but must sentence the juvenile as a habitual offender.[3]

The Illinois law is representative of a trend throughout the United States—to "get tough" with repeat juvenile offenders. Under Minnesota's revised juvenile statutes, effective August 1980, chronic juvenile offenders can be sent to adult prisons and county jails. As of October 1, 1981, there were twenty-nine 16- and 17-years-olds at the adult reformatory at St. Cloud. Similar statutes have been passed recently in California, Louisiana, Delaware, and New Jersey. The Minnesota law is "tougher" than the laws of most states, because it focuses on property offenders rather than on violent offenders. The California law emphasizes murderers. Louisiana transfers juveniles accused of armed robbery,

[1]Federal Bureau of Investigation, United States Department of Justice, *Crime in the United States,* U. S. Government Printing Office, Washington, D. C., 1981, p. 200.

[2]National Institute for Juvenile Justice and Delinquency Prevention, Law Enforcement Assistance Administration, *Juvenile Dispositions and Corrections,* U. S. Government Printing Office, Washington, D. C., 1977, p. 28.

[3]Lee Strobel, "Is Illinois Juvenile Law Fair to Kids?" *Chicago Tribune,* Oct. 17, 1980, pp. 1 and 4.

aggravated kidnapping, and aggravated burglary to criminal court. In 1981 it was estimated that a total of 10,000 juveniles in the United States had been certified as adults and tried by adult courts.[4]

Juvenile Rights

Since 1965, controversy has continued over the broad powers exercised by the juvenile court, the informal procedures followed in juvenile proceedings, and almost unlimited discretion granted juvenile authorities. In 1967 the United States Supreme Court issued the famous *Gault* decision, which requires the court to notify juveniles brought before it of the charges against them, their right to counsel, their right to confront and cross-examine witnesses, their privilege against self-incrimination, their right to a transcript of the proceedings, and their right to review by an appellate court.[5]

Gault was only one decision handed down by the Supreme Court giving juveniles the same rights in juvenile court that exist in adult criminal proceedings. In 1962 *Gallegos v. Colorado* condemned confessions obtained by "secret inquisitorial processes."[6] The decision in *Kent v. United States* held that required elements of due process and fairness must be met and stated that a hearing, effective assistance of counsel, and a statement of reasons must be given to a juvenile.[7] The court in *In Re Winship* ruled that juvenile court proceedings required proof beyond a reasonable doubt.[8] In *Breed v. Jones* (1975), the court stated that the adult standard forbidding double jeopardy applies to juveniles as well.[9]

These various Supreme Court decisions have granted almost every due process right to juveniles as to adults except trial by jury.[10] However, several states do provide trial by jury in children's cases, and the dissenters in *McKeiver v. Pennsylvania* cite the satisfactory experience in those states. Some state courts have decided that a jury trial is a right of juveniles in their jurisdictions.[11]

The Supreme Court decisions in *Gault* and other cases stated that the procedures of the juvenile court are methods whereby juveniles may be sent to correctional institutions. Even though the courts still hold broad powers over children, the result has been procedural changes in juvenile courts throughout the United States. There is now recognition that children possess the same rights as adults according to our Constitution. Yet as late as 1975, thirty-three states

---

[4]Edward Kiersh, "Minnesota Cracks Down on Chronic Juvenile Offenders," *Corrections Magazine,* December 1981, pp. 22 and 28.

[5]*In Re Gault,* 387 U. S. 1, 87 S. Ct. 1428, 18 L. Ed. 2d 527 (1967).

[6]*Gallegos v. Colorado,* 370 U. S. 49 (1962).

[7]*Kent v. United States,* 38 U. S. 541 (1966).

[8]*In Re Winship,* 397 U. S. 358 (1970).

[9]*Breed v. Jones,* 43 L. W. 4644 (1975).

[10]E. Sol Rubin, "The Juvenile Court Needs a New Turn," *Federal Probation,* vol. 45, no. 2, Administrative Office of the United States Courts, Washington, D. C., June 1981, p. 52.

[11]*McKeiver v. Pennsylvania,* 403 U. S. 528 (1971).

and the District of Columbia still legally sanctioned the disposition of juveniles without court proceeding.[12]

STATUS OFFENSES

Definition

Currently the *parens patriae* concept is being challenged, because children who do not commit crimes can be placed under state jurisdiction through use of the category *status offenses*. Status offenses are acts committed by children— truancy, running away, consensual sexual behavior, smoking, drinking, curfew violations, disobeying authority, ungovernability, and waywardness—which would not be considered crimes if committed by adults. In twenty-six states, status offenders are not differentiated from children classified as delinquents and are subject to the same disposition as juveniles who commit a crime. In twenty-five states special categories have been created for status offenders.[13] These include juveniles in need of supervision (JINS), persons in need of supervision (PINS), minors in need of supervision (MINS), and children in need of supervision (CINS).

A Question of Jurisdiction

Many critics, such as Professor Paul Lerman, believe that the creation of the category *status offense* represents a change in America from a juvenile justice system to a juvenile social control system.[14] In 1975 it was estimated that 25 percent of the 29,070 children placed each year in private local residential units were status offenders (including 70 percent of the girls) and another 46 percent were nonoffenders.[15] By 1977 a subsequent national study showed an increase in the percentage of female status offenders to 75 percent of the total number of females in the juvenile system.[16]

The question of the placement of status offenders within the jurisdiction of the juvenile court is not new. In 1967 William Sheridan, assistant director of the Division of Juvenile Delinquency Services, United States Children's Bureau, recommended their removal from juvenile court jurisdiction. At that time a conservative estimate indicated that 26 percent of the 184,000 cases coming before the courts were status offenders.[17]

[12]*Juvenile Dispositions and Corrections,* op. cit., p. 20.

[13]Mark M. Levin and Rosemary C. Sarri, *Juvenile Delinquency: A Comparative Analysis of Legal Codes in the United States,* National Assessment of Juvenile Corrections, Ann Arbor, Mich., 1974, p. 12.

[14]Paul Lerman, "Delinquency and Social Policy: A Historical Perspective,"*Crime and Delinquency,* vol. 23, no. 4, October 1977, p. 383.

[15]"Thousands of Youngsters Jailed for Non-Criminal Acts,"*American Journal of Correction,* vol. 37, no. 3, May/June 1975, p. 18.

[16]Meda Chesney-Lind, "Judicial Paternalism and the Female Status Offender: Training Women to Know Their Place," *Crime and Delinquency,* vol. 23, no. 2, April 1977, p. 121.

[17]William H. Sheridan, "Juveniles Who Commit Non-Criminal Acts: Why Treat in a Correctional System?" *Federal Probation,* vol. 31, no. 1, Administrative Office of the United States Courts, Washington, D. C., March 1967, p. 27.

In 1974 the Juvenile Justice and Delinquency Prevention Act passed by Congress clearly intended that federal funds appropriated to assist state, local, and private juvenile serving agencies be allocated on the condition that status offenders be removed from jails and institutions. However, two days of hearings in September 1977 by the Senate Subcommittee on Juvenile Delinquency proved conclusively that many states had failed to live up to the intent of the act.[18]

In April 1975 the board of directors of the National Council on Crime and Delinquency advocated the removal of status offenses from the jurisdiction of the juvenile court. As Milton Rector, president of the council, said, "This is a national scandal. . . . We spend thousands of dollars a year on each of these incarcerated youngsters only to find that this so-called treatment makes them a continuing problem to themselves and society."[19] The committee of the standards project of the American Bar Associations Institution of Juvenile Administration took the same position.

At least one critic, sociologist Robert Balch, challenged the treatment of "predelinquent" children on ethical grounds. He questioned the practice of subjecting children to various forms of "treatment" even before they have broken a law, confining status offenders indefinitely in reformatories and training schools, and deciding cases on the basis of expediency and individual whim rather than specific violations of law.[20]

Others disagree with the attempt to remove status offenders from juvenile court jurisdiction. In January 1976, Lawrence H. Martin and Phyllis Snyder, Berkshire Farm Center of New York administrators, stated in *Crime and Delinquency* that they opposed removing status offenders from juvenile court jurisdiction for fear that services available to families in stress would be limited. Instead, they advocated more facilities and programs developed at the dispositional stage to provide additional options for children in need of care.[21]

Some objectors to discontinuing the category of status offense have cited research to justify their position. Professor Richard L. Jenkins has stated that a group of delinquent releasees from the Boys' Training School in Iowa did much better than a runaway group (status offenders) in avoiding return to the training school. The group of delinquents returned at a 24 percent rate, compared with a 64 percent rate for the runaways. The conviction rate in adult court, too, was lower for the delinquent group (40 percent) than for the runaway group (61 percent). Jenkins believes that the poor showing of the runaway group resulted from a failure of parenting and, consequently, of socialization.

[18]John Culver, "Culver Hearing Shows States Have Failed to Separate Criminal and Non-Criminal Youth Offenders," *News Release,* United States Senate, Washington, D. C., Sept. 23, 1977, p. 1.

[19]Board of Directors, National Council on Crime and Delinquency, "Jurisdiction Over Status Offenders Should Be Removed From the Juvenile Court: A Policy Statement," *Crime and Delinquency,* vol. 21, no. 2, April 1975, p. 97.

[20]Robert W. Balch, "The Medical Model of Delinquency: Theoretical, Practical, and Ethical Implications," *Crime and Delinquency,* vol. 21, no. 2, April 1975, p. 126.

[21]Lawrence H. Martin and Phyllis R. Snyder, "Jurisdiction Over Status Offenses Should *Not* Be Removed From the Juvenile Court," *Crime and Delinquency,* vol. 22, no. 1, January 1976, pp. 44–47.

Runaways are often unsocialized or undersocialized youngsters who have never developed trust in a parent figure. They have consequently never developed the capacity for loyalty, on which a child's learning of concepts of morality is based. Thus the prognosis for avoiding criminal conviction as adults is less favorable for runaways than for children who commit crimes. If juvenile justice law excludes the "socially maladjusted" (i.e., status offenders), those children most in need of special help are in danger of being systematically deprived of such help.[22]

Deinstitutionalization

The trend toward the removal of status offenders from institutionalization has been slow to gain impetus. Robert Vintor, co-director of the National Assessment of Juvenile Corrections, examined the trends between 1970 and 1974 and concluded that "status offenders referred to juvenile courts have the same, if not higher, probability of being committed to correctional facilities as juveniles with more serious offenses." Vintor cited as reasons the states' budgetary restraints, lack of coordination between state and local practices, state government indifference to status offenders, and lack of executive leadership in juvenile corrections.[23]

Since 1950, statistics regarding the placement of adjudicated youths have uncovered a number of trends, all related in some way to the federally mandated emphasis on deinstitutionalization of status offenders. The percentage of youth in publicly operated correctional facilities has decreased from 79 percent of the total number of children in correctional facilities in 1950 to 52 percent in 1974 (see Table 11.1). The number of children in privately operated correctional facilities increased from 7944 (21 percent) in 1950 to 30,952 (48 percent) in 1974.

[22]Richard L. Jenkins, "Child Psychiatry Perspectives: Status Offenders," *Journal of Child Psychiatry,* vol. 19, no. 2, Spring 1980, pp. 322–324.

[23]Robert D. Vinter, "Trends in State Correction: Juveniles and the Violent Young Offender," *Crime and Delinquency,* vol. 25, no. 2, April 1979, pp. 154–158.

TABLE 11.1
NUMBER AND PERCENTAGE OF RESIDENTS IN PUBLIC AND PRIVATE
JUVENILE CORRECTIONAL FACILITIES
(1950–1974)

	1950		1960		1970		1974	
	No.	%	No.	%	No.	%	No.	%
Public	29,042	79	38,359	84	57,691	87	33,732	52
Private	7,944	21	7,336	16	8,766	13	30,952	48
Total	36,986		45,336		66,457		64,684	

Source: Paul Lerman, "Trends and Issues in the Deinstitutionalization of Youths in Trouble," *Crime and Delinquency,* vol. 26, no. 3, July 1980, p. 280.

As hoped by those people endorsing the removal of status offenders from institutions, the percentage of incarcerated dependent and neglected youngsters decreased from 1974 to 1975. However, an increase in children adjudicated delinquent counterbalanced the decrease insofar as the total population in juvenile correctional institutions.

At the same time, there has been an increase in the number of youths placed in institutions who are labeled as emotionally disturbed. Paul Lerman concludes that these statistics may indicate a shift in labeling rather than a change in children's behavior or the deinstitutionalization of status offenders. Despite the trend toward deinstitutionalization, 74 percent of dependent and neglected youth and 72 percent of emotionally disturbed youth in residential placement in 1974 lived in facilities housing more than 50 children, and 42 to 44 percent lived with 100 or more (see Table 11.2). In 1976 approximately 40 percent of federal Aid to Families of Dependent Children foster care maintenance funds was spent for institutional care, according to Lerman, "primarily because of mental or delinquency problems."[24]

More recent studies do indicate a decrease in the number of status offenders incarcerated in public and private facilities. From 1977 until 1979 there was a decrease of more than 2200 status offenders held in public facilities and more than 1000 held in private facilities. In both instances, the decrease was entirely among girls. This is significant, because girls have been over-represented among status offenders in the past. During the same period there were increases in the number of children held in institutions in both the delinquent and nonoffender categories (see Table 11.3).[25]

[24]Paul Lerman, "Trends and Issues in the Deinstitutionalization of Youths in Trouble," *Crime and Delinquency,* vol. 26, no. 3, July 1980, p. 280.
[25]*Children in Custody, Advance Report on the 1979 Census of Private and Public Juvenile Facilities,* U. S. Department of Justice, Washington, D. C., 1980, table 2.

TABLE 11.2
DISTRIBUTION OF JUVENILES UNDER 18 IN INSTITUTIONS
FOR DEPENDENT/NEGLECTED AND EMOTIONALLY
DISTURBED, BY RESIDENCE AND ADMISSIONS TRENDS AND
CUSTODY/CARE/TREATMENT EPISODES
(1970–1971 and 1973)

	1970–1971				1973			
	Dependent/ neglected		Emotionally disturbed		Dependent/ neglected		Emotionally disturbed	
	No.	%	No.	%	No.	%	No.	%
Residents	43,867	61	28,481	39	36,876	51	34,759	49
Admissions	46,499	56	31,456	44	39,089 (est.)	47	44,492 (est.)	53

Source: Paul Lerman, "Trends and Issues in the Deinstitutionalization of Youths in Trouble," *Crime and Delinquency,* vol. 26, no. 3, July 1980, p. 280.

TABLE 11.3
1979 CENSUSES OF PUBLIC AND PRIVATE
FACILITIES
(Advance Reports)

	1977	1979
Public facilities		
Delinquency offense	37,846	39,455
Status offense	4,916	2,734
Nonoffenders, others	1,334	900
Total	44,096	43,089
Male	36,921	37,063
Female	7,175	6,026
Private facilities		
Delinquency offense	9,484	9,603
Status offense	7,438	6,291
Nonoffenders, others	12,148	12,784
Total	29,070	28,678
Male	20,387	20,505
Female	8,683	8,173

Source: Children in Custody: Advance Report on the 1979 Census of Private and Public Juvenile Facilities, U.S. Department of Justice, October 1980, Table 2.

It is estimated that nearly 500,000 children are detained in the nation's jails and lockups each year—232,342 in jails alone. Studies indicate that 22 percent (46,000) of them committed a status offense or no offense at all. Only 10 percent actually require secure detention. Only fifteen states reported compliance with the provision of the 1974 act.[26]

Evaluations of individual programs designed to deinstitutionalize status offenders have come to the same conclusion. For all sites included in the evaluation (Macon and Cook Counties, Illinois; Pima County, Arizona; Alameda County, California; Spokane and Clark Counties, Washington; and the states of Connecticut, Delaware, and South Carolina), there was a reduction of 43 percent in the use of detention and 50 to 86 percent in the use of postadjudication institutions for status offenders. Some evaluations, however, concluded that the availability of more resources has resulted in more children being referred to the juvenile justice system. They suggest that the net effect may be recategorization of children, widening of the juvenile justice system's jurisdiction, and a decrease in direction from the court.[27]

While the argument about jurisdiction over status offenders has been taking

---

[26]Charles J. Kehoe, "Juvenile Justice Standards: What's in It for the Kids and Us?" *Proceedings of the One Hundred and Tenth Annual Congress of Corrections,* American Correctional Association, College Park, Md., 1980, p. 2.

[27]Irving A. Spergel, Frederick G. Reamer, and James P. Lynch, "Deinstitutionalization of Status Offenders: Individual Outcome and System Effects," *Journal of Research in Crime and Delinquency,* vol. 18, no. 1, January 1981, p. 30.

place, some individual jurisdictions have developed special projects to lower the number of status offenders in their care. The Youth Services Agency of Bucks County, Pennsylvania, cut down the number of status offenders petitioned to court from 1000 in 1975 to 25 during the first 3 months of 1978. The agency used 11 full-time employees and 100 volunteers, who diverted court referrals from probation officers, police, teachers, and parents to public and private resources in the community for housing, counseling, and other services. Each referral was contacted 3 times in the first 3 weeks and then once a month until the youth no longer required services.[28]

DELINQUENT BEHAVIOR

California Youth Authority

A look at statistics about delinquent behavior reveals some similarities to statistics about the adult offender. For example, the California Youth Authority describes the children committed to it as follows: 56 percent of the boys and 61 percent of the girls come from below-average socioeconomic environments. The parents of 57 percent of the boys and 66 percent of the girls were not living together at the time of the youngster's commitment. Neither parent of 24 percent of the boys and 20 percent of the girls had gone farther than the eighth grade. Twenty-one percent of the fathers of the boys and 27 percent of the fathers of the girls has criminal convictions. Achievement scores placed both boys and girls at eighth-grade level in reading comprehension. The average IQ of the boys was tested at 91 and of the girls 92. There was no evidence of a serious psychological disorder in 76 percent of the boys and 54 percent of the girls. Eighty-one percent of the boys and 88 percent of the girls had friends who were adjudicated delinquent. Eighty-seven percent of the boys and 90 percent of the girls did not admit drug use. The median age at the time of the first delinquent contact was 14 years for both boys and girls.[29]

School and Home

At least one study of delinquent behavior specifically examined the relationship between the public school system and juvenile delinquency. Data taken from 618 court files of juveniles appearing in Judge Seymour Gelber's court in Dade County (Miami), Florida, in 1979 indicated that 22 percent of the juveniles were recent school dropouts and more than 50 percent had been truant. More than one-fifth of the charges against the juveniles represented acts occurring on public school property.

The most interesting conclusion of the study was the similarity between

---

[28]James J. Fowkes, "One County's Approach to the Diversion of Youth from the Juvenile Justice System," *Federal Probation,* vol. 42, no. 4, Administrative Office of the United States Courts, Washington, D. C., December 1978, pp. 37, 39.

[29]*Annual Statistical Report, California Youth Authority, 1971,* Sacramento, pp. 12–13.

truancy and delinquency rates among racial/ethnic groupings: for blacks a 58 percent truancy rate and 55 percent delinquency rate, for Anglos a 29 percent truancy rate and a 30 percent delinquency rate, and for Latins a 13 percent truancy rate and a 14 percent delinquency rate.[30]

Not all studies agree with these statistics. An empirical study by researchers Richard Grinnell and Cheryl Chambers published the same year, drawing information from 7793 juvenile cases, revealed little or no relationship between broken homes and middle-class delinquency.[31] However, the overwhelming evidence does indicate that, like adult felons, most juveniles who become adjudicated have been reared in dysfunctional homes, have had few opportunities for individual achievement, and have experienced a number of personal misfortunes.

Self-Report Studies

Some questions have been raised about whether it is wise to use only statistics about adjudicated juveniles to identify characteristics of delinquents. A number of sociologists have used either interviewing techniques or anonymous questionnaires in an effort to measure delinquency. In general, these studies indicate that many people commit delinquent acts which either never come to the attention of authorities or are not officially processed. Austin Porterfield compared a sample of delinquents with college students who had not been adjudicated delinquent and found similar types of delinquency among both groups. Some of the college students were leaders of school organizations and honor students.

Unrecorded incidents of delinquency were found to be frequent in a study involving high school students in three western cities of between 10,000 and 30,000 in population and three smaller midwestern communities. Maynard Erickson and Lamar Empey found many reported offenses that had not been acted on officially among 15 to 17-year-old males in Utah. According to Erickson and Empey, the greater the number of violations reported by the juveniles, the more frequently he had appeared in court. Court records confirmed the distinction between persistent offenders and nonoffenders or one-time offenders and indicated that the most serious violations were committed by the persistent offenders.[32]

JUVENILE COMMUNITY-BASED PROGRAMS

Juvenile community-based programs are operated by both publicly and privately funded agencies, which utilize public schools and local recreation facilities in lieu

---

[30]Seymour Gelber, "Who Is the Juvenile Offender?", *Corrections Today,* vol. 41, no. 6, November/December 1979, p. 14.

[31]Richard M. Grinnell, Jr. and Cheryl A. Chambers, *Criminology,* vol. 17, no. 3, November 1979, pp. 398–399.

[32]Sue Titus Reid, *Crime and Criminology,* Holt, Rinehart and Winston, New York, 1979, pp. 65–67.

of on-campus services. Today community-based programs such as probation, foster homes, halfway houses, and parole are becoming more prevalent within the juvenile justice system.

The greatest impetus for establishing such programs came after endorsement by the President's Commission in 1967. The goal of the movement has been deinstitutionalization, or the use of community-based programs as alternatives to institutions. However, the public's lack of firm knowledge about the programs has hindered their adoption. The result has been only a reduction in the proportion of the youth incarcerated in institutions.

In only eight states in 1974 did the number of juveniles in community-based correctional programs equal or outnumber those in institutions. Only 18 percent of all youth in state juvenile corrections systems were assigned to such programs, in spite of the fact that they were less expensive to operate.[33]

JUVENILE DIVERSION

Overview

One form of community-based program for juveniles is diversion—the process of turning them away from further processing by the juvenile justice system. A diversion program is a resource that provides direct services and referral assistance to children whose status or conduct makes them subject to the jurisdiction of the juvenile court but who are referred to the program in lieu of official processing or incarceration. Basic elements of the program include a standard procedure for referral of candidates from various sources. An immediate determination is made of their eligibility and voluntary acceptance of participation; then a decision is made about placing them in the program. A system is devised for feedback of information on a youth's performance and status in the program to referral sources. Most diversion programs have a service component (i.e., counseling, job placement, educational planning, or emergency foster care).[34]

Diversion was originally intended to be a conscious, policy-based decision to release a juvenile who otherwise would have been arrested and sent to juvenile court. There were a number of possibilities for the diverted youth—release without any further contact with juvenile justice officials, referral to a nonlegal or community alternative providing specific services, and referral to an outside agency without services.

Diversion was initiated to correct a number of shortcomings in the juvenile justice system. It was hoped that most of these deficiencies could be eliminated if the youth had "minimal penetration of the juvenile justice system." Among those deficiencies are denial of due process rights to juveniles; inefficient

---

[33]Rosemary C. Sarri and Robert D. Vinter, "Justice for Whom? Varieties of Juvenile Correctional Approaches," in Malcom W. Klein (ed.), *The Juvenile Justice System,* Sage Publications, Beverly Hills, Calif., 1976, p. 174.

[34]*Juvenile Diversion: A Perspective,* American Correctional Association, College Park, Md. 1972 pp. 7–9.

processing, largely because of a backlog of cases; labeling and stigmatization of youths; failure of the juvenile justice system to reduce recidivism; high costs of handling a multitude of cases; and the failure of communities to assume responsibility for problems of youths.[35]

Police

In most jurisdictions the first handling of a juvenile is assigned to special units of the police, who become involved when an officer observes a suspicious act or when a complaint is filed. In either instance, the police department's juvenile bureau assumes responsibility for the case. Frequently the youth is released if continuance does not seem to be in the best interest of the child or if there is insufficient information to warrant further investigation. This is the first opportunity for a youth to be diverted from the juvenile justice system.

If the police department's juvenile bureau believes further investigation is justified, it has a number of alternatives. It may interview the child and subsequently conduct a full-scale investigation; it may deliver the child to a juvenile detention facility; it may issue an informal or formal (recorded) reprimand and release the child; or it may give a citation to appear at a later time and return the child to his or her parents. The latter two alternatives constitute two opportunities for diversion.

One survey of thirty-seven municipal police agencies revealed that nearly 67 percent had a juvenile diversion program—yet there were few which indicated that rehabilitation was the purpose of the program.[36] One police diversion program in Dallas, Texas, reported that 72 percent of the diverted juveniles experienced improved communication with parents, 63 percent increased their attendance in school, 52 percent made better grades, 29 percent obtained part-time jobs, and 43 percent were actively participating in recreation and hobby programs.[37]

Intake

Once a child is referred to juvenile court, an intake process begins. After an interview, a decision is made whether or not the juvenile should be placed in detention or the case continued while he or she remains at home. If minimal involvement is required, the child may be dismissed, admonished and dismissed, placed on informal probation, or informally referred to a community agency such as a mental health center or Big Brothers/Big Sisters. At the other extreme, a petition may be filed for a court hearing. If the child is physically detained, a

---

[35]Edwin M. Lemert, "Diversion in Juvenile Justice: What Hath Been Wrought?" *Journal of Research in Crime and Delinquency,* vol. 18, no. 1, January 1981, pp. 36–37.

[36]Stanley Vanagunas, "Police Diversion of Juvenile Offenders: An Ambiguous State of the Art," *Federal Probation,* vol. 43, no. 3, Administrative Office of the United States Courts, Washington, D. C., Sept. 1979, p. 50.

[37]Thomas R. Collingwood, Alex Douds, and Hadley Williams, "Juvenile Diversion: The Dallas Police Department Youth Series Program," *Federal Probation,* vol. 40, no. 3, Administrative Office of the United States Courts, Washington, D. C., September 1976, p. 26.

preliminary detention hearing may be necessary to determine whether the information contained on the complaint justifies detention.

The intake officer serves as a kind of "gate keeper." The primary purpose of the intake process is to provide a prepetition screening of complaints in order to determine which cases to divert from or insert into the system. Forty-two states have specifically provided for intake departments in their juvenile courts, frequently as part of the probation department.

Whether intake decision making has actually resulted in diverting youth from the juvenile justice system has been questioned. Assuming diversion is accomplished, there should be an increase in the percentage of cases not referred for adjudication. One study of the New York City Department of Probation reflected such a trend. According to Table 11.4, the percentage of delinquency cases diverted from adjudication increased by 21.5 percent from 1975 through 1980.[38]

Alternatives to Detention

Another point of diversion for juvenile offenders is detention. In 1977 the San Diego County Probation Department substituted a "home arrest" or home supervision program to avoid detention of juveniles who were awaiting court disposition of their cases. Children placed on home supervision were required to stay home and warned that the juvenile officer would arrest them for not being there. From March 1977 until May 1979, there were 2494 juveniles placed on home supervision. Only 33 (1.3 percent) committed public offenses during the

[38]Charles Lindner, "Juvenile Intake Decision Making Standards and Precourt Diversion Rates in New York," *Federal Probation*, vol. 45, no. 2, Administrative Office of the United States Courts, Washington, D. C., June 1981, p. 57.

TABLE 11.4
NEW YORK CITY DEPARTMENT OF PROBATION INTAKE ACTION ON JUVENILE DELINQUENCY COMPLAINTS (1975 through 1980)

Year	Action taken on intake cases	Number diverted	Percentage diverted
1974	24,238	9,586	39.5
1975	25,668	9,774	38.0
1976	24,696	10,618	42.9
1977	22,088	11,025	50.0
1978	21,192	11,437	54.0
1979	18,141	9,553	53.0
1980	16,516	10,076	61.0

Source: Charles Lindner, "Juvenile Intake Decision Making Standards and Precourt Diversion Rates in New York," *Federal Probation*, vol. 45, no. 2, Administrative Office of the United States Courts, Washington, D.C., June 1981, p. 57.

period, and only 504 rule violations took place. An effort was made to provide a ratio of one probation officer for each ten youngsters, and an average of 1.1 personal contacts were made every day with each child. The cost of home supervision was $3200 a year per youth, compared with $15,900 a year for placement in detention at juvenile hall.[39] Similar forms of home detention are being used in St. Louis; Newport News, Virginia; and Washington, D. C. In these communities, however, instead of employing a probation officer, the court pays a guardian to maintain close supervision of a youth during the day when parents are away.[40]

Florida developed an innovative plan in 1975 to provide volunteer substitute homes for status offenders who must be temporarily detained by juvenile authorities. Court personnel recruited adults who agreed to care for children for not more than 10 days, during which a detention hearing would be held. The state division of youth services provided each volunteer home with transportation and emergency medical care for the child. The problems of the children were monitored daily by juvenile court personnel. From March 15 to July 31, 1975, there were 1181 children in volunteer homes for 7506 days—an average stay of 6.4 days per child. During this time only 67 children ran away from their volunteer homes (5.6 percent) and only 18 stole property from their volunteer homes (1.5 percent).[41]

Another form of diversion is "runaway houses." Privately operated but receiving federal funds since 1975, runaway houses provide meals, clothes, job counseling, medical service, family counseling, and temporary shelter to more than 35,000 youngsters annually. Each child voluntarily enters and leaves the program, although some runaway house administrators place a restriction on the number of days a child may remain. By early 1980 there were 165 programs for runaway children, receiving $10.5 million annually in federal funding through the Department of Health, Education and Welfare (now Health and Human Services). A 1980 survey indicated that 59 percent of the youths assisted were females, 66 percent were from 14 to 16 years old, 43 percent returned home, 24 percent were placed in alternative living quarters, and only 11 percent continued running away.[42]

Probation

Probably the most familiar form of diversion is probation. In 1976, there were 328,854 juveniles on probation. Each year 200,000 young people are placed on juvenile probation. The average caseload of a juvenile probation officer is

[39]William G. Swank, "Home Supervision: Probation Really Works," *Federal Probation,* vol. 43, no. 4, Administrative Office of the United States Courts, Washington, D. C., December 1979, p. 48.

[40]Clemens Bartollas, *Introduction to Corrections,* Harper & Row, Publishers, Incorporated, New York, 1981, p. 433.

[41]Jane C. Latina and Jeffrey L. Schembera, "Volunteer Homes for Status Offenders: An Alternative to Detention," *Federal Probation,* vol. 40, no. 4, Administrative Office of the United States Courts, Washington, D. C., December 1976, p. 48.

[42]Greg Mitchell, "For Runaway, a Meal, a Bed—And No Questions Asked," *Corrections Magazine,* vol. 6, no. 2, June 1980, p. 33.

approximately seventy youths. Although a few states have a centralized probation system, most of the 3068 counties in the United States are autonomous
within limits set by state statute. Only six states administer a statewide probation
service; twenty use a combination of probation services provided by the state
and local government together.

In twenty-four states juvenile courts administer services, with the probation
officer serving as an appointee of the judge. The officer's major responsibility
involves three primary tasks: (1) devising an appropriate plan for care of the
child and observing his or her progress to assure that the plan is carried out or
revised; (2) developing and overseeing community resources that can be used by
the child; and (3) counseling young people, family members, and others
associated with the child.

Like adult probation officers, juvenile probation personnel spend an inordi-
nate amount of time completeing tasks for the court without a decrease in
caseloads, thus limiting the time available to supervise and assist the young
probationers. The probation officer undertakes social investigations which
require review of previous reports, interviews, and inquiries within the community. The officer also takes part in preliminary hearings which determine
whether a youth should be released or held in detention. Testimony before
adjudication hearings requires even more time.

Intensive Supervision

A number of experimental programs have been instituted as part of the
probation process. Some that involve intensive supervision are the so-called
tracker and proctor/advocacy programs. *Trackers, proctors,* and *youth advocates*
provide supervision and counseling for two to five probationers. Their responsibilities are indistinguishable from those of other probation officers, except that
they may not be officers of the court and consequently do not possess the same
legal authority.[43]

Massachusetts' community advancement program takes youngsters who have
failed under the traditional version of probation and applies intensive supervision and foster care. Initially it is an attempt to keep the child living at home by
providing intensive supervision. With a caseload of only two to five juveniles,
the officer sees each youth 4 or more times a week and knows where the youths
are 24 hours a day, 7 days a week.[44]

Foster Care

Foster care is a community-based diversionary program frequently used. It
involves the placement of children with parents (not their biological parents)

---

[43]Kevin Krajick, " 'Tracking,' and 'Proctoring' in Utah," *Corrections Magazine,* vol. 6, no. 6,
December 1980, p. 31.

[44]Michael S. Serrill, "The Community Advancement Program," *Corrections Magazine,* vol. 2,
no. 2, November/December 1975, p. 13.

who are paid to care for the children on a temporary or indefinite basis. In 1974 on an average day 8000 adjudicated children were reported in state-funded foster homes. For that year, the cost of maintaining a youth in foster care averaged less than $2500.[45]

Intervention Programs

Researchers have found that a number of family and community intervention programs resulted in an apparent reduction in juvenile delinquency. In studies of both experimental and control groups, James Alexander and Bruce Parsons reported in June 1973 a finding of 21 to 47 percent differences in recidivism rates between experimental groups of delinquents involved in family therapy and various control groups. Each time, the difference was in favor of the experimental group. Walter Fo and Clifford O'Donnell reported in April 1974 on an experimental group designed to be a community intervention program. Paraprofessional "buddies" were used as therapists who offered counseling. Recidivism rates of 38 percent were found among children 11 to 17 years old who had committed "major offenses," compared with a 64 percent for a matched control group.

Studies examining various kinds of counseling programs for juveniles have reported similar success stories. Michael Chandler found a 50 percent lower recidivism rate for delinquent children 11 to 13 years old who were placed in role-playing sessions. Irwin G. Sarason and Victor J. Glanser reported 18 percent and 14 percent recidivism rates for juveniles in modeling and discussion groups, compared with 24 percent for controls.[46]

Youth Services Bureau

A youth services bureau is a noncoercive, independent public or private agency designed to divert children from the juvenile justice system. It is available to parents and children on the verge of trouble and in need of help before their behavior requires judicial intervention. The bureau mobilizes community resources to solve youth problems, strengthen existing resources and develop new ones, and advocate programs to remedy delinquency-breeding conditions. Referral sources may be public welfare departments, mental health centers, police, courts, schools, families, churches, and individuals. Children age 7 to 18 and their families voluntarily work out and use a plan of service designed to avoid referral to juvenile court.[47]

Youth services bureaus were first established in 1958 in Chicago and in Pontiac, Michigan. Following an endorsement by the 1967 President's Commis-

---

[45]Sarri and Vinter, op. cit., p. 175.

[46]Paul Gendreau and Bob Ross, "Effective Correctional Programs: Bibliotherapy for Cynics," *Crime and Delinquency*, vol. 25, no. 4, October 1979, p. 476.

[47]Sherwood Norman, "The Youth Service Bureau," in Povl G. Boesen and Stanley E. Grupp (eds.), *Community-Based Corrections: Theory, Practice, and Research*, Davis Publishing Company, Inc., Santa Cruz, Calif., 1976, p. 126.

sion on Law Enforcement and Administration of Justice, they spread rapidly across the country. A national census in 1972 identified 150 bureaus. The Indiana Juvenile Justice Task Force, funded primarily by The Lilly Endowment, Inc., has helped establish and maintain youth services bureaus in eighteen counties. The commission report anticipated that youth services bureaus would become central coordinating units for all community services for young people. Some of the more innovative bureaus have offered diagnostic services (Hughesville, Maryland), an outpatient medical clinic (Los Angeles, California), and group homes (Omaha, Nebraska, and Las Cruces, New Mexico).

Some people have considered youth services bureaus as a model for all social service delivery systems. Sherwood Norman in his book, *The Youth Services Bureau, a Key to Delinquency Prevention,* stated:

> The Bureau strengthens existing agencies by performing an enabling function rather than by attempting to fill gaps in service. It bridges the gap between available services of youth in need of them by referral and follow-up; it acts as an advocate of a child to see that he gets the services he needs. The Youth Services Bureau is not itself a service agency so much as an agency for organizing the delivery of services to children and their families.[48]

New Pride, Inc.

In Denver, Colorado, a program began in 1972 to divert chronic juvenile offenders to community services. Youths age 14 to 17 with the equivalent of three convictions for robbery, assault, or burglary are eligible. Referrals are made by probation officers, district attorneys, and judges while charges are pending. Both the offenders and their parents must agree to the youths' participation. The program is nonresidential, with most youths residing in their own homes. New Pride, Inc., offers diagnostic services, an alternative school, educational opportunities for learning-disability students, individual and family counseling, and a job development and placement center.

In October 1981 no long-term study had been completed on New Pride offenders, but indications were that recidivism was at a 50 to 55 percent rate for participants during enrollment of 6 months to a year. Seventeen percent were rearrested for robbery, assault, and burglary. Other results include the finding of jobs for 79 percent of the youth although only 20 percent kept their jobs longer than 90 days. Educational achievement of students went up 1.1 and 1.9 grade levels in reading and spelling and 0.1 to 0.9 grade levels in mathematics; and 70 percent of the youths were reintegrated into public schools.

Unexpectedly, New Pride, Inc., had difficulty soliciting offenders from their target population. The LEAA Office of Juvenile Justice and Delinquency Prevention, has initiated a $13.5 million, 3-year effort to replicate New Pride in ten cities—Camden, New Jersey; Providence, Rhode Island; Barton and Pensa-

---

[48]National Advisory Commission on Criminal Justice Standards and Goals, "Youth Services Bureaus," in Gary R. Perlstein and Thomas R. Phelps (eds.), *Alternatives to Prison,* Goodyear Publishing Company, Inc., Pacific Palisades, Calif., 1975, p. 209.

cola, Florida; Chicago, Illinois; Washington, D. C.; San Francisco, Los Angeles, and Fresno, California; and Kansas City, Missouri.[49]

Outward Bound

One of the more innovative diversion programs for youths involves survival experiences, substituting rugged, short-term wilderness trips for incarceration. Survival experiences conducted by Outward Bound are especially well known. This nonprofit agency, founded in the 1960s, has grown into a national program with on-site, ongoing programs in Massachusetts, Colorado, Texas, and California. More than twenty other states have added 2-to-3 week wilderness trips to their correctional programs. The trips, which usually last 3 weeks, can include water rafting, mountaineering, canoeing, sailing, cycling, wilderness backpacking, or desert expeditions. Operators of such programs hope that the wilderness experience will give the youth "something to succeed at."[50]

Outward Bound helps young men and women extend their own self-sufficiency through confrontation with a series of increasingly difficult challenges in a wilderness setting. The director of corrections for the Colorado Outward Bound school states: "Outward Bound is like a rite of acceptable passage of the delinquent into adulthood."

The program begins with an orientation period whereby youngsters are acclimated to the outdoors—practicing rock climbing, fire building, shelter planning, gear packing, and other activities essential for survival. Following orientation, the group of boys and girls begin the expeditionary phase. They start with activities easily mastered by each member of the group—shelter construction, food preparation, etc.—and end with more difficult activities such as rappelling or day-long treks in full gear. All are designed to build self-confidence.

The third phase emphasizes fellowship. The entire program is designed to reconstruct young people's self-images; hence the outdoor experience must be supplemented by interpretation. This is done through a responsive communication network and a continuing supportive relationship with Outward Bound personnel and fellow participants.[51]

Juvenile Restitution

In 1975 another innovative alternative to incarceration began when the "victims program" was established at the juvenile court in Tulsa, Oklahoma. The program sought to bring about restitution to the victims, to assist them in

[49]Suzanne Charle, "The Proliferation of Project New Pride,"*Corrections Magazine,* vol. 7, no. 5, October 1981, pp. 29–32.

[50]Keven Krajick, "Working Our Way Home,"*Corrections Magazine,* vol. 4, no. 2, June 1978, p. 39.

[51]Kristi S. Kistler, Peter M. Bryant, and Gary J. Tucker, "Outward Bound: Providing a Therapeutic Experience for Troubled Youngsters,"*Hospital and Community Psychiatry,* vol. 28, no. 11, November 1977, pp. 807, 812.

recovering lost property, and to personalize crime by bringing victims and offenders together. It served as an instrument through which victims could receive aid and as a means of developing better relations between offender and victim.

The 251 victims involved since its initiation included individuals or households (60 percent), owner-operated businesses (7 percent), managed businesses (26 percent), schools (4 percent), and government or charitable organizations (3 percent). The mean financial loss per victim was $207, and the mean amount of restitution was $127. In addition, 28 hours of personal service restitution was performed for 13 victims. Seventy-five youths completed an average of 37 hours of community service each. Recipients of the community service included schools, libraries, churches, nursing homes, museums, zoos, and social service agencies.[52]

Questions About Diversion

Despite the increasing use of programs for diversion, some critics view them as potentially harmful. They maintain that (1) the expansion of diversionary services often promotes diversion *to* other programs rather than diversion *from* the system; (2) some of the goals of diversionary programs, such as informal procedures and the elimination of stigmatizing labels, are unattainable; and (3) formal diversion is incompatible with due process as dictated in such Supreme Court decisions as *Gault*.[53]

A California Youth Authority evaluation of fifteen juvenile diversion projects concluded that no single type of program, voluntary or otherwise, was optimal for all or even most youths eligible for diversion. Neither was a specific program setting. Researchers suggested instead a series of program and setting alternatives for specific groups. Recommended were (1) outright release (diversion without programming), (2) non-justice system (i.e., private-agency-operated) program on a voluntary basis, (3) non-justice system program on a nonvoluntary basis, (4) justice system (i.e., police- or probation- department-operated) program on a voluntary basis, and (5) justice system program on a non-voluntary basis.[54]

COMMUNITY-BASED RESIDENCES FOR JUVENILES

Halfway House or Group Home

Textbook author Robert Trojanowicz has stated that a halfway house is a "program that attempts to mobilize the resources of the community in an effort

---

[52]Burt Galaway, Marge Henzel, Glenn Ramsay, and Bart Wanyama, "Victims and Delinquents in the Tulsa Juvenile Court," *Federal Probation,* vol. 44, no. 2, Administrative Office of the United States Court, Washington, D.C., June 1980, pp. 42, 44–45.

[53]Bruce Bullington, James Sprowls, Daniel Katkin, and Mark Phillips, "A Critique of Diversionary Juvenile Justice," *Crime and Delinquency,* vol. 24, no. 1, January 1978, p. 59.

[54]Ted B. Palmer and Roy V. Lewis, "A Differential Approach to Juvenile Diversion,"*Journal of Research on Crime and Delinquency,* vol. 17, no. 2, July 1980, pp. 209, 222.

to prevent and treat delinquency."[55] Even though halfway houses have been used only recently on a large scale, the concept is not new. Their early history can be traced to England's Philanthropic Society of London, which opened three cottages for children in 1788. In the United States at about the same time, the Hebrew Orphan Asylum in New York established a home in the community for adolescent girls who had been discharged from the asylum.[56] Rapid development of halfway houses did not begin until after 1960.

Today halfway houses are called group homes, residential treatment centers, or transitional homes. Children placed in halfway houses or group homes generally are those who have no homes, whose parents are incapable or unwilling to care for them, and whose environment may foster delinquent behavior or be harmful to the child.[57] The 1979 census of public and private juvenile facilities revealed that at the end of the year there were 28,678 juveniles in private facilities and 43,089 in public facilities. About four of every five juveniles (22,942, or 80 percent) in the private sector resided in "open" facilities—primarily group homes. The proportions in the public sector were nearly the reverse, with approximately one in four (10,772, or 25 percent) in open settings.[58]

Program Description

Group homes help bridge the gap between institutions and the community or serve as an alternative between the community and incarceration of the juvenile. An effort is made to select an area where the children will be accepted by their neighbors. Thus they can be referred to academic and employment opportunities in the community, community mental health agencies, recreation facilities, evaluation and diagnostic services, and religious organizations. Group homes are staffed by caseworkers or counselors, child care workers, or houseparents and an administrator. These staff members may live in the facility or work 8-hour shifts. In most cases various psychological or psychiatric consultants are also available.

Two areas of concern have continually plagued administrators of group homes —the selection and retention of staff and the training of personnel. Unfortunately many potential employees are motivated by hostility or sympathy rather than a sincere desire to act as a parent to the child. Also, the constant demands by children in these facilities often exhaust the employees. Previously enthusiastic and well-intentioned, they do not have the energy to remain on the job for an extended period. Lack of funds and failure to develop appropriate programs have sorely deprived personnel of much-needed training.

Most community-based programs are dependent financially on state or county

[55]Robert C. Trojanowicz, *Juvenile Delinquency: Concepts and Control,* Prentice-Hall, Inc., Englewood Cliffs, N. J., 1973, p. 266.
[56]Ibid., p. 269.
[57]Martin R. Haskell and Lewis Yablonsky, *Juvenile Delinquency,* Rand McNally College Publishing Company, Chicago, 1974, p. 467.
[58]*Children in Custody,* op. cit., table 2.

per diem payments, grants from public or private sources, and United Way or revenue sharing funds. Budgets may be limited to necessities such as salaries, food, and clothes, with little left for such extras as personnel training. Actually, only a few training programs designed specifically for group home personnel have been developed. A few of note include the workshops offered by Group Care Consultant Services of Chapel Hill, North Carolina; the Teaching Parent Program of Boys Town, Nebraska; and the Training Workshops of The Villages, Inc., of Topeka, Kansas.

The Villages, Inc.

The Villages, Inc., of Topeka, Kansas, is a public nonprofit agency incorporated specifically to develop pilot projects for the housing and care of children. Homes are constructed or renovated, and children are accepted after failure in state institutions or other community-based programs. Each house is staffed by live-in houseparents, who are assisted by social workers, psychologists, and administrators. In contrast to many group homes or halfway houses, the social workers and psychologists do not provide psychotherapy or counseling to the children; instead they assist the houseparents, who assume the primary responsibility for care. If children require therapy they are referred to community resources, as they are for education, recreation, or religion.

Some halfway houses or group homes provide short-term or temporary housing (less than 2 weeks) or specifically require that a child be placed in another setting after a 3-to-12-month stay. The Villages, on the contrary, permits children to remain in their homes as long as care is necessary. Although there is no opposition to children's returning to their biological parents or being placed in foster care or adoption, such change in placement is not mandated or scheduled.

In an effort to retain personnel, preservice and in-service training programs have been developed, using experienced "training parents," experiential workshops, and seminars. Constant efforts are made to retain houseparents by insisting that they take days off to relieve tension. Psychiatric and social work consultants are available, and parents are relieved of such duties as bookkeeping and writing progress reports. The Villages, Inc., makes every effort to develop surrogate families for the children referred by state agencies. Individual house budgets are developed, family vacations are encouraged, and the family is protected as far as possible from institutional routinization.

As of December 31, 1979, there were 200 children who had left the care of the Villages' homes in Topeka and Lawrence, Kansas. Only 7 of these had been institutionalized as adults, and only 7 had been institutionalized for delinquent behavior. More significantly, only 3 had reapplied for welfare assistance as adults—an impressive statistic, because almost 100 percent of the children were welfare recipients at the time of their placement in Villages' homes.

The project, founded by Dr. Karl Menninger, is now expanding its influence nationally through its training program, its development of other group homes throughout the country, and its consultation service to other agencies.

PAROLE OR AFTERCARE

Overview

Like juvenile probation, juvenile parole or aftercare is basically a supervisory and assistance program. The juvenile like the adult, on parole has been released from an institution. The average caseload for juvenile parole officers is sixty-eight, about the same as for adult parole officers. In 1976 there were 53,347 children on parole or aftercare status.

These caseloads, like probation caseloads, do not account for the total time commitment that the officer must make. In addition to supervising juvenile parolees, the parole officer contacts parents and others in the community and writes reports in connection with the release of juveniles. Some differences between juvenile aftercare and adult parole are that juveniles are more likely to be recommended for release by institutional personnel, juveniles do not stay on aftercare status as long as adults, and juvenile aftercare has not yet come under the criticism that adult parole is facing.

In contrast to probation, in forty-three states juveniles in aftercare status are supervised by state parole agents. In five states parole is administrated by state and local officials together. Only two states allow local authorities to administer parole.

Community Treatment Programs

A number of experimental programs have been used as part of the parole process. The community treatment program sponsored by the California Youth Authority, for example, is founded on the classic clinical design prescribing specific types of treatment for specific types of offenders. While its orientation is generally psychological, it departs from traditional personality classifications and defines offenders according to maturity levels. The maturity typology includes nine types of delinquents, classified according to their interpersonal maturity levels and the modes of behavior which typify their interactions with the world. The nine delinquent subtypes fall into three larger groupings, low-, middle- and high-maturity delinquents. Each of the larger groupings, and to some extent the subgroups within them, calls for distinctly different approaches to treatment and control.

Treatment methods regarded as appropriate for a person in any one of the subtypes would be considered highly inappropriate for one in another subtype. Each experimental delinquent is diagnosed before admission and then assigned to a parole agent thought to be skilled in working with that type of delinquent. Thus types of delinquents are matched with types of agents. Each agent has an average caseload of eight to ten children. Contacts may vary from two to five weekly, and they involve full day as well as part-time programming. A given case, for example, may require—singly or in combination—surveillance and firm discipline, individual counseling, psychotherapy, family group therapy, guided group interaction, occasional confinement. or foster home placement.

The latest reported figures show that 29 percent of experimental groups have been parole failures after 15 months on parole. In contrast, 48 percent of control groups fail. Failure means that the parole has been revoked and the child recommitted. The difference in favor of the community treatment program is highly significant. Experimental subjects also showed a significantly higher level of favorable social and personal adjustment, as reflected by psychological test scores.

A striking difference in the other direction was observed with respect to parole suspensions. Suspensions refer to temporary rather than permanent revocations of parole and usually result in a short period of detention. The experimental group had an average of 2.6 suspensions per child, while the control had an average of only 1.4. Furthermore, 61 percent of all experimental group suspensions were the direct result of arrests made by personnel assigned to supervise the experimental group, contrasted to only 25 percent of the suspensions of the control group.[59]

Another innovative program developed for juvenile parolees experiencing adjustment difficulties is the Cregier Outpost in Illinois, which provides an individualized and structured approach for youngsters with behavioral or educational problems in the community. Each child attends a personalized educational program while receiving individual or group counseling. Between its inception in September 1970 and January 1974, there had been 135 youths enrolled. Only nineteen (14 percent) had become recidivists. School attendance had risen 69 percent over the same period.[60]

APPRAISAL

Evaluation

Juvenile corrections is at present facing the same questions as is adult corrections. Martinson and Wilks discovered few positive results from attempts to rehabilitate juveniles, and a review by William Wright and Michael Dixon of ninety-six delinquency prevention efforts revealed that only a few showed significant evidence of success. Wright and Dixon concluded that counseling and social casework had no effect or a negative effect on delinquency rates and that the detached worker or street-corner-gang-worker approach failed to demonstrate positive results. They also concluded that some programs showed "promise or are in need of further evaluation." These were vocational training programs, community treatment projects, programs which use volunteers, and youth services bureaus.

One of the reasons for their optimism in some instances was the lower costs associated with community-based programs.[61] Although Wright and Dixon

[59]Paul Keve, *Imaginative Programming in Probation and Parole,* University of Minnesota Press, Minneapolis, 1967, p. 41.

[60]Guy A. Ruth, "The Cregier Outpost: A Therapeutic Response to the Juvenile Offender," *Federal Probation,* vol. 38, no. 3, Administrative Office of the United States Courts, Washington, D. C., September 1974, p. 49.

[61]William E. Wright and Michael C. Dixon, "Community Prevention and Treatment of Juvenile Delinquency: A Review of Evaluation Studies," *Journal of Research in Crime and Delinquency,* vol. 14, no. 1, January 1977, pp. 54–55.

reviewed evaluations of delinquency programs completed by 1972, later cost comparisons have confirmed their beliefs. In November 1980, the staff of the investigative newsletter *Institutions, Etc.* conducted a state-by-state telephone survey requesting comparative costs of state-operated institutional programs and community-based programs. Ten states did not have figures available or did not operate both types of programs. For the forty states that did provide comparative figures, the national average revealed that juvenile institutional programs cost $17,832 a year per child, compared with a cost of $10,928 a year per child for community-based programs.[62]

Even when success is apparent, researchers cannot be sure of the results, because of the multitude of factors that affect the child. University of Pennsylvania researcher Deborah Denno examined the operation of a Youth Service Center in two South Philadelphia police districts and discovered a 26 percent decrease in arrests during a 1-year period. After careful analysis she concluded that the activities of the Youth Service Center could not be given credit, however, because other factors (such as changes in police arrest practices) were also discovered. Nevertheless, the statistics do indicate a possibility that an effective Youth Service Center can contribute to a decrease in juvenile arrest rates.[63]

The Massachusetts Experience

Today the debate continues over the role of juvenile correctional institutions versus community-based programs. One of the most dramatic examples of the results of this debate occurred in Massachusetts. In the winter of 1972, Jerome G. Miller, at that time director of the Department of Youth Services in Massachusetts, shut down Massachusetts' major training schools and detention facilities. The number of incarcerated juveniles decreased from 1800 to 300.[64] Although the action taken by Dr. Miller was highly controversial, the results from two studies released since 1975 tend to support him. One of these was an LEAA study of the Massachusetts release of juvenile offenders. It revealed that 24 percent of youths released from community programs in 1974 made reappearances in court within a year of discharge, compared with 66 percent of those discharged from institutions.[65]

Preliminary data from a 7-year study being conducted by the Harvard Center for Criminal Justice showed a recidivism rate of 49 percent among those released from institutions, compared with 24 percent for juveniles in community programs. In 1976, four years after the closing of the institutions, 2200 children assigned to the Massachusetts Department of Youth Services were in 200

---

[62]"Juvenile Correctional Programs: Some Cost Comparisons," *Institutions, Etc.*, vol. 4, no. 3, Institutions/Alternatives, Washington, D. C., March 1981, p. 6.

[63]Deborah J. Denno, "Impact of a Youth Service Center," *Criminology*, vol. 18, no. 3, 1980, p. 361.

[64]Michael S. Serrill, "Massachusetts: Its Juvenile System Rehabilitates, Officials Say," *Corrections Magazine*, vol. 1, no. 5, May/June 1975, pp. 33–34.

[65]Rob Wilson, "The Legacy of Jerome Miller," *Corrections Magazine*, vol. 4, no. 3, September 1978, p. 14.

different programs. Of these children, 75 were in secure "intensive care" facilities, 300 were in group care facilities, 220 were in foster homes, and 75 were in programs in other states. Only 220 youngsters were in detention—60 in secure facilities, 90 in less secured "shelter care" facilities, and 70 in temporary foster homes.[66]

Despite the apparent success of Massachusetts' release of juveniles—fewer than 200 were housed in "secure" programs in February 1981— politicians, judges, and probation officers have repeatedly denounced the new system as a "mismanaged hodgepodge of programs that keep poor control of dangerous young criminals."[67]

Many administrators do not agree with Dr. Miller. Joseph Rowan, Florida Division of Youth Services administrator, believes that the four Florida institutions of the Division of Youth Services are as effective as any community-based program. Gerald Hicks, executive director of the Michigan Federation of Private Child and Family Agencies, states there will never be a time when all youngsters can be diverted to community-based programs. Alan Breed of the California Youth Authority was even more dramatic when he stated that what Miller did in Massachusetts was "very tragic and I would hate to see other states imitate it."[68] Obviously, administrators of juvenile programs have not concurred regarding the relative values of community-based programs and incarceration of children.

Nevertheless, South Dakota, Minnesota, Utah, Kentucky, Maryland, and Kansas have begun to place nearly as many youths in the community as in institutions. Vermont closed its only training school in 1978. And even Florida, in spite of Rowan's confidence in the state's institutions, has spent sizeable amounts of money on community-based programs; its $33-million-a-year system includes 17 residential centers and 7 nonresidential centers.

O. J. Keller, former director of youth services in Florida, and chief architect of the community-based programs in that state has said:

> I think we accomplished something in Florida. One of the things we did was to move toward alternatives to large institutions. We set up a comprehensive state system, with state-operated intake, probation, parole, foster care, and counseling services. I still approve of this model. I think community-based corrections is the direction in which to go as far as residential care is concerned and I want to use large institutions as little as possible.[69]

Unresolved Questions

Concern over the inclusion of status offenders within the jurisdiction of the juvenile court has not abated. Although Supreme Court decisions and emphasis

[66]Michael S. Serrill, "Juvenile Corrections in Massachusetts," *Corrections Magazine,* vol. 2, no. 2, November/December 1975, p. 6.

[67]Michael S. Serrill, "Massachusetts: A Harder Line Toward Juveniles," *Corrections Magazine,* vol. 7, no. 1, February 1981, p. 29.

[68]Serrill, "Juvenile Corrections in Massachusetts," op. cit., p. 7. Copyright 1975, by Criminal Justice Publications, 116 West 32nd St., New York, New York 10001.

[69]Bartollas, op. cit., p. 430.

on diversion of youth have attempted to curb the evils of unlimited discretion, fears remain. It is argued that the net effect of the mounting legalization of the juvenile court may be an increase in the volume of nonprosecutable serious offenders, minor offenders, "nuisance" cases, and status offenders with whom the community must deal in some organized way. As the serious offenders are released from legal court action, a groundswell mounts for a more punitive approach. Lowering of the legal age for transfer to adult court is one result; the growing presence of a prosecutional approach is another. There is also fear that the reduction of discretion in the juvenile justice system becomes a warrant to extend control where none existed before. Even the efforts to deinstitutionalize status offenders may have succeeded mainly in stimulating a shift of their custody from public to private institutions and the relabeling of the children. Until the juvenile court relinquishes its hold on children by way of their *parens patriae* philosophy and diversion programs are removed from the juvenile justice system, there may be little chance of a decrease in the number of children who become entangled in the system before committing a crime.

CONCLUSION

No responsible juvenile program administrator will disagree with Mr. Hicks's contention that not all children can be diverted from either temporary or indefinite incarceration. Adding even more questions to the controversy, Professor Lyle Shannon, director of the University of Iowa's Urban Community Research Center, examined 25,000 police reports on more than 6000 persons who grew up in Racine, Wisconsin. The study indicated that half the juveniles who committed felonies merely matured with age and never committed any more felonies. More than half the adults had not committed felonies as juveniles. Professor Shannon asserted that "juvenile delinquency and adult crime are not related in the manner it has been assumed that they are. Some juvenile delinquents become adult criminals . . . but they are not representative as juveniles."[70] After an exhaustive study of 317 Chicago youths over a 2-year period, Charles A. Murray and Lewis A. Cox, Jr., concluded that the elimination of delinquent behavior was a result of getting the boys' attention and then giving them a chance to decide for themselves the most logical method of changing their behavior.[71]

If involvement with the juvenile justice system does not appear to be crucial to the prevention of delinquency, as Dr. Shannon indicates, and diverting youth from physical controls at an early stage is possible, it seems unreasonable to continue the high level of involvement of juvenile justice system personnel. Perhaps a more economical use of time and money would be to establish community support systems in order to prevent more serious problems. At a

---

[70]Lyle Shannon, "Bad Kids, Good Adults," *The University of Iowa Spectator,* vol. 13, no. 5, Iowa City, April 1980, p. 1.

[71]Charles A. Murray and Louis A. Cox, Jr., *Beyond Probation,* Sage Publications, Beverly Hills, Calif., 1979, p. 184.

time of costly inflation and diminished government dollars, future state juvenile services administrators may be forced to bring their programs to the local community. If this is the case, the juvenile programs in the years ahead may pattern themselves after community mental health centers.

EXERCISES

1 Do you believe the concept of *parens patriae* is a contributing factor to the successful treatment of juveniles? Explain your position.

2 Many critics of the juvenile court believe status offenders should be handled by an alternative method, such as family court. Agree or disagree with these critics.

3 Do you believe the United States Supreme Court should require that juveniles receive the same rights as adults? Support your belief with evidence.

4 In your opinion, should the federal government set standards for juvenile courts, such as the maximum age for continuance of jurisidiction, currently being determined by the individual states? Give reasons for your answer.

5 Compare and contrast the juvenile justice system and the adult criminal justice system.

6 Pawlak concluded that courts without detention homes detain juveniles less frequently than courts with detention homes. If we eliminated detention homes, what would you do with juveniles currently being detained?

7 List steps you would suggest to permit the juvenile probation officer to be free for supervision and counseling of the child. Explain.

8 One criticism of the juvenile diversionary system is that the expansion of diversionary services only expands the juvenile justice system itself and does not divert the juvenile from the system. Agree or disagree.

9 Do you believe that group homes should limit the length of stay for juveniles in residence or allow them to remain for an indeterminate period? Give reasons.

10 List your suggestions for the development of alternatives to incarceration and the steps you would take to develop them.

11 Both public and private agencies have been actively involved in the care of juveniles. In your opinion, which sector, if either, should be given priority? Why?

12 There has been much criticism of Dr. Jerome Miller for shutting down Massachusetts' training schools and detention facilities. Do you believe his action was a valid approach to deinstitutionalization of juveniles? Defend your position.

EXERCISE REFERENCES

American Correctional Association, Inc.: *Juvenile Diversion: A Perspective,* College Park, Md., 1972.

Board of Directors, National Council on Crime and Delinquency: "Jurisdiction Over Status Offenders Should Be Removed From the Juvenile Court: A Policy Statement," *Crime and Delinquency,* vol. 21, no. 2, April 1975, pp. 97–99.

Brown, Lawrence D.: "The Development of a Parolee Classification System Using Discriminant Analysis,"*Journal of Research in Crime and Delinquency,* vol. 15, no. 1, January 1978, pp. 92–108.

Bullington, Bruce, James Sprowls, Daniel Katkin, and Mark Phillips: "A Critique of

Diversionary Juvenile Justice," *Crime and Delinquency,* vol. 24, no. 1, January 1978, pp. 59–71.

Calhoun, John A., and Susan Wayne: "Can the Massachusetts Juvenile System Survive the Eighties?" *Crime and Delinquency,* vol. 27, no. 4, October 1981, pp. 522–533.

Charle, Suzanne: "The Proliferation of Project New Pride," *Corrections Magazine,* vol. 7, no. 5, October 1981, pp. 28–34.

————: "Young Offenders Face Their Peers," *Corrections Magazine,* vol. 6, no. 6, December 1980, pp. 38–41.

Chesney-Lind, Meda: "Judicial Paternalism and the Female Status Offender: Training Women to Know Their Place," *Crime and Delinquency,* vol. 23, no. 2, April 1977, pp. 121–130.

Coates, Robert B.: "Deinstitutionalization and the Serious Juvenile Offender," *Crime and Delinquency,* vol. 27, no. 4, October 1981, pp. 477–486.

Collingwood, Thomas R., Alex Douds, and Hadley Williams: "Juvenile Diversion: The Dallas Police Department Youth Services Program," *Federal Probation,* vol. 40, no. 3, Administrative Office of the United States Courts, Washington, D. C., September 1976, pp. 23–27.

Denno, Deborah J.: "Impact of a Youth Service Center," *Criminology,* vol. 18, no. 3, November 1980, pp. 347–362.

Faust, Frederic L., and Paul J. Brantingham: *Juvenile Justice Philosophy: Reading Cases and Comments,* West Publishing Company, St. Paul, Minn., 1974.

Fogel, David: "Institutional Strategies in Dealing With Youthful Offenders," *Federal Probation,* vol. 31, no. 2, Administrative Office of the United States Courts, Washington, D. C., June 1967, pp. 41–47.

Fowkes, James J.: "One County's Approach to the Diversion of Youth From the Juvenile Justice System," *Federal Probation,* vol. 42, no. 4, Administrative Office of the United States Courts, Washington, D. C., December 1978, pp. 37–40.

Fox, Vernon: "A Handbook for Volunteers in Juvenile Court," in Gary R. Perlstein and Thomas R. Phelps (eds.) *Alternatives to Prison: Community Based Corrections, a Reader,* Goodyear Publishing Company, Inc., Pacific Palisades, Calif., 1975, pp. 333–359.

Galaway, Burt, Margie Henzel, Glenn Ramsay, and Bart Wanyama: "Victims and Delinquents in the Tulsa Juvenile Court," *Federal Probation,* vol. 44, no. 2, Administrative Office of the United States Courts, Washington, D. C., June 1980, pp. 42–48.

Gelber, Seymour: "Who Is the Juvenile Offender?" *Corrections Today,* vol. 41, no. 5, November/December 1979, pp. 13–14, 18, and 60.

Gendreau, Paul, and Bob Ross: "Effective Correctional Treatment: Bibliotherapy for Cynics," *Crime and Delinquency,* vol. 25, no. 4, October 1979, pp. 463–489.

"Institutional Programming Reconsidered," in Burt Galaway, Joe Hudson, and C. David Hollister (eds.), *Community Correction,* Charles C Thomas, Publisher, Springfield, Ill., 1976, pp. 25–35.

Jacobs, James B.: "What Prison Guards Think: A Profile of the Illinois Force," *Crime and Delinquency,* vol. 24, no. 2, April 1978, pp. 185–196.

Jenkins, Richard L.: "Child Psychiatry Perspectives: Status Offenders," *Journal of Child Psychiatry,* vol. 19, no. 2, Spring 1980, pp. 320–325.

Kehoe, Charles J.: "Juvenile Justice Standards: What's in It for the Kids and Us?" *Proceedings of the One Hundred and Tenth Annual Congress of Corrections,* American Correctional Association, College Park, Md. 1981, pp. 201–205.

Kiersh, Edward: "Minnesota Cracks Down on Chronic Juvenile Offenders," *Corrections Magazine,* vol. 7, no. 6, December 1981, pp. 21–28.

Kistler, Kristi S., Peter M. Bryant, and Gary J. Tucker: "Outward Bound: Providing a Therapeutic Experience for Troubled Youngsters," *Hospital and Community Psychiatry,* vol. 28, no. 1, November 1977, pp. 807–812.

Krajick, Kevin: "Tracking and Proctoring in Utah," *Corrections Magazine,* vol. 6, no. 6, December 1980, pp. 23–26.

——— "Working Our Way Home," *Corrections Magazine,* vol. 4, no. 2, June 1978, pp. 33–47.

Latina, Jane C., and Jeffrey L. Schemberg: "Volunteer Homes for Status Offenders: An Alternative to Detention," *Federal Probation,* vol. 40, no. 4, Administrative Office of the United States Courts, Washington, D. C., December 1976, pp. 45–49.

Lemert, Edwin M.: "Diversion in Juvenile Justice: What Hath Been Wrought?" *Journal of Research in Crime and Delinquency,* vol. 18, no. 1, January 1981, pp. 34–46.

Lerman, Paul: "Delinquency and Social Policy: A Historical Perspective," *Crime and Delinquency,* vol. 23, no. 4, October 1977, pp. 383–393.

Levin, Mark M., and Rosemary C. Sarri: *Juvenile Delinquency: A Comparative Analysis of Legal Codes in the United States,* National Assessment of Juvenile Corrections, Ann Arbor, Mich., June 1974.

Lindner, Charles: "Juvenile Intake Decisionmaking Standards and Precourt Diversion Rates in New York," *Federal Probation,* vol. 45, no. 2, Administrative Office of the United States Courts, Washington, D. C., June 1981, pp. 53–58.

Lundman, Richard J., and Frank R. Scarpitti: "Delinquency Prevention: Recommendations for Future Projects," *Crime and Delinquency,* vol. 24, no. 2, April 1978, pp. 207–222.

Martin, Lawrence H., and Phyllis R. Snyder: "Jurisdiction Over Status Offenses Should *Not* Be Removed From the Juvenile Court," *Crime and Delinquency,* vol. 22, no. 1, January 1976, pp. 44–47.

Mitchell, Greg: "For Runaways, a Meal, a Bed—And No Questions Asked," *Corrections Magazine,* vol. 6, no. 3, June 1980, pp. 29–35.

Murray, Charles A., and Louis A. Cox, Jr.: *Beyond Probation,* Sage Publications, Beverly Hills, Calif. 1979.

National Institute for Juvenile Justice and Delinquency Prevention: *Jurisdiction—Status Offenses,* U. S. Department of Justice, Washington, D. C., 1977.

National Institute for Juvenile Justice and Delinquency Prevention: *Juvenile Dispositions and Corrections,* U. S. Department of Justice, Washington, D. C., 1977.

Norman, Sherwood: "The Youth Service Bureau," in Povl G. Boesen and Stanley E. Grupp (eds.), *Community Based Corrections: Theory, Practice and Research,* Davis Publishing Company, Inc., Santa Cruz, Calif., 1976, pp. 125–135.

Newcomb, Theodore M.: "Characteristics of Youths in a Sample of Correctional Programs," *Journal of Research in Crime and Delinquency,* vol. 15, no. 1, January 1978, pp. 3–24.

Ohmart, Howard: "The Community and the Juvenile," in Povl G. Boesen and Stanley E. Grupp (eds.), *Community Based Corrections: Theory, Practice, and Research,* Davis Publishing Company, Inc., Santa Cruz, Calif., 1976, pp. 111–123.

Palmer, Ted B., and Roy V. Lewis: "A Differential Approach to Juvenile Diversion," *Journal of Research in Crime and Delinquency,* vol. 17, no. 2, July 1977, pp. 152–165.

Pawlack, Edward J.: "Differential Selection of Juveniles for Detention," *Journal of Research in Crime and Delinquency,"* vol. 14, no. 2, July 1977, pp. 152–165.

Reid, Sue Titus: *Crime and Criminology,* Holt, Rinehart and Winston, Inc., New York, 1979, pp. 531–549.

Reiman, Thomas A.: "Community Corrections in Australia: The Attendance Centre Scheme," *Federal Probation,* vol. 42, no. 2, Administrative Office of the United States Courts, Washington, D. C., June 1978, pp. 50–54.

Rosenheim, Margaret K.: "Youth Service Bureaus: A Concept in Search of Definition,"in Gary R. Perlstein and Thomas R. Phelps (eds.) *Alternatives to Prison: Community Based Corrections, a Reader,* Goodyear Publishing Company, Inc., Pacific Palisades, Calif., 1975, pp. 320–329.

Rubin, Sol: "The Juvenile Court Needs a New Turn," *Federal Probation,* vol. 45, no. 2, Administrative Office of the United States Courts, Washington, D. C., June 1981, pp. 48–53.

Ruth, Guy A.: "The Cregier Outpost: A Therapeutic Response to the Juvenile Offender," *Federal Probation,* vol. 38, no. 3, Administrative Office of the United States Courts, Washington, D. C., September 1974, pp. 43–49.

Sarri, Rosemary C.: *Under Lock and Key: Juveniles in Jails and Detention,* National Assessment of Juvenile Corrections, December 1974.

——— and Robert D. Vinter: "Justice for Whom?" Varieties of Juvenile Correctional Approaches," in Malcolm W. Klein (ed.), *The Juvenile Justice System,* Sage Publications, Beverly Hills, Calif., 1976, pp. 161–200.

Serrill, Michael S.: "The Community Advancement Program," *Corrections Magazine,* vol. 2, no. 2, November/December 1975, pp. 13–16.

———: "Juvenile Corrections in Massachusetts," *Corrections Magazine,* vol. 2, no. 2, November/December 1975, pp. 3–12.

———: "Massachusetts: A Harder Line Toward Juveniles," *Corrections Magazine,* vol. 7, no. 1, February 1981, pp. 29–31.

———: "Massachusetts: Its Juvenile Justice System Rehabilitates, Officials Say," *Corrections Magazine,* vol. 1, no. 5, May/June 1975, pp. 33–36.

Shannon, Lyle: "Bad Kids, Good Adults," *The University of Iowa Spectator,* vol. 13, no. 5, Iowa City, April 1981, p. 1.

Sheridan, William H.: "Juveniles Who Commit Noncriminal Acts: Why Treat in a Correctional System?" *Federal Probation,* vol. 31, no. 1, Administrative Office of the United States Courts, Washington, D. C., March 1967, pp. 26–30.

Spergel, Irving A., Frederic G. Reamer, and James P. Lynch: "Deinstitutionalization of Status Offenders: Individual Outcome and System Effects," *Journal of Research in Crime and Delinquency,* vol. 18, no. 1, January 1981, pp. 4–35.

Swank, William G.: "Home Supervision, Probation Really Works," *Federal Probation,* vol. 43, no. 4, Administrative Office of the United States Courts, Washington, D. C., December 1979, pp. 51–52.

Trojanowicz, Robert C.: *Juvenile Delinquency: Concepts and Control,* Prentice-Hall, Inc., Englewood Cliffs, N. J., 1973.

Vanagunas, Stanley: "Police Diversion of Juvenile Offenders: An Ambiguous State of the Art," *Federal Probation,* vol. 43, no. 3, Administrative Office of the United States Courts, Washington, D. C., September 1979, pp. 48–52.

Vinter, Robert D.: "Trends in State Corrections: Juveniles and the Violent Youth Offender," *Crime and Delinquency,* vol. 25, no. 2, April 1979, pp. 145–161.

―――― and Rosemary C. Sarri: *Time Out: A National Study of Juvenile Correctional Programs,* National Assessment of Juvenile Corrections, Ann Arbor, Mich., June 1976.

Wagner, Robert, and Fred Montanino (eds.): "New Perspectives on Delinquency," *Criminology,* vol. 15, no. 4, February 1978, special issue.

Wilson, Rob: "The Legacy of Jerome Miller," *Corrections Magazine,* vol. 4, no. 3, September 1978, pp. 13–18.

Wright, William E., and Michael E. Dixon: "Community Prevention and Treatment of Juvenile Delinquency: A Review of Evaluation Studies," *Journal of Research in Crime and Delinquency,* January 1977, pp. 35–67.

"Youth Service Bureaus," in Gary R. Perlstein and Thomas R. Phelps (eds.), *Alternatives to Prison: Community Based Corrections, a Reader,* Goodyear Publishing Company, Inc., Pacific Palisades, Calif., 1975, pp. 289–319.

CHAPTER 12

REFLECTIONS FROM THE FIELD

CHAPTER OBJECTIVES

- To review the current status of correctional research
- To examine the use of correctional cost-benefit analysis
- To describe attempts to initiate accreditation in corrections
- To discuss the possibility of penal reform
- To review efforts to prevent crime and delinquency
- To propose a model for a correctional system

INTRODUCTION

Up to this point, this book has been concerned with a system designed to react to offenders—thieves, forgers, robbers, rapists, and murderers. Its focus has been not on those who must be dealt with as dangerous persons, but on those other offenders who, although not dangerous, are ineffectual, impulsive, and frustrated. Correctional personnel must decide which offenders must be incarcerated and which may be supervised in the community, free of prison walls.

Until a determined effort is made to distinguish between the two types of offenders and then to develop a method of redirection designed to suit each type, corrections will continue to stagger along. On the other hand, before the public or legislatures can be expected to support an effort to redirect offenders, correctional administrators must take steps to confirm corrections as a profession. To accomplish this, research must be conducted, accountability for activities must be established, and standards must be implemented. Until these tasks are completed, correctional administrators cannot expect either the public or legislatures to accept and support community-based corrections—probation, jails, work release, furloughs, community-based residences, or parole. This final chapter is devoted to the methods of achieving these objectives.

RESEARCH

The Problem

Criminal justice is facing an evaluation crisis. Although billions of dollars are being pumped into various programs, complaints about their ineffectiveness are prevalent. Demands for evaluation are increasing. The public is troubled by confusion over research methods and strategies, by the shortage of good evaluators, and by indifference on the part of correctional administrators to the need for research.[1] A 1968 report of the Governor's Special Committee on Criminal Offenders for the state of New York stated:

> Unless administrators come to look upon research as an indispensable part of the decision making, policy planning, and treatment processes, there will continue to be no way of telling whether anything we are doing is achieving the objective of the system or whether any new plan is worth acceptance. The integration of research within the post adjudicatory system must be based on a commitment and approach that will permit the ongoing development and refinement of treatment techniques, the accretion of verified political principles, and the accumulation of a precise and extensive criminological knowledge base.[2]

Most practitioners in corrections would not consider investing money in a product, such as a new television set, without assurance that it had been time-tested for performance. Yet not all such practitioners realize the importance of time-testing in their own field.

Regrettably, corrections has assigned a low priority to research, thus substantially handicapping any realistic attempt to improve the effectiveness of correctional efforts. Private industry spends a minimum of 5 percent of its gross expenditures annually on research, including the development of new products; corrections allots a fraction of 1 percent to the same function. Until we know how well or poorly operations or programs are achieving their purposes, hunches or "gut feelings" will continue to be the primary method of managerial decision making, instead of determining facts and planning sound programs.

Past Attempts

Research is the technique by which evaluations are conducted. In corrections there are two basic types of evaluation: outcome and process."Outcome

---

[1]Stuart Adams, "Evaluative Research in Corrections: Status and Prospects," *Federal Probation*, vol. 38, no. 1, Administrative Office of the United States Courts, Washington, D. C., March 1974, p. 14.

[2]State of New York, *Preliminary Report of the Governor's Special Committee on Criminal Offenders*, June 1968, pp. 316–318.

evaluation" is interested in results. Since a major objective of corrections is to reduce crime, the number of people who lead crime-free lives after release is a general indicator of the effectiveness of the system. "Process evaluation" is primarily concerned with ascertaining the degree to which policies and procedures are being carried out. If a halfway house was supposed to provide housing, counseling, and help in job finding, a process evaluation would try to determine whether these tasks were being accomplished or not.[3]

Evaluations of research projects over the last 15 to 20 years reveal a mixture of positive and negative results which frustrate efforts to find valid conclusions. One 6-year follow-up of 1806 federal prisoners released in 1970 discovered that 62.9 percent had been arrested for either criminal charges or parole violations. The risk of rearrest for released federal prisoners is, quite high, according to this report.[4]

Another study, conducted by the Justice Department's Bureau of Justice Statistics, concluded that 64,000 convicts released on parole in 1974 and 1975 reinforced "the traditional view that three-fourths of persons paroled are classifiable as successes."[5] In 1976, new court commitments accounted for more than 75 percent of all prisoner admissions to state institutions. Recommitments of offenders for violations of parole or of other types of conditional release comprised about 15 percent of the total number of admissions.[6] These studies epitomize the problem of validating the results of research, because their conclusions contradict each other.

Although reviews of evaluations of overall correctional programs are not conclusive, controlled experimental designs in selected areas of corrections have shown statistically significant positive effects associated with rehabilitation or cost-benefit ratios.[7] Researcher Stuart Adams in 1967 discovered that 59 percent of the twenty-two experimental studies he reviewed showed either a significant reduction of offender recidivism or a cost-benefit ratio improvement.[8]

Even the use of recidivism rates to evaluate correctional programs has been questioned. A study of federal releasees in 1970, in which researchers varied both the choice of criteria and length of follow-up period, revealed a vast difference in recidivism rates for examined offenders. For example, after 1 year the recidivism rate varied from 29 percent for criterion A (new arrest) to 8.7 percent for criterion D (new prison term). After 6 years the difference had widened to 60.4 percent for criterion A to 27.5 percent for criterion D.[9]

---

[3]E. Eugene Miller and M. Robert Montilla, *Corrections in the Community,* Reston Publishing Company, Inc., Reston, Va., 1977, pp. 266–267.

[4]Peter B. Hoffman and Barbara Stone-Meierhoefer, "Post Release Arrest Experiences of Federal Prisoners: a Six Year Follow-up,"*Journal of Criminal Justice,* vol. 7, no. 3, Fall 1979, p. 202.

[5]"1 in 4 Prison Parolees Fails: Study Reveals," *Chicago Tribune,* Mar. 2, 1981, sec. 1, p. 10.

[6]*Prisoners in State and Federal Institutions on December 31, 1976,* U. S. Government Printing Office, Washington, D. C., February 1978, p. 7.

[7]Adams, "Evaluative Research in Corrections," op. cit., p. 15.

[8]Stuart Adams, "Some Findings From Correctional Caseload Research," *Federal Probation,* vol. 31, no. 4, Administrative Office of the United States Courts, Washington, D. C., December 1967, p. 54.

[9]Peter B. Hoffman and Barbara Stone-Meierhoefer, "Reporting Recidivism Rates: The Criterion and Follow-up Issues,"*Journal of Criminal Justice,* vol. 8, no. 1, 1980, p. 57.

Professor Neal Shover's review of evaluative research published in 1979, failed to draw any definite conclusions about the success or failure of correctional practices. He was convinced that the researchers' lack of objectivity, failure to develop acceptable differential rehabilitation measures, and instincts for self-preservation have prevented conclusive research or the development of acceptable cost-effectiveness determinants.[10] Similarly, Robert Martinson stated in 1971 that "there is little evidence . . . that any prevailing mode of correctional treatment has a decisive effect in reducing the recidivism of convicted offenders."[11]

One thing is clear: Thanks to research, we know that no single policy or program helps all offenders. Consequently the emphasis of both policy and research in corrections should be on particular types of offenders rather than on all of them collectively. The controlled experiments proved to be successful should be developed extensively. For example, the high success rate of "non-self-correcting offenders" placed on probation in lieu of incarceration suggests that people who commit felonies but are not committed to crime as a career are easily deterred by the threat of punishment and exposure to surveillance.[12] Conversely, it has been found that those juveniles highly committed to criminal careers had lower recidivism rates following traditional institutional confinement than did those given early release to their homes with intensive counseling.[13] Finally, Massachusetts studies show that prisoners benefit more from gradual release through halfway houses than from direct release from intensified programs in education or general correctional programs.[14]

Validation of Techniques

As research techniques are applied in the field, efforts should be made to validate them as applicable. Both the professions and the social sciences are without the traditions and the experience by which experimentation is facilitated. In the absence of such traditions, it is difficult to suggest what the necessary elements of an experimental model might be. Some which would seem, logically, to be required, however, are:

1 *Statement of Objectives.* A consensus on objectives is necessary in order to have a logical basis for choosing one approach over another. In many correction-

[10]Neal Shover, *A Sociology of American Corrections,* Dorsey Press, Homewood, Ill., 1979, pp. 307–311.

[11]Robert Martinson, *Treatment Evaluation Survey,* unpublished monograph cited in *Prison Treatment and Parole Survival* by Gene Kassebaum, David Ward, and Daniel Wilner, 1981, p. 309.

[12]W. Ralph England, Jr., "What is Responsible for Satisfactory Probation and Post-Probation Outcome?" *Journal of Criminal Law, Criminology, and Police Science,* vol. 47, no. 6, April 1957, pp. 673–676.

[13]Robert G. Culbertson, "The Effect of Institutionalization on the Delinquent Inmate's Self-Concept," *Journal of Criminal Law, Criminology, and Police Science,* vol. 66, no. 1, March 1975, pp. 88–93.

[14]Daniel P. LeClair, *Community Reintegration of Prison Releasees: Results of the Massachusetts Experience,* Massachusetts Department of Correction, Boston, Mar. 10, 1981, p. 11.

al settings, consensus on objectives is lacking. Correctional workers disagree about whether their main concern is with custody, rehabilitation, vocational education, or some other objective.

2 *Theoretical Assumptions.* There should be a series of theoretical assumptions regarding the nature of the problems that are identified. First we must ask: What are the problems? What causes them? What should be done about them?

3 *Program Strategy.* The set of assumptions chosen should be made operational for action and research. The assumptions should be reduced from abstract to operational terms and translated into the kind of functions which a staff and its organization are expected to perform.

4 *Research Design.* The actual research, ideally, is tied to the other components of the experimental model. It should contribute to knowledge about the particular correctional approach in question.

5 *Research feedback.* Any experimental model should have a feedback system by which all findings could be communicated and their implications assessed for both the researchers and the correctional workers.

Daniel Glaser's interest in research resulted in some practical suggestions for correctional administrators to follow in organizing research programs. He attempted to establish a research base which can justify correctional reform through these five steps: (1) obtain the most complete postrelease information available on offenders under custody or supervision; (2) concentrate presentation of postrelease data on responsibilities that correctional agencies must meet, especially on cost-effectiveness; (3) try to comprehend all circumstances of an offender's current situation and his or her own view of these circumstances; (4) introduce proposals for improvement in corrections that will be most readily supported by the legislature and public; and (5) attempt to discover problems that could be easily remedied.[15]

COST-BENEFIT ANALYSIS

Rationale

Planner Carl Nelson suggests that correctional administrators use a cost-benefit analysis to establish accountability for correctional programs. He believes that such an analysis is a means of comparing correctional program alternatives and discriminating among them on the basis of their net benefits. In some cases a program can be justified as less expensive if it does no worse than traditional institutional settings.

Nelson believes that cost-benefit analysis provides valuable long-term data useful to the government, the public, and correctional administrators. As an example, he compared a house of corrections and a prerelease center in Massachusetts. The house of corrections cost $800 more per inmate than the

---

[15]Daniel Glaser, "Five Practical Research Suggestions for Correctional Administrators," *Crime and Delinquency,* vol. 17, no. 1, January 1970, pp. 32–40.

prerelease center (see Table 12.1).[16] Findings indicate that Massachusetts' prerelease programs reduce by 50 percent the chance that a parolee will have parole revoked.[17] This is true even when there is no decrease in the recidivism rate for inmates from the prerelease center compared with those from the house of corrections. Thus, based on cost-benefit analysis, it is a sound administrative decision to house offenders in the prerelease center.

Application

Cost-benefit analysis can be applied in many ways. Comparisons of costs and benefits can be made (1) among various forms of institutional programs within a single correctional model, (2) between institutional and community-based programs, (3) between diversionary programs and incarceration, (4) between

---

[16]Carl W. Nelson, "Cost-Benefit Analysis and Alternatives to Incarceration," *Federal Probation,* vol. 39, no. 4, Administrative Office of the United States Courts, Washington, D. C., December 1975, p. 49.

[17]Daniel P. LeClair, *An Analysis of Recidivism Among Residents Released From Boston State and Shirley Prerelease Centers During 1972-1973,* Massachusetts Department of Corrections, Boston, August 1975, p. 30.

TABLE 12.1
GOVERNMENTAL COSTS FOR HOUSE OF CORRECTIONS
AND PRERELEASE CENTER

House of corrections		
1. Budget (1972)	$1,580,768	
2. Supplementary budget	52,800	
3. Reported total yearly institutional costs		$1,633,568
4. Personnel not on budget	46,571	
5. Expenditures unrelated to house of corrections	(62,326)	
6. State grants expenditure	27,500	
7. Federal grants expenditure	266,560	
8. Total additional direct program expenditures		278,305
9. Total primary government costs		$1,911.873
Prerelease center		
1. Budget (1972)	$73,970	
2. Personnel not on budget	41,250	
3. Unbudgeted expenses	2,504	
4. Revenue from rent paid by program participants	(7,800)	
5. Total primary government costs		$ 109,924

Source: Carl W. Nelson, "Cost-Benefit Analysis and Alternatives to Incarceration," *Federal Probation,* vol. 39, no. 4, Administrative Office of the United States Courts, Washington, D.C., December 1975, p. 49.

early release and institutionalization for the entire term of imprisonment, and (5) as a means of evaluating new ideas for housing inmates.

By using cost-benefit analysis, correctional administrators can heed information such as that provided by researchers Martinson, Lipton, and Wilkes, who found that early release from institutions results in no noticeable increase in recidivism and that there is no difference in recidivism between adult first offenders classified as medium or as minimum custody.

This form of comparison is especially helpful in judging whether new concepts of corrections are more cost-effective than traditional approaches. Reformer Ernest Van Den Haag believes prisons cost too much because they are too secure. In 1981 a new maximum security prison was estimated to cost $70,000 a bed. To cut costs, Van Den Haag suggests that security prisons be developed which permit private companies to establish factories for the inmates, who, in turn, can be charged for room and board, medical care, psychological services, and educational and vocational opportunities. In addition, they can make restitution and family support payments as well as pay taxes and social security.[18]

At least one state, Iowa, has passed legislation authorizing the lease of facilities on the grounds of any state adult correctional institution to a private corporation for the purpose of operating a "venture" (factory employing inmates or other commercial enterprise). The inmates must be employed at wages equal to those paid to employees in similar jobs outside the institution.[19]

New York's solution to overcrowded conditions was formulated by Benjamin Ward, commissioner in the Department of Correctional Services. It included the conversion of six former drug rehabilitation centers and two former youth facilities into community-based residences. He also opened seven work and educational release centers. Although its prison population increased from 14,000 in 1975 to 20,000 in 1978, New York successfully followed Ward's plan, without using trailers, showers, or dayrooms as cells.[20]

In answer to both the following questions, a cost-benefit analysis could reveal the fiscal efficacy of correctional strategies: Will employing inmates at wages equal to wages of workers in the community and requiring them to pay costs of their care actually reduce costs? Does the conversion of former buildings housing other rehabilitation programs, such as New York's conversion of six drug rehabilitation centers, actually cut costs of construction of new prisons?

Accountability

Accountability can be effected if cost analysis and research are developed in a coordinated fashion. Comparing costs by themselves does not establish any

---

[18]Ernest Van Den Haag, "Prisons Cost Too Much Because They Are Too Secure," *Corrections Magazine,* vol. 6, no. 2, April 1980, pp. 39, 43.

[19]State of Iowa, *Prisons—Employment Opportunities*, 67th General Assembly, House File 57, State of Iowa Printing, Des Moines, 1977, pp. 246–250.

[20]Joan Potter, "A Study in Coping: New York Versus Prison Overcrowding," *Corrections Magazine,* vol. 3, no. 4, September 1978, pp. 63–64.

criteria for correctional program development. But by comparing costs of programs and results of programs (as symbolized by rates of recidivism), cost analysis and research can establish accountability for each program and suggest areas of future program development. The question of accountability is vital to today's correctional system.

For instance, if one considers that probation is 10 to 13 times less expensive than incarceration and more effective, an argument can be made for spending a higher percentage of correctional budgets for increased probation services. Take another example: In a comparative study of three methods of releasing imprisoned felons, the release-at-expiration-of-term group could be said to cost $56,000 for each case, early release to parole could cost $35,000 for each case, and early release to work release then to parole could cost $27,000 for each case. If all three types of release yielded similar recidivism rates, the least expensive would be preferable.[21]

As the amount of available funds decreases, it is essential that the correctional administrator achieve maximum value from each expenditure. At the same time, the active intervention of United States courts in correctional matters has mandated new standards for the civil rights of persons charged with and convicted of crime and has had a strong influence on correctional policies, practices, and procedures. In many cases, court decisions have forgotten correctional traditions and the concept of benevolent purposes. Despite increasingly explosive situations, correctional administrators have been called upon to implement policies to deinstitutionalize corrections. While the abandonment of the traditional model of correctional rehabilitation is long overdue, the question of what model will take its place is far from being answered. The debate concerning the comparative utility of institutional and community-based programs has not ended.[22] It can be resolved only if cost-effectiveness is one criterion for the final judgment.

ACCREDITATION

Historical Precedents

Before achieving public and private support for correctional programs, administrators must take some specific action to polish corrections' tarnished halo. They must recognize where they have failed, admit their mistakes, cast aside ineffective procedures and unrealistic claims, and get rid of the interests that support these impossible premises. It is essential to develop techniques to provide a method of evaluating accountability of correctional programs. Research and cost-benefit analysis are two methods that can be used to achieve program accountability.

[21]Miller and Montilla, op. cit., pp. 267–268.
[22]H. G. Moeller, "Principles of Accreditation for Corrections," *Proceedings of the One Hundred and Fifth Annual Congress of Corrections,* American Correctional Association, College Park, Md., 1976, p. 21.

Another recent attempt designed to establish accountability is the movement to devise a system of accreditation of correctional programs. This idea was preceded by two developments. First, there was concern over the standards themselves (i.e., minimal levels of operation). Second, there was an attempt to apply standards through internal auditing procedures or external examinations.

Establishing accreditation standards for corrections is not new. It has been a longstanding tradition since a national prison association adopted the 1870 Declaration of Principles in Cincinnati. In 1931, the first issue of *The Prison World* contained " The American Jail Standards of Personnel, Plans, and Programs," by Austin MacCormick, then commissioner of corrections for New York City. The National Probation and Parole Association in 1939 published "Model Acts," which stated conditions under which probation and parole should be conducted. In 1946 a manual of suggested standards for a state correctional system was published by the American Prison Association. The first revision of these standards was published in 1954, and in it a plan was proposed for actually applying the standards through self-evaluation. The United Nations, recognizing the need for international standards, issued a list of minimum rules for the treatment of offenders in 1955.[23]

Accreditation Process

The American Correctional Association (ACA) has been a leader in the encouragement of accreditation. In 1975 its Commission of Accreditation for Corrections began developing standards to be applied nationally. Within 2 years, guided by its *By-Laws* and a *Statement of Principles,* the commission developed a manual with approximately 1300 standards for the fields of adult parole administration, community residential services, probation and parole field services, and long-term institutions.[24] The commission established an accreditation process that included five major steps:

1 Upon receipt by the commission of a commitment from a major jurisdiction that all correctional agencies within the system intend to seek accreditation, individual agencies will be admitted to a correspondent's or applicant's status.

2 In the correspondent or applicant status the correctional agency will have 6 months to complete a self-evaluation of its facilities and operations. During the self-evaluation, the agency will receive consultation and assistance from the commission.

3 On receipt of its self-evaluation report by the commission, the agency will be placed in candidate status. During the next 12 months the candidate

[23]Dale K. Sechrest, "The Self-Evaluation and Accreditation Movement in Corrections," *Proceedings of the One Hundred and Fifth Annual Congress of Corrections,* American Correctional Association, College Park, Md., 1976, p. 25.

[24]Sharon J. Winkler and Robert H. Fosen, "Commission on Accreditation for Corrections Marks a First by the Field in Development of Standards," *American Journal of Correction,* vol. 39, no. 3, American Correctional Association, Minneapolis, May/June 1977, p. 16.

correctional agency will be expected to correct deficiencies in policy, procedure, program, and facilities. Again consultation and assistance will be provided.

4 The commission will send a visiting committee to the candidate agency to verify the self-evaluation report and changes which have been made by the agency. In addition, the commission will verify compliance with state and federal standards.

5 The commission will review the report of the committee and, if it is acceptable, will order accreditation status for the candidate agency for a 3-year period.[25]

Since 1975 the self-evaluation and accreditation project by the ACA has resulted in 171 self-evaluation studies, which involve more than 7000 correctional workers in thirty-seven states, the District of Columbia, and the Federal Bureau of Prisons. The 1300 standards in *The Manual of Correctional Standards* were applied largely to correctional institutions. The level of compliance with all standards was below 69 percent.[26]

Standards Development

One innovative result of the work of the ACA's Commission on Accreditation for Corrections is its *Manual of Standards for Adult Community Residential Services.* Published in 1977, the manual suggests standards for halfway houses and prerelease centers in areas such as administration, personnel, program, health services, citizen involvement, out-client services, records, and evaluation.[27]

Standards for juvenile corrections are also being developed by the ACA's Commission on Accreditation for Corrections. As of August, 1979, four such manuals have been published:

1 *Manual of Standards for Juvenile Residential Services*
2 *Manual of Standards for Juvenile Probation and After Care Services*
3 *Manual of Standards for Juvenile Detention Facilities and Services*
4 *Manual of Standards for Juvenile Training Schools*[28]

By 1979 nationally recognized standards had been established by the American Bar Association, the President's Commission on Law Enforcement and the Administration of Justice, the National Sheriff's Association, the United Nations, the National Advisory Commission on Criminal Justice Standards and

[25]Robert H. Fosen, "Accreditation: a New Challenge to the Dilemma," *Proceedings of the One Hundred and Fifth Annual Congress of Corrections,* American Correctional Association, College Park, Md., 1976, pp. 33–34.

[26]Dale K. Sechrest, "The Accreditation Movement in Corrections," *Federal Probation,* vol. 40, no. 4, Administrative Office of the United States Courts, Washington, D. C., December 1976, p. 17.

[27]Commission on Accreditation for Corrections, *Manual of Standards for Adult Community Residential Services,* Commission on Accreditation for Corrections, American Correctional Association, Rockville, Md., April 1977.

[28]Dale K. Sechrest, "The Development and Implementation of Standards for Juvenile Corrections,"*Proceedings of the One Hundred and Ninth Annual Congress of Corrections,* American Correctional Association, College Park, Md., 1980, p. 208.

Goals, and the American Correctional Association. The development of standards by so many organizations was based on three factors: (1) the need to govern the diverse policies and practices of correctional agencies in a consistent and humane manner; (2) recent significant case-law developments establishing the constitutionality of correctional policies, practices, and conditions; and (3) the recognized need to provide the courts with something tangible on which to base their judgments.[29]

The Results

Standards and the accreditation process have resulted in a number of advances. Planning has become more consistent, operational effectiveness and efficiency improved, offender programs upgraded, inmate rights protected, staff professionalism enhanced, and communication and cooperation among correctional practitioners and the community improved. As large numbers of corrections agencies apply for accreditation, it is anticipated that additional improvement will take place.[30]

In the future the problem will not be setting standards for corrections but deciding who will be responsible for setting standards. The leading contenders for this task are the ACA, the American Bar Association, and the United States Department of Justice. In fact, there is even some in-house competition. The ACA's Commission on Accreditation has been funded since 1974 by an LEAA grant of $400,000 a year. In addition, the LEAA, formerly an arm of the United States Department of Justice, funded the ACA's Committee on Standards and Accreditation and announced grants totaling $961,595 to twelve states to assist them in achieving accreditation.

CORRECTIONS REFORM

Reform Process

Corrections' techniques have changed little since the 1790 opening of the Walnut Street jail in Philadelphia. Although some innovative programs exist, the basic structure of corrections remains the same. Any hope for a radical change appears unlikely at present, because neither correctional administrators nor the public are interested in radical change. At best, changes within corrections "must be evolutionary and not revolutionary," as Texas Correctional Administrator George J. Beto stated in a speech in Houston on August 19, 1974.[31] Despite this prediction, reform still should be a goal for corrections. Theoretical-

---

[29]Ernest G. Reimer, and Dale K. Sechrest: "Writing Standards for Correctional Accreditation," *Federal Probation,* vol. 43, no. 3, Administrative Office of the United States Courts, Washington, D. C., September 1979, pp. 11.

[30]Ilene R. Bergsmann, "Correctional Standards Development in the United States," *Federal Probation,* vol. 45, no. 3, Administrative Office of the United States Courts, Washington, D. C., September 1981, p. 50.

[31]George J. Beto, "Correction Change Must Be Evolutionary," *American Journal of Correction,* vol. 36, no. 5, American Correctional Association, St. Paul, Minn., September/October 1974, p. 34.

ly, social reform is a change in society deliberately brought about to reduce the diversion of institutional patterns from particular social values. Reform differs from revolution in that upgrading the social system is not the objective. Rather, the purpose is to reduce discrepancies between generally accepted goals and existing practice.

In practice, reform is not a rational and deliberate process. It moves through a series of accommodations whereby relationships among groups within a system are recast. The ultimate nature of a new accommodation is not predictable, because change agents do not control all other groups and do not realize all the consequences of a problem.[32]

There are two basic types of reform: externally induced and internally induced. Externally induced reform is a strategy that is begun outside the institution. Internally induced reform is change initiated by individuals and groups performing roles and assuming a certain status within the institution. Internally induced reform is more likely to become a permanent part of the administrative process. However, an essential prerequisite is readiness of the administrative process to accept innovation.[33]

To date, primary guidelines for corrections reform have been humanitarian and aimed at diminishing the offender's needless suffering. These guidelines have encouraged a few educational and vocational training classes, an occasional psychiatrist or psychologist, and an additional shower each week. Unfortunately, these efforts toward humane treatment do not lower the recidivism rate significantly.

Hindrances

Professor John Conrad believes there are a number of obstacles to change within the criminal justice system itself. He lists them as (1) the lack of certain and consistent goals (e.g., whether the major goal is punishment or rehabilitation); (2) nominalism, or the verbal support of a program within a half-hearted attempt to actually carry it out; (3) inadequate standards for personnel; and (4) lack of adequate funding.[34] One major impediment to successful program implementation has been the lack of systematic strategies to overcome the problems that prevent penal reform.[35]

One thing is clear: Under the present system reform is difficult because there is resistance to innovation. Correctional personnel are conservative, and their cooperation in reform is seldom sought. Also, offenders may be fearful of change and often resist participation in new correctional programs. Both groups,

---

[32]Robert M. MacIver, *Social Causation,* Ginn and Company, Boston, pp. 291–299.

[33]Elmer Hubert Johnson, *Crime, Correction, and Society,* Dorsey Press, Homewood, Ill., 1974, pp. 624–626.

[34]John P. Conrad, "There Has To Be a Better Way," *Crime and Delinquency,* vol. 26, no. 1, January 1980, pp. 85–88.

[35]Malcolm W. Klein, "Deinstitutionalization and Diversion of Juvenile Offenders: A Litany of Impediments," in Norval Morris and Michael Tonry (eds.), *Crime and Justice: A Review of Research,* vol. 1, University of Chicago Press, Chicago, 1979, pp. 158–159.

even though readily accepting the concept of reform based on humanitarian ideals, are unwilling to accept changes which affect the basic structure of the correctional system. For example, both inmates and correctional personnel oppose elimination of the inmate code. Administrators and correctional officers prefer to maintain a quiet, well-run institution by using inmate control of inmates. In addition, prisoners who prefer to be left alone encourage others to "do their own time," thus minimizing the number of interpersonal relations.

Some difficulties faced in gaining acceptance from correctional personnel are the fault of administrators, many of who do not properly advertise a new program or prepare employees for change. Proposed changes are not communicated from top to bottom. Policymakers initiate change in the system, but lack of consensus within middle management blocks the process. Even professionals, social workers, psychologists, and psychiatrists often contest change in hopes of monopolizing the knowledge of helping techniques.

Another problem is caused by the conditions of offenders' court commitments. Criminals are committed to the care of correctional agencies because they are found guilty of committing a crime. They do not view themselves as being sent to prison for help. They find it difficult to distinguish between correctional procedures designed to punish them and those designed to help them.

"Selling" Change

Before penal reform can be successful, corrections administrators must alter the public's perception of the skills, competence, and potential for success in the field of corrections. Administrators must learn to use the existing communication network to their advantage. Selling a product such as human services should be carried out with the same zeal as selling a commercial product. Media techniques must be developed, and the state and local corrections departments must be willing to spend the time and invest the money to convince the public of the economy of efficient corrections programs.

A Louis Harris poll in 1967 for the Joint Commission on Correctional Manpower and Training discovered that 72 percent of adults polled chose "rehabilitation" over "punishing" and "protecting society" as the main emphasis for corrections. In addition, 77 percent supported the idea of halfway houses, although the figure dropped to 50 percent if put in terms of "a halfway house in your neighborhood." When we do not even know what the public believes today, we are unable to change their opinions or carry out a mandate as a result of those opinions.[36]

The 1980 ACA Congress took for its theme, "Our Challenge: Influencing Public Policy." The members seemed to endorse the underlying message that "if you want to influence public policy, you not only have to assert yourself, but you

---

[36]Gordon Hawkins, *The Prison: Policy and Practice,* University of Chicago Press, Chicago, 1976, pp. 163–164.

have to summon public policy." The approach of "let's package corrections to be a more attractive public policy product" was apparent in many sessions.

Cultivating public interest and support is a prerequisite to successful reform, even if it takes public relations tricks to sell corrections and gain the interest of an uninformed public. Corrections has been unable to climb above its invariable low rung on the ladder of public policy priorities. Undeniably some of the low standing can be attributed to the lack of a nationwide public information campaign.

To bring about long-term positive attention, concern, and understanding on the part of the citizenry, all news media must be used—television, radio, and print. In effect, we must persuade the public to prompt legislators and policymakers to invest in corrections. Corrections professionals can then concentrate on influencing public policy development, ensuring that corrections and the public's best interests are served. Of course, it is inadvisable to attempt to convince the public through a national advertising campaign that corrections can bring speedy relief for society's ills, but properly promoted, corrections can become a household concern.[37]

As correctional administrators polish corrections' reputation through research, cost-benefit analysis and accreditation procedures, they should strive to transmit information to the public. Public education should take place on a statewide and local level. Correctional officials should tell their stories personally through appearances at service clubs, high schools, colleges, and church groups.

The National Advisory Commission on Criminal Justice Standards and Goals has stated:

> Public ignorance of a social problem leads to public rejection of the people who personify that problem. This has been the condition of the public's relationship to crime and delinquency, and until we bring the public into a formal intimate acquaintance with it, the new techniques we professionals develop will not achieve their full potential.[38]

PREVENTION OF CRIME AND DELINQUENCY

Definition

This same Committee states also:

> Delinquency prevention is a process of problem identification, resource analysis, and strategy building aimed at lowering rates of delinquency through the provision of services to persons or groups with specific and demonstrated needs.[39]

[37]Barbara Hadley Olsson, "Making 'Corrections' a Household Word," *Corrections Today,* vol. 42, no. 5, American Correctional Association, College Park, Md., September/October 1980, p. 67.

[38]National Advisory Commission on Criminal Justice Standards and Goals, *Corrections,* U. S. Government Printing Office, Washington, D. C., 1973, chap. 15.1.

[39]National Advisory Committee on Criminal Justice Standards and Goals, *Juvenile Justice and Delinquency Prevention,* Law Enforcement Assistance Administration, United States Department of Justice, Washington, D. C., 1976, p. 25.

Prevention of crime and delinquency has been a hodgepodge of services, involving government departments, privately supported agencies, and volunteer groups. Since the mid-1950s urbanization has necessitated that a wide variety of local, state, and national private and public agencies become involved in crime and delinquency prevention. Unfortunately, efforts remain uncoordinated, and a general lack of communication between agencies remains a hindrance for any concerted effort at prevention.

Prevention Strategies

There are basically two types of crime and delinquency prevention strategies: pre-prevention, which attempts to inhibit crime and delinquency before it takes place, and rehabilitative prevention, which assists persons after they have become involved in the formal criminal and juvenile justice systems. These two types use punitive techniques under the hypothesis that punishment will prevent future deviant acts. Both use methods devised to eliminate potential causes, factors, or motivation before deviant behavior actually takes place; and both types employ mechanical techniques that place obstacles in the path of the perpetrator to make it difficult or impossible to commit a deviant act.[40]

Macrosociological Programs

A number of prevention tactics have developed that approach the problem at different levels. Macrosociological programs—efforts at large-scale social change—have been organized to provide opportunities for more people to achieve socially approved goals. One example is Project Head Start, designed to help culturally deprived children catch up or keep pace in preschool years. The program offers many services, including daily recreational activities, nutritional training, medical and dental care, social work services, psychological services, and parent education. Personnel include both volunteers and professionals.

Other macrosociological projects endeavor to find jobs for the chronically unemployed. Federal laws created the Manpower Development and Training Program in 1962. Between 1963 and 1972 the number of young people in the program grew from 5000 to 150,000. Youth Opportunity Centers and Job Corps are other organizations designed to divert youth from deviant behavior.

Community Programs

At another level, neighborhood and community programs have been designed to prevent deviant behavior by attacking social problems in urban problem areas. A classic example is the Chicago Area Project. In 1933 Clifford Shaw developed a program in six areas of Chicago, coordinating the activities of existing agencies or establishing additional agencies to prevent social problems. Several assump-

---

[40]Robert C. Trojanowicz, *Juvenile Delinquency: Concepts and Control*, Prentice-Hall, Inc., Englewood Cliffs, N.J., 1973, pp. 188–189.

tions underlie this approach: that crime and delinquency cannot be attributed to race or nationality groups, that crime and delinquency can be viewed as conformity to expectations, that deviants in deteriorated areas are not inferior to nondeviants in nondeteriorated areas, that previous practices in preventing crime and delinquency have been unsuccessful, and that local neighborhoods can be effectively organized to cope with their own problems.

Other examples of neighborhood projects are the Mid-City Project in Boston, South Central Youth Project in Minneapolis, Quincy Community Youth Development Project in Quincy (Illinois), and the Los Angeles Youth Project.

Individual Treatment Programs

A third level of attack is dealing with the individual through clinical treatment programs, largely psychological in orientation, which have been developed to prevent deviant behavior resulting from individual pathology. The programs have used psychiatric casework, social group work, and services to families designed to modify attitudes and patterns of behavior.

One project of long standing is the Cambridge-Somerville Youth Study, initiated in Boston in 1936. A group of 325 boys who were provided preventive treatment was matched with an untreated group. There was no statistically significant difference between the two.[41]

School Programs

Still another form of prevention program uses a liaison between police and the schools. Such a program begins when a police officer is assigned to a school as a law enforcement officer and resource person. Educators George Shepard and Jessie James list five objectives of such a program:

1 To establish cooperation in preventing crime and delinquency
2 To increase understanding between police and young people
3 To encourage teamwork in handling problem youth
4 To improve student attitudes toward police
5 To build better police and community relations

Police officers try to reach these objectives by listening to student problems, counseling children, assisting school authorities with deviant behavior, and improving public relations in the classrooms.[42]

The relationship between the schools and crime and delinquency has been examined closely for a number of years. The conclusion was that the longer children remain in school the less likely they will appear in court on a

---

[41]Martin R. Haskell, and Lewis Yablonsky, *Juvenile Delinquency*, Rand McNally College Publishing Company, Chicago, 1974, pp. 420–422, 447–448.

[42]George H. Shepard and Jessie James, "Police—Do They Belong in the Schools?," *American Education*, vol. 3, no. 8, U. S. Office of Education, Washington, D. C., September 1967, pp. 2.

delinquency or criminal charge. Based largely on statistics indicating the number of school dropouts who appear in court, this conclusion is in part the justification for school-police liaison programs. As a result of the same information, there are some direct attacks on the dropout problem itself. Efforts to reduce dropouts have included a work experience program in New York City; an extensive counseling and service program in Hamilton county, Ohio; a combination of individual counseling, group counseling, remedial reading, and remedial mathematics in North Richmond, California; and the forming of a "dropouts anonymous" group in Texas.[43]

Government Agencies

Many governments agencies have programs that contribute to the prevention of crime and delinquency. The Office of Education within the Department of Health, Education and Welfare (now Health and Human Services) originated Upward Bound—a program designed to help youths in secondary school who hope to attend college. The Department of Housing and Urban Development was granted approval to establish the Model Cities Program by the Demonstration Cities and Metropolitan Development Act of 1966. This program permitted the development of juvenile aftercare centers, group foster homes, youth councils, vocational training centers, and unwed mothers' service centers. The LEAA funded the development of similar programs, including one to curb gang violence in Philadelphia and an educational program for parents and offenders. Other federal agencies involved in programs aimed at preventing crime and delinquency include the Department of Agriculture, the Department of Labor, and the Office of Economic Opportunity.

Prevention of Child Abuse

Beginning in the late nineteenth century, activity has been increasing in the prevention and prosecution of child abuse and neglect cases. The National Committee for the Prevention of Child Abuse and Neglect founded by Donna Stone, president of the Stone Foundation, and the Child Abuse and Neglect section of the Department of Health and Human Services, helped to spearhead the emphasis in recent years. Today legislatures and private organizations have brought the problems of child abuse and neglect to the attention of the public in nearly all fifty states. This emphasis was given a major stimulus by the belief in the apparent relationship between abuse and crime and delinquency.

Many states concentrate on four areas: detention through third-party reporting, maintenance of a central register of suspected child abuse and neglect cases, organization of child protection service to investigate reports and provide

[43]William E. Amos and Marilyn A. Southwell, "Dropouts: What Can Be Done?" *Federal Probation*, vol. 28, no. 1, Administrative Office of the United States Courts, Washington, D. C., March 1964, pp. 34–35.

immediate reaction, and availability of court action when the child must be removed from the home. Examples of child abuse and neglect have been listed as malnourishment, lack of supervision, physical abuse, sexual exploitation, lack of medical care, deprivation, immoral or amoral environment, and psychological abuse.[44]

Recommendations

Authors Martin Haskell and Lewis Yablonsky, in their textbook *Juvenile Delinquency,* have suggested that a number of specific steps be taken in an effort to prevent crime and delinquency:

1 Remove legal obstacles and social discrimination against young people reaching adult status. Many young people are frustrated because of an unclear definition of social roles caused by restrictions on participation in adult society even though they may be legally an adult.

2 Improve the educational system to the level where juveniles can motivate themselves, identifying with the educational system and its personnel as a reference group. Individualize the curriculum for noncollege-bound students, with increased emphasis on skill training and on the use of peer groups for stimulation.

3 Minimize the negative labeling effects of court contact for status offenders by limiting the jurisdiction of juvenile courts to acts which would be classified as criminal if committed by adults. Neighborhood councils could be formed, consisting of representatives of the school, social welfare organizations, and parents. Efforts would be made through such councils to support the biological family.

4 Expand helping agencies in the community. Increase the establishment of community-based programs in lieu of confinement in correctional institutions. Although institutions must be retained for juveniles considered dangerous, others can be placed safely in halfway houses, on probation and parole, or on work furlough.

5 Require restitution from juveniles as a condition for completion of their terms on probation, sentences in institutions, or unofficial placement in community-based programs.[45]

Sociology Professor Christopher Sower proposes that a community program be sponsored only if it is within the limits of established standards for all persons and interest groups involved. He calls the proposal "normative sponsorship theory." Sower believes that to achieve a relevant system of crime and delinquency prevention, the various leaders within a community must be identified. They in turn must unite in search of a common goal by identifying areas of agreement and disagreement. The next step should be the implementa-

[44]Trojanowicz, op. cit., pp. 192–195.
[45]Adapted from *Juvenile Delinquency,* 3rd Edition, by Martin R. Haskell and Lewis Yablonsky. Copyright © 1982 by Houghton Mifflin Company. Used by permission.

tion of a program based on these areas, then the development of a constant system of quality control and program updating.[46]

Preventing the Criminal Act

Some efforts toward prevention have concentrated on discouraging the criminal or delinquent act rather than redirecting the perpetrator. Antiburglary campaigns, emphasizing a mass media approach, have alerted homeowners and business owners about techniques such as the use of extra lighting and heavy-duty locks. The number of private security companies has increased throughout the country for the specific purpose of patrolling apartment complexes, housing developments, and business and industrial areas. Neighborhood volunteer patrols have been organized to counteract threatened or actual assaults, vandalism, and break-ins. Former forgers, embezzlers, and shoplifters have offered clinics to educate business owners about steps that can be taken to apprehend or discourage criminals. Check Writer's Anonymous, an organization formed by incarcerated prisoners in Iowa, conducted more than 300 panels during the middle and late 1960s.

Professor Ralph Switzgebel has recommended that a monitoring device be implanted in the brains of convicted felons. In this way, when a crime is committed, law enforcement authorities will be immediately notified of any convicted felon in the geographic vicinity of the criminal act.

Appraisal

To date, except for a few isolated instances, prevention of crime and delinquency has not been accomplished. Funds have been insufficient. Good intentions have been thwarted by inept management. Initial zeal has bogged down. Some successful prevention programs have existed and continued as positive forces in communities when the leadership has been dynamic, when private broad-based support has been maintained, and when careful attention has been paid to the failures of other programs. For the most part, prevention has taken a back seat to putting away. It is hard to convince legislators and the public to appropriate funds and spend considerable time if they are not guaranteed immediate results. Until both groups are willing to work now for future benefits, prevention will remain a secondary priority.

CONCLUSION

One reason for the lack of success of corrections has been the failure of correctional administrators to coordinate efforts. State correctional departments do not coordinate institutional programs and community-based corrections. Missouri was cited as an example in 1976. Vocational and educational programs,

---

[46]Trojanowicz, op. cit., pp. 294–303.

counseling, and other programs existed in institutions. Community service center personnel assisted offenders in St. Louis and Kansas City when they returned to the community by helping them find jobs or housing and by counseling them regarding personal problems such as marriage difficulties. On the other hand, Missouri's prerelease program was small and served only a few inmates. Most offenders were released to the community directly from prison as if no prerelease program existed. Many of those going to St. Louis and Kansas City did not use the community service center. Consequently, many gains achieved in prison disappeared in the sudden move to the community.[47]

It is interesting to note that some states—California, Minnesota, and New Jersey, for example—spend a proportionately large amount of their correctional budgets on rehabilitation staff, although less than 50 percent of their admissions are offenders who have been in prison before. On the other hand, several states spend virtually nothing on rehabilitation, although they have a 75 percent incarceration rate of previously imprisoned offenders.[48]

Variations in recidivism rates among states appear to correlate with the amount of money spent on rehabilitation programs. but allocating money for rehabilitation does not necessarily guarantee that recidivism will decrease. Careful planning is necessary before effective rehabilitation programs can be developed, and it behooves correctional administrators to do this planning and develop such programs. All that has been learned about offender rehabilitation should be applied in order to serve individual inmates best. This means that presentence investigations must be made and diagnostic centers must provide evaluations of offenders' behavior. Probation and other diversionary techniques should be used for all nondangerous offenders, who should then remain in the community unless it is proved that they cannot control their behavior or that they pose a threat.

Maximum, medium, and minimum security institutions are all options that should exist for offenders. Maximum security institutions are available for those considered dangerous and for those unable to control their behavior. Medium security institutions are available for inmates in need of vocational or academic education, work release, or other community-based programs but who still require some structure in order to learn acceptable behavior. Minimum security housing is accessible through halfway houses or contracts with YMCAs, local hotels, and alcoholic rehabilitation centers. These community-based residences are for inmates who do not need structure or close supervision yet are unable to live with their families or by themselves.

Preparing the offender for the community is a major task in today's corrections. Preparing the community for the offender is equally important. In each case, a program must be organized that allows offenders to live as nearly as possible as they will be living after total release.

---

[47]Edgar May, "Profile/Missouri," *Corrections Magazine*, vol. 2, no. 3, March 1976, pp. 58–59.
[48]Vernon Fox, "The Future of Correctional Treatment," in Albert R. Roberts (ed.), *Correctional Treatment of the Offender*, Charles C Thomas Publisher, Springfield, Ill., 1974, p. 313.

The offender's chance for success is diminished if conditions in the prison are totally unlike conditions outside. "Success" in a traditional prison is dependent on abnegation of responsibility for one's actions and passive acceptance of living conditions, food, and medical services. Success outside prison is not measured by these criteria, but by independently meeting one's own needs, working for a living, earning a good wage, having self-confidence, and obtaining prestige in the eyes of other community members. A prisoner who is to attain success after release must be able to make free choices wisely, with decisions that are accepted as law-abiding.

Offenders can benefit from intensive individual and group counseling, vocational and academic education, creative therapy, and other tools. But they must be aware that to live in a free society depends on willingness to work toward goals, make sacrifices, and be responsible for themselves. For this reason a prison system must include opportunities to make decisions and to keep in touch with the outside community.

Offenders must be given the chance to organize their own programs and decide whether vocational, recreational, or clinical experiences are more likely to assist them after release. Programs in which prisoners are given a choice of meals, allowed to make telephone calls, paid minimum wages for work assignments, granted furloughs to visit their families, and make restitution provide a sense of dignity and self-respect. As David Rothenberg, director of Fortune Society, has said, "It's rather absurd to have a program where you give decent treatment of prisoners for a couple of hours a week, and then go back to the routine."[49]

Increased use of work release and furloughs can permit offenders to participate in work experiences and leisure-time activities outside the institution. Prerelease planning can allow them to develop their own release programs, even though supervision is maintained by correctional staff. In each instance the institutional experience should be as much like the community as possible, so that the final transition to community living will not be too sudden. Likewise, parole supervision must be supportive, and each offender must be given ample opportunity to receive help for any problems that develop, including drinking or actual criminal behavior.

Community-based programs (i.e., prerelease centers, furloughs, work release, community-based jails, probation, and parole) must be used for all incarcerated offenders. Their return to the community must be carefully planned, minimizing the self-destructive effects of a door slamming behind a human being whose only possessions are $50.00 and a cheap suit of clothes.

This text expresses optimism about the chances that offenders can be redirected to law-abiding behavior. Each chapter has ended with the belief that incarcerated offenders can be successfully reintegrated into the community or that other offenders can be diverted from institutions and integrated into the

---

[49]"Riots May Be an Established Fact of Life in American Prisons," *The New Mexican,* Santa Fe, N. M., June 25, 1980, p. A-8.

community. Obviously, the optimism is based on an ideal that most men and women desire to be accepted by others, behave properly, and avoid trouble.

The text also assumes that most people will accept offenders into their community as neighbors, employees, and companions. This final chapter implies that the public can be convinced by providing evidence from research and cost-benefit analyses, by establishing accreditation procedures and standards, and by developing an effective education campaign.

In actuality, the mass media can just as easily turn the public against corrections focusing on the community. Political questions will be just as crucial as fiscal issues to acceptance or rejection by legislators. Correctional administrators must take into consideration the public mood that prevails when their message is transmitted. If the mood is characterized by pessimism, an unusual degree of escapism, unwillingness to make personal sacrifices, a decline in confidence in government, anxiety about inflation, and extreme fear of crime, the odds are that success will be lessened in selling community-based corrections.

However, as the reader has probably deduced, the author is an optimist, in part because of his faith in the human spirit as caring, but primarily because of his own successful experiences in selling community-based corrections.

EXERCISES

1 If you were designing a research program for a state correctional department, what questions would you try to answer?

2 List reasons why evaluations of research projects over the last 15 to 20 years contain a mixture of positive and negative conclusions. Explain each reason fully.

3 In the subsection "past attempts" in the beginning of this chapter are three examples of the results of controlled experiments. Write a simulated report using these examples in developing a program strategy for adult offenders.

4 Explain the steps you would take in carrying out Daniel Glaser's five suggestions for correctional administrators to follow in organizing research programs.

5 Agree or disagree with the following statement: "Even if there is no decrease in the recidivism rate for inmates from the prerelease center as compared with those from the house of corrections, based on cost-benefit analysis, it is a sound administrative decision to house offenders in the prerelease center." Defend your anwser.

6 Who should have the responsibility for accreditation of correctional programs—state governments, the federal government, or a private agency? Why?

7 "Public ignorance of a social problem leads to public rejection of the people who personify that problem." Agree or disagree with this statement.

8 Despite statistics indicating high recidivism rates and the poor preparation of criminals for successful functioning in society, correctional techniques are slow to change. Why? Present your answer fully.

9 Should corrections aim for changes in correctional policies or reform—that is, reducing discrepancies between accepted goals and existing practice? Give reasons for your answer.

10 What steps would you take to minimize the effects of the difficulties in achieving penal reform?

11 Develop a statement regarding the direction you believe corrections will take in the next 10 years—more prisons, community-based detention, or programs emphasizing increased freedom for the offender. Give your reasons.

12 List the relative merits and disadvantages of pre-prevention and prevention through rehabilitation. Defend each merit and disadvantage.

13 Evaluate the five steps recommended by Martin Haskell and Lewis Yablonsky to prevent crime and delinquency.

14 Christopher Sower believes that if a relevant system of crime and delinquency prevention is to be achieved the leadership within a community must be identified. Agree or disagree, and give reasons.

15 The author has implied that correctional administrators already possess effective rehabilitation techniques but fail to "put it all together." Do you think this is true? Why or why not?

EXERCISE REFERENCES

Adams, Stuart: "Evaluative Research in Corrections: Definition, Criteria, Methods, and Models," in Povl G. Boesen and Stanley E. Grupp (eds.), *Community Based Corrections: Theory, Practice, and Research,* Davis Publishing Company, Inc., Santa Cruz, Calif., 1976, pp. 235–255.

———: "Evaluative Research in Corrections: Status and Prospects," *Federal Probation,* vol. 38, no. 1, Administrative Office of the United States Courts, Washington, D. C., March 1974, pp. 14–16.

———: "Some Findings From Correctional Caseload Research," *Federal Probation,* vol. 31, no. 4, Administrative Office of the United States Courts, Washington, D. C., December 1967, pp. 48–57.

Allinson, Richard S.: "LEAA: On the Brink of Extinction," *Corrections Magazine,* vol. 6, no 4, August 1980, pp. 34–35.

American Correctional Association: *Proceedings of the One Hundred and Fourth Annual Congress of Corrections,* (Accreditation) College Park, Md., 1975.

Amos, William E., and Marilyn A. Southwell: "Dropouts: What Can Be Done?" *Federal Probation,* vol. 28, no. 1, Administrative Office of the United States Courts, Washington, D. C., March 1964, pp. 30–35.

Bartell, Ted, and L. Thomas Winfree, Jr.: "Recidivist Impacts of Differential Sentencing for Burglary Offenders," *Criminology,* vol. 15, no. 3, November 1977, pp. 387–396.

Beck, James L., and Peter B. Hoffman: "Time Served and Release Performance: A Research Note," *Journal of Research in Crime and Delinquency,* vol. 13, no. 2, July 1976, pp. 127–132.

Bergman, Howard Standish: "Community Service in England: An Alternative to Custodial Sentence," in Burt Galaway, Joe Hudson, and C. David Hollister (eds.), *Community Corrections,* Charles C Thomas Publisher, Springfield, Ill. 1976, pp. 80–89.

Bergsmann, Ilene R.: "Correctional Standards Development in the United States," *Federal Probation,* vol. 45, no. 3, Administrative Office of the United States Courts, Washington, D. C., September 1981, pp. 49–56.

Blackmore, John: "Does Community Corrections Work?" *Corrections Magazine,* vol. 7, no. 5, October 1981, pp. 15–26.

Board of Directors, National Council on Crime and Delinquency: "The Nondangerous

Offender Should Not Be Imprisoned," *Crime and Delinquency,* vol. 21, no. 4, October 1975, pp. 315–322.

Commission on Accreditation for Corrections: *Manual of Standards for Adult Community Residential Services,* Rockville, Md., April 1977.

Conrad, John P.: "There Has To Be a Better Way," *Crime and Delinquency,* vol. 26, no. 1, January 1980, pp. 83–90.

Cressey, Donald R.: "Sources of Resistance to Innovation in Corrections," *Offenders as a Correctional Manpower Resource,* Joint Commission on Correctional Manpower and Training, Washington, D. C., June 1966, pp. 31–49.

Doleschal, Eugene: "Rate and Length of Imprisonment," *Crime and Delinquency,* vol. 23, no. 1, January 1977, pp. 51–56.

Dunbar, Walter: "Goals in Accreditation of Correctional Services," *American Journal of Correction,* vol. 36, no. 5, September/October 1974, pp. 19–20.

Emshoff, James G., and William S. Davidson, II: "Training Prison Inmates as Paralegals: An Experimental Project," *Journal of Crime and Justice,* vol. 8, no. 1, 1980, pp. 27–38.

Englade, Sara G.: "A National Public Awareness Program About Community Corrections," *Corrections Today,* vol. 43, no. 1, January/February 1981, pp. 74–75.

Farrington, David P.: "Longitudinal Research on Crime and Delinquency," in Norval Morris and Michael Tonry (eds.), *Crime and Justice: a Review of Research,* vol. 1, University of Chicago Press, Chicago, 1979, pp. 289–348.

Felkenes, George T.: "Accreditation: Is It Necessary? Yes!" *Journal of Crimal Justice,* vol. 8, no. 2, 1980, pp. 77–87.

Forer, Lois G.: "Moral Failures of the Legal System," *Bulletin of the Menninger Clinic,* vol. 44, no. 5, The Menninger Foundation, Topeka, Kan., September 1980, pp. 457–481.

Fosen, Robert H.: "Accreditation: A New Challenge to the Old Dilemma," *Proceedings of the One Hundred and Fifth Annual Congress of Corrections,* American Correctional Association, College Park, Md., 1976, pp. 31–34.

Fox, Vernon: *Community Based Correction,* Prentice-Hall, Inc., Englewood Cliffs, N. J., 1977, chap. 2.

———: "The Future of Correctional Treatment," in Albert R. Roberts (ed.), *Correctional Treatment of the Offender*, Charles C Thomas Publisher, Springfield, Ill., 1974, pp. 311–326.

Geis, Gilbert: "Ethical and Legal Issues in Experimentation With Offender Populations," *Research in Correctional Rehabilitation,* Joint Commission on Correctional Manpower and Training, Washington, D. C., 1967, pp. 34–47.

Gilbert, Michael J.: "Developing Performance Standards for Correctional Officers," *Corrections Today,* vol. 42, no. 3, May/June 1980, pp. 8–9, 42–43, 52–53.

Glaser, Daniel: "Achieving Better Questions: A Half Century's Progress in Correctional Research," *Federal Probation,* vol. 39, no. 3, Administrative Office of the United States Courts, Washington, D. C., September 1975, pp. 3–9.

———: "Five Practical Research Suggestions for Correctional Administrators, "*Crime and Delinquency,* vol. 17, no. 1, January 1971, pp. 32–40.

Haskell, Martin R., and Lewis Yablonsky: *Juvenile Delinquency,* Rand McNally College Publishing Company, Chicago, 1974.

Hoffman, Peter B., and Barbara Stone-Meierhoefer: "Post Release Arrest Experiences of Federal Prisoners: A Six Year Follow-up," *Journal of Criminal Justice,* vol. 7, no. 3, Fall 1979, pp. 193–216.

———— and Barbara Stone-Meierhoefer: "Reporting Recidivism Rates: The Criterion and Follow-up Issues," *Journal of Criminal Justice,* vol. 8, no. 1, Spring 1980, pp. 53–60.

Hopkins, Arnold J.: "Victim Service Programs in Probation Agencies," *Proceedings of the One Hundred and Tenth Annual Congress of Correction,* American Correctional Association, College Park, Md. 1981, pp. 159–166.

Howell, James C.: "Suggestions for Improving the State-of-the-Art of Evaluative Research in Criminal Justice," *Proceedings of the One Hundred and Fifth Annual Congress of Correction,* American Correctional Association, College Park, Md. 1976, pp. 273–280.

Hylton, John: *Reintegrating the Offender,* University Press of America, Washington, D. C., 1981.

Klein, Malcolm W.: "Deinstitutionalization and Diversion of Juvenile Offenders: A Litany of Impediments," in Norval Morris and Michael Tonry (eds.), *Crime and Justice: A Review of Research,* vol. 1, University of Chicago Press, Chicago, 1979, pp. 145–201.

Korn, Richard R.: "Correctional Innovation and the Dilemma of Change-From-Within," *Canadian Journal of Corrections,* vol. 10, 1968, pp. 449–457,

Lobenthal, Joseph S., Jr.: "Designing Research in Corrections: An Abbreviated Tour Guide," *Federal Probation,* vol. 38, no. 1, Administrative Office of the United States Courts, Washington, D. C., March 1974, pp. 29–36.

Malcolm, Benjamin J.: "Incarceration . . . Rehabiltation or Vindictiveness," *American Journal of Corrections,* vol. 37, no. 1, January/February 1975, p. 21.

Martinson, Robert: "California Research at the Crossroads," *Crime and Delinquency,* vol. 22, no. 2, April 1976, pp. 180–191.

————: "What Works? Questions and Answers About Prison Reform," *The Public Interest,* no. 35, 1974, pp. 22–54.

Menninger, W. Walter: "Rehabilitation—A Correctional Responsibility," *Corrections Today,* vol. 43, no. 4, July/August 1981, pp. 64, 66–67.

Meyer, John C., Jr.: "Change and Obstacles to Change in Prison Management," *Federal Probation,* vol. 36, no. 2 Administrative Office of the United States Courts, Washington, D. C., June 1972, pp. 39–46.

Miller, E. Eugene, and M. Robert Montilla: *Corrections in the Community,* Reston Publishing Company, Reston, Va., 1977, chap. 9.

Moeller, H. G.: "Principles of Accreditation for Corrections," *Proceedings of the One Hundred and Fifth Annual Congress of Corrections,* American Correctional Association, College Park, Md., 1976, pp. 21–25.

Morris, Norval: *The Future of Imprisonment,* University of Chicago Press, Chicago, 1974.

————: "Impediments to Penal Reform," *The University of Chicago Law Review,* vol. 33, no. 4, Summer 1966, pp. 627–656.

Nagy, Thomas J. and Robert L. Fisher: "Meeting the Demand for Repeating Successful Criminal Justice Projects by Using Economics," *The Prison Journal,* vol. LVII, no. 1, Spring/Summer 1977, pp. 28–37.

Nelson, Carl W.: "Cost Benefit Analysis and Alternatives to Incarceration," *Federal Probation,* vol. 34, no. 4, Administrative Office of the United States Courts, Washington, D. C., December 1974, pp. 45–50.

Newton, Anne: *Aid to the Victim,* National Council on Crime and Delinquency, Hackensack, N. J., 1976.

Potter, Joan: "A Study in Coping: New York Versus Prison Crowding," *Corrections Magazine,* vol. 3, no. 4, September 1978, pp. 62–64, 69–70.

Reed, James A.: "Program Evaluation Research," *Federal Probation,* vol. 38, no. 1, Administrative Office of the United States Courts, Washington, D. C., March 1974, pp. 37–42.

Reimer, Ernest G., and Dale K. Sechrest: "Writing Standards for Correctional Accreditation," *Federal Probation,* vol. 43, no. 3, Administrative Office of the United States Courts, Washington, D. C., September 1979, pp. 10–16.

Roberts, Albert R.: "Alternative Strategies to Offender Rehabilitation: A Prison Option System," in Albert R. Roberts (ed.) *Correctional Treatment of the Offender,* Charles C Thomas Publisher, Springfield, Ill., 1974, pp. 5–41. Robison, James, and Gerald Smith: "The Effectiveness of Correctional Programs," *Crime and Delinquency,* vol. 17, no. 1, January 1971, pp. 67–80.

Rosberg, Gary R.: "Community Service Sentencing: Social Restitution to the Community," in Rodger O. Darnell, John F. Else, and R. Dean Wright (eds.), *Alternatives to Prisons,* University of Iowa, Iowa City, 1979, pp. 84–91.

Rowland, James: "Probation and Victim Services," *Proceedings of the One Hundred and Tenth Annual Congress of Correction,* American Correctional Association, College Park, Md., 1981, pp. 187–195.

Ryles, Ruby: "Initiative Public Relations: A Means for Participation," *Corrections Today,* vol. 43, no. 4, July/August 1981, pp. 10–11.

Sechrest, Dale K.: "The Accreditation Movement in Corrections," *Federal Probation,* vol. 40, no. 4, Administrative Office of the United States Courts, Washington, D. C., December 1976, pp. 15–19.

———: "The Development and Implementation of Standards for Juvenile Corrections," *Proceedings of the One Hundred and Ninth Annual Congress of Corrections,* American Correctional Association, College Park, Md., 1980, pp. 205–213.

———: "The Self-Evaluation and Accreditation Movement in Corrections," *Proceedings of the One Hundred and Fifth Annual Congress of Corrections,* American Correctional Association, College Park, Md., 1976, pp. 25–31.

Shepard, George H., and Jessie James: "Police—Do They Belong in the Schools?" *American Education,* vol. 3, no. 8, United States Office of Education, Washington, D. C., September 1967, p. 2ff.

Shover, Neal: *A Sociology of American Corrections,* Dorsey Press, Homewood, Ill., 1979.

Thalheimer, Donald: *Cost Analysis of Correctional Standards: Halfway Houses,* American Bar Association, Washington, D. C., October 1975.

Trojanowicz, Robert C.: *Juvenile Delinquency: Concepts and Control,* Prentice-Hall, Inc., Englewood Cliffs, N. J., 1973.

Van Den Haag, Ernest: "Prisons Cost Too Much Because They Are Too Secure," *Corrections Magazine,* vol. 6, no. 2, April 1980, pp. 39–43.

Vickers, James E., and William H. Kelley: "New Directions for Florida's Correctional System," *Corrections Today,* vol. 43, no. 6, College Park, Md., December 1981, pp. 77–79.

Waldo, Gordon P.: "The Dilemma of Correctional Research," *American Journal of Correction,* vol. 31, no. 6, November/December 1969, pp. 6–10.

Ward, David A.: "Evaluative Research for Corrections," *Prisoners in America,* Lloyd E. Ohlin (ed.), Prentice-Hall, Inc., Englewood Cliffs, N. J., 1973, pp. 184–206.

Weisburg, Susan: *Cost Analysis of Correctional Standards: Alternatives to Arrest,* American Bar Association, Washington, D. C., October 1975.

Wenk, Ernst A., and Colin Frank: "Some Progress on the Evaluation of Institutional Programs," *Federal Probation,* vol. 37, no. 3, Administrative Office of the United States Courts, Washington, D. C., September 1973, pp. 30–37.

Wilkins, Leslie T.: "Evaluation of Penal Treatment," *The American Sociological Review,* vol. 30, no. 1, January 1965, pp. 237–252.

Winkler, Sharon J., and Robert H. Fosen: "Commission on Accreditation for Corrections Marks a First by the Field in Development of Standards," *American Journal of Correction,* vol. 39, no. 3, May/June 1977. pp. 16, 32, and 34.

Wright, William E., and Michael C. Dixon: "Community Prevention and Treatment of Juvenile Delinquency: A Review of Evaluation Studies," *Journal of Research in Crime and Delinquency,* vol. 14, no. 1, January 1977, pp. 35–67.

Zimring, Franklin: "American Youth Violence: Issues and Trends," in Norval Morris and Michael Tonry (eds.), *Crime and Justice: A Review of Research,* University of Chicago Press, Chicago, 1979, pp. 67–108.

EPILOGUE

INTRODUCTION

Corrections involves force—the right to tell persons what to do and what not to do every minute of the day and night. It means keeping them away from family and friends in unpleasant, sometimes disgusting places they do not want to be in, for years or even the remainder of their lives. That kind of power is hard to accept, but it is even harder to use as a force for good. The very word "corrections" gives pause.

It is not just for that unhappy minority of our citizens who are convicted (or accused) of crime that corrections is so important, but for society as a whole. It is society's last line of defense to protect itself against those who will not live by its rules. It is society's last attempt—however halting and misguided—at retribution, deterrence, incapacitation, reparation, and rehabilitation, all in one. The only alternative to corrections is anarchy or death.

Most Americans do not think about how important a well-run correctional system is to their survival, and neither, probably, do most governors, legislators, and mayors. They have to be continually informed, then reminded in terms that they understand and that appear reasonable to them.

Time magazine has accurately stated that the country's penal institutions are a "national disgrace," a "combustible scandal" costing $4 billion a year to operate for a population of 400,000 inmates. This population is two-thirds larger than in 1968 and exceeds safe capacity by 58 percent.[1] Unless sentencing practices are revised radically, there will be more than 750,000 people in custody within 5 years—three-quarters of a million people.

---

[1]Patricia A. Wald, "Corrections—The Unequal Partner," *Corrections Today,* vol. 42, no. 5, September-October 1980, p. 10.

The problems of corrections have become too prevalent and too interwoven with all the rest of the problems of government for simple solutions. Overcrowding, not enough money, bad publicity, a never-ending stream of lawsuits, an uncomprehending judiciary, tyrannical prisoner networks within many prisons, lack of correctional alternatives, and failure of judicial initiative are only some of the problems. To overcome them, each proposed solution needs pubic support from new coalitions of unfamiliar allies.

One of the first tasks that corrections officials will have to complete in order to solve these problems is the cultivation of in-depth knowledge on the part of the public. This involves understanding the significance of corrections, the difficulty of the problems that officials face, where the problems originate, what the possible solutions are, and what corrections officials are trying to do about them. Cultivating the public means a degree of openness and access to corrections personnel and even to prisoners. The public needs to know that decreasing the use of incarceration does not mean decreasing control over the offender. The public must realize the cost-effectiveness of community-based corrections. The public must become knowledgeable about every facet of community-based corrections, from long-range planning through implementation and operation.

The many promising alternatives to incarceration for nonviolent offenders, e.g., community services and restitution programs, are successful only if judges and correctional officials use them. Many of these programs are underused because people do not understand how they operate or because they believe that incarceration is a greater deterrent to recidivism. Yet corrections and the people are not natural enemies; their aims are similar, their needs interdependent. There must be more dialogue between them, however. Corrections can provide valuable feedback by telling the public what can happen to those who offend. Too often, people complain about the shortcomings of corrections programs rather than trying to overcome the problems. The public might well be willing to help conquer these problems if corrections officials would tell them how to help.

"PRACTICAL" APPROACHES TO IMPRISONMENT

Factorylike Prisons

On December 16, 1981, Chief Justice Warren Burger told the Lincoln, Nebraska, Bar Association that we should turn prisons into "factories" with fences around them.[2] Both Minnesota and Kansas have made beginnings. Florida Senate Bill 97, entitled "An Act Relating to Prison Industries," permits the operation of selected correctional industries by nonprofit corporations to be formed specifically for that purpose.[3]

The President's Task Force on Prisoner Rehabilitation also recommended a

[2]"For the Future, Prisons as Factories, Not as Warehouses—Warren Burger," *Criminal Justice Newsletter,* vol. 13, no. 1, Jan. 4, 1982, p. 3.

[3]James E. Vickers and William H. Kelly, "New Directions for Florida's Correctional System," *Corrections Today,* vol. 43, no. 6, November-December 1981, p. 77.

"prevailing wage" or "factory" prison. The prisoner would be paid full market wages for labor but would be required to pay for board and keep, contribute to the support of dependents, and pay taxes and restitution.[4] In 1976 Canada opened a prison with this approach to inmate employment.

Based on the experiences at Coldingly, England, and Tillberga, Sweden, a new plant has been established near Joyceville, Ontario, Canada. Here eighty inmates will be employed in the pilot factory manufacturing metal products such as shelving, lockers, storage cabinets, and lateral filing cabinets. Candidates for jobs will apply in the same manner as in private industry and will meet the same basic requirements set for each position. They will undergo a probationary period of approximately 6 weeks, and promotion will depend on performance, attitude, and aptitude. Hours of work will be similar to those in commercial industry—7 hours a day, 5 days a week. Working inmates will be paid the minimum hourly wage when the pilot project becomes self-supporting, receiving slightly lower wages until then.

The inmate workers will meet all normal requirements for income tax, unemployment insurance, and the Canadian pension plan. They will pay for their own maintenance, and they will face job insecurity. Disciplinary action could result in a return to the general inmate population. All hiring and firing of inmate employees will be determined by a three-person institutional committee. Obviously, the assessment of performance and attitude of inmates working in the plant will be affected by the fact that the program is designed as a training program. Nevertheless, they will be expected to cope with time clocks, production schedules, quality control, and profit margins while incarcerated.[5]

"Real-Life" Solutions

Correctional programs can be similar to real-life situations. In the past, many practical approaches have been ignored. For example, is it realistic to require jobs for parolees and then release them without work clothes or means of transportation to get to work? Is it realistic to release offenders directly from an institution where they stop habitually before doors, waiting for electric buttons to open them, and expect the ex-inmates not to be identified as former criminals? Is it realistic to provide offenders with vocational training but no instruction in filling out job applications, preparing résumés, or interviewing prospective employers?

A study by researcher Alastair MacLeod of inmates from a Montreal penitentiary concluded that recidivism is the result of the absence of meaningful, human relationships at some critical period in the criminal's life. MacLeod termed this absence a "common deficiency factor."[6] Another study similarly

---

[4]Gordon Hawkins, *The Prison: Policy and Practice,* The University of Chicago Press, 1976, p. 123.

[5]Canadian Penitentiary Service Public Affairs Division, "Canada Launches New Approach to Inmate Employment," *American Journal of Correction,* vol. 38, no. 6, November-December 1976, p. 10.

[6]Alastair W. MacLeod, *Recidivism: A Deficiency Disease,* University of Pennsylvania Press, Philadelphia, 1965.

concluded that successful exiting from criminal careers revolved around the establishment of bonds to the "conventional world," i.e., acquiring conventional associates, loved ones, and employment.[7]

Other research has shown that released men whose first residence is with their wives have fewest failures and those living alone have the highest rate of failure. One might assume that those living alone find company in taverns or with ex-felons. Daniel Glaser did discover that ex-prisoners who did not see prison acquaintances succeeded at a 91 percent rate. Those who saw former prisoners succeeded at rates ranging from 79 to 68 percent—the lower rates correlating with more frequent contact. Inmates who made new friends reported that friendships began at work or places of commercial recreation—taverns, restaurants, or pool halls.[8]

Correctional administrators should admit that they are redirecting persons . who have been unable to function effectively in a society in which the vast majority of people are able to cope. Correctional administrator Lawrence A. Bennett suggests that a new objective should be sought by correctional practitioners—the development of improved self-esteem on the part of offenders. He believes that many existing programs can be used to achieve this goal: academic and vocational education, increased social contacts with members of the community, psychotherapy, and post-high school education. The result of a concerted effort to improve offenders' self-concepts would be higher personnel morale, increased program efficiency, reduced disruptive inmate behavior, and better postinstitutional adjustment.[9]

Offender Aspirations

Criminals express high aspirations with little means of achieving them. Most criminals grew up in areas where crime and delinquency were prevalent and have known other criminals most of their lives. They have few ties with the "straight" social world. Their choice of criminal behavior as a means of achieving middle-class aspirations seems logical. Few criminals have known lives free from want of basic needs—job, money, car, and a place to stay. A 1974 study disclosed that 33 percent of the inmate population in state correctional institutions had been unemployed at the time of their offenses.[10] More recent reports on inmates of federal correctional institutions revealed that 56 percent had not finished high school.[11]

Criminals must be integrated into the legitimate social world with opportuni-

---

[7]Thomas Meisenhelder, "An Exploratory Study of Exiting From Criminal Careers," *Criminology,* vol. 15, no. 3, November 1977, p. 331.

[8]Daniel Glaser, *The Effectiveness of a Prison and Parole System,* The Bobbs-Merrill Company, Inc., Indianapolis, 1969, p. 257.

[9]Lawrence A. Bennett, "Corrections Adrift: New Directions Needed," *Corrections Today,* vol. 42, no. 4, July-August 1980, pp. 97, 102.

[10]Law Enforcement Assistance Administration, *Survey of Inmates of State Correctional Facilities, 1974,* U.S. Government Printing Office, Washington, D.C., March 1976, pp. 2–7.

[11]U.S. Department of Justice, Law Enforcement Assistance Administration, National Criminal Justice Information and Statistics Service, telephone conversation, Sept. 21, 1977.

ties to be self-sufficient. What "regular citizen" could succeed today with less than a high school education, no job skills, and few close ties or other resources?

The discrepancy between aspirations and ability to achieve goals should be recognized. Low self-esteem and a lack of conventional social ties should be countered by the development of opportunities that will enable criminals to learn to cope with these problems. A "habituation" program should be created to help them develop a lifestyle plan, including decision making, time structuring, and the cultivation of social relationships. Education, job training and placement should be provided. Community resources should be mobilized to help offenders seek lodging, noncriminal peer group relationships, and other forms of practical, nonpunitive assistance. Both ex-offenders and community volunteers should be used.[12]

Incarceration provides little in the way of concrete help, especially for older offenders. It removes them from society at a point when they are expected to make certain social advances, e.g., obtaining a steady job, getting married, and starting a family. It is regrettable that reintegrative efforts have not been provided for older offenders, because there is evidence that they have less psychological aberrance. Apparently, "burnout" among older offenders occurs with increased requests for assistance.[13]

Corrections programs should help the felon to cope with everyday tension and pressure. Karl Menninger has listed a number of coping devices we all use—smoking, chewing gum, drinking alcoholic beverages, boasting, sleeping, exercising, rationalizing, engaging in pointless activity, fantasizing, daydreaming, and dreaming. For some people, crime is a coping mechanism designed to relieve personal tensions as well as to achieve aspirations.[14]

THE FUTURE OF INCARCERATION

Why Imprisonment?

Only dangerous offenders or those unable to control their behavior should be imprisoned. Community-based programs should be used for all other offenders before incarceration and after. Milton Rector, President of the National Council on Crime and Delinquency, stated in an open letter to Attorney General Griffin Bell:

> The [Justice] department's Bureau of Prisons should . . . establish alternatives for correction in the community for those Federal offenders—the frauds, car thieves, embezzlers, and so on—who are clearly nondangerous . . . change is urgently needed. . . . Most developed countries are now phasing out their use of prisons.[15]

[12]Rosemary J. Erickson, Wayman J. Crow, Louis A. Zurcher, and Archie V. Connett, *Paroled But Not Free,* Human Sciences Press, New York, 1973, pp. 96–105.

[13]Robert Martinson, Douglas Lipton, and Judith Wilks, *The Effectiveness of Correctional Treatment,* Praeger Publishers, New York, 1975, p. 567.

[14]Karl Menninger, Martin Mayman, and Paul Pruyser, *The Vital Balance,* The Viking Press, Inc., New York, 1963, pp. 145–146.

[15]Milton G. Rector, "An Open Letter to Attorney General Griffin Bell," National Council on Crime and Delinquency, Feb. 8, 1978.

Yet as late as 1974, the majority of prisoners in the United States (53 percent) were confined for property offenses; those remaining were incarcerated for assaultive or drug offenses.[16]

When Professor William Nagel reevaluated in 1977 his advocacy of a moratorium on prison construction, he examined the prison population explosion, the inevitable deterioration of existing prisons because of severe overcrowding, and the arguments of the new "hard-line" prison advocates. His findings were: Prison construction policies have little to do with crime rates. The "lock 'em up" solution affords less protection at greater cost than the alternatives. The massive use of incarceration does not prevent or deter crime. The American Correctional Association's opposition to the moratorium is an expedient policy. The conservative states with a "hard-line" philosophy have been faced with higher crime rates than the progressive states. Nagel's conclusion was a restatement of his earlier decision that there should be a moratorium on prison construction.[17]

Prison and jail populations have shown corresponding increases and decreases relative to changes in the general structure of the society. From 1850 to 1880, prison and jail populations increased from 29.1 adults per 100,000 in the general population to 115.2. This did not necessarily represent an increase in crime: it reflected a transfer of people from the poorhouses, which showed a decrease of 217 per 100,000 in 1850 to 132 in 1880. The prison population remained comparatively stable for 60 years, until World War II, when there was a sudden increase to 239.4 per 100,000. After World War II there was a decrease to 98 per 100,000 in 1969. An increase began again in 1972. At the time of the last survey in 1980, the prison population was 140 inmates per 100,000.[18]

Researcher David Biles, in a comparative study of imprisonment rates and total crime rates per 100,000 population refuted Professor James Q. Wilson's statement that "those states incarcerating a large proportion of the population have a lower rate of crime." North Dakota and West Virginia, with imprisonment rates of 27 per 100,000 and 65 per 100,000, have the lowest total crime rates (2337 and 2107 per 100,000 population respectively). States with the highest crime rates (8341 per 100,000 in Arizona and 8152 per 100,000 in Nevada) incarcerate at the rates of 118 and 136 per 100,000.[19] In the United States as of December 31, 1976, the total of state and federal prison populations had reached a level of 263,291, or 123 per 100,000. In striking contrast, Sweden had only 32 prisoners per 100,000, Denmark had 28, and the Netherlands only 18—a decrease from 1972 to 1975 (see Table E.1).[20]

---

[16]Neal Shover, *A Sociology of American Corrections,* The Dorsey Press, Homewood, Ill., 1979, p. 157.

[17]William Nagel, "On Behalf of a Moratorium on Prison Construction," *Crime and Delinquency,* vol. 23, no. 2, April 1977, pp. 154–165.

[18]Margaret Cahalan, "Trends in Incarceration in the United States Since 1880," *Crime and Delinquency,* vol. 25, no. 1, January 1979, pp. 10, 11, 12, and 16.

[19]David Biles, "Crime and the Use of Prisons," *Federal Probation,* vol. 43, no. 2, Administrative Office of the United States Courts, Washington, D.C., June 1979, p. 39.

[20]Eugene Doleschal, "Rate and Length of Imprisonment," *Crime and Delinquency,* vol. 23, no. 1, January 1977, pp. 51–54.

TABLE E.1
PERSONS IN PRISON PER 100,000 POPULATION

Rank	Country	Year*	Prisoners/Population	Rate per 100,000
1	United States	1970	206,531/203,200,000 =	200.0
2	Poland	1972	62,748/ 33,070,000 =	189.7
3	Australia	1972	16,615/ 12,960,000 =	128.2
4	Finland	1972	4,947/ 4,630,000 =	106.8
5	New Zealand	1972	2,643/ 2,850,000 =	92.7
6	Canada	1972	19,668/ 21,850,000 =	90.0
7	England & Wales	1971	39,708/ 48,900,000 =	81.3
8	Denmark	1971	3,350/ 4,800,000 =	69.8
9	Sweden	1971	4,977/ 8,090,000 =	61.4
10	France	1972	31,573/ 51,700,000 =	61.1
11	Italy	1972	27,812/ 54,350,000 =	51.2
12	Japan	1972	49,241/105,990,000 =	46.5
13	Spain	1972	13,826/ 34,680,000 =	39.9
14	Norway	1971	1,432/ 3,870,000 =	37.1
15	Netherlands	1971	2,919/ 13,120,000 =	22.4

*Most recent year for which information was available.
Source: Irvin Waller and Janet Chan, "Prison Use: A Canadian and International Comparison," *Criminal Law Quarterly,* vol. 17, no. 1, Canada, 1974–1975, p. 58.

WHICH PATH TO TAKE?

The Choice Is Imminent

The 1980s may be the most crucial time in the history of corrections in the United States. Public confidence is at a low ebb. Fear generated by rising crime rates and incidents of violence is stimulating demands for repressive punishment. More severe penal sanctions are being enacted by state legislatures and by Congress. By the end of 1980, thirty-seven states had passed mandatory sentencing statutes and fifteen had passed determinate sentencing laws. The predictions made by critics of determinate sentencing, decreased use of parole, and court orders to keep prison populations down have come true.

Prisons are filling up. The overcrowding of nearly all federal and state institutions has reached epidemic proportions. Texas, California, and New York now have more convicts than the United States Bureau of Prisons. The total number of prisoners in the United States has grown from 225,528 on January 1, 1975, to 320,583 on January 1, 1981. Sixteen state prison systems are overcrowded to the extent that 5995 inmates sentenced to state facilities are being held in county jails.[21] As of December 31, 1980, there were 1412 state prisoners housed in Alabama jails, 1267 in Louisiana jails, and 1226 in Mississippi jails. Maryland officials believe that 400 state prisoners will be incarcerated in twenty-four local

[21]Kevin Krajick, "Annual Prison Population Survey: The Boom Resumes," *Corrections Magazine,* vol. 7, no. 2, New York, April 1981, p. 19.

jails for the next 3 years. A Kalamazoo, Michigan, jail is currently housing fifty-two female state prisoners.[22]

Within a few years after the Illinois determinate sentence law was passed, state prison populations had reached 11,557. This was 200 above capacity. State corrections officials were forced to release 800 convicts 90 days earlier than their release dates. These statistics are particularly alarming because 20 percent of the state's prison population had committed nonviolent crimes and had no prior prison commitments.[23]

Forty-three percent of the total state inmate population in the United States were living in overcrowded conditions in the spring of 1981. Three thousand inmates were sleeping on the floors of small cells already occupied by two other men. Correctional administrators fear the worst. Harold Bradley, the Tennessee correctional commissioner stated: "My fear is we'll have an epidemic of riots." Federal judge Lewis Powell ordered the release of 222 named Alabama prisoners as a means to reduce overcrowding.[24]

Another negative effect of determinate sentencing has been demonstrated tragically in California, where it became operative on July 1, 1977. The violent offender is released just as readily at the end of the predetermined time period as is the nonviolent offender. After the determinate sentencing law was passed, 169 prisoners were released upon the expiration of their sentences and 45 percent of them were rearrested within 1 year. Although many of the arrests were for minor offenses such as shoplifting and indecent exposure, two men were convicted of murder, five were convicted of robbery, three for sex crimes, two for forgery, one for auto theft, and one for possession of a controlled substance. Civil commitment procedures have proved inadequate to keep these releasees confined. A legislative solution is being sought, but in the meantime there is an obvious need for some kind of supervision at the time of release from prison.[25]

According to Benjamin Frank, an observer of correctional trends, the venerable prison reform movement in the United States has been replaced by two divergent arguments: One is that the ultimate goal is to keep people out of prison through the use of community-based corrections. The other is that imprisonment is a form of punishment that satisfies the principle of retributive justice.[26]

For inmates who can live safely in the community, open prisons designed as part of a community-based corrections plan will suffice. For others who require

[22]*Prisoners in 1980,* Bureau of Justice Statistics, Washington, D.C., May 1981, p. 3.

[23]Michael J. Mahoney, "The Search for a Better Way to Treat Criminals," *Chicago Tribune,* Aug. 26, 1980, sec. 5, p. 4.

[24]Robert E. Taylor, "Life in Prison," *The Wall Street Journal,* vol. 61, no. 215, New York, Aug. 18, 1981, p. 1.

[25]Walter L. Berkdall, "The Determinate Sentence and the Violent Offender: What Happens When the Time Runs Out?" *Federal Probation,* vol. 44, no. 2, Administrative Office of the United States Courts, Washington, D.C., June 1980, p. 20.

[26]Benjamin Frank, "The American Prison: The End of an Era," *Federal Probation,* vol. 43, no. 3, Administrative Office of the United States Courts, Washington, D.C., September 1979, p. 7.

isolation because of potential violence or uncontrolled criminal behavior, prisons as they exist today must continue.

WHAT KIND OF IMPRISONMENT?

Incapacitation

Drastic changes are difficult because of the widely publicized poor record of the past. Inadequately trained personnel carrying out poorly conceived and minimally supported programs cannot be expected to deliver the services necessary to redirect offenders. But correctional administrators can establish simple and practical goals that do not require a drastic change in institutional programs. Among these are the establishment of an adequate vocational and academic program, improved intergovernmental relations within the state department of corrections, organization of public education programs, modernization of outmoded organizational structures, and provision of adequate preservice and in-service training.

The use of maximum security prisons solely for the repetitively violent criminal would remove threatening inmates from the general prison population and thus allow security measures in other institutions to be reduced.[27] Inmates have stated, "In a closed prison, one spends every waking hour figuring out how to escape. In an open prison, one spends every waking hour figuring out how not to escape." Using maximum security prisons for violent criminals would allow the medium security prison to be open and free to concentrate on the reintegration of offenders into the community. After all, the purpose of the open prison is to place the responsibility for behavior control on the inmates themselves—not on prison personnel. Trying to train people to remain free while they are in conditions of captivity is sheer folly.

In the future, American prison administrators should look toward Denmark, which views incarceration in open prisons as a simple method of punishment. Abandoning the medical or treatment model of corrections, Danish prisons provide punishment in the form of simple deprivation of liberty. Humane conditions exist throughout, including coeducational prisons, conjugal visits which allow for normal sexual relations, frequent furloughs to the community, no inmate dress codes, abundant educational and vocational programs, and short sentences (average 3.4 months).[28]

In the United States the public, legislatures, and correctional personnel are unlikely to accept the economic, humanitarian, and reintegrative advantages of community-based corrections until it is proved that dangerous offenders can be safely locked away in maximum security institutions.[29]

---

[27]Norval Morris, *The Future of Imprisonment,* The University of Chicago Press, Chicago, 1974, p. 88.

[28]Mark Umbreit, "Danish Prisons and Community Alternatives: An American Perspective," *IHHA News,* Seattle, July-December 1979, p. 10.

[29]Simon Dinitz, Dangerous Offender Project, The Academy of Contemporary Problems, Columbus, Ohio, unpublished correspondence, Mar. 14, 1977.

Redirection

This does not mean that correctional administrators should decrease their efforts to deal constructively with offenders while they are in custody. Redirection should be retained as one of several potential useful purposes of correctional efforts. If it is not retained, administrators may discover that their correctional programs will be difficult to implement and absurdly expensive.[30]

Norval Morris suggests two principles on which to build a new model of imprisonment: (1) the substitution of voluntary change for coerced change; (2) the substitution of earlier graduated testing of the prisoner's fitness for increased increments of freedom in place of prediction of parole suitability. "Self-generation requires that the prisoner hold the key to his own prison," says Morris. He advocates using the reception and diagnostic center for estimating the release date and for conducting lengthy discussions with others about the programs which *may* be of assistance to the offender.

Morris recommends that nonviolent offenders be allowed to volunteer for the proposed institutions. They should be randomly selected, finally coming to institutions for a period of 4 to 6 weeks with the option of leaving after that time. Inmates who preferred to stay would be asked to negotiate a contract with prison personnel outlining the programs they chose to attend, parole dates, and various steps they would take on their way out of the institution—furloughs, work release, or transfer to a halfway house. Morris believes the reason for the failure of prisons is that the prisonization theory and the treatment ideology share a common misconception. Both assume that offenders are, to a large degree, passive respondents to outside forces beyond their control, reacting to the pains of imprisonment or being "pushed" toward behavior change by carefully selected treatment techniques.[31]

Correctional administrators must not forget that punishment is one purpose of the criminal justice system and that offenders are placed in prison to keep them away from the community. Yet these administrators can concentrate on behavior rather than on the punishment itself. They must encourage offenders to believe that people are ultimately responsible for their own behavior.

The general statements that prisons are bad for every prisoner or that "nothing works," as Martinson put it, are not true. A study released in 1980, disputing such contentions, agreed with other longitudinal studies reported in the literature: that two-thirds of all ex-inmates did not return to prison. Florida State University researchers Edwin L. Megargee and Barbara Cadow concluded from their study of 1008 admissions to the Federal Correctional Institution at Tallahassee, Florida, that 27.6 percent (278 men) of the prisoners were subsequently reimprisoned and 72.7 percent (730 men) avoided imprisonment. Of the 643 inmates questioned in this study, 84 percent reported that they had "changed for the better." Comparisons of personality tests administered upon

---

[30]Seymour L. Halleck and Ann B. Witte, "Is Rehabilitation Dead?" *Crime and Delinquency,* vol. 23, no. 4, October 1977, p. 382.
[31]Morris, *op. cit.,* pp. 31, 78, and 104.

entrance and upon departure showed improvement to be more common than deterioration.[32]

The Massachusetts Department of Corrections released findings in 1976 regarding recidivists from its state institutions. It was clear that a consistent reduction in recidivistic behavior is occurring in Massachusetts. Thirty percent of all inmates released in 1966 were reincarcerated. They were returned or sentenced to a state or federal correctional institution, a county house of correction, or a jail for 30 days or more. In the year 1971, however, the mean rate of recidivism was 25 percent and it continued to decline to 15 percent in 1977 and 16 percent in 1978 (see Table E.2.).[33]

A 5-year follow-up of Massachusetts prisoners revealed that prisoners released through a prerelease center experienced a lower recidivism rate (35 percent) than prisoners released from other institutions (45 percent) (see Table E.3).[34] The studies firmly demonstrated that furlough programs, prerelease programs, and use of minimum security institutions as transitional residences for prisoners were the most important variables accounting for the reduction in recidivism rates.

Another study by Daniel LeClair of 1719 inmates released from Massachusetts prisons in 1973 and 1974 revealed a significantly lower recidivism rate each year for inmates granted furloughs. In 1973, the rate for the furlough group was 16 percent—considerably lower than the 27 percent rate for the group released

---

[32]Edwin I. Megargee and Barbara Cadow, "The Ex-Offender and the 'Monster' Myth," *Federal Probation,* vol. 44, no. 1, Administrative Office of the United States Courts, Washington, D.C., March 1980, p. 34.

[33]Daniel P. LeClair, *An Analysis of Recidivism Rates Among Residents Released From Massachusetts Correctional Institutions During the Year 1973,* Massachusetts Department of Corrections, Boston, 1976, p. 11.

[34]Daniel P. LeClair, *Rates of Recidivism: A Five Year Follow-up,* Massachusetts Department of Corrections, October 1981, p. 10.

TABLE E.2
RECIDIVISM RATES OF INMATES IN
COMMUNITY PRERELEASE CENTERS IN
MASSACHUSETTS

Year	Rate
1966	30%
1971	25%
1972	22%
1973	19%
1974	19%
1975	20%
1976	16%

Source: Daniel P. LeClair, *An Analysis of Recidivism Rates Among Residents Released From Massachusetts Correctional Institutions During the Year 1973,* Massachusetts Department of Corrections, Boston, 1976, p. 11.

TABLE E.3
RECIDIVISM RATE BY PRERELEASE PARTICIPATION: 5-YEAR
FOLLOW-UP PERIOD

How released	Number	Percent	Recidivism rate
Through prerelease centers	108	(11)	35%
By other institutions	846	(89)	45%
Total	954	(100)	44%

Source: Daniel P. LeClair, *Rates of Recidivism: A Five Year Follow-up,*
Massachusetts Department of Corrections, October 1981, p. 10.

without furlough. The difference for inmates released in 1974 was equally significant—16 percent for the furlough group, compared with 31 percent for the nonfurlough group. By using a prediction device, LeClair also took into consideration (controlled the sample for) selection factors in the process of granting furloughs (see Table E.4).[35] A 5-year follow-up of participation in the furlough program in Massachusetts revealed similar differences (see Table E.5).[36]

A study of recidivism rates of Connecticut offenders concluded that incarcera-

---

[35]Daniel P. LeClair, "Home Furlough Program Effects on Rates of Recidivism," *Criminal Justice and Behavior,* vol. 5, no. 3, September 1978, pp. 254–255.
[36]LeClair, *Five Year Follow-up,* op. cit., p. 8.

TABLE E.4
EXPECTED AND ACTUAL RECIDIVISM RATES, BY
FURLOUGH PARTICIPATION

Group A: Male releasees in 1973	Expected recidivism rate	Actual recidivism rate
Receiving a furlough	25%	16%
Not receiving a furlough	27%	27%
All releasees	26%	19%
Group B: Male releasees in 1974		
Receiving a furlough	24%	16%
Not receiving a furlough	26%	31%
All releasees in 1974	25%	20%

Source: Daniel P. LeClair, *Community Reintegrating Prison Releasees: Results of the Massachusetts Experience,* Massachusetts Department of Corrections, Boston, March 1981, p. 8.

TABLE E.5
RECIDIVISM RATE, BY PARTICIPATION IN FURLOUGH
PROGRAM: 5-YEAR FOLLOW-UP

	Number	Percent	Recidivism rate
Furlough participants	661	(69)	40%
Nonparticipants	290	(31)	52%
Total sample	951	(100)	44%

Source: Daniel P. LeClair, *Rates of Recidivism: A Five Year Follow-up*, Massachusetts Department of Corrections, Boston, October 1981, p. 9.

tion is no better than noninstitutional treatment at preventing recidivism and may actually be worse.[37]

Restitution

In the future the criminal justice system will be as concerned about the victim as it is about the criminal. Each offender will be expected to assume responsibility for the harm caused by his or her criminal behavior. Restitution and victim compensation will be part of the offender's sentence.

Restitution has been defined as a requirement imposed by agents of the criminal justice system by which an offender engages in acts designed to make reparation for the harm resulting from the criminal offense. Restitution is sometimes applied in pretrial diversion programs to provide an alternative to imprisonment and is often a condition of probation or part of a community correction center's program.[38]

Practically, correctional restitution is a process of establishing a relationship between the offender and the victim; it is designed to raise the offender's sense of responsibility to society through personal responsibility to the victim.[39] Although the practice has received increased emphasis in recent years, its origin can be traced to the ancient Greeks and Hebrews, who frequently imposed restitution to increase the severity of the criminal's punishment rather than to aid the victim. The Law of Moses required fourfold restitution for a stolen sheep and fivefold restitution for a stolen ox.[40]

Many states have excluded certain offenders from participation in restitution programs. Maine declared the following ineligible: (1) an offender convicted of a violent crime, (2) an offender who has detainers or cases pending, (3) an

[37]Andrew Hopkins, "Imprisonment and Recidivism: A Quasi-Experimental Study," *Journal of Crime and Delinquency*, vol. 13, no. 1, January 1976, p. 27.

[38]Burt Galaway, "The Use of Restitution," *Crime and Delinquency*, vol. 23, no. 1, January 1977, p. 59.

[39]Romina R. Deming, "Correctional Restitution: A Strategy for Correctional Conflict Management," *Federal Probation*, vol. 40, no. 3, Administrative Office of the United States Courts, Washington, D.C., September 1976, p. 27.

[40]Stephen Schafer, *Restitution to Victims of Crimes*, Quadrangle Books, Inc., Chicago, 1960, p. 3.

offender convicted of an offense in which a firearm or other dangerous weapon was used, (4) an offender who has three or more previous felony convictions, and (5) an offender who is currently a probationer or parolee at the judge's discretion.[41] Maine's restrictions are similar to those of other states.

Two examples of restitution centers exist in Minnesota and Georgia. The one in Minnesota provides a diversion from state institutions for property offenders. Felons are placed in community-based residences whose personnel recognize the right of the victim to be compensated for his or her loss as a result of criminal activity. A restitution contract is negotiated between the victim and the offender. Both control and support are given the offender through group meetings, drug and alcohol monitoring, and intensive parole or probation supervision. Between August 1, 1972, and July 1975, eighty-seven offenders were diverted from various correctional institutions in Minnesota to the restitution center. These offenders completed restitution payments totaling $14,600.[42]

Georgia's program provides inmates leaving prison with four alternative restitution shelter centers in Albany, Atlanta, Macon, and Rome. Each center has a capacity for twenty to forty residents. The offenders work at jobs in the free community, make restitution to the victims of their crimes, and contribute to the cost of their own upkeep. Offenders save money for their release and assume payments for the welfare of their families. Two forms of restitution are required. One is tangible restitution or a cash payment to the victim of the crime. The other is symbolic, i.e., services furnished the victim, such as home maintenance, or unpaid work in community settings such as hospitals, churches, nursing homes, or children's homes.[43] Between July 1975 and December 1976, a total of $126,897 was paid to crime victims by inmates housed in Georgia's shelter centers.

Georgia's program carries out the concept of creative restitution. This is a process by which offenders, with assistance from correctional personnel, find some way to make amends to those they have hurt.[44] Creative restitution may take three forms: (1) monetary payments to victims, (2) service to victims, and (3) service to the general community.

Characteristics of creative restitution: (1) It represents an effort on the part of the offender. (2) The activity has socially constructive consequences. (3) The consequences are related to the offense. (4) The relationship between the offense and restitution is reparative and restorative. (5) The reparation endeavors to leave the situation better than before the offense was committed.[45]

Although restitution is being accepted as a viable reaction to criminal

[41]Charles Sharpe, Director, Maine Restitution Research Project, personal correspondence, May 11, 1977.

[42]Robert M. Mowat, *Final Report: Minnesota Restitution Center,* Minnesota Department of Corrections, St. Paul, September 1975, pp. 5, 7.

[43]Sara Passmore, Public Information, Department of Corrections, Offender Rehabilitation, State of Georgia, unpublished correspondence, Aug. 22, 1975.

[44]Joe Hudson and Burt Galaway, "Undoing the Wrong," *Social Work,* vol. 19, no. 3, May 1974, pp. 313–314.

[45]Albert Eglash, "Creative Restitution: Some Suggestions for Prison Rehabilitation Programs," *American Journal of Correction,* vol. 20, no. 6, November–December 1958, p. 20.

behavior, a number of practical problems in its administration have arisen. Some of these are agreement on the amount of restitution, enforcement of the program, and determination of the degree of victim culpability. At least one observer of restitution programs, Burt Galaway, believes sufficient experience is available to resolve many of the practical issues involved.[46]

As part of this effort, some states have added a victim-offender mediation service, whereby a trained neutral third party facilitates a face-to-face encounter between victim and offender. During the meeting, facts and feelings about the crime are discussed and agreements concerning the conditions of restitution are worked out.[47]

Correctional administrators suggest that the value of including restitution as part of a reintegrative program is fourfold: (1) It requires prisoners to accept responsibility for their actions through the relationship with the victims. (2) It aids the victims themselves. (3) It eases society's pain and desire for revenge. (4) It provides a positive influence on the prisoners. As criminologist Edwin Sutherland stated many years ago, "It is rather absurd that the state undertakes to protect the public against crime and then, when a loss occurs, takes the entire payment and offers no effective remedy to the individual victim."[48]

Victim Compensation and Aid

Another form of assistance to victims is government payment of compensation. In January 1981, twenty-five states were operating state crime victims' compensation programs. Since 1965, when California legislators enacted a compensation law, many other states have passed laws providing funds for medical costs, survivor benefits, loss of wages, and attorneys' fees. The lowest maximum compensation amount is $10,000, applied in ten states. Maryland allows unlimited permanent disability and death benefits, and $45,000 for other injuries.[49]

Physical and financial injuries to victims are easy to see. But victims of crime often suffer injuries that are not observable. They may lose their capacity to trust people. They may be overwhelmed by feelings of guilt and shame. Their relationships with loved ones may be disrupted.

In 1977, there were 40.3 million crime victims in the United States—a rate of approximately 140 per 1000 people. In about 40 percent of all crimes, the security of homes was violated. Approximately 240 of every 1000 households were broken into or had cars stolen.[50]

---

[46]Burt Galaway, "Is Restitution Practical?" *Federal Probation,* vol. 41, no. 3, Administrative Office of the United States Courts, Washington, D.C., September 1977, pp. 3–7.

[47]"Victim-Offender Mediation Service Soon to Be Available in Wichita," *Newsletter,* vol. 8, no. 1, Kansas Council on Crime and Delinquency, Wichita, January 1981, p. 3.

[48]Edwin H. Sutherland, *Principles of Criminology,* J. B. Lippincott Company, Chicago, 1939, p. 576.

[49]John Blackmore, "Paying the Price of Crime," *Corrections Magazine,* vol. 6, no. 5, October 1980, pp. 38–39.

[50]Arnold J. Hopkins, "Victim Service Programs in Probation Agencies," *Proceedings of the One Hundred and Tenth Annual Congress of Corrections,* American Correctional Association, College Park, Md., 1981, p. 159.

Partially in response to the widespread incidents of crime, victim services programs blossomed throughout the United States in the 1970s. They sought to assist victims in their five areas of need: medical treatment, protection, economic restoration, counseling, and information. Victim services programs were operated by district attorneys' offices, law enforcement agencies, private agencies, and probation departments. The State of Minnesota Department of Corrections has programs for battered women, victims of sexual assault, and families of incest offenders.[51]

A typical victim aid program is operated by the Fresno County, California, probation department. Within 48 hours after a violent crime has been reported to a law enforcement agency, a victim counselor tries to contact victims. Crisis intervention counseling is offered. Referrals to helping agencies in the community are made. Assistance during court proceedings is given. Sometimes merely explaining the court process is sufficient; other times the counselor may actually accompany the victim to court. Information is given regarding the state compensation program. Special services may be required, such as moving fearful victims to safer locations, helping clean up residences after a crime has been committed, and attending funerals or family gatherings with victims.[52]

THE FUTURE OF COMMUNITY-FOCUSED CORRECTIONS

Current Status

The growth of community-based corrections has been phenomenal. By 1980 there were thirty-one alternatives to incarceration. Some are commonly known, such as halfway houses, work release, furloughs, and parole. In another class are sentencing alternatives such as restitution, probation, and shock probation. Pretrial diversions constitute a third class. Some of these represent the best in correctional program innovations. A number of cities (San Francisco, Boston, Atlanta, Kansas City, Los Angeles, and Columbus, Ohio) use volunteers to mediate the resolution of cases outside the criminal court. New York permits judges to suspend prosecution for 6 months by ordering the defendant to refrain from crime or to make restitution to the victim. Other diversion projects refer offenders to job placement agencies or drug abuse treatment centers.

Since 1970 the popularity of prerelease programs has grown immensely. It is estimated that there are 2200 prerelease facilities in the country. Six hundred are exclusively for adults and treat 30,000 to 40,000 offenders a day. The United States Bureau of Prisons serves 3000 offenders daily in its community treatment centers. According to 1980 Bureau statistics, 51 percent of all recently released federal prisoners were released through community treatment centers.[53] Federal Bureau prisons have managed to decrease their population from 30,269 at the

[51]*1979–1980 Biennial Report,* Minnesota Department of Corrections, St. Paul, 1980, p. 11.

[52]James Rowland, "Probation and Victim Services," *Proceedings of the One Hundred and Tenth Annual Congress of Corrections,* American Correctional Association, College Park, Md., 1981, pp. 192–194.

[53]John Blackmore, "Community Corrections," *Corrections Magazine,* vol. 6, no. 5, October 1980, pp. 9–10.

end of fiscal year 1977 to 27,112 on November 8, 1978, by using halfway houses and encouraging a decrease in commitments by federal courts.[54] As of July 1, 1980, there were 11,809 men and women offenders living in community-based residences. There were 9791 assigned to work release status and 8926 involved in furlough programs.[55]

Potential Unrealized

Despite the widespread popularity of community-based corrections, its potential has not been realized because of the fragmentation and lack of continuity. As Jerome Miller has said, "The present system is characterized by gaps, duplications, and cross-purposes among the different services and levels of government." The state of Minnesota has endeavored to eliminate the fragmentation by legislating a comprehensive program through a financial payment to counties opting to develop local corrections programs. The state corrections department oversees coordination among counties. Even though fewer than half of Minnesota's county governments have volunteered to enter the program, commitments to state institutions decreased for a while after the legislation was passed.[56]

Fiscal Concerns

Legislation like that passed in Minnesota was subsequently copied in other states, such as Kansas and Iowa, and is essential to the future of community-based corrections. Tax-cutting initiatives, such as Proposition 13 in California, have reduced the amount of state and local funding available. Conservative fiscal policies continue to issue from the federal government.

The largest single source of federal funds for community-based corrections—the Law Enforcement Assistance Administration (LEAA)—was discontinued in September 1981. This organization was created by the Omnibus Crime Control and Safe Streets Act of 1968, which stated, "Crime is essentially a local problem that must be dealt with by state and local government if it is to be controlled effectively." Through 1978 Congress had granted more than $6 billion to be awarded to state and local governments to improve police, courts, and correctional systems; to combat juvenile delinquency; and to finance crime-fighting projects. Under heavy attack in recent years because of alleged waste of money, top-heavy bureaucracy, unproductive programs, and emphasis on law enforcement hardware, the LEAA had been faced with extinction or financial starvation by Congress each time its budget was reviewed.[57] LEAA provided more than 600

---

[54]"Federal Prisons: The End of Overcrowding," *Institutions, Etc.,* Institutions, Etc., Washington, D.C., January 1979, p. 14.

[55]*American Correctional Association Directory 1981,* American Correctional Association, College Park, Md., 1981, p. XII.

[56]Blackmore, op. cit., p. 12.

[57]*The Law Enforcement Assistance Administration: A Partnership for Crime Control,* U.S. Government Printing Office, Washington, D.C., 1978, p. 1.

million for community-based corrections projects. Without these funds, the stimulus for innovative correctional programs will be lacking.

Two observers of correctional trends are reformers William Nagel and Robert Smith, assistant director of the National Institute of Corrections. They believe that state legislators and correctional administrators, disgusted with building new, expensive prisons, will look to community-based corrections as the most cost-effective solution. Encouragement is the assumption of costs by state and local governments of projects previously funded by LEAA, such as the Fort Des Moines Project in Iowa (see Chapter 4).

People who think that the fiscal constrictions represented by California's Proposition 13 will force criminal justice administrators to streamline operations could be badly disappointed. A report from the Rand Corporation suggests that, at least during Proposition 13's first year, the trend was toward a "less humane and less responsive system." Based on extensive budget analysis and interviews in selected counties and cities, they found that "innovation and efficiency in local government have been stymied." Rand reported that many agencies simply did less and did it less well. Police and prosecutors ignored less serious crimes; probation involved fewer services and more surveillance; courts increasingly considered cost in their decisions about due process. The Rand analysis concluded that a criminal justice system more narrowly focused on the more serious cases and harshest penalties may have been just what the proponents of Proposition 13 wanted.[58]

CONCLUSION

"The authors found no significant differences in subsequent arrests or convictions between the two groups." This statement is repeated time and time again as a conclusion to studies of community-based corrections programs. It does not matter whether the study examined work release, parole, or restitution—the conclusion is the same: offenders who are assigned to community-based programs do not commit more crimes than other offenders. Occasionally, as in Massachusetts, the results appear even to favor community-based corrections as a way to reduce recidivism.[59]

In the future, prisons will house only dangerous offenders—men and women who cannot control their behavior or who are potentially violent. Even Karl Menninger has stated, "Some kind of detention is necessary for some people. I think prison terms for some people should even be longer than they are."[60]

Community-based corrections will be used for all offenders who do not pose a

---

[58]Warren Walker, Jan Michael Chaiken, Anthony Jiga, and Sandra Segal Polin, *The Impact of Proposition 13 on Local Criminal Justice Agencies: Emerging Patterns,* Rand Corporation, Santa Monica, Calif., 1980.

[59]John Blackmore, "Does Community Corrections Work?" *Corrections Magazine,* vol. 7, no. 5, October 1981, pp. 18–19.

[60]Karl Menninger, "A Conversation with Karl Menninger," *Psychology Today,* 1968, p. 58.

physical threat to society—if for no other reason than that it is cheaper. Or as Menninger stated,

> "Thousands of others ought not to be in prison at all. . . . They could be out on supervised parole earning a living. . . . What business has a forger in prison? He's not violent. He's not dangerous. Prisons won't keep him from forging checks when he is released. It just keeps him out of circulation for a while. Why not give the forger a suspended sentence, make him report regularly to his parole officer and make him bear all the costs of his forgery? He could make double restitution for the check and pay the state for all expenses of his arrest and trial."[61]

These days it can cost as much as $70,000 a bed to build a prison, compared with $14,400 a bed for a halfway house. The average annual per capita cost of imprisoning a person jumped from $3971 in 1970 to more than $10,000 in 1979,[62] while the cost of maintaining an offender in community-based residences is 25 to 40 percent lower.

At least one study tried to figure the hidden costs of incarceration. Researchers Val Clear, Scott Clear, and Todd Clear calculated that each male inmate in Indiana deprived the state and federal government of $1,828.56 per person for his family every year. These costs included aid to families with dependent children, Medicaid, and food stamps. In addition, the state of Indiana paid $6,055.35 a year to keep each inmate in prison. The total cost to the state and the federal government for each Indiana prisoner was $8,517.65.[63]

Even if determinate sentences were adopted by all states, the options available under the umbrella of community-based corrections would be applicable. Offenders convicted of nonviolent crimes would be placed on probation for a specified period. After serving time in an institution, they would be put under mandatory release. They would be sent to prerelease centers or halfway houses. They would be allowed to use furloughs and work release as they prepared for total freedom.

Corrections focusing on the community will prevail. Enlightened government officials and private citizen groups will be able to convince the general public and the legislature of the efficiency of community-based corrections. As the demand for accountability reveals the cost benefits, legislatures will respond. They will realize the economic advantages of utilizing community resources rather than re-creating a different kind of community in an institution. As the demand for standards in corrections forces in-house cleaning by correctional officials themselves, the public will gain greater respect for corrections practices. As evalua-

---

[61]Reprinted from *Psychology Today* Magazine Copyright © 1969 Ziff Davis Publishing Co., p. 59.

[62]Sam Smith, "State Prisons Bulge; Time Served Shrinks," *Chicago Tribune,* Dec. 4, 1980, Sec. 6, p. 6.

[63]Val Clear, Scott Clear, and Todd Clear, *Eight Million Dollars: The Hidden Costs of Incarceration,* Anderson College, Anderson, Ind., 1977, pp. 1–3, 5.

tions of community-based corrections continue, administrators will discover that recidivism rates are not increasing. Then we will deal with criminals according to Norval Morris's standard: "Power over a criminal's life should not be taken in excess of that which would be taken were his reform not considered as one of our purposes."[64] And we will deal with crime as we do with all other social problems—in the community.

---

[64]Norval Morris and Colin Howard, *Studies in Criminal Law,* Clarendon Press, Oxford, 1964, p. 175.

BIBLIOGRAPHY

Agopian, Michael W.: "Evaluation of Adult Diversion Programs: The California Experience," *Federal Probation,* volume 41, no. 3, Administrative Office of the United States Courts, Washington, D.C., September 1977, pp. 15–18.

"Alaska's Correctional Plan Weathers Criticisms Over Unique Facility," *American Journal of Correction,* vol. 37, no. 2, March-April 1975, pp. 22–24.

Alaska Division of Corrections: *South Central Regional Correctional Institution,* Anchorage, January 1971.

Alders, Donald D., and Peter Hemingway: "Colorado Launches Program Aimed at Reducing Recidivism," *American Journal of Correction,* August 1975, pp. 38–39, 64.

Alper, Benedict S.: *Prisons Inside Out,* Ballinger Publishing Company, Cambridge, Mass., 1974, chap. 5.

American Bar Association, Special Committee on Minimum Standards for the Administration of Criminal Justice: *Sentencing Alternatives and Procedures,* New York, 1968.

American Correctional Association: *Manual of Correctional Standards,* American Correctional Association, New York, 1975.

Banks, Jerry, Terry R. Siler, and Ronald L. Rardin: "Past and Present Findings on Intensive Adult Probation," *Federal Probation,* vol. 41, no. 2, Administrative Office of the United States Courts, Washington, D.C., June 1977, pp. 20–25.

Barnes, Harry Elmer, and Negley K. Teeters: *New Horizons in Criminology,* Prentice-Hall, Inc., Englewood Cliffs, N.J., 1963, chap. 35.

Barnett, Jacob B., and David H. Gronewold: "Confidentiality of the Pre-sentence report," *Federal Probation,* vol. 26, no. 1, Administrative Office of the United States Courts, Washington, D.C., March 1962, pp. 26–30.

Bartell, Ted, and L. Thomas Winfree, Jr.: "Recidivist Impacts of Differential Sentencing for Burglary Offenders," *Criminology,* vol. 15, no. 3, November 1977, pp. 387–396.

Bartollas, Clemens: *Introduction to Corrections,* Harper & Row, Publishers, Incorporated, New York, 1981.

Beckley, Loren A., Christine Callahan, and Robert M. Carter: "The Pre-sentence Investigation Report Program: A Preliminary Report," *Corrections Today,* vol. 42, no. 1, January-February 1980, pp. 10, 12, 15, 20, and 21.

Berkdall, Walter L.: "The Determinate Sentence and the Violent Offender: What Happens When the Time Runs Out?" *Federal Probation,* vol. 44, no. 2, Administrative Office of the United States Courts, Washington, D.C., June 1980, pp. 18–24.

Berkley, George E., Michael W. Giles, Jerry F. Hackett, and Norman C. Kassoff: *Introduction to Criminal Justice,* Holbrook Press, Inc., Boston, 1976.

Berry, Graham: "With Justice for All," *Modern Maturity,* vol. 24, no. 2, February-March 1981, pp. 53–57.

Besharov, Douglas J.: *Juvenile Justice Advocacy: Practice in a Unique Court,* Practicing Law Institute, New York, 1974.

Beshears, Earl: "Translating Policy to Procedure: Participatory Management in Corrections," *Federal Probation,* vol. 42, no. 3, Administrative Office of the United States Courts, Washington, D.C., September 1978, pp. 51–56.

Beto, George J.: "Correction Change Must Be Evolutionary," *American Journal of Correction,* vol. 36, no. 5, September-October 1974, p. 34.

Biles, David: "Crime and the Use of Prisons," *Federal Probation,* vol. 43, no. 2, Administrative Office of the United States Courts, Washington, D.C., June 1979, pp. 39–42.

Blackmore, John: "Community Corrections," *Corrections Magazine,* vol. 6, no. 5, October 1980, pp. 4–14.

Broom, Leonard, and Philip Selznick: *Sociology,* Harper & Row, Publishers, Incorporated, New York, 1963, pp. 114–123.

Brown, Bailey: "Community Service as a Condition of Probation," *Federal Probation,* vol. 41, no. 4, Administrative Office of the United States Courts, Washington, D.C., December 1977, pp. 7–9.

Brown, Lawrence D.: "The Development of a Parolee Classification System Using Discriminant Analysis," *Journal of Research in Crime and Delinquency,* vol. 15, no. 1, January 1978, pp. 92–108.

Burdman, Milton: "Ethnic Self-Help Groups in Prison and on Parole," *Crime and Delinquency,* vol. 20, no. 2, April 1974, pp. 107–118.

Burke, Peter E.: "Prison Reform in Sweden," *American Journal of Correction,* vol. 30, no. 3, May-June 1968, pp. 18–19.

Burns, Henry F.: *Corrections—Organization and Administration,* West Publishing Company, St. Paul, Minn., 1975.

Buss, Hero: *In for Repairs,* National Department of Corrections, Stockholm, Sweden, 1969.

Cahalan, Margaret: "Trends in Incarceration in the United States Since 1880," *Crime and Delinquency,* vol. 21, no. 1, January 1979, pp. 9–41.

Caldwell, Robert G.: *Criminology,* Ronald Press Company, New York, 1965, chaps. 26 and 27.

Calvin, Craig R., and John G. Cull: "Eligibility Determination of the Public Offender," in Richard E. Hardy and John G. Cull (eds.): *Introduction to Correctional Rehabilitation,* Charles C Thomas, Publisher, Springfield, Ill., 1973, chap. 12.

Canadian Penitentiary Service, Public Affairs Division, "Canada Launches New Approach to Inmate Employment," *American Journal of Correction,* vol. 38, no. 6, November-December 1976, pp. 10, 28.

Carlson, Eric: "Field Testing Pre-release Centers," *Corrections Today,* vol. 42, no. 1, January-February 1980, pp. 16, 24–25, 38, and 47.

Carlson, Norman: "Concern Shown—But Problem Goes Unsolved," *American Journal of Correction,* vol. 39, no. 4, July-August 1977, p. 28.

Carney, Francis L.: "The Indeterminate Sentence at Patuxent," *Crime and Delinquency,* vol. 20, no. 2, April 1974, pp. 135–143.

Carney, Louis B.: *Introduction to Correctional Science,* McGraw-Hill Book Company, New York, 1974, chaps. 10 and 13, pp. 2–11, 330.

Carter, Robert M., and Leslie T. Wilkins: *Probation, Parole, and Community Corrections,* John Wiley & Sons, Inc., New York, 1976.

—— and ——: *Probation and Parole: Selected Readings,* John Wiley & Sons, Inc., New York, 1970.

Carter, Timothy J.: "Juvenile Court Dispositions: A Comparison of Status and Non Status Offenders," *Criminology,* vol. 17, no. 3, November 1979, pp. 341–359.

Cavan, Ruth Shonle: *Criminology,* Thomas Y. Crowell Company, New York, 1958, chaps. 14, 19, and 20.

Center for Studies of Crime and Delinquency: *Graduated Release,* Rockville, Md., 1971.

Chaiklin, Harris: "Developing Correctional Social Services," in Albert R. Roberts (ed.): *Correctional Treatment of the Offender,* Charles C Thomas, Publisher, Springfield, Ill., 1974, pp. 294–308.

Chamelin, Neil C., Vernon B. Fo, and Paul M. Whisenand: *Introduction to Criminal Justice,* Prentice-Hall, Inc., Englewood Cliffs, N.J., 1975, chaps. 2 and 3.

Chaneles, Sol: *The Open Prison,* Dial Press, New York, 1973.

Children's Bureau, United States Department of Health, Education and Welfare: *Institutions Serving Delinquent Children: Guides and Goals,* U.S. Government Printing Office, Washington, D.C., 1957.

Clendenen, Richard J., James P. Cullen, and Melvin B. Goldberg: "Legal Assistance to Delinquents," *Federal Probation,* vol. 41, no. 3, Administrative Office of the United States Courts, Washington, D.C., September 1977, pp. 8–15.

Coffey, Alan R.: *Administration of Criminal Justice,* Prentice-Hall, Inc., Englewood Cliffs, N.J., 1974, chap. 12.

Coffey, Alan, Edward Eldefonso, and Walter Hartinger: *An Introduction to the Criminal Justice System and Process,* Prentice-Hall, Inc., Englewood Cliffs, N.J., 1974, pp. 269–277.

Cole, George F.: *The American System of Criminal Justice,* Duxbury Press, North Scituate, Mass., 1975.

"Community Corrections: A Cheaper and More Humane Approach," in George G. Killinger and Paul L. Cromwell (eds.): *Penology,* West Publishing Company, St. Paul, Minn., 1973, pp. 382–388.

Contact, Inc.: *Let the Punishment Fit the Crime,* Lincoln, Neb., May 1978.

Corbett, Jacqueline, and Thomas S. Vereb: *Juvenile Court Statistics,* Law Enforcement Assistance Administration, United States Department of Justice, Washington, D.C., 1977.

Cory, Bruce: "Texas vs. Brother Roloff," *Corrections Magazine,* vol. 5, no. 3, September 1979, pp. 20–24.

Cressey, Donald R.: "Theoretical Foundation for Using Criminals in the Rehabilitation of Criminals," *The Future of Imprisonment in a Free Society,* vol. 2, St. Leonard's House, Chicago, 1965, pp. 87–101.

Crime and Delinquency in California, 1976, Department of Justice, Division of Law Enforcement, Bureau of Criminal Statistics, Sacramento, August 1977.

Culbertson, Robert G.: "The Effect of Institutionalization on the Delinquent Inmate's Self Concept," *Journal of Criminal Law, Criminology, and Police Science,* vol. 66, no. 1, March 1975, pp. 88–93.

Dietrich, Shelle G.: "The Probation Office as a Therapist: Examination of Three Major Problem Areas," *Federal Probation,* vol. 43, no. 2, Administrative Office of the United States Courts, Washington, D.C., June 1979, pp. 14–19.

Dressler, David: *Practice and Theory of Probation and Parole,* Columbia University Press, New York, 1951.

Edwards, George: "Parole," in Sol Rubin (ed.): *The Law of Criminal Correction,* West Publishing Company, St. Paul, Minn., 1963, chap. 15.

———: "Penitentiaries Produce No Penitents," *Criminology, Criminal Law, and Police Science,* vol. 63, no. 2, 1972, pp. 154–161.

Eichman, Charles J.: *The Impact of the Gideon Decision Upon Crime and Sentencing in Florida: A Study of Recidivism and Sociocultural Change,* Florida Division of Corrections, Tallahassee, 1966, research monograph no. 2.

Emshoff, James G., and William S. Davidson, II: "Training Prison Inmates as Paralegals: An Experimental Project," *Journal of Crime and Justice,* vol. 8, no. 1, 1980, pp. 27–38.

England, W. Ralph, Jr.: "What Is Responsible for Satisfactory Probation and Post Probation Outcome?" *Journal of Criminal Law, Criminology, and Police Science,* vol. 47, no. 6, April 1957, pp. 667–676.

Ericsson, Carl Henrik: *Labor Market Wages for Prisoners,* National Correctional Association, Stockholm, Sweden, December 1972, pp. 1–4.

Exemplary Projects, National Institute of Law Enforcement and Criminal Justice, Law Enforcement Assistance Administration, Washington, D.C., September 1977.

Felkenes, George T.: *The Criminial Justice System: Its Functions and Personnel,* Prentice-Hall, Inc., Englewood Cliffs, N.J., 1973, chap. 15.

Figueiria-McDonough, Josefina, and Elaine Selo: "A Reformation of the 'Equal Opportunity' Explanation of Female Delinquency," *Crime and Delinqency,* vol. 26, no. 3, July 1980, pp. 333–343.

Flynn, Edith E.: "Social Planning and the Concept of Reintegration," in Edward Sagarin and Donal E. J. MacNamara (eds.): *Corrections: Problems of Punishment and Rehabilitation,* Praeger Publishers, New York, 1973, chap. 2, pp. 8–17.

The Fortune Society: "Championing the Ex-Offender," *Corrections Magazine,* vol. 1,, no. 5, May-June 1975, pp. 13–20.

Fox, Vernon: *Community-Based Corrections,* Prentice-Hall, Inc., Englewood Cliffs, N.J., 1977.

———: *Introduction to Corrections,* Prentice-Hall, Inc., Englewood Cliffs, N.J., 1977, chap. 5, 10, 12, and 15.

Frazier, Charles E., E. Wilbur Bock, and John C. Henretta: "Pretrial Release and Bail Decisions," *Criminology,* vol. 18, no. 2, August 1980, pp. 162–181.

Fried, Frederick: "Psychiatric Consultation and Adult Probation Case Management," *Federal Probation,* vol. 37, no. 2, Administrative Office of the United States Courts, Washington, D.C., June 1973, pp. 12–14.

Friedman, Sidney, and T. Conway Esselstyn: "The Adjustment of Children of Jail Inmates," *Federal Probation,* vol. 29, no. 4, Administrative Office of the United States Courts, Washington, D.C., December 1965, pp. 55–59.

Fry, Margaret: *Arms of the Law,* Howard League for Penal Reform, Gallancz Publishing Company, London, 1951.

Galaway, Burt, Joe Hudson, and C. David Hollister (eds.): *Community Corrections,* Charles C Thomas, Publisher, Springfield, Ill., 1976.

Galvin, John J.: "Progressive Development in Pre-release Preparation," in Leonard J. Hippchen (ed.): *Correctional Classification and Treatment,* W. H. Anderson Company, Cincinnati, 1975, pp. 221–228.

Gasaway, Donald D.: "The Probation Officer as Employment Counselor, " *Federal Probation,* vol. 41, no. 2, Administrative Office of the United States Courts, Washington, D.C., June 1977, pp. 43–44.

Gibbons, Don C.: *Changing the Lawbreaker,* Prentice-Hall, Inc., Englewood Cliffs, N.J., 1965.

Glaser, Daniel: *The Effectiveness of a Prison and Parole System,* The Bobbs-Merrill Company, Inc., Indianapolis, 1964.

———: "The Prison of the Future," in Robert M. Carter, Daniel Glaser, and Leslie T. Wilkins (eds.): *Correctional Institutions,* J. B. Lippincott Company, New York, 1972, pp. 428–432.

Glueck, Sheldon, and Eleanor T. Glueck: *500 Criminal Careers,* Alfred A. Knopf, Inc., New York, 1930.

Goldfarb, Ronald L., and Linda R. Singer: *After Conviction,* Simon and Schuster, New York, 1973.

Goodstein, Lynne: "Inmate Adjustment to Prison and the Transition to Community Life," *Journal of Research in Crime and Delinquency,* vol. 16, no. 2, July 1979, pp. 246–272.

Gottfredson, Michael R.: "Study of Parole Boards Using Parole Decision Guidelines Confirms a Considerable Reduction in Parole Disparity," *Journal of Research in Crime and Delinquency,* vol. 16, no. 2, July 1979, pp. 218–231.

Graham, Gary, and Herbert R. Sigurdson: "An Organization Development Experience in Probation: 'Old Dogs' Can Learn New Tricks," *Federal Probation,* vol. 44, no. 1, Administrative Office of the United States Courts, Washington, D.C., March 1980, pp. 3–12.

Gray, Charles M.: "Costs of Crime, Review and Overview," in Charles M. Gray (ed.): *Costs of Crime,* Sage Publications, Inc., Beverly Hills, Calif., 1979.

Gula, Martin: *Agency Operated Group Homes,* U.S. Government Printing Office, Washington, D.C., 1964.

Hackler, James C.: "Evaluation of Delinquency Prevention Programs: Ideals and Compromises," *Federal Probation,* vol. 31, no. 1, Administrative Office of the United States Courts, Washington, D.C., March 1967, pp. 22–26.

Hahr, Nicholas: "Too Dumb to Know Better," *Criminology,* vol. 18, no. 1, May 1980, pp. 3–25.

Halleck, Seymour L.: *Psychiatry and the Dilemmas of Crime,* Harper & Row, Publishers, Incorporated, New York, 1967.

———, and Ann D. Witte: "Is Rehabilitation Dead?" *Crime and Delinquency,* vol. 23, no. 4, October 1977, pp. 372–382.

Heilman, Charles E.: "Open Prisons, British Style," *The Prison Journal,* vol. LVIII, no. 2, 1978, pp. 3–17.

Hemple, William E., and William H. Webb, Jr.: "Researching Prediction Scales for Probation," *Federal Probation,* vol. 40, no. 2, Administrative Office of the United States Courts, Washington, D.C., June 1976, pp. 33–37.

Hoffman, Peter B.: "Mandatory Release: A Measure of Type II Error," *Criminology,* vol. 11, no. 1, February 1974, pp. 547ff.

Hood, Robert Allen: "Correcting Correctional Education," *Corrections Today,* vol. 42, no. 3, May-June 1980, pp. 72–73.

Inciardi, James A.: *Careers in Crime,* Rand-McNally & Company, Chicago, 1975.

James, Howard: *The Little Victims,* David McKay Company, Inc., New York, 1975.

Jensen, Richard, and Kenneth L. Westby: "Correction Center Dedicated: Governor Views It As Model for Minnesota and Nation," *American Journal of Correction,* vol. 38, no. 2, March-April 1976, p. 34.

Johnson, Elmer Hubert: *Crime, Correction and Society,* Dorsey Press, Homewood, Ill., 1964, chaps. 25, 26, and 27, pp. 638–704.

Johnson, Richard E.: "Social Class and Delinquent Behavior," *Criminology,* vol. 18, no. 1, May 1980, pp. 86–93.

Jones, Jennifer, and William Thornton: "Women's Liberation and the Female Delinquent," *Journal of Research in Crime and Delinquency,* vol. 17, no. 2, July 1980, pp. 230–244.

Joseph, Herman, and Vincent P. Dole: "Methadone Patients on Probation and Parole," *Federal Probation,* vol. 34, no. 2, Administrative Office of the United States Courts, Washington, D.C., June 1970, pp. 42–48.

Kaplan, John: *Criminal Justice: Introductory Cases and Materials,* Foundation Press, Inc., Mineola, N.Y., 1973.

Kazmier, L. J.: *Principles of Management,* McGraw-Hill Book Company, 1969.

Keldgord, Robert E., and Robert O. Norris: "New Directions for Corrections," *Federal Probation,* vol. 36, no. 1, Administrative Office of the United States Courts, Washington, D.C., March 1972, pp. 3–9.

Kerper, Hazel B.: *Introduction to the Criminal Justice System,* West Publishing Company, St. Paul, Minn., 1972, pp. 327–343, 366–375.

Keve, Paul H.: *Imaginative Programming in Probation and Parole,* University of Minnesota Press, Minneapolis, 1967, 6 and 9.

———: "Sentencing—The Need for Alternatives," *Judicature,* vol. 53, no. 2, August-September 1969, pp. 54–57.

Kiersh, Ed: "Helping Juveniles by Helping Their Families," *Corrections Magazine,* vol. 5, no. 4, December 1979, pp. 54–61.

Killinger, George G., Hazel B. Kerper, and Paul F. Cromwell, Jr.: *Probation and Parole in the Criminal Justice System,* West Publishing Company, St. Paul, Minn., 1976, Pt. II.

Klass, James D., and Joan Karan: "Community Intervention for Reluctant Clients," *Federal Probation,* vol. 43, no. 4, Administrative Office of the United States Courts, Washington, D.C., December 1979, pp. 37–42.

Klein, Helen A.: "Towards More Effective Behavioral Programs for Juvenile Offenders," *Federal Probation,* vol. 41, no. 2, Administrative Office of the United States Courts, Washington, D.C., June 1977, pp. 45–50.

Kuharich, Anthony S.: "The Importance of Training Correctional Officers in Local Jails," *Proceedings of the One Hundred and Third Annual Congress of Corrections,* American Correctional Association, College Park, Md., 1974, pp. 185–188.

Law Enforcement Assistance Administration: *Children in Custody,* United States Government Printing Office, Washington, D.C., 1971.

———: *Children in Custody.* Advance Report on the Juvenile Detention and Correctional Facility Census of 1975, U.S. Government Printing Office, Washington, D.C., October 1977.

————: *1970 National Jail Census,* U.S. Government Printing Office, Washington, D.C., 1971.

————: *Survey of Inmates of State Correctional Facilities, 1974,* Special Report, U.S. Government Printing Office, Washington, D.C., March 1976.

————: Division of Program and Management Evaluation: *Volunteers in Law Enforcement Programs,* Washington, D.C., March 1972.

LeBlanc, Marc, and Louise Biron: "Status Offenses: Legal Term Without Meaning," *Journal of Research in Crime and Delinquency,* vol. 17, no. 1, January 1980, pp. 114–125.

LeClair, Daniel P.: "Home Furlough Program Effects on Rates of Recidivism," *Criminal Justice and Behavior,* vol. 5, no. 3, September 1978, pp. 249–258.

Long, Edward V.: "The Prisoner Rehabilitation Act of 1965," *Federal Probation,* vol. 29, no. 4, Administrative Office of the United States Courts, Washington, D.C., December 1965, pp. 3–7.

Lundman, Richard J., Paul T. McFarlane, and Frank R. Scarpitti: "Delinquency Prevention: A Description and Assessment of Projects Reported in the Professional Literature," *Crime and Delinquency,* vol. 22, no. 3, July 1976, pp. 297–308.

McCarthey, Francis Barry: "Should Juvenile Delinquency Be Abolished?" *Crime and Delinquency,* vol. 23, ïo. 2, April 1977, pp. 186–203.

McGee, Richard A.: "The Jail of Tomorrow," *Proceedings of the American Prison Association, 1939,* American Prison Association, New York, 1940.

MacIver, Robert M.: *The Web of Government,* The MacMillan Company, New York, 1947.

MacLeod, Alastair W.: *Recidivism: A Deficiency Disease,* University of Pennsylvania Press, Philadelphia, 1965.

MacPherson, David P.: "Corrections and the Community," *Federal Probation,* vol. 36, no. 2, Administrative Office of the United States Courts, Washington, D.C., June 1972, pp. 3–7.

McPike, Timothy Kevin: "Criminal Diversion in the Federal System: A Congressional Examination," *Federal Probation,* vol. 42, no. 4, Administrative Office of the United States Courts, Washington, D.C., December 1978, pp. 10–15.

McRae, T. W.: *Analytical Management,* John Wiley & Sons, New York, 1970, chap. 1, 2, 8, 10, and 18.

Maloney, John C., and Frank B. Raymond: "A Standardized Presentence Report: One State's Response," *Federal Probation,* vol. 41, no. 2, Administrative Office of the United States Courts, Washington, D.C., June 1977, pp. 40–42.

Mangrum, Claude T.: "Corrections' Tarnished Halo," *Federal Probation,* vol. 40, no. 1, Administrative Office of the United States Courts, Washington, D.C., March 1976, pp. 9–14.

————: "The Humanity of Probation Officers," *Federal Probation,* vol. 36, no. 2, Administrative Office of the United States Courts, Washington, D.C., June 1972, pp. 47–50.

Martinson, Robert, Douglas Lipton, and Judith Wilks: *The Effectiveness of Correctional Treatment,* Praeger Publishers, New York, 1975.

Massachusetts Department of Corrections: *An Analysis of Recidivism Among Residents*

Released From Boston and Shirley Pre-Release Centers During 1972–1973, prepared by Daniel P. LeClair, Boston, August, 1975.

————: *An Analysis of Recidivism Rates Among Residents Released From Massachusetts Correctional Institutions During the Year 1973,* prepared by Daniel P. LeClair, Boston, 1976.

Massachusetts Research Center: *Highlights from Pre-release Centers: Do They Make a Difference?* Boston, 1976.

May, Edgar: "Profile/Missouri," *Corrections Magazine,* vol. II, no. 3, March 1976, pp. 51–59.

Meisenhelder, Thomas: "An Exploratory Study of Existing from Criminal Careers," *Criminology,* vol. 15, no. 3, November 1977, pp. 319–333.

Menninger, Karl: "A Conversation with Karl Menninger," *Psychology Today,* 1968, pp. 56–63.

————: *The Crime of Punishment,* Viking Press, New York, 1966.

————: "Verdict Guilty: Now What?" *Harper's Magazine,* August 1959, pp. 60–64.

————, Martin Mayman, and Paul Pruyser: *The Vital Balance,* Viking Press, New York, 1963.

Merrill, Francis E.: *Society and Culture,* Prentice-Hall, Inc., Englewood Cliffs, N.J., 1952.

Merton, Robert K.: *Social Theory and Social Structure,* Free Press, Glencoe, Ill., 1957.

Miller, E. Eugene, and M. Robert Montilla, (eds.): *Corrections in the Community,* Reston Publishing Company, Inc., Reston, Va., 1977.

Minor, W. William, and Michael Courlander: "The Post Release Trauma Thesis: A Reconsideration of the Risk of Early Parole Failure," *Journal of Research in Crime and Delinquency,* vol. 16, no. 2, July 1979, pp. 273–293.

Moeller, H.G.: "The Continuum of Corrections," *The Annals of the American Academy of Political and Social Science—The Future of Corrections,* Richard D. Lambert (ed.), January 1969, vol. 383, pp. 84ff.

Morris, Albert: *The Involvement of Offenders in the Prevention and Correction of Criminal Behavior,* Massachusetts Correctional Association, Boston, October 1970, pp. 11–17.

Morris, Norval: *The Future of Imprisonment,* University of Chicago Press, Chicago, 1974.

————, and Colin Howard: *Studies in Criminal Law,* Clarendon Press, Oxford, 1964.

Morton, Joann B.: "Women Offenders: Fiction and Facts," *American Journal of Correction,* vol. 38, no. 6, December 1976, pp. 32–34.

Mowat, Robert M: *Final Report: Minnesota Restitution Center,* Minnesota Department of Corrections, St. Paul, September 1975.

Mutual Agreement Program: Practical Outcome Evaluation, Division of Corrections, Madison, Wisc., July, 1977.

Nagel, William: "On Behalf of a Moratorium on Prison Construction, " *Crime and Delinquency,* vol. 23, no. 2, April 1977, pp. 154–165.

National Advisory Commission on Criminal Justice Standards and Goals: *Corrections,* Law Enforcement Assistance Administration, Washington, D.C., 1972, chaps. 9, 12, and 15.

————: *Juvenile Justice and Delinquency Prevention,* Law Enforcement Assistance Administration, Washington, D.C., December 1976.

National Center for Social Statistics: *Statistics on Public Institutions for Delinquent Children, 1970,* Washington, D.C., 1971.

National Institute of Mental Health: *Community Based Correctional Programs* Rockville, Md., 1970.

Nau, William C.: "A Day in the Life of a Federal Probation Officer," *Federal Probation,* vol. 31, no. 1, Administrative Office of the United States Courts, Washington, D.C., March 1967, pp. 17–26.

Neilson, Dennis W.: "Job Development: The Employer As a Customer," *Federal Probation,* vol. 41, no. 4, Administrative Office of the United States Courts, Washington, D.C., December 1977, pp. 21–24.

Neuman, Franz: *The Democratic and the Authoritarian State,* Free Press, Glencoe, Ill., 1957.

Neuschel, Richard F.: *Management by Systems,* McGraw-Hill Book Company, New York, 1960.

Newman, Charles L. (ed.): *Source Book on Probation, Parole and Pardons,* Charles C Thomas, Publisher, Springfield, Ill., 1958.

———: and Barbara R. Price: "Jails and Drug Treatment: A National Perspective," *Federal Probation,* vol. 40, no. 3, Administrative Office of the United States Courts, Washington, D.C., September 1976, pp. 3–12.

Norland, Stephen, and Neal Shover: "Gender Roles and Female Criminality," *Criminology,* vol. 15, no. 1, May 1977, pp. 87–105.

Novick, Abraham: "Institutional Diversification and Continuity of Service for Committed Juveniles," *Federal Probation,* vol. 28, no. 1, Administrative Office of the United States Courts, Washington, D.C., March 1964, pp. 40–47.

Office of Juvenile Justice and Delinquency Prevention: *Little Sisters and the Law,* Law Enforcement Assistance Administration, U.S. Department of Justice, Washington, D.C., August 1977.

Office of Public Information: *Abstracts from the Annual Report 1971, 17th National Swedish Correctional Administration,* National Correctional Administration, Stockholm, 1971.

Ohlin, Lloyd E.: *Sociology and the Field of Corrections,* Russell Sage Foundation, New York, 1956.

Ozanna, Marg R., Robert A. Wilson, and Dewaine L. Gedney, Jr.: "Toward a Theory of Bail Risk," *Criminology,* vol. 18, no. 2, August 1980, pp. 147–161.

Pacht, Asher R.: "Factors Related to Parole Experience and the Deviated Sex Offender," *Correctional Psychologist,* vol. 3, no. 3, January-February 1968, pp. 8–9.

Packer, Herbert L.: *The Limits of the Criminal Sanction,* Stanford University Press, Stanford, Calif., 1968.

Parker, William: *Parole: Origins, Development, Current Practices and Statutes,* Parole Correctional Project, Resource Document no. 1, American Correctional Association, College Park, Md., 1975.

Parsloe, Phyllida: *The Work of the Probation and After-Care Officer,* Routledge and Kegan Paul, London, 1967.

Perkins, Rollin M.: *Criminal Law,* Foundation Press, Mineola, N.Y., 1957.

Perlstein, Gary R., and Thomas R. Phelps: *Alternatives to Prison,* Goodyear Publishing Company, Inc., Pacific Palisades, Calif., 1975.

Phillips, John C., and Delos H. Kelly: "School Failure and Delinquency," *Criminology,* vol. 17, no. 2, August 1979, pp. 194–207.

Polisky, R. J.: "A Model for Increasing the Use of Community Supportive Services in

Probation and Parole," *Federal Probation,* vol. 41, no. 4, Administrative Office of the United States Courts, Washington, D.C., December 1977, pp. 24–27.

Popper, Hermine I., and Frank Reissman: *Up From Poverty: New Career Ladders for Non-Professionals,* Harper & Row, Publishers, Incorporated, New York, 1968.

Pound, Roscoe: *An Introduction to the Philosophy of Law,* Yale University Press, New Haven, Conn., 1922.

Prassel, Frank R.: *Introduction to American Criminal Justice,* Harper & Row, Publishers, Incorporated, New York, 1975.

Preliminary Report of the Governor's Special Committee on Criminal Offenders, State of New York, June 1968.

President's Commission on Law Enforcement and the Administration of Justice: *Task Force Report: Corrections,* U.S. Government Printing Office, Washington, D.C., 1967.

President's Commission on Law Enforcement and the Administration of Justice: *Task Force Report: The Courts,* U.S. Government Printing Office, Washington, D.C., 1967.

President's Commission on Law Enforcement and the Administration of Justice: "Special Community Programs: Alternatives to Institutionalization," in Robert M. Carter., Daniel Glaser, and Leslie T. Wilkins (eds.): *Correctional Institutions,* J. B. Lippincott Company, New York, 1972, pp. 401–416.

Quiros, C. Bernaldo de: *Modern Theories of Criminality,* Alfonso de Salvio (trans.) Little, Brown and Company, Boston, 1911.

Radzinowicz, Leon, and Marvin E. Wolfgang (eds.): *Crime and Justice, vol. 2: The Criminal in the Arms of the Law,* Basic Books, Inc., Publishers, New York, 1971.

———: *Crime and Justice,* vol. 3: *The Criminal in Confinement,* Basic Books, Inc., Publishers, New York, 1971, pt. II.

Rest, Walter G., and Ellen Jo Ryan: "Group Vocational Counseling for the Probationer and Parolee," *Federal Probation,* vol. 34, no. 2, Administrative Office of the United States Courts, Washington, D.C., June 1970, pp. 49–54.

Richards, Pamela: "Quantitive and Qualitative Sex Differences in Middle-Class Delinquency," *Criminology,* vol. 18, no. 4, February 1981, pp. 453–470.

Richmond, Mark S.: "On Conquering Prison Walls," *Federal Probation,* vol. 30, no. 2, Administrative Office of the United States Courts, Washington, D.C., June 1966, pp. 17–22.

Robison, James, and Paul T. Takagi: *Case Decisions in a State Parole System,* Research Report no. 31, California Department of Corrections, Research Division, Sacramento, November 1968.

Root, Lawrence S.: "Work Release Legislation," *Federal Probation,* vol. 36, no. 1, Administrative Office of the United States Courts, Washington, D.C., March 1972, pp. 38–43.

Roscoe Pound-American Trial Lawyers Foundation: *A Program for Prison Reform in the United States,* Cambridge, Mass., 1972, Final Report.

Roser, Mark C.: "On Reducing Dropouts," *Federal Probation,* vol. 29, no. 4, Administrative Office of the United States Courts, Washington, D.C., December 1965, pp. 49–55.

Rubin, H. Ted: "The Emerging Prosecutor Dominance of the Juvenile Court Intake Process," *Crime and Delinquency,* vol. 26, no. 3, July 1980, pp. 299–318.

Rubin, Sol: *Crime and Juvenile Delinquency: A Rational Approach to Penal Problems,* Oceana Press, New York, 1970.

———: "New Sentencing Proposals and Laws in the 1970's," *Federal Probation,* vol. 43, no. 2, Administrative Office of the United States Courts, Washington, D.C., June 1979, pp. 3–8.

Rumney, Jay, and Joseph E. Murphy: *Probation and Social Adjustment,* Rutgers University Press, New Brunswick, N.J., 1952.

Rutherford, Robert Bruce, Jr.: "Establishing Behavioral Contracts with Delinquent Adolescents," *Federal Probation,* vol. 39, no. 1, Administrative Office of the United States Courts, Washington, D.C., March 1975, pp. 28–32.

Saleebey, George (ed.): *The Non-Prison: A Rational Program,* Institute for the Study of Crime and Delinquency, Sacramento, Calif., 1970.

Savitz, Loenard: *Dilemmas in Criminology,* McGraw-Hill Book Company, New York, 1967.

Scheier, Ivan H., and Leroy P. Goter.: *Using Volunteers in Court Settings: A Manual for Volunteer Programs,* Office of Juvenile Delinquency and Youth Development, Department of Health, Education and Welfare, U.S. Government Printing Office, Washington, D.C., 1969.

Schnur, Alfred D.: "The New Penology: Fact or Fiction," *Journal of Criminal Law, Criminology, and Police Science,* vol. 49, no. 4, November-December 1958, pp. 331–334.

Schoonmaker, Myressa H., and Jennifer S. Brooks: "Women in Probation and Parole," *Crime and Delinquency,* vol. 21, no. 2, April 1975, pp. 109–115.

Schwitzgebel, Ralph R.: *Development and Regulation of Coercive Behavior Modification Techniques with Offenders,* National Institute of Mental Health, Center for Studies of Crime and Delinquency, Rockville, Md., 1971.

Scott, Edward M: "Group Therapy with Convicts on Work Release," in Edward M. Scott and Kathryn L. Scott (eds.): *Criminal Rehabilitation . . . Within and Without the Walls,* Charles C Thomas, Publisher, Springfield, Ill., 1973, chap. XI.

———, and Kathryn L. Scott (eds.): *Criminal Rehabilitation . . . Within and Without the Walls,* Charles C Thomas, Publisher, Springfield, Ill., 1973, sec. 4.

Scudder, Kenyon: "The Open Institution," in David Dressler (ed.): *Readings in Criminology and Penology,* Columbia University Press, New York, 1964, pp. 550–562.

Sellin, Thorstein: *Culture, Conflict, and Crime,* Social Science Research Council, New York, 1938.

Senna, Joseph J.: "Professional Education in Probation and Parole," *Crime and Delinquency,* vol. 22, no. 1, January 1976, pp. 67–76.

Serrill, Michael S.: "Patuxent: Inside 'Clockwork Orange,'" *Corrections Magazine,* vol. 3, no. 4, December 1977, pp. 33–41.

———: "Prison Furloughs in America," *Corrections Magazine,* vol. 1, no. 6, July-August 1975, pp. 2–12.

Shannon, Lyle W.: "A Longitudinal Study of Delinquency and Crime," in Charles Wellford (ed.): *Qualitative Studies in Criminology,* Sage Publications, Inc., Beverly Hills, Calif., 1978, pp. 121–146.

Sheehan, Susan: "Annals of Crime," pt. I, "Prison Life," *The New Yorker,* October 24, 1977, pp. 56ff.

Shover, Neal: *A Sociology of American Corrections,* Dorsey Press, Homewood, Ill., 1979.

Simon, Rita J.: "American Women and Crime," *The Annals of the American Academy of Political and Social Science,* vol. 423, January 1976, pp. 31–46.

Smith, Alexander B., and Harriet Pollack: *Crime and Justice in a Mass Society,* Zerox College Publishing, Lexington, Mass., 1972.

Smykla, John Ortiz: "Does Coed Prison Work?" *The Prison Journal,* vol. LIX, no, 1, Spring-Summer, 1979, pp. 61–71.

Solomon, Richard A.: "Lessons From the Swedish Criminal Justice System: A Reappraisal," *Federal Probation,* vol. 40, no. 3, Administrative Office of the United States Courts, Washington, D.C., September 1976, pp. 40–48.

Spaeth, Edmund B., Jr.: "Directions in Criminal Justice," *Corrections Today,* vol. 42, no. 5, 1980, pp. 36, 70–72.

Spica, Arthur: "The A to Z of the Pre-sentence Report," *Federal Probation,* vol. 42, no. 4, Administrative Office of the United States Courts, Washington, D.C., December 1978, pp. 51–53.

Stanton, John M.: *Success Rates of Male Parolees,* Division of Parole, Bureau of Research and Statistics, State of New York, 1980, processed.

Steele, Eric H., and James B. Jacobs: "A Theory of Prison Systems?" *Crime and Delinquency,* vol. 21, no. 2, April 1975, pp. 149–162.

Steffenmeier, Darrell J., and Renee Hoffman Steffenmeier: "Trends in Female Delinquency" *Criminology,* vol. 18, no. 1, May 1980, pp. 62–85.

Sternberg, David: "Synanon House—A Consideration of Its Implications for American Corrections," *Journal of Criminal Law, Criminology, and Police Science,* vol. 54, no. 4, December 1963, pp. 447–455.

Stollery, Peter L.: "Searching for the Magic Answer to Juvenile Delinquency," *Federal Probation,* vol. 41, no. 4, Administrative Office of the United States Courts, Washington, D.C., December 1977, pp. 28–33.

Stout, Ellis: "Women in Probation and Parole: Should Female Officers Supervise Male Offenders?" *Crime and Delinquency,* vol. 19, no. 1, January 1973, pp. 61–71.

Stratton, John: "A Training Approach for Probation Departments," *American Journal of Correction,* vol. 38, no. 1, January-February 1976, pp. 28–30.

Sturup, Georg K.: *Treating the Untreatable,* Johns Hopkin Press, Baltimore, Md., 1968.

————: "Treating 'Untreatable' Criminals," *Federal Probation,* vol. 36, no. 2, Administrative Office of the United States Courts, Washington, D.C., September 1972, pp. 22–26.

Sutherland, Edwin H., and Donald R. Cressey: *Criminology,* J. B. Lippincott Company, Philadelphia, 1970, chaps. 18, 21, and 26.

————: *Principles of Criminology,* J. B. Lippincott Company, Chicago, 1939.

Swedish Information Service: *Information on Tillberga,* Stockholm, 1973.

Sykes, Gresham M.: *Crime and Society,* Random House, Inc., New York, 1956.

Taft, Donald R.: *Criminology,* The MacMillan Company, New York, 1950.

Takagi, Paul: "The Walnut Street Jail: A Penal Reform to Centralize the Powers of the State," *Federal Probation,* vol. 39, no. 4, Administrative Office of the United States Courts, Washington, D.C., December 1975, pp. 18–26.

Tannenbaum, Frank: *Crime and the Community,* Athenian Press, Ginn and Company, Boston, 1938.

Tappan, Paul W.: *Crime, Justice and Correction,* McGraw-Hill Book Company, New York, 1960.

Tatham, Richard J.: "Detoxification Centers, A Public Health Alternative for the 'Drunk Tank,'" *Federal Probation,* vol. 33, no. 4, Administrative Office of the United States Courts, Washington, D.C., December 1969, pp. 46–48.

Teeter, Negley K.: *The Cradle of the Penitentiary,* Pennsylvania Prison Society, Philadelphia, 1955.

Thomas, Charles W.: "The Correctional Institution as an Enemy of Corrections,"

Federal Probation, vol. 37, no. 1, Administrative Office of the United States Courts, Washington, D.C., March 1973, pp. 8–13.

Thorne, Gaylord L., Roland G. Tharp, and Ralph J. Wetzel: "Behavior Modification Techniques: New Tools for Probation Officers," *Federal Probation,* vol. 31, no. 2, Administrative Office of the United States Courts, Washington, D.C., June 1967, pp. 21–27.

"Thousands of Youngsters Jailed for Non-criminal Acts," *American Journal of Correction,* vol. 37, no. 3, May-June 1975, p. 18.

Trohanis, Pascal Louis: "Developing Community Acceptance of Programs for Children," *Child Welfare,* vol. LIX, no. 6, June 1980, pp. 365–373.

Turk, Austin T.: *Legal Sanctioning and Social Control,* U.S. Government Printing Office, Washington, D.C., 1972.

U.S. Department of Justice: *Attorney General's Survey of Release Procedures,* Vol. 2, Washington, D.C., 1939.

U.S. Bureau of Prisons: *Crime in the United States, Uniform Crime Reports, 1970,* Washington, D.C., 1971.

U.S. Bureau of Prisons: "Prisoners in State and Federal Institutions, 1966," *National Prisoner Statistics,* no. 43, U.S. Government Printing Office, Washington, D.C., August 1968.

U.S. Bureau of Prisons: *Unusual Prisoners in the Jail,* correspondence course for jailers, vol. 8, Washington, D.C.

"Virginia Provides Youth With Wilderness Experience," *Corrections Today,* vol. 42, no. 2, March-April 1980, pp. 62–63.

Waldo, Gordon P.: "Research and Training in Corrections: The Role of the University," *Federal Probation,* vol. 35, no. 2, Administrative Office of the United States Courts, Washington, D.C., June 1971, pp. 57–62.

Waller, Irvin, and Janet Chan: "Prison Use: A Canadian and International Comparison," *Criminal Law Quarterly,* vol. 17, Canada, 1974-1975, pp. 47–71.

Wendorf, Donald J.: "Family Therapy: An Innovative Approach in the Rehabilitation of Adult Probationers," *Federal Probation,* vol. 42, no. 1, Administrative Office of the United States Courts, Washington, D.C., March 1978, pp. 40–44.

Wille, Louis: "Money Against Crime," *Federal Probation,* vol. 26, no. 4, Administrative Office of the United States Courts, Washington, D.C., December 1962, pp. 34–38.

Wilson, Alex: "Self-Help Groups: Rehabilitation or Recreation," *American Journal of Correction,* vol. 31, no. 6, November-December 1969, pp. 12–18.

Wilson, Rob: "Care Is the Magic Ingredient," *Corrections Magazine,* vol. 3, no. 2, June 1977, pp. 3–7.

————: Parole Release: Should Parole Boards Hold the Key, *Corrections Magazine,* vol. 3, no. 3, New York, September 1977, pp. 47–59.

————: "Probation/Parole Officers as 'Resource Brokers,'" *Corrections Magazine,* vol. 4, no. 2, June 1978, pp. 48–54.

Winslow, R.: *Crime in a Free Society,* Winslow Publishers, Belmont, Calif., 1968, chaps. 11, 12, and 13.

Wolfgang, Marvin E.: "Making the Criminal Justice System Accountable," *Crime and Delinquency,* vol. 18, no. 1, January 1972, pp. 15–22.

Wood, William T.: "Multnomah County Probation Teams," *Federal Probation,* vol. 42, no. 3, Administrative Office of the United States Courts, Washington, D.C., September 1978, pp. 7–9.

Wooden, Kenneth: *Weeping in the Playtime of Others,* McGraw-Hill Book Company, New York, 1976.

Wormser, Rene A.: *The Law,* Columbia University Press, New York, 1955.

Wright, Keith C., and John D. Hutchinson: "The Role of Vocational Rehabilitation in the Correctional Setting," in Richard E. Hardy and John G. Cull (eds.): *Introduction to Correctional Rehabilitation,* Charles C Thomas, Publisher, Springfield, Ill., 1973, chap. 10.

Wright, Roberts J.: "Federal Bureau of Prisons Opens New Detention Headquarters in New York," *American Journal of Correction,* vol. 37, no. 5, September-October 1975, p. 32.

Yablonsky, Lewis: *The Tunnel Back: Synanon,* The MacMillan Company, New York, 1965.

Zibners, Harry: "Toward Genuine Communication in a Training School," *American Journal of Correction,* vol. 31, no. 3, May-June 1969, pp. 6–10, 12–13.

Zimring, Franklin: "American Youth Violence: Issues and Trends," in Norval Morris and Michael Tonry (eds.): *Crime and Justice: A Review of Research,* vol. 1, University of Chicago Press, Chicago, 1979, pp. 67–108.

Ziven, Morton: "A Rehabilitation Model for Juvenile Offenders," *The Prison Journal,* vol. VI, no. 1, Spring-Summer 1975, pp. 4–21.

Znaniecki, Florian: *Cultural Sciences,* University of Illinois Press, Urbana, 1952.

NAME INDEX

Adams, Stuart, 299
Alexander, James, 281
Allen, Donald, 139
Allen, Francis, 13
Augustus, John, 26, 32−34, 163

Baker, J. E., 141
Balch, Robert, 270
Banks, Jerry, 119
Beccaria, Cesare, 3, 8
Bell, Griffin, 328
Bennett, James V., 14
Bennett, Lawrence A., 327
Bernado, Thomas, 40
Beto, George J., 307
Biles, David, 329
Bloomberg, Seth, 143
Booth, Ballington, 41−42
Booth, Maud, 41−42
Bradley, Harold, 331
Braun, Fred, 138
Breed, Alan, 290
Brockway, Zebulon, 8, 26, 46
Burger, Warren, 243, 324
Burgess, Ernest W., 244
Burnham, L. P., 34

Cadow, Barbara, 333
Carlson, Norman, 93
Carter, Robert M., 105
Chaiklin, Harris, 129−130
Chambers, Cheryl, 275
Chandler, Michael, 281
Chiricos, Theodore, 203
Clark, Charles Dismas, 43
Clear, Scott, 342
Clear, Todd, 261, 342

Clear, Val, 342
Clemmer, Donald, 56, 128, 158
Coffey, O. D., 96
Cole, George F., 19
Conrad, John, 258, 308
Conte, William, 144
Cook, Thomas, 170
Cooke, Rufus, 34
Cox, Lewis A., 291
Crofton, Walter, 45
Cushman, Robert, 19

Danto, Bruce L., 80
Davis, Rendell, 143
Denno, Deborah, 289
Dershowitz, Alan M., 6
Dixon, Michael, 288−289
Dobrin, Leonard, 203
Dole, Robert, 16
Dressler, David, 107−108
Duffee, Barbara, 146−147
Duffee, David, 146−147
Dye, Larry, 174

Empey, Lamar, 275
England, Ralph, 119
Erickson, Maynard, 275

Fishman, Joseph B., 249−250
Fishman, Joseph F., 78
Fo, Walter, 281
Fogel, David, 6, 261
Foote, Caleb, 12
Fox, Vernon, 169, 252
Frank, Benjamin, 331−332

Frank, Raymond, 159
Franks, Bobby, 244

Galaway, Burt, 338
Gelbers, Seymour, 274
Glanser, Victor J., Jr., 281
Glaser, Daniel, 129, 159, 171, 177, 255, 301, 327
Glick, Henry R., 11
Glueck, Eleanor, 255
Glueck, Sheldon, 255
Goldfarb, Ronald, 95
Gottfredson, Don M., 247
Grant, J. Douglas, 173
Greenburg, David, 11, 140−141
Greenwood, Dorothey, 119
Grindstaff, Gordon, 169
Grinnell, Richard, 275

Hall, Frank, 7
Harty, Robert, 179
Haskell, Martin, 314
Hemmenway, Henry C., 34
Henry II, 29
Hess, Allen, 159
Hicks, Gerald, 290−291
Hodges, Luther, 37
Hoffman, Peter, 254
Holt, Norman, 150, 177, 203
Howe, S. G., 45
Humphries, Drew, 11

James, Jessie, 312
Jenkins, Richard L., 270−271
Jones, David, 57−58
Jones, J. T. L., 218

Keller, O. J., 290
Kennedy, Robert F., 43, 148
Koontz, John, 112

Laune, Ferris, 244
LeClair, Daniel, 153, 335
Leenhouts, Keith, 168
Leopold, Nathan, 244
Lerman, Paul, 269, 272
Lerner, Jay, 254
Lipsett, Laurence, 119
Lipton, Douglas, 17, 119, 121,
    204−205, 303
Long, Huey, 93
Lunden, Walter, 32

McCall, Cecil B., 260
MacCormick, Austin, 305
MacDougal, Ellis, 160
McGee, Richard A., 79
MacLeod, Alastair, 326−327
Maconochie, Alexander, 45
Maher, John, 179
Martin, Lawrence H., 270
Martinson, Robert, 17, 119, 121,
    204−205, 257, 288, 300,
    303, 333
Megargee, Edward L., 333
Menninger, Karl, 8, 95, 286,
    328, 341−342
Miller, Donald, 177
Miller, E. Eugene, 96, 199
Miller, Jerome, 289−290, 340
Moran, John, 7
Morris, Norval, 159, 243, 258,
    333, 343
Mullaney, Fahy, 164
Murray, Charles A., 291
Murton, Tom, 58

Nagel, William, 329, 341
Neithercutt, M. G., 247
Nelson, Carl, 301
Newfield, Jack, 79
Newman, Donald J., 106

Norman, Sherwood, 282
Norton, Robert A., 119

O'Donnell, Clifford, 281
Ohlin, Lloyd, 177
O'Leary, Vincent, 255
Osborne, Thomas Mott, 141

Parsons, Bruce, 281
Perlman, Vee, 249−250
Peterson, David, 57
Porterfield, Austin, 275
Powell, Lewis, 331

Rachin, Richard, 64
Radzinowitz, Leon, 4
Rardin, Ronald, 119
Rector, Milton, 270, 328
Reiss, Albert, 67
Renfrew, Charles, 79
Renteria, Rudy, 150
Rentschler, William, 12
Roosevelt, Theodore, 42
Rothenberg, David, 317
Rowan, Joseph, 290
Rowe, Charles, 126

Sands, Bill, 166−167
Sarason, Irwin G., 281
Saxbe, William B., 197−198
Schwartz, Richard, 159
Schweitzer, Louis, 89
Scioli, Frank, 170
Shannon, Lyle, 291−292
Shaw, Clifford, 311
Shenker, Norris, 43
Shepard, George, 312
Sheridan, William, 269
Shover, Neal, 300
Sigler, Maurice, 262
Siler, Terry, 119
Skolnick, Jerome, 159
Smith, Robert, 19, 341
Smullen, George, 142

Snyder, Phyllis, 270
Sower, Christopher, 305−306
Stanley, David, 257
Stanton, John, 244
Sterling, Joanne, 179
Stone, Donna, 313
Sturz, Herbert, 89
Sutherland, Edwin, 337
Swart, Stanley, 213
Switzgebel, Ralph, 315

Thomas, Charles, 57
Thomas, Wayne, 90
Travisono, Anthony P., 7, 121
Trojanowicz, Robert, 284−285
Turner, Merfyn, 42, 212

Van Den Haag, Potter Ernest,
    303
Velde, Richard W., 79
Vernon, Richard, 226
Vintor, Robert, 271
Von Hirsch, Andrew, 6, 8

Waldo, Gordon, 203
Wallenstein, Art, 19
Ward, Benjamin, 303
Warner, W. Lloyd, 244
Weintraub, Judith, 131
Wilkins, Leslie T., 105
Wilks, Judith, 17, 119, 121,
    204−205, 257, 289, 303
Wilson, James Q., 329
Wilson, Lawrence, 134
Wistar, Richard, 31
Wright, Roberts J., 76
Wright, William, 288−289

Yablonsky, Lewis, 314

Zimring, Franklin E., 7
Zingraff, Rhonda, 57

SUBJECT INDEX

Abscondence, 198–203, 206,
    218, 256
    (See also Escape)
Accelerated Creative Exposure,
    Inc., 130
Accomplices to the Crime, 58
Accountability, 297, 301,
    303–304
Accreditation, 304–307, 310,
    318
    process, 305–306
Ackerman Bill, 9
"Act Relating to Prison
    Industries, An," 325
Adjudication, 46, 75, 87, 267,
    271, 278
    child in need of supervision,
        267, 269
    consensual sexual behavior,
        269
    curfew violation, 269
    disobeying authority, 269
    incorrigible, 267
    juvenile in need of supervision,
        269
    miscreant, 267
    neglected, 267, 272
    persons in need of supervision,
        269
    runaway, 269–271, 279
    smoking, 269
    truant, 267, 269, 274–275
    ungovernability, 269
    wayward, 267, 269
    (See also Juveniles)
Administrative Office of the
    United States Courts,
    118–119

Adoption, 132, 286
    (See also Children)
AFL-CIO, 165, 174
"After care," 287–288, 313
Aid to Families of Dependent
    Children, 272, 342
Alabama, 16, 86, 200, 330
Alachua County, Florida, 82
Alameda County, California,
    273
Alaska, 7, 84, 199, 248, 257
Albany, Georgia, 337
Alcohol:
    alcoholic rehabilitation center,
        19, 54, 193, 223, 316
    alcoholics, 77, 82, 83, 102,
        109, 116, 138, 172, 204,
        214–215, 227, 249, 257,
        337
    Alcoholics Anonymous,
        54–55, 108–109, 129,
        143, 149, 167, 173, 193,
        195, 218–219, 259
    alcoholizer tests, 197, 227
    detoxification unit, 82, 85, 228
    drunkards, 30, 32–34, 59
    (See also Drugs)
America, 4, 8, 11, 25, 30,
    44–47, 56, 77, 83, 135,
    161, 332
American Bar Association, 82,
    112, 270, 306–307
American Civil Liberties Union,
    166
American Congress of
    Correction, 20, 38, 309
American Correctional
    Association, 7, 82, 121,

American Correctional
    Association *(Cont.):*
    202, 212, 238, 246,
    305–307, 309
American frontier, 32
"American Jail Standards of
    Personnel, Plans, and
    Programs, The," 305
American Justice Institute, 19
American Law Institute, 238
American Medical Association,
    82
American Prison Association,
    41–42, 127, 145, 164, 305
American Revolution, 8
American Society of
    Criminology, 166
Andromeda Drug Center, 205
Anglos, 275
Arizona, 9, 60, 138, 238,
    257–258, 273, 329
Arizona Correctional and
    Training Center, 138
Arizona Department of
    Correction, 138
Arizona Pork Producers
    Association, 138
Arkansas, 7, 38, 58, 131
Assize of Clarendon, 29
Atlanta, Georgia, 337, 339
Atlanta Advancement Center, 205
Attica, 58
Attorney General's Survey of
    Release Procedures, 255
Auburn, Alabama, 86
Auburn Prison, 141
Austin-Wilkes Society, 175
Australia, 4, 44–45

Babylonia, 3
Bail, 31, 35, 75, 78, 86, 88–92, 95, 214, 248, 253
  Illinois Ten Percent Plan, 89–90
  percentage bail, 89
  surety, 35
Baltimore, Maryland, 86
Banishment, 4, 29, 44–45
Barton County, Florida, 283
Baylor University, 115
Behavior, violent, 5, 60, 80, 127, 154, 186, 235
Benefit of clergy, 34–35
Bible, 35
Berkshire Farm Center, 270
Bexor County, Texas, Jail, 81, 86
Big Brothers, 165, 277
Big Sisters, 165, 277
Black Culture Group, 143
Blacks, 77, 80, 256, 275
"Bleeding heart," 102
Board of Directors (National Council on Crime and Delinquency), 121, 270
Bond, 35, 61
  bonding company, 89, 172–173
Bonneville Community Correctional Center, 64
Boston, Massachusetts, 26, 30, 34–35, 41, 81, 90, 163, 312, 339
Boston House of Corrections, 32
Boston Municipal Court, 35
Boulder, Colorado, 82
Boulder County Criminal Justice Center, 82
Boys Club, 114
Boys Town, Nebraska, 286
Boys Training School (Iowa), 270
Bread and Roses Too: Reporting About America, 79
Breed v. Jones, 268
  (*See also* Court decisions)
"Bridges," 185–188
Bridgeton, New Jersey, 81
Brubaker, 58
Bucks County, Pennsylvania, 19, 66, 85, 200, 274
Bucks County Prison, 200
"Buddies," 165, 281
Budget, 79, 114, 144, 148, 158, 192, 271
Bureau of Justice Statistics, 16, 256, 299
"Burn-out," 223, 259, 285, 328
By-Laws, 305

California, 9–10, 12, 44, 55, 60, 65–66, 85, 92, 103, 104, 114, 117, 119, 131–134, 146, 150, 173–174, 177–178, 191, 199–200, 203–204, 214, 219, 224, 238, 247–248, 251, 257–258, 261, 267, 273, 282–283, 313, 316, 330, 331, 338–341
California Department of Corrections, 65–66, 173, 178, 204, 224
California Institution for Women, 132
California Parole and Community Services Division, 44, 65–66
California Youth Authority, 274, 284, 287, 290
Cambridge-Somerville Youth Study, 312
Camden, New Jersey, 283
Canada, 27, 127, 166, 207, 212, 218, 326
Canon City, Colorado, 148
Capital punishment, 3–4, 10, 12, 29, 31, 34, 233
  hanging, 80
  (*See also* Punishment)
Caseload, 102, 109, 115–116, 119, 121, 235–236, 246, 248, 252, 280, 287
Central Community Corrections Center, 222
Central referral agency, 61
Chamber of Commerce, 65, 68, 175
Change, 309–310
  "selling," 309
  (*See also* Innovation; Reform)
Chapel Hill, North Carolina, 286
Check Writer's Anonymous 315
Chicago, Illinois, 26, 42–43, 47, 76, 90, 132, 150, 166, 169, 214, 281, 283, 291, 311
Chicago Area Project, 311
Child abuse, 313–314
  central register, 313
  deprivation, 55, 314
  malnourishment, 314
  neglect, 313, 314
  third party reporting, 313
Child care, 178
  child care workers, 285
Children, 32, 40, 46–47, 78, 131–133, 138, 144, 162, 273, 285–286, 290, 312

Children (*Cont.*):
  children's home, 149, 337
  nursery school, 132
Children's Aid Society, 34
Children's Bureau, 47, 269
Chino, California, 146
Chittenden Community Correctional Center, 221
Church, 18–19, 34, 45, 54, 65, 108, 129, 162, 167, 175, 180–181, 186, 188, 193, 207, 212, 214, 217, 226, 281, 284–285, 310, 337
  church circles, 161
  Sunday services, 181
Cincinnati, Ohio, 305
Citizen, 54, 103, 105, 129, 153, 162, 176, 180–181, 206–207, 306, 310, 324, 342
  advisory board, 61, 63, 162, 227
  board of trustees, 227
  handicapped, 130, 144, 226
Citizen Involvement Project, 86
Citizen's Participation Committee, 164
City, 32, 74, 76, 90, 94, 102, 114, 148, 195, 227
  community-relations division, 174
Civic Center Jail, San Jose, California, 81, 314
Civic groups, 175, 180, 188, 193, 216, 227
Civic leaders, 86, 161, 167
Civil rights, 74
  standards, 304, 307
Civil War, 32
Clark County, Washington, 92, 273
Classification, 15, 17, 105, 116, 127–128, 144, 153, 189, 214, 221, 232, 244, 258
  intake classification, 128
  reclassification, 128
  release classification, 128
  team classification, 115–116, 198
"Climate," 142, 185
Clothes, 30, 55, 133, 144, 148, 154, 165–166, 173, 195, 220, 236, 262, 279, 286, 317, 327
Coalition for Prevention of Child Abuse, 130
"Coddling," 209
Code of Hammurabi, 3
Code of Justinian, 29
Coldingly, England, 326

College, 17, 38, 48, 77, 130,
    149, 164, 169, 179, 186,
    201, 218, 233, 310, 313,
    321
  intern, 218
  students, 275
Colorado, 9, 60, 65, 82, 131,
    163, 257, 282−283
Colorado Outward Bound, 283
Columbia, South Carolina, 175
Columbus, Ohio, 42, 339
"Combustible scandal," 270,
    324
  (See also "National disgrace")
Commensurate deserts, 8, 58
  (See also Determinate
    sentencing)
Commission of Accreditation for
    Corrections, 82, 305−307
Commission for the Study of
    Incarceration, 6
Committee on Standards and
    Accreditation, 307
"Common deficiency factor,"
    326
Commonwealth v. Chase, 35
Community, 15, 48, 207, 285
  acceptance, 215
  advancement program, 280
  advocacy programs, 179, 226
Community assistance, 149,
    158−181, 216−217
  development, 160
  rationale, 158−159
Community-based corrections:
  definition, 54
  economic justification, 55, 102
  evaluation, 63−65
  philosophical justification,
    54−55
  public reaction, 63−65
  rationale, 53−58
  statewide program, 60−63
  task, 53
Community contacts, 126, 192,
    197, 327
Community correctional center,
    44, 64, 82, 84, 187, 193,
    212−215, 217, 219−221,
    229, 336
  (See also Residence,
    community-based)
Community interest groups, 61
Community-oriented programs,
    129−130, 214, 226, 228,
    302, 306
Community resources, 43−44,
    54−55, 60, 65, 73−74, 84,
    91, 102−103, 107−109,
    115, 148, 193, 215−216,

Community resources (Cont.):
    218−219, 221, 226, 229,
    232, 252−253, 261,
    280−281, 286, 328, 342
  academic education, 54,
    186−187, 192, 195, 285
  dental clinics, 54, 108, 173
  hospitals, 55, 95, 114, 116,
    130, 180, 216, 219, 337
Community service, 114, 282,
    325
  center, 54, 180, 316
Community service (restitution),
    188, 338
  museum, 284
  nursing home, 284, 337
  (See also Restitution)
Community "success," 197,
    226, 262, 288, 317, 327
Community ties, 53, 60, 95, 188,
    237, 327−328
  "conventional world" bond,
    327
Community treatment center, 43,
    149, 151, 214, 218, 220,
    339
  (See also Residence,
    community-based)
Community treatment program,
    226, 285−288, 312, 335
Commutation, 233
  (See also Sentencing)
Comprehensive Employment and
    Training Act, 130, 172, 221
Congress, 9, 37, 43, 78, 139,
    148, 257, 270, 330, 340
Congress of Corrections, 99th
    annual, 160−161
Conjugal visits, 133−135, 138,
    158, 188, 332
  (See also Visiting)
Connecticut, 47, 60, 77, 82, 84,
    131, 138, 178, 239, 257,
    273, 335
Connecticut Statement of
    Organization and Procedure
    for Granting Parole, 239
"Conning," 208
Constitution, United States, 79,
    268
Contract, treatment, 116
Cook County, Illinois, 273
Cook County Jail, 169
Corporeal punishment, 3, 8, 58
  branding, 31, 35
  lashing, 31
  mutilation, 3, 29, 31, 58
  pillory, 31
  rubber hose, 58
  stocks, 31

Corporeal punishment (Cont.):
  straps, 58
  torture, 10, 58
  Tucker telephone, 58
  whipping, 31
Correctional Association of New
    York, 166
Corrections, 13, 20, 324
  community-focused, 16, 20,
    52−68, 126, 128−129,
    133, 135, 153, 339−341
  department, 189, 238, 260
  planning, 65, 142, 217,
    228−229, 280, 307, 316,
    325
  "practical approaches,"
    325−328
Corrections Task Force, 48, 53,
    81
Cost, 62, 64−65, 204−206,
    223, 226, 303
  cost-benefit analysis, 299,
    301−304, 310, 318, 342
  application of, 302−303
  cost-effective, 64−65, 154,
    226, 234, 300−301,
    303−304, 307, 325, 327,
    332, 341, 342
  cost per day, 77, 88, 226, 234,
    241
  cost reduction, 62, 85, 90, 92,
    102, 119, 153, 188, 207,
    223, 226, 281, 291, 303
Council of State Government,
    27
Counseling, 16, 42, 44, 60, 79,
    83, 85, 90−91, 101,
    107−108, 116, 128, 132,
    135, 140, 146, 149,
    153−154, 165−166, 173,
    177, 179, 194, 205, 212,
    216−217, 219, 220−221,
    232, 248, 261, 266, 274,
    276, 280−282, 286−288,
    290, 299−300, 312−313,
    315, 317, 339
  group, 115, 148, 153, 163,
    179, 220−222, 281, 288,
    312−313, 317, 337
  marriage, 114, 131
    (See also Marriage)
  psychiatric, 140, 312
  psychological, 140, 161, 303,
    311−312
  religious, 140, 149
  therapy, 5, 13, 224
County, 11, 19, 31, 34, 61, 74,
    76, 82, 94, 102−103,
    114−115, 149, 195
  commissioners, 82, 93

County Detention Center, 149
County Home School, 168
Court, 13, 58−59, 93, 112−113,
    117, 189, 204, 233, 268,
    304, 307, 309, 339
  appellate, 268
  44th District Court of
    Michigan, 116
  juvenile, 46−47, 267−271,
    275−277, 279−281, 291
    procedural changes, 268
  police, 163
  secular, 34
Court costs, 102, 112, 188, 205
Court decisions:
  Breed v. Jones, 268
  Commonwealth v. Chase, 35
  ex parte United States, 36
  Gagnon v. Scarpelli, 113, 120
  Gallegos v. Colorado, 268
  Gault, 268, 284
  Greenholtz v. Inmates, 242
  Killits decision, 36
  McKeiver v. Pennsylvania,
    268
  Morrissey v. Brewer, 253
  People ex rel. Forsythe v.
    Court of Sessions, 36
  re Winship, 268
  Williams v. New York, 120
Court order, 79, 107, 253
Court records, 159
Court releases, 59
Creative restitution, 338
  (*See also* Restitution)
Creative therapy, 100, 126, 153,
    266, 317
  art, 86, 128−130, 140
  drama, 128, 130
  music, 86, 128, 130, 140
  wood carving, 139
  writing, 129−130
Cregier Outpost, 288
Crenshaw, 43
Crime, 4−6, 18
  aggravated burglary, 267
  aggravated murder, 234
  armed robbery, 222, 267
  assault, 12, 77, 159, 226, 282,
    315
  assault with intent to commit
    bodily harm, 190
  bribery, 10
  burglary, 227, 254, 282, 315,
    338
  car theft, 328, 338
  check writing, 109
  child molestation, 192
  Class C crime, 61, 63
  embezzling, 10, 315, 328

Crime (*Cont.*):
  extorting, 10, 144
  felony of first degree, 234
  felony with gun, 11
  forgery, 11, 227, 297, 315,
    331, 342
  fraud, 80, 328
  habitual offender, 267
  kidnapping, 10, 190, 268
  lascivious acts, 190, 192
  manslaughter, 254
  mayhem, 190
  murder, 10, 12, 58, 190, 222,
    226, 234, 331
  petty larceny, 77
  poaching, 4
  prostitution, 32, 34, 177, 215
  rape, 7, 10, 12, 58, 80, 190,
    192, 297
  robbery, 10, 190, 227, 254,
    282, 297, 331
  shoplifting, 315
  treason, 190
  vandalism, 77, 315
Crime and Delinquency, 270
Crime Commission, 224
Crime of Punishment, The, 8, 95
Crime prevention, 310−315
  (*See also* Prevention)
Crime Prevention Teen Program,
    Inc., 163
Crime rates, 64, 77, 310, 329
Crime skills, 125
Crimes:
  high, 216
  major, 191, 281, 291
  new, 197−198, 200,
    205−206, 222,
    253−254, 256, 258
  sexual, 106, 134, 331
Criminal, 343
  pattern, 101, 244, 255
  stigma, 159
Criminal Justice Construction
    Reform Act, 16
Criminal justice system, 3, 5, 8,
    11, 13−14, 20, 28−29, 46,
    68, 75, 84, 87, 103, 121,
    125, 159, 162−163, 175,
    177, 181, 188, 214,
    226−227, 260, 308, 333,
    336
  acquittal, 101, 113, 159
  arrest, 177, 203
  citation, 277
  defense, 106
  evidence, 253
  hearing, 162
    preliminary, 253, 280
  indictment, 59, 163

Criminal justice system (*Cont.*):
  jury, 233, 268
  postconviction procedures, 95
  prosecution, 11, 25, 35−36,
    87, 106−107, 225, 260,
    282, 291, 339, 341
  trial, 75, 87, 177, 214
  verdict, 101
  warrant, 248, 253, 256
  witness, 75, 253, 268
Criminologist, 4, 32, 177, 238,
    244, 255
Critics, 66, 102, 121, 161, 173,
    205, 224, 235, 258, 284,
    287
Crofton House, 162−163
Crookston, Minnesota, 85
Cudahy Food Company, 138
Culture shock, 186
Cumberland County Jail, 81
Cummins Prison Farm, 58
Custody, 82, 96, 301
  maximum, 104, 214
  medium, 104, 214
  minimum, 104, 119, 261
  protective, 134
  strict, 45

Dade County, Florida, 274
Dale Carnegie Institute, 129,
    163
Dallas, Texas, 277
Dallas County Jail, 81
Day pass, 153, 186−187,
    197−198, 211
  (*See also* Passes; Transition
    methods)
Death, 235
Declaration of Principles, 20,
    305
"Decompression chambers,"
    212
Deinstitutionalization, 48,
    271−274, 276, 291, 304
  postadjudication, 273
Delancy Street Foundation, 179
Delaware, 43, 77, 117, 267, 273
Delinquency, 47, 237, 272, 275,
    278, 291, 310
  breeding conditions, 281, 327
  low delinquency area, 215
  prevention, 285
  (*See also* Prevention)
  relationship to: age, 127, 159,
    244
    broken home, 275
    honor students, 275
    intelligence level, 274
    school (drop-out), 274

Delinquent, 101, 267, 270, 275, 281
  behavior, 274
  contact, 274
  predelinquent, 270
Delivery of community services model, 179
Democracy in Prison, 143
Demonstration Cities and Metropolitan Development Act, 313
Denmark, 38, 329, 332
Denver, Colorado, 82, 282
Department of Agriculture, 313
Department of Education (Health, Education, and Welfare), 313
Department of Health, Education, and Welfare:
  Child Abuse and Neglect, 313
  Health and Human Services, 174, 279, 313
Department of Housing and Urban Development, 313
Department of Justice, 146, 328
Department of Labor, 171-172, 313
Dependent (juvenile), 267, 272
Deportation, 3
Des Moines, Iowa, 90-91
Des Moines Project, 91-92
Detainer, 148, 336
Detention, 29, 47, 75, 78, 83, 85, 88, 95, 269, 273, 277-280, 287-290, 341
Detention center, juvenile, 47, 168
Determinate sentence, 6-12, 16, 238, 257, 260-261, 330-331, 342
  predictive, 11
  (*See also* Commensurate deserts; Sentencing)
Deterrence, 4-6, 324
  general, 4
  special, 4
Detoxification unit, 82, 85, 228
  "drying out," 82
  (*See also* Alcohol; Drugs)
Detroit, Michigan, 150
Diagnosis, 19, 57, 127, 149, 168, 192, 214, 248, 258, 282, 285, 287, 333
Directory-American Correctional Association, 38
Directory-International Halfway House Association, 53, 212
Disciplinary committee, 144, 198
Disciplinary report, 64, 137, 203, 287, 326

Discretion, 6, 7, 11-12, 16, 20, 109, 140, 169, 190, 260-261, 268, 291
Dismas House, 43, 214
District of Columbia, 34, 38, 129, 162, 174, 197-200, 221-222, 240-242, 246, 250, 269, 279, 283, 306
District of Columbia Department of Corrections, 129, 221
District of Columbia Reformatory, 200
Diversion, adult, 19, 25, 73, 84, 87-93, 95, 214, 302, 311, 337
  citation, 277
  day-time release, 89
  field citation, 88
  postbooking release, 89
  prebooking release, 88-89
  recognizance, 35, 86, 89-91, 214
  station house citation, 89
  third party release, 89
  unsecured bail, 89
Diversion, juvenile, 224, 276-284, 290-291
  expeditionary phase, 283
  formal reprimand, 277
  "house arrest," 278-279
  informal reprimand, 277
  intervention, 281
  modeling, 281
  nonresidential, 282
  Outward Bound, 283
  petition, 277
  prepetition screening, 278
  role-playing, 281
  runaway houses, 114, 279
  service component, 292
  survival experiences, 283
  temporary shelter, 279
  transitional homes, 179, 285
  volunteer substitute homes, 279
  wilderness trips, 283
Division of Juvenile Delinquency Services, 269
"Doing good," 164
  Christianity, 164
Doing Justice, 6
Downey, California, 132
Draper, Utah, 132
Driver's license, 132, 154, 173, 193
Driving instructions, 114
Drugs, 10
  addiction, 32, 60-61, 67, 77, 82, 103, 168, 172, 174, 179, 227, 244, 259

Drugs *(Cont.):*
  "cold turkey," 179
  "hitting up," 140
  marijuana detection kit, 227
  overdose, 58, 214, 234
  possession, 11, 19, 71, 98, 215-216, 218, 224, 227, 234, 247, 249, 251, 257, 331
  rehabilitation center, 19, 54, 179, 193, 303, 339
  related offenses, 11, 116, 140, 148
  saline tests, 197, 227
  therapy, 60, 91, 193, 337
  urine sampling, 227
  (*See also* Alcohol)
Due process, 252-253, 260, 268, 276, 284
  double jeopardy, 268
Dwight, Illinois, 132

Early Release Committee, 244
Economic Opportunity Act, 44
Economic stability, 100, 125, 148
Education, 5, 18, 46, 53-54, 77, 79, 83, 116, 129, 153, 238, 251-252, 300, 303, 328
  academic, 16-17, 95, 128, 140, 216, 219, 232, 266, 308, 315-317, 327, 332
  correspondence course, 140, 202
  high school, 17, 38, 310, 328
  learning, 5, 150, 282, 288
  mathematics, 18, 128, 282, 313
  mentally retarded, 75, 130, 226
  night school, 38
  noncollege bound students, 314
  planning, 87, 90, 149, 154, 160, 276
  reading, 128, 165, 274, 282, 313
  remedial classes, 313
  scholarships, 65
  system, 108
  tutor, 86
  (*See also* College)
Education and Labor Committee—House of Representatives, 18
Effectiveness of Correctional Treatment, 119
Eighteenth century, 46, 228

Elmira, New York
    (Reformatory), 26, 46, 174
Employment, 18, 36–37, 53,
    59, 89, 91, 93, 102, 105,
    108, 112, 115–116,
    119–120, 129, 135, 139,
    146, 148, 152, 159,
    171–172, 180, 193, 206,
    211, 244, 246, 249–251,
    256, 285, 326–327
  barrier, 180
  employee, 57, 77, 93, 116,
    135, 139, 175, 194, 206,
    274, 303, 318
  employer, 30, 54, 101, 107,
    127, 130, 159–160, 172,
    177, 181, 187, 189, 192,
    206, 326
  employment agent, 159, 195,
    220
  ex-offender, 171–177
    New Careers, 173–174
    nonprofessionals, 173, 248
    paraprofessionals, 173
  garnishment of wages, 204
  "shock," 203
  underemployed, 96
  unemployed, 29, 83, 146, 171
  unemployment insurance, 127,
    326
England, 4–5, 25, 29, 34, 40,
    42, 44–46, 101, 212, 285,
    326
  crown, 35, 46
  king, 29
  Parliament, 44–46
  (See also Great Britain)
Enslavement, 29
Entry point, 96, 128
Environment, 55, 102,
    107–108, 128, 181, 188,
    193, 204, 207, 223,
    226–227, 314
  closed, 15
  deteriorated areas, 312
  open, 15, 285
  socioeconomic, 274
Escape, 63–64, 132, 198–199,
    203, 206, 222, 224
  (See also Abscondence)
Ethnic background, 143–144,
    312
Euclid House, 221–222
  open confrontation, 222
Europe, 27, 38
Evaluation, 106, 121, 198–202,
    298, 306
  juvenile, 288–289
  outcome, 298–299
  process, 299
  (See also Research)

Evansville, Indiana, 86
Ex-offender, 166–167, 176,
    212, 221, 248, 327–328
Ex-Offender Coordinated
    Employment Lifeline, 171
Ex-offender employment (See
    Employment, ex-offender)
Ex-parte United States, 36
    (See also Court decisions)
Expiration, 43, 52, 101, 121,
    126, 148–149, 154, 186,
    189, 191, 205, 228, 233,
    235–236, 240, 250, 252,
    254–255, 257, 260–261,
    304
"Exploration in Inmate-Family
    Relationships," 177
Extradition, 249
Eye for an Eye, An, 126

Factorylike prisons, 303,
    325–326
  quality control, 326
  "venture," 303
  (See also Prisons)
Family, 19, 26, 28, 53–54, 57,
    59–60, 67, 74, 80, 85, 87,
    89, 91, 94, 100–102, 105,
    107, 112–113, 127,
    131–135, 138, 146,
    148–149, 153–154,
    159–160, 162, 175,
    177–180, 186, 188,
    193–194, 203–204,
    206–207, 211, 216, 218,
    220, 226–227, 234, 237,
    250, 259, 279–281, 312,
    324, 327–328, 337, 339
  "active family interest," 11
  coordinating committee, 131
  dysfunctional, 275
  family visiting cottages,
    134
  offenses, 77
  outreach methods, 178–179
  planning, 189
  private family placement,
    213
  spouse, 127, 131–132, 134,
    166, 177–179, 188,
    249
  support payments, 107, 119,
    139, 188, 202, 234, 303,
    326
  therapy, 115, 131, 149, 193,
    279, 282, 287
Federal Bureau of Investigation,
    12
Federal Bureau of Prisons, 14,
    16, 36, 38, 43, 76, 82, 93,

Federal Bureau of Prisons
    (Cont.):
    146, 148–149, 171,
    194–195, 199, 222, 242,
    256, 260, 306, 328–330,
    339
Federal dollars, 48, 54, 67
Federal Juvenile Delinquency
    Act, 43
Federal Parole Commission,
    238, 258, 260, 262
Federal Prisoner Rehabilitation
    Act, 37
Federal prisoners, 43, 171, 200,
    328, 339
Federal releasees, 43, 143, 150,
    236, 299
Federal system, 9, 26–27, 43,
    51, 81, 102–104, 126, 136,
    148, 213–214, 217, 224,
    228, 235, 240, 250, 255,
    334
Federal Youth Corrections Act,
    43
Fee for service, 139
Fee system, 29–31, 43, 76
Felon, 6, 34, 37, 58–59, 102,
    115, 133, 154, 162, 179,
    186–189, 192, 214, 224,
    232, 250, 255, 275, 337
Felony, 75, 77, 90, 125, 254,
    261, 337
Female offender, 27, 53, 59,
    74–75, 77–78, 131–132,
    212, 256
Fifteenth century, 29
Filing of cases, 35
Finances, 83, 107–108, 194,
    271, 284
  assistance, financial, 90, 161,
    178, 195
  debts, 109, 339
  incentives, financial, 16
  loan fund, 142, 179
  loans, 127, 173
Fines, 3, 5, 29, 31, 78, 85,
    101–102, 121, 188, 253
Fingerprinting, 58, 254
Firearms, 197, 249
Fiscal constraints, 93, 121, 170,
    271, 286, 308, 315, 325,
    340–341
  funding, 83, 120, 140–141
  revenue sharing, 286
Flat time sentencing, 6
  (See also Sentencing)
Florida, 11, 42, 60, 65, 82, 203,
    214, 241, 246, 248, 258,
    274, 279, 283, 290, 333
Florida Division of Youth
    Services, 290

Florida State Probation and
Parole Services, 65
Florida State University, 333
Food, 6, 76, 134, 138, 166, 205,
212, 279, 286, 317
food stamps, 342
Ft. Des Moines, Iowa, 91, 341
Fort Dodge, Iowa, 42
Ft. Lauderdale, Florida, 214
Fortune Society, 167, 176, 317
Foster community project, 179
Fourteenth century, 35
Fourth Amendment, 235
France, 38, 46
Free community, 145, 186, 219,
229, 233, 317, 337
Freedom, 212–213, 215, 221,
333
deprivation of, 332
restoration of, 45
Free enterprise system,
138–139, 303
(*See also* Prison)
"Free up," 222
Free Venture Prison Industries
Program, 138–139
Free world culture, 58
Fresno County, California, 283,
339
Friends and Families of
Offenders, 178
Friends and Families of
Prisoners, 178
Friends Outside, 178
Friendships, 13, 19, 42, 57, 59,
101, 105, 107, 112, 127,
153–154, 159–160, 164,
185, 187–189, 203–204,
211, 216, 256, 281, 318,
324, 327
fellowship, 43, 283
Fund-raising, 165
Funeral, 138, 193, 339
Furloughs, 18, 27, 38–40, 60,
66, 100, 126, 133, 144,
153–154, 160, 186–187,
189–192, 197, 199, 203,
206, 211, 232, 298, 317,
332, 335, 339–340,
342

Gagnon v. Scarpelli, 113, 120
(*See also* Court decisions)
Gallegos v. Colorado, 268
Gallup Poll, 5
"Games," 179
Gangs, 57, 313
of marauders, 32, 55, 144
Gaol, 28–29
(*See also* Jail)

Gardens For All, 221
"Gate keeper," 278
"Gate" money, 202–203,
235–237, 317
(*See also* Release)
Gault, 268, 284
(*See also* Court decisions)
Geographic area, 103–104, 112,
149, 197, 216
Georgia, 16, 201, 205, 242, 246,
258, 337
"Get-tough-with-criminals," 48,
63, 236, 267–268, 329
"Going soft," 102
Good conduct, 133
"Good moral character," 171
Good time, 10, 233, 239, 261
Good time law, 8, 11
Government, 301, 313, 325,
332, 342
county-state, 103
crimes, 106
employees, 160
executive branch, 103
representative, 141
state, 61, 76, 102–103, 126,
148, 301
Governor, 233, 237–238, 324
Governor's Special Committee
on Criminal Offenders,
298
Great Britain, 8, 40, 127, 212
Greek, 336
Greenhaven, New York, 174
Greenholtz decision, 242
Greenholtz v. Inmates, 242
(*See also* Court decisions)
Group Care Consultant Services,
286
Group counseling (*see*
Counseling)
Group experiences, 57
Group homes, 282, 284–285,
313
craftsmen, 40, 138
Group meetings, 162
Guidance, 101–102, 142, 165
Guided group interactions, 287
Guidelines Project, 164

"Habituation," 328
Half-free status, 206, 224
Halfway house, 26, 43–44,
53–54, 60, 64, 67,
153–154, 162, 175, 179,
187, 191, 211, 213–214,
216–222, 226, 228–229,
276, 284–285, 300, 306,
309, 314, 316, 333, 339,
340, 342

Halfway house (*Cont.*):
homelike atmosphere,
212–213, 218
hostel, 40
"mom and pop," 213, 217,
229
Halfway House Manual, 216
"Halfway in," 60, 188, 214
"Halfway out," 221
Hamilton County, Ohio, 313
Hampton, Florida, 42
Harlan, Kentucky, 44
Hartford, Connecticut, 178
Harvard Center for Criminal
Justice, 289
Hawaii, 26, 131, 242, 258
Head Start, 114, 311
Hebrew Orphan Society, 285
Hebrews, 336
Helping agencies, 180, 314
Helping person, 212
Hennepin County, Minnesota,
167–168
Hennepin County Department of
Court Services, 167–168
Home family, 132–133
Home Mission of Episcopal
Church, 129
"Honeymoon effect," 206
Hope Hall, 42
House of correction, 29–30,
32–34, 301–302, 334
(*See also* Prison)
House of Industries, 41
House of Refuge, 141
House of Representatives, 78
House of Representatives
Education and Labor
Committee, 78
Housing, 42–43, 127, 145, 149,
165–166, 178, 192–193,
195, 205, 211–212, 220,
227–228, 237, 250, 256,
274, 286, 299, 303, 315,
328
problems, 195
Houston, Texas, 307
Huber Law, 27, 36, 85
Hughesville, Maryland, 282
Humane treatment, 18, 38, 53,
95, 307, 332, 341
Humanitarian, 53, 332
Huntsville, Texas, 127
Hutchinson, Kansas, 130

Idaho, 117, 131, 248
Illinois, 9, 11, 15, 90, 103, 118,
126, 131, 132, 138, 175,
177, 190, 198–199, 201,
238, 243, 248, 257, 261,

Illinois *(Cont.):*
267, 273, 283, 288, 312, 331
Illinois Correctional Institution for Women, 132
Illinois Department of Corrections, 126
Illinois Law Enforcement Commission, 261
Illinois State Penitentiary, 177
Illinois Ten Percent Plan, 89–90
(*See also* Bail)
Imprisonment, 3, 15, 31, 55, 57–58, 101, 121, 127, 188, 234, 262, 303, 328–330, 331–339
control system, 55
Improving Victim Services Through Probation, 103
Incapacitation, 4–6, 324, 332–333
Incarceration, 12, 19, 60, 73, 109, 117, 121, 126, 145, 154, 158, 171, 177, 186, 188, 192, 199, 203, 214–215, 226, 290, 300, 302, 328
future, 328–330
Indiana, 9, 11, 47, 86, 117, 131, 200, 204, 238, 257, 282, 342
Indiana Juvenile Justice Task Force, 282
Indianapolis, Indiana, 166
Ingham County, Michigan, 82
"In-groups," 161
In loco parentis, 47
Inmate, 6, 10, 30, 55, 57, 74, 77, 79, 81, 125–154, 158, 177, 186, 188, 195, 201, 204, 206, 235, 239, 241–243, 324
code, 55, 56–58, 224, 309
(*See also* Prison conditions)
council, 141, 143, 144
(*See also* Self-government)
"first term inmate," 191
grievances, 143
Inmate X, 244
median income, 148
panel, 163, 193, 315
(*See also* Public education)
pay, 136–137, 139, 317, 326
experiment, 136–137, 326
savings, 203, 205, 218, 236, 337
Innovation, 307–308
resistance to, 308–309
(*See also* Change; Reform)

Inspectors of the state prison, 26, 41
Institute of Juvenile Administration of American Bar Association, 270
Institutions, Inc., 289
Intake, 46, 55, 116, 153, 178, 277–278, 290, 316
International Halfway House Association, 53, 212
Interstate commerce, 139
Interstate Compact for Supervision of Probationers and Parolees, 250
Iowa, 16, 42, 60, 64–65, 90, 131, 138, 173, 201, 214, 248, 270, 303, 315, 340
Iowa Boys Training School, 270
Iowa Department of Social Services, 173
Iowa Department of Transportation, 173
Ireland, 212
Irish System, 45
(*See also* Parole)
Isaac T. Hopper, 26, 41
Israel, 244
Italy, 3, 8

Jail, 11, 17, 19, 28–32, 36, 38, 41, 47, 54, 73–96, 100–101, 117, 126, 132, 153, 175, 177–178, 187–188, 193, 200, 214, 224, 267, 270, 273, 298, 317, 325, 329, 331, 334
administration, 76–77, 82, 93
almshouses, 46
alternatives, 88–93
chaplain's services, 86
(*See also* Volunteers)
conditions, 30, 78, 108
construction, 79
gatehouses, 29
holding, 75, 253
human squirrel cage, 32
informal settings, 84
inspections, 81
lock-ups, 75, 77–78, 85
metro-jail, 94
personnel, 83–84
sheriff, 25–26, 29, 36, 38, 76, 93, 120
population, 29, 32, 46–47, 76–78, 109, 144, 173
private keepers, 29
program rehabilitation, 83–84
purposes, 75
rationale, 73–76

Jail *(Cont.):*
reform, 32, 81–82, 94–95
regional, 74, 85, 94
rehabilitation, 83–84
as reintegration institution, 82–88
rural, 74
standards, 81–82, 305
state-operated, 77
stockade, 75
suburban, 74
towers, 29
townhouse cellars, 29
"ultimate ghetto," 79
workhouses, 29–30, 32, 46
Jail Center, 82
Jail Management, 96
Jamestown, Virginia, 30
Jaycee Prison Reform Commission, 175
Jaycees, 65, 129, 161, 175
(*See also* Service organizations)
Jewish Community for Personal Services, 166
Job, 16, 19, 43, 83–86, 113, 127, 166, 175, 185, 189, 193, 195, 204, 207, 224, 237, 252, 259, 277, 328
bank, 218, 220
development, 91, 160, 171–177, 195, 215, 248, 282
hunting, 13, 86–87, 108, 145, 158, 165, 169, 173, 198, 219–220, 261, 299, 311, 326
interview, 108, 146, 148, 169, 171, 193, 220, 326
keeping, 86
placement, 19, 90, 148–149, 154, 171–172, 175, 177, 179, 220, 276, 279, 282, 328, 339
private program, 174–176, 185
public program, 172–174, 176, 185
and private industry, 137–138, 148, 158, 172–173, 181, 298, 303
resumés, 108, 326
skills, 5, 44, 129, 328
Job Opportunities in Business Sector, 172
Job Therapy, Inc., 166, 170
John Howard Association, 12, 165–166, 258
Johnson County, Kansas, 130

Johnson County Coalition for
Prevention of Child Abuse,
130
Joint Commission on
Correctional Manpower and
Training, 309
Joyceville, Ontario, Canada, 326
Judge, 4–5, 7–8, 10–11, 25,
29, 32, 34, 46–47, 58, 61,
89, 102–103, 105, 109,
112–113, 117, 159, 168,
188, 191, 233, 257, 260,
267, 280, 282, 290, 325,
331, 337
itinerant, 32
Judicial disposition, 103
Judicial reprieve, 35
Junior League of New York, 132
"Just deserts," 258
Juvenile, 34, 46–47, 62, 74–75,
78, 102, 168, 221, 247,
266–292, 314
community-based corrections,
275–276
corrections, 271–272, 275,
288
court (See Court, juvenile)
delinquent, 267, 270, 281
detention center, 47, 168
diversion (see Diversion,
juvenile)
candidate, 276
emotionally disturbed, 272
evaluation, 288–289
foster care, 132, 280–281,
286–287, 290
homes, 132, 276, 290
jurisdiction, 267, 269–271,
276
justice system, 46, 269, 271,
273, 276, 281, 284, 291
in need of supervision (see
Adjudication)
offender, 27, 77, 221,
266–267, 291
parole (after care), 276,
287–288, 290
probation, 266, 276–277,
279–280, 282, 284, 287,
290
proceedings, 284
recidivism, 289
residence, community-based,
284–286
restitution, 283–284
rights, 268
social control system, 269, 284
status offender, 266,
269–274, 279, 291
testimony, 280

Juvenile (Cont.):
training school, 27, 270, 289,
303
Juvenile Delinquency, 314
Juvenile Justice and Delinquency
Prevention Act, 270

Kalamazoo, Michigan, 331
"Kangaroo courts," 84, 144
Kansas, 16, 60–61, 130,
137–138, 178, 286, 290,
325, 340
Kansas City, Missouri, 166, 214,
283, 316, 339
Kansas Community Corrections
Act, 61
Kansas State Industrial
Reformatory, 130
Kansas State Penitentiary, 130,
137
Kentucky, 44, 60, 117, 131, 214,
248, 290
Kent v. United States, 268
(See also Court decisions)
Killits decision, 36
(See also Court decisions)
Kiwanis, 180
(See also Service
organizations)

Labeling, 277, 284, 291, 314
stigma, 159, 277, 284, 314
La Mesa Penitentiary, 138
Lansing, Kansas, 130, 178
Latin America, 38
Latins, 275
Law, 197, 238, 249
case, 307
common, 35, 101
enabling, 34
legal aid societies, 108
legal counsel, 94, 113, 166,
177, 251–253, 268
legal fees, 339
legal obstacles, 314
legal problems, 107, 148
litigation, 222, 227, 325
public, 29, 278
Law Enforcement Assistance
Administration, 48, 55, 79,
85, 91–92, 120–121, 130,
138, 149, 171–172, 225,
282, 289, 307, 313,
340–341
Law enforcement personnel, 13,
41–42, 61, 74, 76, 80,
88–89, 93–94, 105, 109,
120, 159, 191, 195,

Law enforcement personnel
(Cont.):
206–207, 216, 236, 249,
274, 277, 281, 284,
312–313, 339, 341
"extra work," 206
peace officer organization, 120
Law of Moses, 336
Lawrence, Kansas, 286
Laws of Alfred, 5
Leavenworth, Kansas, 138, 178
Lee County, Alabama, 86
Legislation, 26, 46–47, 60, 63,
102, 134, 189, 250–251,
258, 280, 340
service activities, 142
Legislators, 8, 14, 16, 25, 41,
61, 257, 310, 318, 324,
330, 339, 341
Legislature, 6, 8, 10, 61,
189–190, 197, 224, 241,
257, 260, 297–298, 301,
313, 332, 342
Legitimate opportunity, 203
Leisure time activities, 54, 116,
128, 130, 140, 148, 153,
165, 189, 215, 220
classroom instruction, 128
extracurricular activities, 128
unsupervised activities, 219
Library, 42, 82, 85–86, 95, 114,
219, 284
Life imprisonment, 106, 233
Lilly Endowment, Inc., 164, 282
Lincoln, Nebraska, 325
Lino lakes, Minnesota, 138
Local corrections, 62, 74, 81, 93,
95, 100, 102, 114, 126,
255, 280
Lock-ups (see Jails)
London, England, 42
London Parochial Foundation, 42
Long Island, New York, 42
Lorton Reformatory, 129
Los Angeles, California, 43,
150, 166, 174, 214, 222,
282–283, 312, 339
Los Angeles County Probation
and Parole Department, 174
Los Angeles Youth Project, 312
Los Cruces, New Mexico, 282
Louis Harris Poll, 309
Louisburg, Pennsylvania, 146
Louisiana, 16, 138, 258, 267,
330

Macon County, Illinois, 273
Macon, Georgia, 337
Maine, 9, 117, 131, 139, 198,
238, 246, 257–258, 336

Maine State Prison, 139
Mandatory release (see Release, mandatory)
Mandatory sentencing (see Sentencing)
Manhattan, New York, 42, 89
Manhattan Bail Project, 89
Manhattan Jail Riot, 81
Manipulative techniques (see Supervision)
Man to Man Service, 166
Manpower Development and Training Program, 311
Manual of Correctional Standards, 306
Manual of Jail Management, 82
Manual of Standards for Adult Community Residential Services, 306
Manual of Standards for Juvenile Detention Facilities and Services, 306
Manual of Standards for Juvenile Probation and After Care Services, 306
Manual of Standards for Juvenile Residential Services, 306
Manual of Standards for Juvenile Training Schools, 306
Mark system, 26, 45
Marriage, 17, 83, 114, 131, 148, 194, 207, 220, 237, 244, 249, 328
Maryland, 16, 47, 60, 82, 86, 149, 246, 258, 282, 290, 330, 338
Massachusetts, 26, 34–35, 40–41, 47, 66, 117, 131, 141, 150, 153, 170, 190, 194, 246, 258, 280, 283, 289–291, 300–302, 334–335, 341
Massachusetts Bay Colony, 30
Massachusetts Department of Corrections, 150, 334
Massachusetts Department of Youth Services, 289
Massachusetts Halfway Houses, Inc., 246
699 House, 246
Massachusetts State Prison Colony, 141
McKeiver v. Pennsylvania, 268
(See also Court decisions)
McLennon County, Texas, 115
Media (see Public education)
Mediators, 165, 338
Medical, 61, 65, 75, 77, 338
care, 79, 108, 173, 193, 279, 303, 311, 314, 339

Medical (Cont.):
clinic, 54, 108, 282
doctors, 65, 101–102
examination, 84
illness, 11, 32, 77, 339
services, 95, 317
outpatient services, 137, 306
standards, 82
Mempa v. Rhay, 113, 120
(See also Court decisions)
Men's Residential Correctional Center, 91
Mental health, 48, 192
centers, 60, 102, 195, 277, 281, 285, 292
illness, 5, 18, 32, 75, 77
personality disorders, 83, 128, 172, 236
retardation, 75, 130, 226
service delivery system, 179–180
Metropolitan Correctional Center, 76
Mexico, 138, 166
Miami, Florida, 274
Michigan, 47, 82, 103, 116, 118, 131, 141, 159, 168, 201, 246, 248, 258, 281, 290, 331
Michigan Federation of Private Child and Family Agencies, 290
Michigan State Penitentiary, 141
Mid-City Project, 312
Middle Ages, 4
Middle class, 161, 215, 237, 275, 327
Military, 75, 146
veteran's rights, 148
Military servitude, 4
Milwaukee, Wisconsin, 222
Milwaukie, Oregon, 197
Milwaukie Work Release Center, 197–198, 203
Minneapolis, Minnesota, 312
Minnesota, 9, 16, 27, 60–63, 85, 92, 131, 133, 138, 165, 167, 191, 221, 240, 246, 254, 258, 267, 290, 316, 325, 337, 339–340
Minnesota Community Corrections Act, 61–62
Minnesota Corrections Department, 27
Minnesota State Reformatory, 254
Misdemeanants, 75, 77, 89, 101–102, 114, 163, 179, 188–189, 191–192, 214

Misdemeanor, 32, 75, 77, 90, 125, 165, 254
disorderly conduct, 77
drunkenness, 77, 140, 198, 206, 269
Mississippi, 16, 38, 46, 133–134, 222, 330
Missouri, 7, 34, 115, 179, 258, 283, 315
Missouri Institute of Psychiatry, 179
Mitigating circumstances, 7, 8, 10
"Model acts," 305
Model Penal Code, 238
Money, 13, 127, 136, 138–140, 145–146, 149, 152, 168, 170, 197, 204, 206, 218, 220, 237, 252, 257, 262
Monroe, Washington, 166
Montana, 27
Montgomery County, Maryland, 82, 149
Montreal, Canada, 326
Moritorium, 7, 329
Morrissey v. Brewer, 253
Mothers-in-Prison Project, 132
Move-in-the-dark-of-the-night, 227
Multnomah County, Oregon, 116
Mutual Agreement Program, 245–246, 258
performance goals, 246
(See also Parole contracts)

National Advisory Commission on Criminal Justice Standards and Goals, 17, 19, 82, 87, 243, 250, 252, 306, 310
National Alliance of Businessmen, 172
National Assessment of Juvenile Corrections, 271
National Association of Volunteers in Criminal Justice, 164
National Center on Institutions and Alternatives, 78
National Committee for the Prevention of Child Abuse and Neglect, 313
National Council on Crime and Delinquency, 91, 121, 166, 270, 328
"National disgrace," 324
(See also "Combustible scandal")

National Institute of Corrections, 19, 82, 164, 341
National Institute of Corrections National Information Center, 82, 234
National Institute of Mental Health, 67—68
National Institute of Mental Health for Studies of Crime and Delinquency, 67
National Jail Census, 77
National Law Journal, 7
National Probation and Parole Association, 305
National Sheriff's Association, 82, 94, 306
National Task Force on Corrections, 81
Nebraska, 133, 205, 242, 282, 286, 325
Nebraska Bar Association, 325
Nebraska Center for Women, 133
Nebraska Eighth Court of Appeals, 242
Neighborhood, 193, 222, 227, 259, 285, 312, 318
councils, 314
program, 311—312
(*See also* Prevention)
Netherlands, 329
Nevada, 7, 60, 178, 329
New Careers, 173—174
New England, 139, 220
"New fish," 56—57
New Gate Penitentiary, 8
New Hampshire, 27, 36, 47, 201
New Haven, Connecticut, 82
New Haven, Missouri, 179—180
New Jersey, 47, 60, 81, 131, 191, 248, 258, 267, 283, 316
New Mexico, 58, 238, 257, 282
New Mexico State Prison, 58
New Orleans, Louisiana, 26, 42
Newport News, Virginia, 279
New Pride, Inc., 282—283
Newton, Iowa, 173
New York, 7—8, 11, 35—36, 43, 45—47, 58, 103, 118, 126—127, 131—133, 141, 166, 174, 189, 191, 195, 239, 251, 258, 270, 298, 303, 330, 339
New York City, New York, 26, 41—42, 46—47, 76, 85, 89, 130, 143, 150, 162, 174—175, 195, 214, 222, 278, 285, 305, 313

New York City Commissioner of Corrections, 305
New York City Correctional Facility, 130
New York City Department of Probation, 278
New York Department of Corrections and Services, 303
New York State Reformatory, 26
Nineteenth century, 4, 26—27, 32, 34—36, 41, 79, 313, 329
Ninth century, 5
Nominalism, 308
Nonprofit agencies, 43, 212, 283—284, 286, 325
(*See also* Private agencies)
Nonviolent offender (*see* Offender, nonviolent)
Nonwhite, 90, 151
Norfolk Island, 45
Norman House, 42, 212—213
North Carolina, 7, 37—38, 117, 131, 172, 175, 191, 246, 258, 286
North Carolina Service League, 166
North Dakota, 329
North Richmond, California, 313
Norway, 38
Norwood Law, 8—9
Number, 208

Oakland, California, 44
Odd Fellows Hall, 231
Odyssey House, 162
Offender:
achievement motivation, 203, 274—275
anxieties, 145—146, 194, 222, 318
aptitudes, 220
aspirations, 189, 237, 327—328
attitudes, 113, 150, 188—189, 203, 239
behavior, 207, 220, 241, 288, 327
capabilities, 194, 244
communication skills, 142, 277
coping, 154, 178, 197, 227, 232, 328
depression, 42
ethics, 57
ex-offender (*see* Employment, ex-offender; Ex-offender)

Offender *(Cont.):*
fears, 145—146, 208, 222, 318, 330
health, 93, 250, 306
hopelessness, 80
humiliation, 53, 333
interpersonal problems, 108, 145, 194—195, 207, 220, 223, 309
morale, 134, 327
motherhood, 131—132
pregnancy, 134
nonoffender categories, 272
non-self-correcting, 300
nonviolent, 6, 12—13, 91, 121, 192, 227, 239, 297, 325, 328, 333, 342
petty, 30, 34
problem-solving, 5, 128, 142, 148, 153, 241
psychopathic, 234
rapport building, 116, 223
rejection, 129
semiskilled, 127, 129, 262
short-term, 83
tensions, 134, 139, 195, 203, 206, 227, 232, 286
"trustworthy," 190
unmarried, 201
unreliable, 206
unskilled, 127, 129, 201, 262
values, 5, 48, 113, 188, 271
violent, 4, 6, 12—13, 63, 84, 95, 192, 206, 228, 267, 314, 316, 328, 331—332, 336
voluntary change, 333
Offender Aid and Restoration—USA, 86, 164
Office of Economic Opportunity, 313
Office of Juvenile Justice and Delinquency Prevention, 78, 174, 282
Ohio, 8—9, 42, 46—47, 60, 117, 233—234, 238, 248, 257, 313, 339
Ohio State Legislature, 233
Oklahoma, 131, 136, 174, 283
Omaha, Nebraska, 282
Omnibus Crime Control and Safe Streets Act, 340
Ontario, Canada, 127, 326
Operating public, 161—163
Optimum release time, 235
Orange County, California, 92
Oregon, 60—61, 63, 104, 116, 197, 203, 258
Oregon Community Corrections Act, 61, 63

Oregon State Correctional
    Institution, 197
Oregon State Penitentiary, 197
"Organize the Community to
    Befriend You," 227
Osborne Association, 128
"Our Challenge: Influencing
    Public Policy," 309
"Out of sight, out of mind," 161
Outside Connection, 178
Outward Bound, 283

Parchman Prison Camp, 133
Pardon, 101, 233–234
    (See also Release)
Parens patrie, 46–47, 269, 291
Parent, 46, 270–271, 274–275,
    277, 280
    education, 311, 313
    parent teacher association, 161
Parole, 6, 9–10, 13, 15, 25–27,
    40–47, 52–53, 60, 65, 67,
    87, 101, 129, 133–134,
    148–149, 151, 154,
    159–160, 176–177, 186,
    189, 191, 203, 205, 215,
    220, 227, 232–262, 266,
    314, 317, 333, 337, 339,
    341
    abolished, 257–258,
        260–261
    administration, 161, 237–238,
        251, 257, 260, 305
    advantages, 234–235
    agreement, 249, 258
    aides, 248
    appeal, 243
    board, 7, 15, 105, 189,
        234–235, 237–239,
        242–244, 246, 249,
        251–253, 257–260
        candidate list, 239
        civil service list, 238
        examiner, 239, 241, 243
        independent, 238
        members, 238
        professional, 238–239
    contract, 194, 246, 258, 333
        Mutual Agreement
            Program, 245–246, 258
    criticisms, 235, 257–258
    decision-making, 239,
        251–252
    definition, 233–234
    denial, 242–243
    eligibility, 191, 239–241
    evaluation, 254
    federal, 9
    field investigation, 241

Parole (Cont.):
    hearings, 234, 239, 241–243,
        248, 251–253, 259
    "Illinois Plan," 261
    interstate compact, 250
    interview, 241–242, 248, 259
    Irish System, 45
    juvenile (see Parole, juvenile)
    mark system, 26, 45
    "matrix," 258
    officer, 44, 54, 172, 194–195,
        204, 233, 236, 239,
        248–253, 258, 287
        as helping person,
            248–249, 259–260
        reports, 286–287
        resource broker (see
            Resource broker)
        as rule enforcer, 248, 252,
            261
    panels, 241
    parole d'honneur, 46
    plan, 241
    prediction techniques, 243–245
        actuarial tables, 243, 244
        anamnestic predictions, 243
        base expectancy tables, 243
        categoric prediction, 243
        intuitive prediction, 243
        risk factors, 227, 239, 244,
            250
        success, 159
        "truth group," 244
    preparole: corrections center,
        159
        preparolee, 213
        reports, 141, 159
        (See also Prelease)
    release, 191, 250–251, 254,
        256, 258
        guidelines, 252, 258
    revocation, 215, 234–235,
        248, 250–254, 260, 288,
        302
        procedures, 252–253
    rules, 148, 235, 239,
        249–252, 262
    selection process, 239–246,
        262
    services, 234, 261, 305
    shock, 233–234
    standards, 239–240
    success, 247
    supervision, 234, 237, 239,
        244, 246–250,
        252–257, 259–261
    suspension, 248, 251, 288
    tickets of license, 45
    violations, 12, 253, 255–256,
        261–262

Parole violations (Cont.):
    technical, 251. 256, 261
    word of honor, 46
Parole Correction Project, 246
Parole and Prerelease
    Employment Program,
    173
"Participatory management,"
    142–143, 145
    complaints, 142
    (See also Self-government)
Pascagoula, Mississippi, 222
Passes, 38–40
    (See also Day passes;
        Transition methods)
Patronage plum, 76
Peer group pressure, 217, 219,
    314, 328
Penal code, 101
Penalty, 11, 233, 257, 341
Pennsylvania, 19, 41, 47, 60, 66,
    74, 85, 131, 146, 189, 200,
    248, 268, 274
Pennsylvania Prison Society, 175
Pensacola, Florida, 283
Pentonville Prison, 42
People ex rel. Forsythe v. Court
    of Sessions, 36
    (See also Court decisions)
Peoria, Illinois, 90
Perryville, Arizona, 138
Personal service-restitution, 331
Personnel, 83–84, 306
    activities coordinator, 218
    clinical director, 221
    community coordinator, 195,
        218
    community resources
        developer, 218
    cook, 218
    custodial officer, 16, 64, 93,
        194
    dentist, 65, 311
    selection of, 115, 238
    social worker, 5, 180, 194,
        220, 238, 285–286, 288,
        309, 311
    teacher, 161, 165, 168, 177,
        194, 274
Personnel problems, 223–224
Personnel salaries, 65, 79, 111,
    120, 238, 259
Persons in need of supervision
    (see Adjudication)
Philadelphia, Pennsylvania, 26,
    30–31, 41, 141, 164, 289,
    307, 313
Philadelphia Society for
    Alleviating Distressed
    Prisoners, 31

Philadelphia Society for
　Alleviating the Misery of
　Public Prisoners, 163
Philanthropic Society of London,
　40, 285
Phoenix, Arizona, 138
Phoenix House, 162
Pierce County, Washington, 90
Pima County, Arizona, 273
Plains, 236
Plea bargaining, 7, 106−107
Police:
　investigation, 277
　liaison program, 312−313
　(See also Law enforcement
　　personnel)
Policymakers, 239, 310
Political affiliation, 238, 260,
　318
Political clubs, 179
Politicians, 160, 290
Pontiac, Michigan, 281
Population, institutional, 8, 62,
　65, 77, 80, 84, 88, 94−95,
　223, 324, 329
　cellhouse, 95, 331
　jail, 32, 46, 144, 173
Portland, Oregon, 116, 197
Prerelease, 67, 178, 215
　center, 16, 44, 60, 66,
　　145−154, 212−213,
　　301−302, 306, 317, 334,
　　342
　guidance center, 43−44, 67,
　　148−150, 167, 195, 220
　　(See also Residence,
　　　community-based)
　handbook, 145
　program, 18, 54, 66, 100,
　　125−127, 146−148,
　　150−153, 158, 185, 232,
　　316, 334, 339
Presentence investigation, 91,
　102, 104−106, 108−109,
　120, 192, 241, 244, 246
　social history, 115, 251, 267,
　　280
President's Commission on Law
　Enforcement and
　Administration of Justice,
　43, 48, 53, 81−82, 84, 87,
　160, 238, 276, 281−282,
　306
President's Task Force on
　Prisoner Rehabilitation,
　325
Presumptive sentencing, 6−7
　(See also Sentencing)
Prevention, 310−315
　child abuse, 313−314

Prevention (Cont.):
　definition, 310−311
　detached worker, 288
　macrosociological programs,
　　311
　normative sponsorship theory,
　　314−315
　pre-prevention, 311
　rehabilitative prevention, 311
　strategies, 311
　street corner gang worker, 288
　Unwed Mothers Service
　　Center, 313
Prison, 11, 14, 17−18, 38, 41,
　44, 55−58, 62−64, 66−68,
　75, 83, 100−101, 113,
　125−154, 198, 215, 233,
　253, 256, 267, 270,
　302−303, 330
　closed, 16, 214, 217, 224,
　　234, 332
　coeducational, 332
　communitylike, 185
　conditions, 55−59, 139, 140,
　　144, 206, 212, 224, 234,
　　309
　　homosexuality, 57, 77, 134
　　routinization, 59, 140, 206,
　　　212, 224, 234
　custody, 82, 96, 301
　　custodial rating, 128
　entrepreneurs, 138−139
　factorylike, 138, 303,
　　325−326
　free enterprise, 138−139, 303
　industrial program, 139
　institution based corrections,
　　18, 48, 65, 189, 219,
　　246
　moritorium, 7, 329
　open, 331
　"secure," 219, 290
　"snitches," 58
　wages, 136−137
　　"living wage," 136
　work experience, 127−129,
　　135−141, 158, 161, 171,
　　189, 203
Prison Association of New York,
　45
Prison Community, The, 56
Prisoner, 33, 42, 55, 100,
　125−154, 168, 174, 259,
　317
　aid organizations, 166−167,
　　175−177
　handicapped, 77, 172
　network, 325
　privileges, 107, 129,
　　131−135, 138, 153, 158,

Prisoner (Cont.):
　177−179, 188, 193, 207,
　216, 219−220
　separation center, 146
Prisoner Rehabilitation Act, 43
Prisoners Accelerated Creative
　Exposure, Inc., 130
Prisoners Aid by Citizen Effort,
　Inc., 166
Prisoners Employment Program,
　173
Prisonization, 56−58, 100, 125,
　128, 153, 185, 224, 234,
　333
　"do their own time," 309
　inmate code, 55−58, 224,
　　309
　　(See also Prison conditions)
　intrainstitutional tension, 64
　"new fish," 56−57
　prison culture, 56, 58
　prison neurosis, 57
Prison Journal, The, 143
Prison Reform Commission, 175
Prison World, The, 305
Private agencies, 41, 160, 165,
　212, 226, 272, 274, 285,
　291, 311, 339
　(See also Nonprofit agencies)
Probare, 101
Probation, 6, 13, 15, 25−27,
　32−36, 47, 52, 55, 59,
　65−67, 83, 87, 91,
　100−121, 125,
　159−160, 186,
　191−192, 214, 220, 227,
　233−234, 246, 266, 276,
　298, 300, 314, 317,
　336−337, 339, 342
　administration, 102−104
　advantages, 101−102
　case assignment, 103−104
　case files, 108
　　(See also Caseload)
　conditions, 114
　day-to-day tasks, 108−112
　definition, 101
　evaluation, 118−120
　juvenile, tracker, 280
　　(See also Juvenile,
　　　probation)
　legality, 35−36
　　Killits decision, 36
　officer, 34, 54, 103−105,
　　107−109, 112,
　　114−115, 118, 120, 161,
　　163, 168, 194−195,
　　222
　　selection of, 115
　plan, 105, 109, 113, 116

Probation *(Cont.):*
presentence investigation *(see* Presentence investigation)
rationale, 101
records, 192
relationship, 108−113
"reluctant probationer," 116
revocation, 104, 112−114
(See also Revocation)
rule enforcement, 112, 114
selection, 104−107, 114
services, 103, 114, 119, 121, 305
innovative, 115−118
shock, 117, 339
statutory limitation, 106
supervision, 59−60, 101−102, 104, 119
counseling techniques, 108
executive techniques, 108
guidance techniques, 108
manipulative techniques, 107−108, 143
resource broker, 91, 108, 111, 121, 248
techniques of, 107−108
trends, 114−115
career oriented service, 115
centralized organization, 114, 280
Probational Offender Rehabilitation and Training (PORT), 221
Probation Subsidy Act, 55, 60, 117−118
(See also Subsidy)
Project Culture, 130
Project Head Start, 311
Project Re-Entry, 170
Project Second Chance, 174
Proposition 13, 340−341
"Protecting society," 309
(See also Incapacitation)
Providence, Rhode Island, 283
Psychiatric, 5
counseling, 140, 312
difficulty, 116
nurse, 180
test, 84, 214
Psychiatric Institute Foundation, 221
Psychiatrist, 65, 144, 168, 180, 195, 221, 238, 285, 308−309
Psychological:
abuse, 37, 314
counseling, 140, 161, 303, 311, 312
disorder, 58, 116, 220, 274

Psychological *(Cont.):*
test, 214, 288
Psychologist, 168, 195, 238, 285−286, 308−309
Psychotherapy, 286−287, 327
Public:
general, 5−6, 14, 26, 53, 63−65, 67, 105, 148, 154, 160, 170, 194−195, 197, 204, 218, 224, 227, 239, 276, 297, 301, 332
operating, 161−163
receiving, 162−163
supporting, 161−163
Public advertising, 59, 162
Public agencies, 161−163, 165, 181, 212, 216, 272, 274, 284−285, 291, 311
Public assistance, 54, 102, 108, 116, 206, 220
Public charity, 30
Public education, 160−163, 176, 216, 227, 310, 318, 325, 332
communication skills, 148, 161, 178, 307
methods of, 48, 63, 140, 148, 161−163, 167, 169, 185, 193, 216, 227, 310
coalition building, 162
consultation, 162
inmate panel, 163, 193, 315
media, 48, 144, 161−162, 169, 190, 309
sales kit, 175
special events, 162
tarnished halo, 304
Public humiliation, 3
Public image, 161, 189
Public interest, 93, 310
Public policy, 309
Public pressure, 224−225
Public protection, 204, 206−207, 218, 228, 234
Public reaction, 63−65, 120, 198
Public relations, 63, 142, 218, 224, 227, 310, 312
public relations officer, 162
Public support, 96, 105, 120, 239, 298, 330
Puerto Rico, 34
Punishment, 3−6, 8, 11, 13−14, 20, 28−32, 48, 79, 83, 94, 96, 102, 154, 300, 309, 330, 332−333, 336
capital *(see* Capital punishment)
corporeal *(see* Corporeal punishment)
Purdy Treatment Center, 132

Quakers, 26, 31, 41, 164
Quincy, Illinois, 312
Quincy Community Youth Development Project, 312

Race, 103, 148, 312
Racine, Wisconsin, 291
Rand Corporation, 341
"Real-life solutions," 326−327
"Reasonable probability," 240
"Recall to mind," 35
Receiving public, 162−163
(See also Public)
Recidivism, 6, 17, 42, 65−68, 85, 116, 133, 150−153, 159, 166, 170, 177, 200, 204−205, 224, 226, 229, 251, 254−257, 262, 277, 281−282, 288, 299, 303−304, 316, 326, 334−335, 341
juvenile, 289
Recognizance, 35, 86, 89−91, 214
(See also Diversion)
Record keeping, 221, 223, 306
Recreation, 40, 44, 54, 82, 85, 91, 95, 100, 107−108, 126, 128−129, 139−140, 142, 153, 159, 179, 186, 193, 207, 215−216, 219, 276−277, 285−286, 311, 317, 327
hobbycraft, 40, 128, 130, 139−140, 165, 277
Recruitment, 163, 165, 169−170, 217, 285
(See also Personnel)
"Red houses," 133
(See also Conjugal visits)
Redirection, 18, 20, 297, 317, 327, 333−335
Reentry, 73, 257, 262
Reform, 11, 48, 93, 144, 188, 258, 303, 307−310, 331, 343
externally induced, 308
hindrances to, 308−309
internally induced, 308
(See also Change; Innovation)
Reformatory, 17, 267, 270
Regulations *(see* Rules)
Rehabilitation, 3, 5−6, 8, 11−14, 16−17, 20, 53−54, 83, 121, 129, 135, 142, 190, 193, 201, 241, 260, 270, 277, 297, 301, 308−309, 316, 324

"Rehabilitative ideal," 13,
17–18
Rehumanize, 153
Reintegration, 14, 18–19,
47–48, 52–53, 60, 64,
67–68, 73–74, 80, 83–88,
94, 96, 100–102, 107, 126,
149, 153, 158, 160, 173,
176, 180–181, 186–187,
192, 197, 213, 215,
218–219, 229, 233–234,
248, 252, 261–262, 317,
327, 332, 338
Reintegration centers, 228
Relationships, 55, 59, 128–129,
140, 148, 160, 167,
169–170, 186, 206, 211,
218–219, 336
one-to-one relationship, 107,
162, 166, 175, 338
trusting, 170, 249
Release, 46, 53, 55, 58–59, 66,
83, 117, 128, 145–146,
148–149, 153, 159, 168,
175, 228, 232, 235, 237,
246, 249, 258, 284, 303,
333
classification, 128
conditional, 45, 233, 256
gradual, 186, 333
"hit the streets," 208
mandatory, 53, 149, 205, 215,
233, 235, 254, 261, 342
"muster out," 146
optimum time, 235
plan, 128, 133, 146,
192–194, 220, 246
process of planning,
192–193
postinstitutional mechanism,
228
preconditioning, 207, 213
pretrial release (see Diversion)
questions asked potential
releasees, 191–192
referral service, 258, 276, 282
study release (see Study release)
supervision, 194–198, 246
temporary release (see
Temporary release)
work release (see Work
release)
(See also "Gate" money;
Pardon; Parole)
Religion, 16, 85, 94–95, 100,
103, 112
(See also Counseling)
Reno, Oklahoma, 136
Reparation, 4–5, 102, 197, 324,
336, 337

Research, 17–18, 82, 106, 115,
150, 170, 177, 200, 203,
226, 247, 256, 275, 284,
289, 297–301, 303, 304,
310, 318, 327, 329
correctional, 298–301
design, 301
feedback, 301
program strategy, 301
theoretical assumptions, 301
validation of techniques,
300–301
(See also Evaluation)
Residence, community-based,
26–27, 40–44, 47, 49,
53–54, 60, 64–65, 67, 82,
84, 91, 148–150,
153–154, 158, 162, 187,
191–193, 195, 197, 205,
211–229, 232, 284–286,
298, 303, 305, 316, 340,
342
contracted housing, 193
current status, 212
description, 205, 216,
218–219
development, 215–216
site selection, 213,
215–216, 226, 309
(See also Site selection)
dwellings used, 213, 215–216
evaluation, 225–226
informal structure of,
217–219, 284
juvenile, 284–286
"over-use," 223
personnel, 217–218
problems encountered,
222–225
programs, 218–222
quasi-institutional setting, 213
residents, 214–215
postinstitutional, 215
preinstitutional, 214
satellite facilities, 84
supervision, 217–218
types of facilities, 213–214
community correctional
center (see Community
correction center)
community treatment center
(see Community
treatment center)
halfway house (see Halfway
house)
prerelease center (see
Prerelease, center)
prerelease guidance center
(see Prerelease, guidance
center)

Residence, community-based,
types of facilities
(Cont.):
residential housing unit (see
Residential housing unit)
residential treatment center
(see Residential treatment
center)
Resident Government Council,
144
Residential housing unit, 193,
212–214, 217, 220, 269
(See also Residence,
community-based)
Residential institution, 47, 272
program, 25
Residential treatment center,
228, 285
(See also Residence,
community-based)
Resource broker, 91, 108, 111,
121, 248
(See also Parole; Probation)
Restitution, 3, 6, 16, 102, 112,
114, 119, 121, 129, 188,
205, 218, 283–284, 303,
314, 317, 325–326,
336–338, 339, 341–342
center, 228, 337
community service, 188, 284,
337
creative, 337
constructive consequences,
337
juvenile, 283–284
Retribution, 3, 189, 324, 332, 338
symbolic, 188, 283, 337
tangible, 337
Revocation, 104, 112–113, 119,
214, 235
hearings, 108, 112–113, 235
notice of violation report, 108
procedures, 252–253
technical violations, 114, 119,
251, 256, 261
(See also Parole; Probation)
Revolutionary War, 30–31, 44
Re Winship, 268 (See also Court
decisions)
Rhode Island, 7, 47, 77, 84, 283
Richmond, Virginia, 86, 174
Richmond Center Community
Relations Division, 174
Rikers Island, New York, 130,
174
Riot, 12, 58, 81, 144
Risk Prediction Scale, 104
Riverview Release Center, 173
Rochester, Minnesota, 221
Rochester State Hospital, 221

Rockville, Maryland, 149
Rome, Georgia, 337
Room and board, 137, 139, 195, 202, 241, 303, 326
Rotary, 18, 175
  (*See also* Service organizations)
Royal Navy, 45
Royal Oak, Michigan, 116, 168
Rules, 141, 178, 194, 197–198, 205–206, 212, 217–218, 223–224, 233, 239, 249, 279
  infraction, 112
  "Mickey Mouse," 140
  rigidity of, 140, 206
  (*See also* Parole; Probation)
Runathon to Prevent Child Abuse, 130
Rutgers School of Criminal Justice, 261
Rutgers University, 261

Safe Streets Act, 48
Salient factor score, 244
  (*See also* Parole, prediction techniques)
Salt Lake City, Utah, 64, 222
Salt Lake County, 92
Salvation Army, 114, 127, 166
Sam Houston School of Contemporary Corrections, 127
San Antonio, Texas, 81, 86
San Diego, California, 76, 85, 162, 278
San Diego County Probation Department, 278
San Francisco, California, 26, 42, 166, 179, 283, 340
San Joaquin, California, 81
San Joaquin County Jail, 81
San Jose, California, 81, 132
San Mateo, California, 85, 92, 178
San Quentin, 134
Santa Clara County Women's Residential Center, 132
Santa Fe, New Mexico, 58
"Save Parole Supervision," 257
School, 19, 43, 45, 55, 65, 82, 95, 102, 107–108, 132, 135, 140, 167, 173, 179, 187, 192–193, 198, 211, 213, 215, 217, 219, 226, 237, 246, 274–275, 277, 281–282, 284, 286, 288, 310, 312–314
  diploma, 17

School (*Cont.*):
  drop-out and delinquency, 274
  "drop-outs anonymous," 313
  leaders, 275
  police liaison program, 312–313
School of depravity, 41
Seagoville, Texas, 146
Second Annual Runathon to Prevent Child Abuse, 130
Secret inquisitional processes, 268
  (*See also* Juvenile rights)
Security:
  "high security risk," 190, 200–201
  maximum, 57, 64–65, 126, 212, 216, 228, 303, 316, 332
  medium, 134, 138, 212, 216, 226, 303, 316, 332
  minimum, 75, 134, 149, 216, 303, 316, 334
Self-concept, 135, 203, 234, 283
Self-determination, 227
Self-discipline, 206, 227
Self-employment, 187, 192
Self-esteem, 100, 125, 188, 197, 203, 317, 327–328
Self-evaluation, 305–306
Self-generation, 333
Self-government, 140–145, 158
  cellhouse and, 141–142
  inmate council, 141, 143–144
  institutional, 141–143, 153
  "participatory management," 142–143, 145
  "town meeting," 141–142, 220
Self-help groups, 18, 126, 130, 153
Self-incrimination, 112, 268
Self-management, 130, 140–141, 145, 153, 212, 219, 234, 317
  voucher system, 140–141
Self-preservation, 300
Self-report studies, 275
  anonymous questionnaire, 275
  interviewing techniques, 275
Self-sufficient, 237, 283, 317, 328, 337–338
Senate Subcommittee on Juvenile Delinquency, 270
Sentencing, 35, 61–62, 74–75, 83, 87, 101, 138, 149, 178, 191, 237, 257, 260, 262
  aggravating circumstances, 7–8, 10
  commensurate deserts, 8, 258

Sentencing (*Cont.*):
  commutation, 233
  determinate sentences, 6–12, 16, 238, 257, 260–261, 330–331, 342
  enhancements, 12
  indeterminate sentence, 6–12, 178
  maximum sentence, 233, 240, 250–251
  minimum sentence, 233, 239–240
  mitigating circumstances, 7–8, 10
  predictive, 11
  split sentence, 117
  suspended sentence, 35, 87, 101, 117, 339
  weekend sentence, 83
Sentencing options, 188, 339
Sentencing practices, 6, 9, 62, 117
  flat-time, 6
  mandatory, 6–7
  presumptive, 6–7
Service League of San Mateo, California, 178
Service organizations, 54, 65, 129, 161, 164, 169, 175, 180, 186, 207, 310
Services, 5, 223–224, 228, 247, 274, 276, 282, 292, 311, 316, 341
  human services, 173
  service delivery system, 54
Sesame Street, 132
Seven Steps Program, 166–167, 176
Sex, 103, 127, 134, 168, 220
  sexual abuse, 80, 339
  sexual tensions, 134
Sheriff (*see* Jail, personnel)
Shock parole, 233–234
Shock probation, 117, 340
Sing Sing, 141, 174
Site selection, 65, 138, 159, 179, 215–216, 223, 227–229, 309, 315, 327
  petition, 226–227
  professional resistance, 226–227
  skid row, 215
  war games, 226–227
  zoning, 216, 222, 226–227
Small Business Administration, 129, 175
Social:
  adjustment, 207
  barometer, 3
  code, 28

Social (Cont.):
  debasement, 55−56, 80
  defense, 4
  education, 148
  environment, 18
  events, institutional, 144
  functions, 140, 181, 186, 193,
    198, 215
  groups, 57, 83, 113, 159
  history (see Presentence
    investigation)
  injury, 5
  integration, 180, 207
  order, 206
  problems, 310−311, 343
  roles, 57
Socialization, 237, 270, 327
  customs, 56, 113, 128
  folkways, 56, 128
  mores, 56, 128, 132
  undersocialized, 271
  unsocialized, 271
Socially maladjusted, 271
Social security, 195, 303
Social service program, 86, 129,
  131, 149, 178, 224, 249,
  284
  social services delivery
    system, 185, 282
Society of Friends, 129
Society of Reformation of
  Juvenile Delinquents,
  46−47
Socioeconomic status, 78
South, 236
South Burlington, Vermont,
  221
South Central Youth Project,
  312
South Carolina, 131, 138,
  149−150, 153, 175, 199,
  202, 204, 273
South Carolina Department of
  Corrections, 149
South Dakota, 117, 190, 290
South Dakota State Penitentiary,
  117
"So You Want to Open a
  Halfway House," 64
Special Intensive Parole Unit,
  247−248, 261
Spithead, England, 45
"Split sentence," 117
Spokane County, Washington,
  273
St. Cloud, Minnesota, 254, 267
St. Leonard's House, 43
St. Louis, Missouri, 43, 214,
  279, 316
St. Louis County, Minnesota, 92

St. Louis State Hospital, 179
Standards, 81−82, 94, 103, 118,
  218, 239, 297, 305−306,
  308, 318, 342
  development, 81, 306
Statement of Organization and
  Principles, 239−240
Statement of Principles, 305
Stateville Prison, 15
Status offender, 266, 269−274,
  279, 291
Statutes of Artificers, 46
Stigma, 159, 277, 284, 314
Stillwater, Minnesota, 138, 165
Stillwater Prison Data Processing
  System, Inc., 138
Stone Foundation, 313
"Straight" social world, 237,
  327
"Study and observation," 214
Study release, 38, 54, 85, 95,
  153, 185−208, 211, 215,
  303
  evaluation, 201−202
  selection of participants,
    189−192, 206
Subsidy, 55, 60−63, 94, 103,
  117−118
  comprehensive program, 340
  (See also Probation Subsidy
    Act)
Suffolk County Jail, 81
Suicide, 77, 80
Supervised community visits, 153
Supervised release, 86, 186
Supervised trips, 186, 197, 204,
  206−207, 211
  selection of participants,
    189−192, 206
Supervision, 107−108, 119,
  193, 205−206, 214, 220,
  228−229, 261, 280
  aids (letters, office contacts,
    reports, shakedowns, strip
    searches, telephone calls),
    55, 80, 107, 113, 162,
    194−195, 197, 222, 227,
    317
  (See also Parole; Probation;
    Release)
  contraband, 144
  custodial rating, 128
  follow-up, 206, 248, 282
  intensive, 116, 119, 121, 248,
    280
  mail-in, 104
  maturity typology, 287
  techniques of, 107−108
Supporting public, 161−163
  (See also Public)

Support system, 178, 283, 291
Supreme Court, 3, 36, 79, 113,
  235, 242, 253, 268, 284,
  290
Suspended sentence, 35, 87, 101,
  117, 340
  (See also Sentencing)
Sweden, 38, 40, 188, 326, 329
Symbolic restitution, 188, 283,
  337
  (See also Restitution)

Tallahassee, Florida, 333
Tallahassee Federal Correctional
  Institution, 333
Tangible restitution, 337
  (See also Restitution)
Taxes, 55, 139, 188, 195, 202,
  260, 303, 326, 340
Taxpayers, 149, 161, 188, 205,
  226
Teaching Parent Program, 286
Tehachapi, California, 153
Temporary Asylum for
  Disadvantaged Female
  Prisoners, 41
Temporary release, 27, 36−40,
  95, 185−208, 226, 266
  evaluation, 198−199
  selection of participants,
    189−192, 199, 206
Tennessee, 16, 57−58, 191,
  258, 331
Tennessee State Penitentiary,
  57−58
Texas, 42, 86, 115, 117, 127,
  131, 146, 148, 150, 242,
  277, 283, 307, 313, 330
Texas Department of
  Corrections, 150
Texas Pre-Release Center,
  148
Theatre for the Forgotten, 130
Therapeutic community, 213,
  218, 220−221
Ticket of leave, 45
Tillberga, Sweden, 326
Time, 324
Toastmasters, 129
  (See also Service
    organizations)
Topeka, Kansas, 178, 286
Training, 5, 46, 79, 82, 86, 111,
  118, 120, 132, 142, 144,
  163, 169−170, 193, 235,
  259, 295, 326, 328
  child care worker training, 286
  in-service training, 64, 163,
    286, 332

Training *(Cont.):*
preservice training, 163, 169, 177, 286, 332
Training Manual for Jail Personnel, 94
"Training parents," 286
Transition methods, 185–208, 232, 334
benefits, 202–204
evaluation, 198–202, 204, 211
goals, 187–189
plan, 192–194
procedure, 192–193
rationale, 186
selection of participants, 189–190
supervision, 194–198
Transportation, 44–45, 131, 137, 148, 165, 178, 192, 194, 205, 215, 236, 279, 327
Troy, Missouri, 179–180
"Truth group," 244
Tucker Telephone, 58
Tulsa, Oklahoma, 283
"Turn around," 91
Twentieth century, 27, 32, 67, 78, 139, 228
"Two Studies of Legal Stigma," 159

Uniform Crime Reports, 5, 266
Unions, 54, 139, 165, 180
"union busting," 139, 193
United Kingdom, 188
United Nations, 305–306
United States, 6–7, 9, 13, 16, 27, 34–36, 41, 43, 45, 47, 53, 58, 68, 76–79, 81–82, 85, 115, 127, 133, 148, 166–167, 185, 197–198, 212, 222, 235, 253, 260, 262, 267, 280, 285, 304, 307, 329, 332, 338–339
United States Board of Parole, 262
United States Children's Bureau, 47
United States Courts Administrative Office, 118–119
United States Department of Health, Education, and Welfare, 174, 279
United States Department of Health and Human Services, 174, 279

United States Department of Labor, 171
United States District Court #75, 104
United States Highway #1, 139
United States Parole Commission, 244, 260
United States Supreme Court *(see* Supreme Court)
United Way, 286
University of Iowa, 291
University of Pennsylvania, 289
University of Vermont, 221
Upward Bound, 313
Urban Community Research Center, 291
Utah, 38, 64, 92, 132–133, 198, 222, 248, 275, 290
Utah Division of Corrections, 132
Utah State Prison, 132

Vacaville Medical Facility, 173
Vandenburgh County, Indiana, 86
Vera Institute of Justice, 174
Vermont, 84, 131, 202–203, 214, 221, 248, 290
Victim, 336, 338
aid, 284, 338–339
compensation, 5, 188, 284, 336–339
culpability, 338
services, 5, 284, 337–339
crisis intervention, 338
face-to-face encounter, 338
"Victims program," 283
Vietnam War, 48
Villages, Inc., The, 286
Violent offender *(see* Offender, violent)
Virginia, 30, 60, 86, 131, 174, 248, 258, 279
Visiting, 107, 129, 131–135, 138, 153, 158, 177–179, 188, 193, 207, 216, 219–220
conjugal visits, 133–135, 138, 158, 188, 332
Vocational Rehabilitation, 54, 172, 195
Vocational Rehabilitation Act of 1920, 172
Vocational training, 16–18, 38, 44, 54, 79, 95, 102, 108, 128–129, 135, 140, 153, 173, 177, 186–187, 192, 195, 212, 216, 219, 232, 244, 246, 266, 286, 288,

Vocational training *(Cont.):*
301, 303, 308, 313, 315–317, 326, 332
General Aptitude Test Battery, 171
Volunteer, 54, 65, 85–86, 107, 115–116, 129, 152, 160, 163–170, 178–180, 185, 187, 192–193, 217–218, 239, 258, 274, 288, 311, 328, 339
aid, 116
coordinator, 169
and court system, 167–168
curiosity, 169
families, 132–133
organizations, 161, 166–167, 311
paraprofessionals, 166
professionals, 169
problems, 168–170
selection, 169–170
substitute homes, 279
supervision, 169–170
use of, 164–166
Volunteers of America, 42, 127, 166
Volunteers in Misdemeanor Program, 165
Volunteers in Probation, 168
Volunteer Teacher Program, 168
Voucher system, 140–141
(See also Self-government)

Waco, Texas, 42, 115
Walla Walla, Washington, 144
Walnut Street County Jail, 30, 141, 307
Warden *(see* Personnel, custodial officer)
Washington, 90, 92, 118, 131–132, 138, 144, 198, 226, 248, 257–258, 273
Washington, D.C., 197, 221–222, 279, 283
Washington Department of Corrections, 226
Washington Heights, New York, 42
Washington State Prison, 144
Washington State Reformatory, 166
Watkins, South Carolina, 149
Waupun Correction Institution, 142–143
Welfare, 18, 108, 205, 216, 281, 286, 314
personnel, 105, 161
private assistance, 108

West, 275
Western Europe, 25
West Virginia, 325
Wichita, Kansas, 178
Wildcat Service Corporation,
  174–175
Williams v. New York, 120
  (*See also* Court decisions)
Wilmington, Delaware, 43
  308 West Residence, 43
Wisconsin, 27, 36–37, 47, 60,
  85, 104, 119, 142, 191,
  222, 227, 238, 243, 246,
  248, 258, 291
Wisconsin Board of Charities and
  Reform, 36
Wisconsin Bureau of Community
  Corrections, 104
Woman to Woman, 166
Women, 32, 36, 38, 41, 78, 82,
  85, 91, 114, 117, 131–132,
  137, 161, 180, 256
Women in Crisis, 178
Women Offender Resource
  Center, 174
Work, 17, 19, 29, 45, 59, 67,
  107, 126–128, 175, 187,

Work *(Cont.):*
  193–195, 198, 200, 211,
  217, 219, 244, 256, 277,
  313
  work assignment (*See* Prison,
    work experience)
Work houses (*see* Jail)
Working class, 215
Work release, 16, 19, 26–27,
  36–38, 54, 60, 64–67, 74,
  82–83, 85, 89, 91, 95, 100,
  126, 132, 144, 153–154,
  160, 171, 185–208, 211,
  213, 215, 218, 224, 226,
  232, 298, 304, 316–317,
  333, 339–340, 341–342
  coordinator, 194–195
  earnings, 200, 202–203
  evaluation, 200–201
  housekeeping, 187, 192, 218
  selection of participants,
    189–192, 205–206,
    227
  and self-employment, 187, 192
  work release center, 195,
    211–213, 222, 303
Work time credit, 233

World War II, 37, 42, 139, 146,
  164, 329
Wyoming, 27

YMCA, 149, 193, 207,
  213–215, 316
Youth advocates, 280–281
Youth Alternatives, 174
Youth councils, 174
Youth Crime Control Project,
  162
Youth Opportunity Centers,
  311
Youth Services Agency, 274
Youth Services Bureau,
  281–282, 288
*Youth Services Bureau, A Key to
  Delinquency Prevention,
  The,* 282
Youth Services Center,
  Philadelphia, 289
Yo yo theory, 208
YWCA, 193

Zephyr Products, 137–138